THE NORTHERN SEAS
Shipping and Commerce in
Northern Europe
A.D. 300-1100

THE NORTHERN SEAS

Shipping and Commerce in
Northern Europe A.D. 300-1100

By ARCHIBALD R. LEWIS

Princeton University Press
Princeton, New Jersey
1958

Printed in the United States of America
by Princeton University Press, Princeton, New Jersey

Preface

IN THE last fifty years our knowledge of the lands which surrounded the Northern Seas during the period of the Early Middle Ages has grown immensely. Brilliant historians, archeologists, numismatists, and other scholarly specialists have, by their researches and their hypotheses, greatly widened our knowledge of this period. Four great historians, in particular, have been in the vanguard of those who have stimulated our imaginations and increased our perspective. They are Michael Rostovtzeff, Alphons Dopsch, Alexander Bugge and Henri Pirenne. Rostovtzeff not only pointed out clearly the structure, character and contribution of the Roman world and its relation to our own, but was the first to bring to our attention the importance of that trade route from Baltic to Black Sea, leading across the steppes and rivers of Russia. Dopsch profoundly altered our views of the Germans who invaded the Roman world and in addition was among the first to clearly emphasize the creative side of the Merovingian and Carolingian Ages, which too many historians had dismissed as dark and decadent. It was Bugge who was largely responsible for reassessing the role of the Vikings in European development and who showed how constructive their expansion was for the lands about the Northern Seas. And, finally, Pirenne with brilliant, clear ideas and style gave us an appreciation of the factors at work in the late tenth and eleventh centuries to create the urban centers upon which so much of the later medieval development was to be based. To these four, the author, like all who attempt to unravel the historical riddles of the Early Middle Ages, must humbly offer his thanks and his homage.

To those who would understand medieval Europe the problem of the Northern Seas is of great importance. Much of the Europe which emerged at the end of the eleventh century owed its form and substance to events which took place about the Mediterranean. That, however, is but half the story, for Europe is a dual heritage, and those five shallow arms of the Atlantic—the Bay of Biscay, the Irish Sea, the English Channel, the North Sea and the Baltic— played a role hardly less important than the Mediterranean. They and the rivers which emptied into them carried a commerce and a shipping which influenced Europe as much as did the Middle Sea to the south. It is to a study of these waters and the lands surrounding them that this work is dedicated.

Here it must be emphasized that it is the author's conviction that seas are not barriers now and were not in the Middle Ages. Rather they were highways which connected, influenced and tended to unify the lands whose shores they touched. Thus, in the ensuing pages an attempt has been made to view Northern Europe as a unit which surrounded the Northern Seas, with particular emphasis upon the commerce and shipping which were found there. This method has often resulted in new views, new perspectives on certain aspects of Northern Europe's history. The results may not always be pleasing to historians who have different concepts and ideas. The author can only answer in advance that there is nothing eternal about any historical point of view. Hypotheses based on conditions which actually pertain to only a certain small locality or period of time may be at the root of many of the difficulties and controversies which have marked the study of early medieval history in Europe. The author can therefore only hope in all humility that, in his attempt to give the history of Northern Europe a wider geographical basis and a new maritime emphasis, the result may be a facsimile of the truth. He trusts that his errors will lie more in detail than in substance.

The major problem attendant upon the history of the Northern Seas in this period does not, however, come from clashing hypotheses or misplaced emphasis. Rather it comes from lack of information. How little we actually know of these centuries! We have, for instance, only a few words of Gildas and traditions found in Bede, Nennius and the *Anglo-Saxon Chronicle* to help us learn the facts of early Anglo-Saxon England. Except for the works of Gregory of Tours, our knowledge of Merovingian Gaul comes largely from scattered Saints' Lives and unreliable chronicles of the period or even from some of a later date, like the *Gesta Dagoberti*. For tenth-century France and Kievan Russia we are forced to rely largely on Dudon of St. Quentin and the *Primary Chronicle*, respectively. Our exact knowledge of Scandinavia, if we did not turn to the Eddas and Sagas which were written down later, would be restricted chiefly to the works of Adam of Bremen and the traditions of Saxo Grammaticus. And even the Sagas throw no light upon events taking place in Sweden in the tenth century, which remain a mystery to us.

Happily for us, we can supplement our historical records, meager as they are, with two other sources of information now open to us—

archeology and numismatics. In recent years the spades of the archeologists in Europe have opened up new worlds of comprehension for us. Their excavations have revealed the astoundingly rich cultures of Vendel Sweden and of Bede's England, and are yearly throwing light upon early Irish, Merovingian, German and Baltic history. The historian must, to the best of his ability, try to utilize the information they make available to supplement meager and inadequate sources. In these pages an attempt has been made to do so.

The use of numismatics is equally vital and all too frequently in the past has been neglected by the historical profession. Coins, particularly those buried in coin hoards, can tell us many, many things. Their burial was almost always the result of a catastrophe or invasion which caused their owners to attempt, in this fashion, to safeguard their wealth. So a lack of coin hoards proves little except that a certain period or region enjoyed peace. But, where they are found, such hoards tell us much of commercial and other contacts existing at a particular place at a particular time. Coins located in a specific spot must be regarded as facts more undeniable and specific than the best historical source. Used with care in conjunction with other written and historical evidence, such hoards can do much to clarify these centuries in the Northern Seas.

Finally, a word about tradition. Past historical opinion has been highly critical of such traditions as those found in Irish legends, Norse Sagas, Anglo-Saxon poems, posterior Saints' Lives and the like. Such an attitude is, no doubt, the necessary equipment of the careful historian. But it seems possible that criticism in the past century has tended to be too sweeping, too all-inclusive, too uncritical. The scholarly graveyards of the past are full of the reputations of critical scholars who dismissed as inventions the legends of Homer and the words of the Bible, only to have the archeologists' spades prove their validity at Troy, Cnossus, Ur, Nineveh and the Valley of the Kings. Already the archeologists and numismatists are similarly vindicating much of the material found in *Beowulf* and the Norse Sagas by excavations at Sutton Hoo, Gotland and Uppsala. They are busy doing the same in Ireland and Russia. One must never forget that those who recorded these traditions, a Bede or a Snorri Sturluson, were much closer to the facts in time than those who criticize and dismiss them in our own age. Traditions which can be confirmed by reliable sources, by numismatics or by archeology— or, better still, by all three—can be assumed to rest in part upon fact and can be used as such to round out one's knowledge of these years, often so sparsely documented.

It would be impossible, however, to conclude this brief introduction without noting the author's reliance upon others who have labored so fruitfully in the fields he is entering. Without the insights of scholars and specialists like Collingwood, Charlesworth, Grenier, Lot, Lestocquoy, Musset, Halphen, Ganshof, Vercauteren, Dvornik, Shetelig, Patzelt, Stenton, Bolin, Hodgkin, Nerman, Lopez, Zimmern, Chadwick, Vernadsky and Kostreczewski—to name but a few— this work could not have been written. Particularly outstanding in blending archeological and historical fact have been Salin in France, Arbmann in Sweden, Werner and Jahnkuhn in Germany, Leeds in England and Boeles in Holland. That great historical cooperative effort of Dutch and Belgian scholars, the *Algemeine Geschiennis der Nederlanden,* is another example of the same thing. One can only hope for more such works to broaden our knowledge of the early medieval past of Northern Europe.

In the matter of footnotes and bibliography the author must also beg the indulgence of the scholarly reader. A full bibliography would entail three times the space occupied by these pages. It therefore seemed wiser to omit it. In the footnotes there has been a similar compression. The literature upon some subjects is immense, such as the birthplace of St. Patrick, the reliability of Nennius, the kingdom of Samo, the supposed Varangian foundation of Poland, the role of the Varangians in Russia and the Fair of St. Denis, to give only a few examples. Much of this literature has therefore been omitted in footnotes. Likewise, in the interests of brevity and harmony, the author has generally omitted from his footnotes many of the disagreements with his conclusions found in the works of previous historians. He has, on the whole, contented himself with citing agreements. It can only be hoped that the reader will forgive this presumption in the assurance that the author is well aware of such disagreements and of the reasons which lie behind them.

It is to be hoped, however, that to combine, integrate and re-examine the history of the Northern Seas during these centuries will stimulate and provoke further investigation and hypothesis. If that end is accomplished and the right questions have been asked, the result can only be a better understanding of the beginnings of medieval Europe. Since that is the purpose of all historians, the author must therein rest content.

In conclusion, the author wishes to express his gratitude to the following institutions for assistance in the gathering of materials and preparation of this volume. First, to the Committee on the International Exchange of Persons for a Fulbright Research Grant to Belgium in 1951-1952 and to the University of Texas for financial assistance in the final preparation of the manuscript and publication.

Secondly, his thanks are due for the use of their collections to the University of South Carolina Library, the Princeton University Library and the University of Texas Library. Abroad he must thank the British Museum, the Cambridge University Library and the Library of the Ashmolean Museum, as well as the Bibliothèque Royale in Brussels, the Library of the Stadtsmuseum in Stockholm and those of the University of Lund and the University of Oslo.

Even more important have been the generous help and suggestions of a number of scholars in the fields of medieval history, archeology and numismatics: In England, Mr. M. R. Maitland-Miller of the Dover Museum, Dr. E. T. Leeds, Dr. H. V. C. Sutherland and Mr. J. D. A. Thompson of the Ashmolean Museum and Mr. Philip Grierson of Cambridge University; in Belgium, Mme. Faidler-Feytmans of the Mariemont Museum, Dr. Charles Verlinden of the University of Ghent, Dr. Fernand Vercauteren of the University of Liége, Mr. Alexandre Eck of the University of Brussels and many others; in France, M. Edouard Salin of the Archeological Museum of Nancy, Abbé Jean Lestocquoy and M. Jean Massiet du Biest, archivist of Tours; in Spain, Dr. Mateu y Llopis of the Barcelona Museum and Dr. F. Bouza-Brey of Santiago; in Scandinavia, Dr. Hans Holst and his staff of the Oslo Museum, Dr. Store Bolin of the University of Lund and Dr. Martin Stenberger, Dr. Wilhelm Schwabacker, Dr. Nils Lagerholm and Mr. G. O. Matson of the Stadtsmuseum of Stockholm. He also wishes to thank Dr. Henry S. Lucas of the University of Washington and Dr. Ramon Martinez-Lopez of the University of Texas for valuable suggestions and advice. Above all, however, he is grateful to Dr. François L. Ganshof of the University of Ghent, who for many months gave him constant assistance and encouragement in his researches.

In addition, the author is grateful to his colleague, Dr. R. John Rath, for help and suggestions regarding his manuscript and to Miss Patricia Lewis of Princeton and Mrs. Lelon Winsborough of the University of Texas, who helped prepare it for publication. Finally, he wishes to thank his wife, Elizabeth Z. Lewis, for long hours spent in helping in the final preparation of this work.

Archibald R. Lewis

Austin, Texas
March 1, 1957

Contents

THE NORTHERN SEAS

Shipping and Commerce in
Northern Europe
A.D. 300-1100

1. Northern Europe in the Fourth Century

IN THE FOURTH CENTURY the principal fact of importance to the Atlantic lands stretching from Spain to the Gulf of Finland was the Roman Empire. This had been true for more than three centuries. Its importance was based upon a number of factors. First, this Empire included, from a geographic standpoint, the larger portions of the coasts washed by the gray waters of the Northern Seas. All of Atlantic Spain and Gaul acknowledged Rome's sway, which extended north to the mouths of the Rhine and beyond. So did all Britain up to the Firth of Forth. Only Ireland, parts of Scotland, Scandinavia and the Baltic lay beyond the Pax Romana.[1]

In the second place, by the time of the Early Empire, Rome had taken control of most of those peoples who had boasted a native Atlantic maritime tradition before her arrival. Cadiz, that old Phoenician center for trade in the Atlantic, had passed to Roman control as early as the end of the third century B.C. Caesar had added to the Empire the accomplished mariners of the coasts of Gaul, the Santones, the Morini, the Menapii and the Veneti. Claudius in conquering Britain had added those Celtic sailing peoples who remained still free, while the later absorption of Frisians and Batavians had completed the process. By the mid-second century the Suiones in the distant Baltic, using primitive oared craft, were the only important Northern maritime people not under Rome's rule. And their activity, if we may believe Tacitus, was then confined wholly to the Baltic.

In the third place, and even more significant, Rome's influence, based upon her superiority in organization, government, arms and civilization, gave her culture an immense prestige—one that extended far beyond her borders where her legions and shipping did not penetrate. In the Early Empire, the terms "Rome" and "civilization" were all but synonymous. She was an Atlantic power of prime importance—in fact, the only true Atlantic power of this period.[1]

In the light of such facts, it seems paradoxical to maintain that

---

[1] In this respect, as far as Scandinavia is concerned, see H. Shetelig, *La Préhistoire de la Norvège* (Oslo 1926), pp. 136-64, and L. Musset, *Les Peuples scandinaves au moyen âge* (Paris 1951), pp. 11-13. For Russia, see B. Grekov, *La Culture de la Russie de Kiev* (Moscow 1948), pp 17-19. This is less true of Ireland at the time of the Early Empire. F. J. Haverfield, "Ancient Rome and Ireland," in *Eng. Hist. Review*, CIX (1912), 1-12.

during the first two centuries of the Empire Rome instinctively rejected an Atlantic destiny. But her rulers in general, with the exception of their conquest and retention of Britain, seem to have reacted against the pull exerted by a geography which, from the rivers of Spain and Gaul and the Rhinelands to distant Britain, called her to become an Atlantic power. The reasons for Rome's reluctance are not too difficult to discover. In the first place, the Romans were not maritime-minded. Unlike the Greeks and Phoenicians, who preceded them in the Atlantic, they were and remained continental-minded soldiers and farmers rather than sailors and traders. They seem to have distrusted the sea, even their own Mediterranean. The Atlantic with its tides, its fogs, its tempests filled them with horror. One need only read Caesar's account of his invasion of Britain when he first made the acquaintance of the tides of this British coast and all but lost his naval transport in the process, or follow Tacitus' account of the same tides along the Frisian coasts, or glance at Pliny's writings to catch Rome's distaste for the Atlantic waters.[2] A road the Romans understood and admired. Sea lanes were alien to them.

Second and perhaps more important is the fact that Rome was, as Pirenne has pointed out, essentially a Mediterranean empire. Despite their Atlantic possessions her rulers never forgot this fact. Imperial advances took place north of the Mediterranean basin, it is true, but they were essentially defensive in nature. They were to protect her heartland, the Mediterranean. If we view them in this way, we can appreciate that to a Roman Caesar's conquest of Gaul was not so much an advance toward the Atlantic as a defensive offensive, which by pushing Rome's borders to the Rhine and the ocean, safeguarded the important Rhone valley invasion route and the Garonne route as well—the former then threatened by Ariovistus' Helvetians and earlier by the Cimbri and Teutoni whom Marius had eliminated. Caesar stopped at the Rhine because he needed to go no farther to accomplish his objective. Augustus moved the frontier farther east up to the Danube to protect the Alpine passes leading into Italy and absorbed Lusitania to secure once and for all Mediterranean Spain. He and his successors allowed one defeat to deflect them from a half-hearted conquest of Germany up to the Elbe. The two later extensions of Rome northwards, the conquests of Britain and Dacia under Claudius and Trajan, were similar de-

[2] For example, Pliny, *Natural History*, XVI, 2, ed. Rackham, IV, 388-90.

4

fensive-offensive moves based on a Mediterranean point of view. Britain formed an outer bastion or triangle which defended Gaul and thus the vital Rhone valley route, while Dacia in Roman hands gave extra protection in the Balkans to the Vardar valley route south to the Aegean—a passage which Slavs, Bulgars and Avars were to show was as dangerous to Rome in the East as the Rhone was in the West. To reproach Roman rulers in the Early Empire for not moving their frontiers farther to establish a Vistula-Dnieper line is to misunderstand both their purpose and their basis of rule. They were content to remain Mediterranean. If their attempts to secure and protect this basin led them to the Atlantic, this was accidental and changed neither their purpose nor their character.

This may help to explain a number of curious things. It accounts for the fact that they never bothered to conquer Ireland, though they falsely believed that it lay geographically between Britain and Spain. Its conquest would thus have rounded out their Atlantic possessions and, if we may believe Tacitus, it could have been occupied by one legion.[3] It also explains how they came to believe that Britain, an island, could be protected from invasion by fortifications in the north across its narrowest spot—the famous walls of Hadrian and Severus.

Even more important, this Mediterranean, land-minded, defensive thinking explains the curious pattern of Rome's road system in Spain, Gaul and Britain. In these provinces, Rome's roads ignore the Atlantic almost altogether. Their Gallic road net, for instance, seems to be centered on Lyons at the head of the Rhone valley and leads from there to the vital Rhine frontier and to Rouen and Boulogne, whence is found the shortest possible water passage across the Channel to Britain. Except in the Garonne valley and the Saintognes region, it hardly leads to the Atlantic at all. One gets an impression from studying their roads that the Romans scarcely occupied Brittany.

In Britain one notes the same pattern. Roman-built roads completely avoided Cornwall, which the legions failed to occupy and Romanize, and were only extended into Wales rather late. Neither Channel nor North Sea coasts, save in Kent, boasted roads either. Like their villas and the Romanized British population, their arteries were concentrated in the Midlands and led up to York and

---

[3] Tacitus, *Agricola*, XXIV. M. P. Charlesworth, *The Lost province, or The Worth of Britain* (Cardiff 1949), pp. 4-7.

the Roman Wall of Hadrian, following the sea only for a short distance along the coast of Cumberland.

That this was no accident can be seen by examining Roman Spain as well. In the Iberian peninsula Roman builders again avoided the Atlantic coast. Their routes formed a quadrilateral about the interior of the peninsula. Even the rich mines of Galicia were linked to a road net which led by land to the Mediterranean rather than to the nearby Atlantic. One can understand how in the second century Appian could write that "Romans do not use the Atlantic or the German Ocean except to go to Britain" and Tacitus similarly could speak of the lack of navigation in the North Sea.[4] A comparison of modern and Roman road nets in Western Europe reveals how truly these two writers stated Rome's attitude and practice in regard to Atlantic navigation.

All this does not mean that the Romans completely neglected their maritime interests in the Northern Seas. They saw that sea power here had some value. In A.D. 5 their Atlantic fleet reached the shores of Jutland and the entrance to the Baltic.[5] Agricola maintained a flotilla which he sent around Northern Scotland.[6] Similarly Septimus Severus in his campaigns in Caledonia used naval contingents to good effect. And we know from archeological evidence that some naval forces were regularly stationed at Boulogne and along the coast of Britain to repress the piracies of the Chaucii and keep the sea lanes open.[7] But it would seem that in the Early Empire the Romans used their Atlantic navy as an adjunct to their land forces or as a police force—not as a separate tactical arm. Corbulo, for instance, preferred to dig a canal between the Meuse and the Rhine to ensure his supplies and communications during his campaigns along the lower Rhine and in Frisia rather than to rely upon shipping using the waters of the Channel and North Sea.[8]

Despite this official attitude and policy of the Romans, however, their occupation of Britain and the coasts of Spain, Gaul and Frisia had important maritime results in the Atlantic. In large part, this was due to the economic stimulus they provided in the first two centuries of the Empire. There is not sufficient space in these pages

[4] Appian, *Hist. Rom.*, VI, 1, ed. White, I, 140.
[5] *Res gestae divi Augusti*, ed. Gage (Paris 1935), p. 128.
[6] Tacitus, *Agricola*, X; XXV.
[7] D. Atkinson, "Classis Britannica," in *Historical Essays in Honour of James Tait* (Manchester 1933), pp. 1-12.
[8] J. Breuer, *La Belgique romaine* (Bruxelles 1950), pp. 56-57.

to do more than summarize the remarkable development of these regions under Rome's aegis during this period. First, the Romans introduced new crops, new fruits and new agricultural methods into Atlantic regions, particularly Gaul. Vineyards came to cover the slopes of the Garonne, Charente and Loire valleys. A new villa system changed the agricultural pattern of life in Northern and Western Gaul, the Rhinelands and much of Britain and Spain. New towns arose upon the older tribal centers of these regions. A more cultivated, Romanized British, Spanish and Gallic aristocracy joined the upper classes of the Empire. No doubt, Roman urban centers were in some respects artificial, governmental creations, especially in Britain and Northern Gaul, where they served as residences of a rentier aristocracy that was not productive in an urban sense but drew its wealth from the surrounding countryside. But, in comparison with what had existed earlier, their importance is considerable.[9]

In addition, under Rome much development and new exploitation of mineral resources took place. In Britain this resulted in large-scale production by the Romans of the iron of Kent and the Forest of Dean, of the silver and lead of the Mendips, Flintshire and Derbyshire, of the copper of Anglesey. In Belgium they made use of the iron and zinc of the Meuse region and of the Argonne and exploited iron deposits in the Massif Central. In Noricum and Rhaetia they mined the abundant iron of the Alps. In Spain it was they who first worked on a large scale the copper of Huelva, while Pliny records that they opened up mines of tin, silver, gold and lead in Asturias.[10]

The impact of Roman economic activities was particularly great near those frontiers where, since the time of Augustus, the legions had been stationed. This fact explains the particular growth of the iron industry of Belgium, the Rhinelands, Noricum and parts of Britain that arose to meet the demands of legionary forces for weapons. It also explains why a woolen industry was to be found

[9] See A. Grenier, "La Gaule romaine," in *An Economic Survey of Ancient Rome*, ed. T. Frank (Baltimore 1937), IV, 479-551, and R. G. Collingwood, "Roman Britain," and J. J. Van Nostrand, "Roman Spain," in *ibid.*, III, for full accounts of the early development of these provinces under Rome's sway. See also L. C. West, *Imperial Roman Spain: The Objects of Trade* (Oxford 1929), pp. 30-92, *Roman Britain* (Oxford 1931), pp. 11-108, and *Roman Gaul* (Oxford 1935), pp. 55-191.

[10] M. P. Charlesworth, *op.cit.*, pp. 50-58. J. W. Gough, *The Mines in the Mendips* (Oxford 1936), pp. 1-40. O. Davies, *Roman Mines in Europe* (Oxford 1935), pp. 78-93, 97-106, 141-64. A. Grenier, *op.cit.*, pp. 588-89. T. A. Rickard, "The Mining of the Romans in Spain," in *Jour. of Roman Studies*, XVIII (1928), 129-43.

in parts of Northeastern Gaul and Flanders at such an early date. It is worth noting that agricultural progress in clearing the land seems to have been greater near the frontiers, where demands of soldiers for food as well as clothing and weapons served as a stimulus, than it was farther in the interior of these provinces.[11]

It is this agricultural, industrial and mining activity, especially notable near the frontiers of Gaul and Germany, which helps to explain the growth of an important Atlantic trade during these centuries. That this traffic was not in Roman hands but rather in those of native peoples under Rome's sway does not change its importance. The most vital routes were those short ones which led from Rouen across the Channel to Clausentum (near modern Southampton) and Porchester and from Boulogne to Dover, Richborough and London.[12] From Nijmegen, Fectio and Domburg at or near the Rhine's mouths, however, another active trade route led to London and Britain's east coast,[13] while other traders sailed to Britain from Bordeaux at the mouth of the Garonne and from Corbilo at the mouth of the Loire.[14] In fact, Strabo, writing in the second century, particularly commented on the activity that characterized British commerce with Garonne, Loire, Seine and Rhine. He also reported Spanish, Gascon and Belgian Menapian merchants at Bordeaux, which he said was linked by a route via Narbonne with the Mediterranean.[15] We can thus see that there existed an Atlantic commerce from the coasts of Spain, perhaps extending to Cadiz, that stretched along the Gallic coasts and led to Britain. It is interesting to note that a colony of Gallic and Menapian merchants was to be found in London in this period.[16]

[11] C. E. Stevens, "Agricultural Life in the Later Roman Empire," in *Cambridge Economic History of Europe* (Cambridge 1941), I, 102-6. F. G. Payne, "The Plow in Ancient Britain," in *Archeological Journal*, CIV (1947), 82-109. F. Cumont, *Comment la Belgique fut romanisée* (2nd ed., Bruxelles 1919), pp. 5-39. R. Doehaerd, *L'Expansion belge au moyen âge* (Bruxelles 1950), pp. 9-11. F. W. Walbank, "Trade and Industry Under the Later Roman Empire in the West," in *Cambridge Economic History of Europe*, II, 33-50. A. Grenier, *op.cit.*, pp. 587-91, and R. G. Collingwood, *op.cit.*, pp. 34-41.

[12] R. G. Collingwood, *op.cit.*, pp. 28-33.

[13] C. Jullian, *Histoire de la Gaule* (Paris 1921), V, 138. A. Dopsch, *The Economic and Social Foundations of European Civilization* (New York 1938), pp. 346-47. E. Janssens, *Histoire ancienne de la Mer du Nord* (Bruxelles 1950), pp. 58-59.

[14] L. Bonnard, *La Navigation intérieure de la Gaule* (Paris 1913), pp. 79-83. C. Jullian, *op.cit.*, V, 183, 253, 328. R. G. Collingwood, *op.cit.*, pp. 30-33.

[15] Strabo, *Geography*, IV, 1, 14; IV, 2, 1, ed. Jones, II, 208-16. L. Bonnard, *op.cit.*, p. 29.

[16] R. Doehaerd, *op.cit.*, p. 9.

Nor was this maritime traffic confined to Britain and Roman-held coasts. At the time of Agricola Roman merchants visited Ireland and perhaps Scotland.[17] Even more important was the trade that reached Norway, Denmark and the Baltic by sea.[18] So great was the volume of commerce over this route that Scandinavian archeologists, struck by the number of objects of Roman provenience found in Scandinavian sites dating from the first and second centuries A.D., have called this period the Roman Iron Age in Scandinavia. The maritime route to Scandinavia followed the Frisian and North German coasts to Jutland, where it either crossed the neck of the Danish peninsula or proceeded up along the coasts of the peninsula to the Kattegat, Skagerrak and the south coast of Norway. The largest number of Roman finds of this period come from Jutland and the island of Zealand, but they are found all the way up the Norwegian coast to the Trondheim region as well.[19] This trade was large enough so that a whole series of small trading ports developed from Flanders to the mouths of the Ems and Elbe rivers. Excavation of these centers, like Dokkum and Beetgum, shows they were probably under Roman protection, and the abundant coin hoards found along the coast illustrate their importance.[20] Such coins have been found far up the Norwegian coast as well—though few in number for this period.[21] It seems probable that the Menapian merchants so active in London and on the west coast of Gaul were the intermediaries in this traffic, though some Frisians may have played a trading role here as well.

In general, then, maritime routes which were in operation along

[17] Tacitus, *Agricola*, XXIV. J. R. Curle, "An Inventory of Objects of Roman and Provincial Origin on Sites in Scotland Not Definitely Associated with Roman Constructions," in *Proc. of Soc. of Antiq. of Scotland*, LXVI (1931-32), 277-341.

[18] H. Shetelig and H. Falk, *Scandinavian Archeology* (Oxford 1937), pp. 252-55. E. Janssens, *op.cit.*, p. 59.

[19] See, for example, K. F. Johansen, "La Trouvaille de Hoby," in *Nordiske Fortidsminder*, III (Copenhagen 1923), 23-37, and *Guides to the National Museum, Copenhagen: Antiquity* (Copenhagen 1952), pp. 71-92. O. Brogan, "Trade Between the Roman Empire and the Free Germans," in *Jour. of Roman Studies*, XXIII (1936), 207.

[20] A. Dopsch, *op.cit.*, pp. 346-47. J. Breuer, *op.cit.*, pp. 56-57. H. Willers, *Neue Untersuchungen über die römische Bronzeindustrie von Capua und von Niedergermanien* (Hanover 1907), pp. 45-52. E. Janssens, *op.cit.*, pp. 46-48.

[21] Roman silver coins minted during the Early Empire are rare in Norwegian archeological sites. In hoards found near Oslo and on Norway's west coast are only one coin minted by Augustus, 2 Claudius, 2 Hadrian and 3 Antonius Pius. H. Holst, "Mynter i Norske Funn," in *Nordiske Numismatisk Arsskrift* (1943), pp. 56-101. No gold Roman coins of this period have been found in Norway. H. Holst, *Numismatica Fasc.*, VII (1928), 83-91.

Atlantic coasts to Britain, Ireland and Scandinavia prior to Roman conquest continued afterwards and even increased in importance during the first two centuries of the Empire. At the same time, it should be emphasized that the maritime peoples active earlier, and particularly the Menapii of the northern French and Flanders coast, continued so in the Early Empire.

To stop with this brief description of the Atlantic trade routes would, however, be an inadequate summary of Rome's commerce north of her frontiers. In addition to the maritime traffic which reached Scandinavia, there was an important commerce by land. This followed routes which led from the Rhine and upper Danube to the south coast of the Baltic. The termini were the mouths of the Oder and Vistula, whence by way of Bornholm, Oland and Gotland trade reached the Swedish mainland. Some centers on the south coast of the Baltic may have attained the status of towns, or *poleis*, or at least have risen far above the primitive trade level to be inferred from Caesar's *Commentaries*.[22] It was by way of these routes that the fur-trading Suiones, or Swedes, mentioned by Tacitus as a people possessing considerable naval power, traded with the richer lands to the south,[23] and it is to them that the Marcomanni owed their powerful position as principal intermediaries in the second century.[24] Nor was this all. By the time of Marcus Aurelius, some trade at least was passing by land farther to the east and reaching the lower Danube and the Black Sea. Thus old amber routes, to be so important later, were again in operation by the last years of the second century.[25]

Despite Rome's reluctance to accept a Northern Atlantic destiny, her sway over Atlantic areas began to encourage commerce to Britain, Ireland and Scandinavia from Spanish and Gallic coasts and to the Central and Eastern Baltic by land routes from the Rhine, Danube

---

[22] A. Dopsch, *op.cit.*, pp. 315-16. O. Brogan, *op.cit.*, pp. 210-19. J. Dechelette, *Manuel d'archéologie préhistorique celtique et gallo-romaine* (Paris 1908), pp. 209-11. H. Shetelig, *op.cit.*, pp. 218-28.

[23] Tacitus, *Germania*, XLIV-XLV.

[24] H. Shetelig, *La Préhistoire de la Norvège*, pp. 136-54.

[25] T. J. Arne and O. Almgren, in *Oldtiden*, VII (1918), 210-12. O. R. Janse, *Le Travail de l'or en Suède à l'époque merovingienne* (Orléans 1922), pp. 3-9 G. Turville-Petrie, *The Heroic Age of Scandinavia* (Oxford 1951), pp. 16-18. M. Rostovtzeff, *Iranians and Greeks in South Russia* (Oxford 1922), pp. 181-209. B. Grekov, *op.cit.*, pp. 17-21, mentions hoards of Roman coins of the 2nd and 3rd centuries found in Russian sites. On these coins, the standard work is the monumental one by S. Bolin, *Fynden ac romerska mynt i det fria Germanien*, 2 vols. (Lund 1926).

and Black Sea. If the trade within the Empire was more important, that by land and sea beyond it was not inconsiderable, especially to Scandinavia and the Baltic, and represented a commercial advance over anything found there in earlier centuries. Rome despite herself served as a stimulus to commerce and civilization about the Northern Seas.

There remains the problem of the products which were the objects of trade along these commercial routes. To Britain from Western Gaul went the wine of the Garonne and Loire, the salt of Saintogne and olive oil trans-shipped from the province via Garonne or Rhone-Loire routes.[26] From Spain came metals, particularly tin and gold.[27] From Northern Gaul, Belgium and the Rhinelands were exported manufactured goods.[28] In return Britain seems to have exported metals—iron, copper, lead and silver—and grain and hides to the Continent. Some metalware and pottery reached Britain and the North from factories in Italy and Southern Gaul, particularly in the first century A.D.[29] To the Germans in Germany proper and Scandinavia went the Roman arms, bronze and metal objects which they prized, as well as wine, pottery and money, in return for furs, slaves, amber, feathers and some of the wild beasts which were used in the Roman civic amphitheaters to the south.[30] It is this trade within and without the Empire which explains the active river traffic of the period on Garonne, Charente, Loire, Seine and Rhine leading into the Atlantic and the *collegia*, or corporations, of *nautae* found on most of them.[31] And it is well to note that the maritime trade of this period was mainly carried on, as mentioned earlier, by Gallic

---

[26] H. Pirenne, "Un grand commerce d'exportation au moyen âge: les vins de France" in *Ann. d'hist. écon. et sociale*, v (1933), 228. R. G. Collingwood, *op.cit.*, pp. 110-16. J. Gage, "Gades, l'Inde et les navigations atlantiques dans l'Antiquité," in *Revue historique*, CCV (1951), 203.

[27] F. W. Walbank, *op.cit.*, pp. 43-46. J. Gage, *op.cit.*, pp. 203-4.

[28] E. Janssens, *op.cit.*, pp. 58-59. R. Doehaerd, *op.cit.*, pp. 9-10. F. Rousseau, *La Meuse et le pays mosan en Belgique* (Namur 1930), pp. 6-11. A. Grenier, *op.cit.*, pp. 560-90.

[29] R. G. Collingwood, *op.cit.*, pp. 114-16. I. D. Margary, *Roman Ways in the Weald* (London 1948), pp. 103-271. M. Bresnier, "Le Commerce du plomb à l'époque romaine," in *Revue arch.*, 5th ser., XIII (1921), 67-70.

[30] O. Brogan, *op.cit.*, pp. 196-204. A. Dopsch, *op.cit.*, pp. 315-16. H. Shetelig and H. Falk, *Scandinavian Archeology*, pp. 253-55. P. Boeles, "De terpencultuur tot omstreeks 400," in *Algemene Geschiedenis der Nederlanden*, I (Utrecht 1949), 179-201. M. Bloch, "Les Invasions: deux structures économiques," in *Ann. d'hist. sociale*, I (1945), 37-43.

[31] A. Grenier, *op.cit.*, pp. 565-89. L. Bonnard, *La Navigation intérieure de la Gaule*, pp. 161-213.

merchants: Menapii, Morini and Western Gallic descendants of the Veneti, Santones and others who had once been the intermediaries in the Atlantic between Greeks and Phoenicians and the barbarian lands beyond the Mediterranean. They with some Spanish and Frisian traffickers were the masters of the Northern Seas of the Early Empire.[32]

Then came the decisive and terrible third century which changed the whole character of the Roman world—particularly in its western provinces. After two centuries of peace, civil war, inflation, *bagaudae* peasant risings in the countryside and German invasions wrecked much of the progress which had taken place in the Early Empire. Saxons on the sea and Franks and Alemanni by land swept into Belgium and Gaul as far as the Pyrenees and beyond. It looked as if the Empire would disintegrate. Then slowly but surely the pattern changed. Soldier Emperors, mainly of Illyrian stock, began to re-establish order against great odds. By the time of Diocletian the Empire had been reconstituted. But it was not that which had existed at the time of Augustus, Hadrian or Marcus Aurelius. It was a radically altered world which Diocletian, Constantine and their successors had to face. And it is this Roman world which concerns us and which merits careful investigation—for from it the Atlantic world of Europe of the next eight centuries was born.

The Late Roman world that bordered the Atlantic and the barbarian world beyond it both stood in rather sharp contrast to those existing at the time of the Early Empire. The Late Roman world, for instance, has frequently been described as medieval—perhaps an apt term. At any rate, it seems to have had four salient characteristics. First and most striking is the fact that by the late third and fourth centuries it had become a fortified empire. Gone were the broad-avenued streets, the spacious temples and gardens that marked the Roman urban centers of the earlier Empire in Atlantic Gaul, Britain and Spain. In their place had arisen towns, small in size, hurriedly fortified with huge walls often constructed from the rubble and debris of their former suburbs.[33] On the borders of the Empire

---

[32] Strabo, *Geography*, IV, 2, 1, ed. Jones, II, 212-16. F. Delaruelle, "Toulouse et la route des Deux Mers," in *Annales du Midi*, LXII (1950), 217-18. Tacitus' story of mutinous Usipii who sailed ships around Britain and then were cut off from home by Frisians suggests these latter possessed some naval power. Tacitus, *Agricola*, XXVIII.

[33] On Britain, see R. G. Collingwood, "Roman Britain," *loc.cit.*, pp. 11-12. Concerning the decay of cities in Gaul and Belgium, A. Blanchet, *Les Encientes romaines*

fortifications were not entirely new. Hadrian in England and Domitian in Germany had begun to establish border lines that were continued by their successors. What was new was that now, as in medieval times, the interior was fortified as far as and including the city of Rome itself. It was as if the population of the Late Empire had little confidence in either internal or external peace—even in Britain, which had been all but untouched by invasions in the third century. One finds fortified towns, fortified bourgs, fortified places of refuge, even fortified villas. Everywhere man had lost faith in order.[34]

The second major characteristic of the Late Empire was that it was regimented. In place of the relative freedom of the first two centuries after Augustus, now the heavy hand of the government lay upon society. By Constantine's time and even earlier the state had begun to force its citizens to do what earlier they had been glad to do for themselves—to feed themselves, to clothe themselves, to defend themselves and, above all, to pay the cost of their government. This system of regimentation grew slowly in all fields of activity until *coloni* were bound to the soil, artisans to their trade, soldiers fixed in their occupations, sailors in their ships and *decuriones* in the towns to their unpaid jobs as collectors of state taxes. A constantly growing, burdensome bureaucracy ate at the vitals of the state as the cost of government steadily increased. Only the senatorial nobility, possessing vast estates, escaped their share of the burdens—and they were the one class best able to bear expenses within the Empire. Not all this regimentation was new in the fourth century. It had begun as early as the second when the Imperial government started to interfere in local agriculture and town government. What was new was the extent and completeness of the system.[35] What a contrast to the free years of Claudius or Trajan!

In the third place, the Empire was by the fourth century in the West an agrarian empire. It is true that under Rome the expansion

---

de la Gaule (Paris 1907), pp. 200-336. For this period, for instance, Poitiers was large, yet it was only 40 hectares in extent and contained no more than 12,000 inhabitants. M. Giraud, "Note sur la cité de Poitiers à l'époque merovingienne," in *Mélanges Louis Halphen* (Paris 1951), pp. 271-72.

[34] Grenier sums this up in "La Gaule," *loc.cit.*, pp. 599-60. See also F. W. Walbank, *op.cit.*, p. 51.

[35] On this regimentation, see F. Lot, *La Gaule* (Paris 1947), pp. 397-420. More exact legal record is found in the Theodosian Code. On state factories, see *Code Theodosian*, ed. Pharr, I, 32, 1; IV, 6, 3; X, 20, 1-9; X, 22, 3. On post service, *ibid.*, VIII, 5-6. On general regulations, *ibid.*, XI, 16, 15. On town decurions, *ibid.*, XII, 1, 8-192. On shipmasters and *nautae, ibid.*, XIII, 5, 1-26.

of cities and urban life into Britain and the Atlantic provinces of Gaul and Spain had never really been successful. An element of the artificial, of the superficial, lay behind this urbanization. Never large, these *civitates* were not truly organic but rather centers inhabited by Romanized rentier estate-owners who drew their income not from production in the towns they inhabited but from the countryside. The middle class of merchants lived in towns largely to supply luxury goods or food to such rentiers. Thus, in contrast to later medieval towns, such Roman cities performed no essential economic role and were essentially parasitical upon the countryside— a fact which explains their limited growth. Centers for worship, for administration, for social life, they played little role in production and, where they did, it was chiefly to supply the equally artificial, governmentally created needs of the Roman garrisons on the frontiers. They were a series of little Washingtons or were like towns which have grown up to serve modern American army camps, drawing their sustenance from a governmental or military system instead of arising out of natural needs of the region in which they were located. In the Atlantic provinces of Rome perhaps there were only two cities, Bordeaux and London, both relatively large, which can be said to have been cities in the sense that Pirenne has used the term for the towns of this same area in the twelfth century.[36]

Thus the true economic unit in this portion of the Roman world was not the *civitas* but the villa, or large country estate, and by the fourth century it was these villas that in the West became the real centers of economic life. The towns, with one or two exceptions, steadily declined. Ruined by the civil wars of the third century and further reduced in effectiveness by the regimentation of the fourth, the surviving *civitates* became mere shadows. Those who could, particularly the senatorial nobility, left them for the countryside. An agrarian-dominated society, so much a feature of the Early Middle Ages, was already apparent by the fourth century.[37]

[36] On Bordeaux in this period, P. Courtreault, *Bordeaux à travers les siècles* (Bordeaux 1909), pp. 3-8. On London, which may have had a population of 15,000, W. Page, *London, Its Origin and Early Development* (London 1923), pp. 3-101.

[37] This is particularly true of Roman Britain, where the late 3rd and 4th centuries were a golden age for villas. F. Haverfield, *The Romanization of Britain* (London 1913), p. 77. See also M. P. Charlesworth, *The Lost Province*, pp. 20-26, and R. G. Collingwood, "Roman Britain," *loc.cit.*, pp. 79-86, who give details on the more than 500 Roman villa sites in Britain, dating from this period, which have been excavated. Of most portions of Gaul the same thing is true. R. Koebner, "The Colonization of Europe," in *Cambridge Economic History*, I, pp. 9-10, 25-27. For example,

Fourth and most important of all, the Late Empire in the West was not only fortified, regimented and agrarian, but also defensive in its outlook. This was perhaps its most salient characteristic. Still immensely rich and powerful in relation to the barbarian world that confronted it, it had lost its initiative, ceased to expand and was busy consolidating, holding what it had against external and internal foes. This is the meaning of its interior fortifications, of its border fortresses and of its regimentation as well. It had lost confidence in its ability to stand against the barbarians it felt pushing against its borders and seeping through its frame. It was the victim of a Maginot Line psychology. It even hired its feared enemies, the Germans, as soldiers charged with the defense of its borders, as if it were unable or unwilling to trust its own subjects with this task.

Within this Empire only Christianity had strength and vitality and the capacity for growth. But it is worth noting that by the late fourth century it was a Christianity merged with the state. It stopped at Rome's borders, if it even extended so far in the West. Not the Orthodox Christianity of the Empire but heretical sects showed an ability to pass its borders and reach peoples beyond. It was Nestorianism, Arianism and Monophysitism that affected non-Roman German, Persian and Abyssinian, not the official cult of the Roman world.

To insist that this defensive character of the Empire in its Western provinces was entirely new in the Late Empire would be unwise. As we have noted earlier, the initial expansion of Rome to the Atlantic had about it a defensive character. Once limited objectives had been reached, Roman rulers had refused to push much beyond the Rhine, the Danube or Hadrian's Wall in Britain. The failure to go farther, however, in the earlier Empire had been the result of deliberate policy by Imperial Mediterranean-minded rulers. A Germanicus or an Agricola, eager to push back the frontier and able to do so in his own estimate, had been held back by the authorities in command in Rome who felt that Ireland, Scotland and Germany were not worth taking. There were even doubts on the score of Britain at the time of its conquest. Decisions were made, it would seem, on

---

see account of the villa of Nennig in Luxembourg in J. Vannerus, "La Villa de Nennig," in *Cahiers Luxembourgeois*, II (1932), 187-210. On Spain, see F. W. Walbank, *op.cit.*, pp. 80-81. See also general comments by Lot in *La Gaule*, pp. 384-96. By the 5th century Roman Emperors had noted this strong agrarian trend, *Nov. Majoran*, ed. Pharr, p. 3.

the basis of the wisdom of such advances, not on the basis of an ability to achieve them. The conquest and development of Dacia in the second century under Trajan and afterwards show how vigorous Roman action in this line could still be.

By the fourth century, however, one senses quite another mood. One feels that weakness, not prudence or economy, dictated the Empire's defensive policies. The *élan vital* had departed from the Imperial body politic. This lack of vigor was noticeable not only in Roman civilization's contacts with peoples beyond its borders, but inside the Empire in the West as well. The so-called Celtic reaction in Gaul, Britain, Spain and Belgium, the return to pre-Roman art forms and religion on the part of sections of the provincial population,[38] the fact that it was from Persia via Visigothic South Russia rather than Rome that new vital art forms were now reaching Scandinavia[39]—all these show us a civilization which was losing its grip on populations both within and outside its borders—a civilization resisting stubbornly, even rallying at times, but essentially in retreat from forces and a destiny it could no longer control.

Remembering these salient facts, let us examine the Northern Seas in the fourth century. What is immediately striking is that Rome no longer dominated these waters by default or conquest of maritime peoples as she had in the period of the Early Empire. The change seems to have begun in the course of the third century when, in conjunction with German assaults across the Rhine, Saxon pirates began pillaging the British coast and raided along the Gallic shores of the English Channel, that vital artery linking Britain with Gaul. A new dangerous naval enemy, the Saxon sea-rover, had appeared, forcing Rome to pay new attention to her maritime defenses in the Atlantic.[40]

Along with the Saxon pirate menace still another appeared—one originating in Ireland to the west of Britain. At the time of Agricola in the first century, Ireland had been a barbarous island on the fringe of Rome's Atlantic world, without significant sea power. But by the third century this had begun to change. According to Irish

---

[38] For Britain, F. Haverfield, *op.cit.*, pp. 72-85. The same thing is noticeable in Belgium, where native Celtic religious cults reappear in the 4th century.

[39] Shetelig and Falk, *Scandinavian Archeology*, pp. 200-8, 230-35. M. Rostovtzeff, *Iranians and Greeks in South Russia*, pp. 203-40.

[40] Eutropas, *Brev. hist. Romanae*, IX, 21, in *MGH Auct. Ant.*, II, 162-64. R. G. Collingwood, "Roman Britain" (Oxford 1932), p. 40.

tradition, in 222 the first Irish fleet made an expedition overseas.[41] We know that by 275 the Desi from the southern part of the island had begun to make landings and to settle on the coasts of Cornwall and South Wales.[42] Raids elsewhere proved the Irish, like the Saxons, a serious menace to Rome.

To these two a third was soon added, the Picts of Scotland. It is difficult to say exactly when the Picts took to the sea in significant numbers. But if sources are lacking, excavation of their *brochs*, or fortresses, on the headlands of Scotland's west coast, Isles and east coast show clearly that by the time of the Late Empire they, too, had become an important maritime people.[43] Where they had earlier been savage tribesmen who could be checked by land walls and fortresses and small naval flotillas, they now were formidable adversaries, for their naval prowess and swift ships made it possible for them to by-pass Rome's defenses on the land and strike both the east and the west coast of Britain.[44]

In the Baltic, of course, Scandinavian naval power had always existed independent of Rome, as Tacitus shows.[45] But it is interesting to note that when Goths and associated Northern peoples reached the Black Sea in the third century, they soon took to the sea and with their fleets harried the coasts of Asia Minor and even passed into the Mediterranean after forcing the Dardanelles. They settled down to form their Ostrogothic South Russian kingdom, but their earlier naval actions seem curiously like those of their Scandinavian Varangian successors. In short, in the third century Rome found herself in serious difficulties on the Northern Seas.

The Roman answer to these menaces was typical of her attitude during the period of the Late Empire. She took strong but strictly defensive measures. In the last years of the third century she began to set up a defensive maritime system to hold in check the Saxon

---

[41] W. L. Clowes, *The Royal Navy*, I (London 1898), 59. J. Hornell, "The Curraghs of Ireland," in *Mariners Mirror*, XXIII (1937), 75-80.

[42] F. Haverfield, *op.cit.*, pp. 80-86. T. Kenney, *The Sources for the Early History of Ireland* (New York 1922), p. 148. M. P. Charlesworth, *The Lost Province*, p. 20.

[43] P. H. Brown, *A Short History of Scotland* (rev. ed., Edinburgh 1951), pp. 14-16. J. Anderson, "Notes on the Structure of the Brochs," in *Proc. of Soc. of Antiq. of Scotland*, XII (1878), 117-51.

[44] The Romans probably copied these Pictish ships. Vegetius, *De re militari*, IV, 37, ed. Schwebel, p. 137.

[45] This Baltic naval power is graphically illustrated by the 4th-century Nydam ship discovered in Denmark. Shetelig and Falk, *Scandinavian Archeology*, pp. 353-89. For general development of ships in Norway and the Baltic, see A. W. Brøgger and H. Shetelig, *The Viking Ships* (Oslo 1953), pp. 40-52.

pirates. This system seems to have been started by Carausius, but it was to Constantius Chlorus that its fuller development and elaboration were owed. In Britain a series of eleven maritime fortresses was constructed, stretching from the Wash to beyond the Isle of Wight. They were garrisoned by Roman soldiers and placed under a special commander, the Count of the Saxon Shore—a significant title indeed.[46]

Probably these sensitive defensive positions included, along with their land garrisons, squadrons of swift scouting vessels—known as Pictish ships, according to Vegetius, because of their camouflage or design—which could warn of the approach of raiding flotillas.[47]

Similar fortresses were constructed on the Gallic side of the Channel from the mouths of the Rhine to Brittany, while the main fleet was located at Boulogne in the narrow Straits of Dover. In charge of this fleet and of the shore defenses as far as the mouth of the Seine, according to the *Notitia Dignitatum*, was the Dux of Belgica Secunda. Other fortresses were constructed at key points along the coasts of Normandy, Brittany and Gaul's west coast as far as the Pyrenees, commanded by the Count of Armorica and of the Nervii. It seems possible that only those Channel defenses as far as Grannona in Brittany, which is specifically referred to as "on the Saxon Shore," were directed against Saxon sea-rovers. Those in West Brittany, along Gaul's west coast, and the one we know of in Spain may well have been constructed to defend these regions from Irish raiders.[48] In addition to these coastal defenses and fleets, special river flotillas were maintained on the Rhine and the Seine.[49]

Similar to these maritime defenses were those which archeology shows us were located on Britain's west coast to deal with Irish piratical activity. A series of fortresses and watchtowers were constructed on the island of Anglesey and in North Wales and on both sides of the Bristol Channel, with the most important one at Car-

[46] On the development of the Saxon Shore forts, see the *Notitia Dignitatum Occid.*, XXXVIII, and D. Atkinson, "Classis Britannica," *loc.cit.*, pp. 2-15. Also F. Lot, "Les Migrations saxonnes en Gaule et en Grande Bretagne," in *Revue hist.*, CXIX (1915), 3-6. The latest and most complete survey of this defense system is in M. P. Charlesworth, *The Lost Province*, p. 48 with map.

[47] It seems more probable that these ships were called Pictish because of their design than because they were painted or camouflaged. Vegetius does not, however, explain his use of this term. Vegetius, *De re militari*, IV, 37, ed. Schwebel, p. 137.

[48] *Notitia Dignitatum Occid.*, XXXVII. F. Lot, *op.cit.*, pp. 5-6. D. Atkinson, *op.cit.*, pp. 9-15. L. Bonnard, *La Navigation intérieure de la Gaule*, pp. 229-32.

[49] *Ibid.*, pp. 217-21. *Ammianus Marcellinus*, XVII, 2. These river patrols are mentioned as early as 325 (*Code Theod.*, VII, 20, 4), and again in 365 (*ibid.*).

diff.[50] A flotilla seems to have been maintained at the mouth of the Severn to ward off attacks, as is suggested by the remains of a naval base excavated there.[51] It seems also probable that older Roman fleet stations on the coast of Cumberland just south of the Wall were strengthened against Irish and Pictish attacks.[52]

The only serious gap in Rome's British maritime defenses was along the northeast coast of Yorkshire, where naval defenses perhaps seemed unnecessary in the early fourth century. The great joint Irish-Pict-Saxon attack on Britain in 367 changed this, however, for following Britain's defeat Count Theodosius constructed a series of watchtowers there, probably to warn Britain of Pictish naval approach.[53]

At the same time, Rome withdrew from her exposed positions along the coast of North Germany and Frisia to the Rhine, abandoning the coastal forts she had occupied there in the Early Empire, probably because they were too vulnerable to enemy naval action.[54] All along the Atlantic, then, from the Rhine to the Pyrenees and about the coasts of Britain a new naval defense system had been put into operation—one that matched the river squadrons, fortresses and special armies that defended the Rhine and Danube frontiers.

When one analyzes this Roman system of maritime defenses, however, one is struck by something else besides its completeness. I refer to its strictly defensive character. It is obvious that river flotillas on Rhine and Seine, swift scouting vessels attached to Saxon Shore forts and squadrons maintained in the British Channel and Cumberland were essentially defensive in character. Even the main fleet located at Boulogne was there to guard the narrow Straits of Dover and protect the vital Channel routes that led to Richborough and Dover from Boulogne and to Clausentum from Rouen. The

---

[50] M. P. Charlesworth, *op.cit.*, pp. 20-26, 48-50.

[51] G. Farr, "Severn Navigation and the Trow," in *Mariners Mirror*, XXXII (1946), 67.

[52] The navy which Coroticus, from his center at Dumbarton, used to raid Ireland in the 5th century was probably a survival of this Roman flotilla. H. M. Chadwick, *Early Scotland* (London 1948), pp. 140-53.

[53] E. Janssens, *op.cit.*, pp. 67-69, and "Note on the Roman Coastal Defenses of Britain, Especially in Yorkshire," in *Jour. of Roman Studies*, II (1912), 201-72. The first mention of serious Pictish attacks comes during the great invasion of 367-68, which all but destroyed Roman Britain. See R. G. Collingwood, *Roman Britain*, pp. 42-43.

[54] On the abandonment of Frisia, see P. Boeles, *Friesland tot de Elfde Eeuw* (2nd ed., The Hague 1951), pp. 145-77. See also E. Janssens, *Histoire ancienne de la Mer du Nord*, pp. 63-118.

many shore fortresses with their garrisons and the far-flung watch-tower system proclaim the same doctrine—one of defense, above all. On the sea, also, the Romans emphasized a defense in depth, but essentially a passive defense. Not for them protection by a large active fleet which could carry the war to Saxon, Irish and Pictish shores. In fact, only once do we read of a naval punitive expedition, one which Count Theodosius sent against the Picts of the Orkneys to punish them for their great attack on Britain in 367.[55] In general, the Romans seem to have been content to await naval assault from their enemies, and their defense dispositions emphasize that they were particularly concerned about attacks from the North Sea into the English Channel, since this was their vital lifeline to Britain.

Closely linked to the Atlantic naval defenses and paralleling them in many ways were those which defended Rome's land frontiers along the Rhine and Danube. This defense system, established by Diocletian and Constantine, has been better understood by historians than that upon the coasts. It consisted of three vital sectors. The first was along the Rhine, particularly the mid-Rhine, from which easy invasion routes led via the Moselle and Saverne Gap into the Rhone valley and the heart of Gaul. Along this route were located Rome's most formidable defenses, and the city of Trier which guarded it was, in the fourth century, generally the Imperial capital in the West. The second sector consisted of Noricum, Rhaetia and Pannonia on the upper Danube, guarding the Alpine passes into Italy. Just behind these provinces in Italy lay Milan, which shared with Trier the honor of being the residence of the Western Imperial Caesar or the Emperor. From the time of the dangerous Marcomanni wars of the late second century, this frontier had been considered a particularly sensitive one and was well guarded. And, finally, there was the lower Danube frontier, the special charge of the Eastern Imperial Caesar and closely watched from Constantinople by the Eastern Emperor as well. Since Dacia had been abandoned to the Visigoths by Aurelian, the Vardar route to the Aegean made it particularly necessary to maintain this region in defense readiness.

By the fourth century a newly revised defense system had been established along these frontiers. Again, it was a defense in depth. The outer crust consisted of tribes of barbarian *foederati* like the

---

[55] *Ammianus Marcellinus*, xx, tells of a naval punitive expedition sent against the Orkneys and commanded by Lupicianus, lieutenant of Julian.

Franks living just outside the river frontiers, or in some cases, like a portion of the Franks, just inside them. They were specially charged with the defense of the regions where they were settled. On the Rhine and Danube there were flotillas whose duty it was to patrol these rivers, intercepting small parties of raiders and enforcing the Empire trade controls. They seem to have been particularly useful on the wide stretches of the lower Danube, where no bridge existed, and their importance is attested by the number of provisions relating to them found in the Theodosian Code and the *Notitia Dignitatum*.[56]

Behind these two forces were fortresses manned by the old frontier legions, now degenerated into little more than a fortress militia useful in giving warning of attack or in repelling small raids, but not effective in the case of a full-scale barbarian assault. The serious defenses were those in their rear, fortified cities and camps which contained the mobile field armies of the Empire; elite, mounted troops under commanders who were prepared to bring them into immediate action whenever assaults broke through the outer crust. Trier and Milan owed their importance to the fact that they served as headquarters of such field armies, while in distant Britain York played a similar role. On the land, then, as on the sea, the emphasis was on defense—defense in depth, it is true, but of a nature that was essentially passive rather than active.[57]

To some extent, the economy of the Empire which faced the Atlantic and Northern Europe reflected and was molded by this defense pattern. At first glance this might not seem to be true, for there were two economies in the Late Empire existing side by side, as Piganol and other historians have shown. One was an international economy based on gold, and to some extent silver, and extending from one end of the Empire to the other. Its membership in the Atlantic provinces of Rome was generally confined to wealthy officials, landowners, churchmen and some merchants, largely Syrian and Eastern, and it consisted largely of a trade in luxury products such as spices, wines, and fine silks. These products passed

---

[56] For an example, see *Code Theod.*, VII, 17, 2.

[57] F. Lot, *Les Invasions germaniques* (Paris 1935), pp. 40-49. Fuller accounts are found in H. Parker "The Legions of Diocletian and Constantine," in *Jour. of Roman Studies*, XXIII (1933), 175-89, and H. Nesselhauf, *Die spätrömische Verwaltung der gallisch-germanischen Landen*, in *Abd. der Preuss. Akad. der Wissenschaften. Phil-Hist. Klasse* (Berlin 1938), pp. 320-81.

through the Mediterranean and reached the villas of Western Gaul, the Rhone and Moselle valleys and even Frisia and England.[58]

The other economy was essentially local and affected the mass of the population rather than the few. It was based upon grain and other foodstuffs paid to the Imperial bureaucracy as taxes, and upon certain manufactured articles turned out in the factories, such as arms, clothing and equipment of various sorts to meet the needs of the army and the bureaucracy. It was based upon *corvées* exacted from the population to maintain roads and Imperial post systems and to transport goods and products in kind to the points where they were to be consumed. Though it had its roots in certain aspects of the governmental system found in the Early Empire, it resembled much more that which had developed in Pharonic and Ptolemaic Egypt than that of the time of Augustus.[59]

Such an economy, by its very nature, had to be local in character in Atlantic and Northern regions because goods and foodstuffs could not in these regions be easily transported long distances, as in the Mediterranean, to meet the needs of the troops and others near the frontiers. Thus there gradually developed under the impetus of defense needs and state regimentation a series of five rather distinct economic regions along Rome's borders. The first was along the lower Danube. The second consisted of Noricum, Rhaetia and Pannonia along the upper Danube. The third was to be found in the Rhinelands and Northeastern Gaul. Britain made up the fourth.

[58] F. Lot, *La Gaule*, pp. 384-96. R. Koebner, *op.cit.*, pp. 25-27. M. Bloch, "Les Invasions: deux structures économiques," in *Ann. d'hist. sociale*, I (1945), 34-36. R. S. Lopez, "L'Evolution de la politique commerciale au moyen âge," in *Annales*, IV (1949), 390-92. See mention, for instance, of abundant gold supplies in *Code Theod.*, VII, 13, 7-21; IX, 21, 8; XII, 13, 1-5. In some regions, like Galicia, where gold was rare in the Early Empire, one finds it abundant by the 4th century. I. A. Arias, "Materiales numismáticos para el studio de los Desplazamientos y viajes de los Españoles en España romana," in *Cuadernos de Historia de España*, XVIII (Buenos Aires 1952), 22-47. F. Bouza-Brey, "La Numismatica en Galicia," in *Faro de Vigo*, II (1953), 6-8. On the other hand, gold was rare in Britain, where the prosperous villas used silver money. C. H. V. Sutherland, *Coinage and Currency in Roman Britain* (London 1937), pp. 50-183. A. Evans, "Notes on the Coinage and Silver Currency in Roman Britain," in *Numismatic Chronicle*, 4th ser., XV (1915), 433-519. For a discussion of the international luxury trade of the Late Empire, see A. Piganol, *L'Empire chrétien* (Paris 1947), pp. 275-303.

[59] F. W. Walbank, *op.cit.*, pp. 59-78. F. Lot, *La Gaule*, pp. 380-90. For examples of state factories, see *Code Theod.*, I, 32, 1; IV, 6, 3; X, 20, 2-9; X, 22, 3, and *Notitia Dignitatum Occid.*, II, 62; VIII; IX, 36; X. For *annona* (taxes in kind), *Code Theod.*, XI, 1, 4-21. In the Mediterranean and Orient and along the Danube frontier, money taxes were, however, more normal. *Code Theod.*, VII, 4, 11; VII, 4, 30; VII, 4, 37; XI, 1, 19; XI, 1, 32. For post system and *corvées*, *ibid.*, VIII, 5-6; XI, 16, 15.

And the fifth, somewhat different from the rest, consisted of Western Gaul and parts of Northwestern Spain.

Of these five regions, we have extensive knowledge only about the Rhineland-Eastern Gallic one. And what stands out is the relatively large amount of industry to be found there, though most of it was directed in the interests of the Imperial government. A number of state factories, or *gynecées,* were maintained in various centers. Reims, Tournai, Trier and Metz manufactured cloth,[60] while arms were produced in the state factories at Autun, Soissons, Strasbourg, Amiens, Reims and Trier.[61] As far south as Vienne and Arles, others furnished linen and fine purple garments for the Imperial court on the Moselle.[62] The mines of Central Gaul, the Meuse and the Moselle produced the metal used in these factories,[63] and regimented *collegia* of *nautae* were responsible for delivering foodstuffs produced locally and paid as taxes, as well as the products of these *gynecées,* to points designated by the state.[64]

In centers where state factories existed, and elsewhere as well, other industries were carried on. Most important probably was the glassware made in Cologne, in the Argonne and in parts of Belgium.[65] But of some importance, too, was the manufacture of fine enameled jewelry and of brass and bronze, and in the Argonne[66] and about Trier the *terra sigillata,* or Samian ware. This latter industry survived well into the fifth century in these regions.[67]

Much the same type of industrialism was to be found across the Channel in Roman Britain by the fourth century. At Winchester, Caistor-by-Norwich and Caerwent state cloth factories like those

[60] A. Grenier, "La Gaule," *loc.cit.,* pp. 623-42. F. Lot, *La Gaule,* pp. 397-412.

[61] *Notitia Dignitatum Occid.,* IX, 36. R. Doehaerd, *op.cit.,* p. 12. F. Vercauteren, "Etude sur les civitates de la Belgique Secunde," in *Acad. Roy. de Belgique, Classe des Lettres,* 2nd ser., XXXIII (1934), 440-44.

[62] *Notitia Dignitatum Occid.,* II, 62. A. Grenier, *op.cit.,* pp. 586-87.

[63] *Ibid.,* pp. 588-89. O. Davies, *Roman Mines in Europe,* pp. 78-83. F. W. Walbank, *op.cit.,* pp. 70-73.

[64] L. Bonnard, *La Navigation intérieure de la Gaule,* pp. 161-213. See also *Code Theod.,* VIII, 5, 31; XI, 16, 15.

[65] J. Breuer, *La Belgique romaine,* pp. 111-12. Morn-Jean, *La Verrerie en Gaule sous l'Empire romain* (Paris 1913), pp. 13-25. This glass contains only potassium, which was locally available, and no imported Mediterranean natron. G. Faidler-Feytmans, "Les Verreries des époques romanes et merovingiennes au Musée de Mariemont," in *Revue belge d'arch. et d'histoire de l'art,* X (1940), 13-21.

[66] F. Henry, "Les Emailleures d'Occident," in *Préhistoire,* III (1933), 70-142. A. Grenier, *La Gaule,* pp. 623-42.

[67] J. Breuer, *La Belgique romaine,* pp. 111-12. E. Janssens, *Histoire ancienne de la Mer du Nord,* pp. 58-59. P. Boeles, *Friesland,* pp. 160-76. F. W. Walbank, *op.cit.,* pp. 39-40.

in Gaul were located.[68] Iron mines in Kent and in the Forest of Dean continued to be active, probably to supply the needs of the troops stationed nearby in the Saxon Shore forts or along the Welsh border.[69] As in Gaul, we find developing in these years an important earthenware industry. In the case of Britain, this was centered in Caistor, where cheap, locally produced Samian ware replaced imported varieties.[70] Along with the mining of lead and silver in various parts of the island, an increase occurred in locally produced bronze, brass and pewter.[71]

Much the same situation seems to have existed in Rhaetia and Noricum. There, too, according to the Theodosian Code, a state-directed cloth industry flourished and use was made of the iron mines of the region to meet the needs of the frontier troops.[72] If we knew more about the situation along the lower Danube, we would probably find a similar state of affairs there.

What appears to have happened, then, was that there had developed by this period, in large part under state stimulus, a series of economically autonomous regions active in an industrial sense, producing for a local market and to meet local needs. In an agricultural sense, the same thing took place. Vineyards, for instance, had by the fourth century spread into the Moselle valley, where they did not exist earlier, and this region now produced its own wine instead of importing it from the south and west of Gaul.[73] It has been remarked that in Britain in this period there was clearly a shift from imported wine and olive oil to locally produced beer and tallow.[74] Only the upper Danube region still maintained close economic connections with the Mediterranean regions to the south,

[68] R. G. Collingwood, "Roman Britain," in *ESAR*, III, 104-7. See also *Notitia Dignitatum Occid.*, XI, 60.

[69] O. Davies, *Roman Mines in Europe*, pp. 141-64. R. G. Collingwood, "Roman Britain," *loc.cit.*, pp. 34-46. I. D. Margary, *Roman Ways in the Weald*, pp. 51-260.

[70] R. G. Collingwood and J. R. Myers, *Roman Britain and the English Settlements* (Oxford 1936), pp. 235-39.

[71] M. P. Charlesworth, *The Lost Province*, pp. 50-59. H. Van Werweke, "Note sur le commerce du plomb au moyen âge," in *Mélanges Pirenne*, II (Bruxelles 1926), 655-57. J. W. Gough, *The Mines in the Mendips*, pp. 6-45.

[72] The Imperial government maintained state factories at Sirminum, Aqunicum, Lorch, Salona and Carnutum. F. W. Walbank, "Trade and Industry in the Later Roman Empire in the West," *loc.cit.*, pp. 72, 79. On mining in Illyricum, see *Code Theod.*, X, 19, 8. There seems to have been less isolation from the Mediterranean and more of a money economy along the Danube frontier in the late 4th century than elsewhere in the West. For example of this, see *Code Theod.*, VII, 6, 4.

[73] Ausonius, *Mosella*, XXI, ed. White, I, 226. A. Grenier, "La Gaule," *loc.cit.*, p. 583.

[74] Collingwood and Myers, *op.cit.*, pp. 227-30.

and even there it would be well not to exaggerate such commerce save in the case of luxury products.

The amount of commerce between these three self-contained economic regions—Britain, Northeast Gaul and the upper Danube— by the fourth century seems to have been relatively slight. Some glass produced in Northern Gaul and the Rhinelands found its way to Britain,[75] and we know that at the time of Julian grain from this island was sent across the Channel to feed his armies on the Rhine.[76] The glassware of Cologne also found its way to the upper Danube region.[77] But such traffic was of a minor nature.

It is interesting to find that, save in some luxury items, these regions were equally separate, economically speaking, from the trade world of the Mediterranean.[78] Examination of objects found in archeological sites in Belgium, Frisia and elsewhere in Northeastern Gaul makes this clear.[79] Few are of Mediterranean origin. Even the Rhineland glass of this period, unlike later Merovingian glass, is revealed by chemical analysis to contain no Mediterranean ingredients.[80] British woolens might have some reputation in the heart of the Empire in Diocletian's day[81] but little else from the north seems to have reached there.

Still one more economic region within the Empire facing the Atlantic needs to be considered. That is the region centering about Bordeaux and consisting of Western Gaul and the northern coast of Spain. Our information about this region during these years is scant

[75] R. G. Collingwood, "Roman Britain," in *ESAR*, III, 110-16.

[76] *Ammianus Marcellinus*, XVIII, 2.

[77] L. Musset, *Les Peuples scandinaves*, pp. 11-13. O. Brogan, "Trade with the Free Germans," in *Journal of Roman Studies*, XXVI (1936), 207.

[78] One reason for this lies in measures taken by the Late Imperial government which discouraged trade within the Empire. *Code Theod.*, VII, 16, 1-2. In the 5th century, Eastern merchants were allowed to return. *Nov. Valentinian*, V, 1-2.

[79] See P. Boeles, "De terpencultuur tot omstreeks 400," in *Algemene Geschiedenis der Nederlanden* I (1949), 106-31, and *Friesland*, pp. 160-77, on the rarity of objects of Mediterranean origin—even from Southern France—in Frisian sites of a date later than 260 A.D. See F. Vercauteren, *op.cit.*, pp. 440-44, on the same situation in Belgium and Northeastern Gaul. The cloth of Arras and other parts of Belgium and Flanders mentioned in the late 3rd-century Edict of Diocletian represents an exception, but one found only during the early years of the Late Empire. E. Carus-Wilson, "The Woolen Industry," in *Cambridge Economic History of Europe* (Cambridge 1952), II, 361-62.

[80] E. Salin, *Le Haut Moyen-Age en Lorraine* (Paris 1939), pp. 197-213.

[81] *Edict Diocletian*, XIX, 36. E. Carus-Wilson, *op.cit.*, pp. 362-63. Authorities agree that in the 4th century Britain was particularly isolated from the heart of the Empire. On the other hand, connections between the Danubian frontier regions and Italy and the Eastern Empire remained relatively close. See note 72.

in an archeological sense, but enough is known to show that it underwent less of a break with the past of the Early Empire than the other
regions we have examined.[82] Though its cities suffered cruelly in the
third century, in the fourth they still had some importance. Bordeaux, Saintes, Poitiers and Orléans caused Ammianus Marcellinus
to comment on their role as urban centers as late as 390.[83] Bordeaux
in particular was still rich enough in this century to support schools of
rhetoric whose shining light was the poet Ausonius.[84] The close
connection maintained with Northern Spain and particularly Galicia in
this period is revealed by the spread of Priscillianism in these
regions.[85] Links were maintained still with the Mediterranean via the
Garonne and perhaps the Loire-Rhone route as well, while an active
commerce along the coasts extended to Gibraltar and to distant
Britain and Ireland. Here there lived a prosperous senatorial aristocracy whose wine from vast estates had a certain Northern market.
Perhaps even metalware was produced for more than local needs.
Far enough removed from the frontiers to escape most of the
Imperial exactions and regimentation required to support the border
armies, this region was in a relatively privileged position. But here,
too, in these years localism and separation from the Mediterranean
were the general rule.[86]

The characteristic economic unit of all these northern regions
of the Empire, however, was not a center where state factories
turned out the arms and equipment needed by Rome's frontier
troops, or surviving commercial towns such as London, Cologne,
Bordeaux or Poitiers, but rather the villas. Always strong in these
regions, even in the earlier prosperity of the Empire, by the fourth

---

[82] There has been insufficient appreciation of the *uniqueness* of these sections of
the Western Empire in respect to their freedom from excessive state regimentation.
Jullian generalized from their brilliant villa life (and that of the Moselle region)
to produce a picture, often false, of the entire Roman Gallic West. On their lack of
state cloth and arms factories, see F. W. Walbank, *op.cit.*, p. 71. Did this also apply
to state *corvées* to transport foodstuffs and thus account for the lack of mention of
regimented *nautae* on the Garonne, noted by Renouard? Y. Renouard, "Voies de
communication entre Mediterranée et Atlantique," in *Mélanges Louis Halphen*
(Paris 1951), pp. 589-92. This seems probable. Even sea defenses along the Atlantic
here seem to have been built later than those Saxon Shore forts of the North Sea
and English Channel and are not mentioned until the time of the *Notitia Dignitatum*.
See *Notitia Dignitatum Occid.*, XXXVII.

[83] *Ammianus Marcellinus*, XV, 11.

[84] P. Courtreault, *Bordeaux à travers les siècles*, pp. 8-12.

[85] Jerome, *Epistolae*, CXXIII, 4; CXX, 1. Prosper of Aquitaine, *Chron. ad anno 385*,
in *Patrologia Latina*, ed. Migne, LI, cols. 580-81. C. Barbut, *Priscillian et le Priscillianism* (Paris 1909), pp. 86-87, 185-96.

[86] C. Jullian, *Histoire de la Gaule*, VIII, 210-14.

century villas became the economic unit, par excellence. In fact, this villa system was the direct result of the very economic localism which has been described in preceding pages. But it should also be noted that this was due to more than lack of a money economy and trade connection with the Mediterranean. It was also the direct result of certain policies of the Imperial government itself.

State regimentation of transport, state direction of industry, state policies which bound artisan guilds, merchants and members of the town aristocracies to their tasks and the heavy burden of Late Imperial taxation had the effect of destroying what vitality remained in most urban centers. It also had the effect of driving much of the commerce and industry into the countryside where, protected by the powerful senatorial aristocracy, they could be carried on more freely. In the Late Empire, then, much economic life escaped to the villas of the countryside, just as in the Late Middle Ages the cloth industry escaped from guild regulation to an agrarian world where it could be operated under a "domestic system."[87] This fact explains the paradox of ruined towns and thriving villas so characteristic of Western Gaul, the Moselle valley and Britain in this period.[88] It explains why villas like Chedworth in the Midlands existed as rural factories producing such goods as woolen cloth and tiles.[89] It explains the prosperity of the British countryside in these years.[90] It explains the villa trade of the Garonne region which called forth a class of prosperous colporteurs, who carried their wares for sale some distance away from the source of production. It helps to give us a clue to the wealth of such families as the Aviti and Apollinares in this part of Gaul.[91]

Those historians who have seen in the villa system of the Late Empire in these regions a domanial economy in the later, closed, medieval sense of the word are probably mistaken. The villa system

[87] Concerning privileges given goods produced on large villa estates, see *Code Theod.*, II, 33, 1; IV, 13, 1-3; XIII, 1, 3; XIII, 1, 12.

[88] R. Koebner, "The Colonization of Europe," *loc.cit.*, pp. 9-10. R. G. Collingwood, "Roman Britain," *loc.cit.*, pp. 75-87. In Belgium, however, except in the Meuse valley, villa life declined drastically in this century. Of 400 early Roman villas in Belgium, only 22 were still occupied by the first years of the 4th century and only seven at its close. J. Breuer, *La Belgique romaine*, pp. 109-10.

[89] R. G. Collingwood, *op.cit.*, pp. 78-95, and F. W. Walbank, *op.cit.*, pp. 68-69, describe the industrialized British villas of Chedworth, Darenth and Titsey.

[90] F. Haverfield, *The Romanization of Britain*, p. 77.

[91] See F. W. Walbank, *op.cit.*, p. 69, on the villa at Chiragan near Toulouse. For the Bordeaux region, see Ausonius, *Epistolae*, XXII, ed. White, II, 72-80, and C. Jullian, *op.cit.*, VIII, 213-14.

instead appears to have been much more like the plantation system of Colonial Virginia, nineteenth-century Malaya or the West Indies. For those who worked the land as *coloni* or labored in villa workshops, it was a closed agrarian system, but for the owners, who lived in comfort, it provided the wherewithal to enjoy the luxuries the Empire provided and to send the products of their rural fields and workshops over wide distances. Privileged economically as a result of Imperial enactment and further protected from official interference or taxation by their own private power, the villa owners of Gaul, Britain and elsewhere in the West played an economic role that extended far beyond the boundaries of their estates. Indeed, in the fifth century one Emperor had the wit to perceive this role and complained that traders were illegally deserting cities to carry on their commercial transactions in ports and villas which were free from the Empire's taxation.[92]

In short, what appeared in the Atlantic and Central European provinces of the Empire by the fourth century was a series of economic regions, separate from one another and each composed of relatively highly developed industry and self-sufficient agriculture. These regions, which owed their localism in large measure to the defensive and governmental system established by the Late Roman Emperors, were not essentially part of the Mediterranean world which served Rome as her basis of being. And they depended more and more on an agrarian, villa-type, economic system to supply not only needed foodstuffs but even the industrial products they consumed.

To consider, however, that such economic developments were solely the result of Rome's defense needs near her northern borders or her governmental policies would be untrue. For since the days of Augustus other forces had been at work, effecting a transformation of the economies of Rome's northern provinces facing the Atlantic and Central Europe. It seems probable that even without the pressures of defense and governmental regimentation and intervention something akin to the fourth-century economic situation would have arisen anyway, though perhaps not so speedily. A growing industrialism and separate economic systems were inevitable in Gaul, Britain, the Rhinelands and along the upper Danube as a result of the very success of Rome's civilizing mission, the presence of natural

[92] *Nov. Valentinian,* XXIV.

resources in these portions of Europe and the effect of a geography that led commerce towards the Northern Seas instead of towards the Mediterranean.

A study of industrial and economic developments in the Latin West makes this clear. Let us consider the cloth, pottery and glass industries. In the first century the centers for the manufacture of these three products were in Italy, whence they were exported to lands to the north, even beyond Rome's borders. By the fourth century a local glass industry had sprung up, eliminating Italian imports, in Belgium and the Rhinelands. In the second century a popular and cheap Samian ware was manufactured in Southern France, whence it reached Britain, Northern Gaul and the Rhinelands. By the time of Constantine this industry had disappeared in Provence and instead had taken root farther north in the Argonne and Moselle valleys and in Eastern Britain. The same pattern was repeated in the bronze and brass industries. As for cloth, we find in the Late Empire that Belgium and faraway Britain were centers for fine woolens, where earlier they had contributed little to this industry. Iron production and metal-working followed the same line of development, becoming particularly important to the economies of Britain, the Rhinelands and the Alps. Nor should we ignore the spread of the vine from Southern Gaul north into the Moselle valley in this same period.[93]

Though the third century witnessed a setback to Roman civilization in the Western provinces, there can be little doubt that by the fourth the advance north had been resumed and that it was not mere localism triumphant that produced the industrial and agrarian developments we have noted. They were the effect of an advancing civilization. So, too, in our modern world we see, despite wars and disorders, industries steadily advancing in South America, Africa, Asia and elsewhere—transforming agrarian regions into more self-sufficient economic units which seem to compete successfully with older established industrial nexuses. It was this process, hastened by Rome's official policies, which was at work in the Roman West and helps to account for the situation that existed in the fourth century.

Let us now consider the effect upon commerce in Northern

---

[93] Perhaps the best general account of this spread of industrialism in the Western portions of the Empire is to be found in F. W. Walbank, *op.cit.*, pp. 35-43. On the glass industry and its movement north in Gaul, see Morin-Jean, *La Verrerie en Gaule sous l'Empire romain*, pp. 111-286. Boeles sketches the same process in the manufacture of earthenware, the *terra sigillata*. P. Boeles, *Friesland*, pp. 145-77.

Europe from Spain to Finland of the development of these economic regions in Rome's northern and Atlantic provinces, which were essentially separate from the Mediterranean. Here one must distinguish between the commerce of the Western Atlantic among Gaul, Spain, Britain, Ireland and beyond and that of Central Europe and the Black Sea which still reached the Baltic and Scandinavia by land over the old amber routes.

We might first examine the maritime commerce of the Western Atlantic. By the Late Empire changes had taken place in the nature of this commerce, in those who were its principal intermediaries and in the routes which they followed. Perhaps the most important change was the appearance of numbers of British sailors and merchants as participants in this maritime trade. At the time of Strabo Atlantic shipping seems to have been largely in the hands of Gallic merchants, particularly the Belgian Menapii and Morini, who were prominent merchants along Atlantic coasts from Bordeaux to London. As early as the third century, however, one begins to find sailors from Britain's east coast appearing at Bordeaux.[94]

One reason for this may lie in a decline in Belgian ports at the time of the Late Empire. Not only is this to be seen in Rome's withdrawal from Frisia and her abandoning of such earlier trade centers as Beetgum, Domburg, Fectio and Nijmegen, but farther down the coast toward Boulogne centers like Oudenarde were by this time without importance.[95] Some have felt that the abandoning of these ports was the direct result of a sea invasion of maritime Flanders and Frisia.[96] Others have seen in their decadence the result of raids by aggressive Saxon pirates. But whatever the cause, it is worth noting that all this portion of the Netherlands, in sharp contrast to the Moselle valley near Trier, decayed under Late Roman rule. Not only its ports, but even its villas disappeared. Of the 400 villa sites known to have existed at the time of the Early

[94] P. Courtreault, in *Revue des etats anciens*, X (1922), 240.

[95] V. Guichez, "Topographie des voies romaines de la Gaule belgique," in *Ann. de l'Acad. Roy. de Belgique*, XXXVIII (1882), 181-93. See also E. Janssens, *Histoire ancienne de la Mer du Nord*, pp. 61-64.

[96] Blanchard believes that Flanders, like Holland, was invaded and inundated by the sea in the Late Empire and that this accounts for its decadence. R. Blanchard, *La Flandre* (Lille 1906), pp. 143-46. This seems very questionable or at least an overworked theory. The sand which covers Roman settlement sites on the *terpens* and islets along the Flemish coast was more probably the result of wind-dune action than maritime inundation. More study of this problem, however, is needed before any definitive answer can be given.

Empire, only 22 were still occupied at the beginning of the fourth century and only seven by the end. And these latter were along the Chausée de Bavai and thus faced the Rhine rather than the Channel and the North Sea.[97]

It seems obvious that the disappearance of Menapian and Morini merchants from Atlantic trade after the time of Carausius was closely related to the decadence that affected their homeland as Roman civilization retreated from Frisia to the south. Not all trade from these regions disappeared, as we know from the fact that Rhineland glass still arrived in England in the fourth century and some *terra sigillata* reached Frisia from the same region after 300 A.D. But such commerce was slight in comparison with what had been true of the Early Empire.[98] No doubt merchants from Eastern Britain, which was untouched by those disasters of the third century which so affected the Netherlands, owed their new maritime prominence in some part to the disappearance of merchant competition across the North Sea. Now they themselves sailed their ships to get merchandise which in earlier centuries Gallic merchants had brought to their ports.[99]

Even more interesting is the new commercial maritime impulse to be found in Western Britain during these years. Here the development of Cornwall in the Late Empire is particularly significant. The Early Empire saw Cornwall unimportant from both an industrial and a commercial point of view. Its tin mines lay unworked and the Romans, with their nearest garrison at Exeter, did not even bother to occupy the peninsula. In the third century, however, one notices a change. The tin workings were reopened and, according to Avienus, an active, native British, maritime commerce stirred along Cornish coasts.[100] Was this because of the exhaustion of Asturian Spanish tin deposits, as is sometimes claimed? Or was it

[97] J. Breuer, *op.cit.*, pp. 109-10.

[98] P. Boeles, *Friesland*, pp. 145-73. The same lack of Late Roman wares is noticeable in sites in Jutland, which was earlier an important terminus of a maritime North Sea trade route. See *Guides to the National Museum, Copenhagen: Antiquity*, p. 95.

[99] This may account for hoards of Roman coins which date from this period found along the east coast of Scotland. T. C. Lethbridge, *Herdsmen and Hermits* (Cambridge 1950), pp. 59-64. Also for finds of Rhenish glass and pottery in the same regions, Collingwood and Myers, *Roman Britain and the English Settlements*, pp. 244-46.

[100] M. P. Charlesworth, *The Lost Province*, pp. 50-54. F. Haverfield, "Cornish Tin," in *Mélanges Boissier* (Paris 1903), pp. 251-53. See especially H. O. Hencken, "An Excavation of H. M. Office of Works at Chyrsauster, Cornwall 1931," in *Archeologia*, LXXXIII (1933), 238-83.

because unsettled conditions in the West made Galician tin difficult to obtain? One cannot say.

There can be little doubt, however, that this new British maritime impulse extended far beyond Cornwall. Suddenly we hear of British mariners on the coasts of Northern Spain. Coruña in Galicia was in the fourth century known as Portus Britanniae and a special lighthouse seems to have been built there for British seamen sailing to this distant shore.[101] It seems probable that this new native British activity upon the sea was a reflection of what Haverfield has rightly called the Celtic revival in Britain under the Late Empire—a revival visible in Celtic religious ideas and strikingly apparent in art such as that found at Bath and in the Mildenhall treasure and in Roman British villas.

Nor was this Celtic revival confined to British coasts alone. It was also reflected in and connected with the rise of Irish and Pictish maritime strength in these years. Ireland, for instance, in the fourth century showed clear signs of a stimulus from Roman sources that was the result of an increasingly close connection with the Empire—probably mainly with nearby Britain. A surprisingly large number of bronze and other objects of Late Roman provincial origin have been found in Ireland dating from these years—in contrast to the relative scarcity of those from the period of the Early Empire.[102] Hoards of Late Imperial coins have been discovered in both Galway and central Ireland.[103] This seems to imply that commercial activity reached this remote island.

Similar objects and hoards of Roman coins have also been discovered along the west coast and islands of Scotland, the land of the Picts—particularly at Uist and Islay in the Hebrides and near Loch Ness on the mainland.[104] That a western maritime route extended on beyond Scotland as far as the Norse coast seems probable from the fact that similar Roman objects and coins have been discovered in sites along the rugged Norwegian fjords. One of the most interesting finds there, incidentally, is a silver coin of Constantius Chlorus struck in Aquitaine, thus perhaps linking West Norway with Western Gaul

[101] Orosius, *Hist.*, I, 2, 72.

[102] S. P. O'Riordan, "Roman Material in Ireland," in *Proceedings of the Royal Irish Academy*, LI (1947), 34-82. This article reverses the previous views of Haverfield in "Ancient Rome and Ireland" in *Eng. Hist. Review*, CIX (1912), 1-12.

[103] T. C. Lethbridge, *op.cit.*, pp. 53-56, mentions three hoards of Roman coins in Ireland, two in Galway and one in the center of the island.

[104] On similar hoards in the Orkneys which may have arrived there via *either* the west or the east coast of Scotland, see T. C. Lethbridge, *op.cit.*, pp. 141-63.

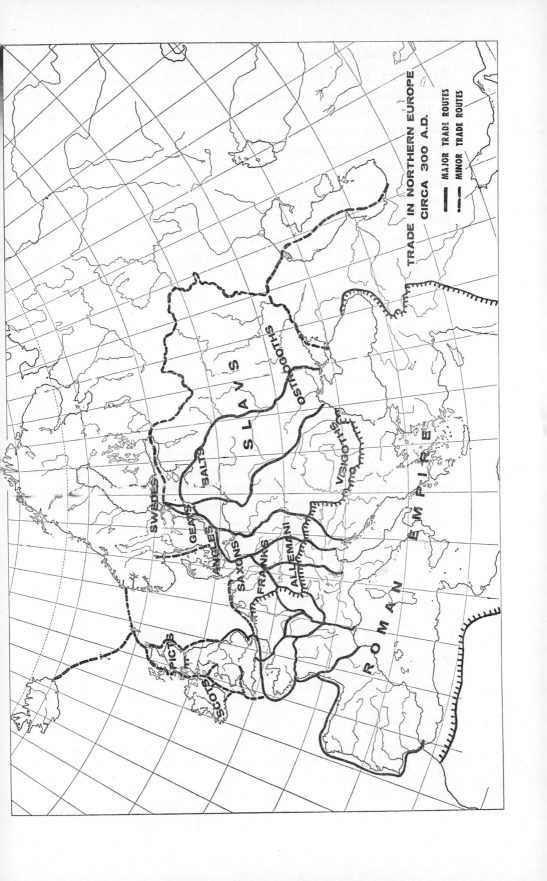

TRADE IN NORTHERN EUROPE
CIRCA 300 A.D.

MAJOR TRADE ROUTES
MINOR TRADE ROUTES

SLAVS

BALTS

SWEDES

GEATS

ANGLES

SAXONS

FRANKS

ALLEMANI

OSTROGOTHS

VISIGOTHS

PICTS

SCOTS

R O M A N   E M P I R E

during the fourth century of the Empire.[105] Even Iceland has yielded Roman coins[106] of this period.

That this Atlantic area, both those regions inside and those outside the Empire, possessed an over-all economic unity can be seen in the coinage in use there during this period. Everywhere from Norway and Iceland to Spain the coin hoards dating from this time which have been uncovered are of silver, and silver only.[107] The Empire in general and the Mediterranean region in particular had, during these years, a bi-metallic system, though gold was most commonly used in international commerce. Why, then, should it be so rare in the Atlantic region? Perhaps one reason lies in the fact that Britain was a great silver producer and thus trade in British hands was carried on in this medium. It is interesting in this connection to note that the silver mines of Melle in Western Gaul, unexploited earlier, were in the fourth century put into operation.[108] But perhaps a better explanation of this silver coinage lies in the fact that the trade transported over Atlantic routes was essentially a trade in non-luxury items carried by small-scale merchants. For such commerce, silver rather than gold was the more useful monetary standard. But whatever the explanation, there can be little doubt that the development of this silver coinage area, so similar to that which appeared in these same regions in Late Merovingian and Carolingian times, marks the establishment of an Atlantic commerce and economic life essentially separate from that of the Mediterranean.

A second important series of commercial routes stretched from the Rhineland-Eastern Gallic regions and the upper and lower Danube overland through Germany and Central Europe to the Baltic and Scandinavia. The old Oder and Vistula amber routes seem to have been those most used for this traffic.[109] And here again,

[105] H. Holst, "Mynter i Norske Funn," in *Nord. Numis. Arsskrift* (1943), pp. 56-101.

[106] These coins, three in number, come from three sites on the southeastern coast of Iceland. Minted by Aurelian, Probus and Diocletian, they probably reached the island in the first years of the 4th century. K. Eldjárn, "Fund of Romerske Mønter pa Island," in *Nord. Numis. Arsskrift* (1949), pp. 1-8.

[107] The exceptions are represented by four rare *solidi* found in Norwegian sites of this period and minted by Constantine, Contantius II, Valentinian and Gratian. They probably reached Norway, however, via Central European routes rather than Atlantic ones. H. Holst, in *Numismatica Fasc.*, VII (Oslo 1928), 83-89.

[108] O. Davies, *Roman Mines in Europe*, pp. 78-84. A. Piganol, "La Problème de l'or au IVe siècle," in *Ann. d'hist. sociale*, I (1945), 45-53.

[109] O. Brogan, "Trade with the Free Germans," *loc.cit.*, pp. 216-24. See particularly the map on trade routes passing through Germany in the Late Empire on p. 217.

as in the case of Atlantic trade, we note certain changes appearing by the fourth century. Up to the third, the sea route which passed by way of Frisia to the mouth of the Elbe or reached Zealand by way of the Jutland peninsula carried the most important share of commercial traffic north to the Baltic. Numerous objects of Roman provenience dating from the Early Empire have been found in Jutland and Zealand and elsewhere also. As already noted, however, the abandoning of Frisia by Rome resulted in the decay of the towns along the North Sea which marked this route. We have little evidence that in the fourth century any Roman trade reached Jutland at all, and little evidence of it is found in sites along the Frisian coast either after 300 A.D.[110]

On the other hand, land routes farther east became relatively more important in a commercial sense, and not only Zealand but the more easterly islands of Oland and Gotland show evidence of having been in closer touch with the Roman world to the south. There was, then, a general shift towards the east of commerce between the Roman Empire and the Baltic.[111]

In addition, still another important route led during these years from the grey Baltic to the south. This was an even more eastern one. It went by way of the Niemen and perhaps the Dvina to the Dnieper and the Ostrogothic kingdom on the Black Sea. From this kingdom this trade route reached the Sassanian Persian realm in the Middle East. It was via this route that the excitingly different animal art of Central Asia reached Scandinavia, bringing tales of the glories of Ermanaric the Ostrogoth to the Baltic to serve as the basis of later Norse legends on this subject.[112]

Analysis of the products which formed the basis of these three trading areas is rather difficult. Our information concerning the Atlantic region is far too scant from a commercial standpoint. We know wine formed the principal export from Western Gaul to Britain and beyond. Probably the salt of the Saintogne was still an important export also. So was olive oil, which was trans-shipped from Southwestern Gaul and originated either in Southern France or in

---

[110] P. Boeles, *Friesland*, pp. 145-77. *Guides to the National Museum, Copenhagen: Antiquity*, pp. 84-97.

[111] L. Musset, *Les Peuples scandinaves*, pp. 11-13. H. Shetelig, *La Préhistoire de la Norvège*, pp. 165-66.

[112] H. Shetelig and H. Falk, *Scandinavian Archeology*, pp. 200-8. J. Musset, *Histoire des pays baltiques* (Paris 1934), pp. 21-22. T. D. Kendrick, *History of the Vikings* (London 1930), pp. 60-61. M. Rostovtzeff, *Iranians and Greeks in South Russia*, pp. 181-209.

Spain.[113] The numerous objects of bronze which have been found in Ireland were either from Gaul or from Britain, most probably the latter.[114] And it seems possible that the iron industry of the Loire valley also furnished a surplus which was exported.[115] From the Rhinelands and Northern Gaul came glassware which reached Britain and lands to the north.[116]

British exports seem to have consisted principally of metals, the tin of Cornwall, the copper of Anglesey, the lead and silver of the Mendips and Flintshire.[117] We also know that British cloth was exported as far south as the Mediterranean,[118] while at times its wheat reached Continental consumers.[119] Spain produced valuable metals also, copper from Huelva and tin, lead, silver and gold from Asturias. Other articles of Spanish export included olive oil and fish.[120] Our knowledge derived from historical sources and archeology is, however, too slight to permit us to be sure that such exports were sent, as earlier, to Bordeaux. Perhaps they formed the return cargoes of those British ships which called at Coruña. Of Irish exports we know little, save that in the early fifth century hunting dogs were shipped from the island to Gaul.[121] It seems probable, however, that hides, slaves and even gold were included in cargoes originating there. The primitive Hebrides, Scotland, Iceland and Norway seem to have sent furs, wild beasts and feathers from sea birds south to Roman markets.[122] All in all, a wide variety of products followed Atlantic routes in this century.

Trade with the free Germans across the Rhine and Danube as far north as Scandinavia was also important in this period, as it had been earlier. Of prime importance were weapons, which formed a major item of export from the Empire, judging from their discovery in large numbers at such a site as Nydam. Other objects of metal, principally of bronze, were also sent north in commerce,

---

[113] Collingwood and Myers, *Roman Britain and the English Settlements*, pp. 244-46.

[114] On the abundant bronze objects of Roman manufacture found in Irish sites, see S. P. O'Riordan, "Roman Material in Ireland," *loc.cit.*, pp. 34-82.

[115] O. Davies, *Roman Mines in Europe*, pp. 78-80.

[116] Collingwood and Myers, *op.cit.*, pp. 245-46. O. Brogan, "Trade with the Free Germans," *loc.cit.*, pp. 216-18.

[117] R. G. Collingwood, "Roman Britain," in *ESAR*, III, 110-14.

[118] Diocletian, *Edict of Prices*, XIX, 36.

[119] O. Davies, *op.cit.*, pp. 97-101. F. W. Walbank, *op.cit.*, pp. 44-46.

[120] *Ibid.*, pp. 46-47, 80-81. Ausonius, *Epistolae*, VI, XXI, ed. White, II, 16-18, 68.

[121] J. B. Bury, *St. Patrick* (London 1908), pp. 31-33.

[122] Collingwood and Myers, *op.cit.*, pp. 245-46.

along with glass and pottery from the Rhinelands which reached all of Germany and the Baltic as well. To these articles of export one should add wine, foodstuffs and probably cloth.[123]

One significant point, however, should be emphasized. In the fourth century, unlike the time of the Early Empire, the source of manufactured articles sent to the Germans was no longer the workshops of the Mediterranean. Instead, those of the Rhinelands, of Gaul, of Noricum and Rhaetia provided the industrial goods sent across Roman borders. Furthermore, while hoards of money dating from this period which have been discovered in Germany and Scandinavia make it clear that silver was the principal monetary unit in German-Roman trade, sufficient gold has been found to indicate that silver was not used exclusively. Unlike the commerce in the Atlantic with Scotland and Ireland, where silver alone was in use, that of Central Europe was sometimes carried on in the more precious gold, though its export may have been more in the form of payments to barbarian soldiers and allies than as a result of commerce.[124]

Imports into the Empire from these regions are harder to catalogue. Amber from the Baltic certainly was one of the major ones. So, too, were furs, wild beasts and slaves. In general, however, examination of both archeological sites and hoards of money in Scandinavia seem to show that, in contrast to the situation in the Atlantic area, the commerce between the Empire and the free Germans was smaller in volume in the Late Empire than it had been at the time of Augustus and his immediate successors and that it steadily diminished as the fourth century progressed.[125]

This trade diminution with the Roman world may account for the increasing importance of the more eastern routes via Niemen and Dvina with the Ostrogothic kingdom of South Russia and

[123] M. Bloch, "Les Invasions: deux structures économiques," in *Ann. d'hist. sociale*, 1 (1945), 43-45.

[124] The following gold coins minted in this period have been found in archeological sites north of the Empire's borders. From Frisia—2 Valens (from Antioch and Constantinople mints), 2 Gratian (Milan and Trier mints) and one Jovinus (Trier mint). P. Boeles, *Friesland*, pp. 502-4. From Germany—one Valentinian (Antioch mint). J. Werner, *Münzdatierte austrasiche Grabfunde* (Berlin 1935), pp. 107-9. From Sweden—2 Constantine, one Valentinian, one Gratian. O. R. Janse, *Le Travail de l'or en Suède*, pp. 12-16. From Norway—one Constantine, one Constantius II, one Valentinian, one Gratian. H. Holst, *Numismatica Fasc.*, VII (Oslo 1929), 83-89. They are found along with silver coins and are predominantly from Italian and Eastern Imperial mints.

[125] O. Brogan, "Trade with the Free Germans," *loc.cit.*, p. 207.

through it with Central Asia, as shown in Russian archeological finds. Along this route furs, honey and slaves were probably in this period, as later, the principal objects of commerce. And it is interesting to note that in Russia, according to Grekov, few hoards of Roman money have been found dating from later than the third century, which seems to show that the commercial connection with Sassanian Persia and Central Asia, rather than that with the Empire via the Crimea and Black Sea, was the important one in the fourth century[126]—a fact that accounts for the artistic impulses which reached Scandinavia from Asian sources in these years.

To sum up, then, examination of trade routes—and of products exchanged beyond Roman frontiers—makes clear a number of things. It shows not only that Roman provinces facing the Atlantic and along the Rhine and Danube in general were economically separate from the Mediterranean world in the fourth century, but that the same was true of regions beyond Rome's borders. Ireland, Scotland and even distant Iceland and Norway were part of an Atlantic trade region linked to Roman Britain, Western Gaul and Northern Spain, while Germany and the Baltic were connected with the Rhinelands and Rome's provinces north of Italy and along the Danube. And a third commercial connection linked the Eastern Baltic with Russia and Central Asia. Already in the fourth century new economic bonds were beginning to draw both Roman and non-Roman lands facing the Northern seas away from their earlier economic connections with the Mediterranean, upon which the Roman world was based. Still formative, still tentative, an Atlantic-North European destiny was being forged.

We have already noted how on land and sea the rulers of the Late Empire met the danger of Irish, Picts, Saxons and Germans by the establishment of a massive defense system along their land and sea frontiers to hold their northern provinces and protect their vital Mediterranean heartland. We have seen how they regimented industry, agriculture and their border populations for this purpose in Britain, Gaul and elsewhere in the West. How did they meet the even more subtle and dangerous economic forces that linked Britain to Scotland and Ireland, or their provinces along the Rhine and Danube to Central Europe and the Baltic? How did they combat economic forces which were inexorably destroying their Empire?

---

[126] B. Grekov, *La Culture de la Russie de Kiev*, pp. 17-18. See also S. Bolin, *Fynden av romerska mynt i det fria Germanien.*

Here lies an interesting mine of information still hardly touched by historians.

At the time of the Early Empire, Rome seems to have welcomed trade across her frontiers. Such commerce does not appear to have been limited except by the ability of barbarian peoples to produce such goods as Rome desired. From an economic and cultural standpoint, much of German Europe was a mere hinterland of the Roman Empire. By the fourth century, however, Rome had come to adopt a different point of view. This may have begun as early as 297 A.D., when a special treaty was negotiated with Persia under which trade between the Empire and the Sassanian Kingdom was restricted to two special points along their frontiers.[127]

In the first years of the fifth century, according to the *Notitia Dignitatum*, a similar system was in force along the Rhine-Danube regulating trade with the Germans. Barbarian peoples passed through two special portals under the regulation of the Counts of Commerce of Moesia and Illyricum.[128] Still another was to be found in Pannonia under the supervision of the Count of Commerce of that province.[129] There is evidence, however, that this system began at least a century earlier. In 329 mention was made of the fact that the decision of the Roman government to break off trade with the Visigoths caused them to sue for peace.[130] And in 369 we have mention of a trade system similar to that outlined by the *Notitia Dignitatum* in effect, since we learn that a treaty with the Goths in that year provided two places where trade between Roman and Goth could legally be carried on across the frontier.[131] It seems most probable that a similar system of controlled trade was also enforced on the upper Danube and Rhine frontiers, since we learn from a law of 367 A.D. in the Theodosian Code that barbarian envoys and delegates entering Roman territory were required to repair to certain specified post stations to procure transport for their journey into the Empire.[132] This law suggests entry control points. A study of the trade routes from Roman territory into Germany in the fourth century suggests that Cologne and Mainz were

---

[127] R. S. Lopez, "L'Evolution de la politique commerciale au moyen âge," in *Annales*, IV (1949), 390-91. *Ammianus Marcellinus*, XIV, 3; XXIII, 3.
[128] *Notitia Dignitatum Orient.*, XIII, 6-9.
[129] *Notitia Dignitatum Occid.*, XI, 86.
[130] M. Bloch, *op.cit.*, pp. 42-43.
[131] Themistius, *Orat.*, X, 135. *Ammianus Marcellinus*, XXVII, 5, 7.
[132] *Code Theod.*, VII, 1, 9.

probably the trade control points for trans-Rhenish trade with the barbarians—a supposition in part borne out in the case of Cologne by other factors. For Cologne, alone of the Rhineland cities, grew larger in this century, which may have been because of the stimulus of trade across the Rhine.[133]

Examination of historical sources, however, makes it clear that the Romans were not satisfied with channeling their trade across frontiers through certain specified points. They placed other obstacles in the way of foreign commerce. A law of the first years of the fifth century, which probably had earlier precedents, forbade Roman subjects to go beyond the Empire's borders or foreigners to enter Rome's boundaries without passports.[134] That such controls of movement were not unusual can be seen from the fact that in the last years of the fourth century the Emperor Honorius even closed all ports of the Western Empire to merchants from the Eastern portion of it—a prohibition that seems to have lasted more than a decade.[135] Other laws of the fourth century limited not only the goods but even the amount of money merchants could carry with them for trade purposes within the Empire.[136]

It is not surprising, then, to note that laws of the early fourth century forbade export of bronze and iron across Rome's frontiers.[137] And in 374 A.D. this prohibition was extended to the export of gold.[138] This law is interesting, since it stated that efforts should be made to *regain* by trade gold which had already passed into the hands of barbarian peoples—surely a bit of mercantilistic thinking. A little later wine, olive oil and *liquamen* (a special fish preparation) were also placed on the forbidden list.[139] While in view of finds in Scandinavian sites of Roman manufactured arms, bronze, etc.—all of which were on the forbidden list—one might well question how effective this system of trade control really was, there can be little doubt as to the intent of the Imperial government which lay behind such prohibitions. For a law of 381 A.D. found in the Theodosian Code lays down the general principles of the Roman government on the conduct of trade with

[133] K. Schumaker, *Siedlungs- und Kulturgeschichte der Rheinland von der Urzeit bis in das Mittelalter*, II (Mainz 1923), 14, 105.
[134] *Code Theod.*, VII, 16, 2.
[135] *Ibid.*, VII, 16, 1.
[136] *Ibid.*, IX, 23, 1-2.
[137] *Ibid.*, VII, 16, 3. *Code Justinian*, IV, 41, 1. *Ammianus Marcellinus*, XXVII.
[138] *Code Justinian*, IV, 63, 2.
[139] O. Brogan, "Trade with the Free Germans," *loc.cit.*, p. 207.

foreign peoples. It states: "Loyal friendly peoples [that is, those friendly to Rome] are allowed to export goods [to the Empire] *from their own regions* upon payment of ⅛ customs levy [15%]. They may purchase from Roman territory *only those which the law allows*. But these shall be duty free."[140]

What this law proposed to do was not only to limit Rome's exports across frontiers, but, by preventing neighboring friendly peoples from exporting to the Empire goods of others, to break up the possibility of prosperous intermediaries developing outside Rome's borders. Seldom has a government consciously followed a more deliberate policy of using trade as a weapon against potential enemies. When one adds to this an interesting law whereby the Empire forbade export of ship plans to foreign peoples—obviously directed against non-Roman maritime peoples,[141]—one sees the extent of Rome's Late Imperial intent to limit, weaken and even destroy the economies of her dangerous neighbors.

In the light of these policies, one begins to understand both the routes whereby in the fourth century Roman goods crossed Germany to reach the Baltic and the nature of the commerce which was carried on. It seems clear that Rome's choice of trade portals in no small measure dictated which routes, during these years, were the more important ones. It is further clear that the diminution of trade reaching Scandinavia as the century progressed was not accidental, but in a large part the result of deliberate Roman policy. In view of this, is it not possible that the ending of the important trade route along the Frisian coast to Jutland was also the result of Roman design, not of other factors? Did it not most probably represent an attempt, in line with the law of 381 A.D., to discourage enemy Saxon sea-rovers by denying them the goods and trade upon which their prosperity and strength seemed to depend? If this is so, it explains the decadence of Menapian and Morini maritime strength, which depended upon this route in such large measure as well.

And it further throws light upon the curious revolt of Carausius at the end of the third century. Carausius was a Menapian who organized a fleet under Roman orders to suppress the Saxon pirates in the North Sea and Channel. Suddenly we find him cooperating with them instead and defying Rome by setting up an independent

---

[140] *Code Theod.*, IV, 13, 8.   [141] *Ibid.*, IX, 40, 24.

Britain with control of Belgian coasts as well.[142] At the same time we know that in 297 the first trade treaty with Persia controlling the foreign trade of the Empire was negotiated. Is it not possible that Carausius' revolt was due to an attempt to set up a similar control or embargo of trade with barbarian-controlled North Sea coasts upon which the prosperity of Carausius' homeland and much of Britain depended? At any rate, his revolt represents the last evidence of Menapian maritime power under the Empire.

It is more difficult to know, however, whether or not Rome applied this system of control of her external trade to the Atlantic commerce from Gaul, Spain and Britain to Ireland and the lands of the Picts. This problem is complicated by the lack of precise information. The *Notitia Dignitatum* contains no information on the subject that applies to these regions, and Britain, the key region in the Atlantic, is not mentioned at all in the Theodosian Code. On the other hand, the law of 381 A.D., already alluded to, certainly would apply to these regions. And we know that in Hadrian's Wall there were two portals specially maintained for trade with the Picts.[143] It also seems probable that two ports, Chester on the west coast and Hull-on-Humber on the east coast, were specifically maintained as centers for maritime trade with the Irish and Picts, respectively.[144]

It is equally interesting to note that certain articles whose export to barbarian peoples was forbidden by the laws of the fourth century —iron, bronze, wine, wheat, olive oil and *liquamen*—were particularly important in Atlantic trade. *Liquamen*, for example, was shipped to Bordeaux from Spain in this period, and wine was the great export of Western Gaul. Furthermore, a provision of the Theodosian Code which ordered ships traveling to foreign nations to furnish officials with their destination seems particularly to apply to the Atlantic.[145] But most impressive proof of the application of these controls to the Atlantic lies in the growth of Irish and Pictish maritime power in these years. The prohibition by Roman law against

[142] D. Atkinson, "Classis Britannica," *loc.cit.*, pp. 1-5. Collingwood and Myers, *Roman Britain and the English Settlements*, pp. 277-78.

[143] *Ibid.*, pp. 245-46. See especially J. R. Curle, "Roman Drift in Caledonia," in *Jour. of Royal Soc.*, XII (1932), 73-78, and "An Inventory of Objects of Roman and Provincial Origin on Sites in Scotland Not Definitely Associated with Roman Constructions," in *Proc. of Soc. of Ant. of Scotland*, LXVI (1931-32), 277-97.

[144] M. P. Charlesworth, *The Lost Province*, p. 50.

[145] *Code Theod.*, VII, 16, 2. Could these ships have included those from Africa which are mentioned as sailing from "expeditionary ports"? See *ibid.*, XIII, 9, 2.

passage by Romans beyond the Empire's frontiers could only have increased foreign maritime activity, for now barbarian peoples had to go to the Empire to procure those products which earlier had been brought them by merchants under Rome's sway. Thus it seems probable that the rise of maritime strength in the Atlantic was the direct result of Rome's own commercial iron curtain.

If this be so, it must, however, be admitted that in general Rome's trade controls were more difficult to apply in Atlantic regions than along the German frontier. Along the Rhine-Danube borders of the Empire, river patrols, fortress troops and the lack of bridges made control of commerce possible to a large degree. Only along the coasts of Belgium, the mouths of the Rhine and in Southeast England was the same thing true in the Atlantic. In this small portion of the Northern Seas, river flotillas, Saxon Shore forts and the presence of the main fleet based on Boulogne would have made any large-scale commercial contacts with North Sea coasts difficult indeed.

Along the coasts of Western Gaul, Northern Spain and Western Britain, however, things were quite different. Rome maintained only a few fortresses on the coasts of Brittany, Aquitaine and Spain —all built late in the fourth century or even early in the fifth. And in Britain the cases of Cornwall and Southwest Wales illustrate her difficulties. Both were officially inside the Empire, but actually outside of effective Roman control. As such, their trade was unsupervised and it seems possible that it was often with Ireland. This would explain the early settlement of Irish colonists here.[146] Their presence may represent a trading more than a raiding settlement—or something like the half-commercial, half-buccaneering settlements of French, Dutch and English in the islands of the Caribbean in the seventeenth century. Something of the same situation may have existed in the small ports of Brittany. At any rate, it seems clear that in general there was less effective Roman control of trade in the Atlantic than in Central Europe during this period—which may account for the fact that there is little evidence that this trade diminished appreciably until towards the end of the fourth century.

Let us now examine the consequences to the lands about the Atlantic of Rome's policies of control of commerce across her frontiers. They were by no means unimportant. To such policies were owed

[146] On these Irish colonies or settlements, see R. Hodgkin, *History of the Anglo-Saxons*, I, 47-48, and F. Haverfield, *The Romanization of Britain*, pp. 80-86.

in large measure the routes followed by trade towards the Baltic during this century and particularly the decadence of the Frisian-Jutland maritime connection. It was also due to Rome's policies that there was a steady diminution of commerce reaching Scandinavia from Central Europe in these years. Certainly the decay of Menapian and Morini maritime strength was also in part the result of Roman restrictions.

But in the larger sense her commercial policy was a failure for the Empire. It could diminish but not destroy the economic links which bound her Central European provinces to the Germanic barbarian world without, while it did little to prevent an Atlantic economic community in the west extending far beyond her frontiers. Worse still, by delivering external trade into the hands of non-Romans, it strengthened the maritime power of the very enemies, like the Picts and Irish, whom it strove to weaken, while it failed to destroy the growing Saxon menace in the North Sea. And in diminishing the commerce that reached the distant Baltic it lessened the prosperity of Scandinavia and so helped to set in motion far to the north that restlessness which already was pushing these Germans towards the Danube and Black Sea and was with Hunnic help to push them into the Empire itself. Behind the *Volkerwanderungen* lies the specter of a Roman economic policy that helped to provoke it.

Nor could Roman frontier armies, naval defenses and trade policies halt the march of civilization across her frontiers, although they were able to weaken the Roman content of that civilization. What is everywhere apparent beyond Britain, Rhine, Danube and Black Sea is that the barbarian peoples were catching up with those who dwelt beneath Rome's rule. The Irish of the fourth century were far advanced over those primitive tribesmen whose island Agricola had believed he could subdue with one legion three centuries earlier. They had been transformed by the material elements of Roman civilization which had reached their shores, and already the seeds of Christianity, so soon to burst into flower, had been planted in their hearts.[147] The painted Picts to the north were not the same barbarians whom Septimus Severus had scorned, but a people capable of building fleets which could raid deep into Roman territory, a folk whose ships even Rome deigned to copy.[148]

[147] Concerning the advances of Ireland towards civilization and the arrival of Christianity in the 4th century, see N. Åberg, *The Occident and Orient in the Art of the Seventh Century*, I (Stockholm 1943), 5-7.

[148] Vegetius, *De re militari*, IV, 47, ed. Schwebel, p. 137.

Even greater advances had been made by the Germanic peoples along the Roman frontiers and in South Russia. To imagine that in the fourth century these Germans were at the level described by Tacitus two centuries earlier is mistaken. The Frisians, Franks, old Saxons, Alemanni and Bavarians were no longer semi-pastoral wanderers, but farming folk settled to the cultivation of their soil. Already they were using the heavy, wheeled, mortar-board plow which made it possible to break virgin soil that the Romans did not have the means to cultivate.[149] Their small, unstable, tribal units had been consolidated into large confederacies under royal families. The idea that *all* these Germans represented a force pressing ceaselessly against Roman territory must also be dismissed as an exaggeration. The Romans obviously did not think so. For already they allowed some of them to enter their Empire as soldiers and to settle along and just inside their borders as trusted *foederati*.

It was the Germans farther north in Scandinavia and Eastern Germany who represented the unstable, nomadic element in these years. It was the Goths, Vandals, Suevi, Lombards and Burgundians who were pressing south towards the lower Danube and Black Sea. And even here the Ostrogoths and Visigoths had made great advances towards civilization. The Goths, Christian and mounted now on horseback in the Central Asian manner, were a far cry from their pagan, Scandinavian, barbarian ancestors, as the Roman legions of Valens were to discover at Adrianople. Already the gap in civilization, as well as in military skill and economic condition, which separated the population of the Empire from the barbarians beyond its borders, while it still existed, was narrower than before.

There remains one final problem to the historian, the types of ships which were in use on the Northern Seas in the fourth century—ships from which all later varieties found on these seas were ultimately derived. To understand the nature of this problem one must go back to the time of the Early Empire. When Caesar arrived in Gaul he found two types of ships in use in the Atlantic from Spain to Norway. The first was the *curragh*, or coracle, a primitive boat of skin stretched over a framework of osiers. Though generally small, some coracles were large enough to be used in coastal ocean voyages.

---

[149] On German agrarian advances, see R. Koebner, *op.cit.*, pp. 30-46. Dopsch in his *Economic and Social Foundations of European Civilization*, pp. 1-240, probably overestimates the advances made by the Germans outside the Empire in the period. On the other hand, M. Bloch in his "Les Invasions: deux structures économiques" in *Ann. d'hist. sociale*, 1 (1945), probably minimizes their accomplishments unduly.

In the fourth century they were mentioned as still in use off Cornwall and in the Irish Sea.[150]

A second type of ship was that employed by the Veneti of Brittany, called the *ponto*. The *ponto*, a much more advanced vessel than the coracle, was a large, carvel-built, flat-bottomed, ocean-going ship. It was of oak construction with high poop and stern and carried leather sails and iron anchors. In this vessel the Veneti navigated to Britain and beyond.[151] To these two should be added a third found in the Baltic, an oared craft constructed of wood, the lineal descendant of the dugout-type of craft depicted in early rock-cut pictures found in Gotland and along the coast of Norway.[152]

There is no assurance that Caesar in destroying the naval power of the Veneti put an end to the building of *pontos* along the Gallic coast. But it does seem true that the Romans introduced into northern waters certain new ship-types of Mediterranean design. One was the *hippago*, a sail-equipped transport vessel used by Caesar in his expeditions against Britain. Another was the *corbito*, a sturdy merchant ship of Mediterranean design well-adapted to the turbulent Atlantic. In addition to these two-oared warship types, the *catopiscus*, or fast scouting vessel, and the *actuana*, or rowing galley, sometimes called the *navis longa*, were introduced by the Romans. All these ships, incidentally, appear to have been carvel-built.[153]

By the fourth century, in addition to sea-going *curraghs*, we have some direct knowledge of other ships in use in the Atlantic. This is because of the discovery at the bottom of the Thames at London of fragments of a Roman ship dating probably from the time of Carausius in the late third or early fourth century. These fragments reveal to us a ship 60 feet in length and 16 feet in width. It was flat-bottomed, constructed of oak and had a false keel. It was carvel-built, with little iron used to hold it together, and carried a mast 10 inches in diameter. Whether or not it was also equipped with oars it is impossible to say. In design this ship seems to have been a mixture of the *ponto* and the *corbito* and was perhaps related to both. Or

[150] J. Hornell, "British Coracles," in *Mariners Mirror*, XXII (1936), 8-9. On these skin boats and their evolution in Scandinavia, see A. W. Brøgger and H. Shetelig, *The Viking Ships* (Oslo 1953), pp. 13-47.

[151] Caesar, *De bello Gall.*, III, 13.

[152] Brøgger and Shetelig, *op.cit.*, pp. 48-51.

[153] Certain frescoes discovered at Hanchia Medina in Tunisia give us an excellent picture of these ship-types. C. de la Roncière and G. Clerc-Rampel, *Histoire de la marine française*, I (Paris 1934), 2-3.

perhaps it was the ship-type known some years later as the *barca*.[154]

Still another ship in use in British waters in these years was a new and different type of war vessel. It was a fast scouting ship which, according to Vegetius, carried a sail and 10 pairs of oars. He called it a Pictish ship, which some have claimed was because it was painted and had camouflaged sails and rigging.[155] It seems, however, more likely that it was so called because it was modeled after similar vessels used by the Picts, which makes one hazard the guess that it was a wooden vessel with lines copied from the coracle-like ship-type still found on the coast of Northumberland. It seems probable that these Pictish ships, like all others in use on the Atlantic in this period, were carvel-built.

In the Baltic, however, by the fourth century a very different type of ship had developed. Thanks to the discovery at Nydam of a ship of this sort dating from about 300 A.D. we know accurately just how these Baltic vessels were constructed. The Nydam ship was clinker-built and was 77 feet long and 11 feet wide. Propelled by 14 pairs of oars, it had oak planks which were held together by iron rivets and fastened to its ribs by ropes. It was steered by a large paddle, had a poorly constructed keel and carried no mast or sail. It had many defects. It was so low amidships that a heavy sea would swamp it and it was very unstable. Furthermore, its oarlocks, which were fastened by ropes to the vessel's frame, were so constructed that the boat could be rowed only in one direction. It was adequate for use in the relatively quiet Baltic, and it probably represents the type of rowing ships that Tacitus mentions as in use by the Swedes. But it was inadequate for use in the Atlantic or even the North Sea.[156] Its many divergences from either Celtic or Roman ship designs are perhaps the best proof that there was in this period little sea connection between the Atlantic and the Baltic regions.

It has generally been assumed that the type of ship used by the Saxon pirates of the North Sea in raiding Roman shores was a vessel modeled after the Nydam ship. That seems, however, highly unlikely. Sidonius, commenting in the next century upon the Saxon

[154] R. E. M. Wheeler, *London in Roman Times* (London 1930), pp. 152-54. Isadore of Seville, as a matter of fact, mentions the *ponto*, but from his description it little resembles that of Caesar's time. Rather it seems more like the *scapha*, with a flat bottom and propelled by both oars and a sail. Isadore of Seville, *Orig.*, XIX, 1, 24.

[155] Vegetius, *De re militari*, IV, 37, ed. Schwebel, p. 137.

[156] H. Shetelig, "The Nydam Ship," in *Acta Archeologia*, 1 (1930), 90-106, and *Scandinavian Archeology*, pp. 353-58.

pirates of his time, mentioned the fact that storms did not bother them, so great was their mastery of the sea. If so, they could not have been using a ship built like that found at Nydam. He further mentioned that their vessels carried sails, and the Nydam ship possessed neither mast nor sail.[157] Finally, it seems highly unlikely that the Saxons, who for several centuries had lived on the North Sea at close quarters with better-built Roman and Celtic ship-types should have used inferior, Baltic-type vessels. Indeed, the express Roman prohibition found in the Theodosian Code against giving barbarian peoples plans of ships[158] shows that such borrowings were common. It seems, then, probable that Saxon pirate ships were modeled on those used by the Picts or Romans, though they may have followed Baltic practice in being clinker- rather than carvel-built. The question, however, remains open to further discussion.

Such was the world of Northern Europe in the fourth century. It was a world moving rapidly towards portentous changes. The new maritime stirrings of Irish, Pict and Saxon coupled with their increased activity upon Atlantic waters, the contacts by land which linked the German peoples on Rome's northern frontiers with the Empire and which were steadily raising their level of civilization, the new Gothic kingdom of South Russia which was increasing the Baltic peoples' contacts with Central Asia—all these were ominous signs for the world of Rome. The Roman world which faced these developments beyond the frontiers, regimented and agrarian, fortified in character, split into regional economies and separate from the Mediterranean, could not long meet the challenge of survival. For its weaknesses were greater than its strength and already in the late fourth century the opening scenes in the next drama of history were being enacted, ending Rome's mastery over lands facing the Northern Seas.

The first blow fell upon the Western Empire along the frontier where Rome had made its greatest defense preparation—the Rhine. In 355 the Franks and the Alemanni pushed through Roman defenses along this river and invaded Northeastern Gaul, sacking a number of cities. Julian, later Emperor, was forced to engage in a difficult campaign, described for us by Ammianus Marcellinus, before he was able to drive the Alemanni back across the Rhine and restore the

[157] Sidonius Apollinaris, *Epistolae*, in *MGH Auct. Ant.*, VIII, 132-33.
[158] *Code Theod.*, IX, 40, 24.

frontier.[159] But he was less successful in his endeavors against the Franks. Despite some victories he found himself obliged to allow many of them to settle on the west side of the Rhine in the largely deserted territory of Northern Belgium.[160] At the same time Saxon raids down the Channel from the North Sea had so increased in number and severity that some of these pirates were able to set up a settlement near Boulogne from which they were not expelled.[161] The Rhine line had been breached and the vital Channel connection linking Britain with Gaul had been weakened.

Dangerous as this situation was for Rome, it was followed by a worse disaster. Britain, its military defenses weakened to support Julian's Rhine campaign, in 363 A.D. was suddenly attacked from all sides. Irish from the east, Saxons from the west, and Picts and Attecotti from north of the Wall fell upon the island in great strength. The Saxons and Irish arrived by sea, and probably the Picts, too, used their naval strength to by-pass Rome's land defenses along Hadrian's Wall. Almost the whole island was overrun and the Roman military commander was slain. It seems probable that to these invasions was added the horror of *bagaudae*-like risings of the servile population who labored upon the soil of the prosperous Romanized villas covering much of Britain. Britain seemed lost to Rome.

At this point, however, the prompt and energetic intervention of Count Theodosius with Continental levies saved the day. He landed troops, defeated the invaders, expelled them from the province and restored its defenses. He did not, however, pay much attention to reactivating Hadrian's Wall as a vital part of Britain's defense

---

[159] C. Jullian, *Histoire de la Gaule*, VII, 172-73. F. Lot, *La Gaule*, pp. 340-44. Julianus, *Opera*, ed. Hertlem, I, 225. A. Piganol, *L'Empire chrétien*, pp. 119-25.

[160] G. Failer-Feytmans, "L'Occupation du sol à l'époque romaine dans le bassin supérieure de la Hain," in *Latomus*, XII (1946), 153-62, and "La Frontière du nord de la Gaule sous le Bas Empire," in *Mélanges J. Marzourian* (Paris 1948), pp. 217-29. See the somewhat different explanation of C. Verlinden in his *Les Origines de la frontière linguistique en Belgique* (Brussels 1955), pp. 50-124.

[161] Saxons attacked this region in 370 A.D. *Ammianus Marcellinus*, XXVIII. Apparently, soon afterwards they established a permanent settlement there. A. Lognon, *Les Noms de lieux de la France* (Paris 1922), pp. 178-95. This probably accounts for the retreat of Rome's Boulogne fleet to the Somme, where it was to be found in the 5th century. *Notitia Dignitatum Occid.*, XXXVIII, 8. On these events, see also J. Dhondt, S. de Laet and P. Hombert, "Quelques considerations sur la fin de la domination romaine et les débuts de la colonization franque en Belgique," in *L'Antiquité classique*, XVIII (1948), 85-97, and J. Dhondt, "Essai sur l'origine de la frontière linguistique," in *ibid.*, XVII (1947), 317-39. Also C. Verlinden, *op.cit.*, pp. 50-73.

system. Such a fortification, easily by-passed from the sea, was neglected. Instead, to guard against future raids from the north he constructed a series of watchtowers along the Yorkshire coast.[162]

Theodosius' energy and efforts, however, could not restore the previous situation to Roman Britain. For what this invasion and its accompanying *bagaudae* risings had fatally destroyed almost everywhere in the Midlands and South Britain was the prosperous villa system—a system which up to this time had been enjoying its golden age. Theodosius could repair defenses and drive out invaders but he could not reconstitute Britain's shattered villa estates. Only near the Saxon Shore forts in Norfolk, Suffolk, the Cambridge region, Kent and about London did this system survive in Eastern Britain, while it was only near the legionary fortresses about Caerwent that it survived in Somersetshire and the Severn river valley. Elsewhere a new, disordered, different age dawned in Roman Britain.[163]

Even the Imperial government recognized the inevitable before the end of the century. Trier, for a century the Gallic capital, was abandoned for the safer city of Vienne, while the mint was in 395 moved to Milan.[164] The way was prepared for the even greater disasters which were to strike Britain and Gaul in the next century.

At the same time that the Empire's defenses were beginning to crumble in the West, a disaster struck the East as well. This calamity was precipitated by the arrival of the Huns. There is not space in these pages to tell the important story of how the Huns moved from the frontiers of China across Central Asia to reach the borders of the Roman world. Nor can we catalogue the effects of their attacks upon

---

[162] *Ammianus Marcellinus*, XXVI, 4; XXVII, 8; XXVIII, 3. Collingwood and Myers, *Roman Britain and the English Settlements*, pp. 284-86. The Picts probably attacked from the sea and thus by-passed Hadrian's Wall, which explains why it was not repaired and re-occupied after 383 A.D. and why instead new watchtowers were constructed south of it along the coast of Yorkshire. T. C. Lethbridge, *Herdsmen and Hermits*, pp. 54-62.

[163] R. Hodgkin, *History of the Anglo-Saxons*, I, 49-50. See also R. G. Collingwood, "Roman Britain" in *ESAR*, III, 75-87, and M. P. Charlesworth, *op.cit.*, pp. 20-26. Judging from finds of *minimi* and *minimissimi*, as a result of this invasion only two areas of Britain escaped disaster, as far as Roman life was concerned. One was in the west about Caerwent, Lydney, Somerset and Dorset. The other was in the east about the Saxon Shore forts at Colchester and in Norfolk and Kent. See P. Hall, "Barbarous Imitations of Fourth Century Roman Coins," in *Num. Chronicle*, 6th ser., X (1950), 233-76. The rest of Central Britain relapsed into the sort of primitive village life shown by excavations at Cranborne Chase. Perhaps the Wansdyke was actually built to protect the surviving Romanized inhabitants of West Britain from such villagers and *bagaudae*. H. J. Fleure, *A Natural History of Man in Britain* (London 1951), pp. 108, 113.

[164] J. Breuer, *La Belgique romaine*, p. 43.

the Sassanian Empire—important as they were. Our interest lies in their direct influence upon Rome. By 370 this nomadic Central Asian people with a snowballing empire, having crushed the Alans and enlisted them in their forces, had reached the newly consolidated kingdom of the Ostrogoths in South Russia. Ermanaric, king of the Ostrogoths, gave battle in vain against these advancing nomads. His forces were destroyed and he himself was slain, while the Germanic and Slavic peoples under his sway were incorporated into the Hunnic host which moved on to the west towards Central Europe.

As the Huns pushed on, the Visigothic kingdom along the Danube was next in their line of advance. This people, alarmed by the fate of their Ostrogothic cousins, in fear sought the protection of Rome and requested that they be allowed to cross the Danube and settle within the Empire where the wide river would give them some protection from Hunnic attack. They were welcomed by the Emperor Valens, who saw in them new contingents for his defense forces.

Having welcomed them into the Empire, however, Valens was foolish enough to allow his officials to oppress them and failed to keep his promises to them. Thus goaded into resentment, the Visigoths rose against their Roman allies and marched on Constantinople. At Adrianople they were met by the Roman legions of Valens in 376 A.D. In the battle that followed the Roman forces were utterly overthrown by the mounted Gothic warriors, and the Emperor himself was among the slain. A whole barbarian people entering the Empire in a mass had destroyed a Roman army and an Emperor and ended the legend of Roman military invincibility. It is true that Theodosius, who succeeded Valens, was able to pacify the Visigoths and transform them, until his death in 395, into loyal *foederati* of the Roman state. He could not, however, wipe out Adrianople, or hide the fact that a victorious German people was now settled upon the soil of the Empire. Nor could he prevent the growth of that vast Hunnic-German-Alanic empire in Central Europe which boded so ill for the future of Rome.[165] The stage was set on the Danube, as in Britain and on the Rhine, for the disasters of the next century.

[165] R. Latouche, *Les grandes invasions et la crise de l'Occident au V° siècle* (Paris 1946), pp. 61-74.

2. The Invasion Period,
A.D. 400-550

FEW PERIODS of European history have been discussed more thoroughly than that which saw the Western Empire overthrown by the barbarian invasions. Since the time of Gibbon these years have had a special fascination for historians. Yet few periods have been so difficult to understand. In part this is due to the fact that troubled years leave few written records to guide us. Nor do peoples in movement leave abundant traces behind them to be uncovered by the archeologist's spade. It is therefore necessary to depend upon scraps of evidence, historical and archeological, in order to piece together an acceptable story of these years of disaster and change in the lands of Europe that bordered the waters of the Northern Seas.

It is also true that only now are we able to realize how complicated were the movements of the actors in this drama of invasion. For instance, historians are now becoming aware how little the names borne by the invaders who entered the Roman world really mean. Tribal groupings in this period were uncertain and unstable in composition, and a similar name does not always mean that a tribe was comprised of the same peoples at all times. One can, as a matter of fact, fairly assume that most of the peoples who moved into the Roman world or into Central Europe during these years were mixed in strain. The Franks, for instance, were a confederation of various Germanic tribal groups. So were the Alemanni. So, too, were the Bavarians, who seem to have been an amalgamation of the Marcomanni and the Quadi. And it is uncertain just what names like Angle, Saxon, Frisian and Jute really stand for—distinct ethnic groups, or a mixture of varying stocks? Who were the Danes? And can we be sure that the Visigoths and Ostrogoths who actually arrived inside the Empire were the same peoples who in the third century were on its borders? Were they not now more probably peoples with a strong mixture of Slavic and Alanic elements after their long residence in South Russia and Dacia? Is it not probable that by the fifth century the Huns were no longer a distinct people of Turkish stock, but rather a mixed group containing Germanic, Slavic and Alanic elements? And how large an Alanic element was to be found in Slavic groups like the White Sorbs and White Croats who spearheaded the advance of the Slavs into Central Europe? None of these questions or conjectures can be answered definitively. But they illustrate the complexity of the problem.

Nor can the invasion period be separated from that which preceded it. Movements which culminated in the fifth and sixth centuries started much earlier. Raids of Irish along the coasts of Western Britain and their settlements in Cornwall and Southwest Wales in the third and fourth centuries were the beginnings of a movement of Celtic peoples which was to end in the colonization of Armorica by the Britons and of Dalriada by the Scots. The passage of Germans into Roman territory to seek employment as soldiers in the Empire's armed forces, the settlement of many of them as *laeti* and auxiliaries within the Empire's borders, simply represented beginnings of events which were to have fateful consequences. Similarly, those Saxon *Gewissae* who settled in Britain in the fourth century, like the Saxon sea-raiders who harried the British and Gallic Channel coasts, were but the initiators of a migration which was to culminate in the fifth and sixth centuries in an Anglo-Saxon England. And the Huns who arrived in Central Europe were but the vanguard of a host of peoples—Slavs, Avars, Bulgars and Hungarians—who were to follow them. All we can say is that by the year 400 A.D. the prelude was over and the curtain rose on the main act already foreshadowed by events of preceding centuries.

The death of the Emperor Theodosius in 395 A.D. was the end of an era. With all his faults, and they were many, he was the last real Emperor of the Roman world who managed to hold together its many discordant parts and who reconciled its divergent interests. He left the Empire to his two unworthy sons, Arcadius and Honorius, who were to live to see the proud power of Rome humbled. Both refused to play the role of generals leading armies in defense of their Imperial heritage. Arcadius instead was content to dwell secure behind the ramparts of his rich and mighty city of Constantinople. Honorius, even more incapable, shut himself up inside the fortress city of Ravenna and left the actual defense and direction of affairs in the Western Empire to Stilicho, his able but unscrupulous German *magister militum*.

There could have been no worse time for the Roman Empire to have been afflicted with weak, do-nothing Emperors. For the situation which existed was fraught with peril for the state. Across the Danube in Central Europe and South Russia the Huns were building up a

Germanic-Slavic empire that stretched from the Rhine to the Urals. Within the Empire in Illyricum the Visigoths, who had been friendly to Theodosius, were now ruled by an ambitious monarch, Alaric, eager for more lands and booty. The troops who defended the Rhine frontiers and Britain and who manned the naval defenses along the Atlantic were few in number. Actually, it was not Roman soldiery but Frankish allied *foederati* who formed the chief defense of Rome's Rhine frontier.

It was the Visigoths who began the disaster. Under Alaric they had taken to plundering widely in the Balkans. They had thus become a menace to the Eastern Empire, and the Emperor Arcadius determined to rid himself of their presence. He therefore summoned their king, Alaric, to Constantinople, loaded him with presents and craftily suggested that he lead his people west into Italy, where the lands of Arcadius' brother, Honorius, would furnish him with rich booty. The forces which Stilicho, *magister militum* in the West, had available in Italy to meet Alaric's forces were insufficient for the task. And so he was forced to draw troops from the vital Rhine frontier. Thus denuded, this frontier could not be held when in 406 Vandals and Suevi moved against it, passing across the Rhine in the vicinity of Mainz. There was no Julian this time to offer battle. All but unopposed, they swept over Gaul, plundering as they went, to settle across the Pyrenees in Spain. The Suevi established themselves in the northwestern corner of the peninsula, the Vandals in the rich province of Baetica which has since borne their name as Vandalusia, or Andalusia.[1]

The sacrifice of the Rhine frontier by Stilicho proved insufficient to protect Italy from the Visigoths, for he was murdered by his craven Imperial master, Honorius. After his death, his army lost interest, and the Visigoths entered Italy without difficulty. Alaric led his warriors to the city of Rome, which he sacked in the year 410.[2] For the first time since Gallic warriors in 390 B.C. had sacked the city, Rome fell to a foreign foe. The shock of this event resounded through the Roman world, and it inspired St. Augustine to write his *City of God* to show his fellow Christians that there was an eternal city more important than the capital on the Tiber which had proved unable to resist conquest.

[1] F. Lot, *Les Invasions germaniques* (Paris 1935), pp. 75-80. Orentius, *Commonitorum*, II, 181. Salvian, *De gubernatione dei*, v, in *MGH Auct. Ant.*, I, 57-66.
[2] R. Latouche, *Les grandes invasions* (Paris 1946), pp. 85-89.

The Visigoths, however, did not linger long in the Italian peninsula. Shortly after taking Rome, Alaric died in Southern Italy. Then their new king, Ataulf, led them west, where they settled in Southwestern Gaul and Spain. There, with Toulouse as their capital, they established in 414 a huge barbarian kingdom as *foederati* of Rome.[3] They performed great services to the Empire in this capacity, crushing the Vandals in Southern Spain and helping the senatorial aristocracy in Gaul by suppressing *bagaudae* risings in Armorica and elsewhere in the province. Nevertheless, their domination of large sections of Gaul and Spain represented a break with Roman governmental continuity, which was never again to be restored in the lands they made their own.

The settlement and conquests of Visigoths, Suevi and Vandals within the Empire set off a chain of events which continued unchecked during the next few years. First the Vandals, defeated by the Visigoths, crossed the Straits of Gibraltar to North Africa. There, under the command of their able, unscrupulous leader Gaeseric, they soon established a kingdom which stretched from the Atlantic to Libya and included the islands of the Balearics, Sardinia and Corsica as well. Taking to the sea, they became redoubtable pirates, interfering with grain shipments to Rome and not hesitating to send a naval expedition which plundered the Eternal City again in 455.[4] To these barbarian conquests another was added in the West when the Roman general, Aetius, settled the remnant of the Burgundian people as allies of Rome in the valley of the upper Saône near the Juras. Soon this settlement grew into a Burgundian kingdom which included all of the Rhone valley.[5] In the West, by the year 450 only Italy and Northern Gaul were still under the direct rule of the Imperial government.

The events related above which took place in Spain, North Africa, Southern Gaul and Italy did not directly affect such northern regions facing the Atlantic as Britain and Northern Gaul. But they had an immense indirect effect. In theory, Britain and Northern Gaul might still acknowledge the overlordship of Rome, but such overlordship was remote and ineffective and cut off from these northern provinces

---

[3] A. Loyen, "Les Débuts du royaume visigothique de Toulouse," in *Revue des études latines*, XII (1934), 68-93. F. Lot, *op.cit.*, pp. 126-28. L. Halphen, *Les Barbares* (5th ed., Paris 1951), pp. 19-21. R. Latouche, *op.cit.*, pp. 90-92.

[4] R. Latouche, *op.cit.*, pp. 93-100.

[5] A. Colville, *Recherches sur l'histoire du Lyon du Ve au Xe siècle* (Paris 1928), pp. 77-204. F. Lot, *op.cit.*, pp. 120-23. R. Latouche, *op.cit.*, pp. 100-2.

by the intervening, newly established domains of the Burgundians, Visigoths and others. In practice, the local Romanized leaders and population of Britain and Northern Gaul found themselves on their own, facing the perils of internal and external disorder. *Bagaudae* risings of their *coloni*, like that led by Tibautto in the Loire valley, added to their difficulties.[6] A famous passage by Zosimus describes the situation graphically: "The barbarians from beyond the Rhine, ravaging everything at their pleasure, forced both the inhabitants of Britain and some of the peoples of Gaul to secede from the Empire. The people of Britain, therefore, taking up arms, freed their cities from the invading barbarians, and the whole of Armorica and other provinces of Gaul, imitating the Britons, liberated themselves in like manner, expelling Roman officials and setting up a civil polity according to their own inclination. The secession of Britain and of Gallic peoples took place during the time of Constantine's usurpation [circa 410], the barbarians rising up in consequence of his neglect of government. Honorius, however, having written letters to the cities of Britain urging them to look to their own safety—took his ease."[7]

The picture painted by Zosimus accurately reveals what happened during the next few decades in Britain and much of Gaul—a period which some historians have aptly described as the sub-Roman period. Local leaders everywhere in these two isolated provinces were left to their own devices. The results varied. In some parts of Gaul, Roman senatorial personalities like Paul, the *magister militum*, or Aegidius or even a general like Aetius took command of the local situation and tried to maintain order in the face of barbarian pressures and local *bagaudae* risings. Elsewhere men like the Aviti and the Apollinares collaborated with barbarian kings and leaders to protect their estates and establish order. In Britain sometimes it was a Romanized Briton like Aurelianus or Artorius, the famous Arthur, who led the forces of order. More frequently, however, judging from Gildas' fragmentary account, it was a Celtic chieftain, only thinly veneered with Roman culture, a Vortigern, a Cunneda or a Coroticus, who assumed local power and resisted both invaders and disorderly elements at home. It must be emphasized, however, that such resistance and such leadership, even the collaboration which was often offered to invaders, was local, fragmentary and spasmodic—seldom coordinated. It is against this general background that we

[6] F. Lot, *La Gaule*, pp. 482-84.
[7] Zosimus, *Hist. nov.* VI, 6-10, ed. Mendelson, pp. 287-92.

must examine in more detail the story of what took place in this portion of the Atlantic Seas in the next few decades.

When the Suevi and Vandals broke through Roman defenses on the Rhine in 406, they let loose a chain of events which was to change the pattern of power about the Northern Seas. Their invasion was followed by Constantine's futile revolt of 410, which, by drawing Roman troops from Britain to the Continent, further weakened Rome's military power in this region. Saxon pirates became more active in the Channel. As early as 370 they had attacked in the vicinity of Flanders and Boulogne, and it is probable that their colony in this area dates from the fourth century.[8] In 406 they were again active here, according to Jerome. A year later they attacked Britain, the event probably alluded to by Zosimus in his account of these years.[9] Under their attacks the Rhine river flotilla seems to have disappeared from history since we hear no further mention of it, while the Roman Channel fleet previously stationed at Boulogne withdrew down the coast and established its base on the river Somme, according to the *Notitia Dignitatum*.[10] At the same time the Franks, paralleling by land the Saxons' advance by sea—and, indeed, perhaps in alliance with them—pushed farther south into Belgium.[11] A beginning was made of breaching Rome's naval defenses in the Channel that linked Britain to the Continent.

At the same time, Irish pirates who were established in Cornwall and South Wales stepped up their assaults upon Western British shores. Under Niall of the Seven Hostages they raided the Severn region in force, an attack which is famous because it resulted in the capture of the young St. Patrick and his being carried to Ireland as a slave. These Irish raids extended into the Channel as well, for Niall is said to have met his death a few years later in an attack near the Isle of Wight.[12] Probably they also extended to Brittany, whose coastal villas burnt by raiders offer archeologists mute evidence of

[8] A. Lognon, *op.cit.*, pp. 178-95. *Ammianus Marcellinus*, XXVIII, 5.

[9] Jerome, *Epistolae*, CXXIII. *Chron. Gallia ad anno* CCCLII, in *MGH Auct. Ant.*, IX, 654.

[10] F. Lot, *La Gaule*, pp. 344-46. The *Notitia Dignitatum*, which cannot have been written later than 428 A.D., places the Roman Channel fleet, which had been stationed at Boulogne, on the Somme in the early 5th century. *Notitia Dignitatum Occid.*, XXXVIII, 8.

[11] C. Jullian, *Histoire de la Gaule*, VIII, 309. See also Jerome, *Epistolae*, CCXXII, on loss of Boulogne, and J. Dhondt, "Essai sur l'origine de la frontière linguistique," in *L'Antiquité classique*, XVII (1947), 320-36.

[12] J. B. Bury, *St. Patrick*, pp. 20-22. J. F. Kenney, *The Sources for the Early History of Ireland* (New York 1920), pp. 148-50.

the fury which the sea brought to these shores in the early fifth century.[13] To Saxon assaults, then, were added Irish attacks which loosened the bonds that linked Gaul and Britain.

Despite these raids, however, it seems probable that some connection between this island and the Continent was still maintained in the first decades of the 5th century. There are a number of reasons for thinking so. According to the *Notitia Dignitatum,* a Roman fleet still remained stationed on the Somme as late as 428. Coin hoards of *minimissimi* also reveal that Clausentum (Roman Southampton) was still occupied during these years.[14] But the most important evidence comes from the Life of St. Germanus. According to this account, in 429 St. Germanus made a voyage from Gaul to Britain (probably via the Rouen-Clausentum route) and traveled as far as Verulam (St. Albans), where he helped the inhabitants to repulse an attack by a band of marauding Picts and Saxons.[15] Evidently passage to Britain was still open to travelers.

By 441-442, though, a change had taken place. In that year a chronicler living in Southern Gaul reported that Britain had been overrun by the Saxons.[16] Certainly this period was a difficult one for the Romano-British inhabitants of the land, since we learn from Gildas that the Britons in 446 addressed a petition to Aetius asking him for assistance.[17] And in 449 or thereabouts, Vortigern in Kent found it necessary to hire Jutish mercenaries who possessed naval vessels to protect his shores from invaders.[18]

These later events help to place for us the time of the disappearance of Rome's Channel fleet. It must have been sometime between 429 and 449 that it ceased to exist, that communication between Britain and the Continent via the Channel all but ended. And it was probably

---

[13] A. de la Bordérie, *Histoire de Bretagne* (Rennes 1905), I, 223-24.

[14] P. Hall, "Barbarous Imitations of Fourth Century Roman Coins," in *Numismatic Chronicle,* 6th ser., X (1950), 273-76 (with a map of the location of all sub-Roman coin hoards in Britain).

[15] Constantius, *Vita Germani,* in MGH *Script. rer. Merov.,* I, 263-65. The town plan of Rouen in the Middle Ages suggests it was continously occupied from Roman times—the only port on the Channel of which this can be true. For plan of city, see F. Ganshof, *Etude sur les villes entre Loire et Rhin au moyen âge* (Bruxelles 1941), p. 131.

[16] *Chron. Gallia,* in MGH *Auct. Ant.,* IX, 660.

[17] Gildas, *De excidio Brit.,* in MGH *Auct. Ant.,* XIII, 34.

[18] F. Lot, "Bretons et Anglais au Ve et VIe siècles," in *Proceedings of the British Academy,* XVI (1936), 9-12, and "Les Migrations saxonnes en Gaule et en Grande Bretagne" in *Revue hist.,* CXIX (1915). See also R. Hodgkin, *History of the Anglo-Saxons,* I, 74-101, F. Stenton, *Anglo-Saxon England* (2nd ed., Oxford 1947), pp. 6-53, and E. Foord, *The Last Age of Roman Britain* (London 1925), pp. 101-216.

during these years that the Saxons, advancing farther down the Channel, established a second colony near Bayeux at the mouth of the Seine.[19] An interesting point concerning this advance is that again it was paralleled by the Salian Franks farther inland, who in 434 were checked in their attacks on Tournai by the *magister militum* of Gaul.[20]

What happened to Rome's Somme fleet? Did it simply disintegrate? Did it retreat to Rouen to join the Seine river flotilla there? Or did it sail to West Britain or Western Gaul, where some Roman naval strength existed? We cannot say. All we can be sure of is that the year 450 saw an end of Roman naval strength in the English Channel.

This brings us to one of the most difficult questions of these years, that which concerns the movement of large numbers of Britons across the Channel into Brittany. The reasons for this movement and exactly how and when it took place have been the subject of much speculation. In general, older historical opinion has tended toward the belief that the movement of Britons into Armorica was the result of the Saxon invasion of Britain—that these Celts were essentially refugees fleeing from Saxon advances into their land.[21] There are, however, serious objections which can be advanced to such an explanation.

In the first place, all evidence seems to show that except for raids, some extending rather far into the interior, the settlement of Saxons in Britain did not take place prior to 450. Instead, as Lot showed long ago, their principal attacks and settlements during this early period were on the Gallic, *not* the English, side of the Channel.[22] Even after 450 there is no evidence that Saxons settled in England by way of the Channel—except in Sussex just across from their earlier colony of Boulogne.[23] Both archeology and our historical sources are in agreement that it was by way of Britain's east coast that the Saxons made their way into the interior, and then only *after* 450.[24] Nor can any

[19] H. Prentout, "Litus Saxonicum, Saxones Bojacassini, Otlinga Saxoni," in *Revue hist.*, CVIII (1911), 285-309.

[20] F. Lot, *Les Invasions germaniques*, pp. 90-95.

[21] J. Loth, *L'Immigration bretonne en Armorique du Vᵉ au VIIᵉ siècle de notre ère* (Rennes 1883), pp. 149-77. See also F. Lot, "Les Migrations saxonnes," *loc.cit.*, and *La Gaule*, pp. 16-17.

[22] Collingwood and Myers, *Roman Britain and the English Settlements*, pp. 352-82.

[23] *Ibid.*, pp. 291-301. F. Stenton, *Anglo-Saxon England*, pp. 16-17. A. W. Wade-Evans, "Further Remarks on the De Excidio," in *Archeologia Cambriensis*, XCVIII (1944), 113-28. T. Hodgkin, *Anglo-Saxons*, I, 61-66. R. Jessup, *Anglo-Saxon Jewelry* (London 1950), pp. 18-26.

[24] On the routes used by the Saxons to penetrate the interior of Britain, see T.

evidence be found that Romanized Britons fled west from this threatened eastern part of the land.

Now we do know that those Britons who colonized Armorica were primitive tribal people coming from Devon, Cornwall, Wales and perhaps Cumberland.[25] They thus left a part of Britain which was completely unaffected by Saxon raids, either directly or indirectly, and under no pressure from them whatsoever.[26] Gildas, our principal source, speaks of them as exiles, never refugees. Even more important is the fact that in moving into Brittany in the mid-fifth century these Britons were entering waters directly exposed to Saxon naval attack, near coasts long spoken of as a "Saxon Shore" and close to the Saxons' advanced pirate base at Bayeux. To believe that a people would move directly into the path of the Saxons if they were trying to escape them strains one's credulity. The theory, then, that the Britons of Brittany were refugees from Saxon pressures seems highly unlikely.

A second theory ascribes the movement of Britons to Brittany to Irish pressures. According to those who advocate this hypothesis, it was the raids of Niall and other pirate Irish chieftains which caused the exodus across the Channel to Armorica.[27] There are, however, strong objections to this idea as well. In the first place, we know that the Irish had been raiding West Britain since the third century and had even established Irish settlements on the shores of Cornwall and South Wales. What new conditions, then, that had not arisen for at least a century, existed in the mid-fifth century to drive the Britons forth? Still more important is the fact that British immigration to the Continent originated from exactly the same places where the Irish had long-established colonies—Cornwall and Wales. How could Britons have left these places if they were in Irish control? Further-

---

Hodgkin, *op.cit.*, pp. 61-62, and F. M. Stenton, *op.cit.*, p. 1740. On the Angles' later routes, see E. T. Leeds, *A Corpus of Early Anglo-Saxon Great Square Headed Brooches* (Oxford 1949), pp. 30-81. Since Frisia was the halfway point of almost all Saxon settlers going to England, the date of Saxon arrival in numbers in Frisia has a bearing on the time they reached Britain. Boeles shows that this was about 450 A.D., based on Frisian archeology. P. Boeles, *Friesland* (2nd ed., The Hague 1951), pp. 181-362. Therefore Saxon colonization of Britain, as opposed to raids, cannot have been before 450, which agrees with Gildas and the traditional account.

[25] J. Loth, *L'Immigration bretonne*, pp. 85-94. F. Lot, *La Gaule*, pp. 483-84. R. Latouche, *op.cit.*, pp. 176-88.

[26] A. W. Wade-Evans, "Further Remarks on the De Excidio," *loc.cit.*, also points out that the West Britons were under no Saxon pressure in this period.

[27] In his most recent discussion of this problem, Lot seemed to veer towards this opinion. F. Lot, *La Gaule*, p. 484. For a contrary view, see R. Latouche, *op.cit.*, pp. 185-86.

more, why should these colonists have left such regions to settle in a Brittany equally open to Irish naval attacks?

The most conclusive objection to the theory that the Irish caused the exodus from Armorica is that as a theory it fails to fit certain historical facts. We know that in the early years of the fifth century there was considerable British maritime strength in the Atlantic quite independent of Roman control. Orosius speaks of British shipping which reached Coruña.[28] Even more vital is information we gain from a letter of St. Patrick. St. Patrick wrote it to a certain Coroticus, whom he addressed as a Roman and a Christian. He reproached Coroticus because this latter, a chieftain who lived near Dumbarton, was raiding Ireland with his fleet and attacking Patrick's Irish Christian converts. Here is direct evidence of contemporary West British naval power.[29] A few years later, about 450, we learn of a certain Cunneda who, coming from the north, drove the Irish out of Cornwall and South Wales. This could only have been possible if Cunneda possessed maritime strength. Instead of evidence that the Irish drove out the British, what we find about 450 is that it is the Britons who are expelling the Irish and launching naval attacks on Ireland.[30] A few years later we hear of them in Brittany.

To account for these facts a different explanation must be found. Perhaps the following comes closest to being satisfactory. About the middle of the fifth century, Britons on their island's western coast who possessed the rudiments of naval organization, and ships inherited from Rome and, in addition, a native maritime traditon of long standing, drove the Irish, or at least their leaders, from their strongholds in Cornwall and Wales. Then, joined by the natives of these regions, and perhaps some of the Irish, they proceeded across the Channel and settled along the shore of Brittany. They were not refugees but invaders and colonists.[31]

[28] Orosius, *Hist.*, I, 2, 72.   [29] St. Patrick, *Epistolae*, ed. White, pp. 26-32.

[30] Charlesworth dates the expulsion of the Irish from Western Britain about 450 A.D. M. P. Charlesworth, *The Lost Province*, pp. 20-40. It is interesting to note that Gildas still speaks of the Britons having a certain Roman discipline. Gildas, *De excidio Brit.*, XIII, in *MGH Auct. Ant.*, XVIII, 34-35. Lethbridge dates the Irish expulsion a little earlier, about 435 A.D. T. C. Lethbridge, *op.cit.*, p. 64. The fact that Caerwent's walls were repaired during the course of the 5th century, most probably because of fear of Irish attacks, makes one hesitate to accept Bury's earlier date of 405 for this expulsion. On Caerwent, see V. E. Nash-Williams, "Caerleon and Caerwent and the Roman Occupation of South Wales," in *Jour. of British Arch. Assn.*, CIX (1929), 59-74. See also on these events, Nennius, *Historia Britonum*, ed. Mommsen, pp. 205-6.

[31] Hencken, who has worked extensively on Cornish archeology, is strongly of this

Their landings were unopposed at first because these shores had been devastated by Irish and Saxon pirates before their arrival[32] and because Rome's Channel defenses had collapsed. Furthermore, the Gallo-Roman inhabitants of the land were weak from *bagaudae* risings and Alanic destruction.[33] Only when these Britons advanced some distance into the interior towards Rennes, Nantes and Vannes did they meet serious resistance from the original inhabitants, aided at times by first the Visigoths and then the Franks.[34]

The expanding West British sea power did not content itself with colonizing Armorica. Some Britons sailed on to Northwestern Spain, following trade routes they had used in the Late Empire, and in Galicia and elsewhere in the neighborhood of Coruña a considerable British colony came to exist which sent its own bishops to Visigothic church councils for several centuries.[35] It should be added that immigration to Armorica probably extended over several centuries, and it is possible that the last wave of colonists, who arrived in the late sixth and seventh centuries, actually *were* refugees from Anglo-Saxon expansion into the Severn region and about Chester—thus giving rise to the historical theory that the earlier Britons were refugees from the Saxons.

In the fifth and early sixth centuries, however, there is no evidence that the Britons were forced out of England. In fact, an early tradition, related by Gildas, tells of a certain Ambrosius Aurelianus who returned from Brittany to help the Celtic natives of the land in their resistance to Saxon invaders, a resistance which resulted in the temporary halt of the invasion at the battle of Badon Hill in 509 A.D.[36] An-

---

opinion. H. O. Hencken, *The Archeology of Cornwall and Scilly* (London 1932), pp. 212-20. But it seems clear that not all the Irish were expelled, for finds of Irish ogam stones dating down to the 7th century reveal Irish presence in Cornwall. *Ibid.*, pp. 223-34. See also K. Jackson, *Language and History in Early Britain* (Cambridge, Mass., 1953), pp. 23-165.

[32] Breton tradition says that they found the shores of Brittany deserted when they landed. J. Loth, *op.cit.*, pp. 176-78.

[33] These last risings, after 435, were crushed by the Franks and the Alans, these latter under a certain King Eochar, who suppressed the *bagaudae* of the Loire region in 448. *Chron. Gallia ad anno 441*, in *MGH Auct. Ant.*, IX, 660. On these Alans, see L. Franchet, "Une Colonie scytho-alaine en Orléanais au Ve siècle," in *Revue scient. fib.*, V (1930), 23-41. F. Lot, *La Gaule*, pp. 482-84.

[34] Gregory of Tours speaks of this Gallo-Roman resistance in *Hist. Franc.*, V, 29-32, in *MGH Script. rer. Merov.*, I, 223-25.

[35] In 572 a Visigothic church council mentions *Mailoc, Britonensis ecclesiae episcopus*. We also find Breton bishops at the councils of Toledo in 653, of Braga in 675 and again at Toledo in 638 and 692. J. Loth, *op.cit.*, p. 176.

[36] F. Stenton, *Anglo-Saxon England*, pp. 3-8, 30-31. According to Gildas, Ambrosius Aurelianus came *from* Brittany to assist the Britons against their Saxon foes. R. Latouche, *op.cit.*, p. 180, and E. Foord, *op.cit.*, pp. 130-72.

other contemporary source bears out the invasion theory of the occupation of Brittany. The Frankish King Theudebert, early in the sixth century, told the Byzantine ruler, according to Procopius, that Angles, Frisians *and* Britons from England, groups he thus *linked together*, were invading his territory. He gave as an explanation the fact that Britain was overpopulated.[37] The movement, then, of British Celts into the peninsula of Armorica and beyond must be recognized not as a matter of refugees seeking safety, but as a full-fledged movement of peoples seeking new homes, as the Germans were doing within the Empire during these years.

There remains one final point of importance, the date of the beginning of this invasion. During these years dates are difficult to fix with any real accuracy. Yet it seems probable that it could not have been earlier than 450 A.D. In 446 a letter from Britain sent to Aetius in Gaul still speaks of the Irish, along with the Picts, as dangerous invaders.[38] We know that it was not until 450 that these Irish were expelled from Cornwall and Wales. In 470 there is mention of a large force of Britons (or Bretons, as we may now call them) under King Riothamus appearing on the Loire, where they were defeated by the Visigoths.[39] And in 463 we hear of a Breton bishop attending a church council in Gaul. Sometime between 446 and 470, or, to narrow it down more closely, between 450 and 463, the movement to Brittany commenced. But it is possible to hazard an even closer guess than this—the year 454. This was immediately after the death of Aetius, Roman Gaul's last considerable military figure, whose prestige probably would have deterred any invader. Even more important, we learn from Sidonius that in 454 Armorica, long in revolt, returned suddenly to her Roman allegiance.[40] What better reason for this change than the sudden arrival of Briton colonists in large numbers on the shores of this province?

But this West British maritime power and expansion about 450 was reflected not merely in expulsion of the Irish from their Cornish

[37] Procopius, *De bello Gothico*, IV, 19-20, ed. Dewing, V, 252-70, contains a famous passage on Britain which was related to him, he says, by Angles who accompanied the Frankish King Theudebert. They claimed that Britain was inhabited by Britons, Angles and Frisians. This latter has puzzled historians. But since we know that Saxons were settled at the time of the Angle invasions in *both* Frisia and England (see Boeles, *Friesland*, pp. 183-246), the Angles thought of them as the same people and called them so. Hence "Frisian" in Procopius' account probably means "Saxon."

[38] Gildas, *De excidio Brit.*, xx, in *MGH Auct. Ant.*, XIII, 36.

[39] Jordanes, *Gaetica*, XLV, in *MGH Auct. Ant.*, V, 118-19. Sidonius also speaks of Bretons on the Loire in this period. Sidonius Apollinaris, *Epistolae*, I, 7, in *ibid.*, VIII, 16.

[40] Sidonius Apollinaris, *Carmina*, VII, in *ibid.*, VIII, 212-16.

and Welsh strongholds, or in expansion overseas to Brittany and Galicia. It resulted in changes in Western Scotland beyond the Roman Wall as well. The late H. M. Chadwick in his last work, a scholarly excursion into the misty, shadowy realm of Celtic history, has shown that about 450 A.D. Romanized Britons advanced beyond Cumberland and captured Scotland right up to the Firth of Forth. This region remained under British control for centuries as the important kingdom of Strathclyde and here St. Ninian built his famous monastery, the White House, which spread Christianity throughout Galway and beyond. In addition, Chadwick showed that in alliance with these Britons an Irish invasion of Dalriada to the north took place, and that it was the occupation of Galway by the Britons and Dalriada by the Scots that broke the power of the Picts on Scotland's west coast and brought peace to the Irish Sea at last. There seems little doubt that Chadwick's picture of British-Irish cooperation after 450 is substantially in accord with the facts as we know them.[41]

In short, what had appeared by 450 or shortly thereafter was the emergence in the Irish Sea of a Celtic thalassocracy which extended from Dalriada to Brittany and perhaps Spain. The Britons, with a rejuvenated maritime spirit, were the senior partners in the thalassocracy, at least at first. The Irish were the junior partners. Though this Celtic maritime empire owed much to surviving Roman tradition in West Britain, it seems to have owed more to that earlier Celtic maritime strength in the Atlantic commented upon in the preceding chapter. It was to endure for centuries, until it forged the Celtic peoples into a cultural area with a common and peculiar set of Christian practices, art, literature and language—as well as a common naval tradition.[42]

Let us now turn to Galicia and Gallic coasts south of Brittany. Here it is interesting to note that up to the time of the invasion of Armorica shortly after 450, these shores do not seem to have been

[41] H. M. Chadwick, *Early Scotland* (Cambridge 1948), pp. 139-53. See also W. D. Simpson, "Stilicho and Early Britain," in *Jour. of British Arch. Soc.*, 3rd ser., VII (1942), 42-52. T. C. Lethbridge, *Herdsmen and Hermits*, pp. 62-64.

[42] In a sense, this marks a return to conditions which prevailed here in the late Bronze Age, when a culture area consisting of Brittany, Spain and the lands about the Irish Sea also took shape. On this earlier culture area, see M. Davies, "The Diffusion and Distribution of Megalithic Monuments of the Irish Sea and North Channel Coastline," in *Antiquaries Journal*, XXVI (1946), 36-43, and V. G. Childe, "Trade and Industry in Barbarian Europe till Roman Times," in *Cambridge Economic History of Europe*, II, 21-24. On connections between Irish art and earlier La Tene culture, see N. Åberg, *The Orient and Occident in the Art of the Seventh Century* (London, 1937), I, 126-29, and T. C. Lethbridge, *Merlin's Island* (London 1948), pp. 121-22.

adversely affected by either Saxon or Celtic sea power. After 454, however, this ceased to be the case. The first mention of Scandinavian pirates along these coasts occurs in 456. In that year a fleet of Heruls made a descent upon the shore of Galicia with seven ships.[43] Three years later Herul attacks were extended down the Spanish coast to reach Baetica near the Strait of Gilbraltar.[44] Four years later, in 463, we hear of Saxon pirates in the Loire region who advanced up the river to besiege Angers.[5] In the next year this city opened its gates to them.[46] Shortly afterwards, in 470, a band of Frankish troops in Roman employ defeated them and drove them from island bases they were occupying at the mouth of the Loire.[47] In 475, however, these Saxons had advanced south to the Garonne, for Sidonius, in a letter dating from that year, informs us that the Visigoths sent their Garonne fleet against them.[48] A little later, at the time of Clovis, we learn that Saxons were again operating at the entrance to the Loire, where they besieged the city of Nantes.[49]

Once established along these shores, the Saxon pirates did not return to their homeland. Rather they soon formed a permanent settlement in the Charente region from which they could harry Gallic shores.[50] They remained there until, towards the middle of the sixth century, they were Christianized and gradually absorbed into the Gallo-Roman population of the region.[51] But until this absorption took place they were a distinct element, still maintaining maritime connections with their kinsmen as far away as Kent.[52]

Thus a study of Western Gallic and Spanish shores between 450

[43] Chron. of Hydatius, in MGH Auct. Ant., XI, 28.

[44] Ibid., p. 31. Note the similarity between these Herul attacks on Spain and those of later Vikings, who also attacked Galicia and Andalusia after plundering Gaul.

[45] Gregory of Tours, Hist. Franc., II, 18, in MGH Script. rer. Merov., I, 83.

[46] Ibid., II, 19, loc.cit.

[47] Jordanes, Gaetica, XLV, in MGH Auct. Ant., V, 118-19.

[48] Sidonius Apollinaris, Epistolae, in ibid., VIII, 152-53.

[49] Gregory of Tours, Liber in gloria martyrum, LIX, in MGH Script. rer. Merov., I, 528-29.

[50] See Salin's analysis of the archeological remains of this Saxon settlement, in E. Salin, La Civilisation merovingienne, I (Paris 1950), 70-76.

[51] Fortunatus, Carmina, in MGH Auct. Ant., IV, 62.

[52] In the cemetery of Herpes one finds brooches made in the same workshops as those found at Sarre in Kent, which date from the middle of the 6th century. E. T. Leeds, Early Anglo-Saxon Art and Archeology, p. 56. On silver money at Herpes which resembles Kentish types, see M. Prou, Catalogue des monnaies merovingiennes (Paris 1892), pp. C-CI. On connections with this region shortly after 550 shown by a Kentish hoard of Merovingian coin ornaments, see P. Grierson, "The Canterbury (St. Martin's) Hoard of Frankish and Anglo-Saxon Coin Ornaments," in British Numismatic Journal, XVII (1953), 39-51.

and 550 shows first Herul and then Saxon pirates active there. And it seems clear that their activities seriously interfered with the commerce which earlier had been carried on all but undisturbed with Ireland and West Britain. It is to these Herul and Saxon pirates, as well as to Breton mariners, that we owe in part the isolation of Ireland and West Britain from the Continent during these years—an isolation which accounts for the divergencies between the Irish and British Celtic church and that of the rest of Europe.[53]

There remains one final point, the question of the relations between those Britons moving into Armorica and Spain and Herul and Saxon pirates off the same coasts. It seems hard to believe that these peoples were always hostile to one another. There is too much coincidence in the timing of invasions by each to be accidental. For instance, the beginnings of settlement by Britons in Armorica coincide with the arrival of the Heruls in Galicia (also a spot where Britons settled). In exactly the same year, 470, we find an army of Britons, or Bretons, under Riothamus on the Loire and a Saxon band besieging Nantes. As Theudebert's later remark implies, there must have been a large degree of cooperation between these two groups of invaders. In the next century such a close collaboration was in evidence when Saxons of Bayeux assisted the Breton chief, Bro-Weroc, in his attacks on Nantes.[54] Was it not probably true earlier as well?

So far our attention has been fixed on naval developments in the English Channel, about the Irish Sea and in the Atlantic between 400-550. But what happened during these years to that portion of Gaul, still loyal to Rome, which lay between the Rhine, the Loire and the Channel? What was its fate, cut off from Britain, on the one hand, and from the Mediterranean, on the other, by the newly established kingdoms of the Visigoths and Burgundians?

It should be noticed in the first place that during the first decades of the fifth century this portion of Gaul and the Rhinelands suffered little from invasion. The Suevi and Vandals passed swiftly through

[53] On these Celtic monastic and church peculiarities, see H. Zimmer, *The Celtic Church in Britain and Ireland* (London 1902), pp. 23-131, and J. Ryan, *Irish Monasticism* (London 1931), pp. 1-25.

[54] The Saxons of Bayeux fought both for and against the Breton chief, Bro-Weroc, when he attacked Vannes, Rennes and Nantes. Gregory of Tours, *Hist. Franc.*, v, 26; v, 29; x, 9, in *MGH Script. rer. Merov.*, I, 221-23, 416-19. One sees the same cooperation in the West Britain of Ceawlin (Colin) and Cerdic. A. W. Wade-Evans, "Further Remarks on the De Excidio" in *Archeologia Cambriensis*, XCVIII (1944), 113-28.

the province without doing much damage.[55] The Visigoths, who entered Gaul from its Mediterranean side, stayed south of the Loire. Save in Flanders, the Rhine frontier stood firm as Franks and Alemanni remained generally in place as loyal *foederati*. The Burgundians, decimated by the advancing Huns in Central Germany and given lands in the Saône valley, stayed quiet and served as auxiliaries in the Roman armies. If the advancing Hunnic Empire in Central Europe looked ominous, it did not, prior to 450, directly menace this portion of the Empire. Perhaps the greatest internal problem, *bagaudae* risings in Armorica, were partially suppressed with Visigoth help.[56]

At this moment the last great Roman general in the West, Aetius, became *magister militum* in Gaul. He seems to have recognized the potential dangers to his province of the uneasy peace that prevailed— to have understood that Visigoths, Burgundians, Franks and Alemanni within Rome's western boundaries, like the Saxon and Irish raiders in the Channel, meant ultimate extinction of Roman authority. At the same time the continued *bagaudae* risings in the Loire valley, led by a certain Tibautto, were undermining public order and prosperity in the heart of Gaul. Aetius, with scanty revenues to pay soldiers and little access to the Mediterranean, had to be more of a diplomat than a soldier to rule Gaul. For a time at least he succeeded.

He persuaded the Imperial government in Italy to pay large sums to Attila the Hun, thus ensuring his benevolence, and hired Alanic and Hunnic mercenaries to keep order in the province.[57] These Alans he quartered in the Loire valley, where they suppressed the *bagaudae* with such ferocity that the devastation they wrought exceeded that achieved by the rebellious peasants themselves.[58] He checked the Franks at Tournai and made them return to their former allegiance, and used the Burgundians to check the Alemanni. By playing one barbarian group against another he kept an unstable peace.[59] Perhaps

[55] Jerome, our chief source on the damage done by this invasion, mentions only Mainz, Worms, Spires and Strasbourg on the Rhine and Reims, Arras, Tournai, Amiens and Toulouse in Gaul as cities sacked by these barbarians. Jerome, *Epistolae*, in *Patrologia Latina*, ed. Migne, XII, cols. 1057-58. G. Kurth, *Etudes franques* (Paris 1919), I, 151. Note that Cologne and the Meuse and Moselle regions escaped damage.

[56] L. Halphen, *Les Barbares*, pp. 19-21. F. Lot, *La Gaule*, pp. 471-75.

[57] On these subsidies, see J. B. Bury, *History of the Later Roman Empire*, I, 271-98.

[58] Y. Kulachovski, *Alany po svedeniiam klassichishik i vizantiishikh pisatelei* (Kiev 1899), p. 38. *Chron. Gallia ad anno 441*, in *MGH Auct. Ant.*, IX, 660. F. Lot, *La Gaule*, pp. 482-84.

[59] F. Lot, *Les Invasions germaniques*, pp. 80-95.

his greatest triumph was at Troyes, where he rallied a Germanic army of Burgundians, Franks and Visigoths to stop the advance of Attila the Hun into Gaul. But this victory was his swan song, for like his predecessor Stilicho he was rewarded for his successes by being murdered by his ungrateful Imperial master. Probably the cause was hopeless anyway. All an Aetius could do in this sub-Roman period in Gaul was to delay the inevitable end.[60]

Within thirty years after his death, Roman Gaul came to this end. Indeed, the disintegration began almost at once. The Britons invaded Armorica, Saxons attacked West Gallic shores, Burgundians fully occupied the Rhone valley, the Alemanni took Alsace. The Visigoths under King Ataulf spread across Central Gaul despite heroic resistance by some local Gallo-Roman magnates. The Franks along the Rhine, sometimes called the Riparians, seeped around the Rhineland cities and advanced into Lorraine and Luxembourg. Other Frankish tribesmen, the Salians, resumed their march towards the Seine. Neither Paul nor Aegidius nor Syagrius, the weak successors to Aetius, could defend their Roman heritage adequately. Roman Gaul was to expire only a few years after Romulus Augustulus, the last Emperor in the West, was deposed by his German mentor in Italy in 476.[61]

The problem in Roman Gaul was not whether it would finally disappear but who would gain the prize. The Visigoths would seem to have had the best chance of succeeding in the sweepstakes of history which were naming Rome's successor to the province Caesar had conquered. They controlled most of the central and western portion of Gaul, areas which were hardly damaged by the disorders that afflicted other sections of the province. They had an able and ambitious leader in King Ataulf. They were the most Romanized of the Germans and had the support of talented Gallo-Roman aristocrats like Avitus. Yet it was not they but the Franks, with few of these advantages, who triumphed.

It was the personal leadership of Clovis which brought the Franks to victory over their rivals in Gaul. Clovis began modestly as a minor Salian princeling in Northeastern Gaul with few assets save an un-

[60] F. Lot, *La Gaule*, pp. 486-93. R. Latouche, *op.cit.*, pp. 108-17.

[61] F. Lot, *op.cit.*, pp. 494-510, and *Les Invasions germaniques*, pp. 120-28. R. Latouche, *op.cit.*, pp. 143-50. See particularly Verlinden's revision of De Marez' views on the Frankish movement into Belgium. C. Verlinden, "Het Kolonization Franke," in *Algemene Geschiedenis der Nederlanden*, I (1949), 30-61. See also E. Salin, *La Civilisation merovingienne*, I, 319-84.

scrupulousness and an energy which were outstanding. His first step was to attack Syagrius, the last leader of sub-Roman Gaul. A victory delivered the northern portion of the province down to the Loire into his grasp. Then he turned on the Visigoths under their new king, Alaric II. Again a single battle near Poitiers sufficed to destroy their dominion. Clovis pursued them south and took their capital of Toulouse, only the intervention of Theodoric the Ostrogoth preventing him from reaching the Mediterranean. The Visigoths henceforth made Spain their kingdom and headquarters, although they kept a narrow strip of land in Southern Gaul bounded by the Pyrenees, the Rhone and the Mediterranean. Then Clovis turned towards the Rhine and at Zulpick defeated the Alemanni, who were advancing north, and forced them to acknowledge his overlordship. In his last days Clovis, who had become an orthodox Christian, contented himself with murdering princely Frankish rivals and consolidating his state. Upon his death in 511 he left a vast kingdom built upon the ruins of Rome's Gallic province and extending beyond into Germany.[62]

His successors as rulers of the Franks continued his work. Seemingly possessed of a fratricidal tendency of a most sanguinary character, and alternately dividing and reuniting their domains, these Merovingian monarchs found time to increase the size of their kingdom. They gobbled up the Burgundian kingdom and advanced to seize Provence on the Mediterranean from the Ostrogoths. They intervened unsuccessfully in the Byzantine-Ostrogothic struggle for Italy. But in the course of this intervention they forced Alemanni, Thuringians and the newly arrived Bavarians of Southeastern Germany to accept their overlordship. It seems probable that even the Saxons of Northern Germany recognized their authority for a time in the mid-sixth century. By 550, then, the Franks had become the most important Continental power in Atlantic Europe, with a realm stretching from the Mediterranean and Atlantic coasts of Gaul into Central Germany. In this period their interests drew them towards the Mediterranean and they made their home in Gaul despite their

[62] The principal source on Clovis is, of course, Gregory of Tours, who wrote after the events he described. The latest revisions of this story are to be found in A. Van de Vijvier, "La Victoire contre les Alemanni et la conversion de Clovis," in *Rev. belge*, XV-XVI (1936-37), and J. M. Wallace-Hadrill, "The Works of Gregory of Tours in the Light of Modern Research," in *Trans. of Royal Hist. Soc.*, 5th ser., I (1951), 25-45. On the events leading up to and including Clovis' victory over the Visigoths at Poitiers, see M. Giraud, "Note sur la cité de Poitiers à l'époque merovingienne," in *Mélanges Louis Halphen*, pp. 271-73. For a brief standard account, see F. Lot, *Les Invasions germaniques*, pp. 130-33.

Germanic blood. But in controlling much of Germany they had Teutonic interests as well, which already forecast the coming of a Dagobert and a Charlemagne in later centuries.[63]

While sub-Roman Gaul was being merged into a greater Frankish kingdom, the eastern and midland areas of sub-Roman Britain were gradually becoming Anglo-Saxon England. Just how the Anglo-Saxons invaded and transformed the major portion of Britain into Germanic kingdoms has long vexed historians. Unlike Gregory of Tours' account of the Frankish conquests in Gaul, there are few historical documents which tell us how the Anglo-Saxons conquered Britain. Only a few fragments found in Gildas, Bede, Nennius and the *Anglo-Saxon Chronicle* throw light on the events of these years— and all these sources have been questioned on various grounds. Happily the resources which archeology and numismatics have made available to us in recent years, not only in Britain but in Friesland and Scandinavia as well, help us to fill certain gaps in our knowledge. We are closer today to a knowledge of the essential facts of Anglo-Saxon movement into Britain than we were twenty years ago, though much remains to be learned.

One fact now seems clear. Though the Saxons' activity along the coasts of Britain goes back to the third century, when the Saxon Shore defense system of Rome began, their actual invasion of the island in force—their colonization, if you will—came rather late. Up to 450 A.D. the main attacks of the Saxons seem to have been directed not against Britain but against the Channel coasts of Northern France, where at Boulogne and at Bayeux in Normandy they formed their first overseas settlements.[64] Certainly they launched raids on Britain in 408, 429 and 441-442 as they had in the fourth century.[65] But, except for certain of them who had long been employed by the Romans as *Gewissae* and a possible foothold established in Essex, near the mouth of the Thames, they left sub-Roman Britain alone. It was not they but the Picts, coasting along Britain's eastern shores in their pirate craft, who were feared as formidable enemies by the

[63] On the development and expansion of the Frankish state after Clovis, see F. L. Ganshof, "Het Tijdperk van der Merovingern," in *Algemene Geschiedenis der Nederlanden*, II (1950) 246-73. Also F. Lot, *La Gaule*, pp. 133-34; E. Salin, *op.cit.*, pp. 55-60; and J. Wallace-Hadrill, *op.cit.*, pp. 131-34.

[64] On this point, see F. Lot, "Les Migrations saxonnes," and "Bretons et Anglais au Vᵉ et VIᵉ siècles," *loc.cit.*, pp. 15-31. Also E. Foord, *The Last Age of Roman Britain*, pp. 141-206.

[65] *Chron. Gallia*, in *MGH Auct. Ant.*, VI, 654, 660. Constantius, *Vita Germani*, XVII, in *MGH Script. rer. Merov.*, I, 263-65.

sub-Roman civilized populace of Britain huddled in the shadow of the Saxon Shore forts in Kent and East Anglia.[66]

The collapse of Rome's naval defenses in the Channel between 428 and 450 made the plight of the Romano-British inhabitants of this part of the island more desperate. They still had their forts along the Saxon Shore to defend them, and some remnants of Roman military units, or at least Roman military traditions, were maintained as late as 428 and even afterwards.[67] They possessed in Kent a leader, Vortigern, who was typical of the sort of local strong man produced by these years in sub-Roman Britain and Gaul. But their contact with the Continent was gone and their naval forces had ceased to exist.[68]

It was at this point, about the year 449, that Vortigern, according to tradition, opened the gates to the Teutonic invaders by hiring several shiploads of Jutish mercenaries under Hengist and Horsa to defend his land against the Picts. No doubt the names Hengist and Horsa are apocryphal, but the event itself has about it an air of verisimilitude. Note that these mercenaries were hired for use against the Picts, but that they were not Saxons. They were Jutes from Scandi- navia, perhaps Jutland. Nor should it surprise us to find Scandinavians so far south. Were not Heruls from the same part of the world to be found a few years later raiding the coasts of Spain? And would not Jutes be safer allies than the neighboring Saxons? It has even been suggested that Franks were included among these mercenaries, certain- ly a possibility. It is clear, however, that their chief purpose was to provide the naval defense then lacking on these coasts. As such, their employment reminds one of a similar purchase of the services of Olaf Tryggvasson along these shores many centuries later.

According to Gildas and later tradition, these mercenaries of Vortigern revolted and established themselves in Kent about 450 with- out too much difficulty. They were soon joined by certain Saxon elements under Aisc, who may have been the actual founder of the Kentish kingdom. About 480 A.D. other Saxon bands arrived on the

---

[66] Gildas, in De excidio Brit., XVII, in MGH Auct. Ant., XIII, 32, tells us of a letter sent to Aetius which mentions only Picts and Scots as invaders—not Saxons.

[67] Though the Notitia Dignitatum still mentions Britain's defenses as late as 428, the Theodosian Code makes no reference to Britain at all. Tradition, however, tells of Britons who defended the Roman shore fort at Andreda (Pevensey) as late at 480. On coin evidence for the late occupation of Richborough, see B. W. Pearce, "The Coins from Richborough—A Survey," in Num. Chron., 5th ser., xx (1941), 57-75.

[68] This lack of contact is best shown by the minimissimi coinage itself, which copies only 4th-century coins. See H. V. Sutherland, Coinage and Currency in Roman Britain (Oxford 1937), pp. 98-105, 122-25.

south coast near Pevensey and established a settlement which was to be known as the kingdom of Sussex. These bands probably originated across the Channel in the Saxon colony of Boulogne. And it is interesting to note that, according to tradition, the local Romano-British inhabitants who were still defending the Roman shore fortress of Anderida resisted their landings stubbornly.[69]

It was not, however, by way of Sussex or Kent that the largest number of Saxon immigrant invaders passed into Britain, but rather by way of the east coast. And excavations in Frisia show us that they reached Britain by way of the *terpens* of the Netherlands—not by crossing the Channel from Saxon colonies like those established at Boulogne. Furthermore, archeology in Friesland allows us to date their invasion with a large degree of accuracy and thus to compare it with the traditional Gildas account.

What *terpen* excavations reveal is that very close to the year 450 there was a large-scale sea invasion of the *terpens* of Frisia by a people whose pottery shows that they came from the low-lying land at the entrance to the Elbe and the Weser—the home of the Saxons. These invaders established themselves so firmly along these coasts that they changed the original Frisian composition of the population to one which was predominantly Saxon in culture. Now Frisia is along the route which, considering the ships in use, must have been followed by Saxons who were moving into Britain, and the date 450 agrees with Gildas' traditional date for the loss of Kent.[70]

Soon after the Saxon conquest of Frisia, archeology reveals their presence on English shores. There they seem to have entered the principal river systems in Eastern Britain, pressing down these streams and other natural land routes. They appear to have by-passed some centers of local British resistance such as Kent, London,

[69] Collingwood and Myers, *Roman Britain and the English Settlements*, pp. 291-320, 352-62. R. Hodgkin, *History of the Anglo-Saxons*, I, 74-101. F. Stenton, *Anglo-Saxon England*, pp. 16-25. T. C. Lethbridge, *Merlin's Island*, pp. 127-29. All these historians stress the uniqueness of Kent in Anglo-Saxon England with its Frankish elements and strong survival of Romano-British culture. On this point, see particularly R. Jessup, *Anglo-Saxon Jewelry* (London 1950), pp. 1-48, and T. D. Kendrick, *Anglo-Saxon Art* (London 1938), pp. 62-68.

[70] Myers, who follows Holwerda, seems to date the Saxon occupation of the Frisian *terpens* too early—in the 4th century. Collingwood and Myers, *op.cit.*, p. 341. Slicher van Bath, who uses the Terpen of Erzinge as his guide, dates the occupation from about 400 A.D. H. Slicher van Bath, "Dutch Tribal Problems," in *Speculum*, XXIV (1949), 319-30. The fuller data of Boeles seems to show that, though there were small earlier Saxon settlements in Frisia, full Saxon occupation of the *terpens* came about 450 A.D. Only after such settlement in Frisia did they go on to England in large numbers. P. Boeles, *Friesland*, pp. 207-50.

the Cambridge region and areas about the Saxon Shore forts in East Anglia. Some reached the upper Thames by way of the Ouse very soon after 450.[71]

In many regions of Eastern Britain, evidence seems to show that this invasion was peaceful—in the nature of a colonization. Elsewhere it was otherwise, and local British inhabitants resisted fiercely and successfully. In fact, we know from Gildas that some Britons under the leadership of Ambrosius Aurelianus and Artorius, who was later famous as Arthur, checked the Saxons at the battle of Badon Hill in 509 and held up their advances in the Midlands and in West Britain for at least half a century. Elsewhere in the east, however, in such regions as East Anglia and Kent a certain amalgamation took place between Romano-British natives and Saxon invaders.[72]

At the same time, from Kent a colony was sent out and established in Hampshire and on the Isle of Wight—interesting because it is the only extension of the invaders beyond Sussex along the shores of the Channel.[73] Gradually new states began to take form in the partially Saxon-Jutish, partially British island. Certainly the most interesting of them was Wessex, a kingdom which from the start seems to have had a mixed population composed of Romano-British subjects of West Britain, Jutes from Hampshire and Saxons who had reached the upper Thames region. If anything, the original dominant element was Celtic rather than Saxon, as can be seen from the names which

[71] F. Stenton, op.cit., pp. 30-31. R. Jessup, op.cit., pp. 18-26. Collingwood and Myers, op.cit., pp. 352-410, contains the fullest account, with a map, of the routes followed. For the archeological basis of any theories on Anglo-Saxon settlement, see the excellent article by E. T. Leeds, "The Distribution of the Angles and Saxons Archeologically Considered," in Archeologia, XCI (1945), 78-85.

[72] On Badon Hill, see Collingwood and Myers, op.cit., pp. 302-24, F. Stenton, op.cit., pp. 3-8, 30-31, and F. Lot, Bretons et Anglais, pp. 9-17. Lot is skeptical of any great survival of Britons in areas colonized by Saxons. F. Lot, op.cit., pp. 17-20. On the other hand, there is much evidence, in addition to coin finds from Richborough, that amalgamation rather than extermination often took place. See, for instance, R. Hodgkin, op.cit., pp. 137-78; and evidence on survival of Romano-British London in R. Wheeler, London and the Saxons (London 1935), pp. 64-66, and F. Stenton, op.cit., pp. 52-57. In Kent both Romano-British techniques in art and the pre-Saxon field system survived. R. Jessup, op.cit., pp. 41-57. The same thing in true in Suffolk, as revealed by the Sutton Hoo finds. R. Bruce-Mitford, "The Sutton Hoo Ship Burial," in Proceedings of the Royal Society of Suffolk, XXV (1949), 23-46. Even in York and Lincoln, both in the Angle—not Saxon—settlement area, one finds some pottery survivals. J. N. Myers, "Lincoln in the Fifth Century," in Archeological Journal, CIII (1946), 85-88.

[73] Collingwood and Myers, op.cit., pp. 397-410. Wade-Evans dates the Jutish colonies in Hampshire and the Isle of Wight from about 514 A.D. A. W. Wade-Evans, "Further Remarks on the De Excidio," loc.cit., pp. 82-109. See also R. Hodgkin, History of the Anglo-Saxons, I, 90-101.

tradition assigns to its first kings, Ceawlin (Colin) and Cerdic.[74] All of this simply seems to bear out what the raids of Britons and Saxons on Gallic coasts reveal, that the relations between these two peoples during these years were often more harmonious than most historians have believed. Indeed, had the story in Britain ended at this point, the island might have settled down to a slow amalgamation of old and new inhabitants not unlike that which was taking place in Gaul.[75]

That this did not happen, that the racial balance was tipped in favor of the Teutonic in England, was due to the arrival in Britain shortly after 500 A.D. of a new Germanic people, the Angles.[76] Unlike the Saxons, the Angles were a Baltic people whose original home appears to have been the Danish peninsula and the islands nearby.[77] Also their movement into Britain was of a different character than that of their near neighbors, the Saxons. Only a portion of the Saxon people left their homes in Germany to settle in Frisia or continue on to England. The greater number remained in Northeastern Germany. On the contrary, the Angles moved as an entire people, leaving their original homeland deserted, though they seem to have included amongst them a certain number of people of Swedish and Saxon-Frisian origin as well.[78] And their migration was something new, a

[74] Wessex represents a particular problem. It seems to have developed late as a separate kingdom and from the start to have represented an amalgamation of Saxon, Jutish and Romano-Celtic populations.

[75] The date of Ceawlin's conquests of Gloucester, Cirencester and Bath, and thus of the Wessex kingdom, was probably the *late* 6th century. A. H. Williams, *An Introduction to the History of Wales* (Cardiff 1944), pp. 76-80. Lot admits the survival of a sizable Celtic population in Wessex, particularly in Dorset, Devon and Somerset. F. Lot, *Bretons et Anglais*, pp. 15-17.

[76] The similarity is striking between the way the Jutish and Saxon advance into Britain was checked at Badon Hill in the 6th century and the way the Danes were checked by Alfred in the 9th century. The Juto-Saxon "Danelaw" established in Eastern Britain, as a result of this victory, did not seem overly dangerous to Gildas as late as 550 A.D. It was the later Angle invasion and settlement that upset the balance between Celt and Anglo-Saxon in the island.

[77] Bede states the Angles left their lands deserted when they came to Britain. Bede, *Hist. eccl.*, I, 15, ed. King, I, 70. His words are echoed by Alfred. *Alfred's Orosius*, ed. Sweet, p. 19. Most important is Procopius' information that they possessed neither horses nor sails for their boats—a perfect description of the Baltic peoples of the Danish islands. Procopius, *De bello Gothico*, IV, 19-20, ed. Dewing, V, 252-70.

[78] H. M. Chadwick, *The Origins of the English Nation* (Cambridge 1927), pp. 17-19, 174-77. Collingwood and Myers, *op.cit.*, pp. 342-51. The Sutton Hoo find shows a strong Swedish element from the Uppsala region present among the Wuffinga kings of East Anglia. R. Bruce-Mitford, *op.cit.*, pp. 17-54. *Beowulf* also reveals a similar Scandinavian-Swedish element. G. Turville-Petrie, *The Heroic Age in Scandinavia*, pp. 40-43. On the Frisian element among the Angles, see E. Wadstein, "On the Origin of the English," in *Skrifter K. Humanistika, Vetensh-Samfundt Reg. Acad. Upsal.*, XXIV (1927), 111-41.

movement of a people southwest from the Baltic towards new homes, rather than following southeastern migration routes which had been the traditional Baltic-Scandinavian ones for centuries.[79]

From historical sources we can date approximately when the Angles reached Britain. Bede tells us that in 545 King Ida established the kingdom of Northumberland.[80] Procopius, however, speaks of Angles inhabiting Britain before 540. Frankish sources in addition reveal a raid by Hygelac, King of the Geats, near the mouths of the Rhine, which took place in the second decade of the sixth century, an event, incidentally, also mentioned in *Beowulf*.[81] Since this raid was probably related to the general movement of the Angles from their Baltic lands to England, it seems safe to say that this migration began between 515 and 540, with 525 a guess as to the exact year. It seems rather probable, however, that it continued over a long period, perhaps a century, with those Swedish elements so noticeable in East Anglia arriving in Britain rather late.[82]

[79] Of the problem of the Varini, or Varni, raised by Procopius' story of a naval battle between them and the Angles, there seems an easy solution. Procopius' account says they lived north of the Rhine. If one substitutes Elbe for Rhine, one difficulty vanishes. It then becomes apparent that the Varini lived, in the early 6th century, north of the Elbe between the Saxons, the Frisians, the Thuringians and the Angles in roughly the area which the Slavic Obodrites occupied about 800 A.D. In 523-526 their king sent an embassy to Theodoric, who was by diplomacy trying to establish a route via the Thuringians to Scandinavia and the Baltic. Cassiodorus, *Variae*, V, 1. Thus the Varini barred the Angles' route south to the North Sea and England. Procopius is relating how the Angles defeated them and opened a way to England, which probably went via the Eider-Schlee route. Some Angles, however, settled near the Varini and, after the virtual extermination of these latter by Slavic tribes in the 6th century, amalgamated with the remainder and are found as late as the 9th century. On these *Varini et Angli* who possessed a special law of their own, see F. Stenton, *op.cit.*, pp. 3-8.

[80] Lot accepts this date of 545 for the founding of Northumbria by King Ida. F. Lot, *Bretons et Anglais*, pp. 1-2. Collingwood and Myers, *op.cit.*, pp. 411-22, place the date somewhat earlier.

[81] Hygelac's raid, the first report we have of Baltic peoples advancing southwest into the North Sea area, is variously dated by scholars. Chadwick dates it about 520. H. M. Chadwick, *The Origins of the English Nation*, p. 18. Kendrick about 516. T. D. Kendrick, *A History of the Vikings*, p. 3. Shetelig believes it took place in 512. H. Shetelig, *An Introduction to the Viking History of Western Europe* (Oslo 1950), p. 3. The source is Gregory of Tours, *Hist. Franc.*, III, 3. It does seem clear, however, that Hygelac's force was the vanguard of what was to become the Angle invasion of Britain.

[82] The defeat of a force of Danes and Saxons near Groningen in Frisia by Duke Lupus of Austrasia between 565 and 574 probably marks the end of this movement southwest from the Baltic in organized form. Fortunatus, *Carmina*, VII, 7, in *MGH Auct. Ant.*, IV, 160. By 600 A.D., when the Franks had stabilized the *status quo* in the Netherlands, the Angle invasion was over. P. Boeles, *Friesland*, pp. 269-77. Interestingly enough, finds of Scandinavian gold *brachteates* in England (almost all from Kent) confirm such dates (circa 515 to circa 575) for the Angle invasion. The first

Archeological discoveries made in Britain add to knowledge gleaned from our sources. They seem to show that the Angles reached a more northerly section of Britain's east coast than was the case with the Saxon migration. The landings of the Angles extended from the mouth of the Humber as far south as the middle portion of East Anglia. From here they advanced into the interior and proceeded up the coast to Bernicia. Their greatest concentration of settlements appears to have been in the Midlands. In their advance they not only overwhelmed British resistance in the northern portion of the island, but seem to have either replaced or amalgamated peacefully with earlier Saxon settlers in parts of East Anglia and Central Britain as well. North of a line running roughly from Oxford to Cambridge through Central and Eastern England they became the dominant group.[83] Thus it seems certain that it was the Angles who upset the balance between Celt and Teuton of which Gildas spoke so confidently after Badon Hill, and who tipped it in favor of the latter. Soon they were to lead this Teutonic element to victory in Mercia and Northumberland, capture the Severn valley and Chester, and sever the land connections which linked Cornwall with Wales and Wales with Strathclyde. But even though they made Britain English, the Angles were not *per se* hostile to the British inhabitants of the land. Even after their arrival, strong Celtic elements remained in Bernicia and elsewhere in Northeastern Britain, while up to the eighth century Celts in Strathclyde and Wales were to fight in alliance with their Angle neighbors in Mercia and Northumberland quite as often as they did against them.[84]

This brings us to a consideration of the pattern of events which occurred during these years in Central European and Scandinavian regions of Northern Europe. What happened in these lands as a result of migration and invasion to the south? Here again, as in the case of England, our knowledge is very scanty indeed—so scanty, in fact,

---

of these *brachteates* come from early 6th century Kentish graves, the last ones from graves dating from the latter half of the century. R. Jessup, *Anglo-Saxon Jewelry*, pp. 121-22, and *The Archeology of Kent* (London 1930), p. 232. On the fact that these *brachteates* are of Swedish rather than Jutish or Angle origin, see E. T. Leeds, "Denmark and Early England," in *Antiquaries Journal*, XXVI (1946), 22-28.

[83] E. T. Leeds, "The Distribution of the Angles and Saxons Archeologically Considered," in *Archeologia*, XCI (1945), 60-75. See also his *Corpus of Early Anglo-Saxon Great Square Headed Brooches*, pp. 3-141.

[84] F. Stenton, *Anglo-Saxon England*, pp. 30-31. A. H. Williams, *op.cit.*, pp. 76-89. F. Lot, *Bretons et Anglais*, pp. 16-17. Collingwood and Myers, *op.cit.*, pp. 411-22. H. M. Chadwick, *Origins of the English Nation*, pp. 17-19.

that without the resources of archeology we would be hard pressed to give even the barest outline of important events.

During the first three quarters of the fifth century, however, it is apparent that the activities of one people—the Huns—were the decisive influence which shaped events from the Black Sea and the Danube to Scandinavia. Even earlier, of course, the Huns had played a vital role by overthrowing the Ostrogothic kingdom of South Russia and driving the Visigoths into the Empire. In so doing, they had undone that Germanization of South Russia which was proceeding under Ostrogothic influence and destroyed the wide dominion which Ermanaric was building in the steppes and forests of Russia west of the Urals.

Now, in the fifth century, the Huns, carrying Ostrogoths and other peoples with them, began to extend their dominion west into Central Europe. Their empire was not essentially an Eastern one, but rather a conglomeration of Germanic, Slavic elements commanded by a Hunnic elite. Certain German tribes, like the Ostrogoths and Gepids, who served them faithfully, almost seem to have had a position of junior partners in their state. Perhaps, then, we would be wise to consider their empire a Germanic-Hunnic affair, rather than exclusively Central Asian. Gradually, as they pushed west, annihilating stubborn enemies like the Burgundians who stood in their way, their empire came to have its center in the Hungarian plain and stretched from the Urals to the Rhine and from the Danube to the Baltic.[85]

Until recently there has been a tendency to paint the Huns of the fifth century as cruel, savage barbarians who menaced the Roman world and ruled by terror. These nomadic warriors have been depicted as little better than the savages whom Ammianus Marcellinus graphically describes at the time of their overthrow of the Ostrogoths. While no one today imagines that the Hunnic Empire was run as an eleemosynary institution, historians have come to temper earlier judgments concerning the Huns' primitiveness and lack of culture. Under King Rugila and under Attila, who succeeded him as monarch in 434, they made great strides towards civilization, as we know from the account of Priscus' embassy to their capital during these years.[86] It is true that their empire represented a menace to the Roman world, one which the Imperial governments to the south attempted to

[85] L. Halphen, *Les Barbares*, pp. 28-35. F. Lot, *La Gaule*, pp. 486-90. G. Vernadsky, *Ancient Russia* (New Haven 1943), pp. 138-42. J. B. Bury, *History of the Later Roman Empire*, I, 290-98.

[86] Priscus, *Frag. hist. Graec.*, IV, ed. Didot, 123-36. J. B. Bury, *op.cit.*, pp. 279-88.

neutralize by payments of immense amounts of gold.[87] But it should be emphasized that in return for these subsidies the Huns on the whole respected the Imperial frontiers and even furnished generals like Aetius with mercenaries who were his most reliable troops. Not until 450 did these warriors become a positive danger when Attila launched two assaults against Rome—one into Gaul and one into Italy. Neither, incidentally, was a success, the first being checked at Troyes, the second resulting in Attila's famous encounter with Pope Leo. Neither the frontiers of the Empire in the West, nor those in the East, then, were broken by Hunnic assault. It seems that the legend of the Hunnic danger to the Roman world has been much exaggerated.

Attila returned from his unsuccessful expeditions to Hungary, where he died in his capital shortly thereafter, in 454. His empire, like most nomadic ones, did not long survive his passing. For a few more years, up to 468, the Huns under Attila's nephews and successors, Dengizik and Enik, continued to threaten the Empire's Danube line. Then revolts split the Hunnic state asunder as Germans and others recovered their freedom. The Huns disappeared from the historical scene, some of them retreating to the lower Danube and Dnieper to become the Bulgars, others moving still farther east to reappear in history as the Magyars.[88]

The disintegration of Attila's empire, however, did not bring peace to Central Europe or to Rome's frontiers. Rather it ushered in a confused period of chaos and new movements of peoples. Though the same golden subsidies were paid by Rome now as earlier, they accomplished little. The Ostrogoths on the middle Danube became particularly dangerous to the Eastern Roman Empire as their raids and ambitions increased. To eliminate this menace, and at the same time revenge Odocer's seizure of power in Italy and the extinction of the Imperial Western line in 476, Constantinople's ruler repeated the tactics which had been used with the Visigoths and encouraged Theodoric to lead his people across the Alps into Italy in 488. Theodoric was only too successful and by 490 had established an Ostrogothic kingdom in Italy, one which included the provinces of Rhaetia, Noricum, Pannonia and parts of Illyricum as well, up to the old Roman Danube frontier. For the next thirty years the influence of this great

---

[87] On these subsidies, see J. B. Bury, op.cit., pp. 271-98, and G. Vernadsky, Ancient Russia, pp. 138-42.

[88] G. Vernadsky, op.cit., p. 151. Chron. Paschal, I, 598.

Gothic monarch was to be of major importance over wide areas of the Mediterranean world and in Central Europe as well.[89]

To fill the vacuum left by the migration of the Ostrogoths into Italy, the Lombards appear to have moved south to take up the lands Theodoric's people had vacated. At the same time, according to Procopius, the Heruls, who were settled nearby, migrated back to Scandinavia through the forests of Eastern Germany. In Scandinavia they were welcomed by the Danes, who gave them homes within their domains, probably in Skanë in Southern Sweden. This migration of the Heruls is interesting because Procopius tells us that on their way north they passed through much territory in Eastern Germany which was completely without population, though they did meet some opposition from tribes, probably Slavic, who in places barred their route. Therefore, about the year 500 A.D., Eastern Germany was an open, underpopulated territory, easily traversed by German tribes passing between the Danube and the Baltic.[90]

This state of affairs was not destined to last long, for into these vacant East German lands new colonists soon pressed, Slavic tribes from farther east. Indeed, it may have been their vanguard who gave the Heruls some bad moments on their way north. We know little of the circumstances behind this Slavic migration. Some have claimed that it was led in the north by the mysterious White Croats and White Sorbs, an Alanic minority controlling a Slavic mass. Others have seen it as a westward extension of the somewhat shadowy empire of the Antas which they feel succeeded the empire of the Huns and the kingdom of the Ostrogoths in Central Russia.[91] But whatever its causes, it was of great historical importance. About 500 A.D. Eastern Germany had been relatively unpopulated. By 550 a solid belt of Slavic tribes extended between the Elbe-Saale line, the Baltic and the Hungarian plain. The Obodrites were located in Holstein, the Rugi, Wilzes and Pomeranians farther along the coast, and other tribes to the south as far as the Carpathians. The south shore of the Baltic between the Vistula and the Elbe was no longer in German hands but was held by Slavic peoples. German tribes who lay in the path

[89] G. Vernadsky, op.cit., pp. 170-91. L. Halphen, Les Barbares, pp. 30-35. R. Latouche, Les grandes invasions, pp. 125-42.

[90] Concerning the Heruls, see Procopius, De bello Gothico, II, 15; O. R. Janse, Le Travail de l'or, pp. 32-34; H. Shetelig, Scandinavian Archeology, pp. 255-57; and G. Turville-Petrie, op.cit., pp. 17-18.

[91] F. Dvornik, The Making of Central and Eastern Europe (London 1945), pp. 277-97.

of this advance to the Saale were either pushed west like the Thuringians and the Bavarians or exterminated like the Varini. A Slavic Central Europe had suddenly appeared.[92]

Meanwhile, along the Danube to the south the Avars, a nomadic Turkish tribe of South Russia, pushed west shortly after 500 to fill the vacuum left by the disappearance of the Huns. In 526 they were on the Bosphorus besieging Constantinople. Later they moved farther west with Slavonic allies to take up their residence on the Pannonian plain. It was their Slavic underlings who expelled the Marcomanni and Quadi from Bohemia and drove them into South Germany, where they became the Bavarians. It was they who likewise exterminated the Gepids and drove the Lombards into Italy in 568, an event which doomed restored Byzantine rule of this province. It was they who were responsible for Slavic penetration into Slovenia, Croatia and Serbia and who prepared the way for later Bulgaro-Slavic occupation of Moesia. A savage, nomadic people, they set up a raiding kingdom on the Hungarian plain which lasted until the time of Charlemagne.[93] By 550, then, in the south as in its northern portion, Central Europe had been tranformed. A solid bloc of primitive Slavic tribes and raiding Avars were located between the Baltic and the Balkans. Extending far to the west, they pressed the Germans into a relatively small area of Southern and Western Germany and isolated the peoples of Scandinavia from their Germanic cousins to the south. Central Europe, now in the possession of a new series of peoples, moved towards a new destiny.

The complicated history of Scandinavia between 400 and 550 A.D., the changes and migrations which occurred there, can be understood only in relation to these developments in Central Europe. For during the years of the Late Empire, as was noted in the previous chapter, it was almost entirely by way of Central Europe that communication and trade were maintained between Scandinavia and the more civilized lands of the Roman Empire and the Black Sea. These routes were land ones extending from the south shores of the Baltic. One

[92] Slavic tribes reached the Elbe in this period, according to Vibrius Sequester, who says, "Albis Suevos a Servetiis dividit." G. Nierdelé, *Manuel de l'antiquité slave*, I (Paris 1923), 65-80, 131. See also F. Lot, *Les Invasions*, pp. 301-4; F. Dvornik, *op.cit.*, p. 14; A. Kroebner, *The Colonization of Europe*, pp. 29-30; and G. Vernadsky, *Kievan Russia* (New Haven 1949) pp. 318-32.

[93] The standard study of the Avars, their expansion and raids, is still H. Howorth, "The Avars," in *Jour. of Roy. Asiatic Soc.*, new ser., XXI (1898), 50-137. See also E. Salin, *La Civilisation merovingienne*, I, 60-61; F. Lot, *op.cit.*, pp. 218-21; and G. Vernadsky, *Ancient Russia*, pp. 170-204.

went by way of the Elbe and Saale to the Rhine and upper Danube. Another followed the Oder and reached the mid-Danube via the Moravian Gap. Still others passed down the Vistula, Niemen and Dvina to reach the lower Danube and Black Sea by way of the Dniester and Dnieper.[94]

In the fourth century the more easterly routes which led to South Russia had assumed a particular importance, since they led to the flourishing Ostrogothic kingdom there. Thanks to them, knowledge of Ermanaric, the Ostrogothic ruler, made him a subject of Norse myth and legend.[95]

When the Huns conquered the Ostrogoths in South Russia and carried them west into Central Europe, they destroyed, or at least seriously weakened, these most easterly routes leading to the Black Sea from the Baltic. But not so those farther west that led to the Rhine and Danube. Under the Huns, contact between Scandinavia and the Baltic was maintained and may even have increased in importance, the best proof being the large volume of gold which found its way to Uppland Sweden, Gotland, Oland and Bornholm, probably as the result of subsidies paid to the Huns and other barbarians.[96] Attila, like Ermanaric, entered Norse legend and story, his half-Germanic empire giving rise to the Niebelungen legend. In contrast to this contact with and interest in Central Europe, the people of Scandinavia played little part at first in the history of Europe farther west. A few Heruls from the north raided Western shores, and some Jutes occupied Kent, but up to 500 A.D. the Saxon invasions of France and England procceded with very little Scandinavian assistance.

Suddenly we notice a change. The Angles from homes on the Baltic

[94] The amber routes to the Baltic across Central Europe have been carefully traced by J. Déchelette, *Manuel d'archéologie préhistorique*, I (Paris 1908), 210. See also V. G. Childe, "Trade and Industry in Barbarian Europe," in *Cambridge Economic History of Europe*, II (Cambridge 1954), 15-16.

[95] R. Schmittlein, *Étude sur la nationalité des Aestii* (Baden 1948), pp. 25-30. F. Dvornik, *op.cit.*, pp. 277-80. G. Turville-Petrie, *op.cit.*, p. 17. C. Brady, *Legends of Ermanaric* (Berkeley 1943), pp. 61-302.

[96] The classic study of this gold, which reached the Baltic in huge amounts between 400 and 500 A.D., is still O. F. Janse, *Le Travail de l'or en Suède* (Orléans 1922). A large part of the Roman gold pieces were turned into ornaments, *brachteates* and ring money and are found in numerous spots in Uppland Sweden, Vastergotland, Gotland, Bornholm and Oland. But much gold in coin form still survived. 666 such coins have been found to date: 245 in Gotland, 203 in Oland, 116 in Bornholm, 60 on the Swedish mainland, 41 in Denmark and only *one* in Norway. They were minted by Emperors from Honorius through Justinian, with the peak period about 500 A.D. Three quarters of them are from Eastern mints of the Empire; one quarter from Western mints. On these coins, see O. R. Janse, *op.cit.*, pp. 14-16, 159-249, and some recent changes in L. Musset, *Les Peuples scandinaves*, pp. 31-33.

side of the Jutland peninsula and the Danish islands began to move in the wake of the Saxons towards Britain's east coast—a movement which was on a mass scale. Hygelac, king of the Geats, appeared as a raider at the mouths of the Rhine. A Swedish element joined the Angles to establish itself in East Anglia.

Nor was this change of interest and migration routes confined to areas outside Scandinavia. In the Baltic itself we find a similar migration of peoples south and west which reversed previous movements towards the southeast. From Uppland Sweden a migration took place down the coast, overwhelming the inhabitants of the gold-rich islands of Gotland and Oland and bringing Swedes as settlers to the now vacant lands of the Angles in Jutland and the Danish islands, where they became known as the Danes.[97] Others followed the inner water route across Southern Sweden to reach the Vik area of Norway and then, joined by those who came by way of Denmark, proceeded up the coasts of Western Norway as far as Nidaros or on to England.

There is much evidence of this sixth-century movement in Scandinavia. Along the shores of Southern Sweden facing the Baltic one finds a whole series of forts, built, no doubt by the Geatish inhabitants of the land against the coastal attacks of their Uppland neighbors. The traditions of the royal houses of Denmark and Norway, who traced lines back through Ingvar to the kings of Uppland Sweden, are equally impressive evidence of this migration. But most interesting is what we can learn from numismatics. Up to 500—or even 550, for that matter—the abundant gold of Scandinavia, either in the form of Roman coins or heavy gold ornaments, was concentrated in the islands of Gotland, Oland and Bornholm and along the coasts of South Sweden. Soon thereafter, however, we begin to find *brachteates*, gold ornaments copied from these coins, in large numbers in Jutland, the Vik region of Norway and beyond on Norway's west coast—as well as some in Frisia and Eastern Britain. If one follows on a map the locations of finds of *brachteates*, one can chart the migration routes

[97] On Gotland's coming under Swedish control about 550, or at least being attacked and sacked by forces from the Swedish Uppland, see H. N. Sonyrwigg, *Gotland under Aldre Medeltid* (Lund 1940), pp. 8-79. See also O. R. Janse, *op.cit.*, pp. 9-11, and B. Nerman, *Det Svenska Rickets Uppkomst* (Stockholm 1925), pp. 90-133. On the movement of the Danes into the Danish islands and Jutland in this period, see G. Turville-Petrie, *op.cit.*, pp. 47-53, for traditions; and E. T. Leeds, "Denmark and Early England," in *Antiquaries Journal*, XXVI (1940), 34-43, for archeological evidence of this movement.

of the people who made these ornaments from the Swedish Uppland down the coast to Denmark, Southern Norway and beyond.[98]

To this archeological and numismatic information can be added that provided by *Beowulf*. This poem contains important evidence on the situation in Scandinavia during this period—evidence which can be dated from the fact that Hygelac, king of the Geats, or Goths, who appears in the poem was an historical, early sixth-century personage mentioned by a Frankish source. Behind the poem lies the story of the struggle of the Geats or Goths of Southern Sweden with their enemies the Swedes of the Uppland and the Danes—a fact which we have already shown is strongly indicated by other evidence. And the poem ends on a note of despair on the part of the author, who laments that the Geats will suffer a sad fate, since they lie between the hostile Frisians and the hostile Swedes.[99] This remark makes clear what happened in Scandinavia. The Geats, or Goths, had probably owed their earlier wealth and power in Scandinavia to the fact that their location in South Sweden and possibly on the islands of the Baltic like Gotland made them natural intermediaries between this region and the south. Now this was no longer true. The routes south which brought wealth were by way of Frisia and the North Sea[100] and thither a Hygelac went to gain wealth; while by by-passing the Geats and establishing themselves in Denmark and joining with new

---

[98] The routes followed in this movement of peoples west and southwest into Denmark and Norway are outlined by *brachteate* finds shown on a map in O. R. Janse, *op.cit.*, p. 131. Since none of these *brachteates* are of Jutish, Norwegian or Angle style, but are Swedish, they must have been carried by invaders or colonists to the sites where they have been found in Denmark and Norway. O. R. Janse, *op.cit.*, pp. 70-103, and E. T. Leeds, "Denmark and Early England," *loc.cit.*, pp. 27-37. That these movements were not peaceful ones can be seen from the fact that along the shores of Southern Sweden and Southern Norway one finds a series of 5th- and 6th-century stone fortresses, or *borgar*, which show the local inhabitants' attempts to defend themselves. L. Musset, *op.cit.*, pp. 31-33.

Other evidence of the Swedish origin of these movements is to be seen in Norway in the similarity between the Ynglinga kings' graves near Tønsberg and those of Vendel Sweden. A. W. Brøgger, *Borrefundet og Vestfoldkongeres graver, Videnskaps-Selskapets Skriftar*, II, *Hist. Fil. Klasse* (Christiania 1916), pp. 83-137. Equally interesting is the similarity between the Swedish-type boat discovered at Sutton Hoo (Baltic perhaps in origin) and the 6th-century, greater Kvalsund boat uncovered in coastal Norway. Brøgger and Shetelig, *The Viking Ships*, pp. 52-60.

[99] *Beowulf*.

[100] The first concrete evidence of these new *Western* routes reaching the Baltic by way of Moselle, Rhine and perhaps Frisia—routes opened perhaps by Theodoric's diplomacy—comes from four coins, dating from about 550 or shortly thereafter, found in Gotland. They are a *solidus* of Theudebert of Austrasia (534-48) and 3 *solidi* of Anastasius, 2 struck by Burgundian mints and one in Ostrogothic Italy. N. L. Rasmusson, "Foreign Coins in Swedish Coin Finds," in *Trans. of International Num. Congress* (1938), p. 325.

allies there like the Heruls, the Swedes by 550 effectively destroyed the strength of their Geatish neighbors.

What *Beowulf* and the resources of archeology reveal, then, is the tremendous effect upon Scandinavia of the Slavic-Avar occupation of Central Europe. By this occupation the Slavs cut Scandinavia off from its sources of trade and wealth and ruined peoples in that region, like the Geats, who owed their power to their position as intermediaries with the south via Eastern European land routes. They thus helped to stimulate a new migration from Scandinavia to England, the Angle invasion, and a movement of Swedes from the Uppland south and west to Denmark, Southern Norway and beyond.

The closing of the older overland trade routes between Scandinavia and the south was a gradual affair. It began about 500, at the time when the Heruls made their way back to Denmark through Eastern Germany. It was certainly not complete by 550, as we know from the fact that right up to that time a number of gold coins of Eastern Roman origin, which presupposes connection with the lower Danube, were arriving in the islands of the Baltic.[101] And we have additional evidence that from the upper Danube land contact with the Baltic region was still possible as late as 530. Our knowledge comes from the discovery of large numbers of silver Ostrogothic coins across the Alps in South Germany as far north as Mainz. These coin hoards seem to show that commerce towards the north extended this far.[102] To this coin evidence we can add information on embassies which reached Ostrogothic Italy in Theodoric's time. They show that the Ostrogothic ruler maintained contact with Scandinavian and Baltic lands, since he sent embassies and letters to the Thuringians, the Esths and to a certain Roila, king of the Vik region of Norway. In conjunction with the finds of Ostrogothic coins in South Germany, they suggest a route leading by way of the Rhine and the Elbe to Southern Norway and Esthonia.[103]

[101] Since coins of Justinian are rare, one can assume that routes linking the Baltic with the Eastern Roman world via Central Europe were all but closed by 530. O. R. Janse, *op.cit.*, pp. 14-16.

[102] To a few early 6th-century gold *solidi* and *trientes* from Italian and other Mediterranean mints found in scattered sites in Germany, one must add the more abundant silver *siliquae* and *demi-siliquae* (26 in all) found mainly about Mainz and the Upper Rhine. All of these silver coins were minted in Ostrogothic and Byzantine Italy. They show an active contact across the Alps with Italy which extended as far as the mid-Rhine. J. Werner, *Münzdatierte austrasische Grabfunde*, pp. 109-33.

[103] Theodoric's interest in maintaining a *land* route across Germany to Scandinavia and the Baltic is shown by his active diplomacy. On his negotiations with Clovis after the latter's defeat of the Alemanni in 506 A.D., see Cassiodorus, *Variae*, II, 41,

Such a route, however, did not long survive Theodoric's death. The arrival of the Obodrites upon the banks of the Elbe and in Holstein and the wiping-out of the Varini cut the last land route south. Henceforth the Baltic was isolated from the south except by a sea route along the Frisian coast to England and the mouths of the Rhine, while the North Sea area surrounded by Scandinavian and Saxon peoples in Frisia, England, Denmark and Norway became a Teutonic thalassocracy as separate from the rest of Europe as the one the Celts had established in the Western Atlantic.[104] Scandinavia, isolated as never before, began a separate political and cultural existence.[105]

It should be noted, however, that even as the Slavs cut the old amber routes to the south, another development along the Swedish coasts was beginning to take shape. This was a movement not south and west towards the North Sea, but directly east from the Swedish Uppland via the Aland Islands to the coasts of the Gulf of Finland and beyond. One may safely view this as the first step towards the establishment of the later famous Varangian route via Lake Ladoga, the Volga and the Dnieper to the Black and Caspian Seas. Archeological remains show that by 550 some Swedes had penetrated along this route as far as Southern Finland.[106] And Byzantine interest in the Crimea under Justinian seems to indicate one southern terminus at least was active. In fact, Jordanes' remark that Cherson was al-

---

and A. Van de Vijvier, *op.cit.*, pp. 138-43. On his negotiations with the Thuringians between 507 and 511, see Cassiodorus, *Variae*, III, 1, in *MGH Auct. Ant.*, XII, 114. On similar negotiations with the Heruls in the same period, see Cassiodorus, *Variae*, III, 2, in *ibid.*, pp. 114-15. On later negotiations with the Varini in 523-526, see Cassiodorus, *Variae*, V, 1, in *ibid.*, p. 143. On relations with the Aestii, who visited his court with gifts of amber, see Cassiodorus, *Variae*, V, 2, in *ibid.*, p. 144. On his connections with King Roila, or Rodulf, of Norway, mentioned by Jordanes, see H. Shetelig, *La Préhistoire de la Norvège*, pp. 185-86. Down to 530, then, Theodoric maintained contact via land routes across Germany with Southern Norway, Southern Sweden (where the Heruls were settled) and the Eastern Baltic.

[104] See Slicher van Bath on the development of a common culture area around the North Sea which included Jutes, Saxons, Angles and Frisians (I would include Danes and Norwegians). H. Slicher van Bath, "Dutch Tribal Problems," *loc.cit.*, p. 324.

[105] L. Musset, *Les Peuples scandinaves*, pp. 32-37, sums up the aspect of this new Scandinavia. See also *Guides to the National Museum, Copenhagen: Antiquity*, pp. 98-103.

[106] On Swedish expansion into Finland in the 6th century, see L. Musset, *op.cit.*, pp. 39-41, and A. Hackman, *Die Alterei Eisenzeit in Finnland*, I (Helsingfors 1905), 30-151. This also included penetration of the coast of Courland in the vicinity of the Gulf of Riga from both Gotland and the Swedish Uppland, as revealed in archeological finds. B. Nerman, *Die Verbindungen zwischen Skandinavien und dem Ostbalticum in der jüngeren Eisenzeit* (Stockholm 1929), pp. 1-24. Note that Jordanes, writing in this period, speaks of the East Baltic as being under German control (i.e., Scandinavian). Jordanes, *Gaetica*, III, 20, in *MGH Auct. Ant.*, V, 59.

ready, in the early sixth century, an important terminus for furs makes one suspect that faintly, but no less surely, a new trade route linking the Eastern Baltic with the Black Sea was coming into being at the very moment when the older ones were closing.[107]

How can one sum up the changes which the period of migrations, ending about 550, brought to the world of Northern Europe? They were startling indeed. The Roman Empire which faced the Atlantic and Northern Seas had disappeared, and in its place new states, new political units, were being born out of travail and confusion. Now Visigoths were in Spain; Franks, Alemanni, Bretons and Burgundians in Gaul and the Rhinelands; Irish, Jutes, Saxons and Angles in Britain. Irish had settled in Scotland, Saxons in Frisia and Swedish peoples in Denmark, Norway and Finland. In Central Europe Slavs had pushed west until they had reached the Atlantic in Northern Germany and established themselves along a line that stretched from the Elbe to the Adriatic. Avars and Bulgars were located in the plains of the lower Danube, and in South Russia the population consisted of Magyars, White Bulgars and Turkish Kazars. The Late Roman world within and without the Empire had been shattered beyond repair. A new and different era was at hand in the lands facing the Northern Seas of Europe.

It has proved difficult in the preceding pages of this chapter to relate with any exactitude the precise movements of peoples who played their part in the drama of the *Volkerwanderung*. It is even more difficult to assess the economic results of these migrations upon the lands of Northern Europe. In part this comes from the scantiness of our sources relating to these matters. But in a real sense the difficulty lies elsewhere. Peoples in movement mean shifting trade routes and changing economic activity. Thus the century and a half from 400 to 550 A.D. is not one in which there are easily discernible economic threads. What one finds true economically in Southwestern Gaul is quite unapplicable to the northeastern portion of this province. Western Britain differs economically from Eastern England and Scandinavia during this century and a half. The economic pattern of the Rhinelands is not that of nearby Noricum and Rhaetia. Remembering these difficulties, then, let us examine the economics that prevailed in Northern Europe during these years of migration and confusion.

[107] Jordanes *Gaetica*, III, 21, in *ibid.*, p. 82.

During the first half of the fifth century, the Continental domains of the Roman Empire which faced the Northern Seas were not too greatly affected in an economic sense by the military and political difficulties which disturbed these regions. This was particularly true of Western Gaul. This region, not really a part of that regimented, state-industrialized section of the province near the Rhine, was little affected by the presence of Saxon raiders in the Channel or barbarian Franks in Belgium. The swift advance of the Vandals and Suevi through the land in 406 on their way to Spain caused damage only in limited areas. The installation of the Visigoths seems to have been a relatively peaceful one. These barbarians, most civilized and Romanized of the invading Germans, appear to have respected the Roman system that they found and to have genuinely tried to preserve it.

As a result, cities like Bordeaux and Poitiers continued their urban life relatively undisturbed. Senatorial aristocrats like the Apollinares, the Aviti and the Rucii hastened to serve the Visigothic kings as they had their Imperial masters before them. The picture painted by Sidonius' letters of a continuing rich, pleasant country life centering around the spacious villa estates of this nobility is probably not an untrue one. The court of Alaric II at Toulouse represented a surprising continuance of Late Roman culture.[108] In this portion of Gaul the Visigoths appear to have kept internal and external order. Only farther north in the Loire valley, where the surviving Roman government was weak, do we find terrible *bagaudae* risings which were only suppressed with Visigothic and then later Alanic help.

South of the Loire an active commercial life continued. An important river traffic plied the Garonne, while commerce with the Mediterranean via Narbonne was not unknown.[109] This latter city, described by Sidonius as being in ruins, may have begun to gain in importance as Syrians and other Oriental merchants, after the ban against their presence in the Western Empire had been lifted, returned with their commerce from distant Syria and Egypt.[110] In striking contrast to

---

[108] Sidonius Apollinaris, *Carmina*, XIX, and *Epistolae*, IV, in *MGH Auct. Ant.*, VIII, 59. P. Courtereault, *Bordeaux à travers les siècles*, pp. 8-10. M. Giraud, "Note sur la cité de Poitiers," in *Mélanges Louis Halphen*, pp. 271-72. S. Dill, *Roman Society in the Last Century of the Western Empire* (London 1899).

[109] Y. Renouard, "Voies de communication entre Méditerranée et Atlantique" in *Mélanges Louis Halphen*, pp. 589-92. F. Delarelle, "Toulouse et la route des deux mers," in *Annales du Midi*, LXII (1950), 217-19.

[110] Sidonius Apollinaris, *Carmina*, XXIII, XXXVIII, in *MGH Auct. Ant.*, V, 60-72. See also A. Dupont, *Les Cités de la Narbonnaise première depuis les invasions germaniques* (Nîmes 1942), pp. 1-53, on the status of these cities. On importations from

the Rhone valley, where a *minimissimi* coinage shows evidence of local commercial stagnation,[111] economic life along the Garonne was still active. The booty Clovis took in Toulouse is some evidence of this fact.[112] No doubt there was a continuation of the decline of cities and economic life, so much a feature of the Late Empire, and the Gallic *solidi* which circulated were of poor quality,[113] but the decline was gentle rather than drastic.

One reason for this continued relative economic health lies in the commerce that still reached these shores from the Atlantic. The story of Patrick makes this clear. St. Patrick, born of a family of minor gentry living in West Britain, was captured by an Irish party of raiders in the Severn region and carried to Ireland as a captive. Escaping from his slavery in Northern Ireland, he made his way to the island's south coast. There he took passage on a merchant ship carrying a cargo of hunting dogs to Gaul. This ship arrived at a Continental port, probably near the mouth of the Loire. St. Patrick made his way with some difficulty through a devastated countryside and finally arrived in Southern Gaul. There, deciding to enter the church, he studied at the monastery of Lerins on the Mediterranean. Ordained, he returned by ship to Britain to visit his family and then, after a return trip to Auxerre, set sail in 431-432 for Ireland and his great work.[114]

The story of Patrick is instructive for a number of reasons. It shows us that merchants from Ireland, carrying what might be termed luxury products, were still sailing to Gaul in these years without difficulty. And St. Patrick's later sea voyages to Britain, then back to Gaul and then on to Ireland show that neither Irish piracy nor Saxon raiders were yet seriously interrupting the maritime commerce of the Western Atlantic to these shores.

To this information from the life of St. Patrick can be added other interesting facts. When St. Germanus made his second voyage to Britain in 447 he seems to have gone by way of Cornwall and West Bri-

the Mediterranean, see Sidonius Apollinaris, *Epistolae*, IX, 12, in *MGH Auct. Ant.*, V, 183-85. C. Jullian, *La Gaule*, VIII, 212-14.

[111] P. Grierson, "Numismatics and History," in *Historical Association* (London 1951), pp. 9-10.

[112] F. Lot, *Les Invasions germaniques*, p. 132. R. Doehaerd, "La Richesse des Merovingiens," in *Studi in Onore di Gino Luzzatto* (Milan 1949), pp. 30-38.

[113] *Nov. Majoran*, VII, 14, speaks of the poor quality of Gallic *solidi*.

[114] J. B. Bury, *Life of St. Patrick*, pp. 20-38, 338-82. N. White, "Life of St. Patrick," in *Proc. of Royal Irish Acad.*, IX (1905). L. Bieler, *St. Patrick, His life and Letters* (Dublin 1949), pp. 102-7.

tain without difficulty, according to tradition.[115] And when St. Melanie died in 439 she seems to have possessed estates not only in Southern Gaul but also in Britain.[116] Archeological sites in Ireland dating from this period even show an increase in manufactured bronze objects of Roman origin—many of which must have come from Gallic workshops.[117] And we know that a stream of Western British and Irish saints appears to have studied at Lerins. It must have been via Western Gaul that they traveled to and from their native lands, bringing back with them those Eastern elements which they found at this monastery and which were to become so conspicuous a part of the life of the Celtic church.[118] A traffic which was important enough for the Visigoths to maintain a fleet on the Garonne as late as 475 was indeed more than occasional in nature.[119]

It also seems highly probable that during these decades this commerce extended along the North Spanish coast as far as Galicia and even beyond, for Orosius in the first years of the fifth century stated that Ireland lay directly opposite Spain, and reported a lighthouse existing at Portus Britanniae (Coruña), built *ad speculam Britanniae*.[120] The traditions of this region which speak of St. Armador coming directly by sea to Medoc, and of the Holy Grail coming to Glastonbury Abbey in West Britain directly from Palestine, may reflect the same active maritime commerce.[121] Down to 450 at least, then, the earlier Atlantic commerce of wine, olive oil and salt exchanged for metals, hides and wild beasts was still in existence.

In Northeastern Gaul and the Rhinelands the story is somewhat different. The economic life which had existed here in the fourth century continued, but on a modest scale. Some areas, as a matter of

[115] *Vita Germani*, XXIII-XXVIII, in *MGH Script. rer. Merov.*, VII, 269-72. Traditions mentioning St. Germanus' visit to Cornwall are found in H. O. Hencken, *The Archeology of Cornwall and Scilly*, pp. 212-18.

[116] M. Bloch, "Les Invasions: deux structures économiques" in *Ann. d'hist. sociale*, I (1945), 32-38.

[117] S. P. O'Riordan, "Roman Material in Ireland," in *Proc. of Royal Irish Acad.*, LI (1947), 101-31.

[118] Contacts with West Britain may have lasted late into the 5th century, for the Pope could communicate with British bishops in 475, and in 480 Constantine, the biographer of St. Germanus, could call the island rich. F. Lot, *Les Migrations saxonnes*, p. 12. On connections between this Celtic world and the Abbey of Lerins, see R. Hodgkin, *Anglo-Saxons*, I, 246-50.

[119] Sidonius Apollinaris, *Epistolae*, in *MGH Auct. Ant.*, VIII, 132-33.

[120] Orosius, *Hist.*, I, 2, 72.

[121] Y. Renouard, *op.cit.*, pp. 8-10. Concerning this gold mined in Galicia during this period and coined by the Suevi at Braga, Merida, León, Baja and Tuy, see F. Bouza-Brey, "La Numismatica en Galicia," in *Faro de Vigo*, II (1953), 6-8.

fact, suffered severe economic dislocation. Even in the fourth century the Channel coast had been exposed to destructive Saxon raids. As Flanders was abandoned in the fifth century and the Channel fleet fell back on the Somme, a paralysis hit these shores. When by 450 all Roman naval power had disintegrated here, with it disappeared the importance of those cities which faced Britain and their trade with that island. Only Rouen clung to a precarious existence.[122] Farther inland, where the Salian Franks were advancing into Belgium, a similar collapse took place. Villas disappeared and even such a city as Tongres does not appear to have survived long into the fifth century.[123] Farther south along the upper Rhine, where Alemanni threatened, a similar depression of economic life ensued. Strasbourg, destroyed by these barbarians in 355, was not rebuilt, and villa life weakened.[124]

On the other hand, there were areas about Cologne in the Rhinelands, in the Meuse and Moselle valleys and farther to the west where something of the earlier order of things prevailed, at least down to 450. Arras, according to Orosius, was still producing wool cloth during these years.[125] And Cologne still contained a Syrian population and produced some industrial wares.[126] Villas still existed along the Moselle.[127] Some exports from the Rhineland region, including glass, *terra sigillata* ware and even objects of Mediterranean origin, still passed up the Rhine to reach Frisia as late as the middle of the fifth century.[128]

More important still was the maintenance of commerce across Rome's borders into Germany and towards the east. When Priscus reached Attila's capital in Hungary, he reported that merchants

---

[122] See continuance of Rouen's Roman city plan in F. L. Ganshof, *Les Villes entre Rhin et Loire*, p. 207.

[123] L. Duschesne, *Fastes épiscopaux de l'ancienne Gaule*, III (Paris 1915), 10-20. L. Breuer, *La Belgique romaine*, pp. 109-10, on disappearance of Belgian villas in the 5th century.

[124] A. Grenier, *La Gaule*, pp. 620-22.

[125] Orosius, *Hist.*, VII, 32.

[126] Morin-Jean, *La Verrerie en Gaule sous l'Empire romain*, pp. 13-26. J. Breuer, *op.cit.*, pp. 109-10.

[127] Trier continued important until taken in 460. G. Keternich, *Geschichte der Stadt Trier* (Trier 1915), pp. 8-51. On the villa of Nennig and its survival into the 5th century, see J. Vannerus, "La Villa de Nennig," in *Cahiers Luxembourgeois*, II (1932), 187-210. The fortified villa of Nicetas also lasted on. E. Salin, *La Civilisation merovingienne*, I, 417-18.

[128] P. Boeles, "De terpencultuur tot omstreeks 400," in *Algemene Geschiedenis der Nederlanden*, I, 200-19. Few gold coins dating from this period have been found in Frisian sites, and these are all from Italian mints. They thus probably arrived here via Alpine passes and the Rhine. P. Boeles, *Friesland*, pp. 502-4.

traded there and that Latin rather than Greek was the language used—which seems to suggest that contacts were still maintained with more westerly portions of the Roman state.[129] Examination of archeological sites similarly shows that in Eastern Gaul during these years Central Asian art motifs and techniques were introduced, such as those used by the workers in the *barbaricini* decoration of jewelry and weapons.[130] It is difficult to say how much export commerce in weapons, glass, pottery and wine from the Rhine into Germany still continued, but it is clear that it had not yet completely disappeared.[131] It is dangerous, however, to assume that the economic life of even those cities which remained was a vital force. The closing of mints in this portion of the West after 395, Salvian's comments on the decadence of Gaul's urban centers[132] and Majoran's plaint that the cities of the Empire were being deserted[133] probably applies with particular force to this region. But it seems fair to say that up to the death of Actius the collapse of the Late Roman economic system here was by no means total.

Farther east along the upper and middle Danube there is evidence that economic conditions were considerably better. The iron industry and perhaps the woolen industry, both of which had been important earlier in Rhaetia and Noricum, continued.[134] So, too, did a rather active trade across the frontier. Here a special factor was at work. During these years of the fifth century both the Eastern and Western Imperial governments paid huge subsidies in gold to the Huns and their associated allies.[135] This money seems to have stimulated economic life. Evidence of this is to be found in the fact that every treaty

---

[129] Priscus, *Fragmentae hist. Graec.*, ed. Didot, pp. 123-36.

[130] *Notitia Dignitatum Occid.*, XI, 71-74. On the new technique used for smelting iron, which came from Central Asia, and which Rutilius mentions being employed in the Alps and Central Gaul, see E. Salin, *La Fer à l'époque merovingienne*, pp. 235-40.

[131] Shetelig mentions bronze and glassware which reached Norway in this period. H. Shetelig, *La Préhistoire de la Norvège*, p. 177. But such products were rare in Scandinavia after 400 A.D.

[132] Salvian, *De gubernatione dei*, V, 21-45, in *MGH Auct. Ant.*, I, 57-66.

[133] *Nov. Majoran*, III. On merchants and traders who avoided the *civitates* in carrying on their business in 446, see *Nov. Valentinian*, XXIV. This was caused perhaps by a new transaction tax levied in 444-445 A.D. *Ibid.*, XV, 1.

[134] *Code Theod.*, VII, 6, 4-5, mentions clothing for troops in Illyrium and the East. On Noricum's iron industry in this period, see E. Salin, *op.cit.*, pp. 335-41.

[135] In 424 Theodosius II paid the Huns 350 lbs. of gold a year. In 434 this rate was increased to 700 lbs. of gold. By 443 arrears in tribute amounted to 6,000 lbs., and the subsidy itself was raised to 2,600 lbs. annually. J. B. Bury, *op.cit.*, pp. 271-98. Such subsidies continued to be paid along the Danube border all through the 5th and 6th centuries.

negotiated with the Huns after 424 contains special provisions which bind the Romans to continue trade with the Hunnic Empire through their specially established trade portals; and there is evidence that the Romans periodically used the economic weapon of trade embargoes to reduce Hunnic pressures.[136] Priscus' account of his encounter with a Roman renegade at Attila's court who told him that he had deserted the Empire because among the Huns he could trade freely is very revealing indeed.[137] So, is the name Commercium, applied about this time to one of Rome's trade portals on the Danube. And, in that connection, we have the case of a Pannonian border city which in 459 begged the barbarian king of the Rugii to resume trade which he had broken off.[138]

The continued maintenance along the Danube of points of control of foreign commerce entering and leaving the Empire,[139] the continuance here of river patrols[140] and the fact that, as earlier, embargoes on the export of strategic goods from the Roman world to the barbarians are found in laws which were enacted during these years are proof of an important continued commerce to the north.[141] Probably the same weapons, metalware, wine and grain which had earlier figured in this trade with Central Europe made up fifth-century exports—these and the huge gold subsidies paid to Attila and others. Imports no doubt consisted of amber, furs, slaves and Roman gold returning to the Empire. One special export we know of was marble, probably from Illyricum, sent north to construct a palace for Attila.[142] It thus seems possible that along the Danube during most of the fifth century, commerce, stimulated by gold that was paid to barbarian peoples, stayed almost as important as it had been in earlier periods.

[136] Ibid. G. Vernadsky, Ancient Russia, pp. 138-51.

[137] Priscus, Fragmentae hist. Graec., pp. 126-30.

[138] M. Bloch, Les Invasions, p. 43.

[139] R. S. Lopez, "L'Evolution de la politique commerciale au moyen âge," in Annales, IV (1949), 390-95, and "The Silk Industry in the Byzantine Empire," in Speculum, XX (1945), 25-26. See also Notitia Dignitatum Orient., XIII, 6-9, and Occid. XI, 86.

[140] On the strengthening of river patrols in Illyricum and Moesia along the Danube in 428 A.D., see Nov. Theod., XXIV, 1-5. See general order of Theodosius II in 410, Code Theod., VII, 16, 2.

[141] In 420 these embargoes were reiterated for certain prohibited goods. Code Theod., VII, 16, 3.

[142] During the 5th century, in contrast to the 6th, amber was plentiful on both sides of the Rhine, and in Hungary as well, on the route to the Mediterranean amber center of Aquileia. This seems to show continuing trade via the Elbe-Rhine and Elbe-Saale routes between the Roman world and Scandinavia. E. Salin, Le Haut Moyen-âge en Lorraine (Paris 1939), p. 161.

Quite different was the economic fate of sub-Roman Britain during these years. It has already been noted that the economy of this island never recovered from the disasters which befell it in the last years of the fourth century, particularly that great invasion of Picts, Scots, Attecotti and Saxons in 363 which ended the prosperous villa system in most of Britain. Thus in the first years of the fifth century there were only certain parts of England in which an advanced economy still remained in operation—one area around the Severn region, where trade was still open to the Atlantic, and one in the east near London and the Saxon Shore forts. It is worth noting that these two separate regions were just those where, according to the *Notitia Dignitatum*, Roman troops were still stationed in Britain.[143]

In the southeast, London, Canterbury and Verulam still enjoyed some life in this sub-Roman period and a few villas continued a precarious existence.[144] In 429, for instance, St. Germanus reported that Verulam was still inhabitable.[145] But there is strong evidence that during these years the economic life of this area was completely local and cut off from contact with either the Continent or other parts of the island. Excavations at Richborough, for instance, reveal that during these years glass from the Rhinelands no longer reached there. And at Richborough, Colchester, Rendenhall (Norfolk) and Gillingham (Kent) finds of *minimissimi* hoards suggest a completely local economy.[146]

In the west of Britain, Caerwent continued to have some urban existence of a sort throughout the century, and its walls show signs of repair to protect it against Irish attacks.[147] At nearby Lydney, too, the pagan temple gives evidence of a certain peaceful continuity of life.[148] But we again find hoards of *minimissimi* at Caerwent, Lydney,

---

[143] *Notitia Dignitatum Occid.*, XXXVIII.

[144] R. G. Collingwood, "Roman Britain," in *ESAR*, III, 58-59. J. Tait, *The Medieval English Borough* (Manchester 1936), p. 3. R. Jessup, *The Archeology of Kent*, pp. 20-24. Collingwood and Myers, *Roman Britain and the English Settlements*, pp. 425-38.

[145] *Vita Germani*, XVII, in *MGH Script. rer. Merov.*, VII, 263-65.

[146] J. Bushe-Fox, *Fourth Report on the Excavations of the Fort at Richborough, Kent* (Oxford 1949), pp. 7-16. B. W. Pearce, "The Coins from Richborough—A Survey," in *Numis. Chron.*, 5th ser., XX (1941), 57-75. P. Hall, "Barbarous Imitations of Fourth Century Roman Coins," in *Numis. Chron.*, 6th ser., X (1950), 233-56.

[147] V. Nash-Williams, "Caerleon and Caerwent and the Roman Occupation of South Wales," in *Jour. of British Arch. Soc.*, XXXV (1927), 59-74.

[148] R. G. Collingwood, *op.cit.*, pp. 58-59.

Bourton-on-Water and Wholebury Camp (Somerset) that suggest a local type of economic existence.[149]

Elsewhere in Britain the picture is even darker. On the south coast a few scattered coin hoards, dating from the very first years of the century, have been turned up near Clausentum (Southampton) and Weymouth Bay (Dorset).[150] Then even *minimissimi* hoards disappear, showing that as the Saxons cut communications with Gaul, this flickering economic life ended. In the north around Chester, York and Lincoln there exists some area of doubt as to economic conditions. No coin hoards have been uncovered here and these cities were always military rather than commercial in character.[151] But it seems possible that they too lingered on as urban centers, as their use of the old Roman city plan and street system in the later Anglo-Saxon period seems to indicate.[152]

When one views all available evidence, then, one is struck by the fact that Roman Britain's economy was swiftly sinking into decay after 400 A.D. No wonder the Theodosian Code, written down about 433, does not even mention Britain. The limited declining economy of the sub-Roman period, and its isolation from the Continent, made it no longer economically or politically part of the Roman world.

So much for the lands in Northern Europe which had been part of the Empire. What of those outside it? In the Atlantic region that means Ireland and Scotland. As far as Ireland is concerned, the evidence seems to show that her primitive economic life declined little. She kept contacts, as we have noted, with Western Gaul and with Cornwall and the rest of Western Britain, and archeology gives evidence of continued import of metal ware from these regions.[153] In Scotland, however, all indication is lacking of any advanced economy at all after 400. No coin hoards and no imported wares have been turned up by the archeologists for this period. One can only hazard that the decadence of economic life in Britain resulted in an even greater decline in the lands north of Hadrian's Wall.

Quite different, however, is the case of Scandinavia and Central

[149] P. Hill, *op.cit.*, pp. 256-73.
[150] *Ibid.*
[151] J. N. Myers, "Lincoln in the Fifth Century," in *Archeological Journal*, CIII (1946), 18-23. R. Jessup, *Anglo-Saxon Jewelry*, pp. 25-26. T. C. Lethbridge, *Merlin's Island*, pp. 60-63.
[152] C. Stephenson, *Borough and Town* (Cambridge 1932), contains a series of medieval town plans that seem to show unbroken continuity between Roman and later medieval town sites.
[153] S. P. O'Riordan, "Roman Material in Ireland," *loc.cit.*, pp. 117-43.

Europe across the North Sea to the east, regions which were part of the Hunnic Empire or were closely influenced by it. We have already noted that during most of the fifth century considerable commerce crossed the Danube frontiers of the Roman world. Excavations in Scandinavia reveal that from the Empire came the vast amounts of gold found in Bornholm, Gotland, Oland and the mainland of Sweden—to make this, as Janse calls it, an age of gold in Scandinavia. There is, then, continuing evidence of Roman economic influence in both Scandinavia and Central Europe.[154]

Here, however, we must pause to consider a paradox. In the fourth century little Roman gold reached Scandinavia, but many wares from foundries and workshops on the Rhine and Danube frontiers did. In the fifth century, though, despite the fact that Roman gold is found in large amounts on Baltic islands and Swedish mainland, there is little evidence of Roman wares there—despite the active commerce that crossed Rome's Central European frontiers. Instead, the metal objects and jewelry of these years in Scandinavia show strong evidence of being under Central Asian influence and seem to be of local manufacture almost exclusively. Vendel helmets from the earliest period in Sweden, for instance, are basically Roman in design, but decorated in quite a different fashion.[155] Scandinavia, despite its Roman gold, seems to have been part of a larger Central European-Russian cultural area extending to the Rhine, an area in which influences from Sassanian Persia and Central Asia were more vital than those emanating from the Roman world. Even more puzzling is the fact that though Roman gold has been found in large amounts in hoards in Scandinavia which date from these years, practically none has been found in Central Europe—in Eastern Germany, in particular—across which it must have passed to reach distant Baltic shores.

Some scholars have attempted to explain this paradox by denying the existence of trade with Scandinavia during these years. To them, the gold found there reached the Baltic not through commerce, but through returning Norse soldiers and others who brought it with

---

[154] See O. R. Janse, *Le Travail de l'or en Suède*, pp. 103-55, as previously noted.
[155] L. Musset, *Les Peuples scandinaves*, pp. 33-37. Rostovtzeff believed this new style to be of Sassanian, Central Asian inspiration. M. Rostovtzeff, *Iranians and Greeks in South Russia*, pp. 181-209. Others have disagreed and seen German and local Scandinavian influences as the dominant ones. All agree it is non-Roman in origin. See H. Shetelig, "The Scandinavian Style of Ornament During the Migration Period," in *Archeologia*, LXXVI (1927), 27-48. For Sweden, H. Arbman, "Verroterie cloisonné et figurine," in *Kgl. Humanist Vitenskaps i Lund Arsber*, XIX (1949-50), 136-70.

them from the Hunnic Empire and the Roman world. While this may be true in some cases, it seems a poor explanation. Perhaps the following is more likely. The Roman world traded across the frontiers with the barbarians of Central Europe, as we know. But the volume of this trade, owing to the decadence of the Empire's economic life and the trade controls in force, was sufficient only to supply the immediate needs of the people beyond the Rhine and Danube. Instead of goods, then, a large portion of the exports sent to Central Europe by Rome consisted of gold in the form of subsidies. It was, however, the furs and amber supplied from Scandinavia, not to mention slaves, which found a ready export market in the Empire. So when Scandinavian traders brought their wares from the north into the heart of Attila's domains, they received for their furs and amber, etc., not Roman-made goods, but Roman gold and perhaps a few wares of essentially Eastern, non-Roman manufacture. This gold they carried back with them to the north. And the lack of gold hoards in Eastern Germany is explainable on the simple basis that these regions were, as we know, largely deserted and without population up to about 500 A.D.

Thus the curious paradox of gold but no Roman wares can be explained, as can the Huns' constant reiteration in their treaties with the Empire that trade be allowed to flow more freely. Obviously, such a trading situation was artificial in the extreme. It depended completely upon Roman bribes and subsidies being paid the non-productive barbarian peoples of Central Europe. And its results were far reaching in causing a hemorrhage of gold which moved north from the Roman world to Scandinavia, there to be used less for productive trade purposes than for the massive jewelry, ring money and ornaments which characterize this age in the Baltic. Certainly those who, with little evidence, speak of a drain of gold to the East in the last years of the Empire have not considered sufficiently the archeological indication that more golden wealth of the Mediterranean world moved north to Scandinavia than east towards China and India.

Such was the situation from an economic point of view in Northern Europe in the first five or six decades of the fifth century. What happened during the next hundred years of the period we are considering? Let us first examine Gaul. We have noted earlier that after 450 rapid changes took place there. From the sea Britons landed to colonize Armorica, while Saxon pirates active along West Gallic coasts made maritime Atlantic commerce all but impossible. A

Frankish conquest overwhelmed sub-Roman Gaul north of the Loire and soon after 500 A.D. destroyed Visigothic dominion over Aquitaine. By 550 the Burgundians had been conquered as well and a new Mero- vingian Frankish empire stretched from the Mediterranean well into Germany.

Curiously enough, Southern and Western Gaul were not very ad- versely affected, from an economic standpoint, by these events. To replace Visigothic or Burgundian rule with Frankish did not, south of the Loire, mean any great change at first. Families like the Rucii and Apollinares shifted their support without too much difficulty to a Merovingian line which had the advantage of being orthodox Catho- lic Christian, not heretical. South of the Loire the villa system con- tinued relatively undisturbed. Cities like Bordeaux, Toulouse and Poitiers continued to exist. The Gallo-Roman aristocracy continued to dominate rural society and to monopolize the important positions in the church.[156] A Fortunatus could find available in many places that cultivated taste and society that he so much craved.[157]

True it was that the Atlantic commerce which up to 450 had reached Western Gallic shores was now in the doldrums,[158] but a new develop- ment more than made up for it—a revival of Mediterranean commerce reaching Gallic shores. Starting in the late fifth century, as Vandal piracy declined, and still more so in the early sixth century, when Justinian's restored Romania stimulated commercial development, trade revived between Gaul and the East. Syrians and Jews and other Easterners again brought their wares to Marseilles, Narbonne and farther inland.[159] Gold, so rare in the fifth century, once more became relatively common. Southern and Central Gaul, which in the fourth century had been essentially separate economically from the Mediter-

[156] F. Lot, *Les Invasions germaniques*, pp. 206-16. P. Courtreault, *Bordeaux à travers les siècles*, pp. 8-12. M. Giraud, *op.cit.*, pp. 7-9. E. Salin, *La Civilisation merovingienne*, I, 116-18. N. Åberg, *op.cit.*, pp. 5-20. L. Desgranges, *Les Apollinaires* (Paris 1937).

[157] See Fortunatus' *Carmina*, which reflect a continuing culture in this part of Gaul.

[158] *Vita Bibiani vel Vibiani Episcopus Santonensis*, in *MGH Script. rer. Merov.*, II, 98, describes difficulties afflicting commerce owing to the piracies of the Saxons and others during those decades. On the other hand, close connections were maintained with Galicia, whose Suevic king asked help from Tours about 550 A.D. P. Davies, *Etudes historiques sur la Galacie et le Portugal*, p. 119. On the richness of this part of Spain in gold, see F. Bouza-Brey, "La Numismatica en Galicia," in *Faro de Vigo*, II (1953), 7-9.

[159] On the Syrians and other Orientals in Gaul in the 6th century, see F. Vercauteren, *Etude sur les civitates de la Belgique Secunde*, pp. 440-51. Also L. Brehier, "Les Colonies d'orientaux en Occident," in *Byz. Zeit.*, XII (1903), and P. Lamprechts, "Le Commerce des Syriens en Gaule," in *L'Antiquité classique*, VI (1937), 34-61.

ranean, now began to be reintegrated with it.[160] A Merovingian economic renaissance, in some ways the Western counterpart of Justinian's
revival in the Mediterranean, made its appearance.

If such was the situation in Southern and parts of Central Gaul,
however, quite different was the economic situation up to 550 in the
rest of the province and in those Rhineland regions which faced the
Atlantic and Northern Europe—not the Mediterranean. In the Rhinelands city life disappeared altogether in centers like Cologne, Tongres,
Bonn, Worms, Mainz, Spire and Strasbourg. Even farther south and
east little of the Roman economy was left in centers like Trier, Verdun, Tournai and Cambrai.[161]

The reasons for this collapse of urban centers are not difficult to find.
They do not lie in the destructiveness of the Frankish conquest, but
rather in the nature of Late Roman economic life in this part of
Europe. As was noted earlier, the industry of this region, centered in
Roman cities; factories for the making of arms, cloth, etc., were completely under state control. So, too, were the arrangements for collect-
ing and transporting foodstuffs, which were the particular responsibility
of the state-controlled *collegia* of river transport shippers. The end
of the Roman governmental system in these regions and its replace-
ment by Frankish rule almost immediately ended this state of affairs.
A system directed towards keeping frontier armies supplied had no
meaning when those armies no longer existed and the Rhine no longer
served as a boundary between two worlds. The Franks did keep going
the Roman forced public-transportation system, which they found
useful. But the rest of Rome's system of *gynecées*, arms factories,
public food storehouses and corporations of *nautae* on the rivers
disappeared almost immediately after Frankish control had been
established. With them disappeared the whole pattern of Late Roman
life in this region.

It is equally interesting to note that in most of northern and
eastern Frankish domains the villa system also soon disappeared.
Like state *gynecées*, the villa system in these regions was dependent
upon a strong state organization to maintain the power of the land-
holding aristocracy over the serf-like *coloni*, while the latter were
responsible for the actual cultivation of the soil and the payment of a

[160] On the *solidi* struck in this part of Gaul, see P. Le Gentilhomme, *Mélanges
de numismatique merovingienne* (Paris 1940), pp. 134-35.
[161] R. Doehaerd, *L'Expansion économique*, pp. 13-14. F. Lot, *Les Invasions germaniques*, pp. 198-206. Lot in F. Lot, C. Pfister and F. Ganshof, *Les Destinées de
l'empire en Occident* (Paris 1940-41), pp. 364-66. E. Salin, *op.cit.*, pp. 429-37.

large portion of their crops to the Empire as taxes. Whenever the government proved disorganized and weak, the villa system came upon difficult days. Immediately the *coloni* rose and proclaimed their independence in the *bagaudae* risings. It was such a rising, in conjunction with invasions and government paralysis, which appears to have destroyed the villa system of most of Britain in the late fourth century. It was a similar weakness that caused revolts in the Loire region and in Armorica in the early fifth century. It was probably a similar lack of governmental control which caused villas to disappear in Belgium during the same period. Now we find an identical state of affairs in most of Gaul north of the Loire and in the Rhinelands. Unsupported by an organized state the villa system collapsed everywhere, as in the case of the villa of Nennig in Luxembourg which has been carefully studied.[162] A few, like the fortified villa of Bishop Nicetas near Trier, survived, but they were exceptions which prove the rule.[163] North of regions like the Vivarais, the Garonne valley and Poitiers where the older system continued, it seems fair to say that by 550 the Roman villa system had disappeared. Just so in our modern world we have seen a plantation system, similarly dependent upon the powers of a sympathetic government, disappear in Mexico, the Dutch East Indies and Burma. New settlements by German invader colonists, important in number in the Rhinelands, Belgium and Alsace and fewer as one approaches the Seine, forced a native population of Gallo-Romans to move towards a new system—the village system which was to characterize the Middle Ages.[164]

In those regions where both villa system and state-regimented industry failed to survive barbarian conquest, an intense localism perforce prevailed, for a village-type society could not at once emerge with any economic strength beyond that needed to subsist. As in sub-Roman Britain, this localism is reflected in coinage. For we find that in this part of Gaul, in the late fifth and early sixth centuries, coins were struck which much resemble the *minimi* and *minimissimi* of Britain. They are small, even tiny silver pieces and have been discovered in the Meuse valley near Namur, on the Marne and even in

---

[162] For examples of this, see report of the Emperor Severus in 465 that *laeti*, *coloni* and slaves had thrown off their yokes in every province. *Nov. Severus*, II, 1.

[163] E. Salin, *La Civilisation merovingienne*, I, 416-18.

[164] W. Von Wartburg, *Umfang und Bedeutung der germanischen Siedlung in Nordgallen im 5. und 6. Jahr im Spiegel der Sprache und Ortsnamen in Vorträge und Schriften* (Berlin 1950). R. Koebner, "The Settlement and Colonization of Europe," *loc.cit.*, pp. 41-50.

the Charente region.[165] At the same time it must not be supposed
that all industry disappeared. It did not. South of Trier and Tournai
the populations which had labored in the now dead *gynecées* survived.
But they turned their industrial skill into new channels, connected, it
is true, with their older occupations. They became moneyers, and
jewelers, and made arms for the warlike Frankish society in which
they lived. But as they continued their older or related trades in the
same regions where they had earlier labored for the Roman state,
a strange thing happened. Their techniques and artistic motifs
changed. We find appearing by the sixth century in Eastern Gaul
and the Rhinelands a new pattern—welding technique for forging
sword blades, superior to and different from that found here in
Roman times—a technique which seems to have arrived from Central
Asia.[166] The system of smelting iron likewise changed from a Roman
to a more primitive method.[167] The jewelry which was made in these
parts of Gaul also altered and became similar in style and design to
that found in South Russia, Germany, Scandinavia and Kent.[168] A
new non-Roman industry and art, like the new non-Roman agricultural system, appeared in these regions of Gaul and Germany.

One observes very much the same situation in Britain in the century following the Saxon invasion of the island—but to an even
greater degree. In Western Britain the area where some local Romanized civilization continued steadily shrunk in size until in only two
places, at Bourton-on-Water (Gloucestershire) and at Lydney, does
one find any remaining *minimissimi*, those symbols of continuing
Roman economic traditions.[169] Gildas in the middle of the sixth
century might call himself a Roman, but barbarous Latin betrayed
him. West Britain had become completely Celtic and even the church
as in Ireland, had come to be organized on a tribal basis. This does
not mean that maritime commerce did not continue in the Irish Sea

---

[165] We find also a few bronze or copper coins. P. Le Gentilhomme, *op.cit.*, pp.
134-35. The rare, small Merovingian silver money of the 5th and 6th century is
found in the Seine, Marne and Oise regions of the north, near Namur in the northeast
and in the Charente region of the west. M. Prou, *Catalogue des monnaies merovingiennes* (Paris 1896), pp. XCVI-CI. Somewhat similar pieces were struck by Burgundian rulers in the same period. A. Blanchet and A. Dieudonné, *Manuel de numismatique française* (Paris 1912), III, 184-85.
[166] E. Salin, *La Fer à l'époque merovingienne*, pp. 167-97.
[167] *Ibid.*, pp. 235-40.
[168] E. Salin, *La Civilisation merovingienne*, Vols. I-II, contain the best description
of these new styles and techniques. See also L. Brehier, *L'Art en France* (Paris 1930),
pp. 46-60.
[169] P. Hill, *Barbarous Imitations of Fourth Century Roman Coins*, pp. 240-54.

and perhaps as far south as Coruña. It did. Tin and copper were still exchanged over wide distances and Cornwall's mines continued active. Ireland, particularly, made some economic advances, as excavations at Lagore clearly show.[170] Irish saints visited Cornwall and Wales for their religious training.[171] But such contacts, commercial and otherwise, within the Celtic thalassocracy were not of sufficient importance during these years either to resuscitate the old Roman urban centers of West Britain or to create new ones in other Celtic regions.

Much the same thing is true in Eastern Britain, which after 450 also underwent continued economic decline. Only at Richborough have *minimissimi* of the sixth century, been discovered, to show continuity, on a strictly local basis, with the Roman past.[172] Elsewhere a Canterbury, a London, a York might continue to have some faint semblance of urban life, but it was very faint indeed. The Juto-Saxon inhabitants of Canterbury, for instance, appear to have lived outside the walls of the old Roman town,[173] while the change of street plan in London when it again became important shows that its population must have all but disappeared by 500 A.D.[174] It is true that certain art motifs in Kentish and East Anglian jewelry imply that some Romano-British traditions of craftsmanship lingered near the Saxon Shore forts.[175] And the continuation of earlier house styles and field divisions reveals the same thing. But, as in the case of Northern Gaul, these survivals are not very impressive.

In contrast to Britain was the Scandinavian world where, down to 550, a stream of gold arrived from the south. Here one finds much evidence of economic growth, on a primitive level, it is true. A native iron industry flourished[176] and the hoards on the islands of Gotland,

[170] F. Haverfield, "Cornish Tin," in *Mélanges Boissier* (Paris 1903). H. O. Hencken "An Excavation at Chysauster," in *Archeologia*, LXXXIII (1953), 83-97, and H. O. Hencken, "Lagore Crannoy, An Irish Royal Residence," in *Proc. of Royal Irish Acad.*, LIII (1950), 17-91.

[171] H. O. Hencken, *The Archeology of Cornwall and Scilly* (London 1932), pp. 212-34, on Irish connections with Cornwall and Brittany in this period. See A. H. Williams, *op.cit.*, pp. 7-71, on connections with Wales.

[172] P. Hall, *op.cit.*, pp. 257-73.

[173] S. S. Frere, *Canterbury Excavations, 1948-1950* (Canterbury 1948-50), pp. 8-11.

[174] R. Wheeler, *London and the Saxons*, pp. 18-51.

[175] R. Jessup, *Anglo-Saxon Jewelry*, pp. 41-57. R. Bruce-Mitford, "The Sutton Hoo Ship Burial," in *Proceedings of the Royal Society of Suffolk*, XXV (1949), 23-56, and R. Hodgkin, *History of the Anglo-Saxons* (3rd ed., Oxford 1952), II 695-734, 749-56, which contains additional and amplifying information on Sutton Hoo.

[176] This is particularly true of Norway. A. W. Brøgger, *Ancient Emigrants* (Oslo 1929), pp. 12-14. On shipbuilding, see Brøgger and Shetelig, *The Viking Ships*, pp. 10-61. On jewelry, O. R. Janse, *Le Travail de l'or en Suède*, pp. 11-183. On

Bornholm and Oland suggest maritime traffic.[177] It is probable that Roman coins and *brachteates* served as ornaments rather than money, as did the beautifully constructed massive jewelry of the period like the Torslunda collars, the sword rings mentioned in *Beowulf* and great golden bowls discovered in Denmark. But, if so, they represented exchangeable wealth, like the ring money found in so many sites. It is hard to believe that something akin to a primitive commercial civilization did not exist here in the late fifth and early sixth centuries.

Commerce to the south survived the fall of Attila's empire, for as late as the time of Justinian gold arrived in this region via Central Europe. But the Avar and Slav advances gradually cut the commercial routes, until at the time of Theodoric, just before 550, only one land connection with the Mediterranean world existed. This one, revealed by Theodoric's diplomatic relations with a king of Norway, the Heruls, the Esths of the Eastern Baltic and the kings of the Varini and Thuringians, went west from the Baltic to the Elbe and then down the Rhine to Italy over Alpine passes. It must have been by this route that the *Aesti* brought gifts of amber to the court of the great Ostrogothic monarch. Then came the final Slavic push across Northern Germany to the Atlantic.[178] Scandinavia found itself cut off from the south except via the sea route along Frisia and by way of the Gulf of Finland and the rivers of Russia.[179] Like the Celtic thalassocracy, the Scandinavian Baltic became an isolated region, economically separated from a world to the south to which it had once been linked in trade.

The economic fate of Central Europe was even more somber by the mid-sixth century. Where the Slavic tribes moved, they brought with them their primitive agricultural system and little else during these years. And the Avars, unlike the Huns, were little interested in trade. Rather, their raiding activities and their domination of their weaker Slavic neighbors condemned this part of Europe to a very

---

technological advances in Denmark, *Guides to the National Museum, Copenhagen: Antiquity*, pp. 98-103.

[177] Judging from finds of gold coins, ring money, etc., the islands of Gotland, Oland and Bornholm were the commercial centers of Scandinavia in this period, closely followed by the Swedish Uppland. O. R. Janse, *op.cit.*, pp. 51-136, and L. Musset, *op.cit.*, pp. 31-37.

[178] See note 103 on this route. On routes leading across the Alps from Italy to Germany, see A. Dopsch, *The Economic and Social Foundations of European Civilization*, p. 349, and J. Werner, *Münzdatierte austrasische Grabfunde*, pp. 23-29.

[179] The best proof of this isolation lies in the lack of finds of amber in 6th-century sites along the Rhine and in Hungary in contrast to its abundance in 5th-century sites. E. Salin, *Le Haut Moyen-age en Lorraine*, p. 161.

low level of economic life for centuries. Archeology makes clear that in this proto-historic period of Slavic settlement little commerce, trade or industry flourished. Many years were to elapse before the situation was to change for the better.[180]

There remains one exception, other than Southern Gaul, to the generally dreary economic picture that Northern Europe presented by the year 550. That exception is the Alpine region of Noricum and Rhaetia. Perhaps this was because, after Theodoric and his Ostrogoths took Italy, they maintained control over these upper Danube provinces of Rome and kept the older Roman economic system in effect. Whatever the cause, it is interesting to note that up to the mid-sixth century both the Roman villa system and some old Roman techniques and industries survived around centers like Augsburg and Regensburg.[181] Furthermore, a connection was maintained via the Alpine passes with Italy, as finds of Ostrogothic and Byzantine *siliquae* and *demi-siliquae* in South Germany as far north as Mainz clearly show.[182] Some of this trade was that which has already been noted as reaching the Baltic via the Elbe up to 550. But more of it probably was following a new route up the Rhine to Frisia, as gold coins struck in Italy which have been found in the Netherlands seem to indicate.[183] This new north-south route to the Mediterranean, the only one still in operation by 550, no doubt explains the expedition of Hygelac to the mouths of the Rhine in these years. He was seeking not just booty but a route to the south. And it explains how the author of *Beowulf* could speak of the Frisians as being hostile enemies on the other side of the Geats.

[180] Again the contrast between the 5th and the 6th century is striking. Earlier, down to about 500, influences from Central Asia and certain objects reached Northern France freely via Central Europe. But neither objects of Avar manufacture nor Avar influences are to be found here dating from the 6th century. E. Salin, *La Civilisation merovingienne*, I, 178-85.

[181] G. Strakosh-Grassman, *Geschichte der Deutschen im Oesterrich Ungarn* (Vienna 1895), pp. 167-68, and F. Lot in Lot, Pfister and Ganshof, *op.cit.*, pp. 101-3. Perhaps the continuance of Roman civilization, almost unique in Europe during this period, explains why Dopsch, who knew this region so well, was so sure that this was true elsewhere. A. Dopsch, *op.cit.*, p. 347.

[182] J. Werner, *op.cit.*, pp. 109-33. E. Salin, *La Civilisation merovingienne*, I, 168-77.

[183] The gold coins minted during this period which have been found in Frisia are as follows: 1 Arcadius (Milan mint), 1 Theodosius II, 2 Valentinian III (Ravenna mint), 2 Marcian, 10 Leo I, 1 Anastasius and 9 Imitations (3 Ravenna and 4 Merovingian), 2 Justin (Constantinople mint) and 4 imitations (2 Italian mints and 2 Merovingian), 8 Justinian (7 Constantinople mint and 1 Italian) and 18 imitations (4 Italian mints and 4 Merovingian). These coins show that contacts between Merovingian Gaul and Frisia began again about 500, but that down to 550 routes leading to Italy were more important. P. Boeles, *Friesland*, pp. 502-13.

Geographically this remark makes little sense. Economically it is revealing and perceptive. The Geats' route to southern wealth *now* lay
via Frisia and the Rhine to Italy. And with the development of this
route the Rhine began to play a new and vital role. No longer was it
a barrier between two rival and hostile economic and political systems.
It was a highway, linking the Mediterranean to Northern Europe—
a role it was to play for many centuries.

Let us sum up, then, the economic changes brought by these years.
In the fourth century an industrialized, separate series of economic
regions in the Northern European portion of Rome's domains faced
a developing, non-Roman north divided into an Atlantic region and
a Central European-Scandinavian area. By 550 this had been completely altered. We know that in most of what had been Rome's
northern provinces the cities, the industries and the villas which made
up her civilization had disappeared and with them most of the commerce which they stimulated. Neither the greater Atlantic trade
area nor the greater Central European-Scandinavian commercial
region survived. Instead, a series of isolated regions appeared about
the Irish Sea, the Baltic, the North Sea and Central Europe. In
only two of these, both connected closely with the Mediterranean—
Noricum-Rhaetia and Southern Gaul—was there any continuation of
Roman economic life. Elsewhere a new economic order was slowly
arising out of the ruin and destruction of the old.

In history as in life itself, an end and a beginning, birth and death,
the new and the old, are often found together. So it is that we can
already see by 550 the outline of a new economic order arising out
of the old. We can catch a glimpse of new trade routes faintly linking
the separate economic systems into which Northern Europe had lapsed.
Some have already been noted. They are the Rhine route linking
Italy with the North Sea, the Frisian coastal route which linked the
Baltic again with the North Sea area, and a few first steps in the
formation of a Varangian route from the Gulf of Finland through
Russia to the Black and Caspian Seas.

But from still another region, Kent, similar commercial traffic
was beginning which was to be of importance in later centuries.
Kent's location at the junction of the Rhine, Channel and North Sea
was ideal for commerce. By the mid-sixth century we have some
evidence that this was resulting in new commercial traffic. Kentish
grave finds of jewelry and other objects show that the inhabitants of

this region were in close contact with the Rhinelands,[184] while sites in Frisia which contain Kentish-type brooches show that this contact extended even farther north.[185] There may even have been some direct contact with Scandinavia via either Frisia or East Anglia, since *brachteates* of a definite Scandinavian origin have been found in Kentish graves.[186] Nor were contacts limited to the north. Irish hanging bowls in Kent similarly show a connection, probably via the Irish Hampshire colony, with the Celtic world to the west[187] and perhaps also with Rouen, the only Roman city on the Channel that seems to have survived.[188] Nor was this all. There is evidence from coins and jewelry that contact was even maintained with the distant Saxon colony in the Charente region on the west coast of Gaul.[189] Thus Kent, in contact with Gaul, the Celtic west, the Rhinelands, Frisia and Scandinavia, was already heralding the new era that was in the process of formation.

One final problem remains, that of the ships in use on the Northern Seas during this period of migrations. Again our information is much too modest for our liking. But it is clear that on the coasts of Western Gaul the same type of ships that were mentioned in our first chapter continued in use. We know nothing of the warships which composed the Visigothic Garonne fleet, or of those employed by the Romans in the Channel, but the types used may have been the same galleys, or *naves longae*, and swift Pictish-type scouting vessels encountered earlier.[190] Since 475 is our last mention of the Garonne

[184] T. D. Kendrick, *Anglo-Saxon Art*, pp. 62-68. R. Hodgkin, *History of the Anglo-Saxons*, I, 74-83.

[185] P. Boeles, *Friesland*, pp. 207-60, 338-59. H. Slicher van Bath, "Dutch Tribal Problems," *loc.cit.*, pp. 131-36.

[186] E. T. Leeds, *Denmark and Early England*, pp. 22-37, and *A Corpus of Early Anglo-Saxon Square Headed Brooches*, pp. 81-216. Amber in Kentish graves, which may have come from Norfolk rather than Scandinavia, is abundant in late 6th-century Kentish graves, though rare earlier. R. Jessup, *Anglo-Saxon Jewelry*, pp. 51-57. H. Shetelig, *An Introduction to the Viking History of Western Europe*, p. 6.

[187] T. D. Kendrick, "British Hanging Bowls," in *Antiquity*, VI (1932), 161-84. F. Henry, "Hanging Bowls," in *Jour. of Royal Soc. of Ant. of Ireland*, LXVI (1936), 209-35.

[188] For example, King Aethelbert of Kent shortly after 550 married Bertha, daughter of King Haribert of Paris, who controlled Rouen in this period. W. Levison, *England and the Continent in the Eighth Century* (London 1946), p. 5.

[189] See E. T. Leeds, *Early Anglo-Saxon Art and Archeology*, p. 56, on similarity between objects found in Kentish graves and those found in the Charente. See also P. Grierson, "The Canterbury (St. Martin's) Hoard," in *British Numismatic Journal*, XXVII (1935), 8-17, on numismatic evidence of Kentish links with Southwestern Gaul.

[190] Sidonius Apollinaris, *Epistolae*, in *MGH Auct. Ant.*, VIII, 132-33.

fleet, we can probably assume that no more warships were built there after this time.

As to merchant ships, however, we are better informed. In the late years of the sixth century there is mention of two types of vessels used by Gallic sailors. One was the *scapha,* or coaster, which Gregory of Tours tells us was used in trade with Spain as far as Galicia.[191] The other was the *barca.* The *scapha* was a flat-bottomed ship with a square stern and a large sail and was used both for river traffic and along the coasts. It seems to have been similar in design to luggers still seen along Welsh and western British shores. The *barca,* on the other hand, was a larger, sturdier vessel not unlike the fourth century Roman ship discovered in London. It appears to have been larger than the *scapha* and probably owed something of its design to the Venetic *ponto* and Roman transport vessels like the *hippago* and *corbito.* Certainly it was carvel-built. Perhaps it was in a *barca* that St. Patrick sailed from Ireland to Western Gaul.[192]

It is less easy to identify the ships used by the mariners of West Britain for passage to Armorica and Portus Britanniae in Spain. One thing, however, seems certain. They were not the sea-going coracles found earlier about the Cornish shores. The vessels in which Coroticus raided Ireland must have been larger, owing something to Roman naval design, and it seems probable, as well, that it was superior ships which enabled Cunneda to expel the Irish from Cornwall and Wales. By the time of Gildas this becomes clear. He speaks of the ships of the Briton exiles going to Brittany as *naves longae,* or Roman-type warships.[193] Coracles were certainly in use for local purposes. But were there other ship types, too? Perhaps there were, the same *scaphae* and *barcae* found on Gallic coasts.

Concerning Irish shipping during these years there is less doubt. Down to 550 the Irish native ship par excellence was the coracle. Sidonius, for instance, mentions Irish pirates cleaving the sea in a sewn skiff—obviously a *curragh.*[194] Irish sea tales of a latter date give

---

[191] Gregory of Tours, *Hist. Franc.* VIII, in *MGH Script. rer. Merov.,* I, 351. L. Bonnard, *La Navigation intérieure de la Gaule,* p. 154. T. C. Lethbridge, *Merlin's Island,* pp. 110-40.

[192] Adamnan, *Vita Columbae,* I, 28, ed. Reeves, p. 131. T. C. Lethbridge, *op.cit.,* pp. 140-77. W. Vogel, "Zur nord- und westeuropaischen Seeschiffahrt," in *Hansische Geschichtsblätter,* XIII (1907), 187-88.

[193] Gildas, *De excidio Brit.,* IV, in *MGH Auct. Ant.,* XIII, 29. Elsewhere in this work Gildas calls them *cyriles* or *cuilae.* W. Vogel, *op.cit.,* pp. 187-89.

[194] On these early coracles, see J. Hornell, "The Curraghs of Ireland," in *Mariners Mirror,* XXIII (1937), 75-93.

us more information concerning this craft. Some of them were of large size, made of three thicknesses of hide, capable of transporting a crew of twenty men and carrying a mast.[195] These ships must have been the type used by Niall of the Seven Hostages on his raiding expeditions. A century later they were still in use along Irish coasts.

Scant as our information is concerning ships in the Atlantic, we know even less about vessels used during these years in the North Sea. We cannot be sure what type of ships Saxons, Jutes and Heruls employed on their raiding expeditions. All we can say for sure is that they were not of the unseaworthy Nydam type, since Sidonius tells us that they bore sails.[196] It seems a fair guess that they were clinker-built craft modeled upon the general lines of those Pictish ships mentioned by Vegetius. They were probably rather large in size, for one source tells us that the Herul raid on Spain in 459 was carried out by 400 men in seven ships.[197] If we may believe such statistics, we arrive at a figure of almost 60 men per ship—approximately the number carried in the early ninth century by the average Viking vessel. Incidentally, the fact that Kent by 550 carried on maritime commerce with places as far away as Scandinavia, Frisia, the Rhine mouths, the Celtic west and the Saxon colony on the Charente seems to show that Kentishmen had superior ships, fully capable of standing up to long sea voyages. Is the later Barset ship the type they employed? Perhaps so.

Our information for the Angles and the Scandinavians of these years in the Baltic and along the coasts of Norway is more precise. This is due to the discovery at Kvalsund and Sutton Hoo of ship remains which date generally from this period. The Sutton Hoo ship and the greater Kvalsund vessel resemble each other closely and are clearly descended from the earlier Nydam ship. They thus represent

---

[195] Dicuil, writing in the early 9th century, tells of large sea-going coracles which sailed to Iceland. Dicuil, *De mensura orbis terrae*, VII, 14, ed. Parthney, p. 44. They are mentioned at the end of the 6th century by Adamnan in Vita Columbae, II, 16, ed. Reeves, p. 189. Legends or sea tales of Bran, St. Brendan, Teigue and the Sons of Coira give us the best descriptions of these coracles. T. Curry, *Manuscript Materials for Irish History* (Dublin 1893), p. 289. J. Hornell, *op.cit.*, pp. 80-93, dates St. Brendan's second voyage about 525-527. See also A. MacDermott, "St. Brendan the Navigator," in *Mariners Mirror*, XXX (1950), 74-80, and the more cautious J. F. Kenney, *The Sources for Early Irish History*, pp. 408-12. For evaluations of Irish navigation in the Atlantic, see the invaluable T. C. Lethbridge, *Merlin's Island*, pp. 80-165, and *Herdsmen and Hermits*, pp. 73-215.

[196] Sidonius Apollinaris, *op.cit.*, pp. 132-33.

[197] Hydatius, *Chron.*, in *MGH Auct. Ant.*, XI, 28. This is about the capacity of the Gokstad ship. H. Shetelig, *Scandinavian Archeology*, pp. 346-56.

another bit of evidence, if more is needed, of the movement of Baltic peoples as far west as Southern Norway and Eastern Britain in the early sixth century. Though the Sutton Hoo ship was not buried until 655, it was already old then and goes back to the sixth century,[198] while the Kvalsund boat dates from about the same period.[199]

From the point of view of construction, both ships had the following characteristics. They were large, flat-bottomed, rowing ships designed in a general way like the Nydam ship. On the other hand, they were better built and their strakes and oarlocks show a better arrangement. They also both contained an improved type of steering oar, instead of a paddle. Despite this, they possess definite Baltic characteristics, as does the Nydam ship. That is to say, they carried no sails and were so low amidships that they were poorly adapted for ocean navigation. Like all Baltic, Scandinavian craft, they were clinker-built. Despite improvement, they were still closer in design to Nydam than to the later Viking Gokstad type.[200] Curiously enough, the Sutton Hoo and Kvalsund ships seem to vindicate the Byzantine historian, Procopius, whose information on Britain has often been considered unreliable. Procopius, who tells us he gained his information from Angles who accompanied Frankish envoys to Justinian's court, informs us in a famous passage that the ships used by the Angles had no sails.[201] He seems rather surprised at this, which may imply that other peoples in Britain—Celts, Saxons and Jutes—did have them. Now the Sutton Hoo ship confirms his statement fully.

One further point on shipping during these years concerns navigation. In general, our evidence seems to point to the fact that, when possible, mariners followed the coastline on their voyages and avoided the open sea. Thus from Coruña or Bordeaux to Britain and Ireland the route traveled passed along the French coast, past Brittany and then across to Cornwall. From Kent to Rouen maritime traffic coasted down the south shores of Britain to the Isle of Wight and then crossed the Channel to Gaul. From Kent to Scandinavia the route was across the narrow seas to the mouths of the Rhine, then

---

[198] C. W. Philips, in *Antiquaries Journal*, xx (1940), 18-32. R. Bruce-Mitford, *The Sutton Hoo Ship Burial* (London 1947), pp. 15, 35-38. Brøgger and Shetelig, *The Viking Ships*, p. 52. T. C. Lethbridge, *Merlin's Island*, pp. 130-37. R. Bruce-Mitford, "The Sutton Hoo Ship Burial," in *Proc. of Royal Soc. of Suffolk*, xxv (1949), 30-45, and R. Hodgkin, *History of the Anglo-Saxons*, 3rd ed., II, 695-756.

[199] On the greater Kvalsund ship, see Brøgger and Shetelig, *op.cit.*, p. 53.

[200] *Ibid.*, pp. 51-60, shows how closely these two ships resemble each other and how they are both descended from the 4th-century Nydam ship.

[201] Procopius, *De bello Gothico*, IV, 19-20, ed. Dewing, V, 252-70.

up along or inside the Frisian coastal islands to the Eider river and via the Jutland peninsula into the Baltic. This explains the value of such locations as Frisia, Hampshire, Kent and Brittany to maritime peoples. It was these that controlled maritime traffic in the Northern Seas.

If this was true of sailing ships, it was even more so of rowing ones, which were the only types then in use in Scandinavia and the Baltic. For rowing ships, the route across the North Sea to England must have been along the Frisian coast, then across the lower end of the North Sea to Kent or the Thames estuary, and then along the eastern shores of Norfolk and Suffolk to the Wash and beyond. It must have been via this route that the Angles reached England, for in their ships the direct route across the North Sea would have been highly dangerous.[202] Similarly, the route whereby Swedish ships reached Southern Norway was along the Swedish coast from the Uppland, past Gotland, Oland and Bornholm and then via Skagerrak and Kattegat to southern Norwegian waters—or alternately by lake and stream across the peninsula of South Sweden to the Kattegat.[203] Thus, in the Baltic, control of the large islands off the Swedish coast and Denmark carried with it control of maritime traffic in these waters. Those who controlled them here, as in the Atlantic, were to become the important trade intermediaries in future years in the Northern Seas.

[202] We know there was a more active navigation linking Norway, Ireland, Britain and Spain together in the late Bronze age than is found in the later Iron age—a fact which bothers Brøgger and Shetelig in *The Viking Ships*, pp. 8-46. Yet there is a rather simple explanation for this. In the earlier period the skin boat or coracle was everywhere in use, including on the coasts of Norway. Riding on top of the waves, it was an ideal Atlantic ocean craft.

When wooden, planked ships were brought into Norway from the Baltic area—and perhaps into Denmark, too—they failed to be as seaworthy in their first stage. The Venetic *ponto* was, as a matter of fact, the only seaworthy, ocean-going, wooden ship in use in the Northeast Atlantic prior to Roman times. Then gradually the Romans introduced their better wooden ships, which had spread to the Saxons and the Picts by the 4th and 5th centuries. The coracle, however, continued in use off Irish and Scottish coasts. On the other hand, the Norwegians and the Angles of Eastern Britain under strong Baltic wooden ship influence, were slow to adopt better wooden ship designs—probably waiting until about 600 A.D. The lesser Kvalsund ship represents the change reaching Norwegian shores, or the marriage of the skin ship with the Baltic wooden plank boat—a marriage which produced the masted Viking ship of later centuries.

[203] See O. R. Janse, *op.cit.* (with map), on routes of travel as outlined in finds of *brachtaetes* in Scandinavia in this period.

3, New Beginnings, A.D. 550-750

TOWARDS THE MIDDLE of the sixth century the lands of Northern
Europe which faced the Atlantic had reached their lowest point
in economic life and civilization since the time of Julius Caesar. They
were divided into a series of isolated cultural and economic regions.
Most of everything that Rome had built in these lands had been
destroyed. Only in South and Central France and along the upper
Danube did much remain of the advanced civilization which had
followed in the wake of the Roman legions. The collapse of Roman
civilization over such a vast area was not, however, entirely a disaster.
With this collapse came an end to those artificial trade barriers, those
swollen defense forces maintained by regimentation and the hated
villa system in most of Northern Europe. Now regions like Germany beyond the Rhine, Ireland, Scandinavia and even the river
valleys of Russia were no longer enemy areas separated from the
world of Rome. In a sense, the century and a half of migrations and
chaos which we have called the invasion period had resulted in a
certain equalization of conditions about the Northern Seas. The
decline of civilization in lands which had been under Rome's sway
was balanced, to some extent, by the relative advance of areas beyond
Roman frontiers. In the period to come, Northern Europe was to start
again, and begin her reconstruction on a more even basis than had
been the case in Roman times.

Furthermore, though not all the gains of Roman times had been
lost, one can observe new forces stirring which were to produce a
better economic and cultural future. Already Kentish mariners were
in contact, from their central position on the trade routes, with the
shores of Western Gaul, the Irish Sea, the Seine, the Rhine, Frisia
and Scandinavia. A trickle of commercial traffic from Italy was crossing the Alpine passes and flowing down the Rhine to Frisia and
beyond. Irish mariners were pushing beyond their Celtic thalassocracy
in the Irish Sea to more distant coasts. A new economic and maritime
epoch was in the first stages of development in the Northern Seas—
one which was to bring with it great advances for Northern Europe.

If one had to sum up in few words the accomplishments of the era
between 550 and 750, one would probably say that these years saw
the gradual fusion of the cultures and economies of isolated regions
in Northern Europe—the development of trade along maritime and

fluvial routes which linked together Spain and Atlantic Gaul, Ireland, Scotland and England, Frisia and Scandinavia. Swedish connections even reached down Russian rivers to the Black and Caspian Seas and the Moslem Middle East. The two centuries saw important steps taken towards the development of a unified region of the Northern Seas, essentially separate from the Mediterranean despite the bond of commerce via Russian rivers, Alpine passes, Southern French valleys and the Atlantic Spanish coast. Though many changes were to take place in Northern Europe after this period, this unity of the Northern Seas was never again to be completely destroyed and was to become one pillar of the Europe of the High Middle Ages. Thus one sees during these two Merovingian centuries some beginnings, different from those of the Late Empire and frequently underestimated by historians, yet of supreme importance for Europe's future.

In the year 550, commerce from the Mediterranean reached Northern Europe largely by way of the Alpine passes and the Rhine, though there was some slight trade passing to the Atlantic by way of the Seine and the Garonne. By the first decades of the eighth century this was no longer the case. The Atlantic, the English Channel, the North Sea and the Baltic possessed a maritime traffic which owed its origin to a commerce flowing north from Spanish coasts and from France between the Garonne and the Rhine, as in Early Roman times. This traffic came from ports at the mouths of the Garonne, the Charente, the Loire, the Seine, the Somme, the Canche, the Scheldt, the Meuse and the Rhine, and the cargoes loaded in these localities reached Ireland, England, Scotland, Frisia, Scandinavia and the Baltic. To understand how this commerce revived, we must examine Merovingian Gaul, from which so large a portion of it originated.

It has already been noted that Gaul south of the Loire and along the Rhone represented a region all but unique. Of the areas once forming Rome's northern provinces, it was one of the few to which the barbarian invasions brought relatively little change. In it neither the economic and social structure of the large landed estates run by a Gallo-Roman aristocracy nor the remaining Late Roman urban centers were destroyed. Instead, under Merovingian rule, as under that of Romans, Visigoths and Burgundians, the old order continued relatively intact in the first years of the sixth century. The Franks, like their predecessors, allowed the Gallo-Roman aristocracy to keep possession of most of their estates, their power and their privileges. They continued to use this aristocracy to fill important positions in church and state. And under them conditions may even have improved for this land-owning class, in the sense that the Franks, with their simpler political system, were unable and even unwilling to continue the regimentation and heavy taxation of the Late Empire. Such policies may well have given more actual freedom to town and landed estate than they had possessed in the fourth century.[1]

Frankish benevolence, however, was not the chief reason for the continuance of the older order of things in this part of Gaul. Rather it was due to the fact that connections with the Mediterranean world increased during these years. In the fourth and early fifth centuries such connections via ports like Marseilles, Arles and Narbonne had been relatively unimportant. Regulations forbidding Eastern merchants to enter the Western Empire and Vandal piracy had reduced the Mediterranean trade of Gaul to a trickle. The stability brought to the Mediterranean West by Theodoric's diplomacy and the decline of Vandal piracy had initiated a change. Justinian's reconquest of Italy, North Africa and Southern Spain—a revived Mediterranean Romania—had further influence.[2] By 550 a certain number of Oriental merchants—Syrians, Jews and Greeks—began to establish themselves again in Gaul, bringing their wares with them.[3] Their presence in Gaul in this century may have been caused in part by the fact that Italy, suffering from ruin brought about by the wars of Justinian and the Lombard invasion, was, temporarily at least, less attractive as a field for commercial enterprise. The studies of Vercauteren, Pirenne, Brehier and Lamprechts emphasize the importance to Gaul of this commerce with the Orient handled by these merchants.[4] So, too, does a reading of Gregory of Tours. All these make it clear that in the

[1] On the continuance of power of the old senatorial families, particularly in Western Gaul, see E. Salin, *La Civilisation merovingienne*, I, 25-30, 411-18. See also N. Åberg, *The Occident and Orient in the Art of the Seventh Century*, I (Stockholm 1947), 5-14, and L. Desgranges, *Les Apollinaires* (Paris 1937). On the resistance of this group to taxation by the Merovingian rulers, see Gregory of Tours, *Hist. Franc.*, IX, 30, and J. Wallace-Hadrill, "The Work of Gregory of Tours in the Light of Modern Research," in *Trans. of Royal Hist. Soc.*, 5th ser., I (1950), 25-33.

[2] On this, see A. R. Lewis, *Naval Power and Trade in the Mediterranean, A.D. 500-1100* (Princeton 1951), pp. 3-53.

[3] L. Brehier, "Les Colonies d'orientaux en Occident," in *Byz. Zeit*, XII (1903), 23-46, and P. Lamprechts, "Le Commerce des Syriens en Gaule," in *L'Antiquité classique*, VI (1937), 152-57.

[4] See particularly F. Vercauteren, *Etude sur les civitates de la Belgique Secunde* (Bruxelles 1934), pp. 186-203. Also H. Pirenne, "Le Commerce du papyrus dans la Gaule merovingienne," in *Comptes rendus de l'Acad. des Inscriptions et Belles Lettres* (Bruxelles 1928), pp. 213-37, and *Mahomet et Charlemagne* (Paris 1936), pp. 1-250.

late sixth century the domains of the Merovingians in Gaul were much more closely integrated with the economic and even the cultural life of the Mediterranean than had been the case in the year 400.

The coinage in use during these years makes this even plainer. In 395 minting of gold had been transferred from Trier to Milan and in the mid-fifth century a Roman Emperor commented upon the bad quality of the Gallic *solidi*.[5] In the Rhone valley *minimissimi* of bronze had appeared, always a sign of localism and economic decadence.[6] Yet in 550 we again find an abundant gold coinage, minted in the form of *solidi* modeled after the Byzantine *nomismata*. Such *solidi* were numerous near the Mediterranean, while elsewhere the less valuable gold *triens* was a favorite. Gregory the Great might complain about the quality of such Gallic coins,[7] but certainly the monetary situation had improved immensely since 450. Everywhere in this part of Gaul mints were turning out a gold coinage,[8] as subsidies from Byzantium, expeditions into Visigothic Spain and renewed Mediterranean commerce brought streams of golden metal into the land.[9] And this gold brought with it those Eastern merchants who exchanged their spices, silks, wine, olive oil and other Oriental manufactured wares for Gallic leather, metals, wood, grain and slaves. Their presence, not only in cities like Bordeaux, Agen, Narbonne, Arles and Marseilles, but even as far north as Tours, Paris, Orléans, Verdun and Trier shows how real this Merovingian economic renaissance was.

If there remains any doubt that Gaul in the mid-sixth century was

[5] *Nov. Majoran*, VI, 14.

[6] P. Grierson, *Numismatics and History* (London 1950), pp. 9-10. A. Blanchet and A. Dieudonné, *Manuel de numismatique française*, III, 184-85.

[7] M. Bloch, "Le Problème de l'or au moyen âge," in *Ann. d'hist. écon. et sociale*, IV (1933), 8-9. On these lightweight *solidi*, P. Grierson, "The Canterbury (St. Martin's) Hoard," in *Brit. Num. Journal*, XXVII (1953), 50.

[8] The fact that after about 600 A.D. the gold coinage of Gaul was no longer struck in royal controlled mints, but by cities, bishops, monasteries and even landowners, is noted by M. Prou, *Catalogue des monnaies merovingiennes* (Paris 1892), pp. LXII-XCV. See also P. Le Gentilhomme, "Aperçu sur quelques aspects du monnayage des peuples barbares," in *Mélanges de Numismatique Merovingienne* (Paris 1946), pp. 103-32. This was probably due to the weakness of the Merovingian state. But it is worth noting that exactly the same thing happened in Galicia, where minting places, including some in villas, multiplied in the late 6th and 7th centuries. F. Bouza-Brey, *op.cit.*, pp. 7-8, and "La ceca suevo visigodo de Valencia del Sil," in *Zephyrus*, IV (1953), 69-78. See also on this coinage, G. C. Miles, *The Coinage of Visigothic Spain* (New York 1952). For a similar situation in England, see G. C. Brooke, *English Coins*, pp. 3-23.

[9] R. Doehaerd, "La Richesse des Merovingiens," *loc.cit.*, pp. 30-46.

linked to the Mediterranean rather than to the Northern Seas, it can be dispelled by examining information provided us by Gregory of Tours. In his works he mentions a total of 45 *civitates* in Merovingian Gaul, most of which he also identifies as *urbes*, or inhabited centers, and all of which were of Roman origin. The greater part were located in the southern or western regions of Gaul, particularly in the Loire, Garonne and Rhone valleys. Of these 45, few were on the Atlantic coast and these mainly in Aquitaine, where Bordeaux, Saintes, Nantes and Vannes seem to have survived despite Breton invasion and Saxon piracy. Along the English Channel only Avranches and Coutances near the Brittany-Normandy border, and Bayeux and Rouen near the Seine, are among those he mentions. In the northeast he names only Tournai, Verdun, Metz and Trier, and in the Rhinelands only Cologne.[10] He comments on city walls surviving only in the case of Paris, Rouen, Tours, Orléans and Bordeaux.[11]

Thus Gaul looked south towards the Mediterranean at the beginning of this period, which explains the Oriental influences found in Merovingian glassware[12] and in the marble work of Aquitaine.[13] Influences arriving from Egypt and the rest of the Byzantine East were the decisive ones. With justification Vercauteren can say that Belgica Secunda, during these years, was but an economic hinterland of Mediterranean Marseilles and received its money, commerce and cultural influences via the Rhone valley, which led to the south.[14]

In addition to this Mediterranean connection, however, it is interesting to note that during these early years of Merovingian times Gallic economic life gradually increased in intensity. Cities like Bordeaux and Poitiers, which had survived the invasion period virtually intact, now began to expand. At least we find new churches built beyond the confines of their Late Roman walls, buildings so extensive that medieval pilgrims on their way to Compostela were to believe them to be the work of the mighty Charlemagne.[15] At

---

[10] F. Vercauteren, *op.cit.*, pp. 347-49.

[11] Orléans kept its walls and its Roman city plan. Gregory of Tours, *Hist. Franc.*, II, 7, in *MGH Script. rer. Merov.*, I, 69, and F. L. Ganshof, *Les Villes entre Loire et Rhin*, plan no. 27. On Bordeaux, see Gregory of Tours, *Hist. Franc.*, v, 29, and F. Vercauteren, *op.cit.*, pp. 347-51.

[12] E. Salin, *Le Haut Moyen Age en Lorraine*, pp. 197-213.

[13] R. Lautier, "Les Eglises de la Gaule merovingienne" in *Journal des Savants*, XXXII (1950), 22.

[14] F. Vercauteren, *op.cit.*, pp. 440-51.

[15] On these new religious foundations outside the 4th century walls at Bordeaux, see P. Courtreault, *Bordeaux à travers les siècles*, p. 8. At Poitiers, P. de la Croix, *Les Origines des anciens monuments religieux de Poitiers* (Poitiers 1906), pp. 9-38.

Bordeaux, Le Mans, Paris, Orléans, Auxerre, Verdun and Maastricht new inns, always a good index of travel and commercial activity, were constructed. Such hostelries about Paris were able to supply the traveler with spices and other Eastern products.[16]

As the current of economic life quickened, it began to reach parts of the Channel coast, Belgium and the Rhinelands which had been all but dead for a century. Soon after 550 Quentovic came into being[17] and Amiens farther south began to take on life.[18] Tournai on the Scheldt increased in importance again.[19] On the Meuse a series of trading places, so located that each was one day's river journey from the other, arose at Huy, Dinant, Liége and Maastricht.[20] This last replaced the defunct Roman center of Tongres nearby on the Chausée Bavai-Cologne. On the Moselle we now find Marsal joining Metz and Trier as an urban center,[21] while along the Rhine Andernach, Mainz, Worms and Cologne became important enough to mint *trientes*.[22] Near the mouths of the Rhine about 600 A.D. Dorestad began to take shape, while Antwerp nearby at the mouth of the Scheldt also appeared.[23] These ports were the result of a new commerce which moved north up the Canche, Meuse, Moselle and Rhine in the late sixth and seventh centuries. Nor was this all. Farther south, between the Seine and Meuse, centers like Cambrai, Soissons, Châlons-sur-Marne, Noyon, Arras and Terouanne show their importance by the fact that they coined money during the years of the seventh century.[24]

[16] W. Schonfeld, "Die Xenodochien im Italien und Frankreich im frühen Mittelalter," in *Zeit. der. Savigny-Stiftung. Kan. Abth.*, XLIII (1922), 133-46. F. L. Ganshof, "La Tractoria," in *Revue d'hist. de Brabant*, VIII (1927), 88.

[17] P. Heliot, "La Question de Quentovic," in *Revue du Nord*, XXIII (1937), 260-65. O. Fengler, "Quentovic, seine maritime Bedeutung unter Merovingern und Karolingern," in *Hansische Geschichtsblätter*, XIII (1907), 216-38.

[18] L. Duschesne, *Fastes épiscopaux de l'ancienne Gaule*, III (Paris 1915), 10-24.

[19] H. Pirenne, "Le Fisc royal de Tournai," in *Mélanges Lot* (Paris 1926), pp. 183-97. P. Rolland, "Le Problème de la continuité à Tournai et dans la Gaule du Nord," in *Ann. d'hist. écon. et sociale*, VII (1937), 248-64.

[20] R. Doehaerd, *L'Expansion économique de la Belgique*, pp. 13-16. F. L. Ganshof, "Het Tijdperk van de Merowingern," in *Algemene Geschiedenis der Nederlanden*, II, (1950) 290-93.

[21] E. Salin, *La Civilisation merovingienne*, I, 429-33. F. Vercauteren, *op.cit.*, pp. 445-49.

[22] F. L. Ganshof, *Les Villes entre Loire et Rhin*, pp. 11-15. K. Schumacher, *Seidlung und Kulturgeschichte des Rheinlands*, 2 vols. (Köln 1924-25), pp. 181-236, 11-47.

[23] P. Boeles, *Friesland*, pp. 270-73. *Chron. Eptarnocens*, in *MGH Script.*, XXIII, 63. R. Doehaerd, *op.cit.*, pp. 13-16.

[24] F. Vercauteren, *Belgique Secunde*, pp. 445-50. M. Prou, *Catalogue des monnaies merovingiennes*, pp. C-CIV. F. L. Ganshof, "Het Tijdperk van de Merowingern," *loc.cit.*, pp. 17-33.

Joined to this new economic activity that resulted in the reinvigoration of old Roman *civitates* and the establishment of new ones was fresh industrial activity. In the same regions where, in the fourth century, the Empire had some of its most important workshops, we find an industrial impetus developing again. One of the new or reappearing industries was the making of glass, centering around Trier and Arras. New Syrian techniques and the use of natron imported from the Mediterranean resulted in a glassware, however, which was very different from that produced in Late Roman times.[25]

The other industry was the production of iron and other metalware. This industry was also new in technique, since it used a system of pattern-welding and damascening sword blades unknown to the Romans, which produced a weapon of such temper that it was prized as far away as Central Asia. Such swords, known as Frankish swords, were far superior to those manufactured elsewhere in the West. Other metal techniques included the production of a type of damascened belt-buckle and ornaments which copied styles and decorative techniques of Germany, England and distant Scandinavia.

Salin has discovered four different areas which produced distinctive arms and metalwork in this part of Gaul in Merovingian times, basing his classification upon ornament styles. One is the upper Rhone-Switzerland area. A second consists of the Meuse region. A third is found along the Moselle, and the fourth near Paris in the Seine-Marne region. He dates the beginning of production as the late sixth century and considers that all four regions were in full flower during the seventh, with the Paris region developing last. He also points out that these regions coincided with those where metal workshops were active in Late Roman times, according to the *Notitia Dignitatum*. Style and technique for working iron and other metals had changed, but the industry's location remained the same, as in the case of glass manufacture.[26] Was there also an important woolen industry still functioning about Arras, or being revived during these years? We do not know, but it seems probable that cloth was produced in commercial domanial *gynecées* near Tournai, where stone continued to be worked and exported also.[27]

[25] E. Salin, *Le Haut Moyen Age en Lorraine*, pp. 197-213. F. Faidler-Feytmans, "Les Verreries des époques romanes at merovingiennes" in *Revue belge d'arch. et de l'hist. de l'art*, v (1940), 17-23.

[26] E. Salin, *La Civilisation merovingienne*, I, 150-214, and *La Fer à l'époque merovingienne*, pp. 169-97.

[27] P. Rolland, "Le Problème de la continuité à Tournai," *loc.cit.*, pp. 84-92. R. Doehaerd, *L'Expansion économique de la Belgique*, pp. 13-18.

Though Northeastern Gaul was rapidly developing as an industrial region during these years, just as it had in the Roman period, it seems possible that industrial life was not unknown in the western part of Gaul either. The Loire iron industry around Nevers, important in the fifth century, seems to have been so again in the late sixth and seventh; place names like La Ferrière on the lower Loire may testify to its continuance.[28] An important marble industry flourished about Bordeaux and Poitiers and was linked in technique to the Near East.[29] Whether the older cloth industry of the Saintogne region survived the invasion period or not is rather problematical.[30] But salt continued to be produced here and at Noirmoutier, just as it did along the Rhine and Moselle. If one may believe a ninth-century tradition, the silver mines at Melle were again in production as early as 635, the year of King Dagobert's gift of a large quantity of lead *ex metellem* to the Church of St. Denis.[31] Since St. Eligius is known to have roofed his Church of St. Paul in Paris with lead at about the same time,[32] this tradition is probably based on fact.

As this commercial and industrial development expanded its field of operations in Merovingian Gaul, it stimulated new use of those rivers which led to the Atlantic. The Rhine, the Moselle, the Meuse, the Seine, the Loire and the Garonne began to carry a burden of goods between the new ports and reinvigorated older Roman urban centers along their banks. In this period it was such river systems, even more than the still remaining Roman roads, which carried most of the commercial traffic[33]—even though the *tractoria*, or Late Imperial post system, survived.[34] For in its emphasis on river traffic this period represents a break with the Roman past. In the Late Empire, for instance, it was not the Meuse but the Bavai-Cologne highway which had been important. Along this highway were clustered the surviving villas of the region and the chief Roman city of this area, Tongres, lay some distance by road from the river. Now by the seventh century we find Tongres abandoned and a new *portus*,

[28] O. Davies, *Roman Mines in Europe*, pp. 85-93.

[29] R. Lautier, *Les Eglises de la Gaule merovingienne*, pp. 70-132. E. Salin, *La Civilisation merovingienne*, I, 211-37.

[30] H. Hauser, "Le Sel dans l'histoire," in *Revue économique internationale*, III (1927), 275-76.

[31] *Gesta Dagoberti*, in MGH *Script. rer. Merov.*, II, 419.

[32] *Vita Eligii*, in MGH *Script. rer. Merov.*, IV, 684.

[33] F. Rousseau, *La Meuse et le pays mosan*, pp. 37-45. Lot, Pfister and Ganshof, *Le Destinées de l'empire en Occident*, pp. 355.

[34] F. L. Ganshof, "La Tractoria," *loc.cit.*, pp. 11-17.

Maastricht, appearing, but on the Meuse.[35] All other settlements and *vici* of Merovingian times were also located on the river systems, not on the old Roman roads of the region.[36] Were this situation confined to the Ardennes, we might consider it accidental, but we find the pattern repeated on the middle Loire. Here around Tours we notice the same shift from villas located along the road system of Roman times to settlements based upon the river systems of the region. Obviously, by the seventh century, it was rivers rather than roads which dictated the economic life of Northern Merovingian Gaul.

In general, there has been a tendency to regard this development or revival of Northern and Western Gaul during this period, its new industrial impetus, its revival of old Roman *civitates* and founding of new ports along the Channel, in Belgium and the Rhinelands, even this new use of rivers reaching the Atlantic and the spread of a gold currency, as an extension of Mediterranean civilization towards the north. Certainly Gaul's firm connection with the revived Romania of Justinian and his successors did play an important role in this process. But it is equally important to understand that this revival represented something more than that. It was also the result of renewed commercial and maritime life in the Northern Seas, a return, in a sense, to the days of the fourth century under certain new conditions. Let us, then, examine the way in which this renewed Atlantic commerce, so potent a force in this revival, reached and affected western Gallic coasts, where, in 550, a number of older centers, never having completely disappeared, lay ready to receive it.

About the middle of the sixth century we begin to hear of commerce reaching along the northern Spanish coast, for Gregory of Tours tells us of a Visigothic monarch who interfered with a merchant fleet from Bordeaux trading with Galicia.[37] Among other products, these ships probably carried wine, for we learn that there was a *fiscus vinitor* located near the island of Oleron where Merovingian monarchs levied dues upon the export of this article of commerce.[38] About the same time we learn that the King of the Suevi who controlled Galicia was in close communication with the shrine of St. Martin of Tours, where he asked for help in curing his son of a dangerous ill-

---

[35] F. Rousseau, *La Meuse*, pp. 37-38. R. Doehaerd, *op.cit.*, pp. 13-15.

[36] R. Koebner, *The Settlement and Colonization of Europe*, pp. 30-51. See also M. Bloch, "Les Invasions: deux structures économiques," in *Ann. d'hist. sociale*, II (1945), 13-28.

[37] Gregory of Tours, *Hist. Franc.*, VIII, 35, in *MGH Script. rer. Merov.*, I, 351.

[38] *Ibid.*, V. 48, in *loc.cit.*, p. 239.

ness.[39] Shortly thereafter we learn that Gallic merchants were sailing as far as Ireland and carrying their wine up the river Shannon to the monastery of Clonmacnois in the interior of the island.[40] A few decades later, in the first years of the seventh century, there is a mention of Gallic sailors and ships in the Irish Sea off the Scottish coast not far from Iona.[41] So important did this trade become that the Irish name for foreigners in general was *Gall*, or Frenchman. Nor was it a one-way traffic. At the time of St. Columba, Irish merchants were trading with Nantes[42] and a bit later were reported selling coarse cloth and shoes on the island of Noirmoutier.[43] Excavations at Lagore in Ireland, going back to this period, seem to show that both these products were of native Irish provenience.[44] Considering these close maritime connections, it is not surprising that it was to Ireland that the young Merovingian Prince Dagobert was carried late in the seventh century to escape assassination.[45] Nor should we be surprised that Irish monks were found in such numbers in the region of Poitou, where the tomb of Merobaudes that has been excavated near Poitiers shows a number of Irish Celtic features. Maritime commerce between Western Gaul and Ireland was now a regular feature of the age.

Hardly less so was western Gallic commerce with British coasts, both eastern and western, though it is possible that this traffic became important only in the seventh century, somewhat later than that with Ireland. It has already been noted that archeology provides proof of a maritime connection between Kent and the Saxon colony on the Charente.[46] Such connections grew, for in the late seventh century we hear of British merchants, probably Anglo-Saxon, appearing at the mouth of the Loire and going to Angoulême, probably

---

[39] P. Davies, *Etudes historiques sur la Galicie et le Portugal*, p. 119.

[40] *Vita Ciarini*, XXXI. For more examples of this commerce, see H. Zimmer, "Über direkte Handelsverbindungen Westgallens mit Ireland," in *Sitz. der Kaiser Prusse Akad. der Wissenschaften* (1909-1910), pp 363-419.

[41] Adamnan, *Vita Columbae*, I, 22, ed. Reeves, pp. 130-31.

[42] Jonas, *Vita Columbani*, in *MGH Script. rer. Merov.*, IV, 97.

[43] *Vita Filiberti*, XLI-XLII, in *ibid.*, V, 603.

[44] Lagore in this period possessed smiths, bronze workers, carpenters, weavers and leatherworkers, as revealed by excavations. H. O. Hencken, "Lagore Crannoy, A royal Irish Residence," in *Proc. of Royal Irish Acad.*, LIII (1950), 83-147.

[45] *Vita Wilfridi auctore Stephani*, in *MGH Script. rer. Merov.*, VI, 21.

[46] See Chapter II and also P. Grierson, "The Canterbury (St. Martin's) Hoard," in *Brit. Num. Jour.*, XXVII (1953), 49-51, on numismatic evidence of a close connection between Kent and western Gallic shores in the late 6th century. See also accounts in *Vita Filiberti*, XLI, in *MGH Script. rer. Merov.*, V, 603, and *Virtutis Eparchi*, X-XII, in *ibid.*, III, 556-57.

to procure wine. About this period we also hear of direct traffic by sea from Tours to England.[47] And in the year 700 our sources tell us of St. Yvri (Ives), who took ship in distant Northumbria and sailed direct to Brittany.[48] Certain similarities between inscriptions found at Poitiers dating from this period and those of distant Northumbria are explainable if we remember that a direct sea connection between these regions had been re-established.

To numismatic evidence, however, we must turn for more confirmation of this maritime commerce than our texts or archeology can provide. In England two treasures of gold coins have been discovered at Sutton Hoo and Crondall which give us further evidence of connections with Western Gaul. These hoards make it clear that England's chief link was with Frisia, the Rhinelands, Quentovic and Rouen. But one coin in the Crondall hoard and six *trientes* at Sutton Hoo which were struck at mints in the Loire and Garonne regions, as well as several Visigothic pieces, appear to emphasize that a connection existed between Southeastern Britain and these Gallic coasts.[49] So, too, does a *triens* coined in the Garonne region which is a direct copy of those of English provenience found at Crondall.[50]

Towards the end of the seventh century and the beginning of the eighth, such numismatic proof becomes more conclusive in nature. A whole series of hoards of silver money found in different locations along the coasts of Gaul from the Rhine to the Garonne, and even at Marseilles, contain Anglo-Saxon *sceattas*. At Bais (Ille et Villaine) in Brittany there are 30 *sceattas* in a treasure of 400 Merovingian silver pennies.[51] At St. Pierre des Etiaux (Cher) in the Loire valley there are 11 English *sceattas* in a hoard of 96 Merovingian silver deniers.[52] Farther south along the Atlantic coast at Plaissac (Gironde)

[47] According to Bede, John the Archchanter sailed directly to Britain from Tours. Bede, *Hist. eccl.*, IV, 18, ed. King, II, 100.

[48] *Vita St. Yveis*, in *Actas Sanct. Boll.*, 6 Oct., III, 405.

[49] On these English gold hoards and particularly the Crondall hoard, see C. H. Sutherland, *Anglo-Saxon Coinage in the Light of the Crondall Hoard* (Oxford 1948), pp. 23-40. On Sutton Hoo, see R. Hodgkin, *History of the Anglo-Saxons*, 3rd ed., II, 695-734, 749-56. See also *British Museum Quarterly*, XIII (1939), 4, and R. Bruce-Mitford, *The Sutton Hoo Ship Burial* (London 1947), pp. 18-27. Probably Sutherland dates the Crondall hoard too late, namely about 660-70. P. Grierson, in the *Eng. Hist. Review*, CXIX (1950), 233, places it between 620 and 630 and that of Sutton Hoo about 655. This latter date is accepted by R. Bruce-Mitford in "The Sutton Hoo Ship Burial," in *Proc. of Royal Soc. of Suffolk*, XXV (1949), 37-41.

[50] P. Le Gentilhomme, *op.cit.*, p. 18.

[51] M. Prou, *Catalogue des deniers merovingiens de la trouvaille de Bais* (Paris 1908), p. 11.

[52] B. de Kerseis, *Bulletin numismatique. Mémories de la Soc. des Ant. du Centre*, XI (1884), 93-107.

we find 12 such *sceattas* in a treasure of 170 Merovingian pennies.[53] And finally at Cimiez, near Marseilles, in a later hoard of over 2,000 deniers which dates from 737, there are 80 English *sceattas*.[54] It is worth noting that these Anglo-Saxon silver coins are rare in Gallic hoards of this period. Save for a sprinkling of them in the Rhinelands and one found with some Merovingian pennies in a small hoard at La Panne on the Flanders coast, they are found only in the four treasures mentioned above.[55] Thus they represent a trail of money leading from Kent and the Thames region, where these *sceattas* were minted, along the Atlantic coasts of Gaul to Bordeaux and even on to Marseilles. They reinforce the evidence of our sources and that of the earlier Crondall and Sutton Hoo finds which testify to maritime commerce along these shores. It is also interesting that we have a source, in addition to the Cimiez hoard, which confirms a direct connection between England and Marseilles; for we learn that Botta, an English merchant of Kent, was settled in this city in the mid-eighth century.[56] On the other hand, there is no proof from money hoards of an economic connection between western British coasts and Western Gaul, perhaps because the archeological history of Cornwall and Wales is still in its first developmental stages. One discovery, though, that of a Merovingian chalice which was turned up near the tin mine of Castel-el-Dinas in Cornwall, may be significant.[57]

Not all traffic from Western Gaul, however, went to English and Irish shores. Some reached Gallic ports along the Channel and the mouths of the Rhine in Frisia. Here again our texts give us some information. At the end of the seventh century St. Filibert bought

[53] E. Cartier, in *Revue numismatique*, XXXI (1851), 19.

[54] There is an important literature on the Cimiez hoard. See especially A. Morel-Fatio, *Catalogue raisonné de la collection des deniers merovingiens des VIIe et VIIIe siècles de la trouvaille de Cimiez* (Paris 1890).

[55] Sutherland believes most *sceattas* are of Anglo-Saxon origin, except for a type he calls Anglo-French, which he believes was minted in part in Gaul, and the late dragon or "woden-monster" *sceattas*, which he attributes to the Frisians. C. Sutherland, *Anglo-Saxon Sceattas in England, Their Origin, Chronology and Distribution* (Oxford 1948) pp. 42-76. Le Gentilhomme believes most are of Frisian origin or copied by the Frisians. P. Le Gentilhomme, *op.cit.*, pp. 73-93. Boeles, however, rejects a Frisian origin for the *sceattas* entirely (even the "woden-monster" type) and says they are Anglo-Saxon. He only admits that very *late* in the 8th century the "woden-monster" type was copied in Frisia. P. Boeles, *Friesland* (2nd ed., The Hague 1951), pp. 160-217. The fact that it is in England that *sceattas* have been found in such numbers—not in Frisia or Gaul—seems to make Boeles' argument decisive.

[56] *Annales Petavini*, III, in *MGH Script.*, XVII, 170. See also W. Levison, *England and the Continent*, p. 7.

[57] H. O. Hencken, *The Archeology of Cornwall and Scilly*, p. 263.

a cargo of olive oil in Bordeaux which he shipped by sea to the monastery of Jumièges on the Seine. It is also possible that the wine which the Bishop of Cahors sent to Verdun at about the same time followed an Atlantic sea route.[58] Even more interesting is the fact that the monastery of Stavelot on the Meuse received from Chilperic III an immunity, the first of which we have knowledge, which permitted this foundation to maintain on the Loire two ports, Sellae and Vagatio.[59]

To such fragmentary evidence can be added what numismatics shows of such routes along the coast from the Garonne to the Rhine. First let us consider certain hoards of coins of this period found in Frisia. The gold pieces discovered in Frisia which reached there prior to 700, unlike those found in England, suggest that little maritime commerce existed between this region and the Channel and Atlantic coasts of Gaul. For instance, not a single Quentovic gold *triens*, a type common in England, has turned up in Frisia. But certain other coins, probably from sites at Domburg, are important. They include a Visigothic *triens* struck at Seville between 612 and 623, a seventh-century gold piece from Rodez and three which came from the Loire region.[60]

---

[58] *Vita Filiberti*, xxxviii, in *MGH Script. rer. Merov.*, v, 602. On this shipment of wine from Cahors to Verdun, see *MGH Epistolae*, I, 208-9. It is also possible that the wine which Gregory of Tours tells us merchants bought in Tours was shipped, in part, to Nantes for the Atlantic trade. Gregory of Tours, *Hist. Franc.*, VIII, 45-46, in *MGH Script. rer. Merov.*, I, 332. Nantes may have been a wine port in 587, for in that year Bro-Weroc carried off the city's wine after its capture. *Ibid.* v, 31, in *loc.cit.*, p. 224.

[59] Pardessus, *Diplomata*, No. 39. On this commerce, see also Imbart de la Tour, "Les Immunités commerciales accordées aux églises," in *Questions d'histoire sociale et religieuse* (Paris 1907), pp. 101-37. The immunities given the monastery of Corbie at Fos on the Mediterranean, which Pirenne has emphasized so much, are *later* than those of Stavelot at Sellae and Vagatio, dating as they do between 657-673. J. C. Levillain, *Examen des chartes de Corbie* (Paris 1902), p. 220.

[60] Of the 7th-century gold pieces minted prior to 700 A.D. which have been found in Frisia, 25 are of local Dorestad and Frisian origin, 27 are from Rhineland mints, 10 from the Meuse valley and 3 from the Rhone valley. There are *none* from England and only 2 from the Seine valley, while 3 from the Loire and one from the Garonne may show a trickle of maritime traffic reaching Frisia from the Channel and western Gallic coasts. P. Boeles, *Friesland*, pp. 511-21. On the whole, however, these coins seem to show what Boeles concludes on other evidence as well: that the Frisians were not active maritime traders until late in the 8th century, and that they did not go to the Fair of St. Denis until about 753, the earliest date at which they were mentioned there. *Ibid.*, pp. 512-19. The only mention of Frisians in England prior to the 8th century is found in Bede's reference to *one* Frisian slave-trader in London in 679. Bede, *Hist. eccl.*, IV, 22, ed. King, II, 122. Their *schola* at Rome dates from 799, seventy years after the establishment of the Anglo-Saxon *schola* there. P. Kletler, *Nordwesteuropas Verkehr, Handel und Gewerbe im frühen Mittelalter* (Vienna 1924), pp. 260-64. One can therefore conclude that the Anglo-Saxons

Farther down the coast, however, from the Seine to Bordeaux, money finds show a more active coastal commerce. At Rouen, for example, a find of 11 deniers dating from the first years of the eighth century includes two coins from Tours, one from Angers and one from Poitou. Nearby a seventh-century Bordeaux *solidus* has been discovered as well.[61] At Bais in Brittany a hoard already mentioned earlier has deniers from Paris, Rouen, Rennes and Orléans.[62] The huge Bauguisière treasure from the Loire valley, of a late seventh-century date and very local in nature, nevertheless includes money from Paris, Orléans, and Poitiers as well as one coin from the Garonne region.[63] Found near this hoard, though later in date, that of St. Pierre des Etiaux contains silver pennies from Paris, Le Mans, Poitiers and one *triens* from Banassac in Southwestern Gaul.[64] In another hoard at Plaissac (Gironde) one third of the coins comes from Poitiers.

A gold treasure of Bordeaux, however, dating from the late seventh century, gives us even more significant evidence. This hoard was buried between 673 and 677. Curiously enough, it consists almost entirely of *solidi*, of which 39 are of Visigothic Spanish origin. Among the Merovingian pieces, we find 3 from Paris, 7 from Rouen, 8 from the Loire region and one gilded *thrymsa* copied from Anglo-Saxon money. In addition it contains a series of *solidi* which were minted along the Garonne and its tributaries and some from both Marseilles and Narbonne. Thus we can see in this one hoard a graphic illustration of commercial routes from Bordeaux along the Atlantic coast of Gaul perhaps as far as England, and via the Garonne to the Mediterranean ports of Marseilles and Narbonne. The presence of that olive oil at Bordeaux which St. Filibert purchased and which probably came from Provence is thus explained. So, too, is that trail of English *sceattas* which leads down Gallic coasts to the Garonne and on to Marseilles.

Nor is that all. Some of the 39 Visigothic coins in this hoard are from the eastern coast of Spain and seem to show that trade went from Narbonne down the Spanish coast to Barcelona and Valencia. But the majority of these Spanish pieces come from the south and west: from Cadiz, Seville, Cordova, Emerita and Merida. They thus give

---

were the great merchants of the Northern Seas in Merovingian times, *not* the Frisians. The Frisians as merchants were a Carolingian phenomenon.

[61] P. Le Gentilhomme, *op.cit.*, pp. 12, 60-64.
[62] M. Prou, *Catalogue des monnaies merovingiennes*, pp. XCIX-CIII.
[63] P. Le Gentilhomme, *op.cit.*, pp. 120-25.
[64] B. de Kerseis, *op.cit.*, pp. 93-107.

indication of routes along Spain's Atlantic coast as far as Cadiz. The maritime traffic which Gregory of Tours described as reaching Galicia a century earlier still existed, then, in the late seventh century and extended as far as Gibraltar.[65] A few scattered coin finds confirm the evidence of Atlantic coastal traffic from Spain already provided by the Bordeaux hoard. A gold piece of Egica, found at Coruña, seems to suggest that the gold mines of Asturias were still in operation in this century,[66] while the Visigothic gold pieces of Sutton Hoo and those found in Frisia suggest that trade from Spain even reached the North Sea.[67] One gold piece struck at Braga in what is now Northwestern Portugal even turns up in Skanë in South Sweden.[68]

Important as the commerce was which came to link Western Gaul with other Atlantic shores, it was less important than that which crossed the Channel to England. We have already noted that prior to 550 some commerce passed to Kent from the mouths of the Rhine and from Rouen. Shortly thereafter there is evidence of an increase in such contacts. King Athelwulf of Kent, for instance, had close enough relations with the Seine area of Gaul to marry Bertha, daughter of King Haribert of Paris,[69] while Theudebert even earlier could claim to have dominion over the Saxon Eucii of Kent.[70] In 595 St. Augustine took a ship in Northeastern Gaul to arrive at Thanet on the Thames.[71]

By the seventh century such contacts had multiplied, as coin hoards

[65] P. Le Gentilhomme, op.cit., pp. 9-10. The Visigothic solidi, very rare in Gaul in this period, are from the following mints: Eastern Visigothic—one Narbonne, one Barcelona, one Saragossa, one Valencia, from the west and southwest—7 Cordova, 7 Merida, 6 Seville, 2 Elvira. Ibid., pp. 42-51. In contrast to this, the contemporary Buis hoard of the Rhone valley shows no coin evidence of contact with either Spain or the northern and western coasts of Gaul. It is almost completely local. Ibid., pp. 120-25. By the end of the 7th century, then, we can assert that the commerce of the Rhone valley was much less active than that of the Garonne valley and the Atlantic coast. Interestingly enough, the sceatta finds of a few years later, already commented on, show the same thing. They reveal a trade route leading down the Atlantic shores of Gaul and the Garonne valley to Marseilles. But not a single sceatta has so far been found in Central Gaul or the Rhone valley.

[66] On this gold piece and the activity of gold mines in Galicia, see O. Davies, Roman Mines in Europe, pp. 97-106, and F. Bouza-Brey, "La Numismatica en Galicia," in Faro de Vigo, II (1953), 7-8.

[67] R. Hodgkin, History of the Anglo-Saxons, II, 695-756. P. Boeles, Friesland, p. 511.

[68] N. L. Rasmusson, "Foreign Coins in Swedish Coin Finds," in Trans. of International Num. Congress (London 1938), pp. 18-35.

[69] W. Levison, England and the Continent, p. 5.

[70] R. S. Lopez, "Le Problème des relations anglo-byzantines," in Byzantion, XVIII (1948), 141. H. M. Chadwick, The Origins of the English Nation, pp. 17-19.

[71] Collingwood and Myers, Roman Britain and the English Settlements, pp. 437-38. F. Stenton, Anglo-Saxon England, pp. 29-35.

reveal. The Crondall hoard, which dates from between 620 and 630, contains money struck at Paris, Châlons, Amiens and Quentovic. The connection with Quentovic must have been particularly close, since seven of the gold coins in this small treasure originated there.[72] Coins from the Sutton Hoo hoard, of a slightly later date, seem more scattered in their origin, but pieces from Paris, Troyes and Laon are included in it, as well as some from Sion, Valence, Arles and Uzes in the Rhone valley which may have reached East Anglia via Gallic Channel ports.[73] Certain isolated finds of Merovingian gold coins in Kent show the same trade connections with Gaul.[74]

Our sources provide fuller information. By the middle of the seventh century, perhaps even as early as 634, an important annual fair had been established by the Merovingian kings at St. Denis, near Paris. To this fair in the seventh century came Saxon merchants and those of Quentovic and Rouen to purchase wine, honey and *garance*, a dyestuff produced in Southern France.[75] In the course of the seventh century we find even more commerce developing across Channel routes as a new port, Hamwith, appears near the site of modern Southampton, connecting the Wessex capital of Winchester with the south coast of Britain. Excavations at Hamwith show that already in the mid-seventh century Merovingian glassware from the Rhinelands or Northeastern Gaul was reaching Wessex via this port,[76] while about this time we learn that Willibald took a ship from Hamwith, which he called an *emporium*, to reach the port of Rouen in Gaul.[77]

[72] P. Le Gentilhomme, *op.cit.* pp. 144-45, and especially C. Sutherland, *English Coinage in the Light of the Crondall Hoard*, pp. 106-31.

[73] P. Le Gentilhomme, *op.cit.*, pp. 143-44. R. Hodgkin, *History of the Anglo-Saxons*, 3rd ed., II, 695-756.

[74] G. C. Brooke, *English Coins* (London 1932), pp. 5-7. P. Grierson, "The Canterbury (St. Martin's) Hoard," *loc.cit.*, pp. 18-31

[75] *MGH Diplomata Francorum et stirpe Francorum*, I, 141, and *Gesta Dagoberti*, XXIV, in *MGH Script. rer. Merov.*, V, 331. Scholars have long had divergent opinions about the fair. See particularly J. Levillian, *Etudes sur l'abbaye de St. Denis à l'époque merovingienne* in *Bibl. de l'Ecole des Chartes* (Paris 1930), and "Essai sur les origines du Lendit," in *Revue hist.*, CLV (1927), 241-76. There seems to be general agreement now that the fair began about 634 A.D. W. Levison, *England and the Continent*, p. 8. In the 7th century it was frequented by northern merchants—Saxons, and men from Rouen and Quentovic—and by Italians, Provençals and Spaniards from the South. Dagobert probably founded this fair to *draw* merchants to Paris. F. Lot in Lot, Pfister and Ganshof, *Les Destinées de l'empire en Occident*, pp. 355-57. Interesting enough, we have no record of Syrians here at all, or of Frisians until 753.

[76] M. Maitland-Miller, "Southampton Excavations," in *Hampshire Field Club Publications*, XVII (1946), 3-11.

[77] W. Levison, *England and the Continent*, p. 6.

Most passenger and pilgrim traffic to the Continent, however, seems to have crossed the Channel at Quentovic, Boulogne's successor, and to have gone by way of Canterbury and London. In 669 Theodore of Tarsus followed this route to take up his episcopal duties in England.[78] And in 718 it was via Quentovic that St. Boniface reached the Continent.[79] So famous did the Channel crossing to Quentovic become, as a matter of fact, that Eddi in his Life of St. Wilfred referred to it as the *via rectissima* for pilgrim traffic to Rome.[80] It was probably via this route that the English, so numerous in Rome that a *schola anglorum* was founded there in 727, traveled to Italy.[81] It is also possible that an active Anglo-Saxon slave traffic operated by way of these Channel routes, even though the laws of Kent expressly forbade it, for we know that St. Eligius in Paris was particularly active in the release of such unfortunates.[82] Is it not also probable that it was via this route that St. Benedict of Jarrow traveled to Gaul between 675-680 to procure masons and glaziers to build a stone church in Northumberland?[83] If so, it accounts for the presence in the treasury of St. Julien of Bourges of the famous Franks' casket which was carved in faraway Northumbria.

Commerce also flowed across the North Sea during these years from Kent and London to Frisia and the mouths of the Rhine. Probably it was never long interrupted, even before 550. Indeed, the very location of Canterbury and London, which face the North Sea rather than the Channel, seems significant in this regard. Again coin hoards provide us with some of our earliest information on this commerce. The Crondall hoard, for instance, contains certain pieces struck in the Rhinelands and Meuse valley from Andernach, Metz and Marsal, as well as *thyrmsae* which are copies of coins found only in Frisia.[84] The later Sutton Hoo treasure contains *trientes* from Muy and An-

---

[78] Bede, *Hist. eccl.*, IV, 1, ed. King, II, 6-8.

[79] Willibald, *Vita S. Bonifatii*, V, ed. Levison (Leipzig 1905), p. 20.

[80] *Vita Wilfridi*, in *MGH Script. rer. Merov.*, VI, 219. W. Levison, *op.cit.*, pp. 5-6. P. Grierson, "The Relations Between Flanders and England," in *Trans. of Royal Hist. Soc.*, 4th ser., XXII (1941), 78-83.

[81] Kletler, *op.cit.*, p. 26.

[82] On the efforts of Pope Gregory the Great to help Angle slaves, *see Gregory I Regestum*, VI, 10, in *MGH Epistolae*, I, 388-95. On 7th-century laws of Kent and Wessex concerning slaves, see F. Liebermann, *Gesetze der Anglo-Saxon*, (Halle 1913), I, 502, 693. On St. Eligius' efforts on behalf of English slaves in Gaul, see *Vita Eligii*, I, 10, in *MGH Script. rer. Merov.*, V, 676-77. See especially W. Levison, *op.cit.*, pp. 8-10.

[83] E. Salin, *La Civilisation merovingienne* I, 209.

[84] C. Sutherland, *Anglo-Saxon Coinage in the Light of the Crondall Hoard*, pp. 80-113.

dernach.[85] On the Continent, in Lorraine, there has been found a Saxon *thrymsa* of this period which may have arrived via this route.[86]

Later in the century our sources add information. In 678 Wilfred reached Rome by sailing across the North Sea to Utrecht and then proceeding down the Rhine and Moselle to Italy.[87] Bede tells of a Frisian merchant in London in 679 who engaged in the slave trade there.[88] At Sutton Hoo among the other archeological remains are some pattern-welded sword blades of a type made only in the Rhinelands and Eastern Gaul,[89] while certain Anglo-Saxon pins found in these latter regions show that reciprocal trade relations existed via North Sea routes.[90]

By the first years of the eighth century such contacts multiplied, as is seen in coin hoards. Not only do we find a *sceatta* in the previously mentioned La Panne hoard,[91] but a large number of such *sceattas* have been found at various Rhineland sites as far south as Mainz.[92] In Frisia some Anglo-Saxon silver *sceattas* have been found at Domburg[93] and others, some of Anglo-Saxon origin and some probably copied from them, have been discovered farther north along the Frisian seacoast.[94] Considering this volume of traffic, no wonder Bede can refer to eighth-century London as an *"emporium* filled with many people coming there by land and sea."[95]

To what extent, one might ask, was this commerce developing in the Atlantic between England and Ireland and the Continent connected with that which arrived in Gaul and Spain from the Mediterranean? We have already noted that Oriental wares and merchants were to be found in Paris, Trier, Orléans and Bordeaux during these

---

[85] *Ibid.*, and P. Le Gentilhomme, *op.cit.*, pp. 143-44.

[86] J. Werner, *Münzdatierte austrasische Grabfunde*, pp. 131-33.

[87] Willibald, *Vita S. Bonifatii*, ed. Levison, p. 16. P. Kletler, *op.cit.*, p. 27.

[88] Bede, *Hist. eccl.*, IV, 22, ed. King, II, 122.

[89] R. Bruce-Mitford, *The Sutton Hoo Ship Burial*, pp. 23-28, and "The Sutton Hoo Ship Burial," in *Proc. Royal Soc. Suffolk*, XXV (1949), 111-15.

[90] H. Zeis, "Ein Fibelfund aus Krefeld-Gillep als Zeugnis für den Rhein weg im frühen Mittelalter," in *Festschrift August Oxé* (Darmstadt 1938), pp. 213-29.

[91] G. Cumont, "Monnaies trouvées dans les gisements côtiers de la Panne," in *Ann. de la Soc. Roy. d'Arch. de Bruxelles*, XXI (1913), 125.

[92] *Sceattas* have been found at six spots in the Rhinelands. J. Werner, *op.cit.*, pp. 30-35 (with map).

[93] Marie de Man, "Que sait-on de la plage de Domburg?" in *Tidschrift voor Munt und Penningkunde* (Amsterdam 1899), pp. 161-72.

[94] P. Boeles, *Friesland*, pp. 359-81. See also the views of Belaiew on *sceatta* finds at Hallum, Frankker and Ter Wispel. N. T. Belaiew, "On the Dragon Series of Anglo-Saxon Sceattas," in *Journ. of Brit. Arch. Soc.*, 3rd ser., I (1937), 35-45. Boeles takes exception to these views and believes these *sceattas* are later than 734-40.

[95] Bede, *Hist. eccl.*, II, 3 ed. King, I, 214.

years. Did the commerce they brought extend farther towards the Atlantic? We know that it did. A monastery like Corbie in 709 received from Fos, near Marseilles, spices and other Eastern wares.[96] Glassmakers around Trier and Arras imported from the Orient the natron they used in making their sodalique-type of glass.[97]

But what of England and Ireland? Did such commerce reach these Atlantic isles? As far as Ireland is concerned, archeological evidence is so scant that we can give no positive answer.[98] On the other hand, historical sources provide considerable evidence of contact between this island and the Mediterranean, probably by way of Western Gaul. The story of the three Irish monks who traveled as far as Carthage in the seventh century,[99] and that of the monk Fidelis who, according to Dicuil, visited the Holy Land,[100] show this clearly. From the pen of Adamnan, on the borders of the Irish Sea, we learn the details of the voyage of Arculf to Palestine and the Near East about 670, an account which was to remain a standard pilgrim guide during the Middle Ages.[101] Similarly there are traditions which relate how seven monks from Egypt and several from Armenia arrived in Ireland.[102] It is not surprising to find a knowledge of Greek, then, in Irish monastic circles, despite the recent doubts that have been raised in regard to the intellectual level of Irish monastery life.[103] Nor does the Oriental influence, so clear in such works of Irish art as the *Book of Durrow* or the Celtic crosses, seem surprising in the light of these facts. There were contacts, many of them, between Ireland and the Coptic and Byzantine East.[104]

Similar influences reached England during these years, as the seventh-century organization of the Anglo-Saxon church, along with

---

[96] J. Levillain, *Examen des chartes de Corbie*, p. 201. H. Pirenne, *Mohammed and Charlemagne* (New York 1938), p. 89.

[97] E. Salin, *Le Haut Moyen Age en Lorraine*, pp. 197-213.

[98] No Merovingian coins or Anglo-Saxon *sceattas* have been discovered to date in Ireland. At Lagore, for example, Hencken has uncovered only some pottery and glass beads from the Continent. H. O. Hencken, "Lagore Crannoy," in *Proc. of Royal Irish Acad.*, LIII (1950), 131-37. The archeology of Ireland and West Britain for that period, however, has only begun.

[99] P. W. Joyce, *A Social History of Ancient Ireland* (London 1920), I, 345-46.

[100] Dicuil, *De mensura orbis terrae*, ed. Parthney (Berlin 1870), p. 71.

[101] Adamnan, "De locis sanctis libri tres," in *Corp. eccl. lat.* XXXIX, 33.

[102] P. W. Joyce, *op.cit.*, p. 413.

[103] A rather deprecating recent study of Irish scholarship is to be found in F. Masai, *Essai sur les origines de la miniature irlandaise* (Bruxelles 1947). See J. Ryan's reply, "Irish Learning in the Seventh Century," in *Proc. of Royal Soc. of Ant. of Ireland,* LXXV (1951), 161-71.

[104] T. D. Kendrick, *Anglo-Saxon Art* (London 1938), pp. 94-103. N. Åberg, *Occident and Orient in the Art of the Seventh Century*, III, 9-11, 124-29.

its cultural life and its art, clearly show. This was due in no small measure to the Byzantine traditions which Theodore of Tarsus brought with him to Canterbury, but it also owed something to constant contacts maintained by cloister and secular clergy with Rome and Italy.[105] Material evidence of such contacts is to be found in England. Archeological sites in Kent dating from the late sixth and seventh centuries have yielded Coptic vases, cowrie shells from the Red Sea and fragments of Byzantine textiles.[106] A coin of Constans II has been discovered in excavations at Richborough.[107] Bede speaks of Byzantine *nomismata*, or golden coins.[108] Most important, however, have been the finds of Oriental goods at Sutton Hoo. There, in a grave which dates from about 655, was uncovered a Coptic bowl, a great silver dish still bearing the control marks of the Emperor Anastasius, nine smaller silver bowls of provincial Byzantine origin and two Greek spoons—all evidence of a connection between Anglo-Saxon England and the Mediterranean-Byzantine world.[109]

Such Oriental wares may have reached Kent and East Anglia via a number of routes. One was by way of the Rhine, following directly across Alpine passes and down the valley past Mainz; another passed from Marseilles up the Rhone, then down the Moselle to reach the North Sea and England. The route from Italy and down the Rhine had been in use since the early sixth century, as we know from the large number of Ostrogothic silver coins discovered in South Germany, and particularly about Mainz. After Justinian's conquest of the Italian peninsula silver coins minted at Ravenna, which have been found at eleven places, show that this route continued in use.[110] So, too, do gold coins discovered in Frisia which were minted in Italy

[105] See the excellent résumés of Byzantine influences in R. S. Lopez, "Le Problème des relations anglo-byzantines du septième au dixième siècle," in *Byzantion*, XVIII (1948), 147-54, and "Byzantine Law in the Seventh Century and Its Reception by the Germans and Arabs," in *Byzantion*, XVI (1946). On the Anglo-Saxon connections with Rome, P. Kletler, *op.cit.*, pp. 26-28.

[106] T. D. Kendrick, *op.cit.*, pp. 62-68, on Coptic vases and Syrian and North African influences in Kent. See also N. Åberg, *op.cit.*, pp. 70-73, and *The Anglo-Saxons During the Early Centuries After the Invasions* (1926), pp. 102-26. T. C. Lethbridge, *Merlin's Island*, pp. 153-54.

[107] B. W. Pearce, "The Coins from Richborough—A Survey," in *Num. Chron.*, 5th ser., XX (1941), 123-36.

[108] R. S. Lopez, "Relations Anglo-Byzantines," *loc.cit.*, p. 156.

[109] R. Bruce-Mitford, *The Sutton Hoo Ship Burial*, pp. 21-27, and "The Sutton Hoo Ship Burial," in *Proc. Royal Soc. Suffolk*, XXV (1949), 83-94. See also F. Stenton, *Anglo-Saxon England*, pp. 60-62.

[110] J. Werner, *op.cit.*, pp. 109-33. These finds include gold *solidi* minted by Phocas and Heraclius and even one by Constans II. All of the *siliquae* and *demi-siliquae*, however, are from the 6th century rather than the 7th.

and the Mediterranean during these years. They include *solidi* and *trientes* struck by Anastasius, Justin, Justinian, Justin II and Maurice.[111] In the seventh century this route was used less frequently, judging by coin evidence. No more Byzantine silver money reached South Germany, and only five gold coins, two of Phocas and three of Heraclius have been found in Frisia. But extensive finds of Coptic bronzes dating from these years in Southern Germany show that some contact was maintained with Italy and the Mediterranean. Similarly, the excavation in Frisia of a number of sixth-century gold coins from Narbonne, Arles and Marseilles seems to indicate that some traffic reached here via the Moselle-Rhône route, though there is little evidence that it did so in the seventh.[112]

There is an equally strong possibility that the Oriental finds in England arrived via Paris, where we know that Syrian merchants and Oriental wares were also to be found during these years, and where Saxon merchants visited the Fair of St. Denis. Or they might have come via western Gallic shores.

Most intriguing, however, is the hypothesis that at least some of the Oriental objects found in Kent and at Sutton Hoo reached these regions via the west coast of Spain. One reason for believing so is information contained in the story of St. John the Almsgiver, Patriarch of Constantinople, who lived in the first years of the seventh century. One passage in this saint's Life tells of a large Alexandrian grain ship which sailed to Britain, or more probably Portus Britanniae (Coruña) in Spain, and there exchanged its wheat for a cargo of gold and tin.[113] A later version says that this vessel came from Constantinople instead of Alexandria.[114] When we learn that the huge Church of Hagia Sophia was built in part of what was called Celtic marble, an ideal ballast for a returning grain ship, one begins

---

[111] P. Boeles, *Friesland*, pp. 513-21.

[112] J. Werner, *op.cit.*, pp. 109-10. E. Salin, *La Civilisation merovingienne*, I, 168-77.

[113] "The Life of St. John the Almsgiver," in *Three Byzantine Saints*, ed. Dawes and Baynes (Oxford 1948), pp. 90-107. R. S. Lopez, "Relations Anglo-Byzantines," *loc.cit.*, pp. 145-46. There are several reasons for believing that Coruña (Portus Britanniae) rather than Cornwall was the place where this ship went. First, it was nearer Byzantine Spain. Second, in the Galician mining regions there would be more need for the grain the ship carried. Third, gold was, in this period, being mined in Galicia, but not in Cornwall. O. Davies, *Roman Mines in Europe*, pp. 95-106.

[114] This later version is found in Ioannis Monarchis, *Liber de miraculis*, ed. Hferer (Würzburg 1884), pp. 7-11. It mentions lead and copper rather than gold and tin. These too, however, were to be found in Spain in this period. See O. Davies, *op.cit.*, pp. 97-101.

to suspect that this legend was possibly based on a certain measure of fact.[115]

The probability of this story is enhanced by other facts. We know that for eighty years, until well into the seventh century, Andalusia was under Byzantine control and that a colony of Byzantine merchants was located at Merida.[116] Such merchants may well have proceeded up the coast to Galicia and even farther. Evidence drawn from the late seventh century coin hoard of Bordeaux, which includes a number of *solidi* struck at Merida, certainly inclines one to such an opinion.[117] So does that coin of Constans II found at Richborough.[118] So, too, does the discovery at Hamwith, from a seventh-century site, of a piece of tortoise shell, although turtles were unknown north of the Canary Islands.[119] If such contact existed, it explains the curious remark of Isadore of Seville that glass of good quality was to be found in Britain though unknown in Italy and Gaul. Perhaps Rhineland glass brought to Western Spain by British merchants was the source of this bit of misinformation.[120] There is one final argument for this route being the one by which many Byzantine objects reached distant England—a negative argument. After the Arab conquest of Spain and Southern Gaul destroyed the prosperity and connections of these regions in the mid-eighth century, we find no more evidence of Byzantine objects reaching English shores—even though the Rhine-Alpine route to the Mediterranean remained open. Not until the tenth century were such influences to reappear in England.[121]

To all this evidence of a commerce developing in the Atlantic, English Channel and North Sea and linking Spain, Gaul, the Rhinelands, England and Ireland, one bit more must be added—in some ways, the most important of all. I refer to the change which took place in these regions from a gold to a silver currency. It has often

[115] *Paulus Silentarius,* ed. Friedlander (Berlin 1912), p. 245.

[116] On the colony of Greek merchants located at Merida in the period and on Byzantine contacts with Spain, see P. Gaudert, "Byzance et l'Espagne visigothe," in *Etudes byzance,* II (1944), 209-13.

[117] The Bordeaux hoard of 673-677 contains 7 coins from Merida—the largest number from any Visigothic mint represented—where a colony of Greek merchants lived during this period.

[118] B. W. Pearce, "The Coins of *Richborough*—A Survey," *loc.cit.,* pp. 83-131.

[119] M. Maitland-Miller, "Southampton Excavations," in *Hamp. Field Club Pub.,* VIII (1948), 6-11.

[120] Isadore of Seville, *Etymologiarum,* XVI, 15.

[121] Lopez, "Relations anglo-byzantines," *loc.cit.,* pp. 143-47, shows that after 700 A.D. there was a lapse in Byzantine influences in England—despite other routes via the Rhinelands by which Byzantine goods and influences could have reached England in the 8th and 9th centuries.

been erroneously stated that this development occurred in Carolingian times. That is not so, though it continued and expanded during the age of Charles Martel, Pepin and Charlemagne. It began in those regions which faced the Atlantic along the coasts of Western and Northern Gaul, England, Frisia and parts of Spain. It seems to have had little to do with the appearance of Ostrogothic and Italian Byzantine *siliquae* and *demi-siliquae* in Southern Germany, since by the late seventh century, when Atlantic silver coinage began, such Italian coins were no longer found north of the Alps—to judge by coin hoard evidence—and since in weight and type this Ostrogothic coinage in no way at all resembled Atlantic silver coins.

Numismatists still need to devote more time to the problems presented by the appearance of this new silver coinage, particularly that which is found in Merovingian Gaul, before any definitive conclusions can be reached. But there is a certain body of agreement which has importance for this study. In the first place, numismatists seem to concur that this silver money represented a development from, or even a degeneration of, Merovingian gold coinage. Secondly, they agree that it appeared in Northern and Western Gaul about the middle of the seventh century.[122] This latter point seems in line with our inference that the silver mines of Melle were reopened at about this time and began an important production of silver again.[123]

British authorities agree that Anglo-Saxon silver pennies, or *sceattas*, also date from about the middle of the seventh century, and were first minted in Kent and in the London area. They also seem to feel that this money represented a development from the rather rare English gold *thrymsa* coinage. It is interesting to note that it is only *after* Anglo-Saxons had despoiled the Celts of those areas where silver mines existed in England—the Mendips, Flintshire Derby-

---

[122] M. Prou, *Catalogue des monnaies merovingiennes*, pp. CIV-CV. Blanchet believes this Merovingian silver coinage began a little after the middle of the 7th century. A. Blanchet and A. Dieudonné, *Manuel de numismatique française*, III, 224-47. Le Gentilhomme would date it a little earlier. P. Le Gentilhomme, *op.cit.*, pp. 18-19.

[123] *Gesta Dagoberti*, LI, in *MGH Script. rer. Merov.*, II, 207. O. Davies, *Roman Mines in Europe*, pp. 85-86. One should be cautious in using the 9th-century *Gesta Dagoberti* as a record of events in the 7th century. On this, see L. Halphen, *Etudes critiques sur Charlemagne* (Paris 1925), pp. 215-17. On the other hand, a contemporary source, the *Vita Eligii*, also mentions lead used to roof a church in this period. *Vita Eligii*, in *MGH Script. rer. Merov.*, IV, 684. Since lead in this period was a by-product of silver production, it seems possible that silver mines in Gaul, probably those of Melle, were again in production in the 7th century. On use of lead, see H. Van Werveke, "Note sur le commerce de plomb au moyen âge," in *Mélanges Pirenne*, II, 301-13.

shire—that we find silver *sceattas* making their appearance. These mines were producing again by the year 700, for Wilfred used lead from them to roof his church in Yorkshire. It was not long after the appearance of *sceattas* in England that copies of them appear to have been minted in Frisia.[124]

There also seems to be a general agreement that there is a close resemblance in style and weight between Merovingian deniers and Anglo-Saxon *sceattas* and later Frisian copies as well.[125] All these facts—a parallel origin from a pre-existing gold coinage, a common style and weight, the parallel appearance of this money on both sides of the Channel and the probability that silver mines were again exploited in both areas at the moment of this silver coinage's appearance—all this seems to bear out our previous evidence, that a close connection existed between Britain and Atlantic Gaul during these years.

This leads to a further question that can have no definitive answer: why did these years see not only the appearance of new silver coins but a parallel disappearance of gold coinage in England, Gaul, Frisia and Spain? This fact certainly indicates that a common economic problem affected all these Atlantic regions during these years. But what was its cause? In general, the usual explanation has been that it was caused by a drain or flight of gold to the East. This seems rather an unsatisfactory explanation. The seventh century saw the opposite phenomenon at work. Foreign gold coins found in England and in Frisia and Northern Gaul show gold moving *north* into regions where it had been unknown for several centuries. So does that coin hoard of Bordeaux, with its Visigothic *solidi*.

Whatever one may think about this question, this new silver money was not necessarily, as is often claimed, a sign of economic retrogression. Like the silver money which appeared as the main currency of Atlantic regions in the fourth century during the Late Empire, it represented an active Atlantic commerce, as well as a separation of

[124] P. Le Gentilhomme, *op.cit.*, pp. 9-20. C. H. Sutherland, *Anglo-Saxon Coinage in the Light of the Crondall Hoard*, pp. 31-103. P. Hill, "Saxon Sceattas and Their Problems," in *British Num. Journal*, XXVI (1949-51), 129-54. G. C. Brooke, *English Coins*, pp. 4-7. Hill believes the *radiate* coinage of the sub-Roman period is connected with the later *sceattas*. P. Hill, "The Coinage of Britain in the Dark Ages," in *British Num. Journal*, XXVI (1949), 115-29. On the reopening and exploitation of silver mines in this period, see the remark by Bede that England had "mines of sundry metals, copper, iron, lead and silver," in Bede, *Hist. eccl.* 1, 1, ed. King, I, 14.

[125] P. Boeles, *Friesland*, pp. 385-97. P. Le Gentilhomme, *op.cit.*, pp. 78-93. N. T. Belaiew, "On the Dragon Series of the Anglo-Saxon Sceattas," *loc.cit.*, pp. 35-45.

these lands from the Mediterranean, with its gold standard.[126] The difference between a silver and a gold coinage lies in the fact that, as Le Gentilhomme has shown, silver *sceattas* and deniers were useful for petty commercial transactions, while a coinage confined to gold *solidi* and *trientes* indicated a luxury commerce without small-scale exchanges.[127] That the Bordelais, Narbonnais and Provenence kept their gold coinage longer than other regions of Gaul may have been caused in part by the fact that they lay nearest to the gold-standard Mediterranean and maintained closer links with it. But it may also in part be due to the fact that the unchanged economy of large Roman villa estates in these regions encouraged a luxury gold coinage and discouraged the use of silver for more simple, mundane exchanges.[128] Thus it may be possible to consider the appearance of silver money as proof of a more active ordinary, though different, commerce in Northern Europe in these years, rather than the reverse.

So far in this chapter we have contented ourselves with a description of the growth and spread of a more active economy in Atlantic Gaul, Spain and the Rhinelands and the extension of commerce from these regions to Ireland and England. But what was the result of this extension upon the economies of these two islands between 550 and 750? What new economic developments took place there?

Let us first examine Ireland in Merovingian times. What is most striking at first glance is that, despite commercial contacts, Ireland during these years remained economically quite primitive. There have been no finds of money dating from this period in any Irish site, leading one to suspect that none was in use. Despite this probable lack of a money economy, however, advances were made which owed something to the island's re-established maritime connection with Western Gaul and Western Britain. It is such contacts which may help to explain in part the development of Irish native craftsmanship at centers like Lagore, where bronze and iron were worked, leather goods were produced and a coarse type of woolen cloth was

---

[126] In a sense, even the late 6th-century, lighter-weight, *solidi* coined in Gaul and copied in England mark off this Atlantic area from the rest of the gold-*solidi* Mediterranean, though much work remains to be done on this problem. See P. Grierson, "The Canterbury (St. Martin's) Hoard," in *British Num. Journal*, XXVII (1953), 50.

[127] P. Le Gentilhomme, *op.cit.*, pp. 67-69.

[128] It seems probable that Spain also kept the heavier Mediterranean weight for her *solidi* until late in the Visigothic period and continued to copy the coins of Valentinian III and Honorius for more than a century. See F. Bouza-Brey, "La ceca de suevo visigodo de Valencia del Sil," in *Zephyrus*, IV (1953), 417-27.

woven.[129] They may explain in part, too, the appearance of an Irish school of stone workers who produced fine examples of Irish ecclesiastical art.

Only one center existed in Ireland during this period that can be considered urban: Cashel. But it must be remembered that Irish monastic establishments like Armagh, Clonmacnois and Glendalough fulfilled many of the functions of towns. The very name the Irish gave them, *cathairs*, or *civitates*, reflects this fact. They were often of great size, containing as many as 3,000 monks and students, and attracting a large secular population which settled near them.[130] In addition to such centers, by the eighth century in Ireland at least two large fairs had come into existence. One of them, the Telton Fair, held near the site of Dublin, attracted many foreigners. The other was the Carmen Fair established near Wexford.[131] Perhaps already the linen industry existed on a commercial scale in the countryside and the island's gold deposits were being exploited.

Across the Irish Sea in Western Britain little remained of that strong Celtic civilization of which Gildas had spoken so confidently. Cornwall continued to exploit its tin resources,[132] but the economy of the Severn region does not appear to have survived the conquest of the land by Ceawlin of Wessex or the Anglian kings of Mercia. Perhaps this was because Anglo-Saxon victories here were followed by an exodus of Celts from this region to Brittany and Ireland, an event which may be the origin of the story of the settlement of the Breton peninsula by refugees from Saxon conquest.[133] We do know, for instance, that some of the Celtic inhabitants were driven from North Wales in the early seventh century by King Edwin of Northumbria and took refuge in Ireland.[134] This exodus may account for

[129] H. O. Hencken, "Lagore Crannoy," *loc.cit.*, pp. 83-97.

[130] On these monasteries, see E. Curtis, *History of Ireland* (London 1912), p. 12. R. Hodgkin, *History of the Anglo-Saxons*, I, 255, and especially H. Zimmer, *The Celtic Church in Britain and Ireland*, pp. 15-16. They are called *cathairs* (*civitates*) in the *Annuals of Tigernach*, anno 716, and the *Annals of Ulster*, anno 715.

[131] On the Telton Fair, see *Annals of Ulster*, II, 167-70, and on the Carmen Fair near Wexford, *ibid.*, pp. 182-83.

[132] F. Haverfield, "Cornish Tin," in *Mélanges Boissier*, pp. 251-55. See also H. O. Hencken, "An Excavation at Chysauster," in *Archeologia*, LXXXIII (1933), 238-83.

[133] On Anglo-Saxon advances westwards in the late 6th and 7th centuries, see F. Stenton, *Anglo-Saxon England*, pp. 30-31, and A. H. Williams, *An Introduction to the History of Wales*, pp. 76-80. On the continued movement of West British saints to Brittany down into the 6th century, see J. Loth, *L'Immigration bretonne en Armorique*, pp. 151-70.

[134] Bede, *Hist. eccl.*, II, 9; IV, 20, 24; V, 24. H. M. Chadwick, *The Origins of the English Nation*, p. 18.

the fact that we have no evidence of any surviving urban vigor in such earlier centers as Caerleon and Caerwent,[135] and only a slight suggestion near the Saxon town of Newport.[136] We do not know whether the iron mines of the Forest of Dean or the copper mines of Anglesey and North Wales continued to be worked during these years, though they probably were.[137] Nor do we know exactly what took place in the Chester region. However, the fact that no money hoards of Celtic Britain in these years have been discovered seems to suggest a rather simple and local economy.

Quite different is what one finds in Anglo-Saxon England, which in 500 had been on a par, economically speaking, with the Celtic West. After 550 we discover many evidences, as in Gaul, of a steady growth and development of economic life. In the mid-sixth century such advanced economy as was to be found in Eastern England had been centered about London and in Kent.[138] Though in Merovingian times these regions remained the most advanced, one can see in these two centuries a spread of civilization along the south coast towards Cornwall and up the east coast as far as Northumbria. The finds at Sutton Hoo reveal the existence, by the mid-seventh century, of a civilization quite as important as that of Kent,[139] and a few short decades later the same is true of Northumbria and Wessex. As civilization spread, so did shipping along this coast of England. St. Ives could set sail for Brittany from Northumbria in 700,[140] while a prince of the Northumbrian royal house could escape by sea to Kent.[141] We find in 680 the Abbot of Jarrow importing glaziers from Gaul,[142] and Bede in the first years of the eighth century in touch with the whole Western Christian world. On the south coast of Britain Hamwith appeared as a settlement of some importance in the last years of the seventh century and was known as an *emporium* in the eighth,[143] while Dorchester, farther west, was called an urban center

[135] On the decadence of these centers after the 6th century, see V. Nash-Williams, "Caerleon and Caerwent," in *Jour. of Brit. Arch. Soc.*, XXXV (1929).

[136] On the economic life of the Severn region near Tidenham, perhaps as early as the 8th century, see C. Fox, "The Boundary Line of the Cyrmni," in *Proc. of Royal Brit. Acad.*, XXVI (1940), 281-82.

[137] L. Salzman, *English Industries in the Middle Ages* (Oxford 1923), pp. 20-43. O. Davies, *Roman Mines in Europe*, pp. 150-64. Bede, *Hist. eccl.*, I, 1, ed. King, I, 14.

[138] F. Stenton, *Anglo-Saxon England*, pp. 52-56.

[139] R. Bruce-Mitford, *The Sutton Hoo Ship Burial*, pp. 23-37.

[140] *Vita St. Yveis*, in *Acta Sanct. Boll.*, 6 Oct., III, 405.

[141] Bede, *Hist. eccl.*, II, 20, ed. King, I, 316.

[142] Bede, *Vita Sancti Benedicti Biscopi*, ed. Plummer (Oxford 1896), I, 368.

[143] M. Maitland-Miller, "Southampton Excavations," in *Hamp. Field Club Pub.*, XVI-XX (1946-50), 3-5, 9-16. W. Levison, *England and the Continent*, p. 7.

a few years later. The seventh-century laws of King Ine of Wessex reveal some concern for commerce and merchants at about the same time.[144]

Even the political history of Britain indicates the spread of a more advanced civilization and economy along Anglo-Saxon coasts. We find that in the late sixth century Kent under King Aethelbert was the political as well as the economic center of England, with this monarch exercising a sort of hegemony over his neighbors. By the first years of the seventh century this leadership passed up the east coast to the East Anglia of Redwine. Then late in the century it moved still farther north to be exercised by Northumbria. In the eighth century, as a more advanced economy spread into the interior, the mantle of leadership moved to Mercia, with Wessex as Mercia's principal rival in the southwest.

The history of Anglo-Saxon coinage reveals the same pattern of development during these years, the same growth up the coasts and into the interior from the Kent-London area. Around 550 the only coins struck in Anglo-Saxon England were barbarous *radiates* which have been found at Richborough.[145] A century later there is evidence in Hampshire, Kent, East Anglia and around London of a native gold *thrymsa* coinage with a certain number of Merovingian gold pieces in use as well.[146] Shortly thereafter, we find silver *sceattas*, which, judging from the hoards, spread far beyond the range of the *thrymsas*, until they are found as far west as the Dorchester region of Wessex and as far north as Whitby.[147] The incidence of discovery of such *sceatta* hoards is probably an indication of the intensity of the economic life of this period in England. In this connection it is interesting to note that *sceattas* have been found in largest numbers in Northern Kent, in Essex and about London and are rarest in Western Wessex, Northumbria and the interior of the island.[148] And we might also add that the diffusion of Anglo-Saxon square-headed brooches, carefully studied

[144] *Laws of Ine*, XXV and XXVI, 1, in C. Attenborough, *The Earliest English Laws* (London 1930), p. 45. See also the *Kentish Laws of Hlothere and Eaduc*, XV, in *ibid.*, p. 21.

[145] P. Hill, "Barbarous Imitations of Fourth Century Roman Coins," in *Num. Chron.*, 6th ser., X (1950), 87-101. B. Pearce, "The Coins of Richborough—A Survey," in *Num. Chron.*, 5th ser., XX (1941), 28-47.

[146] C. Sutherland, *Anglo-Saxon Gold Coinage in the Light of the Crondall Hoard*, pp. 17-59.

[147] J. Allen, "The Coins of Whitby," in *Archeologia*, LXXXIX (1943), 85-86.

[148] C. Sutherland, "Anglo-Saxon Sceattas in England: Their Origin, Chronology and Distribution," in *Num. Chron.*, 6th ser., II (1942), 42-70.

137

by Leeds, follows almost exactly the same pattern as these silver *sceattas*.[149]

All this helps to explain why by 750 in Anglo-Saxon England, as in Gaul and the Rhinelands across the Channel, there had developed a number of centers or ports which can be fairly termed urban centers. By this year Hamwith[150] and Dorchester in Wessex, Rochester and Canterbury in Kent,[151] London on the Thames,[152] Thetford in East Anglia,[153] Lincoln in the Midlands[154] and York in the north[155] had reached urban status. Most of them, as in Gaul, were revived Roman *civitates*, but some seem to have been completely new settlements. Already, as Bede pointed out, London had begun to occupy a special, almost metropolitan position in this England. Men of Kent in 686 maintained a cattle trade thither to supply the needs of the town population.[156] In the early eighth century tolls were levied at London, Thanet and at Fordwich near Canterbury,[157] while a money economy had extended far enough into the interior so that an abbot of Medeshampstede in Lincolnshire could receive from a Mercian earl a money payment of 1,000 shillings and a yearly cash rent for a manor.[158]

This revived economic life of Anglo-Saxon England resulted in part from the stimulus of internal and external trade. But it was the result of a certain industrial growth as well. This is reflected in the exploitation of England's mineral resources. Tin continued to be mined and smelted in Cornwall, and perhaps so was copper in Wales.[159] Concerning other mining activities our knowledge is scantier, though Bede expressly mentioned that England was a land

---

[149] E. T. Leeds, *A Corpus of Early Anglo-Saxon Great Square Headed Brooches*, pp. 80-201, and "The Distribution of the Angles and Saxons," in *Archeologia*, XCI (1945), 78-81.

[150] M. Maitland-Miller, "Southampton Excavations," *loc.cit.*, pp. 3-18.

[151] J. Tait, *The Medieval English Borough* (Manchester 1936), pp. 7-10.

[152] Bede, *Hist. eccl.*, II, 3; IV, 22, ed. King, I, 214; II, 122.

[153] G. M. Knocker and R. G. Hughes, "Anglo-Saxon Thetford," in *Archeological News Letter*, X (July-Aug. 1950), 7-8.

[154] Bede mentions a *praefectus civitatis* at Lincoln in the early 8th century. Bede, *Hist. eccl.*, II, 16, ed. King, I, 296.

[155] York is called a *wic* or *portus* in 680. J. Kemble, *Codex diplomaticus aevi Saxoni* (London 1852), V, 82. Frisians were certainly settled there by the middle of the next century.

[156] *Cartular. Saxon.*, ed. Birch, CXLIX, I, p. 216; CLII, I, p. 220; CLXXI, I, p. 246; CLXXXVIII, I, p. 267; CLXXXIX, I, p. 268. See also C. E. Woodruff, *A History of the Port and Town of Fordwich* (Canterbury 1895), pp. 1-8, 48. J. Tait, *op.cit.*, p. 10.

[157] *Ibid.*

[158] *Cartular. Saxon.*, p. 271.

[159] O. Davies, *Roman Mines in Europe*, pp. 141-64.

of mines. In the seventh century the silver mines of Flintshire and Derbyshire were again producing lead and the silver which was used in *sceatta* coinage.[160] It also seems probable that mines in the Mendips were again in production.[161] To such mineral resources we must add the iron of the Weald of Kent, so actively exploited in Roman times, which continued to produce ore for the Anglo-Saxons of this period,[162] though certainly fine pattern-welded Frankish blades were imported as well. Probably the same mining activity was found in the case of the iron of the Forest of Dean, though additional information on this subject is necessary before we can be certain of it.

We know more of other industries, particularly the weaving of cloth. In Roman times fine cloth, woven in country villas and state factories, had been a specialty of Britain. Perhaps such skills survived the Anglo-Saxon conquest. At any rate, fragments of textiles found in graves in Kent reveal a local cloth industry there by the seventh century.[163] In East Anglia likewise, as shown in Sutton Hoo finds, there appears to have been a type of cloth woven of a special diamond pattern quite different from that found upon the Continent. Can this have been the ancestor of the fine English woolen cloth exported to the Continent at the time of Offa and Charlemagne?[164] That such a weave had more than local significance is shown by the fact that similar cloth has been found far to the north in excavations at Whitby.[165] We do not know where such cloth was produced, but it seems possible that in England, as in Gaul, the finest grades were the product of domanial *gynecées*, especially those located in monastic establishments.

To weaving of cloth should be added certain other handicrafts of the England of this period, such as fine jewelry and goldsmith's work. At least two centers of this craft are known to us: Kent, which produced the finest jewelry of the Early Middle Ages in Europe;[166]

[160] Salzmann, *op.cit.*, pp. 41-42. Note that Wilfrid had lead available to roof his church in Yorkshire. It must have come from the reopening of these mines, which the Romans had exploited earlier. *Vita Wilfridi*, in *MGH Script. rer. Merov.*, VI, 211. See also Bede, *Hist. eccl.*, I, 1, ed. King, I, 14, on statement that Britain possessed lead and silver mines.

[161] J. Gough, *The Mines in the Mendips*, p. 48.

[162] O. Davies, *op.cit.*, pp. 38-43, believes Kentish iron production continued active in that period. See also Bede, *Hist. eccl.*, I, 1, ed. King, I, 14.

[163] B. Brown, *The Arts in Early England*, III, 385-87.

[164] J. Tait, *op.cit.*, p. 10. F. Stenton, *Anglo-Saxon England*, pp. 19-22.

[165] J. W. Crowfoot, "A Textile from Whitby," in *Archeologia*, LXXXIX (1943), 87, 88. For textual reference to English cloth in this period, see E. Carus-Wilson, "The Woolen Industry," in *Cambridge Economic History of Europe*, II, 363.

[166] R. Jessup, *Anglo-Saxon Jewelry*, pp. 30-57.

and East Anglia, hardly behind Kent, judging from the Sutton Hoo treasure.[167] Though the style of each region owed something to foreign influences—Kent to the Rhinelands and Germany, and East Anglia to Vendel Sweden—in both one finds a Romano-British element of craftsmanship which goes back to Late Roman times. Thus, as in Gaul, something of the old survived in the new metal industries. It is also noteworthy that as early as the eighth century at Thetford, near Roman Caistor, a pottery industry was arising which appears to have owed something in design to the Rhinelands and, in its glazing technique, to the Charente region of Western Gaul.[168] At Hamwith rather crude tiles, modeled on those of Roman times, also seem to have been produced late in this period.[169] Glass, however, was not manufactured in England during these years and had to be imported from the Continent.[170] On the other hand, the stone crosses of Northumbria show a native stone-cutting tradition of a high order, while the Frank's casket illustrates the skill of the Anglo-Saxon carver in dealing with whalebone. In metal-working, cloth-making, the production of pottery and fine jewelry and other industries, Anglo-Saxon England began to lay the basis, during these years, of those skills which she was to develop in the centuries to come.

The preceding pages have shown us how economic life quickened during this period in Ireland and England. And as it did, commerce and navigation began to extend towards the north from English and Irish shores along the coasts of Scotland and beyond, reaching the Shetlands, Orkneys, Faroes and Iceland in one direction, and the coasts of Norway in the other. The Irish side of this re-expansion of civilization towards the north has often been represented as religious in nature, a movement based upon the desire to bring Christianity to the heathen Picts and to plant religious hermits on the lonely islands of the North Atlantic. No doubt this is partly true. But this movement had maritime and commercial aspects as well.

It started when St. Columba, following the earlier example of St. Ninnian, sailed from Ireland in the late sixth century, founded his monastery of Iona in the Hebrides and began the conversion of the

[167] R. Bruce-Mitford, "The Sutton Hoo Ship Burial," in *Proc. of Royal Soc. of Suffolk*, xxv (1949), 11-79.

[168] G. C. Dunning, "Dating Medieval Pottery," in *Arch. News Letter*, ix (1949), 6-7. G. Knocker and R. Hughes, "Anglo-Saxon Thetford," in *ibid.*, x (1950), 7-8.

[169] M. Maitland-Miller, "Southampton Excavations," *loc.cit.* (1948), pp. 5-9.

[170] M. Maitland-Miller, *ibid.* (1950), speaks of the discovery in Hamwith excavations of a considerable amount of Continental glassware, some as early as the 7th century in date.

Picts.[171] From this foundation Christianity was to radiate out over all the Celtic North. From the time of Columba throughout the next century Irish mariners and saints pressed on, settling in the northern Hebrides, establishing themselves in the Orkneys, as Irish Øgam stones seem to show, and even reaching the Shetlands in some numbers. Dicuil, for instance, tells us that by 700 Irish hermits were already living in the Orkneys and in Iceland as well.[172] Excavations on this distant Arctic isle have recently borne out Dicuil's information, for they have revealed Irish objects, dating from the seventh and eighth centuries—bronze balls and Celtic pins—at a number of Icelandic sites.[173] This pre-Norse Irish settlement of Iceland is further confirmed by the Irish names of many of Iceland's coastal localities, names which seem to have survived into the Viking period.[174]

Other Celtic mariners appear to have reached the Norse coast, where a number of islands named Papey (the Norse word for Irish priests) disclose an Irish connection with these shores.[175] Nor is archeology lacking in proof of such contact. In Norse graves dating from the late seventh and eighth centuries there are a number of objects which came from Ireland,[176] and it seems that it was by way of such contacts with Western Norway that swords and weapons of Merovingian Gallic manufacture reached this part of Scandinavia.[177] Nor was this commerce a one-way affair, since graves in the Shetlands, Hebrides and Northern Ireland reveal that as early as 600, and not later than 700, certain distinctive "strike-a-light's" of Norse origin were reaching these regions of Celtic Europe.[178] Some idea of the extent of this maritime traffic is revealed by the fact that in the year 729, according to the Annals of Tigernach, 150 Pictish ships were wrecked off the headlands of Ross Cuisini.[179]

Our sources reveal also that most contacts by sea along these routes

[171] Jonas, *Vita Columbani*, in *MGH Script. rer. Merov.*, IV, contains the story of these years.
[172] Dicuil, *De mensura orbis terrae*, ed. Parthney, p. 71. G. Turville-Petrie, *The Heroic Age in Scandinavia*, pp. 94-97.
[173] T. C. Lethbridge, *Merlin's Island*, pp. 85-93.
[174] *Landnámabók*, ed. F. Jansson (Copenhagen 1925), pp. 8-17.
[175] H. Shetelig, *An Introduction to the Viking History of Western Europe*, pp. 46-48.
[176] A. Mahr, *Christian Art in Ancient Ireland*, I (Dublin 1925), pp. 11-53. H. Shetelig, *Scandinavian Archeology*, pp. 271-75.
[177] H. Shetelig, *op.cit.*, pp. 261-63. J. Peterson, *Die Norske Vikingswerd* (Christiania 1919), pp. 59-71. Brøgger notes that West Norway seems to have had a special connection with France in this period. A. W. Brøgger, *Ancient Emigrants*, pp. 20-21.
[178] H. Shetelig, *Introduction to the Viking History of Western Europe*, pp. 7-9.
[179] H. M. Chadwick, *Early Scotland*, p. 46.

were peaceful ones. Only twice during this period do we find record of maritime raids in these waters. The first was in 617 against the island of Eigg and was probably the work of pagan Pictish pirates.[180] The second took place farther south when Egfirth of Northumbria, who had reached the west coast of Britain by conquering Strathclyde in the early seventh century, went on to conquer the islands of Man and Anglesey and to drive the inhabitants of North Wales into Ireland. He then appears to have launched an attack on Ireland itself.[181] Perhaps it was the shipping of his new West British maritime subjects which the Angle king used in his maritime conquests and raids. Except for these two episodes, however, along these western Celtic routes peace was the general rule during these years.

On the other side of Scotland, another Celtic area under Pictish rule shows equal evidence of a maritime renaissance. This region, characterized by curious Pictish round towers, built in Late Roman times but now reoccupied, was not peaceful as was that near Ireland. Rather it was characterized by constant conflict upon the sea. In 580 or 581 the Annals of Ulster speak of a naval expedition sent by Bude I, King of the Picts, against the Orkneys, and indeed when St. Columba visited Bude's court, near modern Inverness, he found a vassal king of those islands there. A century later, in 681 and again in 694, raids were directed against the Scottish mainland by Orkney marauders and the Annals of Tigernach tell us of Bude III's retaliatory expeditions sent thither shortly afterwards. We do not yet fully understand enough of Pictish civilization to be sure exactly how it was related to its Celtic and Anglo-Saxon neighbors. But it is clear from the Øgam stones which abound in this part of Scotland that there was a strong Pictish element not only on Scotland's east coast, but in the Orkneys, Shetlands and Hebrides themselves, and that this Pictish population had by the seventh century again developed a maritime tradition quite as important as that of the Irish.[182]

It therefore seems possible that Pictish as well as Irish mariners ventured to the coasts of Norway, and that when Bede mentions Iceland (Tilli) and the midnight sun found there and says he learned

<hr>

[180] W. Skene, *Celtic Scotland* (Edinburgh 1888), II, 152.

[181] Bede, *Hist. eccl.*, IV, 24; V, 24. H. M. Chadwick, *The Origins of the English Nation*, pp. 16-19.

[182] H. M. Chadwick, *Early Scotland*, pp. 46-48, 139-53. W. Skene, *Celtic Scotland*, II, 3-175, contains the fullest account. The interesting and important collection of Pictish Øgam stones found in the Edinburgh Museum and elsewhere in Scotland needs further study to help clear up the history of these years along Scottish shores.

of this from "certain men of our own age who arrive from these countries,"[183] he is referring to Pictish, not Irish, sailors. That there was such direct contact with Norway in Bede's time seems to be confirmed, interestingly enough, by numismatic evidence, the discovery in a hoard in Rogaland on the west coast of Norway of a *sceatta* minted by Archbishop Egfirth of York between 734 and 766.[184] And it may have been via the Picts that certain Anglo-Saxon influences which Shetelig sees in Norse *brachteates*, cruciform brooches and art forms reached Norwegian shores.[185] Nor can we be sure that at least a portion of the Frankish arms, glassware and bronzes which have turned up in Norwegian graves of this period did not reach there in ships navigated by Pictish sailors.[186] Though such contacts in the seventh and early eighth centuries must still have been occasional rather than constant, there is little doubt that already Pictish and Irish navigators had pioneered new Atlantic routes which had been forgotten since Late Roman times. These routes were to be followed by Norse fishermen and farmers who settled in the Shetlands, Orkneys and Hebrides in the eighth century,[187] and by Viking pirates who followed on their heels a few decades later to plunder the coasts of Northumbria and Ireland.

What was the effect upon Scandinavia and the Baltic of the growth of maritime routes again along the coasts of Northern Gaul and the shores of England, Scotland and the Atlantic isles? And what role did the developing economic life of such regions have upon this remote area of the Northern Seas? In an earlier chapter we have noted how Scandinavia in the mid-sixth century had been isolated from her earlier land contacts to the south by the advance of Slavic tribes and of the Avars in Central Europe. Thus isolated, she began to develop along Swedish coasts her own civilization, called Vendel from the graves of this period excavated in the Uppland region of Sweden and

---

[183] Bede, *Commentary on the Fourth Book of Kings*, xx, 9.

[184] H. Holst, "Mynter i Norske Funn," in *Nord. Numis. Arsskrift* (1943), pp. 101-6.

[185] H. Shetelig, *Scandinavian Archeology*, pp. 271-93. Brøgger notes that Eastern Norway (the Oslo region) seems to have been connected with England. A. W. Brøgger, *Ancient Emigrants*, p. 21. This, however, may have been due to the fact that both Eastern England and Eastern Norway were settled in the 6th century by similar peoples from the Baltic, rather than to any *later* trade connections. On this point, see Chapter II.

[186] G. Gjessing, *Studier i Norsk Merovingertid*, pp. 106-48.

[187] A. W. Brøgger, in *Ancient Emigrants*, pp. 6-18, shows that this emigration began in the 8th century, perhaps earlier, and was, at first, a peaceful one. See also H. Shetelig, *Introduction to the Viking History of Western Europe*, pp. 21-44.

found as well in Baltic islands like Gotland, in Denmark and along the coasts of Southern Norway. Isolated though this culture was from Southern and Central Europe, it was less so from North Sea areas, since it was connected with them via the maritime route which passed down the Frisian coast to the Rhine and across the North Sea to Kent and East Anglia. This route remained open, and by way of it the Angles with their Swedish contingents had traveled to Eastern England in the first years of the sixth century. Down it, too, had sailed Hygelac, King of the Geats, to raid in the Rhinelands about 518. Though the great Anglian migration ended about 550, as late as 574 a mixed group of Saxons and Frisians who were still moving south along it were defeated in Frisia by the Franks.

In the lull that followed the ending of such migrations, and perhaps even during them, some commerce appears to have reached the Baltic via this route, carried by the Jutes of Kent, the Frisians and the East Anglians who served apparently as its chief intermediaries. Such traffic explains the appearance in the Baltic soon after 550 of the fine pattern-welded swords and glassware of the Rhinelands and Northern Gaul.[188] It explains also new artistic impulses in Gotland, Bornholm and the Swedish Uppland which must have originated in Merovingian Gaul, in Germany and in Kent. And it probably explains the Frisian influence which one finds in the runes of the period.[189] Via this route, too, came the rare gold coins of the period found in the Baltic, four in Gotland dating from the sixth century and one in Scania dating from the seventh.[190]

In this traffic the precociously active merchants of Kent appear at first to have taken the lead. One evidence of this is that, of the 20 Scandinavian *brachteates* discovered in England, 17 were found in Kent in graves dating from the late sixth century, the other three being found in scattered sites in the English Midlands.[191] In Frisia, on

---

[188] J. Peterson, *De Norske Vikingswerd*, pp. 37-81. H. Shetelig, *Scandinavian Archeology*, pp. 272-74.

[189] H. Shetelig, *Préhistoire de la Norvège*, p. 178. E. Salin, *Le Civilisation merovingienne*, pp. 199-201, on Merovingian glassware found in Vendel sites in Sweden. Important trade with Sweden from glass-producing regions of Western Germany and Northern Gaul dates from Carolingian, not Merovingian, times.

[190] N. L. Rasmusson, "Foreign Coins in Swedish Coin Finds," in *Trans. of Int. Num. Congress* (London 1938), pp. 18-33.

[191] On these *brachteates*, see E. T. Leeds, "Denmark and Early England," in *Antiquaries Journal*, XXV (1946), 26-34, and R. Jessup, *Anglo-Saxon Jewelry*, pp. 121-22. On similarity between the brooches of Norway and England, see H. Shetelig, *Introduction to the Viking History of Western Europe*, p. 6. Amber, which may be of local Norfolk origin or from the Baltic, is common in late 6th century Kentish graves. R. Jessup, *op.cit.*, p. 51. T. C. Lethbridge, *Merlin's Island*, pp. 159-62.

the other hand, only six such pieces have been discovered, showing that while this region was a halfway house on the route north, it was not at first as important as Kent.[192] Frisia's rather passive role early in this period is further indicated by the fact that Kentish jewelry seems to have exerted an influence upon Frisia, rather than vice versa.[193] As in the case of the later *scoattus*, which Frisia seems to have copied from Anglo-Saxon England, the Frisians at first followed in the wake of their Anglo-Saxon brothers across the North Sea.

After 600, however, one begins to notice a change. Along English coasts, the role of intermediary with the North that Kent had played began to be taken over by mariners from East Anglia, racially closely allied with the peoples of the Baltic. The discoveries of Sutton Hoo make this clear. In this mid-seventh-century grave have been uncovered a large number of objects which are either of Vendel Swedish origin or show strong Swedish influence. They include a cenotaph, shield and helmet which resemble Uppland finds (though richer, since they are of pure gold) and a great golden buckle, drinking horn and purse which show evidence of Swedish craftsmanship. Under these circumstances, is it surprising to find that Beowulf,[194] a Geatic hero, should be known in Anglo-Saxon England, or that the *Widsuth*, a poem whose locale is clearly Denmark, should reach an English audience?

At about the same time, Frisia began to stop being a passive halfway station between Anglo-Saxon England and the Scandinavian north and play a more active role in this commerce. We can probably date the turning point about the year 600 with the foundation of Dorestad by the Franks, which established a port that for centuries was to be active in commerce with Scandinavia. There is a good deal of evidence that Dorestad's foundation, not completely secure until about 689, when it definitely became part of the Frankish Empire, resulted in

---

[192] P. Boeles, *Friesland*, pp. 317-38.

[193] Boeles shows that Scandinavian influence in runes and jewelry was found in Frisia in the 7th century. P. Boeles, *op.cit.*, pp. 338-59. On the more important Kentish influences, see H. Slicher van Bath, "Dutch Tribal Problems," in *Speculum*, XXIV (1949), 323-35, and Boeles, *op.cit.*, pp. 320-33.

[194] On Swedish influences and objects at Sutton Hoo, see L. Lindquist, "Sutton Hoo and Beowulf," in *Antiquity*, XXII (1948), 98-103, and H. Maryon, "The Sutton Hoo Shield," in *ibid.*, XX (1946), 117-48. While Vendel objects of a similar type from Sweden were made of less precious metals in this period, those of Sutton Hoo are of gold. For a full bibliography, through 1952, on Sutton Hoo, see F. P. Magoun, "The Sutton Hoo Ship Burial: A Chronological Bibliography," in *Speculum*, XXIX (1954), 116-24.

increased commerce with the Rhinelands.[195] This evidence is chiefly found in the seventh-century coin hoards of Frisia, which seem to come almost entirely from Rhineland and Meuse mints. Of the 42 *trientes* found here, 27 are from the Rhine, representing coins of Cologne, Mainz and Worms, 5 are from Metz and Trier on the Moselle, and 10 are from the Meuse valley, with Maastricht furnishing 7 of them.[196] The assassination of the Carolingian Grimold by a Frisian at Maastricht in the late seventh century,[197] like the settlement of Frisian merchants at Worms at about the same period,[198] reflects the Frisian interest in trade with the south via these rivers that our coin hoards reveal.

Thus it was Frisians who in the late seventh century probably carried those bronze keys, originating in Franconia, the glassware and swords of the Rhinelands and other such products north to the Hedeby region of the Jutland peninsula and on to the Swedish Uppland.[199] And it is about this time, in 679, that we hear of our first Frisian merchant in England, a slaver who traded in London.[200] By the time Willibald traveled from Frisia to Denmark via Heligoland and the Jutland peninsula, the Frisians probably were handling the bulk of the commercial traffic going to Scandinavia.[201] Frisian merchants had begun to assume the role of the leading commercial people of the North Sea. But not until the eighth century did they completely replace Anglo-Saxon merchants on this route, for Bede could still mention men arriving on the coasts of Northumbria from faraway

[195] P. Boeles, *Friesland*, pp. 269-75. J. H. Holwerda, *De Franken in Nederland*, *Oudheidkundige Medeleelingen*, new ser., v (Leiden 1924), 9-189, and *Dorestad en onze vroegste Mideleeuwen* (Leiden 1924), pp. 5-81.

[196] P. Boeles, *op.cit.*, 513-21. On the similarity between Dorestad coinage and that of Maastricht in the 7th century, see also F. Rousseau, *La Meuse et le pays mosan*, pp. 44-45.

[197] J. Boëhmer and E. Muhlbacher, *Die Regester des Kaiserreichs unter der Karolingern* (Berlin 1908), p. 12. On the long drawn-out struggle which finally saw Frisia up to the Saxon border annexed by the Carolingians, see P. Boeles, *Friesland*, pp. 275-87, 382-86.

[198] P. Kletler, *Nordwesteuropas Verkehr*, p. 68. B. Rohwer, *Der Friesische Handel im frühen Mittelalter* (Kiel 1937), pp. 3-21. H. Jankuhn, "Der fränkisch-friesische Handel zur Ostsee im frühen Mittelalter," in *Viert. für Soz- und Wirtschaft*, XL (1953), 130-72.

[199] G. Arwisson, *Vendelstile. Email und Glas im 7-8 Jahrhundert* (Uppsala 1942), pp. 101-5.

[200] Bede, *Hist. eccl.*, IV, 22, ed. King, II, 122.

[201] *Vita S. Willibaldi*, x, in *MGH Script. rer. Merov.*, VII, 124. They had extended their control to the Weser and beyond by the late 8th century, if not earlier. *Vita Willibaldi*, v, in *MGH Script.*, II, 381.

Scythia, which must have referred to a commerce that reached Russia via the Baltic.[202]

As connections between the Baltic and Frisia and England increased from 550 to 750, the isolation of this remote sea began gradually to end, and it began, too, to merge with that civilization which was advancing north along the trade routes. In Scandinavia, as in Frisia, Gaul and England, certain trade centers arose which reflected this revived commerce. One of the principal new commercial spots was Hedeby, which lay at the base of the Jutland peninsula where commerce from the North Sea passed into the Baltic by way of the Eider river. Already in the eighth century, as is revealed by examination of objects found in excavations, a certain importance had attached itself to this spot.[203] Farther north, in Southern Norway, where trade routes from the Baltic passed through the Skagerrak and Kattegat, we also find some commercial activity about Oslo fjord, where later on Skringissal was to arise.[204] More important, however, were trade routes passing along the South Swedish coast via Bornholm and Oland and Gotland. Gotland itself had a certain commercial importance in the eighth century, not as an urban community like Hedeby, but as an island which seems to have served as a sort of permanent fair in the Baltic, a place where wares from all parts of this sea were exchanged.[205] And, finally at the entrance to the Mälar Sea we find arising the island *portus* of Birka, which provided an entry into all Central Sweden.[206] No doubt Hedeby, the Oslo region, Gotland and Birka were not, in this period, much more than rudimentary commercial centers, handling native Scandinavian products and imported Western European goods on a very small scale, but already they were pointing the way to a more active Scandinavian economic future. Although the gold which had flowed here during the migration period had ended, the graves at Gotland and in the Uppland show a rich civilization and a creative native artistry still at work.

[202] Bede, *Commentary on the Fourth Book of Kings,* xx, 9.

[203] B. Rohwer, *op.cit.,* pp. 12-16. H. Jankuhn, *Ergebnisse und Probleme der Haithabu Grabungen* (Kiel 1939), pp. 51, 78-80. H. Shetelig, *Scandinavian Archeology,* p. 275.

[204] H. Shetelig, *op.cit.,* p. 178. This was not, however, an important trading spot until the late 9th century.

[205] The main proof of Gotland's extensive commerce lies in its coin hoards, which go back to the 6th, 7th and 8th centuries. See pages to come on these hoards. Also O. Montelius, *Kulturgeschichte Schwedens* (Leipzig 1906), pp. 21-118.

[206] H. Arbman, *Schweden und das Karolingische Reich* (Uppsala 1937), p. 24, and especially *Birka, Sveriges Äldsta Handelstad* (Stockholm 1939), pp. 58-67.

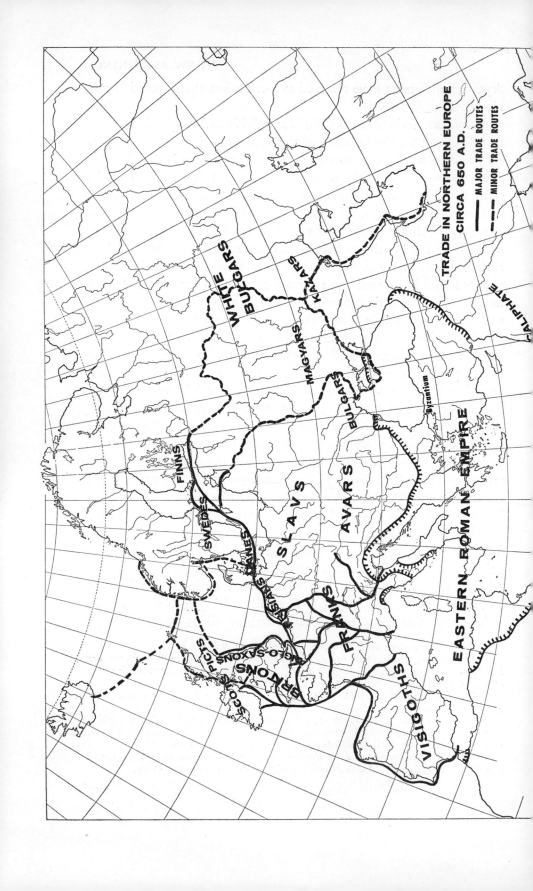

TRADE IN NORTHERN EUROPE
CIRCA 650 A.D.

——— MAJOR TRADE ROUTES
- - - MINOR TRADE ROUTES

FINNS

SWEDES

WHITE BULGARS

KAZARS

MAGYARS

BULGARS

SLAVS

AVARS

FRISIANS

ANGLO-SAXONS

SAXONS

PICTS

SCOTS

BRITONS

FRANKS

VISIGOTHS

EASTERN ROMAN EMPIRE

Byzantium

CALIPHATE

Important as were the commercial relations which linked this Scandinavian world with the North Sea and Western Europe, they were not the only ones which developed between the Baltic and the outside world during these years. Even more significant were those new trade routes which led to the Middle East via the Gulfs of Finland and Riga and the rivers of Russia. We have already noted that towards the mid-sixth century this route began to gain some faint importance. During the next two centuries its development continued. Archeological remains dating from these years, for instance, show that Swedish settlements were firmly established on the Aland Islands on the way down the Gulf of Bothnia to Old Ladoga and the Volga.[207] Similarly, excavations reveal Swedish colonies, or at least contacts, along the Gulf of Riga leading to the Dvina, the Russian trade center of Gnezdovo, the Dnieper and the Crimea. The abundant metalware and jewelry which have been discovered along these Latvian shores came in large measure from Gotland as well as the Swedish Uppland, suggesting that it was from these centers that this impetus originated.[208] Thus it is not surprising that archeologists should find in seventh-century graves on the Swedish mainland armor of a type unknown except in the distant Crimea.[209]

To archeological evidence of these eastern routes and commerce via Russia one must add that which numismatics provides. A relatively large number of Sassanian coins dating from the sixth and seventh centuries have been found in Swedish sites. In the Aland Islands one hoard consists of 25 Sassanian silver dirhems which were coined between 591 and 628.[210] On the island of Gotland, 35 such Sassanian

---

[207] On this penetration of Finland and the establishment of an important trade route between the Baltic and the Volga, see C. A. Nordman, *Kultur Och folk i Finlands forntid* (Helsingfors 1928), pp. 18-126, and A. Hackman, *Die Alterei Eisenzeit in Finnland*, I (Helsingfors 1905), 131-59. It is interesting to note that along the Finnish coast are to be found fortified places, as early as the 8th century in date, which show efforts of the local population to resist this Swedish penetration, particularly in the Vaasa region. L. Musset, *Les Peuples scandinaves*, pp. 33-35, 40-41.

[208] See especially B. Nerman, *Die Verbindungen zwischen Skandinavian und dem Ostbalticum in der Jüngeren Eisenzeit* (Stockholm 1929), pp. 1-41. Nerman shows from archeological evidence that Gotland's influence upon Courland and Esthonia was the most important one, followed by Uppland Sweden and Bornholm and Oland. On these finds, though he dates them too late, see also T. J. Arne, *La Suède et l'Orient* (Uppsala 1914), pp. 58-67. For a later account, B. Nerman, *Sveriges Första Storhetstid* (Stockholm 1942), pp. 15-71, and a résumé entitled "Sweden's Colonies in the Baltic," in *Eurasia Septentrionales Antiqua*, IX (1934), 209.

[209] G. Arwisson, "Armour of the Vendel Period," in *Acta Archeologia*, X (1939), 32-59.

[210] C. A. Nordman, "Schatzfunde und Handelsverbindungen in Finlands Wikingerzeit," in *ibid.*, XIII (1942), 274.

coins have come to light, while they are by no means rare in finds in the Swedish Uppland.[211] In all, 86 such silver Persian coins have been uncovered in Sweden, and a few seem even to have reached Denmark.[212] Nor did Moslem conquest of Persia end this coin export to the Baltic. Rather it increased it, for hundreds of silver Ommiad coins have been found along Baltic coasts, extending even to Norway— most of them in the same regions where Sassanian silver money is also present.[213]

It was perhaps to this trade along Swedish coasts and extending east into Russia and West into the North Sea that was owed the appearance in the late seventh century of a maritime Dano-Swedish empire in this part of the world, that of the somewhat legendary King Ivar Wide-fathom. According to tradition, the nucleus of this empire was South Sweden, Denmark, Bornholm, Oland and perhaps Gotland. In the west it may have included a certain hegemony over the Oslo region of Norway, too. It is interesting to note that, in line with our numismatic and archeological evidence, Ivar is said to have conquered Courland across the Baltic and to have met his death fighting along the south shores of Finland in the Gulf of Bothnia. He is even said, certainly without justification, to have conquered the Saxons of North Germany and a portion of England.[214] In short, tradition here reveals the development of a maritime state in this period which accurately reflects not only the development of a common economic system in the Baltic, but even an effort to control its western and eastern trade exists. This empire did not end with Ivar's death, if we may believe

[211] On finds of Sassanian coins in Gotland, see M. Stenberger, Die Schatzfunde Gotlands der Wikingerzeit, II (Stockholm 1942), 350-461.

[212] On total number found in Sweden, U. S. Linden, "En Upplandsk Silverskatt frön 800-Talst," in Nord. Numis. Arsskrift (1938), p. 124. Though all are early in date, not all Sassanian coins found in the Baltic are pre-Islamic. Some have "Praise Allah" inscribed on them. Ibid., pp. 109-15.

[213] On Swedish finds of Ommiad coins, see ibid., p. 124. They are particularly numerous in Gotland hoards. For example, there are 37 Ommiad coins in the great Stora Velinge hoard. U. S. Linden, "Ein grosser Fund Arabischer Munzen aus Stora Velinge, Gotland," in Nord. Numis. Arsskrift (1941), pp. 74-120. This hoard includes coins minted by the Caliphs Walid, Yezid II, Hisham, Walid II and Merwan II (704-749). Other Gotland hoards, such as those of Foldhagen, Oster Ryfter, Hagvats and Sigsawe, also contain such coins. M. Stenberger, op.cit., pp. 21-24, 63-64, 73-75, 106-10. On Ommiad coins in Danish hoards, see R. Shovmand, Die Danske Skattefund (Copenhagen 1942), pp. 13-17. On the 5 Ommiad coins (all late, 740-50) found in Norway, see H. Holst, "Mynter i Norske Funn," in Nord. Numis. Arsskrift (1943), pp. 72-103.

[214] On the traditions of a Dano-Swedish kingdom of Ivar Widefathom, see F. Balodis, Det Äldsta Lettland (Uppsala 1940), pp. 112-45; B. Nerman, Die Verbindungen zwischen Skandinavien, pp. 13-14, and Sveriges Första Storehetstid, pp. 15-92. See also L. Musset, op.cit., pp. 26-31.

later accounts, but continued down to the time of his grandson, Harold. This latter's death at the battle of Bravalla, which historians date about 750, marked the end of this state and the beginnings of a separation between the political life of Denmark and Sweden.[215]

To the south of Scandinavia stretched the vast expanses of Central Europe, merging at last into the plains of Russia. What did these years of economic growth and expansion bring to this region? The answer is, very little indeed. In Western Germany the Saxons, Thuringians and Hessians under Merovingian control remained primitive and tribal in their political and economic life. The law codes of these tribes seem to make this clear, for they reveal an economy in which there is no money and fines are levied in kind rather than coin, as the tribute of fifty cows paid by the Saxons to their Merovingian overlord shows.[216] There was some trade in Germany which traveled, as noted earlier, across the Alpine passes from Italy, its route marked by hoards of Ostrogothic and Ravenna silver found as far north as Mainz. But it does not seem to have affected areas of North or Central Germany farther east than the Rhine. Rather it continued past Worms, Spire, Mainz and Cologne to reach Frisia and the North Sea. In the next century this trade continued, despite Lombard-Byzantine wars in Italy and the move of the Alemanni south into Rhaetia,[217] as we know from Coptic bowls and other objects of Lombard Italian manufacture found in Southern Germany. But it seems probable that commerce across the Alps via this route decreased in the course of the seventh century.[218]

Farther east there was another route leading to Italy by way of

---

[215] The traditional interpretation of the battle of Bravalla is that it marked the final conquest of Gotaland (the Goths or Geats) by the Swedes and the uniting of Sweden under an Uppland dynasty. See B. Nerman, *Det Svenska Rikets Uppkomst* (Stockholm 1925), pp. 260-68, and H. Sonyrwigg, *Gotland under aldrae medeltid* (Lund 1940), pp. 1-157. This seems doubtful. Rather, perhaps Bravalla marked the break-up of the loose Dano-Swedish Baltic kingdom or confederacy, with Gotland gaining its independence in the process. L. Musset, *Les Peuples scandinaves*, pp. 22-26. G. Vernadsky, *Ancient Russia*, p. 275. G. Turville-Petrie, *The Heroic Age in Scandinavia*, pp. 55-57. Various dates for this battle have been suggested. Perhaps 750-770 A.D. is the best approximation.

[216] F. Lot, *Les Invasions germaniques*, pp. 133-34.

[217] P. Martin, *Etudes critiques sur la Suisse à l'époque merovingienne*, pp. 50-61. On the Alemanni's expansion south into Switzerland in this period, see E. Salin, *La Civilisation merovingienne*, I, 217-53.

[218] J. Werner, *Münzdatierte austrasische Grabfunde*, pp. 109-32, and "Italienischer und koptisches Bronzegeshin des 6. und 7. Jahrhunderts," in *Mnemosynon Theodor Wiegand* (Munich 1938), pp. 63-81. See also G. Lohlein, "Die Alpen- und Italienpolitik der Merowinger im 6. Jhd.," in *Erlanger Abhandh. zur Mittleren und Neuren Geschichte*, XVII (1932), 15-43.

the Brenner Pass, the old Claudia Augusta. Never as important as the Alpine routes farther to the west, it was at no time completely abandoned during these years, as silver Italian coinage and Coptic bowls found in upper Bavaria and Austria indicate. But goods and commerce traveling this route do not seem to have reached far beyond the Danube.[219] Not until the first years of the eighth century did a certain air of bustle begin to appear in this region, reflected in economic provisions of the laws of the Bavarians and the revived importance of such surviving centers as Regensburg.[220] But even then there is little evidence that up to 750 any of this commerce passed north into the German and Slavic lands of Central Europe.

We have, as a matter of fact, only one bit of evidence of trade passing beyond the Rhine and Danube in the Merovingian period. This comes from the story of Samo. Samo, a rather mysterious Frankish merchant, perhaps a sort of seventh-century *courier du bois*, at about the time of Dagobert united the Slavic tribes of Bohemia, and perhaps some to the north as well, into a confederacy. He is said to have massacred Frankish merchants who entered his domains to trade— probably for slaves. With his death, however, his kingdom collapsed and we hear no more of such merchants.[221] Indeed, archeology's failure to find in this part of Germany and Central Europe any coin hoards at all dating from this period seems to point to the fact that trade currents active in the North Sea and Baltic still had made little impression upon this remote region.[222]

North of the probable location of Samo's kingdom in the region bounded by the Elbe and the Saale on the west, and Russia on the east, the Slavs were even less touched by trade currents during these years. Their chief interests appear to have been agricultural and their efforts to have been directed towards putting under cultivation the new lands which they had occupied only since the first years of the sixth century. The simplicity of their economy was due to their neighbors. The Eastern Germans who lived to the west of them were,

[219] J. Werner, *Münzdatierte austrasische Grabfunde*, pp. 76-78.

[220] See *The Laws of the Bavarians*, in *MGH Leges*, III, 294; IV, 38; IX, 7, 13, 15; X, 19-21; XIII, 1, 3; XV, 1-6; XVI, 3, 9-10, 15-16. See also A. Dopsch, *The Economic and Social Foundations of European Civilization*, pp. 350-51.

[221] The sources on Samo are scant. *Chron. Fredegarii*, IV, in *MGH Script. rer. Merov.*, IV, 144-60, and the *Gesta Dagoberti*, in *ibid.*, II, 410. See also V. Chaloupicky, "Considerations sur Samon, le premier roi des Slaves," in *Byzantoslavia*, XI (Prague 1950), 222-39, and G. Vernadsky, "The Beginnings of the Czech State," in *Byzantion*, XVII (1945), 315-28. The most critical account is still C. Verlinden, "Le franc Samo," in *Revue belge*, XII (1933), 1090-95.

[222] J. Werner, *op.cit.*, pp. 77-78.

in these years, as economically primitive as they, and thus insulated them from trade currents flowing up the Rhine to Frisia and beyond. The Bulgars and the Avars, their neighbors to the south, were raiding nomadic peoples whose constant wars similarly cut off these Slavs from the more advanced economy of the Mediterranean-Byzantine world.[223] On the north, along the south shores of the Baltic, where they infringed upon the somewhat more economically advanced Danes and Swedes, they found these Scandinavians had little use for the agricultural products which they had to exchange.[224]

Perhaps the only outside economic contact that these Slavs had was with the Avars, whom they called the Chunni. With them a minor traffic was carried on by way of the Moravian Gap, as we know from a few objects of Avar workmanship which have been found by archeologists in Southern Poland and Silesia. By this route a trickle of amber moved south to Hungary and the Mediterranean. But such exchanges were few indeed. The Slavs of these regions continued to inhabit their fortified villages, or *grody*, and to cultivate their fields until the years of Carolingian and Ottonian revival changed their economy and their history.[225]

In another section of the world of Slavdom, however, new trade currents are to be found. I refer to Russia. The history of Russia in this period is obscure indeed. Casual references to this vast territory by Procopius and certain Byzantine and Arab annalists give us almost the only information we have about that rather mysterious empire of the Antas which seems to have arisen here following the end of the Ostrogothic kingdom and the breakup of the Hunnic state. It appears to have been shattered by the Avars about 550.[226] In its place there

[223] See G. Vernadsky, *Ancient Russia*, pp. 312-24, 327-30, on the low cultural and economic level of this region. The definitive work, however, and interesting in its emphasis upon the fact that the Slavs in the 7th and 8th centuries had a settled agricultural *non-nomadic* economy, is J. Kostryzewski, *Les Origines de la civilisation polonaise* (Paris 1949), pp. 28-32, 102-110. On the existence during these years of a White Croatian kingdom which included at least a part of this region, see F. Dvornik, *The Making of Central and Eastern Europe*, pp. 268-97.

[224] On the lack of contact between the Scandinavians and the Slavs of the South Baltic coast in this period, see W. Vogel, "Zur nord- und westeuropäischen Seeschiffahrt im frühen Mittelalter," in *Hansische Geschichtsblätter*, XIII (1907), 156.

[225] J. Kostryzewski, *op.cit.*, 37-74. A possible 8th-century beginning of Slav merchant contact with Mainz via Fulda is mentioned, however, in *Vita Sturmi*, in *MGH Script.*, II, 369.

[226] On the Antas, see F. Dvornik, *op.cit.*, pp. 277-97, and B. Grekov, *La Culture de la Russie de Kiev*, pp. 17-23. Recent Russian historians have developed an important literature on the Antas with little basis except archeological finds. See particularly V. A. Rybakov, *The Antas and Kievan Russia* (1939) [in Russian], and

seem to have arisen certain confederacies or groupings of Slavic tribes along the upper Dnieper, Don and Volga—in civilization and in economy very much like their Slav brothers in Central Europe. They, too, were separated from the more civilized lands to the south by nomadic tribesmen on the steppes of South Russia: White Bulgars, Turkish Kazars and Magyars.[227]

But in these neighbors they were more fortunate than the Western Slavs. For in the last years of the sixth century one of these nomadic peoples, the Kazars, began to form a strong kingdom north of the Caucasus between the Dnieper and the Volga, with its center at Itil not far from modern Stalingrad. North of them on the middle Volga another stable state arose, that of the White Bulgars. Byzantium under Justinian established firm control of the Crimea about Cherson. Unlike the Avars and Western Bulgars, the Byzantines, Kazars and White Bulgars were interested in trade with the north.[228] So it was that two general trade routes came into existence across Russia leading to the Baltic. One went by way of the Don and Dnieper to reach the Dvina and then followed the Dvina up to the Baltic. The other— much more important, judging from coin hoards—was by way of the Caspian and Volga to Lake Ladoga and the Gulf of Finland. Since the Swedes began to colonize the Aland Islands and the south shores of Finland as early as the sixth century, we can assume this route began about that time, while Jordanes' mention of furs reaching the Crimea seems to imply that the Dnieper route was again in existence shortly thereafter.[229]

There is some evidence that trade north from the Black Sea was more active in the seventh century than in the late sixth. That armor of a Crimean type, already mentioned as found in Sweden, shows such a commerce in existence. So do two large silver dishes found in South Russia, similar to that excavated at Sutton Hoo and bearing

---

B. D. Grekov, *The Formation of Russia into a State* (1945) [in Russian]. See review of their theories in R. Portal, "Quelques problèmes d'histoire russe et slave," in *Revue hist.*, CXCIX (1948), 56-73.

[227] B. Grekov, *La Culture de la Russie de Kiev*, pp. 18-23. N. K. Chadwick, *The Beginnings of Russian History: An Inquiry into the Sources* (Cambridge 1946), pp. 15-106. G. Vernadsky, *Ancient Russia*, pp. 170-204.

[228] F. Dvornik, *The Making of Central and Eastern Europe*, pp. 60-67. G. Vernadsky, *op.cit.*, pp. 205-6, 213-28. A. Vasiliev, *Goths in the Crimea*, pp. 30-97. On their importance to the trade of Byzantium, see A. R. Lewis, *Naval Power and Trade in the Mediterranean*, pp. 33-63, 84-91, 112-20. On the origin of the Kazar State, see the excellent account in D. M. Dunlop, *The History of the Jewish Kazars* (Princeton 1954), pp. 3-57.

[229] Jordanes, *Gaetica*, in *MGH Auct. Ant.*, v, 59.

the marks of Anastasius. One, which dates from 688, was excavated at Poltava along the Dnieper trade route. The other, slightly later in date, was discovered in Perm near the Urals and the Volga route.[230]

But it seems probable that trade originating in Persia and passing north by way of the Caspian and the Volga was more important still. Hoards of Sassanian coins on the upper Volga, dating from the early seventh century, like those found in the Baltic, show the importance of this trade. So does the Ommiad silver which followed swiftly in their wake in an increasing stream of dirhems. Via Lake Ladoga and the Gulf of Finland, by the eighth century a commercial route of some importance had been built up by means of which silver, silks, spices, metals and armor of the East were being exchanged for furs and perhaps slaves, honey and beeswax. The Varangian route between Baltic, Black and Caspian Seas had already been established.

It was this commerce which began to develop favorably located Russian Slavic *grody* into something resembling urban communities, though they remained still rather primitive. Gnezdovo, near Smolensk, is revealed by excavation to have grown in the seventh and eighth centuries to the point where it received goods from the Sea of Azov and the North Caucasus.[231] Even more important was Rotsov on the Volga, where bronze, silver ingots, copper, iron and brass have been found, and where there is evidence of an artisan population which included carpenters, workers in bronze and iron, goldsmiths, silver-smiths and potters. Hardly less important was Old Ladoga, located still farther to the northwest.[232] No wonder Swedish rulers like Ivar Widefathom established colonies in Courland and advanced into the Gulf of Finland. They were securing the Baltic side of important trade routes.

Yet it seems highly probable that such centers as Gnezdovo, Rostov and Old Ladoga, although they owed their importance to trade which reached the Baltic, were not Scandinavian foundations. The all but complete lack of objects of Swedish origin in materials excavated at Gnezdovo, for instance, seems almost decisive in this regard. So, too, does the location of these trading centers. They were *not* near the Baltic, but far inland in Russia, almost as if they were placed by design where distance would make them hard for Viking raiders to reach, but not too far for trade with Scandinavia. Though,

[230] R. Lopez, "Relations Anglo-Byzantines," *loc.cit.*, p. 142.
[231] G. Vernadsky, *op.cit.*, p. 231. B. Grekov, *op.cit.*, pp. 18-28.
[232] *Ibid.*

as Vernadsky suggests, some Swedes may have penetrated far into Russia—even as far as the Black and Caspian Seas—in the course of the eighth century, it seems probable that their economic role within this region was still slight. Only in the Carolingian period were such Varangians to occupy an important commercial position within Russia. It seems wiser to assume that, until then, the trade and industry which helped to found these rising Russian communities were carried on, not by Scandinavian outsiders, but by Slav, Kazar and White Bulgar natives of the land.[233]

From the Atlantic coast of Spain and Gaul, then, to the distant Orkneys and across the North Sea into the pine-fringed Baltic, the commerce of Northern Seas showed new vigor during these years. New ports arose in Ireland, along the English Channel and even in Scandinavia, some revived older Roman centers, some new ones. From the distant Caspian up the rivers of Russia new commercial routes came into being, touching every section of Northern Europe except the lands between Elbe and Dnieper. The world of Rome in the Northern Seas, destroyed by the barbarian invasions, was arising in a new form like the phoenix from his ashes—more youthful, and full of promise for the future.

It is easier, however, to trace these new commercial and maritime routes that pumped economic lifeblood through the arteries of the lands of Northern Europe than to be sure exactly what this lifeblood consisted of. Our information concerning the products that formed the maritime commerce of the Northern Seas during this period is much too scant. We can glean only enough to give us a general idea of the nature of this traffic.

Let us begin with the coasts of Western Gaul and Northern Spain, where Atlantic commerce revived earliest during these years. Here the main export seems to have been wine. It was wine which Gallic ships carried to Ireland[234] and which English merchants arrived to

---

[233] Archeological evidence in T. Arne, *La Suède et l'Orient*, pp. 9-203, shows that the Varangian Swedes did not penetrate further than Courland, Esthonia and Finland until the last years of the 8th century. Grekov also does not mention any Scandinavian objects as having been found in sites at Rostov, Old Ladoga or Smolensk. B. Grekov, *op.cit.*, pp. 18-30. Nor has *one* coin that was minted in Byzantium in these years been found in Baltic hoards. The only basis for belief in an early Swedish penetration into Russia and to the Black Sea is Theophanes' mention of *Rus* ships in 773 A.D. *Theophanes*, ed. De Boor, p. 446. While one need not doubt in the least Scandinavian penetration far into Russia in Carolingian times (circa 800) [see Chapter IV], Vernadsky's ingenious reconstruction of an earlier penetration (*Ancient Russia*, pp. 261-91) must be labeled as unproved for the *Merovingian* period.

[234] *Vita Ciarini*, XXXI, and H. Zimmer, *op.cit.*, pp. 363-400.

purchase and bring back to their British coasts in ships that stopped at Bordeaux, Saintes and Nantes.[235] The *fiscus vinitor* at the mouth of the Garonne is certainly significant.[236] It is probable, too, that wine formed an important portion of the cargoes of the ships which Gregory of Tours tells us traded with Galicia.[237] But the salt of the Saintogne and of Noirmoutier probably also had some importance in commerce.[238] So did olive oil found at Bordeaux, which may have arrived there via Spanish coasts or from Provence via the Garonne.[239] It also seems possible that grain was sent from the Loire region to supply mining regions like Galicia and Cornwall which were without adequate foodstuffs. The story of the Egyptian grain ship reaching these shores and returning with tin is probably significant in this regard.[240] The lead of Melle, heavy and bulky, probably reached Paris as well by sea during these years.[241] It is likely that some luxury items of Mediterranean provenience—spices, papyrus and silks—were also sent north via these Atlantic coasts.[242] *Garance*, or madder, later so much of a specialty of the Garonne region, which Saxon merchants sought at the Fair of St. Denis,[243] may also have figured in West Gaul's export commodities.

As for the Atlantic coasts of Spain, we cannot be sure what products made up their exports. It seems safe to assume, however, that in general they consisted of minerals—the copper of Huelva and the tin, silver, lead and gold of Asturias, as well as of those fish products of Galicia so famous in Roman times.[244] Some products transshipped from the Mediterranean also figured in Spain's Atlantic trade.[245]

Concerning the commerce of Northern Gaul and the Rhinelands there is more information. Wine was bought in Paris by Saxon mer-

---

[235] *Vita Filiberti*, XLI, in *MGH Script. rer. Merov.*, V, 603, and *Virtutis Eparchi*, X-XII, in *ibid.*, III, 556-57.

[236] Gregory of Tours, *Hist. franc.*, V, 48, in *ibid.*, I, 351.

[237] *Ibid.*, VIII, 35, in *loc.cit.*

[238] H. Hauser, *Le Sel dans l'histoire*, pp. 275-76.

[239] *Vita Filiberti*, XXXVII, in *MGH Script. rer. Merov.*, V, 602.

[240] *The Life of St. John the Almsgiver* tells of grain ships in the Atlantic, thus emphasizing the probable value of wheat as a trade commodity in this period.

[241] *Gesta Dagoberti*, LI, in *MGH Script. rer. Merov.*, II, 207, and *Vita Eligii*, in *ibid.*, IV, 684.

[242] See mention of such finds in Kentish graves in B. Brown, *The Arts in Early England*, III (London 1907), 31-89.

[243] *MGH Diplomata Franc. et stirpe Francorum*, I, 141, and *Gesta Dagoberti*, XXIV.

[244] The *Life of St. John the Almsgiver* mentions only metals as objects of trade in these areas—for example, in Galicia or possibly Cornwall.

[245] R. S. Lopez, "Relations Anglo-Byzantines," *loc.cit.*, pp. 141-42.

chants, as well as honey and dyestuffs.[246] And certainly some of the Oriental spices and silks found in this region made their way to consumers farther north, while Coptic bowls may have reached England via the Rhine route.[247] But more important were industrial products produced locally. Those pattern-welded Frankish swords, already in the seventh century found at Sutton Hoo, Taplow and Broomfield,[248] soon were arriving in Scandinavia, on Norwegian coasts and in Sweden.[249] Bronzework from Mainz seems to have had an equally wide export market,[250] as did glassware, which has been found in so many English and Baltic sites.[251] Perhaps more local was trade in cloisonné jewelry and belt-buckles and in salt, which was transported on the Moselle.[252] A trade in stone down the Scheldt from Tournai also had some importance.[253] Whether wine from vineyards in Burgundy and along the Rhine and Moselle, which was to be a major Carolingian export, was already an article of commerce is unknown. But it seems probable that it and local Rhineland pottery were already reaching the lower Rhine and Meuse and perhaps Frisia and beyond. There is, on the other hand, little evidence of cloth exports from these regions during this period. Probably cloth was still being made for local consumption only. There is also evidence that slaves, either those arriving by sea from the north or those from Central Europe, were an important trade commodity, since we hear of their passage along the Chausée de Brunhaut in this period.[254]

Of Ireland's trade we again are all too ignorant. Some of it consisted of wares from the south, transshipped to Scotland and even distant Norway.[255] But other articles of commerce were locally produced.

---

[246] *MGH Diplomata Franc. et stirpe Francorum*, I, 141.

[247] On Coptic bowls in Kent, see R. Jessup, *Anglo-Saxon Jewelry*, pp. 9-51, and on their presence in the Rhine region, J. Werner, *Münzdatierte austrasische Grabfunde*, pp. 76-78.

[248] On Sutton Hoo, see R. Bruce-Mitford, "The Sutton Hoo Ship Burial," in *Proc. of Royal Soc. of Suffolk*, XXV (1949), 61-73. On Kentish sites, R. Jessup, *The Archeology of Kent*, pp. 1-137.

[249] H. Shetelig, *Scandinavian Archeology*, pp. 271-75.

[250] G. Arwisson, *Vendelstil. Email und Glas*, pp. 101-5.

[251] M. Maitland-Miller, "Southampton Excavations," *loc.cit.* (1946-50), on glass from the Continent at Hamwith. G. Arwisson, *op.cit.*, pp. 102-5, on glass finds in Sweden.

[252] For a discussion of metalwork in Northeastern Gaul, Belgium and the Rhinelands in this period, see the works of E. Salin, *Le Haut Moyen Age en Lorraine, La Fer au temps des Merovingines* and *La Civilisation merovingienne*, I-II.

[253] P. Rolland, *Le Problème de la continuité à Tournai*, pp. 250-52.

[254] R. Doehaerd, *L'Expansion économique belge*, p. 10, and C. Verlinden, "Le franc Samo," *loc.cit.*, pp. 117-31.

[255] A. W. Brøgger, *Ancient Emigrants*, pp. 20-24.

Among them were the coarse cloth and leather goods that Irish merchants traded to Western Gaul.[256] Probably gold and hides were also export commodities, as well as linen, later such a specialty of this island.

Britain's exports, on the other hand, seem to have been more varied than those of Ireland. From Cornwall, tin was shipped to many Atlantic regions as well as east to Anglo-Saxon English coasts.[257] Farther north the copper of Wales, like the iron of Gloucestershire, may well have been sent to Ireland and perhaps Gaul.[258] Lead and silver may have also found more than a local market,[259] as did foodstuffs like the cattle brought from Kent to London.[260] One local industry, cloth, was already of some importance, as we know from discoveries made in Kent, at Sutton Hoo and Whitby.[261] At the time of Offa in the late eighth century such cloth was exported to Gaul.[262] It therefore seems probable that it already was reaching Quentovic and the Garonne region, if not elsewhere on the Continent. Also important were fine Kentish brooches which reached Frisia,[263] as well as the less elaborate square-headed brooches which had a wide local English market.[264] Pottery made at Thetford certainly had some local sale in Eastern England.[265]

It seems probable, however, that none of these English exports, important though they were, had as much value for England's external trade as one special commodity—slaves. The ancient laws of Wales specifically mention the slave trade.[266] So, too, do the earliest Anglo-Saxon law codes, those of Kent and Wessex, and the

[256] *Vita Filiberti*, XLI-XLII, in *MGH Script. rer. Merov.*, V, 602-3.

[257] H. O. Hencken, *The Archeology of Cornwall and Scilly*, pp. 110-220.

[258] The Lagore site shows that bronze was used in this period. The copper as well as the tin may have come to Ireland from overseas. H. O. Hencken, "Lagore Crannoy, an Irish royal residence," *loc.cit.*, pp. 131-59.

[259] *Vita Wilfridi*, in *MGH Script. rer. Merov.*, VI, 211, and Bede, *Hist. eccl.*, I, 1, ed. King, I, 14.

[260] J. Tait, *The Medieval English Borough*, p. 6.

[261] J. W. Crowfoot, "A Textile from Whitby," *loc.cit.*, pp. 11-17. E. Carns-Wilson, "The Woolen Industry," *loc.cit.*, pp. 363-64.

[262] F. Stenton, *Anglo-Saxon England*, pp. 19-22.

[263] P. Boeles, *Friesland*, pp. 338-59.

[264] E. T. Leeds, *A Corpus of Anglo-Saxon Great Square Headed Brooches*, pp. 21-173.

[265] G. Dunning, *op.cit.*, pp. 6-7. G. Knocker and R. Hughes, *op.cit.*, pp. 9-11. Maitland-Miller also reports a coarse local pottery and tiles manufactured at Hamwith during these years. M. Maitland-Miller, "Southampton Excavations," *loc.cit.* (1946-50), pp. 3-18.

[266] E. I. Bromberg, "Wales and the Medieval Slave Trade," in *Speculum*, XVIII (1942), 263-69.

latter expressly forbids the selling of one's countrymen overseas.[267] It seems possible that such laws were evaded, for it is as a slaver, purchasing English captives, that we meet the first Frisian merchant in England in 679, and as we know from the famous story of Pope Gregory, Angle slaves were reaching Rome as early as the late sixth century.[268] According to St. Eligius, St. Richardius and others, they were very common in Gaul.[269] The high price paid for a slave in Gaul relative to what he brought in England, coupled with the constant Anglo-Saxon and British conflicts that produced numbers of such miserable captives, combined to stimulate trade in human chattels.[270] Forbidden by English law, condemned by the church, it continued for centuries to be the source of much of England's prosperity.

Farther north an analysis of the spasmodic trade which reached Scotland, the Orkneys, the Faroes, Norway and Ireland is particularly difficult to make. Copper may have been produced from mines in in the Orkneys, and Dicuil's mention of sheep and seabirds on the remote islands suggests that feathers and wool were shipped south to pay for imports.[271] The whalebone of the Franks' casket suggests a fishing industry of some importance along these coasts as well. Distant Norway probably relied on furs and marine products to balance her trade account now, as later.

The Baltic also sent goods to pay for the swords, bronze, glassware and probably wine and foodstuffs which it imported from the Rhinelands and England. Its chief export product was certainly furs. Amber, rare in Continental finds of the fifth and early sixth centuries, but found more abundantly later, was also sent south.[272] Perhaps timber, needed in tree-poor Frisia, was another important export. Some jewelry, like the *brachteates* discovered in Kent and Frisia, may also have been exported to the southwest.[273] To the east into Russia went furs and perhaps iron, which, along with slaves, honey and beeswax, passed into the hands of Kazar traders to reach the Orient.[274] In

[267] C. Attenborough, *The Earliest English Laws*, pp. 21, 45.

[268] *Gregory I Regestum*, VI, 10, in *MGH Epistolae*, I, 388-93.

[269] W. Levison, *England and the Continent*, pp. 8-10.

[270] H. M. Chadwick, *The Origins of the English Nation*, pp. 17-19.

[271] Dicuil, *De mensura orbis terrae*, ed. Parthney, p. 71.

[272] E. Salin, *Le Haut Moyen Age en Lorraine*, p. 161. R. Jessup, *Anglo-Saxon Jewelry*, p. 51.

[273] E. T. Leeds, "Denmark and Early England," *loc.cit.*, pp. 24-31.

[274] On furs from Russia, see Jordanes, *Gaetica*, in *MGH Auct. Ant.*, V, 59. On iron and other metals from the Azov region in early Russian sites, B. Grekov, *op.cit.*, pp. 17-28. Slaves are not mentioned as an export from Russia until about 800 A.D., though they probably were exported earlier. Actually we have no archeo-

return, various fine metal products and some silks and spices reached North Russia and the distant Baltic.

When one analyzes what we know of the products that made up the cargoes which formed the maritime and river commerce of Northern Europe in these years, a number of things seem very clear. In the first place, this trade undoubtedly received some stimulus from Mediterranean and Middle Eastern regions, whether it came via Black and Caspian Seas, Alpine passes, Southern Gallic ports or Spanish Atlantic coasts. But there is little evidence that this stimulus was very great in respect to either material products or money. It seems improbable that the luxury trade from the south in silks, spices, wines, papyrus and manufactured goods—even the silver and gold sent north—was a decisive factor in the trade of Northern Europe during these centuries. Rather, local products apparently formed the bulk of trade cargoes. In part, these consisted of natural products: wine, foodstuffs, metals, salt, timber, fish and furs. In part, they consisted of manufactured articles produced in Northern Europe for local or wider markets. The shoes and woolen cloth of Ireland, the glass, weapons, pottery and metalware of Gaul and the Rhinelands, the woolen cloth and fine jewelry of Britain, the iron products and jewelry of Scandinavia owed nothing to the Mediterranean.[275] In fact, though manufacturing techniques were different in some cases and the routes that commerce followed had changed, it is hard not to find this economic life very similar to that existing in the Northern Seas at the time of the Late Empire. Even the money which was coming into use, the *sceattas* and silver pennies of Gaul, was locally produced from European silver mines and as with the silver area of Late Roman times, by 700 its use separated Northern Europe from the Mediterranean. Important as trade connections to the south were in these years, it seems possible that their influence has been exaggerated by some historians.

Another matter of interest is to attempt to find out who actually carried on this trade, who the merchants of this period were and

---

logical proof of these Eastern wares reaching the Baltic until Carolingian times— nothing, in fact, except some coins.

[275] This point is made forcibly by Postan in his article on Northern European trade in the Middle Ages, which deals rather cursorily with the period covered by this volume. M. Postan, "The Trade of Medieval Europe—the North," in *Cambridge Economic History of Europe*, II, 121-29. See R. Doehaerd, *L'Expansion économique belge au moyen âge*, pp. 7-8, and P. Kletler, *Nordwesteuropas Verkehr*, pp. 107-9.

how they were organized. Here again our information is scanty indeed. We hear of individual merchants like our Frisian in England,[276] or a Samo traveling into Slavic lands,[277] or a trader of Metz going to Trier to procure salt.[278] But we seldom hear of groups of merchants and artisans. No scrap of evidence exists, for instance, of *collegia* in former Roman territory. Perhaps they continued to survive, but more probably they disappeared with the end of Roman authority. A vague reference to guilds appears in the early Anglo-Saxon laws— which is not surprising, since the Anglo-Saxons were the most active traders of the period, but it may mean little.[279] In fact, not until Carolingian times do we find a guild even mentioned by name.

What seems to emerge, then, is a picture of a trade which was free to go where it liked. We find no maritime codes in Merovingian Gaul, certainly the most advanced economic region,[280] and only a few *fisci* levying taxes on trade there and in Southern England.[281] In a late Carolingian document, as a matter of fact, it is mentioned that the Mercian merchants (Anglo-Saxons) were long accustomed to travel freely in Gaul.[282] In England, the Laws of Ine in Wessex and those of Kent contain a bit more evidence. They speak of merchants traveling freely inland, but hold their "hosts (those who sheltered them) responsible for their good behavior.[283] Much the same provisions in the eighth century laws of the Bavarians imply a like attitude.[284] Traders thus seem in this period to have wandered freely on their own account, relatively untrammeled by commercial organizations or by the rather primitive governments which existed at this time.

This impression of generally free trade, so different from the system prevailing in Roman times, is heightened by the fact that these two centuries seem to have been relatively peaceful ones in the region of the Northern Seas. In contrast to the raids, fortifications

---

[276] Bede, *Hist. eccl.*, IV, 22, ed. King, II, 122.

[277] *Chron. Fred.*, IV, in *MGH Script. rer. Merov.*, II, 144-60.

[278] Gregory of Tours, *De virtute S. Martini*, in *ibid.*, I, 656.

[279] E. Coornaert, "Les Gildes médiévales," in *Revue hist.*, CXCIX (1948), 31-33.

[280] R. S. Lopez, *La Politique commerciale*, pp. 397-402. J. M. Pardessus, *Collection des lois maritimes*, IV (Paris 1837), 222-23.

[281] Such as the *fiscus vinitor* mentioned by Gregory of Tours on the Atlantic shores of Aquitaine, and those spots where tolls were levied in England near Canterbury and London.

[282] *MGH Epistolae aevi Karol.*, II, 145.

[283] *Laws of Ine*, XXV, in C. Attenborough, *The Earliest English Laws*, p. 45.

[284] A. Dopsch, *The Economic and Social Foundations of European Civilization*, pp. 350-51.

along the coasts and conflict of earlier centuries, little of an aggressive character can be noted in the Northern Seas for a long period after 550. We do hear of some raids by Northumbrian monarchs in the Irish Sea,[285] of one descent by pirates on the island of Eigg,[286] of conflicts between Pictish overlords and their Orkney vassals[287] and of a few expeditions of the Frisians against the Franks on the lower Rhine.[288] We even know from tradition that Ivar Widefathom lost his life fighting off Karelia.[289] But these are merely local episodes. No naval organization in the Late Roman sense of the word existed. Walls of Roman times in Gaul and Britain were neither repaired nor even used. Only in the lands of Slavdom do fortified *grody* seem to have been the order of the day.[290] It was a lawless age and a violent one, as a reading of Bede or Gregory of Tours shows, but it was not one in which the seas swarmed with pirates. Trade and traders could move more freely and undisturbed than was to be the case again for many centuries.

Still another economic phenomenon appeared during these years which was closely connected with the free and expanding commerce of Northern Europe. I refer to changes taking place in the field of agriculture. It is worth noting that the Romans of the Late Empire had been particularly unsuccessful in this branch of their economy. Their villa system was not, it proved, a very efficient way of handling agricultural development, and their system of state regimentation of the peasantry and high taxes seems to have discouraged production. As a result, depopulation became a problem in the Northern European countryside of the Roman Empire, a trend which even imported German *laeti* and *foederati* could not reverse.[291] The migration period destroyed the villa system except in Southern Gaul and Spain. Even more important, it brought many new settlers to areas like Brittany, England, Gaul, Flanders and the Rhinelands, thus reversing the population trends of earlier times. Slavs, pushing into Central Europe, filled up these rather empty regions as well.[292] But at first these migrations, which caused confusion and difficulties where they oc-

[285] Bede, *Hist. eccl.*, IV, 25; V, 25, ed. King, II, 140-50, 374-82.

[286] W. Skene, *Celtic Scotland*, II, 152.

[287] H. M. Chadwick, *Early Scotland*, pp. 46-48.

[288] P. Boeles, *Friesland*, pp. 269-75.

[289] B. Nerman, *Sveriges Första Storhetstid*, pp. 15-63.

[290] J. Kostryzewski, *Les origines de la civilisation polonnaise*, pp. 102-10.

[291] See, for example, *Code Theod.*, V, 11-15, 17-19.

[292] M. Bloch, "Les Invasions: occupation du sol et peuplement," in *Ann. d'hist. sociale*, II (1946), 20-27.

curred, did not change the agrarian picture for the better to any significant extent.

By the late seventh century, however, after a period of relative peace, we begin to notice certain important changes taking place in Northern European agriculture. These changes have three main aspects. First, they show an extension of agrarian settlement into regions and soils that had been relatively neglected in Roman agrarian practice. Second, they seem to show certain new methods of agriculture coming into use. And third, they are characterized by new individuals and institutions at work in the transformation of the countryside. These changes have been most carefully studied in France by scholars like Bloch, in Belgium by Kurth, in England by the Crawfords and in Germany by many savants with an interest in agriculture. And the regions where in this period we see agrarian changes taking place are equally instructive. They appear to be the Loire valley, the plain of Flanders, the Meuse and Scheldt valleys, the valley of the Ijessel in Holland, the forested regions of Lorraine, the Midlands and eastern portions of Britain and the river valleys and fjords of Norway. Thus they follow no particular racial pattern. They occur among a native Gallo-Roman population in the Loire region, among mixed German-Gallo Roman groups in Belgium, Lorraine and East Britain and among a purer Germanic stock elsewhere.

The first feature of this agrarian change is the utilization of new soils. Here a glance at Roman practices may prove enlightening. In Britain and Gaul, the Romans concentrated their agriculture in those regions which possessed light soils, generally those which had long been under cultivation. Such soils were adapted to their light Mediterranean plows and required little clearing. Only in certain limited areas, such as the fenlands of Eastern Britain and along some parts of their Rhine frontiers, do they appear to have attempted to break the heavy clay soils of the bottom lands or clear the primeval forest of Northern Europe.[293] It was these soils, however, neglected by Rome, which were those now put under cultivation in the late seventh century. Studies in the Cambridge region of Britain show Anglo-Saxon settlements and villages located in just such heavy-clayed

<hr>

[293] C. E. Stephen, "Agricultural Life in the Later Roman Empire," in *Camb. Econ. Hist. of Europe*, I, 102-17. R. Koebner, "The Settlement and Colonization of Europe," *ibid.*, pp. 11-12, 25-27. C. Jullian, *Histoire de la Gaule*, V, 179-94. C. Fox, *The Archeology of the Cambridge Region*, pp. 223-25. Collingwood and Myers, *Roman Britain and the English Settlements*, pp. 340-50.

bottom lands. So, too, does an examination of the Meuse valley and of its tributaries, where one notices Roman villas located near roads on the ridges, but seventh-century farms close to the streams along the valleys of the Ardennes.[294] About the Loire the same pattern of new settlements along the rivers stands in contrast to the location of the Roman agrarian villa system. In Lorraine one notices in this period an expansion of settlement into the forested lands of the Juras and Vosges neglected by the Roman.[295]

Farther north the pattern is repeated. In Zealand and Flanders a beginning was made in diking and the establishment of polders—a development which was, of course, to transform this low-lying coast in later centuries.[296] Farther inland along the Ijessel, one also sees a movement in the seventh century into the heavy clay bottom lands of this river—previously untouched by agriculture.[297] Much farther to the north, along Norway's west coast, archeologists have noted a similar breaking of new land. This was made possible by the advance of settlers into this region of fjords and mountains, hitherto all but uninhabited, and the felling of the primeval forest that covered the valleys.[298]

The main reason why this movement to new lands could be successful lies in the use of improved agricultural implements and practices—the second feature of this change. The Romans had employed, in general, the light Mediterranean plow—really little but an improved digging stick. In the northern portions of Europe, however, we find a new plow coming into use, the wheeled, mortarboard plow. Though this heavy plow was known in Rhaetia in the second century and may have seen some use in Roman Britain,[299] its general

[294] C. Fox, *op.cit.*, pp. 220-31. E. Barger, "The Present Position of Studies in English Field Systems," in *Eng. Hist. Review*, CLIV (1938), 385-409. See especially the pioneer work by H. L. Gray, *English Field Systems* (Cambridge, Mass., 1915). C. Fox, *The Personality of Britain* (Cardiff 1932), pp. 15-84, also contains certain later views on this subject.

[295] M. Bloch, *op.cit.*, pp. 18-20. F. Ganshof, "Het Tijdperk de Merowingern," *loc.cit.*, pp. 286-90. E. Salin, *La Civilisation merovingienne*, I, 168-97, and especially *Le Haut Moyen Age en Lorraine*.

[296] The pioneer work on agricultural patterns in Flanders is G. Marez, *Le Problème de la colonisation franque*, pp. 60-78. See also F. Ganshof, *op.cit.*, pp. 270-302.

[297] B. Slicher van Bath, "Mark, Manor and Village in the Eastern Netherlands," in *Speculum*, XXI (1946), 116.

[298] A. W. Brøgger, *Ancient Emigrants*, pp. 12-14. R. Hodgkin, *History of the Anglo-Saxons*, II, 488.

[299] M. Bloch, *Les Caractères originaux de l'histoire rurale française* (Oslo 1931), pp. 51-57. C. E. Stephens, *op.cit.*, pp. 105-15. F. G. Payne, "The Plow in Ancient Britain," in *Arch. Journal*, CIV (1947), 82-109.

employment over a wider area probably did not occur before the Merovingian Age.[300] Along with this improved plow we also find, perhaps beginning as early as these years, a better system of animal traction—the horse collar. The Romans had employed yokes, a relatively inefficient harness. Probably brought in by invaders from Central Asia, the horse collar changed this system. Now horses hitched to the heavy mortarboard plows could effectively work the heavier clay soils, virgin and rich. These two technological developments, heavy plow and horse collar, thus went together.[301] To them, a third might be added: the three-field system, which made use of the fact that there are summer as well as winter rains in Northern Europe, unlike the Mediterranean region. By taking advantage of this, an extra crop can be raised every other year under a rather complex field-rotation system. There is, however, little proof that the three-field system was in use until Carolingian times, and even then; as Bloch has shown, it was frequently combined with the two-field system in various parts of Gaul. If it already was to be found in these portions of Western Europe, however, it, like the deep plow and horse collar, may lie behind much of the agrarian change we have noted.[302]

Finally, the agencies which were responsible for these changes are worth summarizing. In Roman times the villa was the system whereby agriculture was carried on in most of the regions of the Western Empire, save for those sections where a more primitive, Celtic, small-field system prevailed. The villa system, however, disappeared with the collapse of Rome in all regions north of the Rhone and the Loire. As noted, the village system tended to take its place. It was not, however, this village system which was responsible for new cleared lands and new agricultural practices appearing in the seventh century. Rather it was the monasteries that took the lead. It was they, it would seem, that in the Meuse valley, in Flanders, even perhaps along the Loire, spearheaded a clearing of the forest and brush and a breaking of new ground and introduced improved agrarian techniques which their

[300] F. G. Payne, op.cit., pp. 115-17. M. Bloch, Les Caractères originaux, pp. 58-83.
[301] On the use of the horse collar, see A. G. Hauricourt, "De l'origine de l'attelage moderne" in Ann. d'hist. écon. et soc., VIII (1936), 137-54; L. White, "Technology and Invention in the Middle Ages," in Speculum, XV (1940), 203-31; and C. E. Parain, "The Evolution of Agricultural Technique," in Camb. Econ. Hist. of Europe, I, 127-32.
[302] B. Slicher van Bath "Mark, Manor and Village," loc.cit., pp. 114-17. M. Bloch, op.cit., pp. 31-34. C. E. Parain, "The Evolution of Agricultural Technique," loc.cit., pp. 132-41. H. L. Gray, English Field Systems, pp. 380-432.

neighbors could copy.[303] Elsewhere, in the Ijessel valley of Holland, in Lorraine, in England and in Norway, no agency seems to have been at work except the individual peasant, who, like the American pioneer, began the slow work of hacking down the forest and draining the swamps. In certain regions these individual peasant proprietors, a class new in Europe, helped to mark the way that was to lead to later agrarian growth.[304]

Here caution is necessary. By the eighth century only the first beginnings of the vast clearing job that lay ahead for Europe had been accomplished, and then only in limited areas. Large parts of England and the Continent lay outside the regions where agrarian changes were taking place. Some, like the Seine valley and Central Germany, were not to undergo such agrarian changes until Carolingian times. Others were to wait until the eleventh and twelfth centuries. But at least a certain beginning had been made in this proto-Carolingian late seventh century, a beginning that reversed the Late Roman trend of agrarian depopulation and decadence and marked a path towards the future.

This brings us to a final question concerning this new agriculture—its relationship to the commercial and industrial growth which we know these years brought to the lands of Europe which faced the Northern Seas. Here we notice a striking phenomenon. The places where this agricultural revolution was occurring were just those spots along the Atlantic where commerce was again becoming active, where a silver coinage was found most abundantly and where new ports and revived Roman *civitates* were most in evidence. There seems, therefore, to have been a close connection between new trading settlements along the Rhine, the Meuse and the Scheldt and the new ways of using virgin land and clearing it for agriculture. The same thing is true of Southeastern England, where new trading settlements and an abundant *sceatta* coinage were to be found in just those regions where agrarian change was most rapid. Similarly, Le Gentilhomme has commented upon the fact that gold coins of the seventh century found along the Loire were generally struck in *vici*, or

---

[303] See F. L. Ganshof, *op.cit.*, pp. 260-89, on the role of monastic foundations in Flanders and the Meuse valley. On the prosperous agrarianism in the Loire valley, see P. Le Gentilhomme, *op.cit.*, pp. 95-103.

[304] H. Slicher van Bath (*op.cit.*, pp. 111-18), stresses the free village character of Frisia. On the individualistic nature of Britain's clearing of the forest in these years, see F. Stenton, *Anglo-Saxon England*, pp. 276-89.

villages, thus furnishing apparent evidence of an agrarian prosperity.[305] On the other hand, regions like Western Britain, North Jutland and Eastern Germany which show little commercial or industrial activity seem not to have shared in such agrarian improvements and changes. It will take more detailed studies before an answer can be definitively given to this problem, but at least a provisional hypothesis can be hazarded. That is, that trade, industry and agrarian growth were interconnected in this period. Each stimulated the others, and the presence of each phenomenon was necessary for a general, healthy, steady economic growth.

Another matter of importance concerns the types of ships in use along these maritime trade routes which now flowed unchecked from Spain to Iceland and from the Bay of Biscay to the Gulf of Finland. Here again, as in the case of the commerce, industry, and agriculture of Northern Europe, the accent is on growth, development and improvement. In 550 only the maritime shores of Gaul, Western Britain and Saxon and Jutish England appear to have produced first-class sailing ships capable of long, difficult voyages. Other regions—Ireland, Scandinavia and Anglian Britain—produced inferior vessels, coracles and rowing ships, which were not adequate for maritime traffic in the Atlantic on a large-scale basis. By 700 the situation had, however, changed much for the better.

On the coasts of Western Gaul, the two main types of ships during this period were the carvel-built *scaphae* and *barcae*. Gregory of Tours mentions *scaphae* trading with Galicia in the late sixth century,[306] while it is known that in the seventh a *barca* was manned by Gallic sailors in the Irish Sea.[307] It seems probable that both these wooden ships, as well as the *navis longa* mentioned by Gildas, were used by the Celtic mariners of Britain's west coast.

Across the Irish Sea a different situation prevailed. There, in the first years of the sixth century, the coracle was the main vessel in use. In these craft the Irish proved themselves the most intrepid mariners of the Atlantic prior to the age of the Vikings. Thanks to Irish accounts, we also possess for the sixth and seventh centuries rather precise information about these *curraghs* and the voyages for which they were used. Some of these stories, like those which deal with St. Brendan, are at least partially legendary, but they reveal

---

[305] P. Le Gentilhomme, *op.cit.*, pp. 95-101.
[306] Gregory of Tours, *Hist. Franc.*, VIII, 35, in *MGH Script. rer. Merov.*, I, 351.
[307] Adamnan, *Vita Columbae*, I, 28, ed. Reeves, p. 131.

much concerning these ships. They were, it seems, often of great size, constructed of from 20 to 30 oxhides, two or three hides thick, carrying masts and capable of transporting as many as 20 passengers. In them, Irish mariners made astonishing voyages as far as the Orkneys and Faroes and even sailed direct to Spain.[308] It was in a coracle that St. Columba reached Iona,[309] and in such craft, according to Dicuil, Irish monks sailed to Iceland.[310] Actually, in some respects, a coracle, its light weight enabling it to float upon the waves like a cork, was and still is an ideally seaworthy craft for use in the stormy Atlantic.

About 550, or just before, according to legend, the Irish began to build wooden ships as well as *curraghs*. St. Brendan, for instance, is said to have sailed south on his second voyage in a wooden ship. Here one cannot doubt that legend is in accord with facts, for we know, thanks to Adamnan, that in St. Columba's time the Irish were constructing wooden vessels. Adamnan mentions an astounding number of vessel-types used by the Irish at this time—some of which are unknown to us. They are the *barca, caupullus, navicula, navis longa, navis onera, scapha* and *curragh*.[311] Some, of course, like the *barca* and *scapha*, we have already encountered on Gallic coasts. The *navis longa* we earlier found in Celtic Britain. It is interesting that they appear in Ireland only after reopened trade routes linked the island again with Gaul, and the revived Anglo-Saxon offensive in Britain drove Celts from West British shores to seek refuge in this island. Probably the simplest classification of such ships, however, is that found in the Ancient Laws of Ireland. Three ship-types are mentioned: the *navis longa*, or warship; the *barca*, or ocean-going merchant vessel; and the *curragh*, or coracle. All save the *curragh* were probably carvel-built.[312]

It seems natural that these ship-types should have reached the lands of the Picts in Scotlands, the Orkneys and Shetlands during these years of contact with Irish mariners. Indeed, all through the seventh century, we find mention of *curraghs* about these coasts, where treeless islands made such boats the only practicable ones. They seem to have

[308] J. Hornell, "The Curraghs of Ireland," in *Mariners Mirror*, XXII (1937), 75-93. A. MacDermott, "St. Brendan the Navigator," in *ibid.*, XXX (1950), 74-80. See also the interesting information in T. C. Lethbridge, *Merlin's Island*, pp. 141-89, and *Herdsmen and Hermits*, pp. 13-172.

[309] Adamnan, *Vita Columbae*, II, 16, ed. Reeves, p. 189.

[310] Dicuil, *De mensura orbis terrae*, VII 14, ed. Parthney, p. 44.

[311] Adamnan, *Vita Columbae*, ed. Reeves, contains mention of all these ship-types.

[312] J. Hornell, *op.cit.*, pp. 89-92. W. L. Clowes, *Royal Navy*, I, 56-57. W. Vogel, "Zur nord- und westeuropäischen Seeschiffahrt," in *Hansische Geschichtsblätter*, XIII (1907), 171-74. On similar types on Norway's coast, see H. Shetelig, *Scandinavian Archeology*, pp. 370-76, and Brøgger and Shetelig, *The Viking Ships*, pp. 1-71.

been found along the east coast of Britain, too, as far south as Northumbria, where their lines are still followed, according to Lethbridge,
in the fishing cobbles used along these shores.[313] They may even have
reached Norway. But at the same time we also find larger wooden
rowing ships used by Pictish kings like Bude I and Bude III in their
raids on the Orkneys. Such ships seem to have been masted, swift
warships like the *naves longae* alluded to by Gildas and Adamnan,
and thus constructed along the lines of the Pictish vessels which
Vegetius mentioned centuries earlier. Unfortunately we have little
accurate information on their construction.[314]

Just as better ship-types were spreading to Ireland and the land of
the Picts, the same thing was happening in the North Sea and the
Baltic. As noted earlier, about 550 both the men of Kent and the Saxons
of England appear to have possessed sailing ships, but the Angles and
Scandinavians did not use them. Rather their typical vessel, as shown
by the Sutton Hoo ship and the greater Kvalsund boat found on Norway's coast, was still a rowing craft, improved but not radically
different from the earlier Nydam ship of the Baltic.[315] By 700, however, this had changed. On eastern English coasts sails were in general use. St. Ives, about 700, must have traveled in a sailing vessel
from Northumbria to distant Brittany, since his vessel awaited a favorable wind to set sail.[316] We hear, at about the same time, of Wilfred
sailing directly across the North Sea to Frisia and the mouths of the
Rhine.[317] In the Baltic, archeologists have discovered a carving of
a sailing vessel upon a stone which dates soon after 600.

It is rather uncertain just how this change took place. Better ship
construction may have reached the Anglian shores of Northumbria
via the Celts of the Irish Sea or from Picts to the north. We know
of the activities of the kings of Northumbria in the Irish Sea in the
early seventh century and again in 684-685, when they launched
maritime attacks which must have familiarized them with better
ship-types. In this regard, it is interesting that Bede definitely men-

[313] T. C. Lethbridge, *Merlin's Island*, pp. 100-60.
[314] Bede mentions the *navis longa* in *Hist. eccl.*, I, 15 ed. King, I, 68.
[315] C. W. Philips, "The Sutton Hoo Ship," in *Antiquaries Journal*, xx (1940),
18-42. On the Kvalsund boats, see H. Shetelig and F. Johannsen, *Kvalsundfundet*,
in *Bergens Museum Skrifter* new ser., II, 2 (Bergen 1929), pp. 131-57. On the
Barset ship, see W. La Baume, "Zum Stand unserer Kenntis vom germanischen
Schiffbau," in *Hammaburg*, III (1949), 216-25. See also Brøgger and Shetelig,
The Viking Ships, pp. 51-58.
[316] *Vita St. Yveis*, in *Acta Sanct. Boll.*, 6 Oct., III, 405.
[317] *Vita Wilfridi auctore Stephano*, in *MGH Script. rer. Merov.*, VI, 220. On the
lack of winter navigation, see W. Levison, *England and the Continent*, p. 14.

tions the *navis longa*, or warship.[318] Such improvements in naval construction may have arrived via Kent, which was in close contact with Northumbrian shores in the seventh century, as we know from the story Bede tells us of the prince of Northumbria who fled to Kent by sea.[319] Perhaps both Celtic and Kentish influences lie behind these changes.[320]

We are also uncertain as to how these improved ships came to the Baltic and Scandinavia. The lesser Kvalsund boat provides at least one clue. It has no mast and is still a rowing ship, but its lines resemble those of the narrower coracle-cobble type used by the Celts. Perhaps it, halfway between the greater Kvalsund boat and the later Viking ship of Gokstad, shows the influence of Celts reaching Norway's shores.[321]

But, one might ask, what of ships other than *naves longae* and other clinker-built vessels of this North Sea? What did they look like? Here our Baltic information helps us. At Gotland there are a series of graphic rock-cut pictures of Scandinavian vessels. These were once believed to date from the ninth century. Now Swedish archeologists date them from about 700, or the time of Ivar Widefathom's empire. They give us some valuable information. They show large sailing ships, without oars, clinker-built and constructed like the later Osberg ship of Norway. They are, it would seem, of a type known later in Viking times as a *knorr*, or merchant vessel. They probably give us an idea what the English and Frisian ships of the North Sea looked like during these years.[322] It is interesting, in this connection, to note that Charlemagne's later Dorestad coinage has on one side a clinker-built ship that is not unlike those in the rock pictures of Gotland.

Owing something to Celtic design, then, there appeared along eastern English and Frisian coasts as well as in the distant Baltic a series of clinker-built vessels which carried masts and sails, and which were superior to the earlier rowing ships in use there, though derived in part from them. With their appearance the link between Baltic and North Sea, already noticeable in commerce, is found in ship-

---

[318] Bede, *Hist. eccl.*, I, 15, ed. King, 68, for mention of *navis longa*.

[319] *Ibid.*, 20, in *loc.cit.*, p. 316.

[320] This seems to be the opinion of Lethbridge in *Merlin's Island*, pp. 100-77.

[321] H. Shetelig and F. Johannsen, *op.cit.*, pp. 145-49. See also remarks of Brøgger and Shetelig, in *The Viking Ships*, pp. 60-69.

[322] S. Lindquist, *Svensk Forntidstev*, pp. 204-307. Brøgger and Shetelig, *op.cit.*, pp. 70-72.

types, too. The basis of those swift Viking vessels which were to terrorize Western Atlantic coasts for decades had been already laid in the types of vessels which had developed in Scandinavia and the North Sea.

It would be wise, however, at this point, to discuss one danger which may arise in considering the development of commerce, industry, agriculture and shipping in the lands that surrounded the Northern Seas of Europe during these years. That is the danger of exaggeration. It must be emphasized that vital changes did take place almost simultaneously everywhere along these coasts from Spain to distant Russia, developments that knit these seas and the lands they touched into a common economic system of importance for the years to come. However, it was only the beginnings which occurred during the two centuries considered in this chapter, beginnings whose flowering did not come until much later. Ireland, for instance, despite its commerce and the far-flung voyages of its navigators, remained extremely primitive in an economic sense. It had only one settlement which could be called urban and there is no evidence that money was in common use at all. Not until the time of the Vikings in the ninth and tenth centuries was it to achieve a truly urban civilization, even on its coasts.

To a somewhat lesser extent the same thing is true of England. It did develop during these years a widespread money economy and a number of trade centers such as Hamwith, Canterbury, London and York. But these were located almost exclusively on or near the coasts. The interior of the island remained economically backward, as a reading of the law codes of Kent and Wessex makes abundantly clear. The western coast also made few economic advances. Neither a money economy nor urban centers appeared on these shores during this period. Not until the time of Aethelstan was Britain to achieve anything resembling a really advanced economy.

If that was true of England in Merovingian times, it was even truer of Scotland, Norway and Baltic lands. Some trade did reach Scottish shores, the Hebrides, Orkneys, Shetlands, Iceland and Norway, but how little it amounted to! No money hoards have been found in these regions dating from these years, and no single evidence of a trading settlement. In the Baltic the story is somewhat similar. A certain amount of commerce crossed into the Baltic by way of the Eider at the base of the Jutland peninsula and helped to establish the town of Hedeby. It reached farther to Birka and Gotland. From here, trade continued into Russia to Old Ladoga, Gnezdovo, and Rostov and Central Asia. Thus the basis of later important trade routes was laid. But it is clear that only with great reservations may any of these trade centers be called urban in Merovingian times. Among other things, the all but complete absence of money, except some Sassanian and Ommiad silver coins, is significant.

Similarly, the ports of Northern Gaul, Frisia and the Rhinelands which developed during these years were still only small trading stations. Their age of true growth lay in the future, as did the age of important traffic down the Rhine to Italy or across the Alps to Regensburg and the Slavic East. It was the period of the Carolingians and the Ottos which was to see this part of Europe really grow and develop. Even more substantial Western and Central Gallic *civitates* like Bordeaux, Poitiers and Tours were small and much less important than they were to become in the eleventh and twelfth centuries; while centers like Braga and Coruña had little urban life at all.

In short, compared with the urban centers which were found along these coasts in Late Roman times, those of the Merovingian period were rudimentary and primitive. They contained, as did the industry, shipping and agriculture of the period, seeds of future development that were to surpass the best Rome had to offer, but the seeds had just begun to sprout.

Furthermore, even this limited growth suffered a rude setback by the mid-eighth century—one which destroyed many of the advances in economic life already made. This check to economic development seems to have originated in the Mediterranean, and deserves close attention. As we noted earlier in this chapter, southern Gaul was, in the sixth century, closely linked with the Mediterranean world. A common gold currency and trade via Marseilles, Arles and Narbonne formed these connections. Syrians carrying their spices, papyrus, wine, silks and other goods were the agents of this commerce, and were found in many parts of the land. It was to some extent due to this trade that Gaul recovered from the disasters of the fifth century and that commerce extended again towards the Channel and the Rhine.

Shortly after 600, however, things began to change in the Mediterranean. First, the Persians invaded Syria and Egypt, and on their heels came the Arabs, who conquered these Oriental provinces permanently. This conquest and the resulting struggle between Byzantium and the Arabs interfered with trade between Southern Gaul and the Orient in the course of the seventh century. Fewer and fewer Eastern merchants and goods reached Gallic Mediterranean shores.[323] The Rhone route north, so vital a highway for passage and commerce to the Seine, Moselle and Rhine, gradually ceased to have importance. A slow decay began in cities like Marseilles which had been flourishing earlier. As it did, Lyons, Dijon and Trier along the Moselle decayed as well.[324] The marble trade of Southwestern Gaul dwindled away as its links with the Mediterranean were cut.[325] Importation of natron from Egypt, which was used in the glassware of Northeastern Gaul, came to an end.[326] Perhaps as early as 634 the effects were felt in Northern Gaul, where the Fair of St. Denis was organized to draw not only Northerners but Provençals, Italians and Spaniards towards this part of Gaul. In Frisia, finds of gold coins show trade arriving by way of both Rhone-Moselle and Rhine-Alpine routes in the sixth and early seventh centuries. But after 650 no gold coins arrived from the south of Gaul at all, though those coming from Rhine regions continued down to 700.[327] When in the first years of the eighth century Byzantine trade controls were added in the Mediterranean, commerce practically ceased to reach Southern Gaul at all and was directed instead to Venice, where some of it still passed over the Alps up the Rhine to Frisia.

It was this lack of commerce via the Rhone which may help to explain the *sceattas* of the seventh century that are found down Gaul's west coast and on to Marseilles. Perhaps English merchants were reaching down to Marseilles and even towards Spain in search of Oriental wares no longer to be found in Northern Gaul, just as Frisian merchants were proceeding south to Worms on the same quest. Economically Gaul was being split into a series of separate regions, as its Rhone valley backbone to the Mediterranean disintegrated. Such a hoard as that discovered at Buis from the late seventh century shows how local and regional Gaul's economy had become.[328] And this economic division of the land explains much of the struggle between Neustria, based on the Atlantic and Channel, and Austrasia,

---

[323] See A. R. Lewis, *op.cit.*, pp. 44-97, on the causes of this change.

[324] E. Salin, *La Civilisation merovingienne*, I, 429-33.

[325] R. Lautier, "Les Eglises de la Gaule merovingienne," in *Journal des savants*, XXXIV (1950), 22.

[326] G. Faidler-Feytmans, "Les Verreries des époques romanes et merovingiennes au Musée de Mariemont," *loc.cit.*

[327] P. Boeles, *Friesland*, pp. 513-21.

[328] P. Le Gentilhomme, *op.cit.*, pp. 95-123.

based upon the Rhinelands and Germany. Already the Merovingian state was foreshadowing its later division into France and Germany.

At first, it seems, the failure of Gaul's Mediterranean trade did not seriously hinder the commercial growth of the lands facing the Northern Seas. Some Mediterranean goods reached the Atlantic via the Narbonne-Bordeaux route and some went around Spain. Venice's rise also stimulated early eighth-century commerce across the Alps and up the Rhine.[329] Routes to the Baltic from the Black and Caspian Seas also may have helped to make up for losses in goods which no longer arrived by way of the Rhone. Besides, as has been noted, the larger part of the commerce, industry and agriculture in Northern Europe had little to do with the Mediterranean anyway, and was essentially indigenous. Central and Southern Gaul might decay, but the rest of Atlantic Europe, its trade based on a silver currency and an indigenous economy, continued to flourish.

A second blow, however, proved more serious: the Moslem invasions of Spain and Southern Gaul and the reactions to these invasions. The conquest of Spain in 711 was a serious blow because it resulted in the almost complete extinction of the economic life of the northern coastal region of this peninsula, where small Christian principalities still clung to the mountains of Asturias. By 750 not a single town, not even a bishopric, which had existed in this part of Spain in Visigothic times survived.[330] In some ways the situation was even worse in Southwestern Gaul. Moslem invaders and Basques moving north in their wake wrought havoc in this land of villa estates and rich vineyards. The plundering of Carolingian Frankish soldiery added to the destruction. In a sense, the war that Charles Martel and Pepin waged here was less a battle with the Moslems than a civil war between a Gallo-Roman nobility and a Germanic Frankish state. By 750 the old structure had disappeared, save about Tours and Poitou. Not a bishopric whose borders can be recognized remained in the Garonne valley. The villa system simply collapsed. The older economic life came to an end.[331]

[329] A. R. Lewis, op.cit., pp. 90-93.

[330] P. Le Gentilhomme, op.cit., pp. 146-47. J. F. Bladé, "Géographie politique du sud-ouest de la Gaule depuis la fin de la domination romaine jusqu'à la création de la royaume d'Aquitaine" in Ann. de la Faculté de Lettres de Bordeaux, xxx (1873), 19-106, and especially Etude sur l'origine des Basques (Bordeaux 1863). L. Auzias, L'Aquitaine carolingienne, 778-987 (Toulouse 1937), pp. 1-21. L. Halphen, Charlemagne et l'Empire carolingien (Paris 1949), pp. 141-42.

[331] J. H. Mahn, "Le Clergé seculier à l'époque asturienne," in Mélanges Louis Halphen (Paris 1951), pp. 138-57. P. David, Etudes historiques sur la Galacie et le

Perhaps numismatic evidence can make the situation clear. In the late seventh century and the first years of the eighth, south of the Loire numerous mints had turned out gold coins and silver ones, too. Later in the Narbonnaise, Provence and Southern Aquitaine, such coins show an active economic life. By the time of Peppin III (752-68), only four places in Southern and Western Gaul still were striking coins: Tours, Brioux, Clermont, and Poitiers. In the Rhone valley no mints existed south of Besançon, Lyons and Troyes.[332] In the disastrous years between 711 and 750 the whole southwestern economic anchor of the trade and commerce of the Western Atlantic simply disappeared. From the Loire to Coruña nothing remained. The age of the Merovingians in the Northern Seas was over. That of the Carolingians was at hand.

To this disaster, for a real disaster it was, are probably owed the changes which took place elsewhere in the Northern Seas in the next decades, changes which swiftly reversed the trend towards growth and development noticeable everywhere around the Atlantic, North Sea and Baltic for more than a century and a half. Ireland, of course, was particularly affected by the economic decline on Spanish and West Gallic coasts, where her ships had traded for two centuries. This may explain why her shipping and commerce so swiftly declined, and why she remained unimportant during the Carolingian Age. In England one notices a similar dislocation of economic life. Leadership passed to Mercia, which lay inland and had little connection with Atlantic and North Sea trade. Northumbria declined rapidly and suddenly became an isolated region, as its *sceatta* silver coinage was replaced by a copper mintage of *stykas* of local value only.[333] In the lands of the Picts, that naval power, so noticeable in the seventh century, disappears by the mid-eighth and we hear no more of maritime activities along eastern Scottish coasts for centuries.[334] Even in Frisia a copper *sceatta* coinage like that of Yorkshire makes its appearance, though this section of the domains of the Franks, which was connected with Venice and Italy via the Rhine, suffered least of all.[335] In the Baltic the sea-

---

Portugal (Lisbon 1947), pp. 30-36. C. Sanchez-Albornoz, *Estampas de la vida en León durante el Siglo X* (3rd ed., Madrid 1934), pp. 8-10.

[332] M. Prou, *Catalogue des monnaies carolingiennes* (Paris 1896), pp. CIX-CXII.

[333] G. C. Brooke, *English Coins*, pp. 9-10.

[334] The complete decadence of maritime life along the eastern Scottish (Pictish) coast is a most mysterious affair. We hear nothing of this region for centuries—not even, it would seem, of Viking raids here.

[335] P. Le Gentilhomme, *Mélanges de numismatique*, pp. 90-95.

empire of Ivar Widefathom broke up after Harold Wartooth's defeat in the battle of Bravalla. Out of its fall emerged two kingdoms, a Swedish one in the Uppland which faced Russia and the Eastern Baltic, and a Danish one whose interests lay in Frisia and the North Sea. A new and different era dawned in the Northern Seas which we call the Carolingian Age. Much of the progress of the years 550-700 A.D. was gone. But not all. Enough remained to serve as the basis for further growth in the years of Charlemagne and Louis the Pious.

There remains one final question about this period, perhaps the most important of all. That is, why this age so filled with economic growth and development and agrarian change throughout the Northern Seas should seem to so many historians one of decadence. Perhaps in part the answer lies in the fact that its last years did see the end of that Roman villa-system, gold coinage and society which survived the barbarian invasions and lingered on two centuries more in Spain under the Visigoths and in Southern Gaul under Frankish rule. Perhaps it is because, similarly, most trade from the Orient ceased to reach the Mediterranean shores of these regions after 716. Thus interest in the end of an era in parts of Gaul and in Spain has kept attention from developments elsewhere about Northern Europe. As pointed out, the disaster which overtook the Midi and Spain in the early eighth century did have important repercussions elsewhere about the Northern Seas which caused earlier trends to be reversed in certain areas.

Nevertheless, it seems possible that the feeling among historians that the age of the Merovingians was retrograde rather than progressive, decaying rather than growing, lies in the curious nature of its political and organizational development. This has caused many to be blind to its concrete advances. For the main failures of this age lay in just that political sphere which made it from a governmental point of view curiously inchoate and formless, even chaotic.

Gildas early in the period noted this characteristic of his age when, about 550, he viewed the Celtic princes of his day in Western Britain, and their tyranny and disorder, moral as well as political, caused him to call down his wrath upon them. Similar conditions existed in Merovingian Gaul. One cannot read the pages of Gregory of Tours or Fredegarius without being struck by the curious picture they give of Merovingian kingship, whose representatives divided their domains like booty and murdered each other with savage gusto. Nor do Visigothic rulers seem much better, as the story of Egica's deposition shows. Obviously, by the seventh century, Spanish kings found it as impossible to rule effectively as Frankish ones did. The pages of Bede are just as revealing in this respect. One watches hegemony move rapidly from Kent to East Anglia, to Northumbria, to Merica. One sees the same murders as in Gaul, the same instability and political formlessness. Behind Irish legends lie the forces of disorder, too, and St. Columba, in his early days, seems as much a tribal leader as a religious one. *Beowulf* gives us a glint of light on the political scene in Scandinavia—characterized by the same murders and violence. In Central Europe the strange career of Samo has about it an ephemeral flowering and decay. What seems lacking is order, purpose and political discipline—even a moral ideal. Dagobert, with his prime minister, St. Eligius, strangely Carolingian in his sense of policy and purpose, is a unique figure. And he had no successors. Ivar Widefathom, whom, if we knew more about him, we might consider a seventh-century Canute, seems equally to be an isolated figure in the blood-stained annals of the Danish royal house. One seeks in vain in England for an Offa, an Alfred or an Aethelstan and in Ireland for a Brian Boru. Saints abound, administrators almost do not exist.

The same pattern is true of the church. Gregory the Great, who showed a sense of organization and purpose, had no real successors until the time of Nicholas II in the ninth century. Rare is a Theodore of Tarsus who could rival a Lanfranc as a skillful church administrator. Rather it is Wilfrid and Columba, individualistic wandering saints, who typify the age. The Irish monk was better adjusted to his time than the Benedictine.

Rather than being decadent then, this age was politically and administratively anarchical, inchoate and independent. It had vigor and growth, but it lacked discipline. It was just the opposite of the Roman world which had preceded it. Until rulers, church and circumstances could weld its vigor to some purpose, it was to remain formless and weaker than it should have been, considering its resources —a prey to those within and without who used such resources for their own benefit.

4. The Carolingian Revival A.D. 750-840

IN THE YEAR 752 Pippin was anointed by the Pope, as King of the Franks—the first of his line to hold this august title, though Mayors of the Palace of this Austrasian family had actually governed the Frankish kingdom since 689. This symbolic event signaled the opening of a new era in the lands of Europe which faced the Northern Seas. In a general sense, it coincided with other changes taking place about this time. For in England Mercia was just emerging victorious over Northumbria. In Scandinavia the battle of Bravalla marked the end of the naval empire of Ivar Widefathom. Even in the Orient the Abbassids of Iraq were at this moment achieving the defeat of the Ommiad Caliphs of Damascus, and in Spain a scion of the Ommiads was setting up an independent Emirate of Cordova.

This change in Frankish rulers also coincided with the final disintegration of the old Roman agricultural and social system in Southern Gaul and Spain—a system which had lasted down to the first years of the eighth century. In the chaos and confusion which attended the Moorish invasions of Spain and the Midi and the intervention of Gascons and Carolingians in their turn, the older system of these lands had simply disappeared. Upon its ruins in Northwestern Spain small Christian principalities were painfully arising, while in the Garonne and Rhone valleys and the plains of Septimania, which stretched from Arles to the Pyrenees, a similar period of difficult rebuilding was slowly getting under way. Such was the world in which the Carolingian state, founded—or, rather, consolidated—by Pippin, was beginning its existence.

It would be one-sided, however, to view this Carolingian Age as completely new in character. It did differ from that which preceded it. But in Northern Europe much that some historians have emphasized as essentially Carolingian actually had begun a good deal earlier during the time of the Merovingians. As has already been explained, as early as the seventh century the maritime commerce, the economic life and even the culture of these northern lands had begun to form a region separate from that of the Mediterranean. Certain features generally considered as specifically Carolingian—a silver coinage, a maritime traffic which flowed north from England, Gaul and Frisia into the Baltic, and then down Russian rivers to the Black and Caspian Seas—existed long before Pippin and Charlemagne. So did that trade from the lower Danube and Central Germany which reached Slavic Central Europe. And it is equally true that a clearing of new soil and a changed agricultural system in Holland, Belgium, the Loire valley, England and faraway Norway began before the Carolingians assumed power. So, too, did the extension of Christianity beyond Rome's former borders into Ireland, Scotland, Frisia, Germany and Britain. In short, Northern Europe was in Late Merovingian times already proto-Carolingian, in the sense in which the term is often used. A mighty monarch like Dagobert, insofar as we can see him through the inadequate sources of the period, seems more like Charlemagne than Clovis. Just so his able minister, St. Eligius, reminds one forcibly of Alcuin or a Suger. Similarly, behind the mists of Norse tradition, we sense in Ivar Widefathom something of Canute or Harold Fairhair. The Carolingian Age was new, but the tendencies it represented had long been present about the Northern Seas. They simply reached a certain culmination under this new Frankish line of rulers.

In one respect, however, the situation under which Pippin began his reign was unusual. By 750 economic conditions in Northern Europe had reached their lowest state since 550—particularly in Atlantic Gaul and Spain. That growth and expansion about the Northern Seas, so characteristic of the period from the mid-sixth to the eighth century, had come to a halt at the time of the Moslem conquest of Spain and retrogression had begun. In the last chapter, we have noted some of the causes of this retrogression which ushered in the Carolingian Age, but it might be well to examine them somewhat more fully. This economic decline was the result of the ending of commerce between Southern Gaul and other Mediterranean regions, particularly the Orient. A slow decay, beginning about 640, had culminated by 715 or 720 in the all but complete disappearance of Oriental wares and merchants from the coasts of the Midi, with resultant commercial decay spreading into the interior of France.

Even more important was the devastation and disorganization along Spanish and Gallic coasts that resulted from the Moorish invasion and the Carolingian reaction to it. By 750, the Moslem tide had receded south of the Pyrenees in France, and south of the Douro in Northern Spain. But what remained in the wake of this withdrawal was a shattered economic life and a broken social system. In the small struggling eighth century Christian principalities of Northern Spain little of the Romano-Visigothic order was left. Not a single earlier urban center along these coasts, like Braga or Coruña, showed signs of life.[1] The old Visigothic system of bishoprics, going back to Roman times, disappeared as well.[2] We know of no coins minted during this century in a region which had long been a mining center. In fact, so little is known of this region that it is chiefly from Moorish sources that we are able to piece together the main outlines of its history.

Conditions were little better in France south of the Loire. Cities like Bordeaux, Agen, Toulouse, Cahors and Saintes ceased for all practical purposes to exist. South of Poitiers the bishoprics disappeared.[3] The villa system vanished as the prevailing form of agrarian organization. Stagnation was the order of the day. Examination of the coins struck by Pippin between 752 and 768 illustrates the economic situation in the Midi perfectly, and shows how this section of Gaul had suffered. The only mints still in operation south of the Loire and west of the Seine during these years of Pippin's reign were located at Tours, Brioux, Clermont and Poitiers. In Central France, no money was coined south of Besançon, Lyons and Troyes.[4] There were, then, no longer any centers of economic life sufficiently active to serve as mints in the lower Rhone valley, in Provence, in the Narbonnaise or in the Garonne valley. And no mints existed any longer along the whole western coast of Gaul from the Pyrenees to Brittany. Even as late as 775, in the first years of Charlemagne's reign, when conditions had improved, we find things little better in this part of France. The hoard of Imphy, which dates from this year, and includes coins from widespread areas of the Carolingian west, has in it no coins from the southwest, and only one from the Midi, minted at Arles.[5] As late as 775, then, there are no signs of economic

[1] C. Sanchez-Albornoz, *Ruina y extinción del municipio Romano es España* (Buenos Aires 1943), pp. 19-137.
[2] C. Sanchez-Albornoz, "La primitiva organización monetaria de León y Castilla," in *Ann. de Historia del Derecho Español*, v (1928), 305, and *Estampas de la vida en León durante el Siglo X* (Madrid 1922), pp. 8-10. P. David, *Etudes historiques sur la Galicie*, pp. 30-38. J. B. Mahn, "Le Clergé seculier à l'époque asturienne," in *Mélanges Louis Halphen*, pp. 53-64.
[3] On the destruction of urban life in the Midi, see A. Dupont, *Les Cités de la Narbonnaise première depuis les invasions germaniques* (Nîmes 1942), pp. 131-356; P. Courtreault, *Bordeaux à travers les siècles*, pp. 10-14; J. F. Bladé, *Géographie politique de la sud-ouest de la Gaule*, pp. 81-97; and L. Auzias, *L'Aquitaine carolingienne*, pp. 1-21.
[4] M. Prou, *Catalogue des monnaies carolingiennes*, pp. XCI-CIX.
[5] E. Gariel, *Les Monnaies royales de France sous la race carolingienne* (Strasbourg 1883), I, 3-8.

recovery along the western coasts of Gaul, anymore than there are along the Christian shores of Northern Spain.

These Gallic and Spanish shores, facing the Bay of Biscay, had been in Merovingian times the southwestern pivot of the commerce that appeared throughout the Northern Seas. Thus their collapse was an economic fact of great importance to other regions. This was particularly true of Ireland, for it was to western Gallic and Spanish shores that Irish mariners looked for their supplies of wine and other commodities, of which some were of Mediterranean origin. There, too, they looked for markets for their export goods. With the ending of this trade, therefore, Irish maritime commerce appears to have suffered a blow from which it never fully recovered. After 750, we hear little of Irish shipping in the Atlantic, and, in fact, up to 800 there is no evidence at all of any further contacts between this island and Gaul. Nor are new Oriental or Eastern influences apparent in the Irish art forms. Ireland seems to have returned to an isolated position on the fringes of the European world, whence she had emerged for a brief period in Merovingian times.

Farther north, along maritime routes which the Irish had pioneered, the same economic and naval decadence is noticeable in the lands of the Picts, and along west Scottish coasts as well. From Scotland, Irish monks still traveled as far as the Faroes and Ireland in their light but sturdy coracles[6]—perhaps even to Norway—but we hear nothing of those Pictish fleets which, a century earlier, had been so active off the shores of Scotland and about the Orkneys. Apparently the Celtic maritime tradition simply disappeared. Now it was not Celtic sailors who pushed north, but rather mariners from Western Norway, fisher folk and farmers, who began to probe southwest towards the Hebrides, colonizing this northern island chain of the British Isles—and doing so with little Celtic opposition.[7]

One notices in England, in the late eighth century, certain similar manifestations of decay in maritime commerce and in the general level of economic life.[8] Such a decline may have lain behind political changes there. In Merovingian times, political power had rested with Anglo-Saxon kingdoms which touched upon the sea and drew

---

[6] Dicuil, *De mensura orbis terrae*, p. 44.

[7] A. W. Brøgger, *Ancient Emigrants*, pp. 18-22.

[8] There seems to have been a general, widespread debasement of the silver *sceatta* coinage in this period. W. Levison, *England and the Continent*, pp. 11-12. On the ending of Byzantine influences in England, see R. S. Lopez, "Le Problème des relations anglo-byzantines," *loc.cit.*, pp. 143-51.

power from this fact: first Kent, then East Anglia and then Northumbria. Now we find political leadership moving to Mercia, whose center was far from the sea in the Midlands of Britain. Northumbria declined not only politically, but culturally and economically as well. It could still produce Alcuin in its monastic schools, but he was to have his career in Carolingian Gaul—not his homeland. In place of a silver *sceatta* coinage, we find appearing a copper money of *stykas*, which could have had little value beyond Yorkshire, and which is an example of a new economic localism in this part of England.[9] Such outside economic contacts as were maintained seem largely to have been through foreign Frisian merchants, whom we find established at York in 778.[10] Only a few rare Northumbrian coins dating from this period, which have been discovered on Norway's west coast,[11] give a hint that anything of the trade to the north mentioned by Bede still survived along these coasts. In general, however, the world of Bede appears to have vanished, and a new age in England, as in Ireland and Gaul, was dawning.

Even across the North Sea in Frisia one sees a certain economic decline and localism about 750, similar to what appears to have occurred in Yorkshire. For here, too, one finds a copper coinage, copied from *sceattas*, and of only local value for trade purposes.[12] Farther to the north, in Scandinavia, the political changes which took place about 750 may also have reflected this economic dislocation. As already noted, they consisted in the destruction of the great Dano-Swedish Empire of Ivar Widefathom after the battle of Bravalla. Most Swedish historians seem to believe that this represented a struggle between the Swedes of the Uppland and the Geats of Gotland for dominance over Sweden itself, with the Swedes victorious, thanks to their victory at Bravalla. However, since the forces at the battle, according to tradition, seem to have included Danes and Frisians, it is probable that it represented something more than that—a struggle between that part of Ivar's domains which looked towards the North Sea and that which was linked with Russia, Courland and the Eastern Baltic. Swedish victory, then, may have reflected the fact that by 750 lessening contacts with the west, via the Frisian coast, and increasingly important trade with Russia had tended to split this Scandinavian

---

[9] G. C. Brooke, *English Coins*, pp. 9-10.
[10] *Vita Liutgeri*, I, in *MGH Script.*, II, 407. F. Stenton, *Anglo-Saxon England*, pp. 29-33.
[11] H. Holst, "Mynter i Norske Funn," in *Nord. Numis. Arsskrift* (1943), pp. 101-6.
[12] P. Le Gentilhomme, *op.cit.*, pp. 95-102.

Baltic world in two. One part, Uppland Sweden and a now all but independent Gotland, looked east. A separate Danish kingdom continued to look west towards Frisia, Norway and an Atlantic destiny.[13]

There seems to have been only one area in all the lands of Northern Europe facing the Atlantic that was but little affected by the economic dislocation which we have been describing. It was that part of the Carolingian Empire which was bordered by the Rhine, the Seine and the upper Rhone valleys—a region which we might define as the heartland of this state. In Pippin's time we still find here a number of surviving economic centers important enough to possess mints. These were Dorestad, Strasbourg, Trier, Quentovic, Amiens, Cambrai, Metz, Verdun, Paris, Chartres, Troyes, Lyons and Besançon.[14] Three of them, Dorestad, Amiens and Quentovic, were ports which faced the English Channel and North Sea. The rest, if plotted on a map, seem to form a series of urban centers that lead southwest towards Italy via a series of Alpine passes. These passes, or *clusae* as they were called, were the Great St. Bernard and the Mount Geneva, which communicated with the upper Rhine, and the Little St. Bernard and the Septimer, by which one could reach Italy via Lyons, the upper Rhone, the upper Loire or the lower Seine valley routes.[15] From these passes the Po led directly to Venice, which already in the mid-eighth century had become Byzantium's main trade entrepôt for her commerce with the Latin West.[16] Thus, in the very location of surviving economic centers in Carolingian domains, we can see that a shift in trade routes had taken place, a shift which had begun in the mid-seventh century, but which only now had been completed. Instead of a trade axis that reached Northern Gaul and the Rhinelands via the north-south Rhone valley route from Marseilles, which had been the more popular route in the Merovingian

[13] B. Nerman, *Det Svenska Rickets Uppkomst*, pp. 260-73; G. Turville-Petrie, *The Heroic Age in Scandinavia*, pp. 56-57; G. Depping, *Histoire des expeditions maritimes des Normands* (Paris 1844), p. 40; and B. Nerman, *Sveriges Första Storhetstid* (Stockholm 1942), pp. 45-92, all follow the traditional views. See also F. Balodis, *Det aldsta Lettland* (Uppsala 1940), pp. 1-127. The breakup after Bravalla was followed by the kings of the Westfold in Norway throwing off the Danish yoke, probably about 770 A.D. A. Brugge, *Wikinger* (Oslo 1917), pp. 20-25. H. Shetelig, *La Préhistoire de la Norvège*, pp. 200-1. See especially L. Musset, *Les Peuples scandinaves au moyen âge*, pp. 26-41.

[14] M. Prou, *op.cit.*, pp. CI-CIII.

[15] P. A. Scheffel, *Verkehr-Geschichte der Alpen* (Berlin 1908-14), pp. 1-179.

[16] A. R. Lewis, *op.cit.*, pp. 111-31. R. Cessi, *Storia della Republica di Venezia* (Milan 1944), pp. 13-31, and especially *Venezia Ducale* (Padua 1928-29), pp. 137-89, and "Pacta Venetia," in *Arch. Veneto*, new ser., V-VI (1928-29), 118-51, 217-73.

period, now a northeast-southwest commercial axis based on Venice was predominant. This change, as Vercauteren has pointed out, marks one of the principal differences between the Merovingian and Carolingian periods in this part of Europe,[17] and it was through these *clusae*, or passes, in the Alps that commercial traffic and travelers alike reached Italy and the Mediterranean lands to the south.

To this new trade orientation is probably owed the fact that the Carolingians, unlike the Merovingian monarchs who preceded them, had a vital interest in Italy. It helps to explain, for instance, why Pippin was willing to invade the Lombard kingdom and ally himself with the Pope in this enterprise, and why in 774 Charlemagne annexed Northern Italy to his empire. These Carolingian rulers had a special interest in this region, because Italy was the source of almost all the commerce that linked their domains with the Mediterranean world.[18] We even have one coin hoard that illustrates this new trade orientation—that of Imphy, which we have already mentioned and which dates from 775, the precise time at issue. This hoard, found in Central France, has in it coins from Rouen, Quentovic and Dorestad as well as from Geneva, Lyons, Besançon and Troyes. But it contains only one coin, a silver piece of Arles, from the lower Rhone valley.[19] Evidently, by 775 trade passed rather freely from the Channel and the North Sea towards Italy, but was all but non-existent in the direction of the Midi via the Rhone. One notices a similar shift in travel routes linking England to Rome during these years. During the seventh and early eighth centuries pilgrims and other travelers had reached Rome via the Rhone valley and Marseilles. Now, starting with Unwin in 758, they traveled to Utrecht or Dorestad and Cologne, and down the Rhine to reach Italy via the Alpine *clusae*.[20]

It is, no doubt, this orientation of Frankish commerce which explains why, in 779, Charlemagne can speak of five ports between the Rhine and the Seine—Dorestad, Maastricht, Quentovic, Amiens and Rouen—as the most important in his Empire.[21] These ports, linked to Italy and the Mediterranean world of commerce via the above-mentioned trade routes, naturally were better able to maintain their economic existence than those less favorably located.

[17] F. Vercauteren, *Etude sur les civitates de la Belgique Secunde*, pp. 451-55. R. Doehaerd, *op.cit.*, pp. 16-17.
[18] A. R. Lewis, *op.cit.*, pp. 118-25. R. Cessi, "Pacta Venetia," *loc.cit.*, pp. 130-51.
[19] E. Gariel, *op.cit.*, pp. 3-8.
[20] P. Kletler, *Nordwesteuropas Verkehr, Handel und Gewerbe* (Vienna 1924), p. 28.
[21] On this Diploma of 779, see *MGH Diplom. Karol.*, I, 170.

To this orientation is also owed the importance of the Frisians in the Carolingian period. The Frisians, who had begun to be important as North Sea traders and intermediaries between England and the Continent and Scandinavia and the Rhinelands in the eighth century, under the Carolingians became the leading mariners and merchants in the Northern Seas. Their location was ideal for this purpose. As already noted, they were, in the early eighth century, pushing down the Meuse and Rhine, where in 716 Duke Redbad appeared at Cologne with a fleet. After Charles Martel conquered their homeland, Frisia, in 734, their political independence was ended, but not their power of expansion,[22] which took an economic form. Thus we find Frisians moving down the Rhine to establish a merchant colony at Worms late in the century,[23] and, judging from the similarities between coins of Dorestad and Maastricht, they penetrated south into the Meuse valley as well.[24] In 753 they are found at Paris as merchants at the Fair of St. Denis, which previously had been the preserve of Anglo-Saxon traders.[25] As already noted, in 778 they possessed a merchant colony at York as well.[26] Finally, by 799, their contacts with Rome and Italy were well enough established for them to form a *schola* of pilgrim-merchants there, too,[27] matching the Anglo-Saxon *schola* which had existed in the Holy City since 727. They were by 800, then, well on their way towards becoming the principal intermediaries between Carolingian Europe and the Atlantic regions beyond the Empire: England, Northern Germany and Scandinavia. They had surpassed their chief rivals, the Anglo-Saxons, to become the most important middlemen in the Northern Seas.

At this point it must be emphasized, however, that during the age of the Carolingians, as in other periods, economic conditions did not remain static. A northeast-southwest axis of commerce, linking the heartland of the Carolingians to Italy, remained a fundamental factor of life about the Northern Seas. The area between the Seine and the Rhine continued to be the most advanced economic region of

[22] P. Boeles, *Friesland*, pp. 275-87. E. Salin, *La Civilisation merovingienne* I, 63-64. H. Slicher van Bath, "Dutch Tribal Problems," *loc.cit.*, pp. 326-35. H. M. Chadwick, *The Origins of the English Nation*, pp. 90-103.

[23] P. Kletler, *op.cit.*, p. 8. B. Rower, *op.cit.*, pp. 8-11.

[24] J. H. Holwerda, *De Franken in Nederland*, pp. 38-46. F. Rousseau, *La Meuse et le pays mosan*, pp. 41-45.

[25] *MGH Diplom. Karol.*, I, 43. J. Levillain, *Etudes sur l'abbaye de Saint Denis*, pp. 31-192.

[26] *Vita Liutgeri*, I, in *MGH Script.*, II, 407.

[27] P. Boeles, *Friesland*, p. 407.

Northern Europe during the next decades. The Frisians remained the most important international traders of the Northern Seas. These facts are fundamental to an understanding of this period. But that does not mean that economic conditions and maritime commerce along other shores were unable to escape from the doldrums of the mid-eighth century. Gradually, as the Carolingian Age proceeded and the peace established by the mighty Charlemagne continued for some decades, we can note a revival of commerce and maritime interests along coasts and in regions which seemed dead in 750. By the time Louis the Pious succeeded his father as Emperor in 814, this revival had attained the status of a commercial renaissance throughout the Northern Seas and the lands which faced them—a renaissance which we will now proceed to examine.

This revival of economic life, starting in the later years of Charlemagne's reign, can be seen clearly in Gaul, west of the Seine and south of the Loire. First, we note a revival of commerce in the Rhone valley, as older urban centers there, and in the Narbonnaise, too, again began to coin money. By 781 Arles, Avignon, Marseilles, Uzès, Beziers and Narbonne were centers containing mints, and by 814 had been joined by Vienne as well. In the new Spanish March across the Pyrenees, Barcelona too became a center from which coins were issued. After 814, all these mints continued in operation, as well as one other, Ampurias, near the Pyrenees, between Carolingian Frankish territory and that of Spain. Now a whole series of mints had been re-established in the Midi, from the upper Rhone valley to the borders of Moorish Spain, seeming to testify to a commercial link between Northern Gaul and this section of the Mediterranean, a link which had hardly existed for a century.[28]

There are other signs, however, of the revived economic and maritime importance of this coast, from Marseilles to Barcelona, during these years. In the first years of the ninth century, we hear of Moorish traders bringing spices, silks and other Oriental products to Arles.[29] Shortly before 840, Ibn Khordâdbeh, in distant Bagdad, tells us of certain Rhadamite Jews who set sail from Gaul and reached Egypt and beyond via Spanish Moorish ports, carrying with them as part of their merchandise Frankish swords, and returning west with silks and

[28] M. Prou, *Catalogue des monnaies carolingiennes*, pp. C-CIV. E. Gariel, *op.cit.*, pp. 3-8.
[29] Theodolphus, *Carmina contra iudices*, in *MGH Poeta lat. aevi.*, I, 499.

spices.[30] It seems that it was to such commerce that Louis owed the precious Spanish silk cloth which he presented to the Abbey of Fontanelle.[31] Perhaps it was via this commercial route, too, that Duke William of Toulouse received the brocades and silk garments which he placed upon the abbey altar of Gellone, before he became a simple monk.[32] And it was probably the commercial traffic of this region which lay behind the Carolingian decision, about 800, to build a fleet to protect these coasts.[33] This fleet, under the Count of Ampurias, soon proved powerful enough to enable the Carolingians to defeat a Moorish squadron in 813 and to place the Balearics under Imperial protection.[34]

There can be little doubt that at the time of Louis commerce from this region of the Midi was reaching the Channel coast between Rouen and Dorestad. Two coin hoards seem to make this clear. One, dating from the first years of Louis' reign, has been discovered at Veuillen in the Cher region of Central France. Among its coins are 2 from Ampurias, 3 from Barcelona, 14 from Narbonne, 11 from Arles and 19 from Lyons; thus illustrating a trade route extending from Central Gaul down to the Moslem Spanish border. In this hoard, too, are coins which suggest routes extending to the Channel, the Rhine and the North Sea, for it also includes 4 silver coins from Meaux, 24 from Paris, 5 from Reims, 18 from Cambrai, 7 from Quentovic, 21 from Sens, 12 from Rouen, 12 from Verdun, 3 from Strasbourg, 2 from Mainz, 3 from Cologne and 14 from Dorestad.[35] Lest this hoard be considered exceptional, we have another one, slightly later in date, found at Belvezet not far from Uzès in the lower Rhone valley, which seems to illustrate the same commercial routes as the Veuillen hoard. In addition to coins from the local area, the Belvezet hoard contains 10 coins from Narbonne, and 9 from Barcelona; and the Rhone valley

---

[30] Ibn Khordâdbeh, *Book of Routes*, ed. de Geoje, in *Bibl. Geog. Arab* (London 1899), IX, 114-16.

[31] Angelbertus, *Gesta Abb. Fontanellensium*, in *MGH, Script. rer. in usum scholarum*, II, p. 53.

[32] *Vita Willelmi duces et monarchi gellonensis*, in *Acta Sanct. Boll. Saec.*, IV, 82. See E. Sabbe, "L'Importation des tissus orientaux en Europe occidentale," in *Revue belge*, XIV (1935), 813-23, for a full discussion of this trade in Carolingian times.

[33] On this defense system, see C. de la Roncière, "Charlemagne et la civilisation maritime au IXe siècle," in *Le Moyen Age*, XI (Paris 1897), 131-52.

[34] On naval actions by the Carolingians off these coasts, see A. R. Lewis, *Naval Power and Trade*, pp. 103-6. The Carolingian fleet stayed active until about 830, for in 825 an expedition was sent against Corsica. *Capitula de expeditione corsicana*, in *Capit. regum. Franc.*, ed. Boretus, I, 325.

[35] E. Gariel, *op.cit.*, pp. 60-64.

route north to the Channel and the Rhine is illustrated by 8 silver pennies from Vienne, 7 from Bourges, 4 from Sens, 13 from Paris, 3 from Rouen, 4 from Reims, one from Trier and 3 from Dorestad.[36] Thus we can see in these coin hoards certain evidence of a traffic extending, in the early ninth century, from the north all the way to Spain. This route, our sources tell us, was used particularly by merchants who took slaves south from Verdun to sell in Moorish slave marts.[37]

The information which these hoards provide about a revived Midi trade to the north from Spain is not, however, all that we learn from them. For they both contain another interesting group of coins including some coming from Italy. About one-half of the large Veuillen treasure consists of Italian silver money from three mints and only three: 47 coins from Milan, 26 from Pavia and 195 from Venice. At Belvezet are found 17 silver pieces from Milan and 34 minted at Pavia. Thus another important route, that reaching Central France and even the Midi via the passes of the upper Maritime Alps, the *clusae* of Mount Geneva and the Little St. Bernard, is illustrated by these hoards. And here we note another important point. Not a single coin from the Mediterranean coast between Marseilles and the Tiber is to be found in either of these hoards, nor a single one from Byzantine Italy or Sicily. Lest this be thought accidental, another small hoard found near Luni and dating from this period proves the contrary. This hoard includes a large number of silver coins from various Italian mints, and four from beyond the Alps. They are from Tours, Sens, Mainz and Dorestad.[38] Such coins must have reached Luni via the *clusae* of the Alps, since not a single coin of the Midi is represented here at all. What we find, then, is this. Some commerce reached Northern and Central Gaul via certain Alpine passes leading to Venice and also to Luni. Another commercial route reached Spain by way of the Rhone valley and the Narbonnaise. But there was *no* commerce between the ports of the Midi and either Italian coasts or more

---

[36] *Ibid.*, pp. 65-67.

[37] *Mirac. S. Bertiniani*, in *Acta Sanct. Boll.*, Sept., II, 597.

[38] This hoard at Sarzana, described in Gariel, *op.cit.*, pp. 58-59, is among the most significant he mentions. It illustrates that the Via Francigena rather than the Ligurian coastal road was the one in use in this part of Italy and that it was by way of this road that goods reached Luni (*not* Genoa) from Northern Europe beyond the Alps and from the Po valley. On this route, see R. S. Lopez, "Aux origines du capitalisme genois," in *Ann. d'hist. écon. et sociale*, VI, 430-31. On its significance, see A. R. Lewis, *op.cit.*, pp. 92-93. It is worth noting also that in this period the southern passes in the Maritime Alps between France and Italy were not used. The *clusae* were farther north. G. G. Dept, "Le Mot clusae dans les diplômes carolingiens," in *Mélanges Pirenne*, I, 92-96.

Oriental regions. Thus commerce between these ports of Southern France and the East, so vital in Merovingian times and still found as late as 737, when the Cimiez hoard was interred, no longer existed. Only a Mediterranean trade to Spain linked this coast with the Orient.[39]

This revived economic life in Gaul, however, extended beyond the Rhone valley and the Narbonnaise to the valleys of the Garonne and the Loire, and to the coasts of Western France. Again this is revealed by numismatic evidence. As already noted, at the time of Pippin only four centers were still minting coins in Western Gaul: Tours on the Loire, Clermont in the Massif Central, and Poitiers and Brioux in Poitou—these last two, no doubt, being stimulated by the nearby silver mines of Melle. Yet later, in Charlemagne's reign, we find the old ports and *civitates* of this Atlantic region sufficiently revived so that Avranches and Rennes in Brittany, Bourges, Orléans and Nantes along the Loire, Limoges, St. Maixent, Melle, Angoulême and Saintes in Aquitaine, and Agen and Toulouse along the Garonne all possess mints. To them, the mints of Bordeaux and Dax near the Spanish border were added during the reign of Louis the Pious.[40]

What the revival of these mints seems to show is a renewed traffic upon rivers reaching the Atlantic in this period: Orléans, Bourges, Tours and Nantes illustrating Loire trade; St. Maixent's commerce from Poitiers reaching the ocean via the Sèvre and Niortaise; Angoulême and Saintes showing that economic life was being revived upon the Charente; and Toulouse, Agen and Bordeaux representing trade along the Garonne. Dax, near the Spanish border, and Avranches on the Channel round out the picture.

Our two vital coin hoards of Veuillen and Belvezet provide us with additional information concerning the commerce of these regions. At Belvezet certain coins, one from Nantes and seven from Bourges, suggest a commerce reaching the lower Rhone from the Loire valley, while another route reaching the lower Garonne is illustrated by 11 coins from Melle, 4 from Toulouse and 5 from Bordeaux. That of Veuillen is perhaps more significant. It contains 20 silver pennies

---

[39] On the scant use of ports of Provence in this period, see F. Ganshof, "Note sur les ports de Provence du VIIIᵉ au Xᵉ siècles," in *Revue hist.*, CLXXXIII (1931), 108-13. Contrast this with the activity of ports in the Narbonnaise trading with Spain. A. Dupont, *Les Cités de la Narbonnaise première*, pp. 215-68, and, for a later period, his *Les Relations commerciales entre les cités maritimes de Languedoc et les cites méditerranées d'Espagne et d'Italie du Xᵉ au XIIIᵉ siècles* (Nîmes 1942), pp. 1-138.

[40] M. Prou, *op.cit.*, pp. C-CIII. E. Gariel, *op.cit.*, pp. 60-64.

from Tours, 15 from Bordeaux, 5 from Dax and 2 from Toulouse. Trade from the west and southwest reaching Central and Southern Gaul by both land and river routes is thus indicated.[41]

To this coin evidence we must add information from our sources which similarly shows commercial activity upon the rivers of Western Gaul, especially on the Loire, in the years of the early ninth century. In 834, for example, a charter of Pepin I of Aquitaine gave the Abbey of St. Martin of Tours the right to circulate two ships upon all the rivers of Aquitaine without paying tolls. This charter specifies the Loire, Cher and Vienne in particular as those rivers referred to.[42] By 847 we find that the same general right to navigate freely on rivers in this region had been extended to the Abbey of St. Florentius.[43] Another charter, one granted by Louis the Pious in 834, gave to the monks of St. Mesmer a freedom from tolls at their *portus* on the river Tensu.[44] The commerce of the region helps to explain references to a Jewish colony at Bordeaux in 810 and 848,[45] and contemporary accounts which speak of Nantes and Poitiers as urban centers of some importance during these years.[46]

In addition to this river commerce, we have certain indications that maritime traffic had also revived along West Gallic shores by the reign of Louis the Pious. Such a maritime revival would partly explain why the Spanish Christian kingdom of León, in the early ninth century, had such close political relations with Carolingian monarchs, and why we find such close connections between the coinage and architecture of Galicia and Frankish Gaul during these years.[47] But certainly the best proof of a maritime revival along these shores comes from the fact that Louis the Pious was able to construct ships, and organize naval units at the mouths of the Garonne and Loire, to protect these coasts from the attacks of Norse Viking

[41] E. Gariel, *op.cit.*, pp. 60-67.
[42] *Recueil des actes de Pepin I et II*, ed. Levillain (Paris 1926), p. 61.
[43] *Ibid.*, p. 214.
[44] *Ibid.*, p. 78.
[45] L. Auzias, *L'Aquitaine carolingienne*, p. 248.
[46] J. W. Thompson, "The Commerce of France in the Ninth Century," in *Jour. of Pol. Economy*, XXIII (1915), 863-65.
[47] M. Defourneaux, "Charlemagne et la monarchie asturienne," in *Mélanges Louis Halphen*, pp. 177-84. On the similarity between Asturian money and the Carolingian coinage, especially the *solidi gallicanos* found in Galicia, see C. Sanchez-Albornoz, "La primitiva organización monetaria de León y Castilla," *loc.cit.*, pp. 296-310, and *Estampas de la vida en León*, p. 38. On the economic revival which took place in this part of Spain after 786 and especially in the early 9th century, P. David, *Etudes historiques sur la Galicie et le Portugal*, pp. 30-88. Note that this revival seems to parallel that of Southwestern Gaul.

pirates.[48] Already, then, in the early ninth century, the shores of Western Gaul and Northern Spain, connected again by commerce to Central Gaul and the Mediterranean, had regained something of the prosperity which had been lost in the disastrous years of the early eighth century.

This revival of commerce and maritime traffic, as evidenced along the coasts of Aquitaine, was even more marked during the first years of the ninth century along the Frankish side of the Channel, and farther north in the Netherlands. Here we have already noted the reappearance of Avranches as a place where coins were minted, and therefore of some economic importance.[49] In the region between the Seine and the Rhine, however, there is indication of much more activity of an economic sort. Here, in the heartland of the Carolingian state, revived Merovingian ports and new trading centers became active along the rivers leading into the Channel and the North Sea. On the route up the Canche from Quentovic there were now two other urban centers, Arras and Montreuil-sur-Mer.[50] On the Scheldt were now found a whole series of ports: Cambrai, Valenciennes, Condé, Tournai and Ghent.[51] To the Merovingian trading centers of Dinant, Namur, Huy and Maastricht, now reviving, was added Liege, a new Carolingian foundation.[52] Along the Rhine, there were signs of economic life at Strasbourg, Worms, Mainz, Bonn and Cologne and, nearer its mouths, at Dorestad and Utrecht.[53] The urban conglomerations existing in Merovingian times in this part of Europe thus were

[48] F. Ganshof, in Lot, Pfister and Ganshof, *Les Destinées de l'empire de l'Occident*, p. 468. C. de la Roncière, "Charlemagne et la civilisation maritime," *loc.cit.*, pp. 103-31.

[49] Charlemagne struck money here early in his reign, between 768 and 781. M. Prou, *op.cit.*, pp. C-CIII.

[50] On Montreuil-sur-Mer, see J. Lestoquoy, "Les Origines de Montreuil-sur-Mer," in *Revue du Nord*, XXI (1948), 185-88. Arras had a mint where coins were minted between 768 and 781. M. Prou, *op.cit.*, pp. C-CII.

[51] On these trading places, or *wicks*, see the admirable survey of their development in F. L. Ganshof, "Het Tijdperk van de Karolingen," in *Algamene Geschiedenis der Nederlanden*, II, 350-51. See also R. Doehaerd, *op.cit.*, pp. 18-20, and F. Vercauteren, *Belgique Secunde*, pp. 451-56. Judging from mints in operation, the trading places on the Scheldt were more active in Carolingian times than in Merovingian. M. Prou, *op.cit.*, pp. LXXXIV-CIV.

[52] F. Rousseau, *La Meuse*, pp. 52-66. R. Doehaerd, *op.cit.*, pp. 16-23, and F. L. Ganshof, *op.cit.*, pp. 315-52, contain admirable summaries. On mints here, see not only Prou, but A. Blanchet and A. Dieudonné, *Manuel de numismatique française*, III, 367-401.

[53] F. Rousseau, *op.cit.*, pp. 54-65. On Dorestad, the most important trading place in the region, see J. H. Holwerda, *Dorestad en onze vroegste middel eeuwen* (Leyden 1942), pp. 103-77. On Utrecht, W. Vogel, "Wikorte und Wikinger," in *Hansische Geschichts blätter*, LX (1935), 215-31. On mints, M. Prou, *op.cit.*, pp. LXXXIX-CIII.

equaled and even surpassed during the reign of Louis the Pious. But one notices a subtle difference. In Merovingian times the economic center of the Frankish state lay in Central Gaul, with Aquitaine almost as important, and both regions were linked to the Mediterranean by way of the Rhone. Now, in Carolingian times, despite the existence of urban centers in the valleys of the Loire, Rhone and Garonne—the older Merovingian heartland—the center of the Frankish Empire's economic life had moved north and east towards the Scheldt, the Meuse, the Rhine and the North Sea. This region, connected with Italy rather than with the French Midi, was to remain Northern Europe's economic center for many centuries to come.

One might ponder, at this point, the role of commerce from the Mediterranean which, as we have seen, reached the Carolingian heartland between the Seine and the Rhine by way of Italy and Moslem Spain. Was it a significant factor in the Empire's economy at the time of Charlemagne and Louis the Pious? The political policies of the Carolingians help to give an answer to this question, for they show an interest in and expansion towards these two sources of Mediterranean trade wealth on the part of these rulers. Charlemagne, for example, not only annexed the Lombard kingdom of Northern Italy early in his reign, but also attempted, almost until his death in 814, to add Venice to his Empire and thus gain possession of this great trading city, whose commerce reached Byzantium and so much of the Moslem East.[54] Equally far west, his seizure of the Spanish March from the Emirs of Cordova, and his campaigns and those of his son, Louis, along the coasts of the Narbonnaise and Catalonia, show he was aware of the value to his Empire of this region whence Eastern wares could be procured.[55] There also seems to be no doubt, as Sabbe has clearly shown, that both spices and silk from the Orient reached Gaul and the Rhinelands without any great difficulty during these years. So much was this the case that at Cambrai such spices could be easily purchased, and throughout the Empire, Eastern silks were often worn by men and women of the court and the Frankish aristocracy. Nor can we doubt that the arms, furs and slaves which Jewish and Moslem merchants carried to Spanish trading centers were, like the slaves, timber, arms and metals reaching Venice and

[54] A. R. Lewis, op.cit., pp. 106-11. R. Cessi, Venezia Ducale, I, 31-33.
[55] E. Lévi-Provençale, Histoire de l'Espagne mussulmane (Cairo 1944), pp. 175-78. F. W. Buckler, Harunu'l-Raschid and Charles the Great (Cambridge, Mass., 1931), pp. 18-134.

the Po valley from the north, a significant element in Carolingian economic life.[56]

But it should be emphasized that such commerce was limited by a number of factors, even during the reign of Louis the Pious, when it was probably most important. Commerce with Italy suffered from the fact that it had to be carried on via Alpine passes, which were blocked by snow a good part of the year, and which furthermore made a commerce in *bulk* impossible. In addition, it seems probable that the silver coinages of the Carolingian state hampered trade with this part of Italy and the Mediterranean East, where a gold-standard *dinar* and a *nomisma* currency prevailed.[57] Trade with Moslem Spain gained from the fact that, though Spain was not particularly prosperous during these years, this part of the Mediterranean was, like the Carolingian Empire, on a silver standard, and thus no money difficulties existed. The limited urbanization of Spain and restricted trade with the Orient allowed Spain to serve as a middleman between the Carolingians and the Eastern Mediterranean, and to ship spices and silks north, but such trade could not be developed to any great extent.[58]

As a result, during the period 750-840, trade with the Mediterranean world via Italy and Spain increased until the the last years of Louis the Pious. It did link the Carolingian heartland with the Orient and provide the Empire with needed Eastern wares. But such commerce was limited and less important than some historians seem to believe. The economy of the Carolingian state, like that of its Late Merovingian predecessors, faced the Northern Seas and depended, for its growth and being, upon the lands of Northern Europe, not those which were washed by the blue waters of the Mediterranean.

If we cannot ascribe more than a small portion of the Carolingian economic revival to trade connections with the Mediterranean area, we must look elsewhere for its impetus. Certainly both the revival of old ports along the rivers leading to the North Sea, Channel and Atlantic and the establishment of new ones owed something to the revived industries of the regions in which they were located. This is particularly true of the area between Seine and Rhine where, in Late Roman and Merovingian times, the heaviest industrial concentration

[56] E. Sabbe, "L'Importation des tissus," *loc.cit.*, pp. 813-21.

[57] Carolingian Italy was part of the Mediterranean gold area—and in part also it was bi-metallic as far as coinage was concerned. On the gold coinage struck by Charlemagne in North Italy, see F. Jecklin, "Der langobardisch-karolingisch Münzfund bei Ilanz," in *Mitteil. der Bayer. Num. Gesellschaft*, xxv (1906-7).

[58] E. Lévi-Provençale, *L'Espagne mussulmane*, pp. 113-67.

of Northern Europe was located. It remained true under the Carolingians, with this difference. Such industries began to move gradually north and east from their old Merovingian location. For instance, take the manufacture of glass. In the early ninth century, glass was produced, as previously, about Trier and along the upper Meuse, but its principal center now seems to have been the Rhinelands. Furthermore, this Carolingian glass was different in style and type from that which the Merovingians produced. It had a potassium rather than sodium content, and thus contained none of the Mediterranean natron which had been imported in the sixth and seventh centuries and had given the glass of that period its distinctive chemical structure.[59]

To the new glass industry of the Rhinelands an important pottery product was added, Badorf ware, which was manufactured around Cologne and was probably copied in both the Dorestad region on the lower Rhine and in Eastern England.[60] This Badorf ware was exported in large amounts and has been found plentifully in archeological sites as far away as Hedeby and Birka.[61] It seems to have been used as a container for the wine and perhaps the wheat exported from this part of the Empire.

Even more vital than these two industries, however, was the iron industry of this region. Now, in addition to older centers along the Meuse, the Rhinelands too began to manufacture those fine pattern-welded Frankish swords, famous for their temper and quality, and other arms as well. These specialized products found a ready market in England, Scandinavia, the Baltic and Central Europe[62] and were renowned as far away as Bagdad and Central Asia.[63] Equally important was the bronze and brass industry of the Meuse valley around Dinant, Huy and Liége.[64] This industry furnishes a particularly important insight as to the ease of trade in these years, because though zinc

[59] J. Steinhausen, "Früh mittelalterlich Glasshütten im Trierland," in *Trierer Zeitschrift*, IX (1939), 151-63. H. Arbman, *Schweden und das Karolingisch Reich* (Stockholm 1937), pp. 252-53.

[60] F. Rodemacher, *Karolingische Keramik am Niederrhein* (Vienna 1927), pp. 11-91. F. Fishler, "Frühmittelalterlich aus Duisburg," in *Germania*, XXVIII (1950), 180-84.

[61] H. Jankuhn, "Probleme des reinischen Handels nach Skandinavien," in *Reinische Viertel.*, XV-XVI (1950-51), 131-52, 289-97. H. Arbman, *op.cit.*, pp. 87-115.

[62] H. Jankuhn, "Ein Ulfberht Schwert aus der Elbe bei Hamburg," in *Festschrift Schwantes* (Hamburg 1950), pp. 213-23.

[63] On these Frankish swords taken by Rus merchants to Bagdad, see Ibn Khordâdbeh, *Book of Routes*, ed. de Geoje, pp. 114-16.

[64] F. Rousseau, *La Meuse*, pp. 110-21.

was mined along the Meuse, the other two principal metals used in this ware—copper and tin—had to be brought to this region from other areas of Europe. Probably the tin came from Cornwall and the copper from mines in Saxony.

Even more interesting is the development in this region of a textile industry which produced the famous Frisian cloth. Again, as in the case of the glass, iron and pottery industries, we notice a change in the area where this cloth was manufactured. The finest varieties—the red and blue types—were produced around Boulogne or in and around the newly rising ports along the river Scheldt in Flanders. Some of the coarser varieties, however, were probably woven in Frisia and in certain North German centers like the monastery of Corvey. The name "Frisian cloth," then, does not mean it was a Frisian product, but rather that it was one of the most important wares handled by the active Frisian merchants of the period.[65] These *pallia fresonica* were, incidentally, as famous in the ninth century as the Frankish swords of the Rhinelands. Louis the Pious sent the cloth as a present to the Abbassid rulers of Bagdad,[66] and it has been found in graves of the early ninth century which have been excavated at Birka.[67] It was widely prized inside Carolingian domains as well.[68]

Mining was also an important industry in this part of the Carolingian Empire by the ninth century. The iron mines along the Rhine and Meuse which produced the metal used in the manufacturing of arms were steadily exploited, as were the zinc mines of the Ardennes.[69] Beyond the Rhine, no mineral wealth seems to have been exploited except the copper mines of Saxony. Thus the abundant lead used to roof Carolingian churches of the region, and the silver used in the coinage, must have come from deposits worked in England

[65] H. Pirenne, "Draps de Frise ou draps de Flandre?" in *Viert. für Soz- und Wirtschaft*, VII (1909), 308-37. P. Kletler, *Nordwesteuropas Verkehr*, pp. 109-15. H. Laurent, *La Draperie des Pays Bas en France et dans les Pays Méditerranés* (Paris 1935), pp. 29-37. E. Sabbe, "L'Importation des tissus," *loc.cit.*, p. 832.

[66] R. Doehaerd, *L'Expansion économique belge*, pp. 18-19.

[67] A. Geijer, *Birka*, III, 22-47.

[68] For instance, in Alsace, where Frisian merchants traded it for wine. C. Verlinden, "L'Etat économique de l'Alsace sous Louis le Pieux d'après Ernold le Noir," in *Revue belge*, IX (1934), 217-34.

[69] *Capit. de Villis*, Art. 62, in *MGH Leges*, I, 186. A. Peltzer, *Ländern zwischen Maas und Rhein von der Römerzeit* (Aachen 1904), pp. 32-51. F. Rousseau, *La Meuse*, pp. 100-118. R. Doehaerd, *op.cit.*, pp. 19-20.

and Western France.[70] The salt of Alsace, however, was produced in large enough amounts to serve as an export article.[71]

Such industrial growth was not confined to the Carolingian heartland, important though it was. In Western Gaul, the mines of Melle never ceased their production of lead and silver during these years, though we know less of the history of this industry than we would like to know.[72] Salt, of the coarse maritime sort so prized for curing fish, also continued, it seems, to be produced in the salt pans of the Saintogne region and on the island of Noirmoutier.[73] The iron industry of the upper Loire near Bourges and that of Normandy were producing metal in this period, though probably to meet needs which were largely local in character.[74]

Similarly, farther east along the upper Danube, we find industry of some importance. Here, the mining of iron and the manufacture of arms, important since Roman times, continued under the Carolingians in the mountains of the Austrian and Bavarian Alps. Certainly a portion of the arms which were exported to the Slavs of Central Europe and which reached Venice during these years came from these Alpine workshops.[75] Interesting, too, is the production in this region of a distinctive pottery which was sent north as far as the Baltic.[76] Also busy were the great salt mines of Salzburg, whose production reached a wide market.[77] Such industrial activity helps to explain the importance of centers like Regensburg on the upper Danube which grew steadily throughout this period and which began to match the trading places along the Rhine, Meuse and Scheldt in economic activity.[78]

[70] H. Van Werweke, "Note sur le commerce de plomb au moyen âge," in *Mélanges Pirenne*, II, 508-11. R. Doehaerd, *op.cit.*, p. 20. F. Rousseau, *op.cit.*, pp. 112-19.

[71] A. Dopsch, *Die Wirtschaftsentwicklung der Karolingerzeit*, II (Vienna 1924), 176-77. L. Halphen, *Etudes critiques sur Charlemagne*, pp. 281-82.

[72] A. Blanchet and A. Dieudonné, *Manuel de numismatique*, IV, 334-36.

[73] H. Hauser, *Le Sel dans l'histoire*, pp. 275-77.

[74] O. Davies, *Roman Mines in Europe*, pp. 87-93. It is worth noting that it was not until the late 8th century that the Paris region produced, according to Salin, fine iron belt-buckles. E. Salin, *Le Fer à l'époque mérovingienne*, pp. 173-87.

[75] On this trade in iron and timber which reached Venice in the early 9th century and which the Byzantine Emperor Leo V tried to keep from going to Moslem ports, see A. R. Lewis, *op.cit.*, p. 116. See also H. Oehlmann, "Die Alpenpasse im Mittelalter," in *Jahrbuch für Schweizische Geschichte*, III, 246-49.

[76] H. Arbman, *Schweden und das Karolingisch Reich*, pp. 110-14.

[77] H. Hauser, *op.cit.*, pp. 275-77. A. Dopsch, *Die Wirtschaftsentwicklung*, I, 176-77.

[78] A. Dopsch, *The Economic and Social Foundations of European Civilization*, p. 315.

Connected with this revived and new industrial production and urbanization in the northern portion of Charlemagne's Empire was agriculture. The clearing of the forest, draining of swamp and polder and the introduction of better agricultural methods, which we have noted as starting in the seventh century under the Merovingians, began again in the late eighth and ninth centuries. In Flanders, and along the Meuse, new lands were put into cultivation under Charlemagne and Louis the Pious.[79] In the Seine valley a similar movement was under way, as we know from the full account contained in the precious early ninth-century *Polyptype of Abbot Irminon*. This speaks of new agricultural settlements, or *assarts*, hacked out of the forest by peasant *hospes*, or colonists, and the introduction and use in the region of the horse collar, the deep plow and the three-field system.[80]

Farther south in the Midi, during the reign of Louis the Pious, we find similar evidence of agricultural revival. This region, which had been so badly devastated in the wars and invasions of the eighth century, began to be transformed by Spanish Christian refugee colonists, who were given land there by the Carolingian government. Also active were abbeys like Aniane and Gellone, which established agricultural *cellae*, or settlements, of peasant *hospes* not unlike those described in the *Polyptype of Abbot Irminon*.[81] Perhaps a similar agricultural change also was taking place in the Garonne and Loire valleys during these years, though our information is too scanty to allow us to do more than speculate upon this possibility. The expanded activity of the monasteries of these areas of France, already noted, may also have included agricultural clearing and settlement. We must await further studies on this subject, however, before passing any final judgments.

It is not, however, the development of agriculture in Western Frankish domains but that to the east which seems the more important by the early ninth century. Work begun in Merovingian times in clearing the brush of Brabant and diking the lowlands of Flanders and Holland continued and expanded. But even more significant is

[79] G. des Marez, *Le problème de la colonisation franque*, pp. 60-78, 162-63. B. Slicher van Bath, *Mensch en land in de Middeleeuwen*, II, 98-104, and "Dutch Tribal Problems," *loc.cit.*, pp. 320-24.

[80] On the *Polyptype of Abbot Irminon*, see M. Bloch, "Les Invasions: occupation du sol et peuplement," in *Ann. d'hist. sociale*, II (1946), 20-34, and *Les Caractères originaux de l'histoire rurale française*, pp. 31-57. See also C. Parain, *The Evolution of Agricultural Technique*, pp. 127-41.

[81] Imbart de la Tour, "Les Colonies agricoles et l'occupation des terres désertes à l'époque carolingienne" in *Mélanges Paul Fabre* (Paris 1902), pp. 301-16.

the fact that it was extended down the Rhine and to the east. On both sides of the central Rhine valley, in Hesse, along the lower Moselle, in Luxembourg, in Alsace, and along the river Maine, the first real clearing of the primeval German forest was attempted. New agricultural settlements were established in these forest lands and encouraged by nobility, churchmen and Carolingian rulers alike. We also find this movement spreading along the upper Danube, and German colonists moved down the river valleys towards Hungary. Though this movement was, in general, confined to the Rhine and Danube valleys and those of their tributaries, it affected some other parts of Central and Eastern Germany, too. New monastic foundations on the upper Weser and Elbe, like Corvey and Gandersheim, also began to introduce into these regions, newly won from the Saxons, more advanced agrarian practices. By 800, the Rhine river line, which since Roman days had separated the more advanced West from the more primitive area of Central and Eastern Germany, was being breached by the beginnings of an agricultural advance that linked this area to the more cultivated portions of the Carolingian world.[82]

Two interesting examples of agricultural development in Germany show what was happening as a result of these agrarian changes. One is the spread of the culture of the vine. In Roman and Merovingian times grapes were grown and wine produced in the Moselle valley, but there is no evidence of their being introduced elsewhere. Now we find wine culture spreading rapidly into Alsace, into the Rhinelands, and even into Franconia and the valleys of the Bavarian Alps.[83] Similarly, wheat had not in Roman times been one of Germany's major crops. Now, with new lands cleared for agriculture, we suddenly find it grown on such a large scale in Franconia that a surplus was available for export.[84] One must not, of course, magnify such beginnings into too optimistic a picture of Carolingian agricultural growth in Germany or elsewhere in the Empire. But it does seem clear that some of the large-scale clearing of brush and forest, draining of swampland and fenland, diking of polders, introduction and spread of the horse collar, deep plow and three-field system which took place in

[82] A. Dopsch, *Die Wirtschaftsentwicklung der Karolingerzeit*, Vols. I-II, is the fundamental work on this agricultural advance. See also the excellent summary of Koebner in "The Settlement and Colonization of Europe," in *Cambridge Economic History of Europe*, I, 41-51.

[83] C. Parain, *op.cit.*, pp. 59-60.

[84] Einhard, *Trans. et miracula SS Marcellini et Petri*, in *MGH Script.*, XV, 250. E. Sabbe, "Quelques types de marchands," in *Revue belge*, XIII (1934), 182-83.

Northern Europe under the aegis of these Carolingian rulers probably laid the basis for improvements in the centuries to come.

Along maritime coasts, stretching from the Rhine to the Pyrenees, the revival of urban centers, industry and the new agricultural advances which marked this Carolingian era resulted by the first years of the ninth century in a renewed commerce upon the Northern Seas. This was true even in Northwestern Spain, where simultaneously repopulation of waste lands was taking place in León and bishoprics were being reorganized in Galicia. The similarities in money between this region and Gaul suggest that trade was also gradually reviving along North Spanish coasts in the same manner as along the shores of Aquitaine.[85]

But those who benefited most from this renaissance of commercial traffic were the Frisians, whose location near the mouths of the Rhine and Scheldt enabled them to take advantage of the commerce that developed more heavily here than elsewhere along Carolingian coasts. We have already noted that, as early as the middle of the eighth century, they had replaced Anglo-Saxon merchants and mariners as the chief traders of the Northern Seas, extending their commerce down the Rhine to Worms, down the Meuse to Maastricht and down the Seine to the Fair of St. Denis. Their colony of merchants located at York, and their *schola* at Rome, show that their interests extended to English coasts and even reached faraway Italy before 800.

After 800 there is evidence that these Frisian merchants extended their influence still farther west to the Loire river valley and Aquitaine and perhaps even to the Midi. First, we have the testimony of the Monk of St. Gall, who tells us that Charlemagne forbade the Frisians to export their cloth to Gaul late in his reign.[86] Second, during the reign of Louis the Pious, mention is made of a cargo of olive oil being sent *up* the Rhine.[87] Such a cargo could only have arrived there by sea from Western Gaul, like that which in Merovingian times St. Filibert sent from Bordeaux to the Seine. To these scraps of information numismatic material adds further proof of a maritime traffic reaching Frisia from Aquitaine. Near Nantes, at the entrance of the Loire,

[85] C. Sanchez-Albornoz, *Estampas de la vida en León*, pp. 8-10. On money, see C. Sanchez-Albornoz, "Primitiva organización monetaria de Léon y Castilla," *loc.cit.*, pp. 302-10. J. B. Mahn in "Le Clergé séculier à l'époque asturienne," in *Mélanges Louis Halphen*, pp. 53-64, stresses the monastic element in this land clearing in Galicia.

[86] Mon. S. Gall, *De gest. Caroli Magni*, I, 34, in *MGH Script.*, II, 747.

[87] *Miracula Wandalberti S. Goaris*, in *ibid.*, XV, 368.

have been discovered two gold *solidi* of a type copied in Frisia, prior to 840, from those issued by Louis the Pious. Near Aclum on the Frisian coast in a coin hoard dating from about 840 is a coin of Pepin I of Aquitaine,[88] while similar Aquitainian money is found in a whole series of hoards of this period at Oudwarden, Pingjum, Aalsum, Emmen, and Midlaren nearby.[89] When one also takes into account the fact that the earlier Belvezet hoard on the lower Rhine and the Veuillen hoard on the Loire both contain a number of coins from Dorestad, one becomes aware that trade between the Netherlands and western French coasts must have been considerable—in startling contrast to its rarity in the Merovingian period.[90] The ubiquitous Frisians were now apparently extending their trading interests into areas where earlier they had not penetrated. Nor did they neglect their interests in the North Sea in doing so. For Yorkshire in the ninth century, as in the eighth, continued to lie in their zone of trade, as revealed by the fact that it was the Frisian gold *solidi* of Louis the Pious which served as the model for those gold pennies which Archbishop Wigam of York minted during these years.[91] The Frisians, along the coasts of France, in the North Sea and stretching up to Scandinavia, were the main beneficiaries of the revived commercial traffic on the Northern Seas during the reign of Louis the Pious.

If the Frisians tended in this period to overshadow their earlier rivals, the Anglo-Saxons, as merchant intermediaries along Gallic coasts and in the North Sea, they by no means eliminated them from such commerce. Frisian commercial dominance was greatest in the North Sea and along trade routes leading to the Baltic. Here we find no indication at all of Anglo-Saxon commercial penetration in the Carolingian period. And when we consider the bronze *styka* coinage of Yorkshire and evidence of Frisian economic penetration there, we may consider that it, too, lay in Frisia's commercial sphere.

Farther south in the English Channel and beyond, however, this was much less true. Here a large proportion of the trade between the Carolingian Empire and England was still in the hands of Anglo-Saxon merchants. We know, for instance, that in 753 they were still

[88] P. Grierson, "The Gold Coinage of Louis the Pious and Its Imitations," in *Jaarboek voor Munt-en Penningkunde*, XXXVIII (1951), 211-31.

[89] P. Boeles, "Les Trouvailles de monnaies carolingiennes dans les Pays Bas, spécialement celles des trois provinces septentrionales," in *ibid.*, II (1915), 10-82.

[90] E. Gariel, *op.cit.*, pp. 40-71.

[91] P. Grierson, *op.cit.*, pp. 223-28. G. C. Brooke, *English Coins*, pp. 8-12.

going to the Fair of St. Denis,[92] while the complex trade negotiations between Offa and Charlemagne, in the last years of this century, reveal that they were still exporting English cloth to France. As a result of these negotiations, Anglo-Saxon traders even received a privileged position in Frankish domains, both their persons and their goods being given the Emperor's special protection while they were within his realm.[93] In this period, as earlier, Quentovic seems to have been the most important entrepôt for English travel and trade with Continent.[94]

It seems probable that by the early ninth century England's trade contacts with the Continent multiplied, as the general economic tenor of life quickened on both sides of the Channel. It was probably English ships which transported tin and wine to Yorkshire for Alcuin.[95] Anglo-Saxon vessels were used to carry lead from England to Rouen for a French monastery in 810[96] and a few years later carried a similar cargo to Quentovic (Etaples) for Lupus of Ferrières. Probably, too, we may assume that English mariners brought to Gaul the English cloth purchased by the Abbey of St. Bertin in 800.[97] As late as 841, English merchants were certainly active in trade on the Seine, where their presence is mentioned by Nithard.[98] And the tin of Cornwall, which found a Continental market, seems also from coin hoard evidence to have been handled and shipped by Anglo-Saxon rather than foreign merchants.[99] Nor did all trade with the Rhinelands cease. One coin hoard at Grisons, for instance, contains three English pennies of Egbert of Kent and Offa of Mercia,[100] suggesting that contacts with England were still maintained in this region, where *sceatta* finds of the seventh century had been so common.

We also learn from our sources that there was a resumption in the ninth century of trade in English ships to western Gallic coasts, for

[92] MGH Diplom. Karol., I, 43. J. Levillain, Etudes sur l'abbaye de Saint-Denis, pp. 108-211.
[93] W. Levison, England and the Continent, pp. 108-31. Alcuin, Epistolae, in MGH Epist. Karol. aevi, II, 144.
[94] E. Sabbe, "Les Relations entre l'Angleterre et le continent au Haut Moyen Age," in Le Moyen Age, LVI (1950), 315-42. O. Fengler, "Quentovic," loc.cit., pp. 151-63.
[95] W. Levison, op.cit., p. 8. Alcuin, Epistolae, in MGH Epist. Karol. aevi, II, 226.
[96] MGH Formulae Merov. et Karol. aevi, p. 505.
[97] Lupus of Ferrières, in MGH Epistolae, III, 50.
[98] B. Guerard, Cartulaire de l'abbaye de Saint Bertin (Paris 1877), p. 65.
[99] Coin hoards in Cornwall dating from the 9th century consist almost exclusively of Anglo-Saxon coins. H. O. Hencken, The Archeology of Cornwall, pp. 262-63.
[100] A. Luschin von Ebengreuth, "Beiträge zur Münzgeschichte im Frankreich I," in Neuss. Archiv., XXXIII (1908), 440.

we find English merchants mentioned as arriving at the island of Noirmoutier and at the two Loire ports of Furc and Conches.[101] The Monk of St. Gall confirms this by telling us of Anglo-Saxon traders at the mouths of the Loire at about the same period.[102] Perhaps it was this traffic which accounted for the Carolingian money in two coin hoards dating from the mid-ninth century that have been found in Cornwall: one at Trewhiddle, a penny struck by Louis the Pious;[103] and two in the Penard hoard, minted by Charlemagne and Lothair.[104] Some English merchants may have traveled farther along Atlantic Spanish coasts into the Mediterranean itself, for there is a suggestion of English ships at Narbonne and Marseilles during the last years of Charlemagne's reign.[105] Again numismatics provides us with some indirect evidence of contacts with Moslem lands, probably Spain, for late in the eighth century Offa coined a golden dinar, unique in British monetary history, that would have been useful in trade with the Moslem Mediterranean.[106] In general, evidence of economic activity during these years at Porchester in Devon, just across from Carolingian Avranches, in Cornwall and in the Bristol Channel near the old site of Caerwent seems to indicate that this region, close to western French coasts, was even more active than had been the case in Merovingian times.[107] In short, though the Frisians were the most important merchants of the Carolingian world, they did not completely replace the Anglo-Saxons, particularly in commerce which passed across the Channel and revived along the coasts of Western Gaul and Britain.

Evidence of an indirect nature of commercial contacts between England and the Carolingian Empire is even more conclusive. Earlier,

---

[101] *Ex emertairi miraculis S. Filiberti*, in *MGH Script.*, IV, 603.

[102] Mon. S. Gall, in *ibid.*, II, 731, 75.

[103] H. O. Hencken, *Archeology of Cornwall*, pp. 262-63. J. Rashleigh, "An Account of Anglo-Saxon Coins Found at Trewhiddle," in *Num. Chron.*, new ser., VIII (1868), 137-49.

[104] J. Allen, in *Num. Chron.*, VIII (1946), 236.

[105] Hucbaldus, *Vita Sancti Lebuini*, in *MGH Script.*, II, 757, and *Annales Petavini III*, in *ibid.*, XVII, 170.

[106] M. Bloch, "Le Problème de l'or au moyen âge" in *Ann. d'hist. ècon. et sociale*, V (1933), 15-31. F. Stenton, *Anglo-Saxon England*, pp. 232-33. G. C. Brooke, *English Coins*, pp. 41-50. Is this the *mancus* mentioned in *Cart. Saxon*, I, 409? In Galicia in 796 a charter mentions a *gold* dinar. *Cartulario de Santo Toribo de Liebano*, in *Bull. Acad. Hisp.* XLV (1923), 69.

[107] On Dorchester as a trading spot the later story of the first Viking raid there is revealing, since it mentions that the pirates were mistaken at first for traders and that Dorchester possessed a port-reeve. Florence of Worcester, *Chronicle*, ed. Thorpe (London 1848), I, 162.

in Merovingian times, English *sceatta* coinage seems to have served as the model for the silver deniers minted in France. In 755, 781 and 794 Pepin and Charlemagne reformed the coinage of their state, setting up each time a new basis for the weight of their silver pennies. Meanwhile the English coinage of the Heptarchy degenerated steadily, reaching its nadir in the *stykas* minted in Yorkshire. When Offa, in the last years of his reign, reformed English money, he directly copied the monetary system of Charlemagne, and this Carolingian standard was maintained by Egbert of Wessex when leadership of the Heptarchy passed to his state.[108] Thus England in this period, like the northern Christian kingdoms of Spain, followed the lead of the Carolingian Empire in its coinage system, while earlier it had been the other way around.

One other bit of evidence of a political sort may throw light upon the importance of this Carolingian commerce and its connection with the England of the late eighth and ninth centuries. When Offa became ruler of Mercia, his kingdom lay in the Midlands, far from the coasts which communicated with Carolingian shores. Offa, however, moved south to take control of London and Kent, which he added to his realm. But he never seems to have bothered with Northumbria. Can it be that the riches which London's and Kent's contacts with the Continent made available to him were their main attraction for him?[109] It seems very possible. And when he died, it was Wessex—of all the Anglo-Saxon kingdoms, the one closest to France—which took over political dominance of the Heptarchy, even adding Kent to its realm as well. Cannot we see here, too, the influence of the revived and advancing commerce and trade with Carolingian shores, playing a role in the Anglo-Saxon political scene?[110]

By Late Carolingian times England, linked to the Continent by a growing commerce, began to show other signs of recovery from the economic setbacks she had suffered in the mid-eighth century. In general, the economic centers which were active in Bede's time—London, Rochester, Canterbury, Hamwith and York—still remained the important ones. But we can begin to discern a certain shifting of gravity, in an economic sense, towards the western and southern parts

---

[108] On the reform of England's coinage, see W. Levison, *England and the Continent*, pp. 11-12, and G. C. Brooke, *English Coins*, pp. 29-31, 41-50. J. Tait, *The Medieval English Borough*, p. 11, and F. Stenton, *op.cit.*, pp. 225-53.

[109] On Mercia's expansion, see F. Stenton, *op.cit.*, pp. 205-7, and R. Hodgkin, *History of the Anglo-Saxons*, II, 387-88.

[110] F. Stenton, *Anglo-Saxon England*, pp. 230-41. R. Hodgkin, *op.cit.*, pp. 403-10.

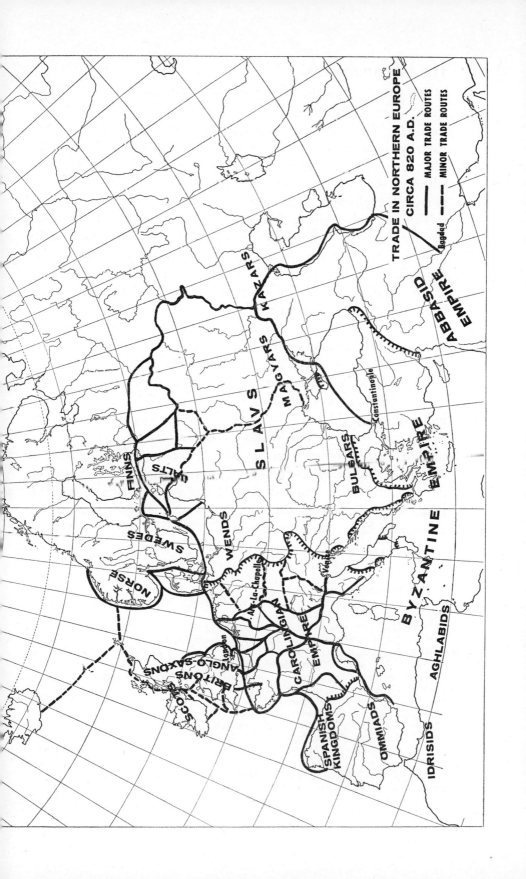

TRADE IN NORTHERN EUROPE
CIRCA 820 A.D.

MAJOR TRADE ROUTES
MINOR TRADE ROUTES

Baghdad

ABBASID
EMPIRE

KAZARS

SLAVS

MAGYARS

Constantinople

BULGARS

BYZANTINE EMPIRE

AGHLABIDS

IDRISIDS

FINNS

BALTS

SWEDES

WENDS

NORSE

Aix-la-Chapelle

Venice

CAROLINGIAN EMPIRE

BRITONS

ANGLO-SAXONS

SCOTS

SPANISH KINGDOMS

OMMIADS

of the island. Thus, in the Midlands, Offa's capital of Tamworth seems now to have reached the status of an urban center,[111] and some commercial life is apparent near Caerwent on the Bristol Channel.[112] Equally, in Wessex, the rise of Egbert's kingdom to Anglo-Saxon leadership suggests that this region was sharing more fully in an advanced economic life than had been the case earlier, particularly as regards exploitation of its mineral resources of tin and silver.[113]

This revived economic life was by the first years of the ninth century reflected in England's industrial development. One of its principal industries was the manufacture of cloth, as in Merovingian times. This was now a valued Anglo-Saxon export, as we know from the negotiations on this subject between Offa and Charlemagne,[114] and mention of its being exported across the Channel to the Abbey of St. Bertin in 800.[115] Probably as early as 800 these *pallia anglisca*, which rivaled the famous *pallia fresonica*, were prized in the commerce of the Northern Seas. We cannot be certain, however, just where this cloth was produced. The best guess, based on later evidence, would seem to be the eastern and southeastern area of Britain. To this cloth industry we should add iron production, centering, as of old, in the Forest of Dean and the Weald of Kent.[116] Silver and lead were produced now principally in the Mendips, though the operation of Flintshire and Derbyshire mines may have continued to some extent. Mendip production was undoubtedly the source of the lead which reached Carolingian Channel ports in these years, while Offa's silver coinage probably owed something to the production of Midland mines.[117] Tin, judging from coin hoards, was more actively exploited in Cornwall in the early ninth century than had been true earlier,[118]

[111] F. Stenton, *op.cit.*, p. 245.
[112] C. Fox, "The Boundary Line of the Cyrmni," in *Proceedings of the British Academy*, XXVI (1940), 281-82.
[113] O. Davies, *Roman Mines in Europe*, pp. 153-64.
[114] Alcuin, *Epistolae*, in *MGH Epist. Karol. aevi*, II, 144.
[115] B. Guerard, *Cart. de l'abbaye de Saint Bertin*, p. 65. Sabbe believes that the "Frisian" cloth of Carolingian times was of English origin. E. Sabbe, *Les Relations économiques entre l'Angleterre et le continent*, pp. 178-84. There seems no reason to doubt, however, that in this period, as later, *both* Frisian (or Flemish) cloth and English cloth were prized exports. On the difference between English cloth discovered at Whitby and that of Flanders found in graves at Birka, see J. W. Crowfoot, "A Textile from Whitby" in *Archeologia*, LXXXIX (1943), 87-88.
[116] L. Salzmann, *English Industries in the Middle Ages*, pp. 40-61.
[117] J. W. Gough, *The Mines in the Mendips*, pp. 40-49. H. Van Werweke, *Note sur le plomb*, pp. 655-58.
[118] O. Davies, *op.cit.*, pp. 141-45. H. O. Hencken, *The Archeology of Cornwall*, pp. 260-65.

and North Wales and Anglesey probably still produced valuable copper.[119] Some pottery continued to be made at Thetford in East Anglia.[120] Nor did the earlier tradition of fine jewelry and goldsmith's work, noticeable in Kent and East Anglia, disappear in Carolingian times, as we know from the splendid present of golden vessels sent to the Pope by the royal house of Wessex.[121] In general, however, the impression is given that England's level of industrial life was somewhat lower than that prevailing in the Carolingian Empire. Although important, English industry, like Anglo-Saxon maritime activity, was now playing a secondary role to that of the realms of Charlemagne and Louis the Pious. Similarly, we find few parallels between the agrarian growth of the Carolingian Empire and agricultural activities across the Channel in England. There is no evidence in Britain, for instance, of organized efforts to clear the forests by monastic establishments, nobility and rulers. What we do find is rather a slow steady pushing back of the primeval woods, and an occupation of the heavier bottom lands of Wessex and certain other areas of the Midlands and Western Britain.[122] Advances in the field of agriculture were thus of a gradual rather than spectacular nature, and occurred only in certain limited areas of the island.

This brings us to the problem of Ireland. Did this revival of economic life in Britain and along the western Gallic coasts result in a similar improvement of Ireland's depressed state? It is hard to say. There is no record of any Irish shipping reaching western Gallic ports during these years, as it had in the seventh century. In fact, we know that it was on an English vessel that two Irish travelers sailed to the mouth of the Loire early in the ninth century.[123] On the other hand, there is evidence of revived connections between Ireland and the Continent. About 800, according to Einhard, the Kings of Ireland placed themselves under Charlemagne's protection.[124] Irish scholars like Dicuil, John the Scot and many others reached the Carolingian Empire, to rise to scholarly eminence there. The coins in the

---

[119] The small Penard hoard in Wales probably reflects this copper trade. Note that it contains French coins of the Carolingian period. J. Allan, in *Num. Chron.*, VIII (1946), 236.

[120] G. M. Knocker and R. G. Hughes, "Anglo-Saxon Thetford," *loc.cit.*, pp. 6-7.

[121] Anastasius Bibliothecarus, in *Vita Rom. Pont. CVI*, ed. Migne, sec. 575.

[122] F. Stenton, *Anglo-Saxon England*, pp. 276-89. H. L. Gray, *English Field Systems*, pp. 203-51. C. Fox, *The Archeology of the Cambridge Region* (Cambridge 1923), pp. 209-301.

[123] Mon. S. Gall, in *MGH Script.*, II, 731.

[124] Einhard, *Vita Karoli*, in *Script. in usum scholarum*, p. 19.

Delganey hoard, the earliest discovered in Ireland after Roman times, reveal by the fact that some of them are from Aquitaine that some commerce with Gaul was still being carried on, although whether by native Irish merchants or foreigners it is impossible to say.[125] The fact that Norse Viking raiders followed their descents upon Irish coasts with attacks upon Noirmoutier and the shores of Aquitaine may also be significant. Perhaps they were but following recognized maritime commercial routes south to these coasts. Probably it would be fairest to guess that by 800 a certain maritime commerce had been re-established between Ireland and the Continent, but that the Vikings, who arrived earliest of all along Irish coasts, nipped this nascent revival in the bud.[126] It seems certain that after 820 such maritime commerce as Ireland possessed was essentially Viking rather than native in character.

There remains the question of Carolingian commerce in another direction, that which went from the Empire's heartland east and northeast towards the Baltic and the lands of the Slavs. We have already noted the fact that during these years in Germany an agricultural change was taking place that resulted in a clearing of the primeval forests along the upper Danube, the upper Weser and the Main, and in the establishment of new, pioneer-like agricultural settlements in these regions. In addition, we have commented upon the industrial activity that was to be found during this period about Regensburg and in the Bavarian and Austrian Alps. There is evidence that this brought about some new commerce, reaching Slavic and Avar lands farther east, in a region which had been all but devoid of commerce since the sixth century. Our best source for this information is the famous Carolingian Capitulary of Thionville, dating from the first decade of the ninth century. This document speaks of certain frontier posts which were established along the Carolingian borders to control trade with the Slavs and Avars; merchants were forbidden under this act to carry past the posts certain objects, such as arms, which were on the contraband list. Posts established to control trade with the Slavs were located at Bardowic, Schlesel, Magdeburg, Erfurt, Haberstadt, Forchheim and Bamberg. Those that controlled trade down the Danube to Avar lands were located at Linz and Re-

[125] John Evans, in *Num. Chron.*, new ser., XXIV (1882), 61-79.
[126] Kendrick believes that the early 9th century was Ireland's golden age, although he admits the island's political weakness. T. D. Kendrick, *History of the Vikings*, pp. 274-75.

gensburg.[127] The establishment of these posts is proof that some trade at least now reached the Slavs and Avars via Eastern Germany. But we have even more evidence of this fact. Certain provisions of the Laws of the Saxons, which date from 802, mention merchants specifically,[128] and evidence from the reign of Louis the Pious shows that an over-land trade route from Duisburg on the Rhine reached Magdeburg on the Elbe by way of Corvey and Gandersheim.[129] Farther south in Central Germany we find as early as the late eighth century mention of Slavic merchants coming to trade at Mainz by way of Fulda and the valley of the Main.[130] Still farther south the testimony of the Laws of the Bavarians, with their emphasis on commerce,[131] is rein-forced by the fact that in this period at least some of the peculiarly styled Bavarian pottery of this region was reaching the Baltic[132]— thus showing some trade with Slavic lands. After the destruction of the Avar kingdom by Charlemagne, and the subsequent advance of Moravian and German colonists into the middle Danube area,[133] there is evidence that contacts between Carolingians and Bulgars increased, including those of a commercial nature.[134]

But it would be unwise to overemphasize the importance of this trade to Slavic Central Europe prior to 840. Some existed, but gen-erally on a minor scale—certainly not enough to bring any great pros-perity to the lands of Eastern Germany through which it passed. These areas still remained almost completely agricultural in their economy. The best proof of this lies in the fact that only two places in Germany east of the Rhine coined money up to the end of the reign of Louis the Pious: Regensburg and Corvey. And the charter that Louis granted Corvey for this purpose expressly stated that the right was given to the monastery because so few merchants arrived to bring money there.[135] Nor do archeological finds in Silesia and Poland, dat-ing from these years, seem to give evidence of any considerable traffic

---

[127] *Capitulary of Thionville*, in *MGH Leges*, Cap. I, no. 44.

[128] *Leges Saxonicum*, III, IX, LXI, in *MGH Leges*, III, 50, 68, 78.

[129] P. Kletler, *Nordwesteuropas Verkehr*, pp. 47-55.

[130] *Vita Sturmi*, in *MGH Script.*, II, 369.

[131] A. Dopsch, *Economic and Social Foundations of European Civilization*, pp. 351-53.

[132] H. Arbman, *Schweden und das Karolingisch Reich*, pp. 110-14.

[133] On the struggle with the Avars, see H. Howorth, "The Avars," in *Jour. of Royal Asiatic Soc.*, new ser., XXI (1880), 790-98. See also J. B. Rose, "Two Neglected Paladins of Charlemagne, Eric of Friuli and Gerold of Bavaria," in *Speculum*, XX (1945), 184-91.

[134] On the complex situation created by the end of the Avar kingdom, see F. Dvornik, *Les Slavs, Rome et Byzance* (Paris 1928), pp. 1-76.

[135] Böhmer-Muhlbacher, *Regestum*, I, 329.

beyond Germany's frontiers into Slavic Central Europe.[136] A beginning was certainly made in the establishment of trade routes across Germany into Slavic lands, but it was only a beginning, and did not become important until the tenth and eleventh centuries. Germany east of the Rhine remained in 840 what it had been earlier, an agrarian region whose economic and commercial progress still lay in the future.

In rather sharp contrast to the trickle of trade to the east via overland routes through Central Germany is the maritime traffic that passed towards Scandinavia and the Baltic by way of Frisian and North German coasts. This trade had had some importance in Merovingian times, as we have noted. Now, in the late eighth and early ninth centuries it probably represented the most valuable external commerce of the Carolingian Empire. The ubiquitous Frisians, settled along the coasts of Holland and North Germany from Dorestad to the Eider, served as the main intermediaries along this route.[137] But it seems probable that at least some of this commerce was handled by Danes, who had settled in some numbers in Dorestad,[138] and by Saxon merchants from Hamburg.[139] The actual route by which most commerce reached the Baltic seems to have been inside the Zuyder Zee and the Frisian islands, past Heligoland, and on to the mouth of the Eider river on the lower part of the Jutland peninsula.[140] From here, most traffic crossed the Danish isthmus via the Eider and Schlee rivers to reach Hedeby on the Baltic side. Then it proceeded along the coast of Sweden to Birka at the entrance of the Malar Sea near the modern city of Stockholm.[141] Dorestad was the principal southern terminus,[142]

[136] On the lack of objects of German origin found in Slavic sites in Central Europe dating from this period, see J. Kostryzewski, *Les Origines de la civilisation polonaise*, pp. 102-10.

[137] On the Frisians as traders with Scandinavia, see H. Poelman, *De Handel van Noord-Nederland gerunde het Merovingische en het Karolingische Tijdperk* (The Hague 1908), pp. 60-69. P. Kletler, *op.cit.*, pp. 53-74. E. Wadstein, "On the Relations Between Scandinavians and Frisians in Early Viking Times," in *Saga Book of the Viking Society* (1933), pp. 163-79. Especially full are the accounts of B. Rower, *Die Friesisch Handel im frühen Mittelalter* (Kiel 1937), and H. Jankuhn, "Der fränkisch-friesische Handel zur Ostsee im frühen Mittelalter," in *Viert. für Soz- und Wirtschaft*, XL (1953).

[138] On the Danes in Dorestad, see Rimbert, *Vita Anskari*, XVII, XXI, XXIV, in *MGH Script.*, II, 693-709.

[139] *Ibid.*, p. 709. They were certainly there in 873, according to the *Annales Fuldenses*. On this, see W. Vogel, *Zur nord- und westeuropäischen Seeschiffahrt*, p. 160, and P. Kletler, *op.cit.*, p. 69.

[140] This was the route traveled by St. Willibrod in the 8th century. *Vita Willibrodi*, x, in *MGH Script. rer. Merov.*, VII, 127. It was that used by Anskar in 826. P. Kletler, *op.cit.*, pp. 46-48.

[141] This route was followed by Anskar on his voyages to Birka. In the 11th cen-

Hedeby the most important trading center towards the middle of this route,[143] and Birka its major northern destination.[144] All three had long been trade centers, going back to Merovingian times, Dorestad having been founded about 600 and Birka and Hedeby having shown some commercial importance by the eighth century. In the Carolingian era, however, it was not until 806 that Hedeby was definitely called a *portus*,[145] while not until Anskar's first visit to Sweden in 826 do our sources reveal that Birka had grown sufficiently to be designated as urban.[146] Besides these three, there soon arose a whole series of trading centers. North of Dorestad lay the Frisian center of Dokkum, large enough to boast a Carolingian *prefectus* during these years.[147] Farther north still, at the mouth of the Weser, we find a *portus* appearing at Bremen, where Anskar moved after the destruction of Hamburg in 845.[148] At the mouth of the Elbe lay Hamburg, important enough in Anskar's time for its merchants to travel to Hedeby itself.[149] Near Hedeby on the Baltic, a little to the south, was Reric, a trading center of the Slavic Obrodites, called a fortress in Carolingian sources.[150] And on the way to Birka in the Baltic lay the island of Gotland, which some commerce from the Carolingian Empire also reached, judging from archeological evidence.[151]

Not all commerce followed the Hedeby-Birka route. On the Atlantic side of the Jutland peninsula some traders branched off to pass the *vicus* of Ribe and proceed north towards Norway.[152] More, per-

---

tury, Adam of Bremen reported that such a trip from Hedeby to the Malar Sea took five days—a fast sail indeed. Adam of Bremen, *Descrip. Insulae Acquilonis*, XXI.

[142] On Dorestad, see J. H. Holwerda, *Dorestad en onze vroegste middeleeuwen* (Leyden 1924), and *Opgraven van Dorestad, Oudheidkundige medelallingen*, new ser., XI (1930).

[143] On Hedeby, the definitive studies are H. Jankuhn, "Ergebnisse und Probleme der Haithabugrabungen 1930-39," in *Zeit. für Gesellschaft für Schleswig-Holsteinische Geschichte* (Neumünster 1949), and *Die Ausgrabungen in Haithabu 1937-39* (Berlin 1943).

[144] On Birka, see H. Arbman, *Birka* (Stockholm 1939).

[145] H. Jankuhn, "Ergebnisse der Haithabugrabungen," *loc.cit.*, pp. 4-5.

[146] *Vita Anskari*, in *MGH Script.*, II, 703.

[147] P. Boeles, *Friesland*, pp. 385-86.

[148] P. Kletler, *op.cit.*, p. 103. E. de Moreau, *St. Anschaire* (Louvain 1930), pp. 63-67.

[149] V. Kellerman, "Die Hamburger Stadtbefestgungen im frühen Mittelalter," in *Hammaburg*, III (1949), 180-96. P. Kletler, *op.cit.*, pp. 102-3.

[150] W. Vogel, "Emporium Reric," in *Festskrift Halvdan Koht* (Oslo 1933), pp. 85-93.

[151] On the relative unimportance of Gotland's trade in the 9th century, see H. Arbman, *Schweden und das Karolingisch Reich*, pp. 16-17, and B. Nerman, *Die Verbindungen zwischen Skandinavien und dem Ostbalticum*, pp. 60-85.

[152] *Vita Anskari*, in *MGH Script.*, II, 711. P. Kletler, *op.cit.*, p. 104.

haps, traveled an inland Baltic route north from Hedeby and, by way of the Kattegat, to Skringissal on the Oslo fjord, which was already an important entrepôt in the ninth century for furs and other products which reached it from points along the Norwegian coast.[153] Such were the principal trade centers of Scandinavia in Carolingian times. But, in addition to these, there existed a series of smaller trading points known as *bjorkeys*, located along Norwegian and Swedish shores from the Lofoten Islands in far Northern Halagoland to the Gulf of Finland. Scandinavian scholars have indulged in much speculation concerning the *bjorkeys*, which, like Birka in Sweden, seem all to have been located at the head of a fjord or other waterway leading into the interior. The general consensus seems to be that these *bjorkeys* were so named because they were trading spots of a rather primitive nature where goods were gathered for shipment down the coasts to more important commercial centers.[154]

Another much-discussed problem has been the role of the Frisians in the establishment and development of Scandinavian urban centers like Hedeby, Birka and Ribe, and of the *bjorkeys* as well.[155] Some have claimed a Frisian origin for all of them, including the *bjorkeys*. It seems more likely, however, that while the Frisians played a major role in the foundation and growth of such ports as Hedeby and Ribe, the Scandinavians themselves, as well as Saxon and Slavic merchants, were equally important—particularly as regards Birka and the *bjorkeys*. Though the Frisians were the principal merchants traveling to the Baltic in Carolingian times, they were by no means the *only* maritime traders active along these coasts.[156]

However, trade routes reaching Birka and the island of Gotland

[153] O. A. Johnsen, *Tønbergs Historie*, I (Oslo 1929), 16. New excavations at Kaupanger near Larvik seem to have turned up the actual site of ancient Skringissal. We await final archeological reports on this, however.

[154] On these *bjorkeys*, see O. A. Johnsen, "Le Commerce et la navigation en Norvège au moyen âge," in *Revue hist.*, CLVIII (1936), 388-89, and E. Wadstein, "Birka och Bjorköratt," in *Namn Och Bygd*, II (1914), 92-113.

[155] On the Frisian theory, see E. Wadstein, "Vara forfader och Gamla Friserna," in *Svensk Hist. Tidskrift*, LII (1952), 163-89. Also N. T. Belaiew, "Frisia and Its Relations with England and the Baltic Littoral in the Dark Ages," in *Jour. of British Arch. Soc.*, XXXVII (1931), 209-15.

[156] One special reason for rejecting a Frisian origin for the *bjorkeys* is a lack of coin evidence. Carolingian Dorestad coinage has been found in the Danish peninsula near Hedeby. E. Nobbe, *Münzfunde des 8.-10. Jahrhunderts aus Schleswig-Holstein* (Frankfort on Main 1924), p. 5. Such coins have been found in some numbers along the Norwegian coast, especially the gold *solidi* of Louis the Pious. H. Holst, "Mynter i Norske Funn," in *Nord. Numis. Arsskrift* (1943), pp. 52-112. But they have not been found in Sweden or elsewhere in the Baltic. Hence it is doubtful if these trading spots were all, or even in part, of Frisian origin.

through the Baltic did not stop there. Some, at least, crossed this sea to Courland, where trading settlements existed at Apolloné and See-burg and at Truso, which lay to the south at the mouth of the Niemen river in East Prussia. Anskar mentions the first two as being under Swedish control until just prior to his second visit to Birka in 850, when they gained their independence from their Swedish masters. He tells us how they were raided by Danish pirates and reconquered by a Swedish expedition.[157] Archeological excavations confirm Anskar's account in many respects. They show us that all three were Swedish colonies, or at least under strong Swedish influence, from 650 to 850. They thus probably represent Swedish settlements established on the eastern shores of the Baltic at the time of Ivar Widefathom, as tradition tells us. Their remains indicate that they were closely related in culture to Gotland and the Swedish Uppland, whence this colonization probably originated.[158]

In Carolingian times, however, the important trade routes from Birka and Gotland were not those which reached the shores of Courland and Samland. Rather they led to the Bay of Riga and the Gulf of Finland and on to the Black and Caspian seas. We have already noted that these routes through Russia had some influence even in Merovingian times, when they led to Old Ladoga, Rostov on the Volga and Old Smolensk on the Dnieper. Now they increased in importance. By Carolingian times they seem also to have changed slightly. The route to Southern Russia started by way of Dvina and, after reaching the Dnieper near Smolensk, continued by way of Kiev until it reached the Black Sea and the Crimea. The northern Varangian passage started in the Gulf of Finland and continued to Lake Ladoga. There the route branched. One of the branches passed by way of Old Ladoga to Novgorod, connecting there either with the upper Dnieper or with the upper Volga via Rostov. The other branch went by way of Lake Onega and Belozero to the Volga and down to the Caspian. Novgorod's importance probably came from the fact that from it one could easily reach either Volga or Dnieper routes.[159]

[157] E. de Moreau, *St. Anskaire*, pp. 95-98. G. Vernadsky, *Ancient Russia*, pp. 338-40.
[158] B. Nerman, *Die Verbindungen zwischen Skandinavien und dem Ostbalticum*, pp. 60-120, and his *Sveriges Första Storhetstid*, pp. 1-142, contain information on archeological finds at Apolloné, Seeburg, Truso and other sites. See also L. Musset, *Les Peuples scandinaves*, pp. 42-43, and H. Arbman, *Schweden*, pp. 23-24.
[159] On these routes into Russia, see W. Vogel, "Zur nord- und westeuropäischen Seeschiffahrt," *loc.cit.*, pp. 162-66; H. Arbman, *Birka*, pp. 22-30; and L. Musset, *op.cit.*, pp. 67-69. See also T. J. Arne, *La Suède et l'Orient* (Uppsala 1914), pp. 1-206, and *Det Stora Svitjod* (Stockholm 1948), pp. 8-75.

The question as to whether Swedish Varangian traders penetrated these routes far into Russia before the time of Rurik, and during the reigns of Charlemagne and Louis the Pious, has been much discussed by scholars. The actual facts upon which an opinion can be based are few in number. The first is information which comes from the *Russian Primary Chronicle*, embodying as it does early traditions about the foundation of the Kievan kingdom. It states that Russian, Finnish and Baltic peoples and the Russian *grody* expelled the Rus, or Varangians, living there, and only called them back later in Rurik's time, when they needed their military and organizing ability.[160] This clearly seems to indicate that *prior* to Rurik, Swedes had at least reached such centers as Novgorod, Belozero and perhaps Polotsk. Other information from Byzantine and Moslem sources is equally specific. A Byzantine source tells us of certain Rus Kagans and Varangian chieftains who in 839 reached the lower Don, and were sent back to Scandinavia by way of Constantinople and the Frankish Empire.[161] Even more to the point is information from the pen of the Arab annalist, Ibn Khordâdbeh. Writing in the early ninth century before 840, he mentioned traders, whom he called Rus, who sailed up the Don and down the Volga and, accompanied by Slavic servants, carried *foxskins, slaves and Frankish swords* to trade as far as Bagdad.[162] Without attempting to assert, then, that these Varangian Swedes, or Rus, founded either the trade routes leading to the Baltic or the cities along them, which were all of pre-Carolingian date, it seems clear that Scandinavian infiltration into Russia preceded Rurik by a half-century or more.[163] It also seems clear that some Varangian traders had already reached the heart of the Moslem East early in the ninth century.

But there is still another source of information concerning the commerce flowing along these routes to the Moslem East which can be exploited to add to what we can learn from our scanty historical records. That is the coin hoards of the Baltic, which if properly interpreted, add immensely to our knowledge of the events of these years. More than 50,000 Moslem silver dirhems have been discovered in Swedish hoards alone dating from these centuries, and thousands more have been unearthed in Denmark, Norway and along the

---

[160] *The Primary Chronicle*, ed. Cross, p. 144.

[161] *Annales Bertiniani*, in *MGH Script.*, I, 435.

[162] Ibn Khordâdbeh, *Book of Routes*, ed. de Geoje, pp. 114-16.

[163] For archeological evidence of the infiltration into Russia, see T. J. Arne, *La Suède et l'Orient*, pp. 61-74, and G. Vernadsky, *Ancient Russia*, pp. 266-91, 301-7. See also N. K. Chadwick, *The Beginnings of Russian History: An Inquiry into the Sources* (Cambridge 1946), pp. 1-134.

southern and eastern shores of the Baltic. When classification and study of all of them have been completed, they will give us a precious picture of the Eastern contacts of the Baltic. But even now enough has been done with certain hoards to provide us with some interesting information.

In our last chapter, we noted that the presence of Sassanian silver dirhems at a number of points seems to show that the Varangian trade routes were already functioning as early as the first years of the seventh century. When we approach the Carolingian Age, we can gather from our coin information that this commerce increased in volume, since we find numerous hoards containing Ommiad silver dirhems. Such Ommiad coins are particularly numerous in Gotland and Swedish Uppland sites. In Gotland, four separate hoards of Arabic coins contain Ommiad silver pieces; in one case, a coin minted as early as 716; in another, a coin struck in 718-719; and in the other two cases, coins which were minted in 739 and 741.[164] In still another great Gotland hoard, that of Stora Velinge, which has been carefully studied, we find, among more than 4,000 Arabic dirhems dating from the eighth to the tenth century, a total of 37 Ommiad coins. These include dirhems minted between the years 708 and 749 by the Caliphs Walid, Yezid II, Hisham, Walid II and Merwan II.[165] Lest this be considered unusual, another coin hoard of the ninth century, this time found in the Swedish Uppland, also includes a large number of Ommiad pieces minted between the years 705 and 746 by the Caliphs Walid, Hisham and Walid II.[166]

The same type of information is provided by the sparser Arab silver hoards excavated in Denmark. There, too, Ommiad coins have been uncovered, one minted as early as 705 and the rest continuing through the first half of the eighth century.[167] Even in Norway a few finds of Ommiad coins have been made, one from the Ostfold region bearing the date 742-743, and three from Sogne, coined in Mesopotamia about the mid-eighth century.[168] If one allows for a certain time to elapse between the minting of such coins and their arrival in distant

[164] These hoards are those of Oster Ryfter, Hagvats, Sigsawe and Folhagen. M. Stenberger, *Die Schatzfunde Gotlands der Wikingerzeit*, II, 21-24, 63-64, 73-75, 106-10.

[165] U. S. Linder-Welin, "Ein grosser Fund Arabischer Münzen aus Stora Velinge Gotland," in *Nord. Numis. Arsskrift* (1941), pp. 74-120.

[166] U. S. Linder-Welin, "Ein upplandst Silverskatt från 800-Talet" in *ibid.* (1938), pp. 172-217.

[167] R. Skovmand, *De Danske Skattefunde* (Copenhagen 1942), pp. 13-17.

[168] H. Holst, "Uter-og Innerlanske Mynter i Norske Funn, Nedlogtfor ar 1100," in *Nord. Numis. Arsskrift* (1943), pp. 56-112.

Scandinavia, it is still apparent that the flow of commerce from the East to the Baltic and beyond was not interrupted in the first years of the Carolingian era.

Nor is this all. These coin hoards include even more dirhems minted by the earliest Abbassid Caliphs after 754, and they increase in volume down to those which date from the last years of the Caliph al-Mamun. Some idea of how much more abundant Abbassid coins are than Ommiad in these hoards can be furnished by a few examples. In the great Gotland Stora Velinge hoard are 37 Ommiad dirhems, but a total of 1,247 Abbassid coins.[169] On the Swedish mainland, over 700 Abbassid coins have been found, against a mere handful of Ommiad ones.[170] Furthermore, comparison of the minting dates of Abbassid dirhems found here reveals an interesting curve. Those coined by early Abbassid rulers are not rare, but the most numerous are those minted by Haroun-al Raschid and al-Mamun, who were contemporaries of Charlemagne and Louis the Pious, respectively. A few coins of al-Mutawakkil dating from about 850 then appear, followed by a complete cessation of Moslem dirhems minted in the second half of the ninth century, until a new flood of dirhems bearing a date of 890 or later appears in our hoards.[171] Exactly the same thing is true of dirhems found in Norway. There we find a certain number of coins minted by Haroun-al Raschid. Then a break appears until new coins bearing a late ninth-century or tenth-century date turn up in the finds.[172]

There is still another point of interest. Information derived from dirhems found in Swedish Uppland and Norse hoards permits us to identify the mints from which they came in the Moslem East. The Ommiad and Abbassid coins came from one area of the Middle East alone. Except for one coin struck in Damascus, all the rest came from mints in Iraq and Western Persia, especially the Persian province of Tabaristan on the south shores of the Caspian Sea. On the other hand, few of those, which must have arrived later in Scandinavia, since their date of minting reveals them to have been struck after 890, came from these regions. Rather they are from Samanid Turkestan, and not from Western Persia and Iraq.[173]

[169] U. S. Linder-Welin, "Ein grosser Fund Arabischer Münzen aus Stora Velinge," loc.cit., pp. 78-96.

[170] U. S. Linder-Welin, "Ein upplandst Silverskatt," loc.cit., p. 124.

[171] U. S. Linder-Welin, op.cit., p. 80, contains a graph of these coins based on the time they were minted.

[172] H. Holst, op.cit., pp. 60-72.

[173] In the Uppland hoard from the Swedish mainland, noted above, the Kufic

These coin hoards give us other precious information as well. If one accepts their evidence, there is very little proof that much contact was maintained during these years between Scandinavia and Moslem Spain along Atlantic routes, either by way of Ireland or by way of the Carolingian Empire. For only four Western Moslem coins minted prior to 840 have been found in all Scandinavia. One of them, a coin of Abdār-Rahman I of Spain, dating from 776-777, comes from Uppland Sweden.[174] The other three, one a Spanish coin of 769 and two Iddrisid Moroccan ones of the ninth century, come from Norwegian sites.[175] In contrast to the great trade which these coin hoards reveal as existing in Carolingian times with Iraq and Western Persia via Russia, that with the Moslem Mediterranean areas is shown to be all but non-existent.

How can we, then, sum up our evidence derived from these coin finds and reconcile it with information from our other sources? First, these hoards show that there was, via Varangian routes, a commercial contact with the Orient which started in Merovingian times and continued without interruption until the death of Louis the Pious. Second, they illustrate a steady increase in this commerce right down to the end of Louis' reign. Third, they show that such trade went by way of the Volga to Moslem Persia and Iraq via the Caspian, and there only. The fact that not a single Byzantine coin minted in Carolingian times is found in the Baltic explains the silence of Byzantine sources concerning this Swedish penetration of Russia. Obviously, until 840 no Rus traders were arriving in Byzantine-controlled regions on the Black Sea. Instead their penetration was, as both the *Primary Chronicle* and Ibn Khordâdbeh state, along the Volga route as far as Iraq.[176]

Even more important, these coin hoards show clearly that an expulsion of the Varangians prior to Rurik actually took place—an expulsion, incidentally, that is independently corroborated by Anskar as far as Seeburg and Apolloné in Courland are concerned. For only

---

coins are from mints in Wasit, Western Persia, Iraq, Samarkand and especially Tabaristan. See map of these mints in U. S. Linder-Welin, *op.cit.*, p. 123. On mints represented by Norway's Kufic coins, see H. Holst, *op.cit.*, pp. 71-82.

[174] On Swedish finds, see U. S. Linder, *op.cit.*, p. 121.

[175] On such coins in Norway, H. Holst, *op.cit.*, pp. 56-112. Shetelig much exaggerates the importance of these few Western Moslem dirhems found in Norse sites. H. Shetelig, "Arabiske Mynter Paa Vestlandet," in *Oldtiden*, III (1913), 25-32.

[176] These Rus merchants carried Frankish swords for sale in the Moslem Middle East. Leo V was, we know, attempting to keep such weapons from reaching the Moslem East in Carolingian times. See A. R. Lewis, *op.cit.*, pp. 111-31.

this can explain why, after their peak about 830-840, Abbassid coins which bear a date later than 850 no longer reach Scandinavia, and even during this last decade from 840 to 850 only in a trickle. Obviously, a rising of the Slavs, Chud and Finns cut the trade routes to the Orient until they were opened again by Rurik and Oleg and the silver flood resumed its flow to the Baltic, although now from Byzantium and Turkestan, not Western Persia or Iraq. And our Byzantine source which speaks of Rus who returned to Scandinavia via such a roundabout route proves valuable, too. For it enables us to date this rising and cutting-off of trade routes at about 839—a fact which would agree with our coin hoard evidence. These Rus Kagans sought to return by way of Constantinople and Frankish lands, then, for a very simple reason. The risings of the Slavs and others in North Russia against their compatriots that cut off trade routes through to the Baltic gave them little chance to reach home the way they had come. They chose the only possible alternative.

There was still one other series of maritime routes reaching Scandinavia besides those already discussed in preceding pages. These passed from Norway's west coast through the Western Atlantic by way of the Shetlands, the Orkneys and Hebrides to the coasts of Scotland and Ireland. Earlier we noted that the disappearance of Pictish shipping and the equally sudden decline of Irish maritime strength by 750 all but destroyed the economic life of regions touched by these routes. A few Irish saints in their coracles, according to Dicuil, were still sailing as far as the Orkneys and even Iceland, where remains of their occupation have been discovered, but these were just remnants of what had been more active Celtic contacts. Instead, what seems to have happened in the late eighth century was not Celts sailing north, but rather a movement of fishermen and farming folk south and west, going from Norway by way of the Shetlands and Orkneys to the Hebrides. Probably better Norwegian ships, adapted to the Atlantic, made this migration possible. But whatever its cause, the results are plain to see in excavations made along the route, which show a peaceful penetration of these islands between Norway and the British Isles taking place even before 800.[177] And it seems possible that at least a portion of those objects of Irish origin found in late eighth-century graves, like the Carolingian silver coins on

[177] T. C. Lethbridge, *Herdsmen and Hermits*, pp. 90-102. H. Shetelig, *An Introduction to the Viking History of Western Europe*, pp. 21-44. A. W. Brøgger, *Ancient Emigrants*, pp. 7-24. See also T. C. Lethbridge, *Merlin's Island*, pp. 85-103, on proof of Irish in Ireland during this period.

Norway's west coast, arrived there via this route, now in Norse hands.[178] The first steps towards that more violent contact which the years after 800 were to see between Celt and Viking on the coasts of Ireland were already taken in these last years of the eighth century.

Trade routes reaching the Baltic from the Orient, bringing increasing numbers of silver dirhems, account for the importance of commerce between this region and the Carolingian Empire. They help to explain the economic role which Frisian merchants played in this Empire, since it was they, more than any others, who tapped this wealth with their maritime shipping, which linked Dorestad and the Rhinelands with Hedeby, Birka and the Baltic. These routes may also throw light upon the reasons for the existence at Birka of those rich merchants whom Anskar mentions. It was probably due in part to the riches of the Baltic trade that Charlemagne spent so much of his reign subduing the Saxons of North Germany. In so doing, he was protecting his access to Baltic markets by gaining firm possession of adjacent shores. As in the case of Northern Italy and the Spanish March, it seems that Charlemagne's Saxon policy rested in part upon economic considerations.

We might also attribute currency changes which took place late in Charlemagne's reign to the importance of Carolingian Baltic trade. These changes in the weight of the Carolingian silver penny have rather mystified some historians. But if we consider the influence exerted upon Charlemagne's Empire by silver dirhems from the Baltic, as well as those from Moslem Spain, the problem is solved. For Charles in his last currency reform was only adopting the same weight for his silver money as that possessed by Abbassid coins, which during his reign reached even beyond the Baltic. Interestingly enough, such coins bore in Arabic a motto from the Koran glorifying Allah. Even this fact influenced Carolingian coinage a little later, during the reign of Louis the Pious. For we note that this monarch struck a silver penny which bore the counterclaim, "Christian religion"—no doubt, a numis-

---

[178] On Irish objects found in Norwegian archeological sites dating from this period, see A. W. Brøgger, op.cit., pp. 20-21, and H. Shetelig, Scandinavian Archeology, pp. 261-85. Carolingian coins of this period in Norway have been found mainly in the Oslo region. They include 15 coins, of which 4 are gold solidi of Louis the Pious. The west coast has revealed only 10 Carolingian coins as yet. Of these, 5 were found in Sogne and 4 in Trondelag. H. Holst, op.cit., pp. 56-112. Contrary to Shetelig's opinion, it seems probable that these coins, found in twelve scattered sites, arrived in Norway as the result of trade rather than piracy. Furthermore, the lack of Anglo-Saxon coins seems to emphasize that it was via Frisia and to some extent Ireland—not England—that trade reached Norway's coasts in these years.

matic bit of religious counterpropaganda.[179] One more interesting point. When Louis the Pious—for reasons of prestige, most probably —struck his gold *solidi*, he minted them at Dorestad for use in this northern trade, and only along this North Sea route towards Scandinavia have they and copies made from them in the early ninth century been discovered.[180] Probably of all the commerce which is found in the Carolingian era about the Northern Seas, that leading to the Baltic was in volume and value the most important to the Carolingian Empire.

When we take up the question of the products which were exchanged in Northern Europe during this period of the Carolingian Empire, we become aware that our knowledge is considerably greater than it was for Merovingian times. It is worth noting, however, that such commerce differed little from that of the earlier period. Again it seems principally to have consisted of the natural products of each separate area from Spain to Finland. There seems little doubt, for instance, that it was the wine of Western Gaul that drew Frisian and Anglo-Saxon merchants to these Atlantic shores. In 753 it was wine which still brought them to the Fair of St. Denis.[181] And it seems probable that at the Fair of Troyes, that early ninth-century predecessor of the later Fairs of Champagne, wine was also a principal exchange item.[182] By these years, however, a major source of wine was the Rhine and Moselle regions. Frisian merchants were seeking wine when they traded in Alsace early in the ninth century.[183] And it was wine which found its way north to Dorestad and on to Hedeby and Birka, in those Rhineland "Birka" jars which have been found in such abundance by archeologists at these Baltic trading centers.[184]

[179] On this point, see the important article by S. Bolin, "Muhammed, Karl den Store och Rurik," in *Scandia*, CXII (1939), 185-232. An English translation is to be found in *Scandinavian Economic History Review*, I (1953), 5-39.

[180] On these coins and their imitations *and* the places where they have been found, see P. Grierson, "The Gold Coinage of Louis the Pious and Its Imitations," in *Jaarboek voor Munt-en Penningkunde*, XXXVIII (1951), 211-31.

[181] *MGH Diplom. Karol.*, I, 43.

[182] A. Dopsch, *Die Wirtschaftsentwicklung der Karolingerzeit*, II, 198, contains information on this fair. See also J. W. Thompson, "The Commerce of France in the Ninth Century," *loc.cit.*, p. 885. It is worth noting that it is near the location of this fair that we find the Veuillen coin hoard, which contains specimens from the most widespread number of mints of any of the French Carolingian hoards noted by Gariel—including a large amount of money struck in Italy. This seems to confirm the importance of trade reaching this area and this fair about 820 A.D.

[183] C. Verlinden "L'état économique de l'Alsace," in *Revue Belge*, IX (1934), 217-34.

[184] On these "Birka jars" at Hedeby, see H. Jankuhn, *Die Ausgrabungen in Haithabu*

But if wine formed one great export north to England, Scandinavia and perhaps even Ireland, there was still another: wheat. Since Scandinavia was too far north to grow wheat, flour had to be imported. Now, we know that sufficient grain was produced in the newly cleared lands in Central Germany for grain merchants to be important at Mainz, where a Frisian colony also existed at this time.[185] It thus seems probable that these Frisians shipped flour and grain north to Scandinavia in the so-called Birka jars, as well as wine. Charlemagne's prohibition against grain shipments to Denmark was, then, an effective economic weapon to use against his dangerous northern neighbors. We know little of honey, the sugar of the Early Middle Ages, beyond the fact that it was a product sought by merchants attending the Fair of St. Denis.[186] Where it was produced in Carolingian times, however, and the extent of commerce in it remain unknown. Nor can we do more than suppose that leather and leather goods were still being exported from Ireland. Olive oil, found on the Rhine, which arrived by sea,[187] may also have had a wide market, but evidence is lacking. Similarly, our knowledge is scant on the timber trade; but timber must have been an important item of shipment from Scandinavia to the Frisian coast, which, though humming with maritime activity, was treeless. Until more evidence is found, however, we are reduced to supposition on this subject.

If the products of the soil—wine, wheat, honey, leather and timber —were widely traded during this Carolingian era, so was Northern Europe's mineral wealth. The silver and lead of England and that of Melle were transported long distances by sea, as we know from cargoes of lead which reached the Carolingian shores of the English Channel and from the number of Carolingian churches whose

---

1937-39, pp. 176-82. On their presence in Frisian sites, see P. Boeles, *Friesland*, pp. 430-38. On Birka, see H. Arbman, *Schweden und das Karolingisch Reich*, pp. 10-35. In this connection, one should note that about 840 Anskar found a woman at Birka who possessed wine. E. de Moreau, *St. Anskaire*, pp. 60-64.

[185] An account of the Franconian grain trade and the Frisians' connection with it, as well as their connection with the wine export of Alsace, is found in E. Sabbe, "Quelques types de marchands du IXe et Xe siècles," *loc.cit.*, pp. 182-84. But in general there has been insufficient emphasis upon this grain trade between Scandinavia and Germany in the 9th century. Somewhat later, flour was, according to the *Egils Saga*, a principal export to Norway from England. H. Shetelig, *Scandinavian Archeology*, pp. 305-8. It seemed probable that in this period the Frisians handled this trade up the Rhine to Frisia and on to Scandinavia.

[186] *MGH Diplom. Karol.*, I, 43.

[187] *Miracula Wandelberti S. Goaris*, in *MGH Script.*, xv, 368.

roofs were leaded.[188] The tin of Cornwall, and perhaps that of Bohemia, also found wide export markets.[189] Alcuin's sending of a cargo of tin, along with wine, to the Abbey of Lindesfarne in Yorkshire is a case in point.[190] The copper used in making brass and bronze during this period also must have been transported from distant regions—either from western British shores or from Saxon mines via the Dortmund-Duisberg route.[191] Iron was exported, we know, from a number of places: the upper Loire, Normandy, Lorraine, the Rhinelands, the Meuse region and the Alps.[192] It was also mined, outside the Empire, in Kent and Gloucestershire in Anglo-Saxon Britain,[193] and at numerous places in Norway and Sweden, where deposits were particularly rich.[194] No doubt such iron was exported beyond local areas and reached regions like Northern Italy, Southern France, Slavic Central Europe, Ireland and certain Baltic areas lacking iron resources. Salt was, we know, produced both for local purposes and for export on the west coast of Gaul, in Alsace, along the upper Danube and perhaps in Saxony, near Luneville, where it was later exported to the Baltic.[195] Stone, perhaps that special stone of Tournai, figured in the trade negotiations between Offa and Charlemagne.[196]

To natural products of soil and mine should also be added manufactured goods as articles of commerce in Carolingian times. Such goods were produced in the main in three separate regions, which might be considered by the early ninth century the workshop areas of the Northern Seas. One was the heartland of the Carolingian state between the Seine and the Rhine, the most important of the three. The other two were England and the area of the upper Danube.

One of the principal exports from the Carolingian heartland was

[188] On the trade in lead, see H. Van Werweke, "Note sur le commerce du plomb au moyen âge," in *Mélanges Pirenne*, II, 508-11.

[189] On the coin hoards of Cornwall which show overseas contacts, see H. O. Hencken, *op.cit.*, pp. 262-63, and J. Rashleigh, *op.cit.*, pp. 137-49. On bronze objects of the Meuse country which must have been made from imported tin, see F. Rousseau, *La Meuse*, pp. 100-18.

[190] Alcuin, *Epistolae*, in *MGH Epist. Karol. aevi*, II, 226.

[191] See F. Rousseau, *op.cit.*, pp. 112-17, and A. Peltzer, *op.cit.*, pp. 32-45.

[192] O. Davies, *Roman Mines in Europe*, pp. 87-95. F. Rousseau, *op.cit.*, pp. 110-21. A. R. Lewis, *op.cit.*, p. 116. H. Jankuhn, "Ein Ulfberht Schwert," *loc.cit.*, pp. 213-21.

[193] L. Salzman, *English Industry in the Middle Ages*, pp. 10f., contains information on the production of iron and iron weapons and tools in this period.

[194] On the iron industry in Norway, see A. W. Brøgger, *Ancient Emigrants*, pp. 12-14, and H. Shetelig, *Scandinavian Archeology*, pp. 250-73. On Sweden, see O. Montelius, *Kulturgeschichte Schwedens* (Leipzig 1906), pp. 1-154.

[195] H. Hauser, *Le sel dans l'histoire*, pp. 275-77. A. Dopsch, *op.cit.*, pp. 176-77.

[196] F. Stenton, *Anglo-Saxon England*, pp. 219-21.

glassware, produced near Trier, between Bonn and Cologne in the Rhinelands and perhaps farther west in Gaul. As in the period of the Late Empire and of the Merovingians, much of this glass was exported to England and to Scandinavia, and perhaps along trade routes which reached Western Gaul as well.[197] Pottery, the Badorf ware of the Rhinelands,[198] and the bronze and brassware of the Meuse valley were also articles of export.[199]

More important than these industrial products, however, was the manufacture of fine swords and other arms. Charlemagne forbade, as we know, export of arms to the Slavic East,[200] and, judging from both our sources and finds made by archeologists in the Scandinavian world, such Frankish swords were particularly prized by the Vikings.[201] They were produced in some quantity along the lower Rhine near the present industrial area of the Ruhr, and perhaps also in the Meuse valley. They were carried by Scandinavian merchants as far as Bagdad.[202] According to the Monk of St. Gall, they were the treasure of the Frankish kingdom, and the export which the Vikings most desired. [203]

And, finally, this area of the Carolingian Empire produced fine cloth, the so-called *pallia fresonica,* an export hardly less prized abroad than the arms. Manufactured in Flanders, Frisia and parts of Northern Germany, it was carried by Frisian traders south to Alsace, west to Aquitaine and north to the Baltic.[204] It has been found in early ninth-century graves in Birka, and may be identified even in fragments by its special weave.[205] It was prized highly enough for Louis the Pious to think fit to include fine grades of it among the presents he sent to the Caliphs of Bagdad, or gave to members of his own court.[206]

Only second in importance as an industrial region during this period was Anglo-Saxon England. Its chief export of a manufactured nature seems to have been a fine grade of cloth which was the subject

[197] J. Steinhausen, "Früh mittelalterlich Glasshütten im Trierland," in *op.cit.,* pp. 151-63. H. Arbman, *Schweden,* pp. 26-36.

[198] F. Rodermacher, *Karolingische Keramik am Niederrhein,* pp. 11-83. H. Jankuhn, *op.cit.,* pp. 215-17.

[199] F. Rousseau, *La Meuse,* pp. 210-21.

[200] *MGH Leges,* II, Cap. I, no. 44.

[201] J. Peterson, *De Norske Vikingswerd,* pp. 59-71. H. Jankuhn, "Probleme des reinischen Handels nach Skandinavien," *loc.cit.,* pp. 289-97.

[202] Ibn Khordâdbeh, *Book of Routes,* pp. 114-16.

[203] Mon. S. Gall, *Gesta Karoli Magni,* in *MGH Script.,* II, 753.

[204] H. Pirenne, "Draps de Frise ou Draps de Flandre?" *loc.cit.,* pp. 308-37. P. Kletler, *Nordwesteuropas Verkehr,* pp. 109-15. H. Laurent, *op.cit.,* pp. 308-35.

[205] A. Geijer, *Birka,* III, 22-47.

[206] Mon. S. Gall, *Gesta Karoli Magni,* in *MGH Script.,* II, 762.

of negotiations between Offa and Charlemagne and probably was sent principally to Gallic coasts.[207] England also had a budding pottery industry at Thetford which was, however, largely local in importance.[208] It, too, produced arms from the iron of Kent and the Forest of Dean which had more than local value. Its jewelry and fine metalwork were still highly prized abroad.[209] If England during these years seems to have been less industrial than the Rhinelands and the regions of the Meuse and the Scheldt, perhaps this is because our evidence concerning its industrial accomplishments is still slight. Some of its production—for instance, its fine cloth—undoubtedly seriously rivaled that of Flanders in international markets.

Finally, we have the upper Danube region. Here the ancient iron industry of Roman times still continued, and during this Carolingian era merchants were shipping arms down the Danube to the Avars and across the Alps to Venice and Northern Italy.[210] Here there was already an important pottery industry.

Even Scandinavia, during this period, began to show signs of a rather advanced industrial economy along some lines. Finds of ships buried there reveal a skill in shipbuilding hardly matched elsewhere about the Northern Seas.[211] Its jewelry also was of a fine quality.[212] But particularly significant was its iron industry. The Scandinavians do not seem to have produced the fine pattern-welded swords that made the Rhinelands famous, but their iron tools, found in numerous excavations, and exported to Russia and Baltic coasts, indicate that they were smiths of no mean skill.[213] Even in distant Ireland there is evidence of some industrial skill in the manufacture of fine bronze objects, which were exported as far as Norway.[214]

To such industrial wares, mineral and natural products, which no doubt formed the bulk of long-range commerce in Carolingian times, should also be added objects of a luxury nature. One of the most im-

[207] Alcuin, *Epistolae*, in *MGH Epist. Karol. aevi*, II, 144.
[208] G. M. Knocker and R. G. Hughes, "Anglo-Saxon Thetford," *loc.cit.*, pp. 7-9.
[209] Anastasius Bibliothecarus, in *Vita Rom. Pont.* CVI, sec. 575.
[210] *MGH Leges*, II, Cap. I, no. 44.
[211] On this development, see the excellent account in Brøgger and Shetelig, *The Viking Ships*, pp. 104-51. This also contains an excellent survey of Norse iron tools, technology and industrial arts in this period.
[212] *Ibid.*
[213] On the magnificent jewelry produced in Viking times, see the plates in M. Stenberger, *Die Schatzfunde Gotlands*, II, 250-306.
[214] A. Mahr, *Christian Art in Ancient Ireland*, I (Dublin 1932), 83-118, contains a study of this bronze work. See also H. O. Hencken, "Lagore Crannoy," *loc.cit.*, pp. 159-71.

portant was furs. These appear to have come mainly from Scandinavian and Russian forests. Our Arabic sources tell us they were one of the principal products carried by Scandinavian traders to Iraq.[215] They also reached the Carolingian Empire. We have mention, for instance, of "Pontic beaver" used by Louis the Pious.[216] Verdun seems to have been a center for this trade in pelts, many of which were sent on to Moslem Spain.[217]

Still other types of imports consisted of spices and silks, which were, if anything, found more abundantly about the Northern Seas during the reign of Louis the Pious than they had been in later Merovingian times. Spices and silks appear to have arrived via three routes: from Southern France, where they were brought by Jewish and Moslem Spanish intermediaries; from Italy, where they arrived from the Byzantine and Eastern Moslem world; and from the Baltic, which they reached via Varangian Russian routes. Probably most arrived via Venice and Northern Italy. But, as Sabbe has shown, the abundant spices available at Cambrai during these years, and the fact that the upper classes of both the Carolingian Empire and Anglo-Saxon England often wore silk, illustrate that this commerce was a valuable one.[218]

Finally, we come to the slave trade—which might be considered in part a luxury trade, and in part a trade in natural products. However we classify it, there can be little doubt that it continued in these years to be important. Slaves were in general sent to Moslem lands, either those of the Mediterranean or farther east. Along the Varangian routes to Persia and Iraq slaves were one of the major articles of commerce,[219] and were exchanged for silver dirhems, spices, silks and other Oriental products. Others, mainly Slav in origin, reached Venice from Central Europe by way of the Alpine passes and from there were shipped to various points throughout the Mediterranean.[220]

---

[215] Ibn Khordâdbeh, *Book of Routes*, p. 114.

[216] Angelbertus, *Gesta Abbatium Fontanellensium*, in *MGH Script.*, II, 53, 397.

[217] On this fur trade, see R. Henning, "Der nordeuropäische Pelzhandel in den älteren Periode der Geschichte," in *Viert. für Soz- und Wirtschaft*, XXIII (1930), 283-317.

[218] See E. Sabbe, "l'Importation des tissus," *loc.cit.*, pp. 583-91, for a full discussion of the evidence of Eastern silks and spices reaching the Carolingian Empire and England during these years.

[219] The Rus merchants who visited Bagdad carried slaves with them. Ibn Khordâdbeh, *Book of Routes*, p. 114.

[220] On the Venetian slave trade, see *Liber Pont.*, ed. Duchesne (Paris 1886), I, 433, and *Codex Carolinus*, ed. Gelzer, *Epist.*, LXXV. See also Muratori, *Annali d'Italia*, XXXVIII, 960, and A. Mez, *The Renaissance of Islam* (London 1937), p. 159.

Still others were sent to Moslem Spain in a trade dominated by Jewish slave traders operating from Verdun, a eunuch center, or from Narbonne and other southern French ports.[221] Though efforts seem to have been made by both the church and the Carolingian rulers themselves to suppress this commerce,[222] it remained of great importance during the reigns of both Charlemagne and Louis the Pious.

At this point, we reach one of the most significant and most disputed questions concerning the economy of Northern Europe during Carolingian times: to what extent was this region which faced the Northern Seas isolated from the more advanced Byzantine and Moslem worlds to the south of it? Our evidence makes it clear that such isolation was by no means complete. As we have seen, spices, silks and other Oriental wares reached Northern Europe from the East during this period, and arms, fine cloth, slaves and furs certainly were sent south in payment for them—particularly to Moslem lands. But it must be stressed, as was done earlier in this chapter, that except in the case of Northern Italy, the Carolingian Empire and other Northern European regions were essentially separate, even during the reign of Louis the Pious, from the Byzantine gold *nomisma* region and the Arabic gold *dinar* areas of the Central and Eastern Mediterranean.[223] Their chief contacts to the south were with Moslem areas possessing a silver coinage, Spain in the West and Persia and Iraq in the East. And, if one considers, as we have just done, the products that made up most of the cargoes which were traded widely in Northern Europe, it is clear that most of the economic development of this area during these decades owed little to contacts with Moslem silver areas. In only one region—Scandinavia—is there coin evidence, for instance, of a favorable balance of trade with regions to the south.

Perhaps the best evidence of the essential separateness of Northern Europe from the gold *dinar* and *nomisma* regions of the Mediterranean is found in its coinage. This coinage, north of the Alps, remained a silver one, as it had been in Late Merovingian times. It was influenced, we have noted, by the dirhem silver standard of

---

[221] On the slave trade to Spain in this period, see A. R. Lewis, *op.cit.*, pp. 180-81, and H. Pirenne, *Mohammed and Charlemagne*, pp. 180-206.

[222] W. Levison, *England and the Continent*, pp. 8-10. *Codex Carol.*, ed. Gelzer, *Epist.*, LXXV.

[223] This explains why such products as natron for glassware and papyrus, and the Syrians from Egypt and the Near East who brought them to Gaul in Merovingian times, were not found in Western Europe in this period. On the causes of this, see A. R. Lewis, *op.cit.*, pp. 88-131.

Persia, or perhaps Spain, but not by Mediterranean gold monetary systems. Had there been close economic bonds between this world and the Eastern Mediterranean, we might well have found a gold currency development in the Carolingian Empire and elsewhere north of the Alps. Such, however, was not the case. In an isolated hoard like that uncovered at Hon in Norway, which dates from this period, we note gold coins, but they are treated as jewelry, not as currency.[224] Offa's gold dinars represent an experiment which had no successors in immediate Anglo-Saxon monetary history,[225] save the gold *solidi* of Wigham of York, copies of those struck in Frisia by Louis the Pious.[226] Even Louis' *solidi*, while of gold, were coined from supplies that he may have procured, not through trade, but as tribute payments from the Princes of Beneventum,[227] and these *solidi* were coined and circulated about the North Sea in a region *completely* separate from the gold *dinar-nomisma* areas in the Mediterranean.[228] Even the *mancus* mentioned in English documents appears to have been a money of account, worth 30 shillings, derived from a light South Italian coin known as the *mancus solidus*. There is no evidence that such a *mancus* means an Arab gold *dinar* until the term was applied to such coins in the late tenth or the eleventh century.[229] There were gold supplies to be found in Carolingian times in Northern Europe, as we know from the gold which was paid Vikings in Frankish Danegelds later in the century, and the gift of gold vessels sent to the Pope by the Kings of Wessex somewhat earlier. Even Gotland hoards dating from Carolingian times contain some objects made of this metal.[230] But such gold was seldom used in monetary form.

[224] H. Holst, *On the Coins of the Hon Find* (Oslo 1931), pp. 1-14, and "Hon Funnet," in *Norges Inskrifter Med. de Ingoe Runny* (Oslo 1952), pp. 33-57.

[225] On Offa's dinar, see M. Bloch, *Le Problème de l'or* pp. 13-20; W. Levison, *op.cit.*, p. 12; and F. Stenton, *Anglo-Saxon England*, pp. 232-33.

[226] G. C. Brooke, *English Coins*, p. 12.

[227] P. Grierson, in "The Solidi of Louis the Pious and Their Imitations," *loc.cit.*, pp. 217-31, deals with these coins and Wigham's copies of them struck in York. On the large sum of gold sent Louis the Pious as tribute by the Princes of Beneventum in 812 and 814, amounting to 30,000 *solidi*, see *Ann. Reg. Franc.*, anno 812 and anno 814, in *MGH Script. in usum scholarum*, II, 137, 141.

[228] See P. Grierson, *op.cit.*, pp. 211-311, on the areas, all of them about the North Sea, where these gold *solidi* have been found. The only exceptions are the two which have been discovered in La Vendée near the mouth of the Loire.

[229] On the *mancus*, see P. Grierson, *Carolingian Europe and the Arabs, The Myth of the Mancus* (which the author was kind enough to show me in manuscript form).

[230] On gold in non-monetary form at Gotland, which probably represents a survival of the earlier gold hoards buried here between 400 and 550 A.D., see M. Stenberger, *Die Schatzfunde Gotlands*, II, 311-78. Only four Arabic dinars dating from this period have been found in Sweden, which shows how little gold arrived here from the Moslem East.

To note that Northern Europe during these years was on a silver standard, not a gold one, and to emphasize, therefore, its essential economic separation from the Eastern Mediterranean, do not automatically mean, however, that its economy lagged or that it was principally agrarian. Regions possessing silver coinage have often been highly advanced in their economies. Witness, for instance, classical Greece prior to Alexander, Abbassid Iraq or modern examples like China and Mexico. Possession or lack of possession of a gold money, however important it may be in explaining or showing separation from gold currency regions of the Eastern Mediterranean, is irrelevant in assessing the degree of economic advance of Northern Europe during this Carolingian era. Only examination of the regions themselves can give us the answers we seek.[231]

At this point a word of warning is necessary. The answer one reaches as to the degree of economic advance in Carolingian times depends to a large extent upon which decades betwen 750 and 840 A.D. one examines. In general, it seems that many historians have made the all but unconscious assumption that the economy of Carolingian times was static. They have thus indiscriminately applied data from Pippin's reign to the period of Louis the Pious, and vice versa. Such practices have frequently resulted in a rather false picture of both periods. For the economy found in Northern Europe in 840 little resembled that of 770. In 770, as we have noted earlier, important economic life about the Northern Seas was almost completely restricted to a small region between the Seine and the Rhine and the coasts of Southern Britain across the Channel, with commercial routes which carried a trickle of trade to the Baltic and on through Russia or across the Alpine passes to Italy.

How different is the picture which emerges by the end of the reign of Louis the Pious! Agrarian changes had transformed large areas of Germany, Southern France, the Seine Valley, Flanders, Asturias and parts of England. Ports had revived in the Narbonnaise, Aquitaine and the valley of the Rhone, a revival that reached Asturian shores. Germany, east of the Rhine, begin to play a more important economic role in commerce. Trade revived in Britain, and again reached Ireland. Scandinavian and Frisian coasts, thanks to the arrival of Arab

[231] The error in interpretation is clear in A. R. Lewis, *Naval Power and Trade,* pp. 80-140, which confuses a silver coinage with agrarianism in Europe north of the Alps. See also the comments of A. Dopsch, in "The Agrarian Institutions of the Germanic Kingdoms from the Fifth to the Ninth Century," in *Cambridge Economic History of Europe,* I, 186-93.

silver dirhems, were filled with economic activity as new ports dotted the shores of the North Sea and the Baltic, from the Rhine to Birka and beyond. Varangian routes across Russia showed new activity. This is the world which the Carolingian era *ended* by producing, and to this world we will devote our attention in the next few pages.

One of the first questions to consider is the relationship in this age between rising trading places and expanding industry and commerce, on the one hand, and agrarian advances on the other. Was there a connection between them? Here, as was the case in our earlier discussion of this problem, we must note an important fact. It was in just those portions of the Carolingian world where evidence is most obvious of a movement toward a clearing of the forest and introduction of better agricultural methods that new trading centers arose, and old ones revived, by the early ninth century. Urban trading centers in Frisia, along the Scheldt, in the Meuse valley, in the Rhinelands and in Southern France all developed in the vicinity of regions showing agrarian growth and advance. In England, we notice the same thing. It is Midland and Western Britain which show evidences of economic growth by the time of the reign of Egbert of Wessex. Similarly, here again is found indication of a better, expanding agricultural economy. Even the maritime advances apparent off Norway's coasts seem to have been linked to an agricultural colonization movement to the Orkney and Shetland Islands. The answer seems obvious. There was a close relationship between these two movements, and one, the agricultural, aided the other, the commercial.

More difficult, however, is a proper estimate of the degree of economic advance which was reached by Northern Europe by 840. We must not exaggerate the maturity attained during these late Carolingian decades. In comparison with towns of the Roman Empire, for instance, the ports and *wicks* of this period were but small settlements, of wood construction, which were generally located in places convenient for trade. The nucleus of such a *portus* might be the remains of an older Roman walled city, like Canterbury or York in England, or Rhineland centers in Germany, or some French Carolingian *civitates*. Or such a *portus* might arise around a fortress, like Dorestad, or Utrecht in Holland, or Birka in Sweden. Or perhaps a monastery or episcopal residence, like those of Tours, Liége, Verdun or Noirmoutier, might serve as the nucleus about which a trading settlement would grow. Sometimes, as in the case of Hedeby, there seems to have been no pre-urban nucleus at all. Such nuclei in themselves were probably not as important as they were to be in the eleventh century, however, for this was not an age of fortified trading centers, such as we find in Late Roman times or during the High Middle Ages. Instead, excavations show that the typical Carolingian *portus* was surrounded by a palisade of wood and little else, except in a few spots like Eastern Germany, Russia and parts of Scandinavia, where unsettled conditions made protection more necessary. Until the late ninth century, trading centers in Carolingian times, as in the Merovingian period, were the products of a relatively peaceful age. Simple and probably primitive, they resembled the first settlements of Colonial America more than those of the Late Middle Ages.

And what of the inhabitants of these trading centers, these pre-bourg bourgeois? Did they also represent an early stage in economic development? It seems probable that they did. Many efforts have been made, as a matter of fact, to qualify the inhabitants of such a *portus* in Carolingian times as essentially agrarian, pertaining to the manor, or proto-urban. Probably, however, no fixed generalization concerning them is possible. As we have already noted, the economic connection between agriculture and commerce was close in this period, and the line separating inhabitants of a *wick* or *portus* from those dwelling in the nearby countryside was probably rather blurred. There were, as Sabbe points out, merchants of importance who lived in centers like Birka and Mainz, or who had important status,[232] like those of the Canterbury *cneuhts* guild,[233] or who traveled with servants, like the Rus who reached Bagdad.[234] There were also simple peddlers who wandered from place to place, carrying on petty commerce.[235] There were servile peasants, belonging to Rhineland monasteries, who, as Van Werweke has shown, transported wine for these establishments north, from land they owned in the region of viniculture.[236] There were others who, like the Sainteurs of the Loire region, can be described, according to Imbart de la Tour, as partly agents of their monastery, and partly merchants carrying on trade for themselves.[237] We find

[232] E. Sabbe, "Quelques types de marchands du IXe et Xe siècles," *loc.cit.*, pp. 180-86, contains an excellent description of such merchants.

[233] On the *cneuhts* guild of Canterbury, see J. Tait, *The Medieval English Borough*, pp. 15-30. C. Gross, *The Guild Merchant* (Oxford 1890), I, 188, and E. Coornaert, "Les Gildes médiévales," in *Revue hist.*, CXCIX (1950), 36-40.

[234] Ibn Khordâdbeh, *Book of Routes*, p. 114.

[235] For examples of such peddlers, *Ex miracules S. Germani*, in *MGH Script.*, xv, 9, and *Ex Andrea valdi Floriacenses miraculis S. Benedicti*, in *ibid.*, p. 496.

[236] H. Van Werweke, "Comment les établissements religieux belges se procuraient-ils le vin au Haut Moyen Age?" in *Revue belge*, II (1923), 289-97.

[237] Imbart de la Tour, *Les Immunités commerciales accordés aux églises*, pp. 13-52.

Frisians and Rhadamite Jews[238] who are merchants traveling over international routes and who carry with them expensive luxury items. Many varieties of men of differing status engaged in commerce during these years and lived in trading centers. The age of the Carolingians was, as Dopsch has emphasized, one of mixed economies, existing side by side.[239]

How interesting it is, and how disturbing, too, for those who demand economic precision and clearly defined status, to contemplate the fact that the Frisians, who were probably the principal indigenous merchants of the north during these years, *at home* lived in an agrarian, non-servile, peasant society in the intervals between their long commercial voyages![240] They were, in other words, only part-time merchants. How equally confusing it is to find that the island of Gotland, that permanent fair in the center of the Baltic, had no commercial settlements upon it at all, as far as we can discover![241] Like New England in colonial times, where a farming, fishing folk proved themselves capable of also being merchants and mariners who visited the shores of the seven seas, so in Carolingian times a man might be either a peasant or merchant, a farmer or commercial *voyageur*, depending upon the circumstances. The economic rule concerning those who carried on commerce in the Carolingian era was that there was no limitation to man's economic pursuits.

One is forced to reach a somewhat similar conclusion as to the status that industry attained during these years. It has probably been over-emphasized that industry was domanial in character.[242] Indeed, it was

---

[238] On these Rhadamite Jews, see, in addition to Ibn Khordâdbeh, J. Rabinowitz, *Jewish Merchant Adventurers* (London 1948).

[239] A. Dopsch, *Naturalwirtschaft und Geldwirtschaft in der Weltgeschichte* (Vienna 1930), pp. 250-315.

[240] The Frisians seem to have had no urban settlements, except perhaps Dorestad, in their homelands, and Dorestad seems to have been more a Frankish than a Frisian foundation, until Dokkum reached urban status at the time of Louis the Pious. See P. Boeles, *Friesland*, pp. 300-415, and J. H. Holwerda, *Dorestad*, pp. 31-202. Their settlements or urban quarters all seem to have been *outside* Frisia, in York, along the Rhine and in Scandinavia. Perhaps in this period "Frisian" was a vague term, meaning only an inhabitant of the North Sea coast from the Scheldt to the coast of Denmark. However that may be, the Frisians were not an urban people in their homeland in Carolingian times. See also the recent article by D. Jellema, "Frisian Trade in the Dark Ages," in *Speculum*, xxx (1955), 15-34.

[241] On Gotland's peculiar status, as shown by location of huge silver hoards here, see M. Stenberger, *op.cit.*, pp. 5-429. Also S. A. Anderson, *Viking Enterprise* (New York 1923), pp. 10-15. Unlike the Frisians, however, the Gotlanders appear in this period to have been a passive rather than an active commercial people, whose island served as a permanent international fair in the Baltic.

[242] Bloch points out that natural and domanial economies were never completely

in most cases, though our information for saying so is limited. But it seems difficult to believe that manufacture of glass, fine cloth, pottery and arms, which had a wide export market, was not centralized either near or in some *portus*. The role which monasteries played as centers for cloth manufacture and production of other merchandise has, for instance, also been insufficiently stressed. Some monasteries undoubtedly were industrial, wealth-producing centers—a fact which accounts for the attacks they suffered at the hands of Viking raiders. And, in addition, even domanial industry was by no means closed. Probably in most regions it was already producing goods which were exported by neighboring ports over wide distances. For instance, could such an industry as mining have been domanial? Obviously not.

Nor does our evidence show a complete lack of organization in the commerce and industry of this Carolingian era, though apparently it was still of a rudimentary sort. It is probably significant that a Carolingian law forbade the organization of guilds[243] and that we find some evidence, during this period, that Frisians and Anglo-Saxons were already formed into organized trading groups.[244] It also seems probable that the *marchands d'eau* on the Seine, late in this period, were the descendants of those earlier *collegia* which flourished there in Late Roman times.[245] And are we to doubt that those chapmen whom the English Laws of Alfred later report to be traveling in groups were not already embryo merchant guildsmen?[246] Nor need we be surprised to find Rus merchants already going to Bagdad, in the same manner as their Varangian descendants were to go to Constantinople.[247] Even the Rhadamite Jews already seem to have been an organized group.[248] The first steps towards later merchant and artisan guilds had been taken by the first years of the ninth century.

To sum up, by 840 the economy of the Carolingian era was still in an early stage of development, as far as its urban life, industry and commerce were concerned. But it was far more than a closed, domanial

---

closed during this period. M. Bloch, "Economie-nature ou économie-argent—un pseudodilème," in *Ann. d'hist. sociale*, I (1939), 7-16.

[243] *MGH Leges*, I, 37. And this prohibition was reiterated later in the century in *MGH Leges* I, 375, 553.

[244] E. Coornaert, *Les Gildes médiévales*, pp. 31-50.

[245] On these *marchands d'eau*, see J. W. Thompson, "The Commerce of France in the Ninth Century," *loc.cit.*, pp. 885-87. Perhaps the mysterious *cappi* whom Thompson finds in Northern France in these years were similarly organized.

[246] *Laws of Alfred*, in C. Attenborough, *The Earliest English Laws*, pp. 42-43.

[247] Ibn Khordâdbeh, *Book of Routes*, pp. 114-16.

[248] J. Rabinowitz, *Jewish Merchant Adventurers*, pp. 115-71.

economy in the sense that this term is so often used, and already it was developing rapidly towards a new future. If one can see in the economy of the Merovingian Age a beginning of economic life and growth, that of the Carolingians represented, by 840, a halfway point towards the more fully achieved urbanization and economic life of the twelfth century. An international commerce composed of many products—natural, manufactured and imported—existed already in the lands of Northern Europe. Trading places were on their way to becoming towns. Industries were developing beyond the domanial stage, particularly mining, glassmaking, metalworking and cloth manufacturing. Extensive clearing of forest lands was changing the face of Europe, and ushering in a new and better agricultural system. New organizational groupings of merchants, and perhaps artisans as well, were forecasting future developments along that line. Without exaggeration, it can be said that a comparison between Merovingian and Carolingian times, except in parts of Southern Gaul and Spain, is entirely in favor of the later period. What had begun as a growth, formless and free, between 550 and 750 had, after a brief mid-eighth-century decline, emerged as an economic system acquiring form and character. The cultural renaissance which took shape during these years was to prove more important than those sparks which had burst into flame in Merovingian times in various localities to produce such figures as Gregory of Tours, Venantius Fortunatus, Isadore of Seville and the venerable Bede. The earlier period had showed it could produce such figures, but only as individuals and in certain localities. In Carolingian times we find, on the other hand, culture expressed more broadly by *schools* of art, of literature and of culture on a wide scale.[249] In economy, as in culture, with the Carolingian Age we begin the great institutional development of medieval Europe.

Nowhere is the contrast between Northern Europe in Merovingian and in Carolingian times more strongly marked than in the field of government regulation and control of economic life. As has been noted earlier, the Merovingians did not regulate their currency, their trade or any feature of economic life of their age, except when something of the Roman system survived within their territory—a *fiscus*,

---

[249] On this monetary anarchy, which seems to have extended to Visigothic Spain as well, see M. Prou, *Catalogue des monnaies mérovingiennes*, pp. LXXXIV-CIX, and P. Le Gentilhomme, *Mélanges de numismatique mérovingienne*, pp. 3-120. On England's similar uncontrolled coinage, see C. Sutherland, *Anglo-Saxon Gold Coinage in the Light of the Crondall Hoard*, pp. 11-17, and "Anglo-Saxon Sceattas in England," in *Num. Chron.*, 6th ser., II (1942), 251-63.

for instance. They were willing to grant immunities which stripped them of what little governing power they possessed, and by the seventh century allowed anyone who so desired to coin money within their domains. Nor is there evidence that the Anglo-Saxon rulers of that period were any more aware of the economic functions of government, except in the most rudimentary sense of the term. But how different the age of the Carolingians proved to be in this respect in all of Northern Europe!

The first step towards this new governmental interest in economic affairs came in 755, when Pippin reformed the silver currency of his kingdom, setting up a standard of 22 *solidi* to one pound of silver. In 781 and 794, Charlemagne continued to adjust the silver coinage of the Frankish realm, finally establishing a new standard, probably influenced by the Moslem dirhem, which was to last for centuries in Western Europe. In 803 and 805 he issued regulations forbidding the counterfeiting of his silver pennies, followed by additional decrees concerning his coinage in 808 and 809. His son, Louis the Pious, showed an even greater interest in the money of the Empire, for he issued regulations on this subject in 819, 825, 826, 829 and 832.[250] Altogether, in the course of some thirty years these two Carolingian monarchs issued nine capitularies concerning the minting of coins. Nor were they alone in this interest, for across the Channel numismatic evidence shows an almost equal concern on the part of Offa and Egbert with the establishment of a pure and abundant silver money modeled on the standard of the Carolingians.[251]

The economic interests of Charlemagne and Louis the Pious did not, however, stop with mere regulation of their coinage. During these years they began to regulate the external commerce of the Empire as well. This seems to have been accomplished through the establishment, in certain main Carolingian ports, of an official known as a *prefectus*, in charge of the foreign trade. In Quentovic, for instance, we learn of such an official, who appears to have conducted trade negotiations with Offa concerning English commerce with the Empire,[252] and we also hear of a *prefectus* of Dokkum in Northern Frisia, per-

---

[250] E. Gariel, *Les Monnaies royales de France sous la race carolingienne*, I, 21-35. M. Prou, *Catalogue des monnaies carolingiennes*, pp. XLIX-LV. See also the admirable summary of these regulations in F. Vercauteren, *Etudes sur les civitates de la Belgique Secunde*, pp. 453-58.

[251] C. F. Keary, *Catalogue of English Coins—Anglo-Saxon Series*, I, XXIII-XXVI. G. C. Brooke, *English Coins*, pp. 13-31, 41-50.

[252] *Ex miraculis S. Wandrigeseli*, in *MGH Script.*, XV, 408. *Gesta Abbatium Fontanellensium*, in *Script. in usum scholarum*, p. 46.

haps in charge of commerce to the Baltic.[253] Our sources reveal similar officials in both England and Scandinavia during this period, the *wic gerefa*, or port-reeve, of Dorchester, mentioned in 787,[254] and the *prefecti* whom Anskar found in Birka and Rimbert in Hedeby in the early ninth century.[255] Thus we see the *state* interested in commercial matters everywhere throughout the Northern Seas, and officials established in important trading entrepôts to carry out certain trade policies. To such evidence of new official concern with trade one should add the fact that Charlemagne[256] built a lighthouse at Boulogne to aid navigation, and in his capitularies attempted to establish legislation governing maritime commerce.[257]

Did this Carolingian interest in commerce go further? Did Charlemagne and Louis the Pious establish a commercial policy for their Empire, as Lopez suggests, and attempt to direct its commerce to strengthen their state?[258] It seems probable that they did, though here our evidence is scattered and not always conclusive. We can see such a Carolingian system of trade controls best in Italy, where Charlemagne several times used trade blockades in his attempt to force Venice to accept his overlordship.[259] We can see them in his maintenance of the *clusae* in the Alps over the Great and Little St. Bernard, the Septimer and Mount Geneva passes.[260] Indeed, it is possible that Carolingian regulations, inherited from the defunct Lombard kingdom, had the effect of channeling all trade to Italy from the north over these particular passes. And we know that Charlemagne's Capitulary of Thionville set up a series of trade portals along his eastern frontier to control commerce with the Slavs and Avars, to whom he forbade export of arms.[261]

[253] P. Boeles, *Friesland*, pp. 385-86.

[254] Florence of Worcester, *Chronicle*, in *Mon. Brit. Hist.*, p. 509.

[255] *Vita Anskari*, XXXI, in *MGH Script.*, II, 747. H. Jankuhn, "Ergebnisse und Probleme der Haithabugrabungen 1937-39," *loc.cit.*, pp. 55-56.

[256] M. Bouquet, *Recueil des historiens de la France* (Paris 1878), V, 60-61.

[257] *Capitularia regum Francorum*, ed. Boretus, I, 319, art. 17.

[258] On this problem, see R. S. Lopez, "La Politique commerciale au moyen âge," *loc.cit.*, pp. 17-18. Lopez stresses that such regulations north of the Alps and Pyrenees were a new development in Carolingian times.

[259] On these efforts, see A. R. Lewis, *op.cit.*, pp. 118-20.

[260] *Capitulary of Pepin*, in *MGH Leges*, II, 201. See also G. Bognetti, *Nota per la storia del passaporto e del salva condotte* (Pavia 1933), pp. 20-35. On the difficulties with Byzantine officials that Boniface and his companions encountered while traveling to Rome, see W. Levison, *England and the Continent*, p. 14. On the passes used between Italy and the north in this period—the Great St. Bernard, the Mont Cenis and the Septimer—see G. G. Dept, "Let Mot clusae dans les diplômes carolingiens," in *Mélanges Pirenne*, I, 92-96.

[261] *Capitulary of Thionville*, in *MGH Leges*, Cap. I, no. 44.

Towards the north we have evidence from Charlemagne's trade wars with Offa in 784-785 and 793-794, ending in a trade treaty, that he was willing to invoke and use economic pressures to regulate the Empire's commerce with England.[262] And we have some bits of evidence that he did the same as regards trade to the Baltic, on one occasion putting an embargo on exports of grain to Denmark. Perhaps the story, told by the Monk of St. Gall, that Charlemagne forbade the export of Frisian cloth to Gaul shows an attempt to put pressure upon these traders, who, as the chief merchants to Scandinavia, were too friendly with his Danish enemies.[263] He was interested enough in control of traffic to this region, at any rate, to refuse St. Luitger's request to be allowed to travel to Denmark on an evangelical mission.[264] It appears, then, that Charlemagne controlled trade with Italy, with Slavic and Avar lands, with England and with the Baltic. A Carolingian trade control system, modeled after that found in the Byzantine Empire and Lombard Italy was, after 800, evidently being established on the borders of Charlemagne's Empire.[265]

It also seems possible that trade with Spain, both Christian and Moslem, was similarly controlled from the Frankish kingdom of Aquitaine, ruled, until his father's death, by Louis the Pious. The only traces of such a system, however, seem to have no earlier date than the reign of Charles the Bald. If such a system was established, it seems probable, from coin evidence, that Narbonne and Dax were the control points for traffic to Moslem and Christian Spain, respectively.[266] Thus one sees, about 800, trade controls established along the borders of the Carolingian Empire, covering commerce with Italy,

[262] R. Hodgkin, *History of the Anglo-Saxons*, I, 389-92, and J. Tait, *op.cit.*, p. 10, sketch these trade wars between Offa and Charlemagne. See also *MGH Leges*, V, Formulae 37.

[263] Mon. S. Gall, *Gesta Karoli Magni*, I, 34, in *MGH Script.*, II, 747.

[264] *Translatio S. Vitri*, ed. Stentrup, pp. 79-83.

[265] This explains those "merchants of the palace" who are mentioned in *Formulae*, in *MGH Leges*, V, 314-15. Their functions were copied from Byzantium and indeed the control and distribution by Louis the Pious of fine Flemish cloth among his courtiers was an aping of similar controls of fine silks by the Emperors in Constantinople. H. Laurent, in "Marchands du palais et marchands d'abbaye," in *Revue hist.*, CLXXXIII (1938), 211-23, seems to confuse such regulation with a lack of regular commerce in this period.

[266] Coin hoards dating from Louis' reign, such as those found at Veuillen and Belvezet, contain coins from mints stretching down to Narbonne and Dax, but no farther. This seems to suggest that they both were trade portals like Boulogne, Dorestad and Quentovic. On these hoards, see E. Gariel, *op.cit.*, pp. 41-70. We lack the capitularies, however, of the kingdom of Aquitaine of Louis the Pious until the time of Pepin I and Pepin II. Hence little trace of such trade controls with Spain exists in the sources.

Slav lands, the Avar realm, Scandinavia, England and perhaps Spain. The age of completely free commerce in the Northern Seas was at an end. The age of trade controls, dead since Late Roman times, had returned.

Did Anglo-Saxon England similarly control its export and import commerce? It seems possible. In 778, for instance, Frisian traders were expelled from York, an interesting example of discrimination against foreign merchants.[267] Some provisions of Anglo-Saxon laws, forbidding the export of slaves and horses, also are suggestive.[268] But England was, no doubt, less advanced than the Continent in matters of trade control during these years, while Scandinavia reveals little evidence of commercial regulation.

This Carolingian Age of economic advance, of increasing state control of commerce and currency in Northern Europe, saw one other event of great importance take place in the Northern Seas in the first years of the ninth century. It saw the beginnings of Viking aggression. The causes of these Viking assaults upon Europe, south of the Baltic, will be dealt with fully in another chapter, but at least a few points are worth considering here. The first is that these Viking attacks began innocently enough with an advance of Norwegians, Swedes and Danes down the major trade routes which reached their shores in the late eighth century. We have already noted that this period saw a pre-Rurik advance of Scandinavians along Varangian routes into Russia, and that it saw Norse colonists establishing themselves in the Atlantic island chain that stretched towards Scotland and Ireland. Evidence from Dorestad, which shows Danes peacefully established there, too, in the early ninth century, also suggests a pre-Viking penetration, from Denmark, of this sea route past North German and Frisian coasts. As confirmation of the fact that initial contacts between Scandinavians and their neighbors to the east and to the south were generally peaceful, one has the later story of the first Viking descent on Dorchester in 787. There the port-reeve and inhabitants went down to the shore to meet the Norse ships, thinking they belonged to peaceful traders, only to discover their error when they were attacked and slain.[269] Evidently Scandinavian merchants were not unknown in these waters— only raiders were unexpected. Dicuil similarly implies that not until 795-796 did Viking assaults force Irish monks to leave their settle-

---

[267] *Vita Liutgeri*, in *MGH Script.*, II, 407.
[268] C. Attenborough, *The Earliest English Laws*, pp. 38-43.
[269] Florence of Worcester, *Chronicle*, in *Mon. Brit. Hist.*, p. 509.

ments in the Orkneys and Hebrides and seek safer homes.[270] Nor does our evidence from Russian sources imply any great friction between Scandinavian and native Slav, Chud and Finn, until the Scandinavians' expulsion well into the ninth century, about 839 or 840. Viking violence, then, seems to have flared up suddenly after a period of peaceful contact and commercial intercourse.

The Norse attacks were begun in 787 with the above-mentioned raid on Dorchester, and a second in 793, equally unexpected, upon the Abbey of Lindesfarne in Northumbria.[271] Following them, the Norse seem to have concentrated their raids initially upon the coasts of Ireland, where Thorgisl of the Westfold played a cruel and violent role as leader of these Viking pirates.[272] Soon they were extending their attacks farther south, to reach the coasts of Aquitaine, where Noirmoutier, at the mouth of the Loire, was raided with regularity between 814 and 819.[273]

The Danes, on the other hand, first concentrated their attention on the Frisian coast, near the mouths of the Rhine, and only later, as Carolingian resistance weakened, extended them south along the Channel to reach the Seine.[274] But, except in Ireland, a special case, these early raids caused little real damage, and not until after the death of Louis the Pious did the great Viking assault on the Carolingian Empire and England begin.

The main reason why these raids were not at first so serious lies in the swift reaction of Charlemagne and Louis to the danger they represented. About 800, after word of raids on Ireland, Aquitaine and England had reached him, Charlemagne began the construction of a naval defense system along his shores.[275] He started with the establishment of a fleet, some of whose ships we know were being built at Ghent in 811,[276] and stationed it at Boulogne, which commanded the vital entrance from the North Sea into the Channel. He also fortified

---

[270] Dicuil, *De mensura orbis terrae*, p. 44.

[271] On Alcuin's efforts to make Offa and Charlemagne present a united front to these Scandinavian raiders after their first attack on Lindesfarne, see Alcuin, *Epistolae*, in *MGH Epist. Karol. aevi*, II, 53.

[272] H. Shetelig, *An Introduction to the Viking History of Western Europe*, pp. 49-55.

[273] T. D. Kendrick, *History of the Vikings*, pp. 10-13. H. Shetelig, *op.cit.*, p. 105.

[274] P. Boeles, *Friesland*, pp. 386-90.

[275] *Ann. reg. franc.*, in *MGH Script.*, I, 187, and Einhard, *Vita Karoli Magni*, in *MGH Script.*, II, 452.

[276] C. de la Roncière, "Charlemagne et la civilisation maritime au IXe siècle," in *Le Moyen Age*, XI (1897), 142-48. See also J. de Vries, *Die Wikinger in de lag landen bij de Zee* (Harlem 1923), pp. 98-99.

Ghent at the mouth of the Scheldt, and built defenses to protect the Rhine and also the Meuse. Other forts were built farther south along the Channel in Normandy to protect this coast as well from pirate assaults.[277] At about the same time, at least as early as 810, his son Louis built ships at the mouths of the Loire and Garonne to protect western Gallic shores.[278] Within a decade, then, the Carolingians had swiftly built a naval defense system for the Empire from the Rhine to the Garonne.

What is interesting about this naval defense system of Charlemagne and of his son Louis is the fact that it closely paralleled that of the Romans four centuries earlier along these shores. Like the Romans, Charlemagne stationed his main fleet at Boulogne to guard the Strait of Dover. Like them also, he supplemented this protection with defenses near the mouths of the Rhine, the Seine, the Loire and the Garonne. But one finds it hard to understand why he neglected to defend the North German and Frisian coasts in the same way. Perhaps he doubted the loyalty of the Frisians, who had so many Scandinavian contacts, and that of the recently conquered Saxons as well. At any rate, we know that only once, in the year 806, did he use his fleet in conjunction with his army in the war he was waging against the Danes. During his other campaigns on the borders of Jutland, in 808 and 811, his ships remained at Boulogne in a defensive role.[279] Perhaps, like the Romans, Charlemagne did not understand the offensive use of naval power.

After his death the Viking naval threat remained a real one, as we know from pirate raids launched on Frisia and Aquitaine. Thus Louis the Pious, as revealed by a number of capitularies, felt it wise to keep up a system of naval defenses along his shores.[280] It was this naval power which enabled him to win an important victory over a Viking force, probably Norse, which in 820 was raiding near the mouths of the Loire in Aquitaine and in Normandy.[281] To these defenses was also probably owed the absence of additional raids along these shores for more than a decade.

Although Louis seems to have defended his Empire with naval con-

---

[277] C. de la Roncière, op.cit., pp. 143-46.

[278] Lot, Pfister and Ganshof, Les Destinées de l'empire en Occident, p. 468, and W. Vogel, Die Normannen und das Fränkische Reich (Heidelburg 1906), pp. 56, 138.

[279] C. de la Roncière, op.cit., p. 207.

[280] These capitularies were issued in 815, 820, 821, 835, 837 and 838. J. W. Thompson, The Commerce of France in the Ninth Century, p. 860.

[281] H. Shetelig, op.cit., p. 108.

tingents and a fixed system of naval defenses, he relied on something else, too—diplomacy. He appears to have given protection to an unsuccessful claimant to the Danish throne, a certain Harold, and to have awarded him and his followers Carolingian fiefs in Frisia and near the mouth of the Weser in Saxony. This assured him of naval allies who would aid in defending these vital shores, though it established a bad precedent for the future. Temporarily at least, it succeeded well enough, and for a brief time Harold even gained control of Denmark, though he proved too weak to hold it.[282] After Harold's death, Danish raids began again in 835 and 838,[283] but even then it is interesting to note that Horick, the Danish king, listened sympathetically to Carolingian protests against such piracy, and tried to do something to stop them.[284] In short, Louis seems to have adopted the method used successfully by the Romans in defense of their frontiers—that of establishing barbarian peoples inside their state to defend it against other barbarians outside, and of relying upon diplomatic pressures to keep neighboring peoples friendly. In this respect, Louis' encouragement of Anskar in his mission north to Denmark and Sweden, in which this latter tried to bring Christianity to Danes and Swedes, is most enlightening.[285] It helps to explain why, almost until Louis' death, the Viking menace to his Empire remained a minor one and why economic progress could continue along Carolingian coasts.

There remains one final question, that concerning the ships in use on the Northern Seas during this Carolingian Age of economic growth and expansion of maritime commercial intercourse. Curiously enough, in general our knowledge concerning this subject is less than it was for the Merovingian period. Only a few scraps of information are available, most of them rather unsatisfactory in nature.

Along Carolingian shores two distinct areas of ship construction seem to have existed by the ninth century—Frisia and the North Sea area, on the one hand, and western Gallic waters, on the other. In Western Gaul it seems probable that older carvel-built *scaphae* and *barcae* survived into this age. *Scaphae* are mentioned in charters of Louis the Pious and Pepin I of Aquitaine as being active along

---

[282] P. Boeles, *Friesland*, pp. 387-91. R. Hodgkin, *History of the Anglo-Saxons*, II, 490-92.

[283] P. Boeles, *op.cit.*, pp. 391-94. T. D. Kendrick, *History of the Vikings*, pp. 194-97.

[284] H. Shetelig, *op.cit.*, pp. 108-10.

[285] *Vita Anskari*, XXIX-XXXIII, in *MGH Script.*, II, 703-42.

the rivers and coasts of Western Gaul,[286] and the *barca* is mentioned later in the ninth century by Hincmar of Reims and the *Annales Vedastes*.[287] Probably, then, it was used still earlier in the century.

On the other hand, the famous ship-money coinage or Dorestad reveals that the Frisians used quite a different type of clinker-built vessel.[288] Later Alfred expressly distinguished between these "Frisian ships" and those he was constructing for his navy in England. Our best contemporary account of these vessels, however, comes from a passage in Rimbert's *Vita Anskari*, where the writer describes Anskar's voyage north to Hedeby from Cologne in such a craft. He mentions that the ship was built with two cabins, a feature which King Harold of Denmark, traveling north with Anskar, found so inviting that he deserted his own Viking ship to enjoy the accommodations that such a cabined vessel provided.[289] Evidently the Frisians' ships were, in comfort at least, superior to those of their Scandinavian neighbors.

Of the warships which Louis the Pious and Charlemagne built to guard their shores, however, we know nothing. Were they the *naves longae* mentioned in the *Ancient Laws of Ireland*? Or did they resemble the fast Byzantine and Arab *dromons* of the Mediterranean? The fact that Carolingian fleets operated, in the early ninth century, in the Mediterranean from Genoa and Ampurias makes it possible that they used Mediterranean ship designs for their Northern fleets.[290] But this must remain little more than a possibility.

Our knowledge of British and Irish ships of this period is even more disappointing. Irish coracles still reached the Orkneys and Shetlands, we know.[291] But what of British ships? There is only the probability that those of the North Sea resembled the Frisian *kogges* and those of the Channel and western British coasts were like the *barcae* and *scaphae* of Gaul.

On the other hand, it is during this period that our knowledge of Scandinavian ships becomes more extensive, thanks to the discovery of two ninth-century examples, the Osberg and Gokstad ships, in excavations along Oslo fjord. These two are very different. The

[286] J. Levillain, *Recueil des actes de Pepin I et Pepin II*, pp. 61, 170, 214.
[287] W. Vogel, *Zur nord- und westeuropäischen Seeschiffahrt*, pp. 188-89.
[288] M. Prou, *Catalogue des monnaies carolingiennes*, pp. 1-21, contains information on these coins. They seem to resemble coins also bearing ship pictures which were found in Norway later in the century. On these coins, see Brøgger and Shetelig, *The Viking Ships*, p. 182.
[289] *Vita Anskari*, XXI, in *MGH Script.*, II, 709.
[290] On these fleets, see A. R. Lewis, *op.cit.*, pp. 105-6, 132-33.
[291] Dicuil, *De mensura orbis terrae*, p. 44.

Osberg ship, which was a beautifully constructed craft, seems to have been essentially a yacht used by its owner, Queen Asa, for cruising in relatively quiet coastal waters. It had a strong keel and carried both a sail and 15 pairs of oars. It used a fixed rudder as well. It was 64 feet long and 15 feet wide amidships. Slender and graceful in design, its fine lines and beautiful carvings make it one of the loveliest discoveries that archeologists have revealed to us from the Viking Age. But in essence its low beam amidships rendered this vessel Baltic rather than Atlantic in character.[292]

If less beautiful, the ninth-century Gokstad ship, on the other hand, gives us a better example of Scandinavian advances in ship-building, and helps to make clear why the mariners who used such a ship were the terror of West European coasts during the next century. This vessel was a sturdy, ocean-going craft, 80 feet long and 19 feet wide amidships. It had a strong external keel, a high prow and a mast which fitted into a wooden block. It carried a large square sail and, in addition, had 16 pairs of oars. The keel was constructed of oak, the ribs of curved beech and the mast of fir. It was clinker-built, like all Scandinavian ships, caulked with cowhair, and it had a rudder and tiller fixed to one side of the stern. Inside it was half-planked, with an elevated deck section both fore and aft. It was capable of carrying a crew of 40, or a total of from 60 to 70 persons in all. The Gokstad ship was seaworthy throughout and extremely maneuverable.[293] It explains how Viking raiders could suddenly appear on foreign shores without warning, as they seem to have done in the case of their raid on Lindesfarne Abbey in 793. For in such a ship the open sea held no terrors for Viking mariners. And upon such vessels their superiority in the Atlantic during the next centuries was to rest.

During these years of the ninth century, however, Scandinavia used other types of ships besides those found at Osberg and Gokstad, as we know from our sources. There was the *knorr*, a sturdy, oarless merchantman, which we have found depicted in Gotland rock sculptures and which was probably modeled after the Frisian merchantman.[294] There was the *skuta*, or fast scouting ship, perhaps basically

[292] A. W. Brøgger, "The Osberg Ship," in *Saga Book of the Viking Society*, x (1919-24), 91-108. See also Brøgger and Shetelig, *op.cit.*, pp. 151-66.

[293] N. Nicolaysen, *The Viking Ship Discovered at Gokstad* (Oslo 1882). See especially the latest views on this craft in Brøgger and Shetelig, *op.cit.*, pp. 104-51. On the very similar Tune ship, see *ibid.*, pp. 147-51.

[294] On the *knorr*, or *knarr*, see Brøgger and Shetelig, *op.cit.*, pp. 233-36. They

of Celtic origin,[295] and the *karfi*, a small vessel used on lakes and rivers in Russia and interesting because its name, derived from the Greek *karabos*, shows some Byzantine influences reaching the Baltic during these years.[296] And, finally, there was the dinghy, which, though of wood, seems to have followed the lines of the Celtic coracle.[297] Altogether, then, by the ninth century the Scandinavian peoples, either by copying other maritime craft or developing their own ship-types, had become the leading shipbuilders of the Northern Seas, with craft capable of carrying them wherever the grey waters of the Atlantic beckoned.

Such is the story of Northern Europe and the Northern Seas during this Carolingian Age. It is a tale of revival, reconstruction and advance in the ninety years that separated Pippin's assumption of the throne from the death of his grandson, Louis the Pious. We have seen, during this period, a revival of older trading centers and a development of new ones, an agrarian advance and great institutional developments. It was an age which saw in Northern Europe a beginning of commercial regulation by governments, the first organized naval establishments since Roman times and a beginning of guild and merchant associations. Though Northern Europe developed links with the Mediterranean during this period, it seems clear that the world of the Carolingians faced north rather than south, much more than had been the case in Merovingian times. Its economic center also was moving to the northeast towards Germany and a Baltic region which now boasted a commerce and silver arriving there from Russia and the Orient. In short, it was a period in which Scandinavia again became closely connected with the cultivated world to her south and one in which commerce flowed more freely from Spain to Finland and on to the Caspian, in contrast to meager beginnings in Merovingian times.

This new integration of the Northern Seas, this new maritime traffic that linked the Baltic firmly with North Sea and Caspian, this northeast orientation of Western Europe's commerce, held danger for many parts of Northern Europe. It did stimulate commerce by

---

deny a similarity between this ship-type and the Frisian *kogge* or *kugge*. *Ibid.*, pp. 236-37.

[295] H. Shetelig, *Scandinavian Archeology*, pp. 370-72.

[296] On the *karfi*, which as a type probably included vessels as large at the Gokstad ship, see Brøgger and Shetelig, *op.cit.*, pp. 173-77, and H. Falk, *Altnordisches Seewessen* (Heidelberg 1912), pp. 90-94.

[297] H. Shetelig, *op.cit.*, p. 370.

bringing Oriental wares and silver far to the West. But in the process the Irish, Anglo-Saxons and Carolingians, like the Kazars and White Bulgars of Russia, raised up in Scandinavia dangerous neighbors. By 800, these Scandinavians had added to trading the occupation of piracy. Russian Slavs and Baltic Chuds and Finns appear to have answered this challenge, about 840, by expelling the Varangians from their territories. Charlemagne and Louis the Pious, on the other hand, faced this Viking threat by setting up naval defenses, establishing export controls about their Empire and using a wise diplomacy to keep such piracy in check. Except in Ireland, up to 838 or 840 these measures kept the Danes in the North Sea and the Norwegians along the Atlantic routes farther west relatively harmless, while preserving the economic advantages gained from commercial contacts with Scandinavia. But Ireland was already a warning of what could happen. When, in 840, the Carolingian Empire fell into the hands of weak, quarreling monarchs, when England lost the strong directing hand of Egbert of Wessex, a new day dawned in the Northern Seas. The coasts of England and the Carolingian Empire now lay open to Viking assaults. Soon, in Russia as well, Rurik and Oleg were to inaugurate a new aggressive Varangian advance which reached Berdea in the Caucasus and the walls of Byzantium itself. By 840 the Carolingian era had ended. A cruel, dangerous age began— the age of the Vikings—an age which was to see the work of Offa, Egbert, Charlemagne and Louis the Pious checked, challenged and endangered by the Ragnar Ladbroks, the Ruriks and the Hastings, who, sword in hand, plowed the seas to lay the foundations of a new and different Northern Europe.

5, The Viking Assault, A.D. 840-911

THE DEATH of Louis the Pious in 840 began a new era in Northern Europe, one that might be called the age of the Viking assault. Though the beginnings of the Viking attacks went back to about 790, and though they were to continue long after 911, it was these eight decades that witnessed the major events in that movement of Scandinavian peoples down trade routes east and west to the heart of England, Ireland, France and Russia. By 911, the major patterns of Viking expansion had taken shape. The Norse were established in Iceland, the Faroes, the Shetlands, the Orkneys, the Isle of Man, and along the coasts of Ireland, and were moving into Westmoreland and Cumberland. The Danes had occupied and then lost Frisia, and were established in the Danelaw and in Normandy. The Swedes had advanced down the rivers of Russia to establish the kingdom of Kiev, and were favored traders in mighty Constantinople.

Meanwhile, under the impact of this assault, the Carolingian Empire had been shattered, one portion becoming Germany, soon to be ruled by the Ottos, the other a France already troubled by a Capetian-Carolingian rivalry that was not to end until about the year 1000. England by 911, rid of the rival Anglo-Saxon royal houses of the Heptarchy, was now led by the House of Alfred of Wessex, which was slowly but surely reconquering the land from the Danes. A united Scottish kingdom had just emerged under Kenneth MacAlpine. A new Europe, which was to continue through the Middle Ages, had appeared in the wake of Scandinavian assault.

The nature of this Viking age has long engaged the attention of historians, who have found it difficult to explain. In the first place, many aspects of it, particularly the movement of Swedes east into Russia, still seem obscure. Even more perplexing is the fact that, though the major outlines of the migrations of the Danes, Swedes, and Norwegians from their Scandinavian homelands are easily apparent, in detail these movements seem mixed in character. Danes as well as Norwegians, for instance, appeared in Ireland, and the great Danish army of Ubbe, Hastings and Gudrum, which invaded England in 865, contained some Norse elements. The majority of the Scandinavians who settled in Normandy seem to have been Danes, yet Rollo and the leading elements were of Norwegian origin. A Swede was the first Northman, it seems, to discover Iceland, and there were a number of Swedes among the original colonists there, who were mainly Norse. Similarly, both Norwegians and Danes appear to have participated in the Swedish movement into Russia. Thus movements of peoples from Scandinavia east and west can only be identified in a general way with a particular people or section of this northern Viking world.

Even harder to untangle are the causes of these Viking attacks and migrations. Many explanations, of both a general and a specific nature, have been attempted. It has been pointed out, for instance, that migrations from Norway, Denmark and Sweden differ in their initial phases of development. It has been emphasized that the Norwegian movement was, from the start, essentially one of colonization, generally peaceful in its penetration and occupation of the Orkneys, Shetlands and Hebrides. Only later on, in Ireland and in attacks upon the Atlantic coasts of France, did it become piratical and violent.[1] Then, in their settlement of Iceland and Greenland, the Norse reverted to their peaceful, colonizing role.

On the other hand, it has been emphasized that the first contacts between the Danes and regions to the south—in this case, Charlemagne's Empire—were violent political ones—a reaction of the Danes to Charlemagne's conquest of Saxony and to his advance to the southern borders of the Danish kingdom.[2] And Denmark, it is said, concentrated on political expansion during the entire Viking period, as is seen in the character of the great Danish invasion of England, in the Danes' duchy in Frisia and in the careers and conquests of Svein and Canute.

The Swedes, however, are said to have pushed east into Russia because they sought trade and economic riches to be gained from commerce with Byzantium and the Moslem East, and thus to have

---

[1] On the earlier, peaceful phase of Norse expansion, see A. W. Brøgger, *Ancient Emigrants*, pp. 1-33, and *Oler Norske bosetningen på Shetland-Orknøyene* (Oslo 1930), pp. 7-61. See also H. Shetelig, *An Introduction to the Viking History of Western Europe*, pp. 5-23, and "Les Origines des invasions des Normands," in *Bergens Mus. Arbok Hist. og Rekke* (Bergen 1932), pp. 315-61.

[2] On the political clash that lay behind the Danes' contacts with Frisia, see J. C. Steenstrup, *Normaneere* (Copenhagen 1878), pp. 28-43; J. de Vries, *Die Wikinger in de Lage Landen bij de Zee*, pp. 50-103; and W. Vogel, *Die Normannen und das Fränkische Reich*, pp. 30-139. See also P. Boeles, *Friesland*, pp. 286-89.

had no essential colonizing or political objective.[3] Much has been made, perhaps too much, of the peaceful trading nature of the Swedish Varangian movement into the heart of Russia. Neither the Byzantines, nor the Kazars, nor the White Bulgars, nor the Moslems of the Caspian, who felt the full fury of the Varangians' attacks, would care, I believe, to attach too much significance to their peaceful trading intentions. And can one say, from what we know, that an Askold, a Rurik, an Oleg or a Sviatoslav were less booty-minded and piratical than a Thorgisl, a Gudrum, a Hastings or a Rollo? For whether they moved east or west, whether their homes were Norway, Denmark or Sweden, all these Viking leaders and their followers sought new riches—the degree of their commercial spirit depending upon the nature of the opposition they met and the particular opportunities available. They were all traders at times as well as raiders and colonists, but the element of force seems to have been ever present in their movements. Granting, then, that some general differences between Swedish, Norse and Danish expansion are to be found, we would be wiser not to exaggerate such differences. Rather our emphasis should be upon viewing the whole Viking expansion as one common movement.

Another equally unsatisfactory suggestion is that which sees in the Viking attacks and expansion the result of a certain political consolidation of Scandinavian kingdoms which drove forth those who did not wish to submit to it.[4] For the initial period down to 911, this seems directly opposed to the facts. The first Viking movement from Norwegian and Danish shores took place before 840, which is to say, before there were any signs of political consolidation in Norway, and at a time when Denmark was gripped by an unsual degree of civil war and anarchy in which no political power seems to have been effective. After 840, when the really great attacks upon Western European coasts began, attacks which lasted until 870 or 880, Norway still was just beginning to be united by Harold Fairhair, and Denmark

[3] On Swedish expansion and its causes, see B. Nerman, *Sveriges Första Storhetstid*, pp. 92-114, and T. J. Arne, *Det Stora Svitjod*, pp. 5-130. Also F. Balodis, *Handelswege nach den Osten und die Wikinger in Russland* (Stockholm 1948), pp. 36-152.

[4] The source of this theory seems to be the tradition held by Iceland's colonists that they fled to Iceland to escape the tyranny of Harold Fairhair. See the *Heimskringla*, *The Saga of Harold Fairhair*, VI, and *The Egils Saga*, IV. Since Iceland was not settled until 870, after most Viking expansion had already taken place, this theory has little basis as regards an earlier period in the 9th century.

had no political unity at all; in fact, Denmark was not united until the next century by Harold Bluetooth.[5]

We know little about Sweden in this period. But precious information that comes to us from Anskar's and Rimbert's voyages gives us little evidence that the traditional Swedish monarchs of Uppsala, prior to Olaf late in the ninth century, had any more authority than their Danish and Norwegian counterparts to the west. The fact that the Swedish king consulted his nobles and advisors before deciding whether or not to allow Anskar, on his second visit, to proselytize for Christianity, the civil war in which a Danish fleet intervened in favor of a rival claimant to the throne, and the inability of the Swedish monarch to protect Birka, his principal trading center, from piratical exactions—all these suggest that Sweden was a weak, decentralized state in which the monarchy was essentially powerless. And what little we know of Swedish history suggests that this weakness continued down to the time of Olaf Skottkonung.[6] The theory that royal consolidation drove forth Viking raiders must be considered untenable.

What remains? Only one explanation: that desire for gain lay behind the whole Scandinavian expansion—gain in the widest sense of the word, including land, commerce and booty—in short, wealth. The sort of wealth which seems to have reached Scandinavia in trade prior to 840—Irish manufactured products and Carolingian coins and goods in Norway, Carolingian products in Denmark and Sweden and Moslem coins everywhere—emphasizes the generally peaceful nature of this early expansion. After 840 it was in part the weaknesses of Scandinavia's neighbors which caused this movement to take a more violent form. In the West a quarreling Ireland, an England which was divided under the Heptarchy and a Carolingian Empire rent by the civil wars of the sons of Louis the Pious all provided too good a chance to be neglected. In the East the disunited Finnish, Baltic and Russian tribes and *grody* provided a similar opportunity—not to mention a weak Kazar state and a Byzantium under Moslem naval attack in the Mediterranean.

If weaknesses on the part of their neighbors explain in part the Vikings' warlike expansion, so do the weaknesses of the governments in their own homelands. What is striking in reading the accounts we

---

[5] On disorders in Denmark, see L. Musset, *Les Peuples scandinaves*, pp. 61-64, and J. de Vries, *op.cit.*, pp. 98-120. See also H. Shetelig, *Viking History*, pp. 5-20.
[6] These episodes are to be found in Rimbert, *Vita Anskari*, in MGH *Script.*, II, and E. de Moreau, *St. Anskaire*, pp. 21-85.

possess of Scandinavia during this period is the fact that these Vikings treated each other as they did their so-called enemies. We see Danes raiding Birka and extracting ransom there, just as they did at Dorestad or Paris. Oleg seems to have been as savage in his treatment of a rival like Askold as Danish invaders were to Edmund the Martyr. Danes and Norse in Ireland slaughtered each other at Carlingsford Lough with a savagery as revolting as that used by Thorgisl in dealing with the Irish. Norse Vikings from the Hebrides seem to have had no compunctions about raiding Norway itself. And the feuds of the Icelandic peasant aristocracy, as related in such a saga as the *Burnt Njal*, make their treatment of captured monasteries in Francia understandable. In a sense, Viking cruelty, raids and piracy were the reflection, the extension, of a situation caused by the lack of law or orderly government in their own countries, rather than the reverse. As long as such anarchy existed at home, so did the violent phase of Scandinavian expansion.[7]

In addition to political weaknesses at home and abroad, an additional factor of an economic nature which we find suddenly appearing in Scandinavia about 840 may have given a special impetus to Viking expansion westwards. I refer to evidence from coin hoards of a stoppage of trade between the Baltic and the Moslem East for more than a decade. As noted in the last chapter, coins found in Scandinavia seem to show that, after a rising tide of commerce with the East until 840 or thereabouts, for thirty years little Eastern trade existed. And we have noted also that the *Primary Chronicle* definitely states that the Varangians were expelled from Russia at about the same time that Byzantine sources tell us that Varangians in South Russia had to return home by way of the Mediterranean. Not until the later years of the ninth century do coin hoards in Scandinavia show renewed commerce with the East, with Samanid Central Asia, which coincides with information in the *Primary Chronicle* to the effect that by then Rurik and Oleg had reopened trade routes through Russia to the Black and Caspian Seas. This cessation of Eastern trade to the Baltic, shown by our sources and coin hoards to have taken place about 840, coincides with numismatic evidence from Norwegian coin hoards of a different sort. Here we find hoards containing Carolingian money minted as late as the end of the reign of Louis the Pious, but not after that.

[7] There has been insufficient probing of the psychology that lay behind Viking attacks.

Norwegian Carolingian coin hoards end when Abbassid silver seems to cease reaching the Baltic and the Norwegian coast.[8]

What this appears to show is the following: Scandinavian commerce with the Carolingian Empire, which continued, despite pirate raids, until 840, was dependent upon supplies of Moslem silver dirhems and other Eastern wares that could be exchanged for cloth, weapons, glassware, wine, and other products which were brought to Scandinavia mainly by Frisian merchants. When the Scandinavians, owing to the closing of Eastern trade routes, could no longer pay for these products, commerce with Western coasts languished, as can be seen by the ending of Carolingian silver money reaching Norway. The answer was to take by force what could no longer be gained by trade. Thus the great Norse-Danish assaults on the West in the 840's, 850's, 860's and even 870's may well have been economically induced by the temporary closing of trade routes through Russia to the Moslem East. This may account, too, for the curious episode that occurred during Anskar's visit to Birka in 852, when the Swedes there, having furnished little booty to the Danes who took the town, blithely directed them across the Baltic to Apolloné and Seeburg.[9] It is almost as if they were saying, "You seek wealth. Well, reopen the routes to the East. Reconquer those people who expelled us, and you will find it. And good luck to you." Until a Kievan state had been established by Rurik, Askold, Dir and Oleg, and new supplies of silver and Oriental goods could reach Scandinavia, Viking piratical excesses continued. After that date they began to slacken.

Thus, having attempted to probe the basic causes of the Viking attacks in the East and West, let us examine the actual course of these invasions in some detail. Initially, prior to 840, the main arena in which Viking activity took place was Ireland. A first attack on Irish shores in 795 was followed by others in 807, 812, 813, 820, 821 and 823. Finally, they became yearly affairs. A contemporary Irish chronicler could say that no harbor or landing place was without its fleet of pirates. By 831 the plundering of the interior of the island began. Larger Viking fleets, numbering up to 60 sails, appeared. Sometime between 830 and 839 the arrival of Thorgisl, of the royal family of

[8] H. Holst, "Mynter i Norske Funn," in *Nord. Numis. Arsskrift* (1943), pp. 56-71. A. W. Brøgger, "Angel-Saksiske mynter frä VIII og IX arhundrede i Norden," in *Norsk Hist. Tidskrift*, 5th ser., I (Oslo), 8-19. English coins from this period found in Norway are very, very few indeed, much fewer than those from the Carolingian Empire.

[9] *Vita Anskari*, xxx, in *MGH Script.*, II, 713.

the Westfold, made this invasion almost an official Norse affair. Under Thorgisl's leadership a number of coastal points were fortified, including Dublin in 841. Actual Norse settlement in Ireland began. Thorgisl, assisted by his able wife, plundered great interior monasteries like Clonmacnois and made himself, though a heathen, Abbot of Armagh. Perhaps this action rallied the Irish against him, for we know that he was killed in 845 and the Norse advance into the interior was temporarily checked.[10]

Connected with the attacks of Norse Vikings on Ireland were their raids farther south along the coasts of Western France, particularly about the mouths of the Loire and Garonne, where Irish trade had long been active. The introductory raid in this region was carried out in 799, and was beaten off by natives of Aquitaine with some losses to the invaders. Then, in 814-819, attacks began again, concentrated, it would seem, upon the islands of Noirmoutier and Ré.[11] Thanks to the naval preparations of Louis the Pious along these coasts, a second victory over Viking pirates was gained in 820.[12] Thus checked, the Vikings remained quiescent along western Gallic shores until 838, when they again raided Aquitaine. This attack seems to have coincided with a joint Viking-Cornish assault upon Wessex. The invading force, which was badly mauled by Egbert, represented the first assault on these shores of England since the raid on Dorchester in 787.[13]

Soon after the death of Louis the Pious, Norwegian attacks via Ireland upon western French coasts increased in severity. In 843 and 844 a very large Viking force reached the Loire from the Westfold, captured and plundered the port of Nantes, and passed the winter on the island of Noirmoutier. In the spring of 844, the Vikings proceeded down the coast to plunder in the Garonne region.[14] Then they continued along Spanish shores to Galicia, where they attacked Gijon and Coruña. Beaten off by the Christian Spanish, they turned south with 100 ships, attacked Lisbon and raided as far as Cadiz and Seville. Though they gathered much booty, their attacks on Moslem

[10] T. D. Kendrick, *History of the Vikings*, pp. 276-85. H. Shetelig, *Viking History of Western Europe*, pp. 49-55. A. N. Clerigh, *The History of Ireland to the Coming of Henry II* (Dublin 1922), I, 688-715. F. Lot, *Les Invasions barbares*, pp. 175-78.

[11] T. D. Kendrick, *op.cit.*, p. 193. W. Vogel, *Die Normannen und das Fränkische Reich*, pp. 64-65.

[12] H. Shetelig, *op.cit.*, p. 108.

[13] T. D. Kendrick, *op.cit.*, pp. 227-28.

[14] H. Shetelig, *op.cit.*, pp. 111-12. *La Chronique de Nantes*, ed. Merlet (Nantes 1896), pp. 14-18, tells how Nantes was taken in 843. See also *Annales Engol.*, anno 843, in *MGH Script.*, XVI, 484, and *Chron. Aquit.*, in *ibid.*, II, 253.

Spain cost them 30 ships, and they returned to winter near the mouth of the Garonne.[15] Apparently it was this raid of 844 on Moorish Spain which caused the Emir of Cordova to send an envoy to treat for peace at a northern Viking court—probably that of Thorgisl in Ireland.[16] The death of Thorgisl in 845, and the resultant check to Norse aggression in Ireland, seem to have coincided with a certain lull in Viking attacks upon western Gallic shores. But already, in their raids upon the Loire and Garonne regions, we can see signs ominous for the future. We can see the beginning of the establishment of permanent Viking pirate fortresses upon islands like Noirmoutier and Ré, from which Viking raiders, who spent the winter there, could launch attacks far into the interior. Along these shores the second phase of Viking raiding had already begun by 845—a phase much more dangerous than the occasional coastal raids which had afflicted these regions during the reigns of Charlemagne and Louis the Pious.

While Norse Vikings were moving into Ireland and proceeding south to attack Aquitaine and Spanish coasts, their Danish brethren were moving down the North Sea towards Frisia. The plundering activities of the Danes may have begun as early as 793 and 794, when the Northumbrian Abbeys of Jarrow and Lindesfarne were sacked by pirates. It seems probable, however, that these raids were launched from Norway's Westfold rather than from Denmark. If so, the first Danish piracy of which we have record took place in 804 in the course of Denmark's war with Charlemagne. In this year the Carolingian ruler began to move north of the Elbe, fortified the bourg of Itzehoe there, and allied himself with the Slavic Obodrites, whose port of Reric (later Lübeck) was a commercial rival of Danish Hedeby. Gotfried, the Danish king, replied by destroying Reric, and built a wall across the Danish peninsula, called the Dannevirke, and sent a Danish fleet to raid Frisia. This fleet forced the Frisians to pay 100 pounds of silver as ransom or tribute. Gotfried's death in 810, and the strength of Carolingian naval preparations and defenses, ended raiding for a short period. But, when the Franks attacked Jutland in 815, the Danes replied with naval attacks which ravaged the banks of the Elbe in 817. Peace between the two opponents was concluded in 819, but a small

---

[15] On these raids on Spain, see sources collected in *Rerum Normannicarum fontes Arabici*, ed. Seippel, 2 vols. (Oslo 1896-1928). See also H. Shetelig, *op.cit.*, p. 139, and R. Dozy, *Recherches sur l'histoire et la littérature en Espagne* (Leyden 1888), II, 252-56.

[16] *Ibid.*, pp. 267-78. It seems probable that this envoy visited Queen Aud's court in Ireland, but he may have gone as far as Norway or Denmark.

Danish flotilla appears to have made an unsuccessful raid upon the coast of Flanders and the Seine region in 820.[17]

For some years after this, civil war in Denmark claimed Danish energies, and Louis the Pious took advantage of the situation. He intervened by supporting one royal claimant, Harold. In 826, with Louis' blessing, Harold sailed from the Rhine to Denmark, carrying with him Anskar, who was to be the first great Christian apostle to the Danes, and who in 829 proceeded on to Birka to launch the Christianization of Sweden at the Swedish king's request. Harold was bound to Louis by more than good will and support for his claim to the Danish throne, for the Carolingian ruler granted him a fief at Rustringen, at the mouth of the Weser, in the hope of making this region a buffer between Denmark and Frisia.[18]

At any rate, until 834 Louis' diplomacy assured peace. In that year, however, Harold lost his kingdom and was succeeded by Horick as the Danish monarch. Strife between Louis and his sons also gave opportunity for Danish intervention in Frankish waters. As a result, in 834 a Danish attack was made upon Dorestad by way of Utrecht. Dorestad seems to have been partially burnt and was required to pay a heavy sum as a ransom to the Danes. For the next four years, Danish raids continued and reached Frisia and the mouths of the Rhine. Dorestad was raided repeatedly, and in 836 a Danish flotilla attacked Antwerp and Witla near the mouth of the Scheldt. The next year the Danes raided the island of Walcheren. Perhaps these Danish pirates were acting as allies of Lothair, Louis' eldest son, who was then revolting against his father.[19]

Efforts were made to conclude peace in 836, after Danish ambassadors had been murdered in Cologne by an outraged populace. Negotiations continued through 837 and 838, with envoys from the Danish king declaring that Horick had commanded the execution of the Viking leaders who were responsible for attacks on Frisia. But they added the ominous demand that Louis cede the land of the Obodrites on Denmark's borders to the Danish king. Instead, the Carolingian Emperor appears to have refused, and in 837 and 838 strengthened his naval defenses. This proved unnecessary, since in the latter year a

---

[17] P. Boeles, *Friesland*, pp. 286-90. J. de Vries, *op.cit.*, pp. 98-121. H. Shetelig, *op.cit.*, pp. 106-8.

[18] H. Shetelig, *op.cit.*, p. 108. R. Hodgkin, *History of the Anglo-Saxons*, II, 490-93. See also *Vita Anskari*, in *MGH Script.*, II.

[19] J. de Vries, *op.cit.*, pp. 122-80. P. Boeles, *op.cit.*, pp. 390-91. T. D. Kendrick, *op.cit.*, pp. 194-96.

storm destroyed the Danish fleet again on its way to Frisia. Louis'
death in 840, however, changed the situation. Lothair, who succeeded
him as Emperor, needed peace in Frisia, for he was busy quarreling
with his brothers, Charles and Lewis. To gain peace with Denmark,
then, in 841 he ceded to Horick the island of Walcheren. The beginnings of the Danish Frisian duchy had been laid, and land far inside
the Frankish state was now under Viking control. A new era had
begun.[20]

The intensive Danish raids between 834 and 840 which we have
just described seem to have affected no other portion of the Carolingian Empire except Frisia. But they did result, it would seem, in certain attacks launched on England across the Channel. In 834, for
instance, Danish Vikings attacked the island of Sheppey at the mouth
of the Thames. In 836, perhaps in conjunction with raids on Frisia,
a Viking force landed in Southern Britain and defeated King Egbert
of Wessex. In 840 Hamwith (Southampton) was raided, but the
Danes were beaten off. They returned a year later to win a victory at
Romney Marsh. Now we find pirates in the waters of the English
Channel, probably because the Frankish fleet at Boulogne was no
longer operative. At least, we hear no more of Frankish naval defenses after 838. The way lay open for Danish attacks in the waters
of the Channel and beyond.[21]

The 840's, thanks to lessening defenses, saw the tempo of Viking
assaults increased along the shores of the Carolingian Empire. These
attacks, mainly by the Danes, began in 841, when a pirate fleet under
Asgeir (Oscar) sailed to the Seine and raided Rouen and the nearby
Abbey of Jumièges.[22] Probably it was this same force which won a
victory at Romney Marsh in England and ravaged Lincolnshire and
East Anglia. During the next year a similar series of raids, even more
serious, took place on both sides of the Channel. A pirate fleet attacked
London, then proceeded across the Channel to sack Quentovic and,
returning to England, plundered Rochester on its way home.[23]

Successes like this seem to have emboldened the Danish pirate

[20] J. de Vries, op.cit., pp. 180-215. H. Shetelig, op.cit., pp. 108-10. F. Stenton,
Anglo-Saxon England, pp. 237-40. F. Lot, op.cit., p. 128.

[21] T. D. Kendrick, op.cit., pp. 227-29. R. Hodgkin, op.cit., II, 475. F. Stenton,
op.cit., pp. 241-42.

[22] H. Shetelig, op.cit., pp. 111-12. T. D. Kendrick, op.cit., pp. 197-99.

[23] F. Stenton, op.cit., p. 242. R. Hodgkin, op.cit., II, 494-98. H. Shetelig, op.cit.,
pp. 79-83. Viking raids on England, however, do not in these years appear to have
been directed primarily against British shores. They were essentially by-products of
raids on Frisia and of attacks launched on French Channel coasts.

bands. For in 845 Ragnar Ladbrok, of the Danish royal house, sailed up the Seine with a force of 120 ships to surprise Paris. In so doing, he defeated an army which Charles the Bald hastily gathered to oppose him, and extorted a sum of 7,000 pounds of silver from the Carolingian monarch before he departed. The first of the notorious Danegelds had been paid these raiders, a bad precedent for the future.[24] In the same year another pirate band, either Danish or Norse, which was established on West Gallic shores in pirate nests, raided the Charente region and sacked the city of Saintes. In 847 Brittany was attacked, while in the next year both Bordeaux and Melle, far in the interior of Poitou, felt the fury of the assaults of Viking bands, who then pressed on to raid Périgueux.[25] In 851 and 852 Asgeir established raiding headquarters on the island of Oisella near Rouen at the mouth of the Seine. From this base, raids were launched as far inland as Beauvais.[26]

During this period England was not spared. A large-scale series of raids were made on her shores. One was by a fleet of 350 ships under Rurik of Frisia which seized and sacked London and Canterbury, only to meet defeat at the hands of King Aethelwulf of Wessex when the Danish forces advanced inland. Other Viking raiders were checked in Devonshire and at Sandwich in Kent, where they lost nine ships.[27] But they did establish one of their fortified pirate bases on the island of Thanet, from which they would raid the interior in future years.[28]

While these increasingly menacing Viking pirate attacks were being launched against the shores of England and the Atlantic and Channel coasts of France, other Danes were increasing their holdings in Frisia. In 841 they had been ceded Walcheren. In 845 and 846

[24] T. D. Kendrick, *op.cit.*, p. 203. H. Shetelig, *op.cit.*, pp. 112-13. On these Danegelds, see E. Joranson, *The Danegeld in France* (Rock Island, Ill., 1924).

[25] L. Auzias, *L'Aquitaine carolingienne*, pp. 246-48. Viking raids here were facilitated by the constant hostilities between Charles the Bald and Pepin II of Aquitaine which made it impossible for either of them to concentrate upon the Viking menace.

[26] H. Shetelig, *op.cit.*, pp. 113-14. T. D. Kendrick, *op.cit.*, p. 206.

[27] T. D. Kendrick, *op.cit.*, pp. 229-30. R. Hodgkin, *op.cit.*, II, 494-98. On Aethelwulf's great victory over the Vikings see the *Anglo-Saxon Chronicle*, anno 851, and F. Stenton, *Anglo-Saxon England*, p. 243. The victory over the Viking raiders at Sandwich by Aethelstan, King of Kent, where they lost 9 ships, may be the first evidence we have of an Anglo-Saxon fleet in existence in the 9th century. On this, see *Anglo-Saxon Chronicle*, anno 851, and R. Hodgkin, *op.cit.*, II, 584.

[28] The establishment of permanent bases on Thanet and Sheppey between 851 and 855 marked a new stage in Viking actions along English shores. On this, see R. Hodgkin, *op.cit.*, II, 497-98, and T. D. Kendrick, *op.cit.*, p. 229. These bases seem to have been used not only by Danish raiders but also by a certain Frisian element from the new Danish principality of Frisia across the North Sea. *Lindesfarne Annals*, in *MGH Script.*, XIX, 506.

they continued attacks upon nearby Dorestad. Finally, in 850 Lothair of Lorraine ceded this port and surrounding regions to Rurik and Gotfried. A full-scale Danish Frisian principality was at last a reality.[29]

Though they were successful in Frisia, the Danes were less so in Germany. In 845 a Danish expedition sacked the thriving *portus* of Hamburg, forcing St. Anskar to seek refuge in nearby Bremen. They then ventured up the Elbe into the interior of Saxony, where a force of local nobles hastily opposed them, beat them badly and drove them from the land. This raid, incidentally, is almost unique during this period because it was followed by a protest to the Danish king by Lewis, the Frankish ruler of Germany. Horick restored the booty taken at Hamburg in an attempt to make amends to Lewis for this raid, only to be murdered the next year, as anarchy descended upon the Danish kingdom.[30]

Meanwhile, in distant Ireland the Danes were also busy. In 849, a large Danish fleet, probably composed of pirates who had been operating off French coasts, sailed to Ireland. After a struggle with the Norse Vikings who were already established there, in 850 and 851 they defeated their Norwegian brothers and took Dublin, the Norse capital. In the course of this struggle, the first sea battle of which we have knowledge in this Viking period was fought on Carlingsford Lough and the Norse were badly beaten. But not for long. In 853 a new Norse fleet sailed from the Westfold to Dublin, commanded by Olaf, a kinsman of Thorgisl. He defeated the Danes, ejected them from Ireland, and re-established the Norse dynasty in Dublin, which was long to continue as a power in Irish affairs.[31]

At this point, it might be well to summarize the results of the dozen or so years of Viking raiding which had followed the death of Louis the Pious. By 852 or 853, Danes and Norwegians had advanced far

---

[29] J. de Vries, *op.cit.*, pp. 122-215, contains the best account of the establishment of a Danish duchy of Frisia under a branch of the Danish royal family. On it see also W. Vogel, *Die Normannen und das Fränkische Reich*, pp. 108-18; T. D. Kendrick, *op.cit.*, p. 201; and H. Shetelig, *op.cit.*, p. 110.

[30] F. Lot, *Les Invasions*, p. 129, and T. D. Kendrick, *op.cit.*, p. 203. See also H. Shetelig, *op.cit.*, p. 118, on the envoys sent by King Horick of Denmark to Lewis the German. On this raid and its effects on St. Anskar, see E. de Moreau, *St. Anskaire*, pp. 60-71.

[31] H. Shetelig, *op.cit.*, pp. 59-61. R. Hodgkin, *op.cit.*, II, 489-90. F. Lot, *op.cit.*, pp. 177-78. The struggle during these years between the Danes and the Norse in Ireland seems to have been the first evidence of such friction between Danish and Norse Vikings who were attacking Irish, French and British shores. It was but a temporary affair, however, as the close cooperation between Olaf of the Westfold house and Ivar the Boneless of Denmark soon showed.

down the trade routes leading from their native lands. They had established two advanced bases: the Norse, that of Dublin, under the control of the royal house of the Westfold; the Danes, a Frisian principality, under Rurik and Gotfried of the Danish royal family. In addition, their fleets had attacked practically every major port in the Atlantic region as far as the Mediterranean: Hamburg in Germany; Dorestad, Antwerp and Witla at the mouths of the Rhine; Quentovic, Rouen, Nantes, Saintes and Bordeaux in France; Coruña in Galicia; Lisbon, Seville and Cadiz in Spain; London, Rochester, Sandwich and Hamwith in England. In addition to their permanent colonies in Ireland and Frisia, they had established permanent bases or fortified pirate strongholds at the mouths of the Thames, the Seine, the Loire, the Charente and the Garonne rivers, settlements which in Western France were already known as *Dani*.[32] From these places, where the pirate bands wintered, they were now beginning, in 853, a systematic plundering of the interior.

Furthermore, while at first these bands of pirates, under sea-kings like Asgeir, Hastings and the sons of Ragnar Ladbrok, were amorphous groups, gradually this began to change. Instead of moving from Thames to Loire, to Garonne or Seine, as opportunities for plunder presented themselves, they began to assume some organized form on a more or less regional basis. Our sources begin to speak of these pirates, who were mainly Danes, as Seine Vikings, Garonne Vikings, Loire Vikings, with certain definite leaders and certain characteristics. They were developing a unique fighting and organizing ability. Already in the 850's there were being formed along the coast of Western Europe the units which would all but conquer Anglo-Saxon England in the 870's.

In 853 the second phase of Viking assaults on France began with attacks which proceeded up the main rivers far into the interior. In this year, Loire bands of pirates moved upriver to seize Nantes and take Poitiers, Angers and Tours. In 854 it was Blois' turn. In 856 Orléans, which had resisted successfully until this time, succumbed in turn, and the Vikings withdrew to their new island base at Besse

[32] It was such permanent fortresses as Oisella on the Seine, Thanet and Sheppey at the mouth of the Thames, Besse on the Loire and other *Dani* along western Gallic coasts that made the Vikings so hard to deal with. Note the similarity between such spots and similar Saxon settlements along the same coasts in the 5th and 6th centuries. On these, see Chapters I and II.

near Nantes. Two years later, in 858, we find them again attacking Poitiers, Tours and Blois.[33]

Meanwhile, the bands on the Seine had not been inactive. In 856 they captured Paris and went on to sack Bayeux, Evreux and Chartres in 858. Charles the Bald, the French king, was at last stung into action and made an attempt to seize their island fortress of Oisella on the Seine. But his attempt proved fruitless. Then he had what seemed to be a good idea. A large Viking army under Weland had appeared on the Somme and had attacked Amiens and raided the coast near Thérouanne. In 860 Charles hired this Viking band for 5,000 pounds of silver to attack the troublesome Seine pirates and eliminate them. Weland and his men proceeded to the Seine, but, instead of keeping their bargain, extorted an additional 6,000 pounds from the Seine Vikings, and then joined them. For some months they continued raids on the Seine as far as Paris, and then in 862 departed in their dragon ships.[34]

The Loire region, however, remained peaceful for a few years after 858. This lull was not due to the defeat or discouragement of Loire bands but to their presence elsewhere. Starting in 859, the leaders of these freebooters, Hastings and Bjorn, took their sea-rovers on what was perhaps the most famous Viking expedition of the century—their great Mediterranean raid. They started from Western France and sailed along the coasts of Spain. In Asturias the Vikings were repulsed, and they suffered some losses in attacking Seville and Cadiz on the Guadalquivir. But, undismayed, they continued on and, after sacking Algeciras and Necour on the African coast, proceeded into the Mediterranean. On their way north they raided Catalonia and the Balearics, and wintered in 860 on the island of Camargue, from which they launched attacks on a number of cities in the Rhone valley. Then, in the spring, they continued to Italian shores, where they raided Luni, Pisa and Fiesoli. Some of them sailed into the Eastern Mediterranean, where they plundered as far as Egypt and may even have reached the Hellespont. Then they sailed west again, returning past Gibraltar and fighting a Moorish fleet at Medina Sidonia, suffering some losses. In 862 the raiding band that survived returned to its Loire bases.[35]

[33] T. D. Kendrick, op.cit., pp. 206-7. H. Shetelig, op.cit., pp. 114-15.

[34] On these years, see F. Lot, "La grande invasion normande de 856-62," in Bibl. de l'Ecole des Chartes, LXX (1908), 301-18.

[35] On this greatest Viking raid into the Mediterranean, see A. A. Vasiliev, The Russian Attack on Constantinople in 860 (Cambridge, Mass., 1945), pp. 49-65.

There they were joined by contingents of Somme and Seine Vikings and again proceeded to raid the Loire, which had now had four years of respite from their depredations. Some Frankish leaders, like Count Robert the Strong, who was in charge of the defenses of this region, resisted—or, rather, bought off these Vikings with 6,000 pounds of silver. Others, like Pepin II of Aquitaine, joined them. Pepin II appears to have actually accompanied them on a raid up the Garonne as far as Toulouse.[36] Equally cooperative was Duke Salomon of Brittany, who joined them in an attack on Le Mans. Under the circumstances, it is not surprising that Nantes, Angers and Bordeaux suffered heavily again, and that Orléans and Poitiers were burnt by freebooters, who ravaged the Rouergue and Poitou. During these years, the only region to escape serious damage was that of the Charente, where castles were built in 864 to resist the Vikings[37]— the first we know of in France. Elsewhere trouble continued, as new bands of pirates under the famous sea-king, Hastings, arrived.[38] In 867 came the death of Robert the Strong, who had won some successes against their attacks, and the Vikings again advanced into the interior. They took Bourges in 867, and Orléans the next year. Bordeaux became so unsafe that Bishop Frotaire fled the city, while, with Breton help, Vikings again sacked Angers. Finally, in 874 they sailed away.[39] After twelve years of conflict, the great Viking assault on Western Gaul was over, though some bands remained to vex Aquitaine as late as 882.

During these years of concentrated attacks by pirate bands in the Loire valley and Aquitaine, the Seine region was not left unmolested. In 864, Charles the Bald tried to deny passage up the Seine to the Vikings by constructing a fortified bridge at Pîtres. A fleet of 50 Scandinavian ships, however, proved Charles' work useless by forcing its way through this barrier and raiding upriver as far as Paris.[40] Only a Danegeld payment of 4,000 pounds of silver persuaded them

[36] J. Calmette, "Le Siège de Toulouse par les Normands," in *Annales du Midi*, XXIX (1917), 171-83.

[37] Ademar de Chabannes, *Chronicle*, III, 19, ed. Chavannon (Paris 1897), p. 137.

[38] L. Auzias, *op.cit.*, pp. 325-38. F. Lot, "La Loire, l'Aquitaine et la Somme de 862-66: Robert le Fort," in *Bibl. de l'Ecole des Chartes*, LXXV (1916), 473-516.

[39] On the flight of Bishop Frotaire from Bordeaux, see John VIII, *Epistolae*, in *Patrologia Latina*, ed. Migne, CXXVI, no. 36. On the last years of these great raids on Western Gaul, L. Auzias, *op.cit.*, pp. 347-58.

[40] H. Shetelig, *op.cit.*, p. 116. F. Lot, *op.cit.*, pp. 510-16. T. D. Kendrick, *op.cit.*, pp. 210-14. On the fortified bridge at Pîtres, F. Lot, "Le Pont de Pîtres," in *Le Moyen Age*, XI (1905), 207-15.

to decamp. In 876, others returned again to attack in the Seine region. Since Charles the Bald was in Germany and could not defend his realm, he paid them another 5,000 pounds of silver and bought peace. A year later he died, leaving a kingdom still troubled by Viking attacks, despite the 21,000 pounds of gold and silver which had been paid these raiders during his reign.[41]

The comparative lull which settled over the Seine region after 862, and which finally affected Western France in 874, was not due to successful resistance offered the Vikings by the inhabitants and rulers of France. It was primarily the result of Viking interest and raiding activities being shifted to a different quarter—Anglo-Saxon England. England had been raided several times between 834 and 851, and though two pirate bases had been established by the Danes at the mouth of the Thames, on the islands of Thanet and Sheppey, in general, the country had not suffered severely from Viking attacks up to 865. Some small-scale raids on Wroken, a few coastal descents on Northumberland and an attack on Winchester in 861 were all that had taken place.[42] Perhaps the great victory of Aethelwulf of Wessex over the Danish invading host in 851 had convinced these Vikings that England was better able to protect herself than France across the Channel.

However that may be, in 865 they were ready to try again, and for the next thirteen years their attack on England represented a major Viking effort. This great assault of the Danes has been thoroughly examined by a number of historians. It will suffice here to give only its main outlines. It appears to have differed in a number of ways from Viking attacks on France, even that twelve-year assault on Aquitaine which took place between 862 and 874. In the first place, the forces used were almost completely Danish and were composed of veterans of twenty years' fighting along Gallic shores. Secondly, it seems to have been carefully organized, more so than was usual in Viking expeditions, and was under the command of the three sons of Ragnar Ladbrok: Ingvar, Halfdan and Ubbe, Duke or Prince of Danish Frisia, all of whom were experienced commanders. In the third place, this Danish army does not seem to have had as

---

[41] F. Lot, *Les Invasions*, pp. 127-28. W. Vogel, *Die Normannen und das Fränkische Reich*, pp. 214-18. H. Shetelig, *op.cit.*, pp. 116-18. On these Danegelds, E. Joranson, *The Danegeld in France*, pp. 1-137.

[42] See T. D. Kendrick, *op.cit.*, p. 230, and H. Shetelig, *op.cit.*, pp. 80-81, on these scattered attacks prior to the great Danish invasion.

its objective a mere series of raids and the gathering of booty, but rather the orderly and systematic conquest of the whole of Anglo-Saxon England. In the scope of its planning, the discipline and experience of the Viking soldiers who engaged in it and the size of its forces, the great Danish assault on England, which began in 865, was unique in the Viking annals of the ninth century.[43]

The Danes launched their attack upon that section of England least able to resist, the east coast. In 866 they landed in East Anglia without difficulty and seized horses there for attacks farther inland. They then proceeded to York, where, after defeating the Northumbrian Anglo-Saxon kings who opposed them, they set a puppet ruler upon the throne of Yorkshire. They wintered in Mercia near Nottingham. In 868 they returned to Yorkshire and took it over completely, making it into a Danish kingdom. Meanwhile Mercia and Wessex, the strongest Anglo-Saxon kingdoms, joined together to check the Danish host as it advanced south, and purchased peace. But the Danish leaders were interested in little more than a truce. They turned southeast to capture East Anglia, where they slew King Edmund the Martyr, and East Anglia was added to Yorkshire as a center of Danish power. Then they turned on Wessex and in 871 took and occupied London. The Kings of Wessex, first Aethelred and then his brother Alfred, fought valiantly a series of nine battles on the upper Thames. The best they were able to do was to check the Danes and gain more breathing space with a money payment. With Wessex temporarily out of the fight, the Danes turned their attention to Mercia. In three years they had driven King Burhed from his kingdom, occupied one half of it themselves, and turned the other half over to an Anglo-Saxon puppet ruler.

Then the Danish host split into two parts. One portion of the invading army, under Halfdan, settled down to organize Yorkshire and the famous Five Boroughs of Mercia into a Danish colony or kingdom. The rest of the invaders, with East Anglia and London as their bases, turned to finish off Alfred and his kingdom of Wessex in 875. The next three years saw Alfred in deadly peril a number of times, his forces at one point being reduced to a small band that was pushed into remote Somerset by the advancing Danes. But then the tide turned abruptly. Alfred began to win victories, and in 878 forced the defeated Danes at Chippenham to accept peace, Chris-

---

[43] On the composition of this force, which may even have included a Frisian contingent, see F. Stenton, *op.cit.*, pp. 242-43.

tianity and Alfred as undisputed King of Wessex and one half of Mercia.[44]

Alfred's defeat of the Danish army of Gudrum in 878, and the settlement of the Danish invading host in Yorkshire, the Five Boroughs and East Anglia—the so-called Danelaw—by no means ended the difficulties of Wessex. Alfred realized that his position was still a precarious one. In facing this fact, he found an interesting answer to his defense problem. He decided to build a navy. In making this decision, Alfred showed himself the first non-Viking ruler since Louis the Pious able to comprehend that against the Danes and other Vikings his realm was indefensible without naval power. Perhaps he was not the first king of the line of Wessex to comprehend this fact; according to the *Anglo-Saxon Chronicle*, in 851 there may have been a small fleet located at Sandwich which defeated the Danes and took nine ships. If so, it disappeared soon afterwards. Alfred, then, started from scratch in 875, when he constructed a small fleet of seven ships.[45] After 878 he rebuilt his navy. It had little success in 881 and 884 when he used it to engage Danish naval vessels.[46] But by 885, his navy seems to have been strong enough to take a more active role, sailing to Danish East Anglian shores and there defeating a Viking force which was raiding his part of England, despite Gudrum's peace treaty of 878. Though this fleet was badly beaten on its return voyage when it met a superior Danish maritime force, the value of such a navy was not lost on Alfred.[47] And so in 897, according to the *Chronicle*, he built warships according to his own design which were unlike either Frisian or Viking ships and which, having 30 oars to a side, were large indeed. He manned these vessels, it seems, with Frisian sailors, then the best non-Scandinavian mariners of the Atlantic.[48] Though these monster warships were of rather uncertain seaworthiness, they represented the nucleus of the

[44] In general, it is the account of F. Stenton in *Anglo-Saxon England*, pp. 242-65, which has been followed. See also the somewhat fuller and more detailed one by R. Hodgkin in *History of the Anglo-Saxons*, II, 522-72. Also valuable are T. D. Kendrick, *op.cit.*, pp. 230-42, and H. Shetelig, *op.cit.*, pp. 79-85. On Alfred's battles in West England in the 870's, see A. F. Major, *Early Wars in Wessex* (Cambridge 1913), pp. 136-242.

[45] R. Hodgkin, *op.cit.*, II, 583.

[46] *Ibid.*, p. 574.

[47] *Ibid.*, p. 584. F. Stenton, *op.cit.*, pp. 260-64. T. D. Kendrick, *op.cit.*, pp. 240-44.

[48] On these ships, which probably started the trend towards the high-built *drekkars*, or dragon-ships, of the 10th and 11th centuries, see R. Hodgkin, *op.cit.*, pp. 284-85; H. Shetelig, *Scandinavian Archeology*, pp. 372-73; and especially Brøgger and Shetelig, *The Viking Ships*, pp. 178-79.

Anglo-Saxon navy which was to flourish under his successors. Surely Alfred deserves the title of the founder of the British fleet.

Thanks to this navy and to his other wise defense measures, such as the building of boroughs throughout the land, Alfred continued to operate successfully against the Danes during the rest of his reign. In 882 Vikings raided his shores again, and in 885 an even larger force attacked Rochester and invaded Kent. When Gudrum, despite his treaty of peace, joined in the attack, Alfred used the opportunity not only to defeat the invaders, but to advance north and recover London from the Danes of the Danelaw. Gudrum made peace in 886 at the cost of some of the southern portion of his domain. In 892 another attack took place, this time by a larger Viking force of 80 shiploads of Somme Vikings and 253 shiploads of Seine Vikings under the command of the formidable sea-king, Hastings. This force, just defeated in the Low Countries by King Arnaulf of Germany, landed in Kent and attacked the Thames region. Danes from the Danelaw and East Anglia joined in, sending a fleet to ravage Devon. Alfred himself defeated the Viking invaders in the west. His son, Edward, smashed the Danish army in Kent and finally destroyed most of their ships on the Thames. By 896 peace had been re-established, and the great period of Danish invasions of England was over.[49] Only slight disorders in 910, during the reign of Edward the Elder, who succeeded Alfred, marked a recurrence of the Danish menace. But Edward's great victory at Tettenhall ended this danger.[50] By 911 it was the Danish kingdom of York, not the House of Wessex, which was on the defensive, and the Danelaw was being reconquered from its new inhabitants.

During these final years of the ninth century when Alfred in England, having defeated the great Danish host of Gudrum, was slowly moving towards the offensive, the last great Viking raids took place on the Continent. These attacks were made, in general, far into the interior in regions from the Somme to the Elbe, which had, up to this point, escaped serious molestation. In fact, between 852 and 879 our only record of Viking activities along these shores concerns raids in 858 and 862 in Saxony, and one attack down the Rhine as far as Cologne, launched in this same year by the Danish rulers of Frisia.[51]

[49] F. Stenton, op.cit., pp. 262-67. T. D. Kendrick, op.cit., pp. 241-45. H. Shetelig, Viking History of Western Europe, pp. 85-87.

[50] F. Stenton, op.cit., pp. 315-20.

[51] W. Vogel, op.cit., pp. 160, 193. T. D. Kendrick, op.cit., p. 207. H. Shetelig, op.cit., p. 118.

In 879, however, the situation changed. The death of Baldwin, Count of Flanders, a valiant warrior who was not to be trifled with, removed one enemy whom the Viking raiders feared.[52] The defeat of Gudrum's army by Alfred in 878 left a number of freebooters who were unwilling to take up homes in the Danelaw, and were thus eager to resume a career of piracy in a new area.

It seems, however, that the situation in Frisia, where the Danes had been peacefully settled as rulers since 852, had a great deal to do with this last period of great Viking attacks upon the Carolingian Empire. For here there seems to be evidence that, by the 870's Danish control of this region was in jeopardy. In 873 friction between Frisians and Danes, its origins obscure, resulted in the death of the nephew of Rurik, the ruler of this Danish duchy. And when in 875 Rurik himself died, Frisia appears to have risen in revolt. The Viking armies who arrived in this region then may well have been called in by the Danes of Frisia to help them maintain their position in the land.[53]

At any rate, in 879 a large Viking force sailed to the Scheldt and established itself at Courtrai, which was fortified as a base. From there these raiders penetrated into the Meuse region, sacking and burning a number of thriving centers. So dangerous were their activities that a number of the inhabitants of Tournai, near the Viking fortress of Courtrai, fled to Arras and Noyon to escape their depredations. When in 880 they penetrated as far inland as Théon on the Sambre, Duke Louis of Saxony tried to stop them, only to meet defeat. Even a check at Sancourt by Louis III had little effect. Instead, a large band invaded Saxony itself in this same year and routed an opposing force composed of the Saxon duke, twelve Saxon counts and two bishops.[54]

It was along the lower Rhine, Meuse and Scheldt, however, from bases established at Courtrai, Ghent and Condé, that the Viking danger was most serious. New bands joined the original invaders and in 881 Danish forces, commanded by Gotfried and Siegfried, advanced into the interior to set up a fortified camp at Asseult. From there a two-pronged attack was launched towards the interior. One

[52] F. L. Ganshof, *Les Origines du Comté de Flandre* (Brussels 1948), p. 17.

[53] On the rather complex situation in Frisia during this period, see J. de Vries, *De Wikinger in de Lage Landen bij de Zee*, pp. 263-85, and P. Boeles, *Friesland*, pp. 388-91.

[54] F. L. Ganshof, *op.cit.*, pp. 17-19. H. Shetelig, *op.cit.*, pp. 119-21. R. Doehaerd, *L'Expansion économique belge*, pp. 21-23.

group of Vikings raided Meuse centers like Maastricht, Liége, Aix-la-Chapelle and Metz. Another proceeded in force up the Rhine to plunder Bonn, Cologne and Strasbourg.

These raids finally roused the sluggish Charles the Fat, King of Germany. He gathered together a large Imperial force and besieged the Viking host in its fortress at Asseult in 882. But the result was worse than indecisive. Instead of seeking a solution by force of arms, Charles conceded Frisia to Gotfried and Siegfried, which was perhaps their real objective, paid the raiders a Danegeld of 2,080 pounds of silver, and allowed them to depart peacefully with 200 ships loaded with plunder. This seems to have encouraged rather than discouraged the invaders, naturally enough. New forces of Vikings appear to have taken the place of those paid off by Charles' Danegeld, and Gotfried began to claim new territory which he wished to add to his Frisian realm, perhaps hoping to found a Danelaw in the Low Countries. Attacks, therefore, continued. But the tide began to turn. A Viking force which was invading the Deventer region of Holland was defeated in 883, and another pirate army, advancing down the Rhine as far as Duisburg, was checked by a German force commanded by Count Henry and the Bishops of Mainz and Wurzburg. In the next year Archbishop Robert of Bremen defeated the Danes and drove them out of Northern Frisia. Gotfried, still encamped on the lower Rhine, meanwhile advanced upriver with large Viking forces to capture Cologne, Andernach and Sinzig, where there was wine that he desired to seize. He was, however, murdered by the Franks and his army invading Saxony was annihilated. The invaders retreated, and in 885 departed, leaving the lands along the North Sea from the Rhine to the Elbe free of Danes for the first time since 840.[55]

Nevertheless, this end of Danish power in Frisia, along the Rhine and in North Germany by 885 did not end the Viking menace to the Low Countries. Pirate bands still occupied fortresses on the lower Scheldt, Yser and Lys like Ghent, Antwerp and Louvain. More successful resistance to their attacks in the interior may have discouraged their piratical proclivities, but it seems probable that the

[55] T. D. Kendrick, op.cit., pp. 214-15. H. Shetelig, op.cit., pp. 119-21. On the fortified camp at Asseult, see "Ascola," in Oudheidkunige Medeelingen, new ser., XI (1930), 73-81, and J. Vanerus, "Asseult et non Elsoo" in Bull. de l'Acad. Roy. Belge, X (1932), 147-68. On the fortified camp at Louvain, probably established in 884, see H. Vander Linden, "Les Normands à Louvain," in Revue hist., CXXIV (1924), 64-81. See also F. Lot, op.cit., pp. 129-30. On the Danish loss of Frisia, see J. de Vries, op.cit., pp. 280-313, and P. Boeles, Friesland, pp. 391-92. On Viking raids into the Meuse region, see F. Rousseau, La Meuse et le pays mosan, pp. 68-69.

lull which descended upon this region was less the result of opposition than of greater opportunities existing elsewhere. In 882, for instance, the Viking bands of Asseult, whom Charles the Fat had bought off with a large Danegeld, sailed to the Somme and, after ravaging this region, moved south towards the Seine and Oise, which had been free from raids since 876. Carloman, the Carolingian ruler of France, much alarmed, bought them off with a huge Danegeld of 12,000 pounds of silver. His death in 889, which the Vikings felt relieved them of their oath to him, and the chance for richer booty encouraged them to reopen hostilities. In 885 there gathered at the mouth of the Seine the largest Viking army since the great Danish host which had invaded England in 865. It appears to have consisted of 700 shiploads of freebooters, numbering perhaps 40,000 men, commanded by the experienced sea-king, Seigfried.[56]

In the spring the army advanced up the Seine, seized and sacked Rouen and reached Paris. But Paris bravely resisted and, though under siege, refused the Vikings passage up the Seine. In 886 a large relieving force arrived under the command of Charles the Fat, now Emperor of a reunited Frankish state. Instead of attacking the Viking forces, however, this incompetent ruler paid them a large Danegeld and allowed them to pass by Paris and proceed on to plunder in Burgundy. By 889, after three years of ravaging Eastern France from Lyons to Flanders, the raiders returned north by way of Paris, where this time they were bought off by Count Odo, who was in command of the city. A part of this host then moved west to plunder St. Lô. The rest returned to the Low Countries, where they established themselves in Brabant in their large fortified base of Louvain.[57]

Their appearance at Louvain, however, seems to have goaded the local nobility of Flanders at last into action. Count Baldwin II of Flanders acted vigorously and drove them from their fortresses along the lower Scheldt. And the able Arnaulf, King of Germany and successor to the unworthy Charles the Fat, gathered a large force and advanced to meet them in Brabant. In the battle of the Dyle which followed, the Vikings suffered a bad defeat and were glad to abandon their Netherlands bases and sail to England, where

[56] This figure is a gross exaggeration, but the Viking force must have been of considerable size.

[57] T. D. Kendrick, *op.cit.*, pp. 212-20. H. Shetelig, *op.cit.*, pp. 118-19. See Abbo's interesting contemporary account of the siege in Abbonis, *De bello Parisiaco*, II.

they engaged in the battles of 892-896 that were waged by the Danes against Alfred. For the first time since 879, the Carolingian state north of the Somme was freed from the presence of Scandinavian invaders. The Danish Viking menace along these shores had ended, as it had in England.[58]

This end of attacks in England and farther north along the North Sea did not, however, free France from Viking depredations. There the problem of these pirate freebooters remained a serious one for two more decades. Though our sources for this period are obscure, it seems clear that anarchy contributed to the continuance of the Viking menace in this area by making concerted action, such as that taken by an Alfred or an Arnaulf, impossible. Viking pirate bands thus remained established at the mouths of the Seine, the Loire and along the Oise. Though they seem to have left the Garonne and Charente regions alone, and to have bothered Spain little except for a raid on Galicia in 903, they were active in the rest of Northern and Central France. Despite Carolingian-Capetian feuds, however, little by little the feudal forces of France began to re-establish order. In 898, defeats at the hands of King Charles the Simple and Duke Richard of Burgundy drove the Oise Vikings to seek refuge at their Seine base. In 903 an invading force, probably composed of Loire Vikings, was defeated when it tried to seize Tours, though it successfully plundered Bourges.[59]

By 911 the chief remaining Viking forces were those of Rollo, who commanded the Seine Vikings. Rollo attempted to take Chartres, which was protected by forces under Robert, Count of Paris, Richard, Duke of Burgundy, and Ebles, Count of Poitou. His attack was beaten off.[60] He therefore was glad, upon his retreat to his Seine base, to make peace with Charles the Simple, a peace in which he was granted Normandy as a fief. Normandy, a sort of French Viking Frisia, had at last been established.[61]

[58] On this final assault on the Netherlands, see F. L. Ganshof, "Het Laat-Karolingische Tijdperk," *Algamene Geschiedenis der Nederlanden*, II (1950), 370-73, and his *Les Origines du Comté de Flandre*, pp. 19-20. See also H. Vander Linden, *op.cit.*, pp. 70-81.

[59] T. D. Kendrick, *op.cit.*, pp. 221-23. A. Eichel, *Charles le Simple* (Paris 1899), pp. 60-90.

[60] On this battle, which broke the power of the Vikings in Central France, see W. Vogel, *Die Normannen*, pp. 397-98, and J. Lair, *Le Siège de Chartres par les Normands* (Chartres 1897).

[61] The fundamental studies on the final establishment of the duchy of Normandy are H. Prentout, *Essai sur les origines et la fondation du Duché de Normandie* (Paris

The granting of Normandy to Rollo and his band did not, however, bring peace to France. Between 919 and 939 Rollo attempted to increase his Seine fief by allying himself with the remnants of the Loire Vikings, and thus to add Brittany, Maine, Nantes and the Norman Bessin to his lands. He also extorted at least one more Danegeld from the French ruler. But such activities were only the last gasps of the old order of things. The Norse and Danes in Rollo's duchy were fast becoming Gallicized and, by the middle of the tenth century, had formed not a Danelaw, as in England, but rather a French Norman feudal principality, whose importance lay in the future.[62] With the emergence of this Normandy the Viking Age ended in France, as it had already done in England, Germany and the Low Countries.

The Scandinavian invading tide of conquest and destruction, largely Danish in origin, which reached its climax between 852 and 892 along the coasts of England and the Carolingian Empire and then gradually subsided, was not the only activity of importance during these years. Farther west, in Ireland and in the Atlantic, other important events were taking place during the decades which followed the initial consolidation of a Norse Irish kingdom in Dublin in 852.

For twenty years after the establishment of this Norse kingdom, its ruler was Olaf of Westfold. But as early as 856 a Danish Viking contingent arrived under Ivar the Boneless, an able leader. When Olaf left Ireland to die in his native Norway in 871, Ivar succeeded him, until he died in his turn in 874. A period of disorder followed, with the Irish throne passing for certain periods to the control of Danes of the Northumbrian royal family, and then reverting to Norse control. Perhaps it was these Scandinavian divisions which gave the native Irish a chance to reassert themselves. They seem at any rate to have expelled some of the Viking settlers and to have regained control of Dublin itself for a decade prior to 911.[63]

To view this last half of the ninth century in Ireland, however, as a period in which the major event was the struggle of the native Irish

---

1911), and *Etude critique sur Dudon de St. Quentin* (Paris 1916). See also R. Douglas, *Rollo of Normandy* (London 1950), for a later interpretation.

[62] On these final Viking flickers in France, or perhaps first Norman beginnings, see T. D. Kendrick, *op.cit.*, pp. 223-24; H. Shetelig, *op.cit.*, pp. 127-31; F. Lot, *Les Invasions*, pp. 145-46; and P. Lauer, *Louis IV d'outre-mer* (Paris 1900), pp. 8-79.

[63] *Codaz Gaedhil re Gaillaibh* (*The Wars of the Gaedhil with the Gael*), ed. Toad (London 1867), is the fundamental source on events in Ireland during these years. See also T. D. Kendrick, *op.cit.*, pp. 285-91, and H. Shetelig, *op.cit.*, pp. 62-70.

against the Viking invaders is to misunderstand this era. What appears to have taken place is a surprising mingling of Celts and Northmen. Many Norse settlers intermarried with the Irish and adopted the Irish tongue, and we find some Irish so attracted to Norse ways that they became known as the *Gall Gaidall*, or foster sons of the Scandinavian invaders.[64] This same process of amalgamation of racial stock also was proceeding apace on the Isle of Man, in the Hebrides and perhaps also in the Orkneys and Shetlands.[65] The Norse who attacked West Britain in the first years of the tenth century, and who began to colonize Westmoreland and the Chester region, contained a large Celtic element.[66] Similarly, the native Irish of Ulster whose raids reached British coasts during these years were semi-Norsified.[67]

All this explains the nature of the Scandinavian colonization of Iceland, which seems to have begun about 870. When the first Norwegian colonists, Lief and Ingvar, reached this island, they found the Irish already there. Indeed, it is worth noting that Lief proceeded to Iceland only after he had raided along Irish shores, so it is possible he learned of its existence from Irish sources. Apparently a large number of the first settlers who arrived after Lief were of Celtic blood, too. The initial settlement of Iceland, then, can be fairly termed a joint Norse-Irish affair.[68] Later a larger contingent of colonists arrived direct from Norway—according to tradition, escaping the tyranny of Harold Fairhair.[69] How much, though, of later Icelandic civilization can be ascribed to Irish influence is a subject on which there is little agreement. But it is significant to note that the Sagas, Icelandic in origin, are found in a region where Irish narrative and epic traditions

[64] Jean Young, "A Note on the Norse Occupation of Ireland," in *History*, xxv (1950), 21-28.

[65] See H. Shetelig, *op.cit.*, pp. 43-45, on the mixed elements found in these islands. Also T. C. Lethbridge, *Herdsmen and Hermits*, pp. 90-102.

[66] Both A. Bugge, "The Norse Settlements in the British Isles," in *Trans. of Royal Hist. Soc.* (1921), pp. 173-221, and A. Eckwall, *An Introduction to the Study of Place Names* (Cambridge 1924), pp. 33-34, emphasize that there was a strong Celtic element among these Norse settlers in Western Britain.

[67] See *Chron. Scotorum*, anno 906, ed. Hennessey (London 1860), p. 181, and *The Annals of Four Masters*, anno 905-909, ed. O'Donovan (Dublin 1856), II, 575-81, on these fleets and the mixed Celto-Norse element which composed them.

[68] On the Irish element in Iceland, see K. Gjerset, *History of Iceland* (New York 1924), pp. 12-20, and T. D. Kendrick, *op.cit.*, pp. 337-38. See also, as a more contemporary source, *Lândnamabôk*, ed. Jónsson (Copenhagen 1925), and T. C. Lethbridge, *Merlin's Island*, pp. 85-103.

[69] On the tyranny of Harold Fairhair, which according to tradition in the *Heimskringla*, *The Saga of Harold Fairhair*, drove a large group of Norwegians to Iceland, see G. Turville-Petrie, *The Heroic Age in Scandinavia*, pp. 112-18. See also K. Gjerset, *op.cit.*, pp. 5-21.

were no doubt strong, while such literary productions seem missing in Sweden, the home of a purer Scandinavian stock. Probably Irish literature, like Irish traditions of seamanship and navigation, played a larger role in Norwegian civilization in the Western Atlantic than some historians have been willing to admit.

So far in this chapter we have confined our attention to Scandinavian advances into the North Sea, Channel and Atlantic as far as Spain and Ireland. But a second and equally important expansion of Scandinavian peoples was taking place during this period—that into Russia, down as far as the Black Sea and the Caspian. This advance is known as that of the Varangians, and it resulted in the establishment of the kingdom of Kiev, the first Russian state, late in the ninth century. Unfortunately, unlike our information concerning Western Scandinavian movements, our knowledge of this eastward expansion is slight indeed. The *Russian Primary Chronicle*, containing traditions written down long after the events described took place, and certain scraps of information from Byzantine and Arab sources are all we have to enlighten us. Unfortunately, too, much of the information that Russian archeologists have available which might throw light upon this subject has either not been made known to the scholarly world or has been interpreted in an overly nationalistic fashion. There has been an attempt among Russian scholars to minimize the role of a Scandinavian element in the formation of the first Russian state. Nevertheless, when we grant these difficulties, we can still discern the broad outlines of development down to 911.

About 840 or thereabouts, the first period of contact between Scandinavians from Sweden and the lands that lay across the Baltic came to an end. In part, this connection was with the coast of Courland, where Apolloné and Seeburg were early Swedish colonies or were under strong Swedish influence. Archeology reveals, however, that other such settlements existed on eastern Baltic shores. Among them were Daugmalé, near the present city of Riga at the entrance to the river Dvina, and Trekala and Jersika, in the interior, which were also either Swedish colonies or had been under strong influence from the Uppland and Gotland since the eighth century. Farther south two centers had arisen in the lands of the Prussians, or Samland, as the Swedes called this region. They were Ebling and Truso, near the mouths of the Vistula and the Nieman. Probably in Carolingian times they, too, had been under Swedish influence.[70] But more important was the region of the Gulf of Finland and the Aland Islands, which connected with the Upper Volga by way of Old Ladoga and Belozero, or communicated by way of the Lovat river and Novgorod with either the Volga or the upper Dnieper near Smolensk, and then with the Caspian and Black Seas.

As noted in a previous chapter, the routes leading into Russia and on to the Orient via the river Dvina or the Gulf of Finland were the more important ones. Routes to Samland and other Baltic shores had but a local commercial value in the ninth century. That is the only possible conclusion which can be drawn from Ommiad and Abbassid silver coin hoards found at Gotland and in the Swedish Uppland, which were the termini of the Dvina and Gulf of Finland routes. Once inside Russia, however, it is clear that down to 840, the Volga trade route was the main one in use, and Ibn Khordâdbeh tells us that Russian merchants carried their wares down it as far as Iraq.[71] The route down the Dnieper, on the other hand, as we have noted, seems to have been in little use in Carolingian times.[72] Thus early Scandinavian settlement apparently was confined largely to such centers as Rostov, Belozero, Old Ladoga, Novgorod and perhaps Smolensk and Polotsk in North Russia. Some finds of early ninth-century Scandinavian material at Belozero and Rostov seem to confirm this fact.[73] So, too, does the *Primary Chronicle*, which speaks of the earlier expulsion of Varangians by Slavs, Kritches, Mervians and Chuds—all peoples of Northwestern Russia near the Baltic.[74]

Then, about 839 or 840, as the *Primary Chronicle* makes clear, came the expulsion of these Swedes from Russia, which included the loss of their eastern Baltic lands as well. We have already noted how coin evidence in Scandinavia confirms this expulsion[75] and how

[70] See B. Nerman, *Die Verbindungen zwischen Skandinavien und dem Ostbalticum*, pp. 60-138, and *Sveriges Första Storhetstid*, pp. 11-168, for archeological evidence on these settlements, which appear to have come to an end about 900 A.D. See also F. Balodis, *Det Aldsta Lettland*, pp. 146-265. For a contemporary source, see *Alfred's Orosius*, ed. Sweet, pp. 19-21.

[71] Ibn Khordâdbeh, *Book of Routes*, ed. de Geoje, p. 114.

[72] The almost complete lack of Byzantine coins buried in Swedish coin hoards (save for a few rare 9th-century ones in Birka graves) prior to the 10th century makes this clear. This is in strong contrast to the discovery of thousands of Sassanian, Ommiad and Abbassid ones.

[73] T. J. Arne, *La Suède et l'Orient*, pp. 62-233, contains much evidence of Norse materials in archeological finds in North Russian sites. Unfortunately this evidence needs to be brought up to date.

[74] *The Primary Chronicle*, ed. Cross, p. 144.

[75] See Chapter IV on this point.

it can be dated by the 839 return of Varangian Russians to Scandinavia by way of Constantinople and the Frankish Empire.[76] And we have noted that Anskar's account of the expulsion of the Swedes from Apolloné and Seeburg prior to 852[77] is in agreement with the *Primary Chronicle's* statement, which adds these Baltic Letts, or Chuds, to those peoples who "expelled the Varangians across the sea and governed themselves and founded *grody*."[78]

About 852, however, we find the Varangians returning to the lands across the Baltic. Again Anskar's account, which states that first the Danes attacked Apolloné and Seeburg and then a Swedish army reconquered them, gives us precious information as to the probable date of the Scandinavian return to North Russia.[79] Exactly how this return took place is unknown. The *Primary Chronicle* seems to imply, however, that it soon resulted in a re-establishment of the Scandinavians in the lands of the Chuds, Slovenians, Mervians, Ves and Krivichians—that is to say, in Courland and about such trading centers as Novgorod, Rostov, Belozero, Polotsk and perhaps Smolensk.[80] The *Primary Chronicle*, however, goes on to imply that the Slavic tribes of the Dnieper and Don valleys—specifically, the Poldanians, Severians and Viatchians—paid tribute to the Kazars during the years immediately after 850.[81]

In what capacity did the Varangians return to Russia, either the Swedes or the other Scandinavians associated with Rurik in his occupation of Novgorod and North Russian *grody?* To most Russian historians, these Varangians were nothing more than hired mercenaries who were called in by the *dans*, or assemblies, of the North Russian cities to assist in their fighting. They were "confederates" of the Slavs, as indeed Constantine Porphyrogenitus expressly states and as the word *Varyang* seems to mean.[82] To Scandinavian historians, on

---

[76] *Annales Bertiniani*, in *MGH Script.*, II, 434.

[77] *Vita Anskari*, XXX, in *ibid.*, p. 713.

[78] *The Primary Chronicle*, p. 144.

[79] *Vita Anskari*, XXX, in *op.cit.*, p. 713.

[80] *The Primary Chronicle*, p. 144.

[81] *Ibid.* Vernadsky believes that in the 9th century, perhaps starting about 833 A.D., the Kazars controlled Kiev and the Dnieper valley, exercising this control through their Magyar allies or vassals. G. Vernadsky, *Ancient Russia*, pp. 330-33. This view seems to be generally shared by Cross and Dvornik. See S. F. Cross, "The Scandinavian Infiltration into Russia," in *Speculum*, XXI (1946), 510-14, and F. Dvornik, *The Making of Central and Eastern Europe*, pp. 60-61.

[82] On the remarks of Constantine Porphyrogenitus, see Constantine Porphyrogenitus, *De administrando imperio*, ed. Bonn, pp. 75, 79. For an extreme position which practically ignores the Scandinavian element in the formation of Russia, see B. Grekov,

the other hand, they were essentially conquerors and the directing force which politically and economically organized the first Russian state and welded together dissident Slavic peoples and trading centers into a workable political system.[83] Probably the truth lies somewhere between these two views. Sometimes, as we know from the reconquest of Courland, related by Anskar, the Varangians returned through force. Sometimes, as in the case of a Rurik or an Askold, the Varangians were partly "confederates" and partly conquerors. There can be little doubt, however, that they were not hostile to the mass of the population, and we know that Scandinavian merchants and adventurers who settled in these Russian cities did so only in alliance with the ruling Slavic merchant class there. Probably, as in the case of the Norse in Ireland, there was a practically inevitable merging and blending of Slavic and Scandinavian elements and interests almost from the start.[84] Such figures as Askold and Dir, for instance, who moved south to take over Kiev from the Kazars and then proceeded to open the Dnieper route south to the very walls of Constantinople in 860, must have been invited by the Kievan population to do so.[85] The suggestion that Kiev called them in to open trade routes and

---

La Culture de la Russie de Kiev (Moscow 1948). More moderate, but still Slavophile and tending to minimize Scandinavian contributions, are A. Eck, "En relisant le Porphyrogénète" in *Mélanges Bidez*, 1 (Brussels 1934), 342-49; F. Dvornik, *op.cit.*, pp. 65-67; and V. Gitermann, *Geschichte Russlands* (Zurich 1944), pp. 34-39.

[83] For an extreme Scandinavian position, see T. J. Arne, *Det Stora Svitjod*, and especially A. Bugge, "Die nordeuropäischen Verkerswege im frühen Mittelalter und die Bedeutung der Wikinger," in *Viert. für Soz- und Wirtschaft*, IV (1906), 181-243. More moderate but still inclining in this direction are the early articles of S. F. Cross, "Medieval Russian Contacts with the West," in *Speculum*, X (1935), and "Yaroslav the Wise and the Norse Tradition," in *ibid.*, IV (1929).

[84] For the most judicious accounts, see G. Vernadsky, *Ancient Russia*, pp. 333-44, and S. F. Cross, "The Scandinavian Infiltration into Russia," in *Speculum*, XXI (1946). To them should be added N. K. Chadwick, *The Beginnings of Russian History, An Inquiry into the Sources*. On the date of Rurik's entrance into Russia we are reduced to conjecture. It was after the time of Anskar (circa 852) and before 880. Perhaps the late 850's represent a good possibility. It has been claimed that Rurik was a Dane of the royal Danish family who held Frisia and that his successor, Oleg, was a Norwegian. This is possible but seems unprovable. No doubt the *Varyangs* were of mixed Scandinavian origin, but it is hard to believe the Swedes did not form a majority of those entering Russia.

[85] Askold's and Dir's attempt to open a trade route to the south via the Dnieper was not a success, judging from the almost complete lack of 9th-century Byzantine coins found in hoards in the Baltic and Scandinavia. On the other hand, a renewed flood of Arabic silver reaching the north from Samanid Asia seems to show that the Volga route was again active commercially after 860 or 870. The failure of Askold and Dir to open a route from Kiev may explain their failure to hold this center when it was attacked by Oleg a little later.

protect the lower Dnieper valley against nomadic Magyars, settled on South Russian steppes, seems a likely one.

By 860, then, the Scandinavians had penetrated again far into Russia, partly as rulers, partly as allies of the Slavs, or perhaps both at the same time. Now, however, they were established not only in North Russia near the upper Volga, in a state which was in the process of formation from a Novgorod ruled by Rurik and Oleg. They were also in charge of the Dnieper valley region, centering around Kiev, where Askold and Dir appear to have become the rulers. These two centers of Varangian power seem to have lasted down to about 880.[86]

Between 880 and 882, however, Oleg, ruler of Novgorod, ended this state of affairs. He gathered together in the north a mixed force consisting of Varangian Scandinavians, Finns and Slavs, and, marching south, seized Kiev and murdered his rival Askold. Thus emerged the Kievan Russian state.[87] From Lake Ladoga and the Gulf of Finland, east to the lands of the White Bulgars and Kazars on the middle and lower Volga, and south to the steppes of the Ukraine, a single Varangian Russian realm had arisen.

Of Oleg's rule in Kiev, during the years immediately following his establishment of a unified Russian state, we know very little. In the course of his consolidation of his kingdom, however, he appears to have sent forces towards the southeast to open trade routes to the Moslem East. Probably the Varangians whom Arab sources mention in 880 in the Caspian went there under his direction.[88] He may even have led attacks on the Magyars to the south along the lower Dnieper, and have been partially responsible for their movement west into Transylvania in 899 and their eventual settlement on the plains of Hungary a little later. It also seems that he extended his overlordship west, along the trade route that led to Prague via Ruthenia, and thus included in his domains the lands of the White Croats, particularly after the Magyars smashed the Moravian Empire of which White Croatia formed a part.[89] This seems particularly probable, since in 906 we have mention of *Rugi*, or Russian merchants, arriving at Raf-

---

[86] *The Primary Chronicle*, p. 145.

[87] *The Primary Chronicle*, p. 146, is our source. Note that the *Chronicle* says Oleg moved south against Kiev with a *mixed* force of *Slavs, Finns* and *Varangians*. Dvornik believes this took place between 880 and 882. F. Dvornik, *op.cit.*, pp. 67-69. Vernadsky thinks about 878. G. Vernadsky, *op.cit.*, pp. 363-70.

[88] B. Dorn, "Caspia: über die Einfälle der alten Russen in Tabaristan," in *Mem. Acad. Imp. des Sciences de St. Petersburg*, XII (1897), 31-128.

[89] F. Dvornik, *op.cit.*, pp. 63-65.

felstein on the upper Danube, who must have passed along the Ruthenian Central European route.[90]

To his activities and expansion of Kiev's influence in his earlier days, must be added Oleg's great expeditions south against Byzantium and the Caspian. In 907 he may have appeared with a fleet before Constantinople,[91] as Askold and Dir had done earlier in 860, and in 907 and 911 he negotiated very favorable trade treaties with the Byzantine Empire for his Rus merchants, who traded south in the Black Sea as far as Constantinople.[92] A few years later, in 910, he led an expedition into the Caspian Sea and attacked Moslem cities on its south shores. Much of this force was massacred by Kazars and Moslems on the way back to the mouth of the Volga, but the campaign at least reveals the power that the new Kievan state possessed.[93] By 911 the existence of Oleg's principality had resulted in the reopening of Baltic trade with Constantinople, the Crimea, the Kazars, the Caspian and even west via Prague with South Germany. Certainly Kievan Russia was the greatest accomplishment of Scandinavia in an age filled with mighty deeds by these Viking expansionists.

Let us now turn our attention from the movements and accomplishments of Scandinavian peoples in the East and West during this period to Scandinavia itself. As we have already emphasized, the main Scandinavian kingdoms existing in 840 were the two which developed out of the empire of Ivar Widefathom after 750—Denmark and Sweden. Under Horick, in 840, Denmark appears to have had a certain political unity, but Sweden less so, with regions like the island of Gotland and even the southern provinces of Gotaland all but independent, and Swedish colonies across the Baltic no less free from control exercised by the Swedish kings of the Uppland. In Norway, across the Kattegat and Skagerrak from Denmark, lay the Ingvar kingdom of the Westfold about Oslo fjord. It seems to have gained its independence from Danish overlordship some time in the late eighth century, shortly after the break-up of Harold Wartooth's empire.[94] Under able rulers, Harold Whiteleg and Halfdan the Black, grandfather and father, respectively, of Harold Fairhair, the West-

[90] MGH Capitularia, II, 249-50.
[91] A. A. Vasliev, "The Russian Attack on Constantinople in 907," in Dumbarton Oaks Papers, IV (1953).
[92] The Primary Chronicle, pp. 149-52, 163. G. Vernadsky, Kievan Russia, pp. 22-30. F. Dvornik, op.cit., pp. 66-67.
[93] B. Dorn, "Caspia," loc.cit., pp. 71-89. G. Vernadsky, op.cit., pp. 25-33.
[94] A. Bugge, Wikinger, pp. 20-25. G. Turville-Petrie, op.cit., pp. 25-33.

fold kingdom was beginning to assume a certain overlordship along the Norwegian coast. As early as 831, for instance, it was this Westfold royal line which produced Thorgisl, Norse leader in Ireland, and his successor, Olaf, King of Dublin.[95]

Soon after the death of Louis the Pious, Denmark disintegrated as a kingdom, particularly during the period of anarchy which followed Horick's assassination in 854.[96] When Ottar and Wulfstan, for instance, sailed past Danish shores late in the century on their voyages to Hedeby, they reported that the Danish kingdom consisted of the Danish islands, Scania, and some control over Hedeby, with Jutland and Bornholm both independent.[97] Jutland seems to have been under Norwegian influence.[98] It is true that Frisia, from 840 to 885, was in the hands of a Danish royal house, like the Danelaw kingdom of Northumbria after 867.[99] But no political consolidation, either in Denmark or in overseas Danish possessions, appears to have taken place prior to the late tenth century in the time of King Harold Bluetooth.[100]

In contrast to the disintegration of Denmark, these years found a different process at work in Norway and Sweden. We can see this more clearly in Norway, thanks to abundant Saga evidence. There, starting about 860, Harold Fairhair, the Ingvar King of the Westfold, began to consolidate the various parts of Norway into a united kingdom. To do so, he formed an alliance with the jarls of the northwestern coast around Trondheim and, with their aid, gradually reduced Sogne, More, Rogaland and Hordaland to submission. He

---

[95] L. Musset, *Les Peuples scandinaves*, pp. 78-80. Almost the only written source for Norway's early history is *The Saga of Harold Fairhair*, as recorded much later by Snorri Sturluson. The royal graveyards of the Westfold kings do, however, seem to show that the Oslo region was the most important in Norway during this period. On these grave finds, particularly Queen Asa's, see Brøgger and Shetelig, *The Viking Ships*, pp. 50-138. On the connection between Thorgisl and Olaf the White of the royal Westfold line and Norse conquests in Ireland, see T. D. Kendrick, *History of the Vikings*, pp. 274-85, and H. Shetelig, *The Viking History of Western Europe*, pp. 55-61.

[96] On the disintegration of the Danish kingdom in the early 9th century, see E. Arup, *Danmarks Historie* (Copenhagen 1925), I, 60-122; L. Musset, *op.cit.*, pp. 81-84; and J. de Vries, *op.cit.*, pp. 128-46.

[97] *Extracts from Alfred's Orosius*, ed. Sweet (Oxford 1893), pp. 8-16.

[98] On the close marriage connections and political links between Harold Fairhair and the rulers of Jutland and Gorm the Old of Denmark, see G. Turville-Petrie, *op.cit.*, pp. 111-15, and S. A. Anderson, *Viking Enterprise*, pp. 12-13.

[99] On the Danes in Frisia, see J. de Vries, *op.cit.*, pp. 126-260. On the role of the Danish royal line in the English Danelaw, see F. M. Stenton, "The Danes in England," in *Proc. of British Acad.*, XII (1923), 203-46, and "The Scandinavian Colonies in England and Normandy," in *Trans. of Royal Hist. Soc.*, XXVI (1945), 1-12.

[100] L. Musset, *op.cit.*, pp. 82-85. E. Arup, *op.cit.*, pp. 123-45.

broke the power of the independent jarls along those shores in a great naval battle at Haffsfjord in 892, a battle in which Viking settlers in the Faroes and Orkneys appear to have supported the West Norwegian nobility.[101] As a result, Harold extended his overlordship to these islands, whose piracies he punished.[102] He may even have been obeyed in Iceland, many of whose inhabitants had fled there to escape his rule in Norway. By 911 he also appears to have extended his power to Jutland by marriage, and thus to have gained control over the important Kattegat-Skagerrak route leading to the Baltic and the riches of the East. Though Icelandic tradition has presented him as a tyrant, there seems little doubt that he brought order to Norway for the first time in its history and laid the foundations of the later Norwegian kingdom.[103]

The same process of consolidation was probably going on in Sweden, though lack of information hides the situation there from us. Sweden seems to have been weak and disunited at the time of Anskar's second visit about 850, but already the forces of integration were reviving, as we can see by the reconquest of Courland about 852 by the Swedish royal house. When later in the century Wulfstan sailed from Hedeby to Truso, he found that Gotaland and Blekinge in South Sweden now belonged to the Kings of Uppsala, though Bornholm and probably Gotland were still independent.[104] About 900, however, we learn that Olaf, a great Swedish king, had expanded his power over Hedeby and the Danish islands, Bornholm and perhaps Gotland. The Baltic had by 911 again become a Swedish lake.[105] It was to remain so until Henry the Fowler of Germany broke the Swedes' power in Hedeby in 934, and a new Danish royal house, that of Gorm the Old, began rebuilding an independent kingdom of Denmark.

[101] L. Musset, op.cit., pp. 78-82. G. Turville-Petrie, op.cit., pp. 110-16. T. D. Kendrick, op.cit., pp. 108-13. A. Bugge, Vikingerne, II, 215-17. In the Snorri's later account of the famous battle of Haffsfjord, which won Harold Norway, there is a 9th-century skaldic fragment apparently embedded. On this, see The Saga of Harold Fairhair, in Corpus Poet. Boreale, ed. Vigfusson and Powell (London 1883).

[102] The Saga of Harold Fairhair recounts how this ruler sent an expedition west to suppress the piracies of Norse Vikings in the Faroes and Orkneys. On this, see G. Turville-Petrie, op.cit., pp. 114-16. Shetelig has doubted the authenticity of this tradition. But recent archeological evidence from Høbn, the principal Viking port in the Orkneys, shows that this settlement was actually destroyed in the late 9th century, thus seeming to confirm the Saga evidence.

[103] L. Musset, op.cit., pp. 54-61. A. Bugge, op.cit., pp. 216-17.

[104] On this, see Alfred's Orosius, ed. Sweet, pp. 14-18.

[105] H. Arbman, Schweden und das Karolingische Reich, p. 23. Adam of Bremen, Gesta Hammab. Pont. Eccl., I, 48. On runic evidence of Swedish control, see H. Jankuhn, Ergebnisse und Probleme der Haithabugrabungen, pp. 12-13.

By 911, then, out of Scandinavian weakness and political disunity we find two distinct kingdoms arising, that of Harold Fairhair, and that of Olaf of Sweden. Between them, they divided the older Danish kingdom. It is well worth noting, however, that in so doing, each monarch paid careful attention to controlling trade routes that led to his particular kingdom. Harold, by his overlordship of Jutland, assured himself of free access into the Baltic. Olaf, by taking Hedeby and the Danish islands, assured himself of control of the Eider-Schlee route across lower Jutland into the North Sea.

This can hardly have been accidental, and it seems, therefore, that the work of consolidation of these two monarchs was as important in ending Viking aggression as the resistance to Viking raids offered by Alfred the Great, Arnaulf or local leaders like Robert the Strong and Baldwin II of Flanders. Orderly government in Scandinavia, particularly in Denmark, where the largest body of Vikings seems to have originated, had the effect of destroying at its source that disorder in which, as we have noted, the Viking pirate spirit had had its origins. Thus Harold's suppression of piracy in the Orkneys, Shetlands and Hebrides, like Olaf's seizure of Hedeby and the Danish islands, struck at the roots of Viking raiding practices. Both monarchs seem to have understood that such pirate raids were a danger to the security of their own trade and of their kingdoms. In suppressing them, they were helping to make possible a new and more peaceful age, the age of the Ottos and the House of Alfred which was to dawn in the Northern Seas in the tenth century.

In the preceding pages we have considered the history of these years around the Northern Seas of Europe from the standpoint of the Scandinavians, who, as invaders and colonizers, moved east to the Caspian and Black Seas, and west as far as Spain and Iceland. This was the principal event of the period from 840 to 911 A.D., but not the only one. There remains the story of how the Carolingian Empire disintegrated under the impact of these invasions, only to re-emerge as the nucleus of a new medieval Europe.

The death of Louis the Pious marked, in a sense, the end of the Carolingian Empire. Even before his death, Louis had divided his state among his sons, giving France to Charles, Germany to Lewis, and to his eldest son, Lothair, a central portion, stretching from the North Sea to Rome, that carried with it the title of Emperor. Charles' realm was in turn subdivided into France proper and the kingdom of Aquitaine under Pippin I and Pippin II. Even before Louis died, this division gave rise to serious conflicts which weakened the political fabric of the Carolingian state. After his death, it resulted in almost constant civil wars waged among his heirs. These wars were one of the chief reasons for Viking successes, for it is clear that the invaders took advantage of the contending factions in planning and executing their raids on Frankish shores.[106]

By the 870's a new political pattern had emerged. Lothair's central region had broken to pieces. A part of it had been added to the lands ruled by Lewis the German. But the major portion had disintegrated, too weak to stand alone, and since that time it has been a cause for conflict between France and Germany. Northern Italy had become independent and free of any effective Carolingian control.[107]

France, which was doubly torn by internal disputes between Charles the Bald and the vassal kings of Aquitaine, and by wars which Charles waged with his brothers Lewis and Lothair, likewise lost strength and cohesion.[108] The temporary unity of the Carolingian Empire in 885-886 under the weak, unworthy Charles the Fat proved but an illusion. For Arnaulf, able though illegitimate, succeeded Charles in Germany, while France continued in the hands of another branch of the Carolingian line.[109]

In France another struggle soon began—one between the Frankish Carolingians and a rival noble family, the Capetians, who held Paris and had distinguished themselves in the struggles waged against the invading Northmen. It gave rise to a new civil war which was to last down to the end of the tenth century. It is not surprising, then, that in the late ninth and early tenth centuries France was the happy hunting ground of Viking raiders, for it could not, under the circumstances, maintain any central government at all, and by 911 was already a country essentially feudal in nature.[110]

[106] The standard study of these last days of Louis the Pious is still W. Simpson, *Jahrbücher des fränkischen Reiches unter Ludwig des Frommen*, 2 vols. (Leipzig 1874-76). See also F. Lot and L. Halphen, *Le Règne de Charles le Chauve*, 2 vols. (Paris 1909-11). For difficulties in Aquitaine between Charles the Bald and Pippin I and II, see L. Auzias, *L'Aquitaine carolingienne*, pp. 270-350.
[107] On Lotharingia and other middle portions of the Carolingian Empire after 840, see M. Chaume, *Les Origines du Duché de Bourgogne*, I (Dijon 1925), 3-121, and R. Parisot, *Le Royaume de Provence, 888-1038* (Paris 1907), pp. 1-112. On Italy, see L. M. Hartmann, *Geschichte Italiens im Mittelalter*, III (Gotha 1908-11), 18-259, and R. Cessi, *Venezia Ducale*, 2 vols. (Padua 1928-29), pp. 23-58.
[108] F. Lot and L. Halphen, *Le Règne de Charles le Chauve*, I, 83-197.
[109] See particularly, L. Auzias, *op.cit.*, pp. 328-43, on this struggle in Aquitaine.
[110] On this rather melancholy period, see A. Eichel, *Charles le Simple*, and E. Faure, *Eudes, Comte de Paris et Roi de France, 882-898* (Paris 1893).

Nor need it surprise us that the fleets which Charlemagne and Louis the Pious had built in the Midi to protect those shores from Moorish Spanish attacks simply disappeared after 840. The Moors, like the Vikings on the Atlantic side of France, again took to raiding the coast along the Mediterranean.[111] By 872 they had established pirate nests at Maguelonne, Garde Frainet and in the Alps, which helped to cut France off from contact with the Mediterranean.[112]

On the other hand, the Carolingian kingdom of Germany, in 840 the weakest and least economically advanced portion of the Empire, remained politically the strongest. Germany suffered from no civil war in these years, maintained communications with Venice over the Alps and possessed able rulers in the persons of Lewis and Arnaulf. As a result, the German kingdom continued to grow.[113] Politically, in addition to absorbing portions of Lotharingia, it expanded east towards the Danube, where the destruction of the Avar kingdom by Charlemagne had left a vacuum to be filled. Allied with Slovak princes like Moimir, German colonists continued their movement east into Hungary and Croatia.[114]

Then the Slavs broke with the Germans. Rastislav of Moravia drove his erstwhile German allies out of the Hungarian plain, and by 862 had built up a Greater Moravia, covering most of the central Danube valley and Bohemia. When Lewis the German attempted to check the growth of this Slavic state to the east by allying himself with the Bulgars, Rastislav countered with a Byzantine alliance. Sviatapolk, Rastislav's successor, further increased the power and extent of this Greater Moravian kingdom by expanding his power over White

[111] The Moslems of Spain began again to attack southern French coasts in 838 with a raid against Marseilles. A. Vasiliev, *Byzance et les Arabes* (Brussels 1935), I, 186. They increased the tempo of such raids throughout the 9th century and into the 10th. See R. Poupardin, *Le Royaume de Provence sous les Carolingiens* (Paris 1901), pp. 240-60, and A. Duprat, "La Provence dans le Haut Moyen Age," in *Bouches du Rhône, Encyclopédie Départementale* (Marseilles 1923), II, 33-36. On the Narbonnaise, see A. Dupont, *Etudes sur les civitates de la Narbonnaise*, pp. 200f.

[112] On Garde Frainet and Moslem strongholds in the Alps, see R. Poupardin, *Le Royaume de Bourgogne* (Paris 1907), pp. 86-112, 250-54. See also G. Patrucco, "I Saraceni i Piemonte et nelle alpi orientale," in *Bibl. della Società Stor. Subalpini* (Pinerola 1908), XXXII. On all these developments and their significance as well as on the possible advance Moslem base at Maguelonne, see A. R. Lewis, *op.cit.*, pp. 146-47.

[113] The standard work dealing with this period is still E. Dummler, *Geschichte des ostfränkischen Reiches* (3rd ed., Leipzig 1887-88).

[114] On the eastward expansion of the Germans and their relations with the Slavic Moravian state of Moimir, see F. Dvornik, *Les Slavs, Byzance et Rome* (Paris 1928), pp. 15-132, and *The Making of Central and Eastern Europe*, pp. 16-19. See also G. Vernadsky, "Greater Moravia and White Croatia," in *Jour. of American Oriental Soc.*, LXV (1945), 237-48.

Croatia on the other side of the Carpathians. But to Arnaulf, now ruler of Germany, this first great Slavic empire in Central Europe represented a danger, and so in 899 he encouraged the Magyars, who had just been expelled from the steppes of South Russia, to move as his allies into the Hungarian plain. Under a double assault from German and Magyar, Greater Moravia disintegrated.[115] In its place a new Hungarian nomadic raiding state appeared on the Tisza, a state which in the course of the tenth century was to spread chaos by attacking across Central Europe, even to Germany.[116] But up to 911 Germany was still a relatively united state, free from serious internal or external disturbances. Unlike France, then, this kingdom, of which Henry the Fowler was elected ruler in 918, was still potentially powerful, with its five great national duchies well-organized, its church submissive and its feudal elements as yet unformed.

Such were the main maritime and political events which took place in Northern Europe from 840 to 911 A.D. We have seen how Scandinavian Viking fleets moved south and west to set up a Viking Normandy in France, a Danelaw in England, a temporary Danish Viking state in Frisia, a Norse kingdom in Ireland and a Norse colony in Iceland. We have viewed the gradual emergence of two strong states in Scandinavia, Norway and Sweden, as well as a Varangian Slavic kingdom in Russia. We have seen how, by the end of this period, the Irish rallied to expel the Norse from some of their holdings in Iceland and how Alfred and his son, Edward the Elder, laid the basis of a strong England under the House of Wessex. We have seen how the Carolingian Empire split into a weak France, a strong Germany and weaker middle region, but still found strength to eject the Danes from Frisia and the other shores they invaded, except Normandy. We have viewed in Central Europe the rise of a raiding Magyar state on the bones of a shattered Greater Moravia. But we may well ask ourselves about the effect upon the economy of the regions which faced the Northern Seas of all these changes, attacks and wars—disorders not seen in Northern Europe since the invasion period. Was the economic progress that had been registered in the Carolingian Empire, Offa's England and Scandinavia between 750 and 840 lost dur-

[115] F. Dvornik, *op.cit.*, pp. 16-19, and *Les Légendes de Constantin et de Méthode* (Prague 1930), pp. 249-83. On the Magyars, see C. Macartney, *The Magyars in the Ninth Century* (Cambridge 1930), and E. Csuday, *Geschichte Ungarns* (2nd ed., Berlin 1899), pp. 3-98.
[116] R. Lüttich, *Ungarnzüge in Europa im 10. Jahrhundert* (Berlin 1910), pp. 20-254. F. Dvornik, *The Making of Central and Eastern Europe*, pp. 16-23.

ing these years of disorder? Did Viking assaults, civil wars and Moslem attacks along the coast of the Midi destroy the economy which had arisen during the early ninth-century Carolingian renaissance?

Perhaps one approach to the problem is to view the eastward and westward Scandinavian migrations from a somewhat different standpoint than that adopted by many historians. The Vikings were pirates, destroyers and plunderers, but they were at the same time colonizers, organizers and merchants. They took by force riches from the trading places and monasteries which they attacked in Western Europe, but they traded, too, when that policy brought better results. For instance, it is worth noting how often during the period of their greatest raids they considered trading to be in their interest,[117] and how many times we can find evidence of their commercial instincts coming to the fore. Charles the Bald in his Capitularies found it necessary to forbid his subjects to trade with the Vikings. He particularly prohibited trade in arms and horses in the Edict of Pîtres, issued in 864,[118] and reiterated such prohibitions in 876.[119] Yet, in 873, we find the Danish leaders in Dorestad, Siegfried and Halfdan, making peace with Germany to secure trade with the Rhineland region.[120] In the same year, Viking bands allowed the trade of captured Nantes to continue, and even evacuated the city on market days.[121] In 882 at Asseult, after peace had been proclaimed, the Vikings threw their fortress open to commerce.[122] According to Dudo, Rollo realized the need for trade on the part of his Seine Vikings.[123] Wine, as well as arms and horses, was a major Viking trade interest. For that reason, in 885, Gotfried of Frisia tried to procure it farther down the Rhine.[124] It was paid as part of Frankish Danegelds during these years. At the height of their power, the pirate bands on the Seine launched raids to secure it.[125] As a bulk commodity, it was probably more often gained by commerce than by theft. In fact, one might well ask to what extent the

[117] See the estimate of T. D. Kendrick, *History of the Vikings*, pp. 3-18, on their trading proclivities, particularly about the Irish Sea.

[118] See the *Edict of Pîtres*, xxv, in *MGH Capitularia*, II.

[119] J. W. Thompson, *The Commerce of France in the Ninth Century*, pp. 862-63.

[120] *Annales Xanten*, anno 873.

[121] J. W. Thompson, *op.cit.*, pp. 862-63.

[122] *Annales Fuldenses*, anno 882, in *MGH Script.*, I, 397. R. Doehaerd, *op.cit.*, pp. 18-20.

[123] *Ibid.*

[124] Dudo of St. Quentin, *Hist. Normann.*, II, 7.

[125] *Annales Bertiniani*, anno 861, *Script. in usum scholarium*, p. 80. J. W. Thompson, *op.cit.*, p. 865.

fortified Viking bases at the mouths of rivers were commercial rather than mere military and naval centers.

In England, too, even during the days of the great Danish attack of 865-878, trading with the invaders went on. Alfred, like Charles the Bald, found it necessary to insert into the peace treaty with Gudrum a provision forbidding trade between his subjects and the Danes, particularly in slaves.[126] Later provisions of the laws of Anglo-Saxon rulers, in echo of Viking times, forbade export of horses.[127] Even in Germany, if we may believe the Monk of St. Gall, Vikings came to the court of Lewis the German to seek the highly prized swords of the Rhinelands.[128]

Still more revealing is numismatic evidence. In their homelands the Scandinavians appear, in this period, to have dealt in silver on the basis of weight and to have eschewed the use of coins in trade. Indeed, all Danegelds were paid then, as we know, on a weight basis.[129] Yet in Western Europe the Vikings almost immediately began to mint coins of their own. The money which the sea-king, Siegfried, struck in Quentovic,[130] those coins which Gudrum minted in London immediately after his conquest[131] and those struck in the late ninth century by the Danish rulers of York[132] must have been intended for use in commerce with a population accustomed to coined money. In Frisia, for instance, during Danish occupation, copies of the gold *solidi*

---

[126] *Treaty of Alfred and Gudrum*, v, in C. Attenborough, *The Earliest English Laws*, pp. 100-3.

[127] *Treaty of Alfred and Gudrum*, IV, in *ibid.*, p. 101.

[128] Mon. S. Gall, *Gesta Karoli Magni*, in *MGH Script.*, II, 737.

[129] On this use of money by weight or as ring money (or *hacksilver*), see S. Greig, "Vikingtidens Skattefund," in *Univ. Oldsakssamlungs Skrifter* (Oslo 1921), pp. 113-19. See also H. Shetelig, *Scandinavian Archeology*, pp. 271-73. An example of such a hoard in bullion or jewelry is the Hon find, mainly gold, where the coins were obviously used as jewelry. Too much, though, has been made of the fact that the Vikings, especially in Scandinavia, always measured silver by *weight*. They had scales and ring money, but they also used coins as coins—especially the Samanid ones, which they and the Russians even imitated at times rather crudely. And the carefully clipped and cut coins found in almost every hoard reveal that they understood the need for fractional coinage, too. What they did not do was to mint any coins of their own in Scandinavia in this period. And this may have been because they were still politically backward, rather than economically so.

[130] On the Cuerdale hoard, which contains five rare coins struck by Viking sea-kings and which dates from between 902-920, see E. Gariel, *op.cit.*, pp. 140-46.

[131] G. C. Brooke, *English Coins*, p. 33, contains information on Gudrum's London coinage.

[132] *Ibid.*, pp. 9-10, 34-37. Until the Danish conquest, Yorkshire's copper *stykka* coinage was entirely local in its distribution and different from that found in the rest of England.

of Louis the Pious continued to be coined, perhaps as late as 890.[133] Furthermore, it is significant that none of the coins paid Viking raiders in Danegelds or seized as booty are to be found in Scandinavian coin hoards of this period.[134] Perhaps some returned in bullion form.[135] But it seems more probable that they found their way back into the hands of the native inhabitants wherever the Vikings stopped and wintered along Western European coasts.[136] Without claiming, as Thompson does, that the Vikings of this period stimulated trade, it is undoubtedly wrong to picture them as mere destroyers of commerce. Probably their purchases stimulated commerce in some regions, while their raids reduced it in others.

Such a theory explains some anomalies which appear in our sources for these years. It explains how ports like Rouen and Nantes could be sacked so repeatedly and still recover again in time for another raid. It shows how an abbey like Noirmoutier could be raided on an almost annual basis without ceasing to be inhabited by monks. Furthermore, it is well to remember that Carolingian trading centers were extremely simply built. Of wood construction for the most part, they were easily burnt, but equally easily rebuilt. Merchants with mobility could thus bury their wealth as a hoard in time of danger and take refuge in safer places until the Viking raiders passed on. Indeed, we know that merchants of Tournai moved to Noyon,[137] and those of Dorestad to Xanten,[138] in just this fashion during pirate attacks, returning to rebuild their homes and start again. It seems possible that too much of our information on Viking plunderings comes from monkish chroniclers, who had a natural hatred for these freebooters because they were pagans and therefore tended to exaggerate the destructive side of their activity.

[133] P. Grierson, "The Gold Coinage of Louis the Pious and Its Imitations," *loc.cit.*, pp. 301-9. See also P. Boeles, *Friesland*, pp. 386-94.

[134] This curious but most significant fact has not been sufficiently noted by historians. On this lack of Frankish or English coins struck in the 9th century after 840, see H. Holst, "Mynter i Norske Funn," in *Nord. Numis. Arsskrift* (1948), pp. 56-112.

[135] The exception is the Hon hoard, whose gold coins were really used as ornaments, not money. But there are Samanid silver coins struck in the late 9th and early 10th centuries in coin hoards along Norwegian coasts. H. Holst, *op.cit.*, pp. 58-79.

[136] We know from the graves at Birka that cloth from the West (probably Frisian) as well as arms—that is to say, objects of Western *manufacture*—were in this period reaching Scandinavia. A. Geijer, *Birka*, III, 22-47. Literary evidence from a passage concerning the late 9th-century battle of Haffsfjord tells us of Flemish cloaks and Frankish arms in Norway, too. See *The Saga of Harold Fairhair*, in *Corpus Poet. Boreale* (1883). Despite Viking raids in this period, the balance of trade was probably still in favor of Western lands and against Scandinavia, especially Norway.

[137] P. Rolland, *Le Problème de la continuité à Tournai*, pp. 147-50.

[138] R. Doehaerd, *op.cit.*, pp. 23-24.

Nor was this curious mixture of raiding and trading on the part of Scandinavian Viking invaders confined to Western Europe. It was just as characteristic of the Varangians in the East. Oleg was capable of raiding Constantinople in 907 and of concluding a trade treaty with the Byzantines in the same year.[139] He could also lead an expedition against Moslem cities in the Caspian region at the same time that coin evidence and Ibn Fadlun's account show us that trade was being carried on between Rus and Moslem worlds.[140] Wealth was what the Varangians sought, and they seized it by violence or gained it by commerce indiscriminately. Probably that careful division between piracy and trade maintained by some historians and economists is more a matter of theory than of historical fact.

Perhaps we can understand the Viking attitude better if we examine the more recent past. If one looks at the Elizabethan Age, in which a Drake or a Hawkins could on the same voyage raid the Spanish plate fleets and sell negro slaves to Spanish plantations, one finds the Vikings more understandable. Or we might take a later example, the eighteenth-century English practice of mixed plundering and trading in India, in which Clive and Hastings distinguished themselves— not to mention our own American Salem privateers. To sum up, the Scandinavians in their advance east and west were not only colonizers, but merchant adventurers also. Sometimes the merchant was uppermost in their approach to outsiders, sometimes we see only the pirate adventurers. Generally there was in their makeup, as in that of most foreign expansionists, something of both.

In addition to all this, it must be remembered that, by 870 and 880, Viking advances east into Russia had reopened the trade routes to the Orient. As a result, Samanid silver, as our Baltic and Scandinavian coin hoards reveal, again flowed into the Baltic, accompanied by Oriental wares as well. Thus a special economic impetus was added once more to the trade of the Northern Seas, stimulating not only the commerce of Scandinavia itself but also that of the shores of England, Ireland, Frisia and Germany which were close enough to feel the effects of this traffic. Even before the tenth century, the East-West trade through the Baltic that had helped to stimulate Carolingian economic life was flowing again, and helping, no doubt, to neutralize the effects of Viking destructiveness.[141]

---

[139] *The Primary Chronicle*, ed. Cross, pp. 149-52.
[140] B. Dorn, "Caspia," *loc.cit.*, pp. 38-91. G. Vernadsky, *Kievan Russia*, pp. 22-30.
[141] For a map showing the locations in Northern Europe at which Samanid and

Such generalities as the foregoing, however, will not serve to do more than illuminate our problem. For only when we examine specific areas of Northern Europe during these seventy years of Viking activity can we come to any conclusion as to the economic results of the Viking assault upon Europe. Only then can we decide whether, economically speaking, the results were positive or negative.

Let us start with that portion of the Carolingian Empire north of the Loire and west of the Rhine, where the larger part of the mints were to be found during the reign of Louis the Pious and where the Empire's major industry, commerce and economic life centered. Up until 879, when the last great Viking attacks took place, or roughly until the death of Charles the Bald in 877, evidence seems clearly to show a continuation of economic activity throughout this region. This is perhaps most dramatically revealed by the development of new mints under Charles the Bald, though in part their appearance was the result of the weakness of the central government. During his reign many places minted silver deniers. We find in the Meuse region—Mouzon, Verdun, Dinant, Namur, Nivelles, Huy, Visé, Bastogne, Tongres, Maastricht and Aix-la-Chapelle; on the Scheldt—Cambrai, Valenciennes, Tournai, Courtrai, Condé and Ghent; along the Flanders coast and its hinterland—Bruges, St. Omer, Quentovic, Amiens, Attigny, Arras and Thérouanne; along the Seine and its tributaries—Rouen, Paris, Melun, Meaux, Compiègne, Evreux, Châlons-sur-Marne, Chartres, Troyes, Sens and Laon; in the Loire valley—Angers, Blois, Orléans, Le Mans, Tours, Nantes, Bourges and Nevers; in the upper Rhone-Saône region—Lyons, Vienne, Dijon, Autun, Besançon and Chalon-sur-Saône. To these forty-nine mints—many of them in operation, it would seem, for the first time during this period—should be added those in other parts of France. From the Rhone to the borders of Spain, we find money still coined at Nîmes, Arles, Uzès, Beziers, Toulouse and Narbonne. In the southwest we find mints at Limoges, Clermont, Agen and Dax, near the Spanish border. Such information, of course, covers Charles' entire reign from 840 to 877, roughly forty years.[142] In the later years, we learn from the Edict of Pîtres in 864 that there were ten places in which money was to be coined. They were Quentovic, Reims, Rouen, Paris, Sens

other Moslem coins have been found, see S. Bolin and J. Carlsson, *Historisk Atlas* (Malmö 1947), p. 10. This map, however, underestimates somewhat the number of such finds in the British Isles, especially in Ireland.

[142] M. Prou, *Catalogue des monnaies carolingiennes*, pp. LXXXIX-XCIV.

and Châlons-sur-Marne in the north, Orléans along the Loire, Châlon-sur-Saône on the upper Rhone, Melle in the southwest and Narbonne in the south.[143] There is no assurance that other mints were not functioning in 864 as a result of this Edict, however. These were merely the *official* mints.

To this evidence of economic life can be added much more from our sources, pertaining particularly to Northern France. In the Edict of Pîtres, previously mentioned, we find information that new markets were being opened in Charles' kingdom.[144] Two years later, in 866, to raise a Danegeld of 4,000 pounds to pay off the Vikings, a tax of one-tenth of their income was levied on the merchants of the realm, who were numerous and wealthy enough to assume this burden.[145] There is mention, between 861 and 879, of merchants of Verdun, on the Meuse, who were trading with Moslem Spain.[146] Near Visé, farther north, zinc mines continued in operation during this period, while the iron industry of this region, at least partly rural in character, continued.[147] Along the Scheldt, both the cloth industry and trade in general seem to have been active. A *portus* near the Abbey of St. Bavon at Ghent is mentioned between 850 and 875,[148] and we find another abbey, St. Wandrille at Thérouanne on the Scarpe, busy producing cloth.[149] So was the nearby monastery of St. Riquier.[150] Between 845 and 855, merchandise in large amounts was reported to be reaching Tournai by water.[151]

Farther south cargoes of lead were reaching Reims in 845,[152] St. Omer in 855,[153] and were imported to Quentovic (Etaples) by Lupus of Ferrières in 852 for his monastery at St. Josse.[154] Reims seems to have been particularly rich, judging from the evidence of a flourishing industry and outside commerce. The goldworkers of this city had such

[143] *MGH Leges*, II, 315.

[144] *Capitulary of Kiersy*, in *ibid.*, p. 302.

[145] *Annales Bertiniani*, in *Script. in usum scholarum*, p. 81, and *MGH Leges*, II, 361. See also F. Vercauteren, *Belgique Secunde*, pp. 453-58, and J. W. Thompson, *op.cit.*, pp. 885-87.

[146] J. W. Thompson, *loc.cit.*

[147] F. Rousseau, *La Meuse*, pp. 115-19.

[148] *Martyrologum Usnardi*, in *Acta Sanct. Boll.*, June, VI, 513.

[149] Einhard, *Trans. S. Marcellini*, in *MGH Script.*, XV, 261.

[150] Hariulf, *Chron. de St. Riquier*, ed. Lot, p. 308.

[151] Milon of St. Armand, *Vita S. Arnaudi*, in *MGH Poeta Latini aevi Carol.*, III, 589.

[152] H. Van Werweke, "Note sur le commerce du plomb," in *Mélanges Pirenne*, II, 653-54.

[153] *Ibid.*

[154] Lupus of Ferrières, *Epistolae*, in *MGH Epistolae*, VI, 23.

a reputation for skill that Lewis of Germany had them make precious objects from gold which he furnished them.[155] In 852 Hincmar mentioned that Reims contained both shops and merchants, while voyagers and pilgrims passed through the city in such numbers from England that towards the middle of the century a special hospice was built for them.[156]

Farther south along the Seine we hear, in 841, of 28 merchant ships[157] and of the importation of cloth from Flanders and the Boulogne region.[158] In 845 one source speaks of Paris as an important market,[159] while a Paris house of merchants there, perhaps *marchands d'eau*, are mentioned in 860, 861, 866 and 877, during the very period of intensive Viking activity on the Seine.[160]

On the Loire, in 869, mention is made of a fleet of merchant ships.[161] Nantes, despite raids in 853 and 868, still had importance[162] and a coin from this city is to be found in a hoard at Arras dating from as late as 880-896.[163] Poitiers is called a populous city in a contemporary source,[164] and evidence is clear that the nearby mines at Melle continued in production.[165] In 848 we find merchant shipping at the mouth of the Oust.[166] Still farther south, Bordeaux in 848 contained a large Jewish population and was strong enough to resist a Viking pirate attack successfully.[167]

There is no need to multiply such examples further. For it is clear that along the Meuse and the Scheldt, between the Scheldt and the Seine, in the Seine valley and along the Loire, there was a continuation of economic activity during the period of early Viking raids. Even in Southwestern France, for which our knowledge is less complete, it would seem that little slackening of economic life occurred during

---

[155] Flodoard, *Hist. rem. eccl.*, III, 20-21. F. Vercautern, *op.cit.*, pp. 77-80.

[156] Hincmar of Reims, *Opera*, ed. Migne, in *Patrologia Latina*, CXXV, col. 775. Flodoard, *Hist. rem. eccl.*, III, 10.

[157] Nithard, *Historia*, II, in *MGH Script.*, II, 658.

[158] R. Doehaerd, *op.cit.*, p. 17.

[159] *Miracula S. Germani*, ed. Mabillon, in *Acta Sanct. Saec.*, III, 106-9.

[160] J. W. Thompson, *op.cit.*, pp. 874-76. See H. Pirenne's objections in "À propos de la hanse parisienne des marchands d'eaux," in *Mélanges Charles Bemont* (Paris 1913), pp. 530-64.

[161] *Ex odonis miracula S. Mauri*, in *MGH Script.*, XV, 498.

[162] *Ibid.*

[163] E. Gariel, *op.cit.*, pp. 107-12.

[164] Falcon, *Vita Filiberti*, L.

[165] O. Davies, *Roman Mines in Europe*, pp. 85-86. A. Blanchet and A. Dieudonné, *Manuel de numismatique française*, IV, 334-36.

[166] A. de la Borderie, *Histoire de Bretagne*, II, 315-17.

[167] *Annales Bertiniani*, anno 848, in *Script. in usum scholarum*, p.36.

the early years of the reign of Charles the Bald. How else can one explain not only the growth of new mints in places like St. Omer or Bruges,[168] but the evidence of new markets and concern for weights and measures in the 864 Edict of Pîtres?[169]

After the great Viking attacks between 879 and 892 in the Flanders region, and during the presence of Viking bands on the Seine, Oise, and Loire up to 911, what evidence do we have of continued trade and commerce? Here, it is worth noting, our sources are scantier. But they show a certain economic continuity. In the Meuse region, according to Rousseau, the damage done by the Vikings was easily repaired and Maastricht, Dinant, Huy and Namur all coined money between 879 and 892.[170] Bruges seems to have completely escaped damage.[171] The destruction of Tournai has been exaggerated, since we find it referred to as a *portus* and trading place of some importance in 898. Noyon, to which some Tournai merchants fled during the Viking attacks, appears to have developed as a trade center during this period, and in 901 possessed a fair.[172] Quentovic, far from being destroyed, continued as a center of some importance and coined money up to the middle of the tenth century.[173] Archeological evidence from both Ghent and Antwerp seems now to show that at least their castles continued to be occupied throughout the period of the Viking invasion and immediately afterward,[174] while the failure to repair the damage done to the Abbeys of St. Pierre and St. Bavon may have been due more to the fact that their lands were seized by the Counts of Flanders than to any economic prostration attendant upon Viking raids.[175] In 885-886 Paris was described as a city whose population

---

[168] Blanchet and Dieudonné, *op.cit.*, pp. 183-370.

[169] *Edict of Pîtres*, in *MGH Leges*, II, 315.

[170] F. Rousseau, *La Meuse*, pp. 61-71.

[171] F. L. Ganshof, *Les Origines du Comté de Flandre*, pp. 17-18. Perhaps because its castle was built as early as 879, if not earlier. R. Doehaerd, *op.cit.*, pp. 24-25.

[172] P. Rolland, *Le Problème de la continuité à Tournai*, pp. 253-60, and *Les Origines de la commune de Tournai*, pp. 27-35. On the lack of a break in Arras' development, see R. Doehaerd, "Note sur l'histoire d'un ancien impôt, le tonlieu d'Arras," in *Bull. de l'Acad. d'Arras* (1943-46). On other towns of this region and their continuity during these years, see P. Rolland, *La Continuité à Tournai*, pp. 273-80.

[173] O. Fengler, "Quentovic, seine maritime Bedeutung," in *Hansische Geschichts-blätter*, XIII (1907), 183-91. See also E. Sabbe, "Les Relations économiques entre l'Angleterre et le continent," in *Le Moyen Age*, LVI (1950), 186-88.

[174] I am indebted to the kindness of Profs. Ganshof and Van Werweke for the opportunity to examine excavations at the castle of Ghent. These seem to show that here, as at Antwerp, there is an unbroken continuity of occupancy from Viking times in the late 9th century up through the 10th century.

[175] F. Ganshof, *op.cit.*, pp. 19-20.

was softened by Eastern luxuries, rich attire, silks and gems.[176] Rouen survived into the first years of the tenth century, when it was referred to as a commercial center of importance with which English merchants traded.[177] Particularly significant is the fact that churches at Reims, Soissons, Tournai and Liége were repaired during these years, and one was actually rebuilt in 881 in the midst of the invasions.[178] Since the lead used in such repairs had to be imported from England, this is a most interesting example of continued economic life.

There is less information in our sources concerning Western France. One bit, however, may be significant. It is a letter sent to the Abbey of St. Martin of Tours by Alphonse of Castile in 904, in answer to one from the abbey which requested that he buy jewels owned by this shrine and so enable it to raise funds to fortify the bourg of Tours. In this letter we find mention of Bordeaux as a *civitas* which possessed a fleet that sailed as far as St. James of Compostela in Galicia.[179] If authentic, this letter reveals that in 904 Tours was in communication with Bordeaux and that the latter was trading with Spanish coasts as far as Galicia. One particular reason for accepting its authenticity is the fact that we hear in 938 of cups and other objects from France in Galicia, perhaps the very ones mentioned in 904.[180] And in early tenth-century documents, one dating from 900 at Braga, and one from 905 in Galicia, we find mentioned French money, or *solidi gallicanes*, in use in this part of Spain.[181] Obviously commerce was not destroyed along western French coasts. A France completely ruined by the great Viking raids of 840-911 seems far removed from the facts.

It is coin hoards, however, which make most clear what happened

---

[176] Abbonis, *De bello Parisiaco*, II, verses 596-601. J. W. Thompson, *op.cit.*, p. 886.

[177] Dudo of St. Quentin, in *Hist. Normanni*, in *Soc. des Antiq. de Normandie*, XXIII (1883), 224.

[178] H. Van Werweke, *op.cit.*, pp. 662-65.

[179] *Bibliothèque Nationale; Mélanges Colbert*, XLVI, 97. On the authenticity of this letter, see B. d'Hijo, "Recherches sur l'histoire du royaume asturienne," in *Revue hist.*, LII (1949), 86-90, and M. Defourneau, *Les Francs en Espagne au XIe et XIIe siècles* (Paris 1940), pp. 63-65. On the whole, it seems wise to consider that it is either authentic or represents an authentic tradition.

[180] See C. Sanchez-Albornoz, *Estampas de la vida en León durante el Siglo X*, pp. 30-40, for products in use in this part of Spain.

[181] C. Sanchez-Albornoz, "Primitiva organizacìon monetaria de León y Castilla," in *Ann. de hist. de derecho español*, V (1928), 306-16, and *Estampas de la vida en León*, p. 38. These *solidi gallicanes*, according to the documents, were to be found only in Portugal and Galicia along the Atlantic coast, while the interior used Roman or Moslem silver coins. Hence it would seem that Portugal and Galicia were linked to the Atlantic world of Northern Europe, while the rest of Christian Spain was tied to the Moorish, Mediterranean economic world. This also marks this part of Spain as similar to France, where localism also was triumphant in the interior.

in this part of the Carolingian Empire during this period. In the last chapter, we noted that many coin finds, interred just prior to 840 in Frisia, reveal the existence of commerce between this region and western Gallic shores. Two hoards, later in date, show that the traffic continued down to about 880. One, from La Haye, dating from the 870's, contains coins from Dorestad, Mainz, Strasbourg and Reims, but also some from Rennes and Orléans.[182] More significant, though, is that of Zelzate, buried about 880. It contains an interesting Moslem silver dirhem minted in 866, and money from Lyons, Reims, Sens, Laon, Paris and Amiens, but it also has coins minted in Orléans, Rennes and Aquitaine.[183] Apparently, then, some maritime traffic from Frisia still reached Aquitaine as late as 879 or 880.

Farther south along the coast, two other coin finds give us equally interesting information. The first is the great coin hoard of Glizy, buried near Amiens about 880-882 and thus contemporaneous with that of Zelzate. This hoard has been carefully analyzed by Vercauteren. It contains many coins from the local region: 114 from Quentovic, 74 from Amiens, 27 from St. Quentin, 8 from Arras, 14 from Soissons, 2 from Beauvais, 4 from Attigny, 3 from Cambrai, 2 from Châlons-sur-Marne, 4 from Sens. It also contains deniers from Flanders and the Meuse region, including: 5 Bruges, 2 Ghent, one Tournai, one Thérouanne, one Condé, 3 Valenciennes and one Thion from the Scheldt; and 3 Maastricht, 3 Visé, 2 Gembloux, 2 Nivelles, one Dinant, and one Namur from the Meuse. From the Seine region, we find: 35 Rouen pieces, 31 St. Denis, 21 Paris, 9 Chartres, 4 Auxerre, 2 Autun and 3 Meaux. From the Loire valley: 2 coins from Angers, 7 from Le Mans, 4 from Orléans and 2 from Nantes. Thus this part of France in 880 was still in touch with the Scheldt and Meuse valleys of Belgium, the Seine and Marne and even the Loire.[184]

A nearby hoard at Arras, perhaps a decade later in date, gives us an idea of the trade of this region after the great Viking raids of 879-892 had ended. This find includes money minted by Charles the Bald,

[182] E. Gariel, op.cit., pp. 72-75.

[183] On the Zelzate hoard, see J. Dhondt and A. Van de Walle, "La Trouvaille de monnaies carolingiennes de Zelzate," in Handel der Maatshaft voor Geschiedenis en Oudheidkunde te Ghent, IV (1949), 1-21, and P. Naster, "Trouvaille de monnaies carolingiennes à Zelzate," in Revue belge de numis., LXII (1950), 203-24. Note that two gold solidi of Louis the Pious, minted in this region, have been found in La Vendée, thus confirming such contacts from the other end. P. Grierson, "The Solidi of Louis the Pious and Their Imitations," loc.cit., p. 302.

[184] F. Vercauteren, "L'Interpretation économique d'une trouvaille de monnaies carolingiennes," in Revue belge, XIII (1934), 750-62. E. Gariel, op.cit., pp. 95-106. Vercauteren overemphasizes the localism of this hoard.

Louis II, Louis III and Eudes. Its silver deniers from local mints in North Central France include 200 coins from Arras, 23 from St. Denis, 15 from Reims, 9 from Soissons, 8 from St. Quentin, 7 from Corbie, 13 from Courtessin, 5 from Amiens, 17 from Laon, 4 from Quentovic, 8 from Paris, 2 from Compiègne, 2 from Dijon, one from Autun and one from Auxerre. Belgian mints are but sparsely represented, but we find one coin each from Tournai, Valenciennes, Dinant and Visé. More numerous are those from the Loire valley, which include 8 coins from Le Mans, 10 from Orléans, 6 from Blois, 3 from Bourges, 3 from Clermont-Ferrand, one from Nantes and one from Rennes. Evidently there was little change in the trade of these shores as a result of the Viking invasions of 879-892.[185]

On the other hand, when finds dating from this period and located farther inland are examined, they show a different character. A Compiègne hoard, which appears to have been buried after the Glizy hoard but before that of Arras, contains 36 coins from Rouen, 29 from Quentovic, 34 from Reims, 19 from Paris, 10 from Laon, 6 from St. Quentin, 5 from Meaux, 5 from Compiègne, 4 from Chartres, 5 from Sens and 3 from St. Etienne—all from this area of France. Belgian centers are represented by only 3 coins: one from Ghent, one from Namur and one from Dinant. A single Nantes denier represents the Loire region.[186] A somewhat later small hoard at Blizy near Arques-sur-Aube which appears to date from 890 contains 10 coins from Rouen, 10 from Paris, 8 from Verdun, 2 from Reims, one from Sens, one from Metz and one from Marsalla. Equally local is the composition of the nearby hoard of Mourray from this period, while that of Etampes, interred in a region between Paris and Orléans, though it contains coins from 26 different mints, includes only those from the Seine and upper Loire valleys, except for a few pieces from Quentovic, Amiens and Le Mans.[187]

This increasing localism is also revealed in hoards of the Loire valley, dating from this period and slightly later. Of particular interest are the two Courbaton hoards, which were buried about 900 and therefore are approximately contemporaneous with that of Arras, previously described. They contain money minted by Charles the Bald, Louis II, Louis III, Charles the Fat and Eudes. In the greater Courbaton hoard, which contains over 12,000 silver deniers, coins

[185] E. Gariel, *op.cit.*, pp. 107-12.
[186] *Ibid.*, pp. 85-86.
[187] *Ibid.*, pp. 81-84.

292

minted by Charles the Bald come from a fairly wide area in Central France, including money from Angers, Orléans, Auxerre, Tours, Blois and Paris, and one coin from Valenciennes. Those minted by Louis II and Louis III come only from Tours and Blois. Those of Eudes, from Angers, Orléans, Blois, Châteaudun and Tours, with one from Paris. By Eudes' time this coin hoard reveals a completely local economy.

The second Courbaton find is even more striking. It contains coins minted by Charles the Bald from Angers, Auxerre, Arras, Bayeux, Blois, Cambrai, Chartres, Courtessin, Le Mans, Orléans, Rouen, Reims, Tours and Thérouanne. Those dating from the reigns of Louis II and Louis III come from Troyes, Blois, Tours and Marsalla. Those coined by Eudes are from mints located at Orléans, Angers, Blois and Tours only. Thus localism is shown to have been prevalent by 900 in the upper Loire region.[188]

Farther west one also can see in coin finds evidence of a creeping localism beginning even earlier than the last years of the ninth century. A hoard found at Angers, for instance, dating from the very last years of the reign of Louis the Pious contains the following coins: 20 from Melle, 2 from Tours, 2 from Bourges, one from Nantes, one from Rennes, 4 from Sens and one from Meaux.[189] A later coin hoard from Brioux near Melle, in Poitou, interred in 870, has only coins struck at Melle or in Aquitaine, except for a single silver one minted in Italy at Pavia.[190] Even more local is the hoard of Bonnevaux in Poitou, dating from the first years of the tenth century. It contains coins minted over a long period, including those of Charles the Bald, Carloman, Eudes and Charles the Simple. Those coined by Charles the Bald came from a wide area in France, from Toulouse, Sens, Le Mans, Bourges, Mouzon, Reims and Thérouanne. Those minted in Carloman's time are from Toulouse, Limoges and Melle. Those of Eudes' come only from Limoges and those dating from the reign of Charles the Simple only from Melle.[191]

These coin hoards, whether in Northern, Central or Western France, clearly supplement information from other sources. They show that up to 879, particularly along the Channel coasts and the lower Rhine, commerce continued active as far as Aquitaine, and

---

[188] *Ibid.*, pp. 86-95.   [189] *Ibid.*, pp. 68-69.

[190] *Ibid.*, pp. 75-81. In this hoard we find one coin of Louis II of Italy, minted at Pavia, the only Italian money found in any of these hoards. It may show some trade crossing the Alps into France as late as 850 or 860.

[191] *Ibid.*, pp. 124-27. This hoard also contains one coin of Carloman minted at Toulouse, and one of Louis the Fat minted at Arles.

until this date there is little evidence of economic decline. But increasingly after 880, the economy of Poitou, the Loire valley, the Seine and the interior of Picardy became essentially local in nature. This tendency may have appeared even earlier in Western Gaul than it did in the northeast, which, up to 900 at least, still maintained some external trade beyond the local region.

But even more surprising is another fact that these coin hoards seem to show: almost no commerce existed between either Northern or Western Gaul and the Mediterranean and Italy during the reign of Charles the Bald or later. For we find no mints south of Lyons or Poitou represented in the abundant coin hoards of the period, whether they be in Frisia, Picardy, the Seine region, the Loire or even Poitou.[192] The force, then, making for increasing localism seems to have come not from the Atlantic as much as from the Mediterranean. This breakdown of Mediterranean and Italian connections is in contrast to that shown in hoards dating from the reign of Louis the Pious. And it seems to absolve the Vikings from any important role in depressing French economy during these years. In fact, not a single mint along the French coast from Nantes to the Rhine ceased operating despite Viking assaults, while the region nearest the North Sea—and thus the trade with Scandinavia—remained the most active of all. By 900 France's economy was as local, viewed from the interior, as it had been in 700 and for the same reason—the lack of trade via the Rhone and the Midi with either Italy or the Mediterranean. Atlantic commerce, however, was more active and formed the only link between separate economic localisms in the various parts of France.

East of Carolingian France lay Germany, which had begun prior to 840 a slow but steady economic advance. The years that followed the death of Louis the Pious saw this progress continue. This is particularly noticeable along the Rhine, where trading centers like Utrecht and Dorestad as well as Cologne, Andernach, Bonn, Trier and Strasbourg appear to have continued to exist. Apparently Danish control of Frisia stimulated the commerce of this region. In 845, for instance, we find important merchants at Bonn.[193] New trading centers appear as well. Xanten was one, and Frisian traders in 863 sought

---

[192] With the three exceptions, slight in nature, mentioned in the above notes. Whether this economic localism helped to produce feudalism, which was its political counterpart, or the feudal anarchy of the period in France helped to produce the localism is a difficult problem that still remains to be solved.

[193] *Ex translatione SS Chrysaute et Dariae*, in *MGH Script.*, xv, 375.

refuge there from Viking attacks. So, too, was Birten, where we find Frisian merchants in 880.[194] Duisburg also achieved more important urban status during this period.[195] Dorestad, it is true, declined, and by 882 its place was taken by nearby Deventer. But it was not destroyed. Rather its *portus* filled with sand, though it continued to be a center of local trade up to the end of the tenth century.[196] Some of Dorestad's commerce may have shifted to nearby Thiel as well as to Deventer in the 880's.[197] Thus, continued commerce along the Rhine and the growth of new centers marked these years. Coin hoards like that at La Haye and Zelzate show that commerce reached Frisia from as far south as Strasbourg during this period.[198] Nor is there any evidence that this progress ceased after the expulsion of the Danes from Frisia, for money of Strasbourg minted during the reign of Louis the Child in the first years of the tenth century has been found in large amounts in coin finds in Northern Frisia, while copies made from these coins circulated freely throughout this area as well.[199]

The Rhinelands' continued economic development during these years, however, was clearly due to more than an impetus from trade which reached the North Sea and Frisia. It was also the result of continued connection with Italy, and particularly Venice, via passes of the Alps which remained open and active commercially right down to 911.[200] This Italian trade explains why Hathumode, Duchess of Saxony, and Gerhage, Abbess of Gandersheim, in the late ninth century possessed fine Oriental silk robes[201] and how a Bishop of Mainz, according to the Monk of St. Gall, could live surrounded by luxurious objects from the Orient. And it equally explains why a Bishop of Constance, writing to Lewis the German, made mention of Oriental prod-

---

[194] R. Doehaerd, *op.cit.*, pp. 23-24. On Frisians found at Mainz and the town's importance, see *Annales Fuldenses*, in *MGH Script.*, I, 363, 403, and Mon. S. Gall, *Gesta Karoli Magni*, in *MGH Script.*, II, 475. On the flight of Frisians to Xanten and Birten, see P. Kletler, *op.cit.*, p. 95.

[195] P. Kletler, *op.cit.*, p. 49, *Vita Anskari*, in *MGH Script.*, II, 709.

[196] J. H. Holwerda, *Dorestad*, p. 21. Dorestad's mints continued to coin money until about 850.

[197] Deventer is mentioned as a *portus* in 877 and 882. *Ex vita Lebuini*, in *MGH Script.*, II, 364, and *Annales Fuldenses*, in *MGH Script.*, I, 377. On Thiel, see H. Poelman, *op.cit.*, p. 118, and P. Boeles, *Friesland*, pp. 440-42.

[198] E. Gariel, *op.cit.*, pp. 72-75. P. Naster, *op.cit.*, pp. 203-24.

[199] At Pinjum and other places in Frisia, Strasbourg money coined during the reign of Louis the Child (901-911) has been found in coin hoards. P. Boeles, *Friesland*, pp. 443-48.

[200] On this commerce across the Alps, see J. Tyler, *The Alpine Passes* (Oxford 1930), pp. 147-48, and A. R. Lewis, *op.cit.*, pp. 178-80.

[201] On these and other such cases, see E. Sabbe, "L'Importation des tissus," *loc.cit.*, pp. 822-31.

ucts arriving over the Alpine passes.[202] In contrast to Southern France, Southern Germany, between 840 and 911, was in contact with both the world of the Mediterranean and that of the Northern Seas.

Though traffic along the Rhine remained the most important in Germany, some also flowed east from the Rhine across Saxony to the upper Weser and the Elbe. Along this route Paderborn, Gandersheim and Magdeburg, of some importance during the reign of Louis the Pious, became more so in the late ninth century.[203] Some commerce also existed along the upper Danube, perhaps stimulated by the existence of the Greater Moravian kingdom. In 887, for instance, we learn that Charles III exempted the merchants of Passau from customs duties,[204] and in 906 at Raffelstein we hear of Bohemian and Rugi (Russian) merchants arriving to trade.[205] It would seem that the important land route which Masudi and Ibn Jacub were to describe later in the century already existed in this period, linking the upper Danube to Prague, Cracow and Kiev.

Even more important was the sea route to Scandinavia via Frisian coasts. To this commerce Northern Frisia owed its continued growth all through the period of Viking raids. In this region we find, for instance, continued minting of gold *solidi* copied from those of Louis the Pious, possibly as late as 890.[206] Here, too, places like Dokkum, Leewarden and Stavoren were growing into urban centers during these years.[207] Moreover, silver dirhems are found in coin hoards of the time, revealing continuous trade contacts with Scandinavia. Farther north, Hamburg and Bremen also benefited from this traffic to the Baltic and the river trade of the Elbe and Weser. In 888 Bremen was called a *portus* and was given the right to coin money by Arnulf.[208] Hamburg down to 845 traded, we know, with Hedeby.[209] In that year it was destroyed by Danish raiders. But it seems to have soon regained its importance, and the Saxon merchants whom we find in Hedeby in 873 probably came from Hamburg,[210] as well as those

---

[202] Mon. S. Gall, *Gesta Karoli Magni*, in MGH Script., II, 337-38, and MGH *Formulae*, p. 415.

[203] P. Kletler, *op.cit.*, pp. 49-55.

[204] E. Patzelt, *Die Fränkisch Kultur und der Islam* (Baden 1932), p. 223.

[205] MGH *Capitularia*, II, 449-50.

[206] P. Grierson, *op.cit.*, pp. 301-8. P. Boeles, *Friesland*, pp. 423-25.

[207] *Ibid.*, pp. 421-38.

[208] Bremischer, *Urkedunbuch in auftage der Senats der frien Hanestad Bremen* (Bremen 1873), pp. 4-27.

[209] *Vita Anskari*, in MGH Script., II, 709.

[210] *Annales Fuldenses*, anno 873, in MGH Script., I, 385. W. Vogel, *Zur nord- und westeuropäischen Seeschiffahrt*, p. 160.

whom Ottar found slightly later in Skringissal in Norway. [211]

It is from Scandinavia, however, that we gain our chief information concerning trade with the Rhinelands via the shores of North Germany. Excavations at Hedeby, for instance, have shown that the important Badorf ware which was produced near Cologne and copied in Frisia and used to ship wine and grain to the north arrived in this part of Denmark without interruption throughout the years of the late ninth and early tenth centuries. Finds of Badorf ware, interestingly enough, overlap in Hedeby with Pingsdorf ware from the Rhinelands, which began to be produced only in the first years of the tenth century. Thus this pottery indicates continuous trade between the Rhine and the Baltic.[212] At Birka, in Sweden, excavations also reveal this pottery in unbroken chronological sequence.[213] To pottery one must also add export of Frisian cloth. This is mentioned in the early Norse account of the battle of Haffsfjord fought in 892 by Harold Fairhair.[214] But, again, archeology affords us our best evidence of its presence in Scandinavia. At Birka, in a series of graves dating from the late ninth and early tenth centuries, we find forty examples of these textiles in an unbroken series.[215] Fine weapons and glass were further products sent north from the Rhinelands. The Monk of St. Gall mentions the arrival of Vikings seeking fine swords at the court of Lewis the German.[216] Archeology reveals that such arms, particularly the Ulfberht swords, which were produced along the lower Rhine, were exported widely and reached Norway, Denmark, Poland, Ireland and the eastern coasts of the Baltic.[217] Glass has been found at Hedeby and Ribe in Denmark and at Birka and in the Uppland region of Sweden.[218]

In short, the earlier trade from the Rhinelands east to the Elbe and north to Norway and the Baltic not only continued during this period, but seems to have increased in volume. Though Germany was connected with Venice and the Mediterranean, it seems that it was

---

[211] *Alfred's Orosius,* ed. Sweet, p. 19.

[212] On this pottery found in continuous sequence in Frisian sites, see P. Boeles, *Friesland,* pp. 423-28. And in Hedeby, see H. Jankuhn, "Probleme des rheinischen Handels nach Skandinavien," in *Rheinische Viert.,* XV-XVI (1950-51), 115-23, 231-45, and *Die Ausgrabungen in Haithabu 1937-39,* pp. 176-83.

[213] H. Arbman, *Schweden und das Karolingische Reich,* pp. 40-63.

[214] *The Saga of Harold Fairhair,* in *Corpus Poet. Boreale.* A. Bugge, *Vikingerne,* II, 215-17.

[215] A. Geijer, *Birka,* III, 22-26.

[216] Mon. S. Gall, *Gesta Karoli Magni,* in *MGH Script.,* II, 347.

[217] These swords also appear in unbroken sequence in sites dating from the mid-9th to the mid-10th century in the Baltic and beyond. H. Jankuhn, "Ein Ulfberht Schwert aus der Elbe bei Hamburg," in *Festschrift Schwantes,* pp. 171-75.

[218] H. Arbman, *op.cit.,* pp. 36-86.

primarily this commerce to the north which accounted for the continuous growth of centers for the manufacture of pottery, glass, and arms near Cologne and the new ports along the Rhine and in Frisia, as well as for the activity of Hamburg and Bremen. Unlike France, except for ports on the Meuse and Scheldt, which may have shared in this northern commerce, Germany's economic life appears to have been stimulated during the period of Viking invasions and raids and to have developed towards the prosperity which she was to know in the days of the Ottos.

The best view, however, of the effects upon economic life of the Viking invasions is found in England and Ireland. Here there are no complicating factors, such as the existence or non-existence of trade with the Mediterranean in the case of Germany and France. England, all but conquered by the Danes in 878, and Ireland, heavily infested by them as early as 850, show whether this Viking penetration was a constructive or destructive economic force.

Up to 840 England seems to have escaped most of the first Viking raids which affected Ireland and Frisia. Under the leadership of Egbert of Wessex, like the Carolingian Empire, she made considerable progress from the low point she had reached by 750. In early ninth-century England, commerce increased with Carolingian ports from the Rhine to the Garonne. Her older trading centers, like London, Rochester, York, Canterbury and Hamwith, continued to exist, while new ones arose at Winchester and Tamworth. English cloth, like the produce of the country's tin, copper and lead mines, was sent to the Continent in exchange for the wine of the Garonne and Loire and the manufactured wares of the Rhinelands and Northern France. Though the Frisians were the main traders of this Carolingian era, Anglo-Saxon merchants were the next most important ones, probably still in advance of the rising class of Scandinavian traders and their older rivals, the Irish and the French of Aquitaine.

England, from 840 to 865, unlike France, remained relatively unaffected by Viking activities, except for occasional raids and the establishment of Danish bases on islands at the mouth of the Thames. During these years her trade with the ports across the Channel may have increased. English lead was shipped to Quentovic (Etaples) and other Continental ports.[219] Copper and tin reached the Carolingian

[219] H. Van Werweke, *op.cit.*, pp. 655-62.

Empire, too.[220] So many English pilgrims made their way to Rome that, as we have noted, Hincmar built them a special hostel at Reims.[221] Yorkshire was so closely connected with Frisia that, between 837 and 854, Archbishop Wigmund of York coined copies of the gold *solidi* of Louis the Pious.[222] Judith, daughter of Charles the Bald, married two Kings of Wessex in succession and was the stepmother of Alfred the Great.[223] Wessex's wealth, much of it in gold which probably came from Ireland, was the source of the gold vessels which King Aethelwulf sent as gifts to the Pope in 855.[224] Contacts with Rome and Italy were very close. English merchants were probably among the pilgrims whom we know went there in 862-863,[225] and members of the Mercian royal family, escaping the Danes, established residence in Italy.[226] The *mancus*, a coin found in England as a money of account in the late ninth century, appears to have been derived from the *mancus solidus*, an Italian Byzantine coin of light weight minted about 850 in Beneventum.[227] In fact, England in some ways seems less isolated from the Mediterranean in this period than does Carolingian France.

Then came the great Danish invasion of 865-878 which at its conclusion saw one half of Britain under the rule of the House of Wessex and the other half, including London, ruled by Danes of York and Gudrum of East Anglia. One might expect that the devastation attendant upon these years would have caused a break in England's economic growth. But such does not appear to have been the case. From 878 to 911, and even *during* the invasions themselves, there are continued signs of economic life. For instance, London, immediately upon its capture by the Danes, issued coins for Gudrum in the year 872.[228] When Alfred recovered it in 886, he immediately made

---

[220] Especially to the Meuse region, where it was needed to make brass and bronze-ware. F. Rousseau, *La Meuse*, pp. 115-19.

[221] Flodoard, *Hist. rem. eccl.*, III, 10, 79.

[222] P. Grierson, *op.cit.*, pp. 304-7. G. C. Brooke, *English Coins*, pp. 22-30.

[223] P. Grierson, "The Relations Between England and Flanders Before the Norman Conquest," in *Trans. of Royal Hist. Soc.*, 6th ser., XII (1941), 215-43.

[224] Anastasius Bibliothecarus, *Vita Rom. Pont.*, CVI, ed. Migne, col. 575.

[225] *Mirac. S. Vedasti*, in *Acta Sanct. Boll.*, Feb., I, 821, and *Mirac S. Bertini*, in *ibid.*, p. 597.

[226] T. D. Kendrick, *History of the Vikings*, p. 238. On the many other Anglo-Saxon contacts with Rome in this period, see P. Kletler, *op.cit.*, pp. 37-39.

[227] On the *mancus*, mention of which was made in a number of documents and charters in Anglo-Saxon England during these years, see P. Grierson, *Carolingian Europe and the Arabs, the Myths of the Mancus.*

[228] G. C. Brooke, *English Coins*, pp. 33-34.

it a borough,[229] and we know that in 889 he and Aethelred, the under-king of Mercia, gave Bishop Werfeld of Mercia a building there for the buying and selling of goods.[230] Alfred also established a mint in London, as he did at Gloucester and Oxford upon their reconquest.[231] Canterbury in 868, during the invasions, is referred to as a *portus,* and there is mention of a merchant in a royal grant to a thegn there.[232] From Canterbury, in this period, also comes our first mention of a guild in England, the so-called *cneuhts* guild located there.[233]

Alfred's treaty with Gudrum in 878 also seems to show that trade with the Danes was a usual practice among members of the Anglo-Saxon host, particularly trade in slaves, which had to be prohibited.[234] The provision in his Laws that groups of merchants proceeding inland should account to the folkmoot for members of their party is also an interesting commentary on commercial expansion inland beyond the sea ports, where it had previously been centered.[235] It seems highly probable, as a matter of fact, that the new *burgs,* or boroughs, which he and his Mercian sub-king built and which his son Edward continued to establish resulted in greater security for internal trade, as well as protecting Wessex and Mercia from Danish attacks. Thus we find money minted almost at once in new boroughs like Oxford and Gloucester,[236] and even an obscure one like Oxfurze, newly built in Mercia, exacted money payments for the upkeep of its fortifications.[237]

By the time of the reign of Edward the Elder in the first years of the tenth century, the economic growth of Central and Western England is striking. Edward struck coins at Oxford, Gloucester, Hereford, Shrewsbury, Chester, Hertford, Maldon, Stafford and Tamworth— all new or recreated centers for minting of coins in this part of England.[238] We see that he, more than his father, attempted to regulate trade by trying to draw all commerce to the official trading centers of

---

[229] R. Hodgkin, *History of the Anglo-Saxons,* II, 576-77.

[230] *Ibid.,* pp. 78-80.

[231] *Ibid.,* pp. 80-82. *Cartul. Saxonicum,* ed. Thorpe, p. 409.

[232] *Cartul. Saxonicum,* p. 519.

[233] R. Hodgkin, *op.cit.,* pp. 80-82. *Cartul. Saxonicum,* p. 409.

[234] *Treaty of Alfred and Gudrum,* v, in C. Attenborough, *The Earliest English Laws,* p. 101.

[235] *Laws of Alfred,* XXIV, in *ibid.,* p. 79. J. Tait, *The Medieval English Borough,* p. 19.

[236] R. Hodgkin, *op.cit.,* pp. 80-82.

[237] J. Tait, *op.cit.,* pp. 20-21.

[238] F. Stenton, *Anglo-Saxon England,* p. 332.

his realm, where a royal official, the port-reeve, already mentioned in Alfred's time, could supervise all transactions.[239] To this evidence of internal economic growth should be added the increased exploitation of silver and lead mines in Derbyshire, Flintshire and the Mendips and intensive working of the Cornish tin mines.[240]

Alfred also seems to have interested himself in affairs outside England. We have already mentioned his fleet, which no doubt gave security to English merchant shipping. But we also find him hiring Frisian sailors to man his vessels[241] and entering into a marriage alliance with his neighbor across the Strait of Dover, Baldwin II of Flanders.[242] His son, Edward, continued this diplomacy by marrying his daughter to Charles the Simple, King of France.[243] Overseas English trade and contact were not interrupted even by the Danish invasion itself, for we learn from Carolingian capitularies issued between 866 and 876 that a need was felt in France to curb the greed and desire for gain of English merchants.[244] Again, between 880 and 890, we learn of English pilgrims, probably including merchants, who were passing through the Meuse region on their way to Rome.[245] So numerous were such English travelers and so strong the ties in this period binding Britain to Rome that in 884 special privileges were given to the English *schola* in the Holy City, which probably included merchants as well as pilgrims and churchmen.[246] Already Anglo-Saxon merchants seem to have occupied that privileged position that they were to hold in Italy in the early tenth century, according to the *Honorantiae Civitatis Papiae*.[247]

Nor was Alfred content with these contacts with Italy, Frisia, Flanders and France. He showed an equally unusual interest in establishing commerce and contact with Scandinavia and the Baltic. It is from his additions to his translation of Orosius that we learn of the voyages of two merchants, Ottar, a Norwegian, and Wulfstan, an Englishman. Ottar's took him to the White Sea and then along the Norse coast to Skringissal and Hedeby. Wulfstan sailed from

---

[239] *Laws of Edward I*, in C. Attenborough, *The Earliest English Laws*, p. 115.

[240] L. Salzman, *Medieval English Industry*, pp. 40-51.

[241] *The Anglo-Saxon Chronicle*, ed. Plummer, I, 190.

[242] R. Hodgkin, *op.cit.*, p. 634.

[243] E. Stenton, *op.cit.*, pp. 339-40.

[244] *MGH Epistolae Karoli aevi*, IV, 190.

[245] R. Doehaerd, *L'Expansion économique belge*, pp. 24-25.

[246] R. Hodgkin, *History of the Anglo-Saxons*, II, 637. P. Kletler, *op.cit.*, pp. 40-41.

[247] On these privileges, see *Honorantiae Civitatis Papiae*, in *MGH Script.*, XXX, 2, and R. S. Lopez, "Les Relations anglo-byzantines," *loc.cit.*, pp. 152-53.

Hedeby to Truso in Samland at the mouth of the Vistula. Both men evidently voyaged to England since Alfred included their tales in his book. Thus, even during continual conflicts with the Danes of the Danelaw, we see evidence of a direct connection established between Alfred's England and the Baltic—interesting, because it is the first Baltic-English contact of which we have proof since the time of Sutton Hoo. And this contact was established by a merchant bearing the English name of Wulfstan![248]

Moreover, signs of economic development are not confined to Alfred's England. They are found in the Danelaw itself. The Danish population which settled in Yorkshire, East Anglia and the Five Boroughs between 871 and 879 was certainly joined in the next decades by a number of peaceful Danish colonists. This population no doubt more than balanced the losses in these regions during the invasion years of 865-878 and even later. The newcomers also seem to have stimulated economic and maritime development. Thetford, for instance, a production center for pottery in East Anglia since the eighth century, began large-scale manufacturing of glazed ware only after the Danish settlement in 869 in this part of Britain, while the first coins minted in this town date from the last years of the ninth century.[249] Similarly, in York, which had had only a local *styka* coinage of copper and the gold pieces of Archbishop Wigmund, we find a silver coinage appearing, struck by its Danish kings on the model of that of Wessex.[250] Norwegian sources also tell us of trade which reached England, either the Danelaw or Alfred's kingdom, during this period. For about the year 900, according to the *Egils Saga*, dried fish and furs were being sent to England from Western Norway in return for wheat, cloth and metals.[251] Thus trade with Norway, attested by Ottar's story in Alfred's *Orosius*, is confirmed by a Saga source, while the discovery on Norway's west coast of English bronzework dating from the late ninth century,[252] gives added weight to the *Egils Saga* information. Interestingly enough, the evi-

[248] On these voyages, see *Alfred's Orosius*, ed. Sweet, pp. 12-24.

[249] On the Danish settlements in England, see F. Stenton, "The Scandinavian Colonies in England and Normandy," in *Trans. of Royal Hist. Soc.*, 4th ser., XXVII (1945), 1-12, and *Anglo-Saxon England*, pp. 511-18. See also W. G. Collingwood, *Scandinavian Britain* (London 1908), and A. Mawrer and F. Stenton, *Introduction to the Survey of English Place Names* (Cambridge 1925), pp. 51-138. On Thetford in this period, see G. M. Knocker and R. G. Hughes, "Anglo-Saxon Thetford," *loc.cit.*, pp. 6-9.

[250] G. C. Brooke, *English Coins*, pp. 33-45.

[251] *Egils Saga*, XVII, ed. Jonsson, pp. 47-49. A. Bugge, *op.cit.*, pp. 230-31.

[252] H. Shetelig, *Scandinavian Archeology*, pp. 271-72.

dence from this source that English cloth was being exported abroad is a vital bit of information, since it shows that the Anglo-Saxon woolen trade, important in Offa's time and in the early ninth century, survived the struggle with the Danes.

To all this must be added information from Anglo-Saxon coin finds interred along England's south coast just before, during, and just after the Danish invasion. The first hoard which we will consider is one dating from 875, found at Trewhiddle in Cornwall near a tin mine. It consists of 114 coins. Of these 56 are Mercian, one minted in Offa's reign, but the majority are from the time of Burghed (839-874). Twenty are from Wessex, none dated earlier than 800 and most of them minted by Aethelwulf (837-857). Six coins are from Canterbury and one from York. Gold and silver ornaments of Saxon design were discovered with these coins, and the hoard also contains one coin minted by Louis the Pious.[253] This hoard seems to reflect trade between Cornwall and all of Western, Southern and Central Britain, as well as some Continental connections. Just north of Cornwall, in Wales, the tiny Penard hoard, dating from about 850, contains but three coins. One is a Wessex coin of Egbert. Of the others, however, one was minted by Charlemagne and one by Lothair—perhaps furnishing us precious information about the foreign connections enjoyed by this copper-producing region.[254]

Farther to the east, in South England, we find four more interesting coin hoards. The first is the Sevington hoard, buried about 871-872. It contains ten Mercian pennies minted between 796 and 870, five from Wessex and five from East Anglia.[255] To the southeast, a larger find of about the same date was discovered at Dorking. Included in it are 30 Mercian pennies, 22 East Anglian coins, 86 from Canterbury in Kent and 550 from Wessex, mainly from the period 837-866. There is also one denier minted by Pippin I of Aquitaine.[256] The nearby Gravesend find, dating from 874-875, is quite similar in composition, containing 400 Mercian coins, mainly those minted by Burghed (852-874), 57 East Anglian pennies, 61 from Wessex and one minted by Louis the Pious.[257] Finally, there is the Croydon hoard of 874-875. In it are 200 Mercian coins (many of Burghed), 112

[253] J. Rashleigh, "An Account of Anglo-Saxon Coins and Gold and Silver Ornaments found at Trewhiddle," in *Num. Chron.*, 3rd ser., VIII (1868), 137-49.
[254] J. Allen, in *Num. Chron.*, new ser., VIII (1948), 236.
[255] J. Rashleigh, in *Num. Chron.*, 3rd ser., VIII (1868), 150.
[256] *Ibid.*
[257] *Ibid.*, p. 151.

East Anglian (Aethelred and Edmund the Martyr) and 19 Wessex (Aethelred and Alfred). It also contains some Carolingian pennies, one of Louis the Pious and several minted by Charles the Bald, and one rare Byzantine coin from Syracuse in Sicily. Finally, it includes three Kufic Moslem dirhems.[258] These hoards all seem to testify to a wide internal English trade and some commerce with the Carolingian Empire and even with Italy. Furthermore, the Moslem dirhems seem to show Kentish commerce with the nearby Viking island bases of Thanet and Sheppey, for such dirhems must have arrived by way of the Baltic.

From the period immediately after the Danish invasions of England we have only two coin hoards, both found along the northwest coast, where invasions from Norse Ireland took place in the early tenth century. The first, discovered near Chester and dating from 901-910, contains 40 coins. They consist of Anglo-Saxon money minted by Edward the Elder and Danish coins from York, suggesting trade between Chester and both of these sections of England.[259]

Nearby has been discovered one of the largest and most controversial of all medieval coin finds, the famous Cuerdale hoard. Dating from sometime between 902 and 920, it contains over 7,000 silver coins. They deserve careful analysis. Like the nearby Chester hoard, this hoard has large numbers of Anglo-Saxon and Anglo-Danish silver pennies—over 400 from Mercia, Canterbury and Wessex mints, including many coins of Edward the Elder—and, in addition, 2,000 Danish-minted coins from York and East Anglia. Among these Danish coins are five of peculiar interest. They appear to have been struck by Viking sea-kings, and two of them from Quentovic were minted by Cnut, a Danish pirate raider and brother of the famous Siegfried.

Even more important is the fact that an immense number of foreign coins are to be found in this hoard, including 750 Carolingian deniers coined by Charles the Bald, Carloman, Charles the Fat, Eudes, Raoul and Louis the Child of Germany. Of these, 560 are from Melle. More exotic are some odd pieces: one coined by a Bishop of Arles, and more than a dozen from Italy, among them 11 Lambert, one Berengar and several struck by the Carolingian Louis II. And, finally, we find 31 Kufic Moslem dirhems.[260]

---

[258] *Ibid.*, pp. 151, 302.
[259] J. Peacock, in *Num. Chron.*, 3rd ser., II (1861-62), 305-10.
[260] On the Cuerdale hoard, see E. Gariel, *op.cit.*, pp. 70-78. J. Rashleigh, *op.cit.*, pp. 151-52.

Now it is possible that this hoard, or at least its nucleus, represents a Viking treasure, and that this accounts for the fact that coins from nearly every mint from the Garonne to the Rhinelands, as well as coins from Italy, are found in it. But it seems difficult to believe that the Anglo-Saxon, Anglo-Danish or Moslem dirhem pieces could have been accumulated by piracy. In fact, the coins represented in this hoard give a perfect picture of trade which we know, from other sources, reached England during these years—from Italy, from France, from the Rhinelands—and of an important internal trade as well. Even the large number of Moslem dirhems, which must have arrived from the Baltic, reflects commerce, too. If it be true, then, that the Cuerdale hoard is of trade rather than pirate origin, it suggests the extent of England's commerce by the end of the period under discussion.

One Irish hoard of slightly earlier vintage, found at Delganey and dating from 835, is of interest to us in connection with the Cuerdale and Chester finds. This hoard, like that of Cuerdale, contains some French coins. It has 86 Anglo-Saxon pieces from Mercia, Canterbury and East Anglia, the same districts represented in the Cuerdale find. But, in addition, it contains a rare Italian coin, minted by Pope Leo III.[261] Perhaps it is a pilgrim hoard. But the distribution of its coins is the same as that of our two English hoards, later in date, on the other side of the Irish Sea. These parts of Ireland and of Britain apparently continued an economic life relatively unchanged by the Danish invasions.

In sum, England during this period presents a surprising picture of continuous economic development from the Carolingian era right up to 911. English commerce, as revealed in sources and coin hoards, extended all the way to the Mediterranean. It seems clear that the Danish invasion and settlement in the Danelaw did not hinder this growth, but instead stimulated it, so that by 911 England had recovered from the devastation of the invasion years and made additional progress. She was, in the early tenth century, well on the way towards becoming a great maritime trading region linked with France, Germany, Italy, Ireland and Scandinavia. She seems to have recaptured that eminence in trade that she had enjoyed in the Northern Seas in Late Merovingian times, but which she had lost to the Frisians and the Carolingian Empire in the late eighth century. She was well advanced towards the position which she was to assume under Aethelstan and his immediate successors.

[261] J. Evans, in *Num. Chron.*, 3rd ser., XXXI (1882), 61-70.

Across the Irish Sea, Ireland in this period possessed many of the economic characteristics of Britain, though our sources are much too meager to allow us to speak as definitively about Irish developments. Both the Viking control of Irish coasts and the relaxation of this control in the first years of the tenth century had definite effects upon Ireland's economy and maritime development. The first was the establishment of at least one urban trading center, the Norse capital of Dublin.[262] The second was a continuation and expansion of Ireland's commerce with England, France and Scandinavia. About 900, for instance, we learn of wine in Ireland which must have been imported from France.[263]

We have evidence from the *Egils Saga* that trade with Norway was active.[264] To this information from our texts should be added archeological evidence of activity of a commercial sort along the Hebrides-Orkney-Shetland route leading to Scandinavia. Excavations at Høbn in the Orkneys reveal a Viking port which was active in the late ninth century,[265] while farther south, on the island of Eigg off the Scottish coast, graves contain fragments of textiles similar to those Agnes Beier has found in such abundance at Birka, including what is probably Frisian cloth.[266] Traffic with both England and France is, of course, revealed in the somewhat earlier Delganey hoard. No doubt, it continued active after 840 as well, which may account for the settlement of Norse and Celts from Ireland on England's west coast during these years, and for the close political connections maintained between Dublin and the Danish kingdom of York.[267]

Equally interesting is evidence of Irish maritime power in this period. This was not all in Viking hands, though raids on England

[262] J. Ryan, "Pre-Norman Dublin," in *Jour. of Royal Soc. of Antiq. of Ireland,* LI (1949), 64-66.

[263] On evidence of trade between Dublin and France which brought wine to Ireland, see *Hail Bridget,* ed. Meyer (Halle 1905), p. 15.

[264] *Egils Saga,* XVII. A. Bugge, *op.cit.,* pp. 274-75.

[265] Accounts of recent excavations at Høbn, seen by the author only in popular form, show an important Viking settlement there which was destroyed in the late 9th century, probably by Harold Fairhair, if we accept Saga tradition. A. W. Brøgger, *Ancient Emigrants,* pp. 147-49. For earlier Høbn finds, see H. Shetelig, "The Viking Graves in Britain and Ireland," in *Acta Archeologia,* v (1945), 5-6.

[266] The graves at Eigg contain not only woolen textiles similar to those found at Birka, but even linen similar to that found in Swedish graves of this period. A. Geijer, *Birka,* III, 14-17. G. C. Crowfoot, "Textiles from a Viking Grave at Kildonom," in *Proc. of Royal Soc. of Antiq. of Scotland,* LXXXIII (1948-49), 24-28.

[267] A. Eckwall, *Introduction to the Study of Place Names,* pp. 30-36. Jean Young, "A Note on the Norse Occupation of Ireland," in *History,* XXV (1950), 28-30. On the Dublin ruler's interest in the kingdom of York, see H. Shetelig, *Viking History of Western Europe,* pp. 62-70.

from Irish Norse-held shores certainly provide an indication of such maritime power in the early years of the tenth century. We do have mention in 891, however, in the *Anglo-Saxon Chronicle*, of certain Irish monks who reached Cornwall in a coracle.[268] And a few years later native Irish pirates from Ulster were raiding British coasts.[269] In general, then, the Vikings seem to have stimulated, rather than destroyed, Irish economic and maritime development.

There is also the very interesting matter of the presence of gold in Ireland. In this respect, Ireland in this period was all but unique in Western Europe, where gold was rarely found, except in England and Frisia. An Irish poem dating from about 900, *The Adventure of Laeghaire Mac Crimithain*, gives us significant information about Ireland's wealth in this metal. The poem mentions a shield with rims of gold, a gold-hilted sword, gold chessmen, the gold and silver of Connaught and a payment made in silver and gold.[270] Now, gold is rare in England in its natural state. Yet in the ninth century we find it there. Archbishop Wigmund of York coined golden *solidi*. Aethelwulf of Mercia sent gold vessels to the Pope.[271] Edward the Elder coined gold pennies.[272] Is it not possible, then, that English gold came from Ireland?

The source of such gold in Ireland is, however, uncertain, though the poem mentioned above suggests that it came from Connaught in the west—perhaps alluvial in nature. But there may have been still another source; barrow-robbing. Modern excavations of Irish graves have revealed much prehistoric gold in the form of ornaments. The Norse and native Irish of this period seem to have discovered this, too, for in 863 we find mention of the fact that Lorcan, King of Meath, with the *Gall*, or Norse, was breaking open the mounds of New Grange, Dowth and Knauth.[273] Perhaps Irish gold, in part, came from such a source.

To the northeast of England and Ireland, across the North Sea,

[268] R. Hodgkin, *op.cit.*, II, 641.

[269] *Cron. Scotorum, anno* 906, ed. Hennesey, p. 181. *The Annals of Four Masters, anno* 905-909, ed. O'Donovan, II, 575-81. See also *Three Fragments of Annals*, ed. Curry, p. 233.

[270] "The Adventure of Laeghaire Mac Crimithain," trans. K. Jackson, in *Speculum*, XVII (1942), 381-87.

[271] G. C. Brooke, *English Coins*, p. 12. Anastasius Bibliothecarus, *Vita Rom. Pont.*, CVI, ed. Migne, col. 575.

[272] D. F. Allen and G. C. Blunt, in *British Num. Journal*, XXV (1945-48), 15-41, 83-126.

[273] *Three Fragments of Annals*, p. 152. *Annals of Ulster, anno* 862, ed. Hennesey (Dublin 1897), II, 373.

lay Scandinavia and the Baltic, from which the hardy Viking mariners of this period originated. How did this region's economy fare as a result of the Scandinavian expansion east and west? From sources we gain very little light on this question. The accounts of Ottar and Wulfstan, contained in *Alfred's Orosius*, do tell us something. Ottar lived in Halagoland on Norway's west coast, from which, according to Saga evidence, commerce was already maintained with Ireland and England. Ottar mentions a trading expedition to seek walrus tusks and other Arctic products in the White Sea and along the northern coast of Norway. With a cargo gained there, and furs and reindeer skins received as tribute, or *finns kaup*, from the Lapps, he sailed south along the coast to Skringissal, a trading place on the Oslo fjord where Saxon and Frisian traders brought goods. He continued on to Hedeby in the Baltic.[274] Wulfstan tells us of a voyage from Hedeby along the south shores of the Baltic to Truso and Elbing in Samland, where he traded his merchandise to friendly natives for horses.[275] Somewhat earlier, we learn from Rimbert and Anskar of trade routes reaching Ribe, Hedeby and Birka, already places of some commercial importance. The *Vita Anskari* also mentions the Courland towns of Seeburg and Apolloné.[276] Thus our sources speak of trade routes and centers at Skringissal, Ribe, Hedeby, Birka, Truso, Elbing, Apolloné and Seeburg during these years. Hedeby and Birka were both large enough to have an urban official, a *comes* or *prefectus*, in charge of their trade as the monarch's official representative.[277]

From archeology and numismatics we learn much more. Archeology shows us that Skringissal was not yet an actual town, since no remains of it have been found, but rather a fair, or pre-urban trading place where merchants came at certain periods of the year.[278] On the other hand, it reveals the presence, unmentioned in our sources, of a number of settlements or towns located in Courland near the mouth of the river Dvina and the land of the Semigallens—all probably under Swedish influence at this time.[279] It further reveals that Ribe, to some extent,

---

[274] *Alfred's Orosius*, ed. Sweet, pp. 16-19.

[275] *Ibid.*, pp. 19-21.

[276] *Vita Anskari*, xxx, in *MGH Script.*, II, 713.

[277] On these trade officials and the Scandinavian rulers' interest in trade, see *Vita Anskari*, xxxi, in *ibid.*, p. 714, and H. Jankuhn, *Ergebnisse und Probleme der Haithabugrabungen*, pp. 55-56.

[278] H. Shetelig, *Scandinavian Archeology*, p. 275.

[279] In addition to the urban centers of Seeburg (Grobina) and Apolloné, the Cours appear to have had another at Kuldiga. A fourth was the Semigallen center

and Birka and Hedeby, in particular, were important trading centers. Excavations at Hedeby have uncovered remains of glass, pottery, jewelry, metalware and arms which came from the Rhinelands, and thus prove it to have been in this period an important middleman in commerce between the Baltic and European coasts to the south.[280] Similarly, in graves at Birka of the late ninth and early tenth centuries are to be found, as we have noted, Rhineland pottery, glass, metalware and fragments of what must have been the famous *pallia fresonica*. Trade here attested to earlier by Anskar apparently continued without interruption. In Birka, too, graves reveal evidence of Oriental textiles from the late years of this Viking period.[281]

Coin hoards, however, found in Finland, on the Swedish mainland, in Gotland, Denmark and Norway are more conclusive as evidence of connection with the East. Judging from these hoards, prior to 911 contact between the Baltic and Byzantine areas was limited, since almost no Byzantine coins have been discovered dating from these years. The exceptions, found in the Hon hoard in Norway, are gold Byzantine *solidi* that probably arrived there from the West, *not* the East.[282] But starting about 880, judging from dates of coin minting, silver dirhems again began to reach the Baltic. Gotland hoards show this clearly. In the great Stora Velinge hoard there, which has been carefully analyzed, the peak period of Moslem dirhem importation seems to have been in the last years of the ninth and the first years of the tenth century. Such coins are interesting for still another reason. They show that little trade existed with Western Persia or

---

of Daugmalé (Portus Semigallorum) near Riga at the entrance to the Dvina. In addition, the Lettgalliens had two interior settlements, Trekala and Jeriska. There were altogether, then, six centers of urban size in this part of the Baltic. B. Nerman, *Sveriges Första Storhetsid*, pp. 3-135, and "Swedish Colonies in the Baltic," *loc.cit.*, pp. 17-21. See especially F. Balodis, *Det Aldsta Lettland*, pp. 146-265. Swedish influence here, judging from archeology, lasted only until about 900 A.D.

[280] H. Jankuhn, *op.cit.*, pp. 91-115, is still the best account of Hedeby's importance in this period.

[281] On Birka, see H. Arbman, *Schweden und das Karolingische Reich*, and *Birka*, which sum up the available archeological evidence.

[282] H. Holst, "Hon Funnet," in *Norges Inskrifter Med. de Yngoe Runny* (Oslo 1952), pp. 132-39, and especially his *On the Coins of the Hon Find* (Oslo 1931), pp. 7-18. See also S. Grieg, "Vikingtidens Skattefund," in *Univ. Oldskamps. Skrifter*, II (1929), 182-98, on the other objects besides coins found in the Hon hoard. On the lack of Byzantine coins dating from this period in Swedish hoards, the evidence is summed up in N. L. Rasmusson, *Foreign Coins in Swedish Coin Finds* (London 1938). On Finland, C. A. Nordman, "Schatzfunde und Handelsverbindungen in Finlands Wikingerzeit," in *Acta Archeologia*, XIII (1942), 273-92. On Denmark, see R. Shovmand, *De Danske Skattefund*, pp. 15-141. On Norway, H. Holst, "Mynter i Norske Funn," *loc.cit.*, pp. 56-112.

Iraq, where Rus or Varangian trade seems to have centered prior to 840. They show contact instead via the Volga with Samanid centers in Eastern Persia and Turkestan.[283] A similar story of revived trade with Samanid domains is revealed by coin finds in Sweden and Denmark.[284] Even more interesting are the sparser coin hoards, containing Samanid silver of this period, along the coasts of Norway. Such hoards, at Grimstead, Grimsby, Holte and Traen, show a commerce from the Eastern Baltic which traveled out into the Atlantic all the way up the Norwegian coast.[285] Ottar's voyage from Halagoland to Hedeby is thus graphically illustrated by successive finds containing Samanid silver. And the presence of dirhems in places like Western Britain, in the Cuerdale hoard, on the Thames in the Croydon hoard, and in Frisia in the Zelzate hoard and others, seems to indicate trade routes continuing south as far as Frisia and England during these years.

This brings up several interesting problems. The first concerns the nature of Scandinavia's trade during these years with both the East and Western Europe. We know that immense sums were paid Viking raiders in Danegelds. Yet, except for some gold Frisian *solidi*, hardly a single Anglo-Saxon or Carolingian coin minted after 840 has been found in Scandinavian coin hoards dating from these years. Those found on Norway's coast were minted prior to 840. Yet Samanid silver is plentiful all through the Baltic and in Norway, and found even in Frisia and England. We know, however, that many products from Western European trade centers reached this northern region. What can this mean? It would seem to show that the balance of trade between Scandinavia and Western Europe was entirely in the latter's favor during this Viking period, and that it took all the available Danegelds, plunderings and even extra dirhems that the Scandinavians possessed to pay for Western products which reached the north. On the other hand, it seems that trade to Samanid Asia, if not Byzantium, was in favor of the Varangians, hence the presence of this silver in such large amounts in Baltic and other hoards.

[283] U. S. Linder-Welin, "Ein grosser Fund Arabischer Münzen aus Stora Velinge," in *Nord. Numis. Arsskrift* (1942), p. 80.

[284] N. L. Rasmusson, *op.cit.*, pp. 130-40. R. Shovmand, *op.cit.*, pp. 11-14.

[285] H. Holst, *op.cit.*, pp. 8-12, sums up the evidence of these hoards. Especially interesting is the early Grimstead hoard, buried about 955. It has 2 coins struck by Harun al-Raschid, one by Mamun, one by Mutawakkil, and one by Mutamid. There is then a break, followed by 48 Samanid dirhems minted between 892 and 921. The nearby Teisen hoard contains 6 Abbassid dirhems and then, after a break, 10 Samanid coins minted between 899 and 931.

The second problem concerns the island of Gotland, whose economic status seems extremely peculiar from a number of points of view. Archeology shows that no communities or trading towns existed during these years on Gotland. Excavations also show no trace of Western wares here, so abundant at nearby Birka, and no trace of Western European coins either.[286] What archeology does reveal is an immense amount of Samanid silver coins in many hoards dating from this era. Furthermore, Anskar, who made two trips to Birka, does not even mention Gotland's existence. How can we account for these facts?

One possibility is that Gotland was not a trading community but a fair which was visited by merchants from the Eastern Baltic only. Thus the lack of towns and the absence of Western European coins and wares would be explained. Since in the period from 840 to 870 coin hoards here reveal little trade with Russia and the East, Anskar's silence concerning it during his second trip, if not his first, would be explainable also. But even granting the plausibility of such an explanation, much remains to be understood about Gotland, particularly why Arab silver coins are found mainly in the north, center and west of the island, in locations different from those where in later centuries we find so many English and German coins.

Our third problem is the status, during these years, of the Baltic coasts from Courland all the way to Hedeby. Our information concerning them is extremely limited up to 900. We know of Wulfstan's voyage to Truso.[287] We know of Danish and Swedish attacks on Apolloné and Seeburg.[288] It seems probable that these coasts were, by 900, under the control of Olaf of Sweden. But that is all our sources tell us. From archeology, other than the existence of certain cities in Courland, we only know that some Frankish swords of the Ulfberht type and some Swedish metalware and jewelry reached these coasts.[289] But we hear nothing of the Slavic inhabited shores from the Vistula to Denmark. Wulfstan does not even mention Wollin, later so important,

[286] M. Stenberger, *Die Schatzfunde Gotlands der Wikingerzeit*, II, contains full information on Gotland's coin hoards and other finds dating from these years. See also H. Jankuhn's summary of archeological evidence for Gotland and the entire Baltic from a trade standpoint, in "Sechs Karten zum Handel des 10. Jahrhunderts in Westlichen Ostseebecken," in *Archeologia Geographica*, I (1950), 8-16. He concludes (*op.cit.*, p. 15) that Gotland's role in *Western* trade, in contrast with that of Hedeby and Birka, remained slight until *late* in the 10th century.

[287] *Alfred's Orosius*, ed. Sweet, pp. 19-21.

[288] *Vita Anskari*, xxx, in *MGH Script.*, II, 713.

[289] H. Jankuhn, *op.cit.*, pp. 8-16. B. Nerman, "Swedish Colonies in the Baltic," *loc.cit.*, pp. 17-18, and *Sveriges Första Storhetstid*, pp. 35-142.

and only a little Bavarian pottery in Birka suggests trade via these lands to the north.[290] The rise to economic importance of South Baltic regions which attended the appearance of Miezko's Poland evidently was still in the future, and by 911 this area was still relatively untouched by economic growth and change.

Still farther to the east lay the Varangian Kievan state of Russia, which was formed by Rurik and Oleg in the late years of this period. Concerning its economic status, however, we know very little. Archeology has not revealed sufficient evidence. Byzantine and Moslem historians and annalists like Constantine Porphyrogenitus and Ibn Fadlan tell us much more about the tenth century than the ninth. What we learn, largely from *The Primary Chronicle*, is mainly the broad political outlines of the formation of a Kievan state which united the northern *grody* about Novgorod with the southern ones about Kiev and the upper Don and Dnieper valleys. This was not completed until about 880, and perhaps its consolidation awaited Oleg's reign in Kiev about 900.

Behind this consolidation, however, we can dimly see the development of a Kievan commercial policy and economic interest. The Varangian rulers of this city seem to have been particularly active in opening up trade routes from their kingdom to Byzantium, the Moslem East and possibly Germany. The expedition of Askold and Dir to Byzantium in 860 may have been such an effort. If so, it was unsuccessful, probably because the Magyars, settled on the steppes of the Ukraine, made the Dnieper route south impossible. When in 899 these nomads were expelled from this region, or at least moved west to Hungary, we find Oleg leading another great expedition south, according to *The Primary Chronicle*, reaching Constantinople in 907. In this year, and in 911, trade treaties were negotiated at last with Byzantium, and commerce between Russia and Constantinople, as well as with Cherson on the Crimea, began.[291] The lack of Byzantine coins in the Baltic prior to 911, then, was apparently due to the fact that little trade reached Russia up to this time from the Byzantine Empire. After 911, Byzantine commerce and industry were to be decisive elements in the development of Russian civilization.

---

[290] On certain pottery which reached Sweden and *especially* Gotland from Pomerania in the late 9th and early 10th centuries, see H. Arbman, *Schweden und das Karolingische Reich*, pp. 110-14. Careful analysis of hoards of Pomeranian silver dirhems might tell us more, however. On the abundance of such hoards, see map in Bolin and Carlsson, *Historisk Atlas*, p. 10.

[291] *The Primary Chronicle*, pp. 149-52.

In addition to opening trade routes to the Black Sea, we find Oleg doing the same towards the west, taking over White Croatian territory north of the Carpathians after the collapse of Greater Moravia about 900. Then we suddenly find Russian and Bohemian merchants in 906 reaching Raffelstein on the upper Danube.[292]

The situation as regards trade with the Moslem East seems more complex. As soon as the Varangians were re-established in North Russian *grody* in Rurik's time, the Volga route was reopened to reach Samanid Turkistan via White Bulgars and Kazars. This route and trade, as we know from Ibn Fadlan, a little later provided the Russian Varangian merchants with silver dirhcms[293] and the silks from China and Turkistan that are found in late ninth-century Birka graves.[294] From Baltic coin evidence, it would seem that this route was in full operation again by about 880.[295] But such trade with Samanid Turkistan aided Kiev little. It by-passed the Dnieper to travel up the Volga route to Novgorod instead. Thus we see Oleg attempting to reopen trade with Western Persia and Iraq via the Caspian as early as 880. This attempt was unsuccessful, as coin evidence in the Baltic shows. Therefore, immediately after his success in opening trade with Byzantium, Oleg led a large expedition to the Caspian, and in 910 attacked Moslem cities in the Caucasus and along Caspian shores.[296] We know this expedition ended in disaster and coin evidence shows that trade with this part of the Moslem East was not reopened, though that with Turkistan proved very lucrative. By 911, then, Russia had established new trade routes from Kiev with Constantinople and Germany, and via the Volga had reached Samanid Asia. Only the older trade to Western Persia and Iraq via the Caspian remained dormant. And Russian commerce, reopened or established for the first time in the early tenth century, made possible the great growth of the Kievan state and its economy of which we have evidence after 911.

Our final question concerns the ships used in Northern Europe by

[292] *MGH Capitularia*, II, 249-50.

[293] B. Dorn, "Caspia," *loc.cit.*, pp. 38-121, sums up the evidence from Arab sources on Varangian activities in this region. See also D. M. Dunlop, *op.cit.*, pp. 100-81.

[294] A. Geijer, *Birka*, III, 26-47. On the sources of these silks, the fundamental work is still E. Pariset, *Histoire de la soie* (Paris 1865), II, 169-86. Pariset points out the importance of Isphahan and Samarkand and Ré in Persia and Turkistan as sources and distributing points. Coin evidence in Baltic hoards, incidentally, bears him out.

[295] B. Dorn, "Caspia," *loc.cit.*, pp. 89-117.

[296] G. Vernadsky, *Kievan Russia*, pp. 25-33.

Scandinavians and others during this period. The major ship-types remained those we have already discussed in our chapter on the Carolingian era. The swift Viking craft of the Gokstad ship-type were used by Scandinavians from Ireland to the coasts of Spain, along the shores of France, England, Germany and in the Baltic. Of shallow draft and carrying many oars, these boats could be taken far up the rivers of Western Europe, while their sturdy frame, seaworthiness, and sails made them ideal for use in the open sea as well. Possession of such warships was, no doubt, the principal reason for Viking pirate successes.[297] But we also find in this period the sturdy merchant ship, or *knorr*, which was used, for instance, to take Ottar on his voyages along the Norwegian coast, or for carrying colonists to Iceland and which, with modifications, was no doubt found in the Baltic as well.[298]

The other principal ship-type was Frisian, which Alfred carefully distinguished from that used by the Scandinavians. We have little information concerning these vessels except that we find them upon the Dorestad coinage of the ninth century. They seem generally to resemble the *knorrs* and to be ancestors of the later North Sea *kogges*.[299] Either the *knorr* or the *kogge* was probably the type of ship used in this period by English merchant seamen like Wulfstan. In Ireland, on the other hand, it seems probable that, in addition to the coracles mentioned in 891,[300] Viking ships, warships and *knorrs* were in use, even by independent Irish seamen of Ulster, in the early tenth century.

The coasts of France, like those of England and Ireland, were under strong Viking influence during these decades. And it is interesting to note that French marine terminology has since borne strong evidence of this fact, employing a number of words which are of Scandinavian origin. But it seems probable that older maritime traditions were not completely displaced. In the late ninth century we still hear of *barcae* built along the French Atlantic coasts,[301] and it seems probable that

---

[297] See Chapter IV and Brøgger and Shetelig, *The Viking Ships*, pp. 81-151.

[298] *Ibid.*, pp. 233-35.

[299] *Ibid.*, pp. 236-37.

[300] R. Hodgkin, *History of the Anglo-Saxons*, II, 641.

[301] There were levies of ships for coastal defense still raised on France's west coast as late as 865, according to W. Vogel, *Die Normannen und das Fränkische Reich*, p. 210, and *barcae* continued to be built along French shores. On this problem, which needs more attention, see W. Vogel, "Gab es vor dem 9. Jahrhundert kleine Schiffahrt an der Atlantische Koste Frankreichs," in *Hansische Geschichtsblätter*, XLII (1937), 185-88.

the Bordeaux fleet, navigating as far as Galicia in 904, was composed of *scaphae* and *barcae*, as of old.[302]

Though Scandinavian ship influences were predominant in the Northern Seas in this period, followed in order by Frisian *kogges*, Anglo-Saxon ships, French *barcae* and a few Irish coracles, the great revolution in ships took place in England. This was the building by Alfred the Great of a new, huge type of warship, which, our sources tell us, was not like either Frisian or Viking ships. Carrying 60 oars, these ships at first did not prove very seaworthy. Perhaps their inspiration came from the *dromons* of the Mediterranean. But they represented a trend towards larger warships which was to culminate in the great dragon ships, or *drekkars*, of Canute and Olaf Tryggvasson of the early eleventh century.[303]

Farther to the east, in the South Baltic and in Russia, we have additional ship information. We cannot say much about the ships used by Slavs and Chud along non-Scandinavian Baltic shores during this period. Such naval power as they possessed may have been modeled on that of Scandinavia. More probably they used small ships, *skutas* and *karfis*.[304] But concerning Russia our information proves fuller. It is clear that the Varangians made no use of ship-types found farther west. Nor did they develop significant naval strength in the Black Sea. Their ships, Byzantine sources tell us, were the small *karabos*, of solid hollowed-out logs, which could be carried around the Dnieper rapids on the way to Byzantium and the Black Sea.[305] Such a vessel was probably native to Russia and could easily be destroyed by superior Byzantine warships. Even the naval terminology in use by Varangians in these regions seems to have been Greek rather than Scandinavian.[306]

[302] On the mention of a fleet at Bordeaux in 906, see *Bibliothèque Nationale; Mélanges Colbert*, XLVI, 97.

[303] *Anglo-Saxon Chronicle*, I, 190. In an excellent discussion of the later Norse *drekkars*, or super-warships, Brøgger and Shetelig suggest that Alfred's innovation consisted not just in making his ships bigger and longer but also higher, so that those who manned them could more easily clear the decks of their opponents from above and board their adversaries' ships more easily. See Brøgger and Shetelig, *The Viking Ships*, pp. 186-232.

[304] The problem of Slavic shipping in the Baltic—a shipping underrated by many maritime historians—remains a difficult one. In the 10th century it was considerable, witness the Jomsburgvikings, and even more so in the 11th century. It seems probable in this period that the seagoing Wends and Balts copied at first the *karfis* of their Scandinavian neighbors. On these *karfis*, see Brøgger and Shetelig, *op.cit.*, pp. 173-76.

[305] On the *karabos* (or *korabli*, in Russian), see H. Falk, *Aldnordisches Seewesen* (Christiania 1906), pp. 90-94, and Brøgger and Shetelig, *op.cit.*, p. 175. Also J. C. Steenstrup, *Normanerne*, I, 353.

[306] On the fact that Byzantine naval terminology, not Norse, was used in Kievan Russia, see B. Grekov, *La Culture de la Russie de Kiev*, p. 13.

There is one other point of maritime importance during these years to be explored.That is navigation. The Vikings of the Atlantic, by the late ninth century, had replaced the Irish as the most intrepid mariners of the Northern Seas. They began, for instance, to sail long distances out of sight of land. Their trips to Iceland and direct from Denmark to England show this clearly. How they navigated so far from land is an interesting problem. De Winter suggests that they used celestial navigation and may even have known the secret of the compass.[307] They used prevailing winds to the best advantage and knew how to tack before the wind, as Ottar's voyage proves.[308] They may have derived some of this knowledge from their contacts with the Irish, though this is a very controversial point. If so, they perfected this type of sailing. Yet it still seems probable that, up to the tenth century, even Viking ships preferred to travel, as before, along the coasts, and open-sea navigation remained the exception rather than the rule.[309] Only in the tenth century did their skill in this type of sailing permit them to make those great voyages that carried them to Greenland and America.

How can one sum up this age of Viking assaults and expansion in Northern Europe? One can, I think, say that by raiding, colonizing and trading in lands which stretched from Spain and Iceland to the Black and Caspian Seas, the Scandinavians changed the political basis and history of Northern Europe in every region they penetrated. But it needs to be emphasized that, even in maritime affairs, their influence, while dominant, was never all-pervasive. Frisian and Anglo-Saxon shipping, Western Gallic mariners and even Irish sailors from Ulster continued to ply the Northern Seas as peaceful merchants. The Anglo-Saxons under Alfred, and perhaps some Irish, even disputed control of the sea with the Vikings. In Russia a Slavic ship tradition continued, and in the Black Sea Byzantine naval power remained

[307] H. De Winter, "Die Nautick der Wikinger," in *Hansische Geshichtsblätter*, XLII (1937), 173-84.
[308] On Ottar's use of tacking before the wind, see *Alfred's Orosius*, ed. Sweet, p. 17. On a similar feat performed by Columba off the Scottish coast in the 6th century, see Adamnan, *Vita Columbae*, II, 15, ed. Fowler, p. 84. On the use of prevailing, seasonal winds to sail directly west from Norway to the Faroes and Iceland, see A. W. Brøgger, *Ancient Emigrants*, pp. 24-25.
[309] At first the Vikings almost always proceeded along the coast to launch their raids—for instance, the Danes went to Frisia and *then* raided the French Channel and England. Likewise, the Norwegians went first to the Orkneys and Hebrides, then to Ireland and then raided Western France and Spain. On this type of coastal navigation, see W. Vogel, "Zur nord und westeuropäischen Seeschiffahrt," in *Hansische Geshichtsblätter*, XIII (1907), 191-94. On the other hand, some raids, like that on Lindesfarne early in the 9th century, may have been launched directly across the North Sea.

predominant. It would be well, then, not to overestimate the importance of the Vikings in the Northern Seas during these years.

In answering the question as to whether the Vikings were a constructive or destructive economic force, one might adopt a middle ground. The Viking raids were destructive up to 911 and did damage to commerce, particularly in France, where in some regions they continued for several decades after 911. But by this date, even in France, regions like the Garonne and northeastern coasts were recovering rapidly, and signs of economic life along the Loire and Seine marked the beginnings of the revival which was to appear here about the year 1000. In the case of France, however, it seems probable that the economic effect of the ending of all trade with Italy via the Alps, and the Mediterranean via the Midi, was more important than Viking raids as a source of economic decadence and localism.

Elsewhere in Northern Europe, it is clear that by 911 the Vikings had stimulated rather than depressed economic life. This seems particularly true in England, Germany and Ireland, as well as in Scandinavia, while in Russia, by reopening trade routes, they laid the basis for future growth and prosperity. Already by the tenth century, then, they had helped to form a trading region which extended from Ireland and England to the Black and Caspian Seas. In this sense, despite their plunderings and destruction, the Scandinavians during these years proved a force as constructive in Northern Europe's economic and maritime progress as either Charlemagne or Louis the Pious.

6. The Age of the Ottos and the House of Alfred, A.D. 911-985

WHEN THE AGE of the Vikings ended in the first years of the tenth century, there followed a period of quite a different character which lasted three-quarters of a century. It led up to the final expression of Scandinavian maritime and political force in Northern Europe, the Danish empire of Svein and Canute. It saw the leadership of the Northern Seas in the hands of Anglo-Saxon England and Ottonian Germany, with surprising strength being revealed in Miezko's Poland, Boleslas' Bohemia and Sviatoslav's and Vladimir's Kievan Russia. In England, Germany and Slavic Europe we find concentrated the principal centers of political power, economic development and cultural leadership. And here, too, were laid foundations for future growth.

This does not mean that the peoples of Scandinavia no longer figured in Northern European affairs, for they certainly did. They remained the dominant element in Normandy and along Gallic shores, in the towns they had founded on the coasts of Ireland, in faraway Iceland— even increasing their importance during this period. Their mariners pushed west from Iceland to reach Greenland and America. Their strong Norwegian kingdom continued, and a new one arose in Denmark. From trading centers like Hedeby, Birka and Gotland they continued to tap the trade of the Orient and to serve as middlemen along routes leading to Wollin, Russia, Ireland and England. They did not cease to penetrate Russia as merchants or as Varangian mercenaries useful to a Kievan ruling family which was still Scandinavian in blood and feeling. They formed the maritime element which held Slav, German, Anglo-Saxon and Irish worlds together. But they ceased to be what they had been in the late ninth century and what they were to be again under Canute, the dominating force in these worlds. That role was played by Aethelstan's England, Otto's Germany and Slavic Central and Eastern Europe.

On the other hand, from a maritime and economic point of view those regions which were of primary importance in this tenth century were just those where the Vikings had earlier been most active, directly or indirectly. By 911 one can clearly see the outlines of a unified Northern world stretching from Ireland in the West to Russia in the

East. It included within its scope Anglo-Saxon England, Northern and Central Germany, the Baltic and Scandinavia. These regions, which faced the north, were joined by trade routes that were in large measure the result of previous and still continuing Scandinavian enterprise. This enterprise had helped to form about the Northern Seas a single, great trading area where Samanid silver held sway, and where its stimulus invigorated Irish town, English borough, German *wick*, Meuse *portus* and Slavic *grody* alike. The development of the Northern Seas in Roman, Merovingian, Carolingian and Viking times was culminating in this tenth century. If the political and military age of the Vikings ended around 911, the economic era they had ushered in was in full flower later in the century.

A major point of interest concerns the center of gravity of Northern Europe in this period. Three regions were particularly active: the area of the Baltic, Otto's Germany and Anglo-Saxon England. All three had had importance in Carolingian, even Merovingian, times. But now their destinies merged in a new fashion, as Northern Europe's center of gravity moved north and east again from that region between the Seine and Rhine where it had rested under Charlemagne and Louis the Pious. In the first years of the ninth century one can speak of a Carolingian renaissance, of a culture centered about Aix-la-Chapelle, around which were clustered the Spain of Alphonse the Chaste, the kingdoms of Ireland, the England of Offa and Egbert, and the Baltic of Swedish Ingvar rulers of Uppsala. In the tenth century, Ottonian Germany was the heart and center of the Northern world, but now the existence of a more independent England of Aethelstan, a strong Norway of Harold Fairhair, a Baltic which saw Miezko's Polish state appear and a powerful Kievan Russia indicated that cultural and economic life had become more widely diffused. Otto's Germany was Northern Europe's center now, but it had more serious rivals than Charlemagne's Empire ever had. This fact may explain why the Ottonian renaissance, important though it was, never dominated Europe as the previous Carolingian one had done. Otto's Holy Roman Empire never matched that of Charlemagne in authority and influence. And so it was not difficult towards the end of this century for Svein and Canute, representing a new Danish kingdom, geographically located in the center of this Northern Seas trading area, to snatch leadership from the faltering hands of the great Otto's successors. The Danes' fleets, their state, and their interests probably represented the Northern Seas more effectively than did those of the German monarchs to the south of them. But this Danish Empire, like that of the Ottos, also reflected the new northern and eastern orientation of the Europe which faced the Northern Seas.

Another point is worth emphasizing about Northern Europe during this period. That is the degree of connection between it and the world of the Mediterranean, where the advanced economies and cultures of Byzantium and Islam held sway. Seldom had Northern Europe ever been so separate from the Mediterranean to the south, particularly as it was in those decades between 911 and 955. We have noted how, in Late Roman, in Late Merovingian and in Carolingian times, the Northern Seas had communicated with the Mediterranean via southern French ports, Alpine passes and the Atlantic coasts of Spain. We have also emphasized the relative unimportance of such connections to Northern Europe's industry, maritime expansion and commercial development. But now in the early years of the tenth century, with the possible exception of England, we see even these slight connections with the south via Alps and Midi reduced to almost zero. Some commerce may have flowed north from Atlantic Spain, which kept links with the Mediterranean, but not elsewhere in the West. Moslem pirates, established along the shores of Southern France and in the Alps, seem to have effectively isolated France from Mediterranean trade currents.[1] And Hungarian raiders who plundered Southern Germany and Northern Italy for a half century after 900 interfered with routes which went north over Alpine passes to Germany.[2] Not until Otto's victory of Lechfeld had stopped Magyar interference with trade over Alpine passes, and not until the expulsion of the Moors from Garde Frainet in 972, were these routes reopened. Until this time the main connections with the East were perforce by way of Kievan Russia. Thus the northern and eastern orientation of these years is, in fact, the result of this separation of Northern from Southern Europe, as well as of developments which took place around the Northern Seas themselves.

It seems probable also that this separation explains, in part, France's political and economic unimportance during this period.[3] Cut off from

---

[1] On the causes of this state of affairs, see A. R. Lewis, *Naval Power and Trade*, pp. 177-82.

[2] On the destructiveness of Magyar raids which extended into Northern Italy in these years, see R. Lüttich, *Ungarnzüge in Europa im 10. Jahrhundert* (Berlin 1910), pp. 15-147 and L. M. Hartmann, *Geschichte Italiens im Mittelalter*, III (Gotha 1911), 151-283.

[3] On this rather obscure period in French history, see P. Lauer, *Robert Ier et Raoul de Bourgogne, rois de France* (Paris 1910), and *Le Règne de Louis IV d'Outre-mer*

Mediterranean contacts save by way of Atlantic Spain, beyond trade routes in the Northern Seas which terminated in Ireland, England and Ottonian Germany, France's ports that faced the Atlantic from the Pyrenees to the Scheldt played a very minor economic role. Not until the last years of the tenth century were they to begin to recover the economic importance which they had had at the time of Louis the Pious and Charles the Bald and to move forward to their greater future destiny. In short, the years from 911 to 985 were a period of growth in the lands facing the Northern Seas, but of an uneven growth. Economic life and culture expanded in Ireland, England, Germany, Scandinavia and the Slavic East, but moved slowly and locally in France. Only gradually did the world of Charles the Simple, of Louis d'Outremer, of Hugh Capet progress towards that of Louis VI and Philip Augustus.

England, of all the regions which showed progress and growth during this period, was the area where development was most continuous and uninterrupted. The progress which we noted in the last chapter as occurring here in Alfred's time continued under his successors. The story of Anglo-Saxon England during these years in part is the story of the slow reconquest of the Danelaw and of its integration with a strong centralized state. We have already noted how this reconquest began in the late ninth century under Alfred, who regained London and Essex from the Danes. During the reigns of Edward the Elder and his sister, Aethelfreda of Mercia, the Anglo-Saxon advance continued, after Danish attacks had been beaten off at Tettenhall in 910. By 917 Derby, one of the Danes' five fortress boroughs in the Midlands, was regained, along with Colchester in Suffolk. By the end of Edward's reign all East Anglia had been added to his kingdom.[4]

When the able Aethelstan succeeded his father on the English throne the advance did not slacken. By 927 he had seized York, which since 919 had been an independent Viking kingdom under the Norse royal house of Dublin. Aethelstan, however, seems not to have felt powerful enough to retain this conquest and incorporate it into his kingdom. Instead he gave it as a vassal kingdom to Eric Blood-Axe, the son of Harold Fairhair of Norway, with whom he was

---

(Paris 1900). See also F. Lot, *Les derniers Carolingiens, Lothaire, Louis V, Charles de Lorraine* (Paris 1891).

[4] T. D. Kendrick, *History of the Vikings*, pp. 246-50. F. Stenton, *Anglo-Saxon England*, pp. 314-17.

closely allied. But he did force the Welsh to pay tribute and ravaged Scotland by land and sea in 934. Such displays of force seem to have alarmed Aethelstan's neighbors and, as a result, in 937 an invading army of Scots and Norse Dublin Vikings landed on the west coast of his kingdom and challenged his power. He gained a great victory over them at Brunaburgh, and this threat subsided.[5]

When Aethelstan died two years later, in 939, and his kingdom passed to his son, Edmund, the Norse Vikings of Ireland returned to the attack. A large army under King Olaf Guthridson of Dublin retook York, and even occupied the five Danish boroughs of the Midlands. Apparently, however, these Dublin Norse proved unpopular with the Danish population of North England, for after Olaf died in 943 the Five Boroughs returned to their Anglo-Saxon allegiance. In York, Ragnald, brother of Olaf, was forced to share the throne with Olaf Sithricson. In 944 Edmund advanced north and expelled both from England, and went on to conquer Strathclyde, which now paid him tribute. The rule of the House of Wessex in York, however, still proved tenuous. In 947 Eric Blood-Axe returned from Norway and regained this Danish kingdom, only to be forced out again in 949 by Olaf Sithricson, who returned from Dublin with a large force. Eric in turn, in 952, won out over his Irish rival and regained York. Apparently these disorders weakened Scandinavian rule there. So it was that when in 954, Eadred, of the House of Wessex, moved north with an army, he was able to defeat Eric Blood-Axe easily at the battle of Stanmore. York fell again into Anglo-Saxon hands, where it was to remain, and the last vestige of the Danelaw's political independence in England disappeared. From Scotland to the Channel, the House of Wessex reigned supreme.[6]

A number of factors explain how the House of Alfred was able, in fifty years, to reconquer the Danelaw and add it to the Anglo-Saxon realm. In the first place, the rulers of this line appear to have been men of real ability. The level of leadership provided by Alfred,

[5] On this battle of Brunaburgh, see *The Battle of Brunaburgh*, ed. Campbell (Cambridge 1930), and William of Malmesbury, *Gesta regum*, in *Roll Series*, I, 151. On Aethelstan's conquest of York in 927, see F. Stenton, *op.cit.*, pp. 250-52, and T. D. Kendrick, *op.cit.*, pp. 248-52.

[6] On the changes which took place and the confused years from 936 to 954 in York and the Danelaw, see A. Mawrer, "The Redemption of the Five Boroughs," in *Eng. Hist. Review*, XXXVIII (1923), 215-47, and M. Beaven, "King Edmund I and the Danes," in *ibid.*, XXXIII (1918), 13-41. Also F. Stenton, *op.cit.*, pp. 352-58, and T. D. Kendrick, *op.cit.*, pp. 252-57.

Edward the Elder, Aethelstan, Edmund, Eadred and Edgar evidently was of a high order. Aethelstan in particular appears to have possessed outstanding ability. In the second place, as they advanced their borders northwards, these kings were careful to organize their conquests, establishing fortress boroughs and integrating their conquests carefully into their kingdom.[7] To them was owed England's centralized shire system. Thirdly, they were always careful not to offend the sensibilities or the local political institutions of the Danes who were settled in the regions that they reconquered. Frequently it would seem that this Danish population therefore preferred their rule to that of the Scandinavian House of Dublin. Able to keep their lands and customs undisturbed under the rule of an Aethelstan or an Edgar, they resisted the advance of the House of Wessex only spasmodically.[8]

To these factors we must add one other, the use of naval power. The House of Alfred, unlike all other non-Viking monarchs of this period, seems to have understood the value of a navy. Thus Alfred's successors continued and even improved the fleet he founded. In 909 we find it used by Edward the Elder, who gathered ships from central and western coasts to concentrate them in Kent, as a protection against the Danish maritime forces who menaced his kingdom.[9] In 934 Aethelstan used naval flotillas to raid Scottish coasts and weaken his enemies.[10] He probably employed a fleet to aid the Duke of Brittany against the Loire Vikings in 939.[11] He used it to destroy a large

---

[7] The new boroughs of Alfred and his successors have been the cause of much investigation and discussion. Among the latest see C. Stephenson, *Borough and Town* (Cambridge 1923), and J. Tait, *The Medieval English Borough* (Manchester 1936). See also R. R. Darlington, "The Early History of English Towns," in *History*, XXIII (1948), 108-43.

[8] On the treatment received by the Danes of the Danelaw at the hands of Anglo-Saxon rulers and their swift absorption into English life, see F. Stenton, *op.cit.*, pp. 354-58, 511-18, and especially his "Scandinavian Colonies in England and Normandy," *loc.cit.*, pp. 1-12. See also H. Shetelig, *The Viking History of Western Europe*, pp. 87-104. Interesting in this regard, though it deals largely with a later period, is A. Bugge, "The Norse Settlements in the British Isles," in *Trans. of Royal Hist. Soc.*, 4th ser., IV (1921), 215-53.

[9] Aethelward, *Chron.*, ed. Saville, pp. 482f. Ships were used against the Danes again in 912. F. Stenton, *op.cit.*, p. 320.

[10] W. L. Clowes, *The Royal Navy* (London 1897), I, 15-16. F. Stenton, *op.cit.*, pp. 354-56.

[11] He certainly used his fleet to ravage Flemish coasts during the period when he was backing Louis IV d'Outremer in France. Flodoard, *Annales rem. eccl.*, ed. Lauer, p. 72, and Richer, *Historia*, ed. Latouche (Paris 1930), p. 152. On the use of this fleet against the Loire Vikings between 936 and 939, see P. Lauer, *Louis IV d'Outremer*, p. 117.

Danish force which raided Sandwich in the same year.[12] Nor was the navy abandoned after his death. For we hear in Edgar's time that this king sailed his fleet to Chester after his coronation, and there received homage from four vassal kings.[13] Divided into three permanent squadrons—one for the North Sea, based on Sandwich, one in the English Channel, and one in the west—this navy, until Aethelred's time, gave Anglo-Saxon shores security from foreign attack.[14] It was as much responsible for the power of the House of Wessex during these years as were orderly governmental institutions and borough fortresses.

This political and naval strength of Britain is reflected in the foreign policies and contacts maintained by the House of Alfred, particularly by Aethelstan. Judith, daughter of Charles the Bald of France, after her marriages to two Wessex kings, took Baldwin I of Flanders as her third husband. This Flanders alliance was strengthened when, between 893-899, Alfred married one of his daughters to Count Baldwin II. Sixty years later, in the middle of the tenth century, Count Arnaulf could still speak of the friendship that linked Flanders and Anglo-Saxon England.[15]

Close marriage ties also were established during these years with France. Edward the Elder married a daughter of Charles the Simple and, after the latter had been deposed in 929, his son, Louis, came to England, where he was raised in exile. Aethelstan assisted this nephew, known in history as Louis d'Outremer, to regain his French throne, and supported him with a fleet against an invasion of France by Otto I.[16] But he was equally determined to maintain ties with the other principal French political factions and married his sister, Eadhild, to Duke Hugh Capet. Farther to the west in France, when Duke Richard of Brittany was driven from his lands by Normans and Loire Vikings, the English monarch gave him asylum in Britain and helped him in 939 to return to Brittany and expel the invaders.[17]

[12] This may have been the first true naval battle in English history. See P. Gosse, "Piracy," in *Mariners Mirror*, XXVI (1950), 339.

[13] Florence of Worcester, *Chron.*, ed. Thorpe, I, 142-43. F. Stenton, *op.cit.*, pp. 364-65.

[14] W. L. Clowes, *op.cit.*, p. 41.

[15] On these marriage alliances, see P. Grierson, "The Relations Between England and Flanders Before the Norman Conquest," in *Trans. of Royal Hist. Soc.*, 4th ser., XII (1941), 85-94. See also *The Memorials of St. Dunstan*, ed. Stubbs, p. 360.

[16] P. Grierson, *op.cit.*, pp. 87-91. P. Lauer, *Louis IV*, pp. 100-86. F. Stenton, *op.cit.*, pp. 339-40.

[17] On these alliances, see F. Stenton, *op.cit.*, pp. 341-44.

Nor did Aethelstan neglect North Sea coasts. He married his daughter, Edith, to Otto I of Germany and so gained the friendship of the other powerful ruler of Northern Europe.[18] And he was particularly concerned with getting and keeping the friendship of Harold Fairhair of Norway, who appears to have shared an anti-Viking policy which led him to cooperate with the English king. Harold sent Aethelstan a fine ship as token of his friendship, and in return Aethelstan not only gave York to Harold's son, Eric Blood-Axe, but seems to have raised another child of his, Haakon the Good, as his foster son.[19] Even the troublesome Norse kings of Ireland were diplomatically handled by this monarch through the marriage of one of his sisters to Sihtric, ruler of Dublin.[20] Thus in Aethelstan's time all his neighbors—Brittany, France, Flanders, Germany, Norway and Ireland—were linked by diplomatic marriages and friendship to the English royal house.

Wise leadership, a good governmental system, a strong navy and close relations maintained with overseas neighbors help to explain why England's economy continued the improvement which had begun under Alfred and Edward the Elder right down to the later Danish invasions of 980. We noted in the last chapter that one indication of this economic growth is to be found in the establishment of new mints under Alfred and his son. This continued, for in Aethelstan's time, we hear of fourteen mints in operation in Kent and Wessex, eight of which were newly established during his reign. In the Midlands fourteen new minting places, in addition to that of York, now coined money in the name of the Wessex king.[21] There is also some indication of the economic importance of various boroughs and towns of England in the number of moneyers in each important trading center. We find that during these years London had 8 moneyers, Canterbury 7, Winchester 6, Lewes 2, Hamwith (Southampton) 2, Wareham 2, Exeter 2, Shaftsbury 2 and each other port or borough one.[22] Such evidence seems to show that in Aethelstan's time the economic life of Western and Southern England, where the principal

[18] Ibid., pp. 342-43. R. Kopke and E. Dummler, Kaiser Otto der Grosse (Leipzig 1876), pp. 20-53.

[19] William of Malmesbury, Gesta regum, in Roll Series, I, 149. L. Musset, Les Peuples scandinaves, pp. 80-82. The ship Harold sent may have been a drekkar, or long-ship. Brøgger and Shetelig, The Viking Ships, p. 180.

[20] Anglo-Saxon Chronicle D, anno 925.

[21] J. Tait, The Medieval English Borough, pp. 27-28.

[22] Laws of Aethelstan, II, 15, in C. Attenborough, The Earliest English Laws, p. 135.

mints were located, was more vigorous than elsewhere in the land. By Aethelred's time, late in the century, the number of mints almost tripled, now totaling 75, with many moneyers at work in various of them.[23] Furthermore, we note under Aethelstan a concern for the regulation of coinage, demonstrated by his prohibition against the minting of coins except in a borough, the penalty for violation being the loss of a hand by the counterfeiter.[24]

Regulations on coinage were supplemented by the English monarch's attempts to order trade during these years. We have already pointed out that sufficient trading places existed in Britain so that Edward the Elder could attempt to force traveling merchants to conduct their trading in a *portus*, where it could be supervised by the port-reeve, a royal official.[25] Aethelstan continued this regulation at first for goods having a value of 20 pence or more.[26] It apparently could not be enforced, however, for in later laws he eliminated the prohibitions against trade outside a *portus* and trade on Sunday.[27] This seems to imply that commerce was already outgrowing the official bounds of recognized boroughs as a money economy moved into the countryside. At any rate, by the time of Edgar we find trade in the country, as in the boroughs of the land, recognized as legal.[28] We can understand how England was developing into a land which could furnish 155,000 pounds of gold and silver in Danegelds alone to Svein and Canute.[29]

Another interesting aspect of the Anglo-Saxon economy during these years is the country's possession of gold and the minting of a gold coinage. Except for Ireland, England seems to have been unique in this respect. Anglo-Saxon wills contain mention of much gold, and we know that later in the century considerable of this precious metal was paid Danish rulers in Danegelds.[30] Offa and Wigmund of York had coined gold in England earlier, but this had no immediate

---

[23] G. C. Brooke, *English Coins*, p. 65-66.

[24] *Laws of Aethelstan*, II, 14, in C. Attenborough, *op.cit.*, p. 135. On the similarity between these and other regulations concerning coinage and Byzantine regulations, see R. S. Lopez, "Relations anglo-byzantines," *loc.cit.*, pp. 159-62.

[25] *Laws of Edward I*, I, in C. Attenborough, *op.cit.*, p. 115.

[26] *Laws of Aethelstan*, II, 12, in *ibid.*, p. 135.

[27] *Laws of Aethelstan*, IV, 2, in *ibid.*, p. 147.

[28] *Laws of Edgar*, IV, 5, in *ibid.*, p. 149.

[29] G. C. Brooke, *English Coins*, pp. 66-68.

[30] D. Whitelock, *Anglo-Saxon Wills* (Cambridge 1930), contains evidence of much gold in the private possession of individuals in Anglo-Saxon England in this period. On the gold paid in Danegelds after 980, often considerable, see J. H. Ramsay, *Foundations of England* (London 1898), pp. 339-42.

follow-up. Under Edward the Elder, however, gold pennies appear to have been minted.[31] And the will of Eadred in 955 directed that 2,000 *mancusi* of gold be coined from supplies he had available and be donated to religious institutions in the name of charity.[32] Somewhat later Aethelred II also coined gold pennies.[33] We have already suggested that English gold came from Ireland, where its source may have been Connaught or grave plunderings, and in this connection it is interesting to note that in a coin hoard of this period from Lancashire gold bars have been discovered.[34] Since this find is located in a region through which the natural trade routes leading to Ireland passed, the supposition that most Anglo-Saxon gold supplies came from there is strengthened. Some gold in this period may also have come from mines in Wales. It seems certain, however, that Moslem gold dinars were *not* the source of England's gold supply, despite the use of the term *mancus*. As already noted, the word *mancus* as used in these years bears no relation to the dinar, but was a money of account, worth 30 shillings, and was modeled upon the Byzantine *mancus solidus*, or lightweight coin of Beneventum and Southern Italy.[35] Nevertheless, the plentiful gold supply of England in this period is unusual and may be an index of its prosperity.

Historical sources supplement the preceding economic information. In the tenth century, York, according to a Life of St. Oswald, had become an important trading city. It contained a large merchant colony, the majority of which was of Danish extraction.[36] Cambridge was a center of the cloth trade where Irish merchants arrived in 975 to sell *sagi*, or woolen cloaks.[37] Thetford nearby is revealed by archeological evidence to have continued as a manufacturing center

[31] P. Grierson, *Carolingian Europe and the Arabs, The Myth of the Mancus,* pp. 1-19.

[32] *Liber Mon. de Hyde,* ed. Edwards, in *Roll Series,* I, 154.

[33] P. Grierson, *op.cit.,* pp. 3-8. See find of 10th-century gold penny at Anglesey in J. Fisher, in *Cambrian Archeological Assn.,* XXIII (London 1917), 268.

[34] It is worth noting that during Aethelstan's reign the Welsh paid a tribute of 20 lbs. of gold and 200 lbs. of silver. William of Malmesbury, *Gesta regum,* in *Roll Series,* I, 148. Perhaps this gold came from Ireland or even from native Welsh gold deposits.

[35] P. Grierson, *op.cit.,* pp. 1-19. In the 11th century, though, not the early 10th, the word *mancus* definitely referred to the dinar, hence the confusion in terms. On this 11th-century *mancus,* see A. R. Lewis, *op.cit.,* p. 248. See also *Laws of Canute,* II, 1, on the fact that important thegns were to pay the king 50 *mancusi* of gold to receive from him their possessions.

[36] *Vita S. Oswaldi,* in *Historians of York,* in *Roll Series,* I, 454.

[37] J. Tait, *op.cit.,* p. 10. On the importance of Worcester in this period, see F. E. Hamer, *English Historical Documents,* pp. 22-23.

for pottery that was distributed all over Eastern Britain.[38] London was already of international commercial importance, and merchants from France, Normandy, Flanders, the Meuse valley and Germany came there to trade.[39] It seems probable that merchant guilds already existed in London as well as in Canterbury and Winchester.[40] In Western England, in 956, we hear of Welsh traders and sailors at the mouth of the Wye.[41] Evidence is available of much exploitation, during these years, of the tin mines of Cornwall,[42] as well as of the silver and lead mines of the Mendips, Flintshire and Derbyshire,[43] and the iron deposits of Kent and Gloucestershire.[44] There is even evidence that an important slave trade continued to exist, particularly in Wales.[45]

While England was developing new commercial centers and mints for the emission of its silver coinage, its agriculture was continuing to expand as well. Danish settlements in the Midlands, Yorkshire and East Anglia increased the population of the countryside, as did Norse-Irish colonies in Lancashire and Westmoreland.[46] But it was in Western and Southern England, around the new boroughs and mints established by the House of Alfred, that the evidence is strongest of continued clearing of the forest and agrarian growth. Here the progress noted in Carolingian times definitely continued during the

[38] G. Dunning, "Dating Medieval Pottery," in *Arch. News Letter* (1949), pp. 5-6.
[39] On this famous toll of London, see F. Liebermann, *Die Gesetze der Anglo-Sacksen* (Halle 1907), I, 232.
[40] C. Gross, *The Guild Merchant*, I, 178-81, 186-88. Coornaert believes such guilds already had commercial significance. E. Coornaert, "Les Gildes médiévales," in *Revue hist.*, CXCIX (1949), 38-41.
[41] C. Fox, "The Boundary Line of the Cyrmni," in *Proc. of British Acad.*, XXVI (1940), 281-82. On a possible occupation of Caerlon in this period, see Gerald Cambriensis, *Itinerary*, v.
[42] Note coins minted from the reign of Aethelstan through that of Canute found in Cornwall near the tin workings in this period. H. O. Hencken, *Archeology of Cornwall and Scilly*, pp. 263-64.
[43] On the working of silver mines, see O. Davies, *Roman Mines in Europe*, pp. 150-64. On British lead shipped as far as South Germany, see *MGH Epistolae selectae*, III, 50.
[44] O. Davies, *op.cit.*, pp. 154-64. Gloucester in the 11th century was particularly important as an iron center. *Domesday Book*, I, 162. No doubt this went back to the 10th century, too. So, too, was Kent in Oswin's time.
[45] On the slave trade of these years and efforts to stop it, see *Laws of Aethelred*, II; V, 2; VI, 9, in F. Liebermann, *Gesetze*, I, 239, 254, and A. Hadon and W. Stubbs, *Councils and Ecclesiastical Documents Relating to England and Ireland* (Oxford 1873), III, 173-75. See particularly also E. I. Bromberg, "Wales and the Medieval Slave Trade," in *Speculum*, XVII (1942), 283-85.
[46] On these settlements, see F. Stenton, "The Danes in England," in *Proc. of British Acad.*, XIII (1927), pp. 183-87, and *Anglo-Saxon England*, pp. 511-18. See also his "Scandinavian Colonies in England and Normandy," *loc.cit.*, pp. 1-12.

course of the tenth century, resulting in increased food production and a growing village population.[47]

Coin finds are rare, generally speaking, for this period in England, since peaceful conditions prevailed, but a few from the northern and western portions of the land gave valuable information of an economic sort which supplements our knowledge from other sources. In Lancashire, a hoard at Haukirke, somewhat later in date than that of Cuerdale, contains coins from some of the same mints on a smaller scale. It has in it money minted by Alfred and Edward the Elder from Canterbury, some Anglo-Danish pennies from East Anglia and York, a few Charles the Bald deniers from France, one Provence silver penny and one of Berengar from Italy.[48] In Anglesey one gold Anglo-Saxon penny has been unearthed, probably of Edgar, dating about the middle of the century,[49] while in Cornwall a small hoard at St. Austel contains nine pennies minted from the time of Aethelstan to that of Edgar. Nearby several scattered Aethelred II coins have also been uncovered.[50] The west coast of Britain thus seems to have been in touch with a large portion of England, with France and even with Italy, judging from this slight coin evidence. In Yorkshire a single hoard found at Goldsborough, dating from about 927, contains a number of coins struck by Alfred and Edward the Elder from various mints, and in addition several Kufic dirhems that must have come from the Baltic.[51]

So far our attention has been fixed mainly upon England's internal agricultural, industrial and commercial growth in the tenth century. But coin hoards and sources alike seem to show that this growth was related to a foreign commerce, too, carried on by merchants reaching England from Ireland and the Continent: Danish, German, Flemish, Walloon, French, Norman, Welsh and Irish traders. Evidence from abroad makes even clearer the extent of this Anglo-Saxon overseas commerce.

In the direction of Ireland and in the Irish Sea, England's commerce was particularly important. We have already noted Welsh

[47] On this continued clearing of the soil, see C. Fox, *The Archeology of the Cambridge Region*, pp. 230-360, and C. S. Orwin, *The Open Fields* (Oxford 1938), pp. 1-86. On rural prosperity—even a money economy in the countryside—see F. Stenton, *Anglo-Saxon England*, p. 475.
[48] J. Rashleigh, in *Num. Chron.*, new ser., II (1861-62), 56.
[49] J. Fisher, in *Cambrian Archeological Assn.* (London 1917), p. 268.
[50] H. O. Hencken, *op.cit.*, pp. 262-64.
[51] *Archeological Journal*, XVI (1859), 187.

merchants at the mouth of the Wye in 956, and Irish traders visiting Cambridge in 975 to sell cloth. Such commerce helps us to understand how in 934 Wales could pay Aethelstan 34 pounds of gold in tribute.[52] Other evidence from Ireland speaks of the Norse merchant, Hrafr Hlyrickfarer of Limerick, who sent ships to trade with England during this period.[53]

It is coin finds in Ireland, however, which best help to show the extent of this commerce. Such coin hoards are rare in the ninth century. They become more common in the tenth and contain large numbers of Anglo-Saxon and Anglo-Danish silver pennies, the latter mainly from York. One hoard, interred at Lugga in County Meath between 920 and 930, contains several Wessex silver pennies.[54] A second, slightly later in date, in Kildare contains nine Anglo-Saxon coins minted by Edward the Elder and Aethelstan.[55] Still another, dating from about 940, from Ballytore in Kildare contains 60 Anglo-Saxon and Anglo-Danish pennies, including money minted by Ragnald and Olaf at York.[56] A fourth, from Armagh, has at least one Aethelstan and one Olaf of York penny in it and thus is approximately contemporaneous with the Ballytore find.[57] A fifth, from Claremont, near Dublin, contains two coins minted by Aethelstan and four from York.[58] Fuller are two later hoards. One is from Lough Lynn in County Meath. Dating from 959, it has 27 Anglo-Saxon coins from the reigns of Aethelstan, Edmund, Eadred and Edgar, as well as some Anglo-Danish ones minted at York.[59] Finally, a large, contemporaneous hoard from Antrim in Ulster contains 107 Anglo-Saxon pennies minted in the reigns of English kings extending from Aethelstan to Edgar (927-959).[60] These coin finds seem to show that commerce was most active from England to Dublin and the surrounding region, where the majority of these hoards are located, but that some reached

---

[52] The tribute sent Aethelstan was even more diverse, according to William of Malmesbury. It included 25,000 cattle, 20 lbs. of gold (either locally produced or from Ireland), 300 lbs. of silver and some falcons. William of Malmesbury, *Gesta regum.*, in *Roll Series*, I, 148. It shows how prosperous Wales was in this period.
[53] T. Walsh, *The Norsemen in Ireland*, p. 23-30.
[54] A. Smith, in *Num. Chron.*, 3rd ser., III (1863), 217.
[55] J. Lindsay, *Heptarchy*, p. 125.
[56] J. Lindsay, *A View of the Coinage of Ireland* (Dublin 1839), p. 139.
[57] J. Lindsay, *Heptarchy*, p. 122.
[58] *Ibid.*, pp. 123-24.
[59] J. Lindsay, in *Num. Chron.*, 3rd ser., VI (1866-67), 305-7.
[60] J. Lindsay in *Num. Chron.*, 2nd ser., II (1843-44), 154-57. See the even earlier Kirkcudbright hoard of about 900 A.D., which contains some *stykas* from York, one Carolingian denier, one dirhem and some Mercian pennies. H. Maxwell, in *Proc. of Royal Soc. of Antiq. of Scotland*, XLVII (1912), 12-31.

Ulster as well. They may help to explain why Aethelstan found it wise to marry his sister to the Norse King of Dublin, and why English monarchs of this period maintained strong naval forces in the Irish Sea.

Coin evidence shows, however, that this English contact did not end in Ulster, but extended north to the Hebrides and Scottish coasts. A hoard on the island of Islay, buried about 950 to 960, contains five coins minted by Acthelstan and 83 by Edgar.[61] One from Portree on the island of Skye, farther north, which is roughly contemporaneous, contains 106 Anglo-Saxon and Anglo-Danish coins. And a third, from Inchkenneth, dating from the last years of the tenth century, includes large numbers of coins minted by Anglo-Saxon monarchs from Aethelstan to Aethelred.[62]

These Hebrides and Scottish coin hoards containing English money probably reveal the route used by some of the commerce which we know traveled between England and Norway and even Iceland in this period. We have already noted how the *Egils Saga* speaks of shipments of dried fish, furs and tallow to England in return for wheat, honey and cloth early in the tenth century. Much later, at the time of Olaf Tryggvasson, we learn again from the Sagas of two Northern Norwegian merchants, Sigrid and Hough, who traded with England, too. And in 991 the trade provisions of the treaty which Aethelred the Unready made with Olaf Tryggvasson reveal the importance each side attached to such commerce. Again, however, we can find in coins the proof of such contacts, since there are, in at least three hoards, in the Trondheim, Rogaland and More regions of Norway's west coast, coins minted by Edgar and Edward II (875-878). Iceland's contacts with Britain in this period are likewise revealed by a number of finds which include money minted in Aethelstan, Edgar, Edward II and Aethelred.

Nor was England's commerce inactive with the Continent. We have already mentioned the famous Toll of London, which speaks of men of Rouen, Ponthieu, Flanders, the Meuse and Germany who came to trade in London in the late tenth century at the time of Aethelred II.[63] Other evidence shows this was but a continuation of earlier tenth-century trade which crossed the Channel and went north to Britain

---

[61] W. Scott, in *ibid.*, XXIII (1889), 314-35.

[62] *Ibid.*, IX (1843-44), 208-18. Note that these hoards from Western Scotland, along with the Antrim hoard in Ireland dating from about 960 A.D., seem to show the growth of a maritime route as early as 900 A.D. from the Irish Sea north to the Hebrides and beyond.

[63] F. Liebermann, *Gesetze*, I, 232.

from coastal ports between Rouen and the Rhine. In the first years of the century, for instance, Dudo of St. Quentin mentions English merchants at Rouen.[64] It is interesting to note that when William Longsword, Duke of Normandy, coined money there between 927 and 943, he modeled his pennies on Anglo-Saxon ones minted in East Anglia, thus showing English contacts.[65] Farther up the coast was Quentovic, which for centuries had been a principal port in cross-Channel traffic. In 938, after he had recovered his throne with English help, Louis d'Outremer made an effort to rebuild this port, no doubt to encourage commerce with Britain.[66] Tenth-century Wissant, Guines and Boulogne also owed their existence to a cross-Channel trade, which apparently included a rather active traffic in slaves.[67] And still farther north, the coinage of St. Omer and St. Winnoc, minted during this period, showed, like that of Rouen, definite English influences.[68]

Farther north we have evidence of English tenth-century contacts even prior to the 991 mention of men of Flanders and the valley of the Meuse trading with London, for English coins of this period have been discovered at Maastricht, Liége and Namur.[69] Even far-away Germany shows traces of this influence, for we have mention in Southern Germany of tin, copper, and lead procured in Britain,[70] while at Regensburg on the Danube fine English cloth, the em-broidered *opus angliscum*, is mentioned in sources dating from this period.[71]

[64] *Dudo of St. Quentin*, in *Soc. des Antiq. de Normandie*, XXIII (1887), 7.

[65] A. Blanchet and A. Dieudonné, *Manuel de numismatique française*, IV, 302. One sees contacts between Normandy and western British shores in the Norman denier in the Inchkenneth hoard of the Hebrides. See *Proc. of Royal Soc. of Antiq. of Scotland*, IX (1843-44), 208-18.

[66] Flodoard, *Annales*, anno 937 and 938, ed. Lauer, pp. 69, 72. Richer, *Historia*, ed. Latouche, I, 140. Quentovic was active enough as a port to have six coins in the Inchkenneth hoard mentioned in the note above.

[67] On Boulogne, see *Vita S. Bertulphi*, in *Acta Sanct. Boll.*, Feb., I, 688, and Bouquet, *op.cit.*, IX, 65. On Guines in the 10th century, see Hariulf, *Chron.*, IV, 23, ed. Lot, p. 241. Shifting sands which silted up these harbors made them all unusable at various times in this period. P. Grierson, "The Relations Between Flanders and England," *loc.cit.*, pp. 280-88. E. Sabbe, "Les Relations économiques entre l'Angle-terre et le continent," in *Le Moyen Age*, LVI (1950), 183-95.

[68] On this coinage, see Blanchet and Dieudonné, *op.cit.*, p. 302.

[69] R. Doehaerd, *op.cit.*, pp. 25-26.   [70] *MGH Epistolae selectae*, III, 50.

[71] On this cloth, see *Diplom. Angl. aevi Saxoni*, ed. Thorpe (London 1865), pp. 178-79. The number of times that English goods, merchants and pilgrims were mentioned as being in Flanders, the Meuse region and South Germany in this period makes one feel that it was by way of Boulogne, Quentovic, Guines and Wissant and then via the Rhine and Alpine *clusae* that Anglo-Saxon England communicated with Italy and the Mediterranean.

Nor were these contacts confined to France, Germany and the Low Countries. They continued on to Italy and the Mediterranean throughout the tenth century, as Italian coin evidence in England has already suggested.[72] The *Honorantiae Civitatis Papiae* reveals that the English were specially privileged among European merchants by being allowed to come to Italy to purchase silks, spices and other Eastern wares at Pavia.[73] And we know that this commerce was not a one-way affair, for we find mention of an Italian merchant who in this period was passing through the Meuse region on his way to England.[74] Such trade contacts, unusual in Northern Europe during these years, help to explain the Byzantine influences which reached tenth-century Britain. The forms of Aethelstan's legal enactments, his use of the term *basileus* and his commercial regulations reflect a surprising knowledge of Byzantine forms and procedure.[75] The *opus angliscum*, or fine embroidered English cloth of the period, resembles Byzantine textiles, while the tenth-century school of Win chester shows traces of direct Byzantine art influences.[76] Were the *dromons* of the English fleet copies of Byzantine naval vessels? Perhaps they were. Under the circumstances, need it surprise us to learn that a Persian contemporary geographer could say that England was the mart of the Rûm (Italians, probably), where they went to trade?[77]

It is more difficult, however, to ascertain whether or not English merchants were trading with western Gallic coasts. The presence

[72] In addition to certain Italian coins found in English and Irish coin hoards, mentioned in the last chapter, we find 14 in the Cuerdale hoard. These include one Louis II of Italy, 11 Lambert and one Berengar. E. Gariel, *op.cit.*, pp. 140-46. The Haukirke hoard in Lancashire also has in it one Berengar penny. Note that all these coins are *silver* rather than gold.

[73] *Honorantiae Civitatis Papiae*, in *MGH Script.*, XXX, 2. It seems probable that English trade with Italy was facilitated because Anglo-Saxons alone of North European peoples possessed the *gold* which was necessary to purchase the fine grades of Byzantine silks available at Pavia. On the use of gold in Italian trade with Byzantium in these years, see R. S. Lopez, "The Silk Industry in the Byzantine Empire," in *Speculum*, XX (1945), 35-40, and M. Lombard, "L'Or mussulman du VII⁵ au XII⁵ siècle," in *Annales*, II (1947), 153-54. See also R. S. Lopez, "Relations anglo-byzantines," *loc.cit.*, 150-54.

[74] M. Mignon, "Les Arts de tissu," in *Manuels d'histoire de l'art* (Paris 1929), pp. 126-27, 169-70.

[75] R. S. Lopez, *op.cit.*, pp. 154-55. *Diplom. Angl. aevi Saxoni*, ed. Thorpe, pp. 178-79.

[76] R. S. Lopez, *op.cit.*, pp. 154-55. *Diplom. Angl. aevi Saxoni*, ed. Thorpe, pp. 178-79.

[77] England, according to this Persian geographer, is the mart of the Rûm (Italians) and the Andalusians. On this, see R. S. Lopez, "Still Another Renaissance," in *Amer. Hist. Review*, LVII (1951), 4-5.

of French, Aquitainian and Provençal coins in western British hoards like Cuerdale and Haukirke suggests that they did.[78] So does Aethelstan's interest in placing a friendly duke upon the throne of Brittany.[79] But direct evidence is lacking. On the other hand, a small coin hoard of the late tenth century discovered at Roncesvalles seems to show that Anglo-Saxons were reaching Northern Spain in these years, though whether as merchants or pilgrims to Santiago de Compostela it is impossible to say. This hoard contains seven silver pennies minted by Aethelred and one bronze *styka* from Yorkshire. The pennies are from mints in London, Rochester, Totnes and Exeter, and thus seem to indicate connection between Spain and southern and western British ports.[80] We must await more evidence of such traffic, however, before coming to any final conclusions.

It is England's trade with the Baltic which shows the greatest development of all her foreign trade with the Continent. We have already noted that, according to a contemporary source, York contained a large number of Danish merchants and that the Goldsborough Yorkshire hoard contains dirhems that must have arrived via the Baltic.[81] Coin evidence from this region itself is even more conclusive. For several centuries, except for Wulfstan's famous voyage, there is little evidence of Anglo-Saxon connections with this part of Europe. Such commerce had been, in Carolingian times, a monopoly of Frisian and Saxon traders. Not so now. In Danish Bornholm and Gotland coin hoards we suddenly find large numbers of English tenth-century coins—not, as in the case of Norway and Iceland, of an occasional variety, but rather numbering in the hundreds. In Danish finds they begin with those minted in the reign of Edward the Elder and continue in unbroken sequence until Aethelred's time.[82] In Gotland one hoard, that of Hagvats, which dates from 995, contains six English

---

[78] The Cuerdale hoard contains immense numbers of western Gallic coins, including some 560 from Melle and even one late coin minted by the Bishop of Arles. E. Gariel, *op.cit.*, pp. 140-46. The Haukirke hoard has one Provence denier. J. Rashleigh, in *Num. Chron.*, II (1842), 56. Interestingly enough, the Tarbat, Ross-shire hoard of circa 960 also contains 10 Aquitaine coins. D. McLain, in *Proc. of Soc. of Antiq. of Scotland*, XXIII (1889), 340-47. Does this show a route to the Mediterranean by way of the Garonne as in Late Merovingian times?

[79] P. Lauer, *Louis IV*, p. 117.

[80] F. Mateu y Lopis, "El hallazzo de 'pennies' ingleses en Roncesvalles," in *Principe de Viana*, XI (1950), 201-10.

[81] *Archeological Journal*, X (1859), 187.

[82] The coin hoards in Denmark which contain Anglo-Saxon money are largely in Zealand, Bornholm and Scania (now Swedish; in this period, Danish). R. Shovmand, *Die Dansk Skattefund frä Vikingetiden*, pp. 17-20.

pennies, starting with one coined by Aethelstan and ending with early coins of Aethelred II.[83] Even Finnish hoards, far to the east, contain some English money of this period.[84] To this coin evidence we must add the discovery of Anglo-Saxon jewelry in excavations at Danish Hedeby. Thus, in the course of the tenth century, the existence of a large Danish population in Eastern England resulted in the development of a trade with Denmark, probably centering in York, which brought to British shores commerce from the Baltic, and prepared the way for the even greater Anglo-Danish connection which we are to find in the days of Canute in the next century.

In summation, between 911 and 985 England's economy developed rapidly inside its borders, but even more rapidly did its commerce assume international importance. Towards Ireland and Denmark such commerce seems to have been particularly active. But it also reached Norway,[85] Iceland,[86] Spain, the French coasts, Flanders, Germany, and even Italy. Aethelstan's diplomacy was perhaps but the reflection of Anglo-Saxon England's international commercial importance. She was in this period the greatest trading nation in the Northern Seas.

If the progress made by England in this century seems surprising, that of Ireland is hardly less so. For it was during these years that she at last achieved a truly commercial civilization. It is hard to separate this progress from the presence of a Norse element along the shores of the island, controlling its seacoast fortresses and handling its main contacts with the outside world.[87] For, in the course of the tenth century, the Norwegian element in Ireland, which had seemed to be weakening and in danger of complete expulsion, again gathered strength. In 913 or 914 a large, new Norse contingent arrived in Ireland and began to reconquer its coasts. In 916, we hear of Dublin again falling into Scandinavian hands, and shortly thereafter Norse control and Norse fortresses were established, or re-established, at Water-

---

[83] M. Stenberger, *Die Schatzfunde Gotlands*, II, 73-75.

[84] On Anglo-Saxon coins found in Finland, see C. A. Nordman, *Anglo-Saxon Coins Found in Finland* (Helsinki 1921), pp. 3-21. They are found in 12 hoards, mainly in the southwestern part of Finland on the route leading to Novgorod.

[85] Anglo-Saxon coins have been found mainly in west-coast Norwegian hoards and those from this period begin with some struck by Edgar the Peaceful. H. Holst, "Mynter i Norske Funn," in *Nord. Numis. Arsskrift* (1943), pp. 101-6.

[86] One single Aethelstan minted coin has been found by itself in Iceland, and in the great Gaulverjabaer hoard there are 2 early ones—one coined by Edgar, the other by Edward II (975-978). K. Eldjarn, "Gaulverjabaer Fundet," in *Nord. Numis. Arsskrift* (1948), pp. 39-50.

[87] On this point, see a contemporary Irish estimate of the Norse in *Wars of the Gaedhil with the Gael*, I, 41-46, 50.

ford, Limerick and Cork. In 919 the High King of Ireland, Niall, was badly beaten by the invaders when he attempted resistance.[88]

Not all Irish native forces, however, were destroyed. In Ulster some Irish independent naval traditions seem to have survived, for we learn of mariners from these shores who, in 939, launched an attack on the Viking-controlled Hebrides.[89] And in 941 King Muirchertach Leathercloaks was powerful enough to force the Norse of Dublin to pay tribute to him.[90] This, however, was but an interlude, for soon afterwards Norse successes were so great that for almost forty years the native Irish were forced to pay tribute to the Vikings, and even accept a Norse ruler or official in every Irish village.[91] Not until about 980 did the native Irish again come to the fore, when a new reaction against the Scandinavians was led by the Irish High King, Maelsechnaill, who temporarily took Norse Dublin and prepared the way for Brian Boru and his victories over Scandinavian colonizers of the island.[92]

There can be little doubt that this Norse domination brought a certain prosperity to the land. Dublin, when it was attacked by King Muirchertach in 941, was surrounded by a wall and was rich enough to pay him tribute in *gold*, colored mantles and foodstuffs for his men.[93] Norse Saga evidence shows it to have been considered a particularly rich trading center.[94] And in 989, when the city was retaken by the native Irish under King Maelsechnaill, it again paid heavy tribute, one ounce of gold per house, which seems a tremendous sum.[95] Nor was Dublin the only important town. Waterford, Wexford, Cork and Limerick all developed into trading centers in this century.[96] When it was taken in 968 by the Irish, Limerick contained, according to our sources, jewels, gold, silver and fine Oriental silk cloth.[97] It

---

[88] On this return of Norse strength after a new expedition arrived from Norway, see H. Shetelig, *The Viking History of Western Europe*, pp. 66-70. See also *Annals of Ulster*, anno 918, and J. Young, "Note on the Norse Occupation of Ireland," in *History*, xxv (1950), 26-30.

[89] *Annals of Four Masters*, anno 939.

[90] *The Circuit of Muirchertach*, ed. Hogan (Dublin 1901), pp. 20-21.

[91] *Wars of the Gaedhil with the Gael*, I, 51.

[92] H. Shetelig, *op.cit.*, pp. 70-71. J. Ryan, "Pre-Norman Dublin," in *Jour. of Royal Soc. of Antiq. of Ireland*, I (1949), 68-73.

[93] J. Ryan, *op.cit.*, pp. 66-68. *Circuit of Muirchertach*, pp. 20-21. J. Young, *op.cit.*, p. 15.

[94] *Egils Saga*, XXII. A. Bugge, *Nordeuropäischen Verkehrswege*, p. 275.

[95] J. Ryan, *op.cit.*, p. 74. H. Shetelig, *op.cit.*, pp. 75-76.

[96] J. Ryan, *op.cit.*, pp. 66-67. T. Walsh, *Norsemen in Ireland*, pp. 25-30.

[97] *Wars of the Gaedhil with the Gael*, I, 51.

had merchants like Hfafr Hlyrickfarer who owned ships trading to England and Iceland.[98] Its commerce continued after its conquest by the Irish, since we learn that it paid an annual tribute of 365 tuns of wine to its conquerors which must have come from outside of Ireland.[99] An Irish contemporary poem of this period characterized the Norse as "sailing across the sea, certainly the gluttony of the Norse and their commerce."[100] Nor did they only trade. In the interior they cultivated the soil and helped produce surpluses of wheat and honey which were exported to Iceland and Norway.[101] Perhaps it was their influence that helped to develop the rural flax and linen industries for which Ulster soon became famous, and the dyed, red and blue *sara* cloth of the Waterford region, as well as the renowned Irish red leather goods.[102]

It is this industry and commerce which explain the development in this period of a money economy in Ireland. There is constant mention of gold and silver—in Limerick, when it was taken by the Irish in 968, and in Dublin in 941 and 989, when tributes in gold were levied on the city. Even in the countryside the same thing seems true, for Irish sources speak of a tax of one ounce of silver per year, paid by Irish householders to their Norse overlords.[103] Coin hoards in Ireland, particularly those found near Dublin, mainly in the countryside, show clearly that the silver existed for payment of such taxes.

As we have shown, Ireland's principal trade seems to have been with England, a fact amply attested to by coin finds. But it also had wider commercial contacts that linked it, by way of the Hebrides route, to Norway and even Russia. The *Laxdaele Saga* mentions a certain Gilli the Russian who purchased an Irish princess as a slave in Ireland and sold her in Iceland,[104] while the Oriental silks found in Limerick probably arrived there via the Baltic.[105] Again, however,

[98] T. Walsh, *op.cit.* A. Bugge, *The Royal Race of Dublin*, pp. 19-21.

[99] *History of Ireland*, in *Irish Text Society*, III, 238.

[100] "National Characteristics," in *Zeitschrift für Keltik Phil.*, ed. Meyer (1897), I, 112. See also the early 10th-century comment that the Norse "had the gift of habitation and commerce," in *Book of Rights*, ed. O'Donovan (Dublin 1847), p. 241.

[101] *Book of Rights*, p. 221. On the Irish trade in honey, see P. Joyce, *Social History of Ireland*, II, 100-10. On leather production, see *Keltische Verträge*, III, 127, and *Ancient Laws of Ireland*, IV, 149. See also an excellent summary on the Norse as husbandmen in J. Young, *op.cit.*, pp. 13-15.

[102] *Annals of Ulster*, II, 420-28, describes the linen trade in rural districts. See Joyce, *op.cit.*, pp. 111-13, on *sara* cloth.

[103] *Wars of the Gaedhil with the Gael*, I, 51.

[104] *Laxdaele Saga*, XII, and A. Bugge, *Nordeuropäischen Verkehrswege*, p. 275.

[105] The fine silks and other Oriental wares found in captured Limerick are believed

Scandinavian contacts are more amply proved by coin finds than by any other evidence. In a number of tenth-century Irish hoards, most of which contain Anglo-Saxon money, as we have shown, we find dirhems as well. This is true of hoards found at Claremont, Derry, Antrim, Drogheda, Lugga and Kildare.[106] Similarly, in hoards in the Hebrides and Scotland, on the route leading to Scandinavia, Moslem dirhems are to be found on Islay, in Kirkcudbrightshire and on Skye.[107] The Kirkcudbrightshire hoard alone contains 15 of these Oriental coins, which must have arrived here from the Baltic via Scandinavian intermediaries.[108]

More difficult is the problem presented by Irish commerce with the Continent, particularly with France and Spain. The fact that wine was to be found throughout the tenth century in Ireland makes it clear that such a commerce existed, probably with western French coasts, while Limerick's agreement to furnish the Irish 365 tuns of wine a year suggests that such trade must have been a regular one.[109] A number of tenth-century hoards at Mullboden in Kildare, and at Lough Lynn in County Meath, for instance, contain French deniers.[110] Equally interesting, in this respect, are Hebridean and Scottish finds. That of Inchkenneth of the late tenth century contains six coins from Quentovic and one from Normandy, a region where we know Irish slaves were to be found in this period.[111] That of Tarbat in Ross-shire, dating from 960, contains ten Aquitainian coins minted by Louis III.[112] And here we note an interesting and perhaps significant fact. All these hoards in Ireland and Scotland contain Anglo-Saxon money. But those which contain Samanid silver coins have almost no French deniers, and vice versa. It would seem, therefore, that trade with

---

by Shetelig to have come from Spain. Though this is possible, coin evidence suggests that, more likely, they arrived in Ireland from the East via the Baltic and Russia.

[106] The hoards at Lugga and Kildare each contain one Moslem dirhem. The Claremont hoard has in it 2 dirhems and that of Drogheda an unspecified number.

[107] The Kirkcudbright hoard contains one dirhem, and so does that discovered at Islay.

[108] On the 15 Moslem dirhems in the Portree hoard, see A. B. Richardson, in *Proc. of Soc. of Antiq. of Scotland*, XXVI (1891-92), 132-55.

[109] *History of Ireland*, in *Irish Text Society*, III, 238.

[110] *Num. Chron.*, new ser., XII (1871), 3, contains a brief account of the 6 Carolingian-type deniers found in the Mullboden hoard. On the Lough Lynn hoard see J. Lindsay, in *Num. Chron.*, new ser., VI (1866-67), 305-7. The earlier Delganey hoard also contains French coins.

[111] On the 6 Quentovic and one Norman deniers of this hoard, see *Proc. of Soc. of Antiq. of Scotland*, IX (1843-44), 208-18.

[112] W. Scott, in *Proc. of Soc. of Antiq. of Scotland*, XXIII (1889), 314-35.

France was in the hands of a different group of merchants than trade with Scandinavia.

Concerning commerce with Christian and Moslem Spain we are reduced to conjectures. Perhaps Vikings from Ireland participated in those small raids on Spanish Galicia that took place in 910, 926, 951, and 964, and in the two large ones which in 968-970 and 984 severely ravaged these coasts, the latter raid resulting in the sack of Lugo.[113] But there is no evidence that this led to commercial contacts. It seems more probable, therefore, that the Oriental wares, including silks, which the native Irish took as booty in Limerick in 968 came there from the Baltic rather than Spain, and that trade contacts with the Iberian peninsula must be regarded as rather problematical. Even granting this qualification, however, it must be admitted that Ireland in this period developed almost as rapidly as England, and enjoyed a commerce which stretched from the coasts of France north via the Hebrides as far as Iceland and Scandinavia. She again occupied a position of maritime importance in the Atlantic which she had not known since the days of the sixth and seventh centuries.

The other lands of the Western Atlantic colonized by the Norse also showed some signs of economic development during this period. The finds of Anglo-Saxon, French and Scandinavian coins in the Hebrides and on the west coast of Scotland indicate that close contacts were maintained with England, Ireland, France and Norway, while the textiles in graves on Eigg reflect trade as far as Flanders and the Baltic. Even the harbor at Høbn in the Orkneys, which had flourished in the ninth century and was then destroyed, probably by Harold Fairhair, late in that century, was in operation again in the tenth.[114] But the rest of Scotland, particularly its east coast, seems to have lagged far behind Ireland and England.[115]

Not so Iceland. By 930 its population, settled on small farms or homesteads about Reykjavík, had probably reached 20,000 or 30,-000.[116] Though no urban settlements existed, the Icelanders certainly

---

[113] H. Shetelig, op.cit., pp. 38-40. F. Lot, Les Invasions, pp. 160-61.

[114] Recent excavations at Høbn, accounts of which I have seen only in popular form in British periodicals, make it clear that despite its destruction in the late 9th century, Høbn was again an active port and settlement in the 10th—probably the Orkney way-station between Scandinavia and the Irish Sea.

[115] The mystery of the lack of commerce reaching Scotland's eastern coast, that classic land of the Picts, remains a perplexing one. Why we have no evidence of either Danes or Norse settling or trading there it is hard to say. Perhaps they did, but left no record or remains of their activities.

[116] L. Musset, Les Peuples scandinaves, p. 61.

engaged in commerce. The chief products that they shipped abroad seem to have been furs, a coarse cloth called *wadmal*, sheepskin coats and falcons. Tradition states that in 980-982 their first cargo was exported to Norway, consisting of cloaks and rugs of *wadmal* and sheepskin coats, six of the latter selling for one øre of silver.[117] Other trade, as noted, linked this island with England and Ireland. Slight evidence in the form of Anglo-Saxon coins and Samanid silver dirhems confirms Saga traditions of English and Scandinavian trade contacts.[118] But voyages to Norway and the British Isles did not content these hardy Icelandic mariners. They moved west into Arctic seas in search of polar bears and walrus, and by 900 appear to have discovered Greenland. By 985 Eric the Red had established on those remote shores a small colony, one that was to last almost five centuries.[119] By 985 Viking trading areas had extended all the way to the coasts of North America.

While England, Ireland and other Northern Atlantic regions were thus developing an increasing tempo of maritime activity and economic life, Ottonian Germany was gradually becoming the other great political and cultural center of Northern Europe. Unlike Anglo-Saxon England, however, the early years of the tenth century did not bring Germany political success at first. Rather they were difficult ones which saw arising on her eastern borders a serious menace, the Hungarians. In our last chapter we explained how the Magyars, called in by Arnaulf, had destroyed the Moravian kingdom and established themselves on the plain of Hungary. By 911 they had begun a career of raiding from their bases on the middle Danube which carried them on long, destructive sweeps far into Italy and Central Germany. Their raids of 924 and 926 proved especially devastating, and much of the agricultural expansion of the Germans into the valleys of lower Bavaria and Austria was checked and the work of German peasant colonists undone.[120] Cities like Pavia in Northern Italy[121] and Stras-

---

[117] O. Tønning, *Commerce and Trade in the North Atlantic 850 A.D. to 1350 A.D.* (Dissertation, Univ. of Minnesota, Minneapolis 1936), pp. 14-16. This information is based primarily upon traditions found in the *Harold Ericson Saga*, xx.

[118] The Gaulverjabaer hoard of 1020 has certain coins in it dating from these years, especially 5 Hedeby coins and 5 Samanid dirhems, which must have come from Scandinavia and the Baltic. The first were minted between 940 and 980, the second from 870 to 942. K. Eldjarn, "Gaulverjabaer Fundet," *loc.cit.*, pp. 40-50.

[119] On the discovery and settlement of Greenland, see K. Gjesset, *History of Iceland* (London 1923), and E. F. Gray, *Leif Eriksson* (Oxford 1930). See also the interesting views of Lethbridge in *Herdsmen and Hermits*, pp. 103-36.

[120] On these raids, see R. Lüttich, *Ungarnzüge in Europa im 10. Jahrhunderts*

bourg on the upper Rhine were sacked and partly destroyed.[122] Areas as widely separated as Bavaria, Swabia, Franconia and Champagne felt the fury of their attacks.[123]

Henry the Fowler, Duke of Saxony, who in 918 had been elected King of Germany, realized the necessity for taking action. To protect North Germany from Hungarian raids, he began the construction of fortresses, or bourgs, much on the order of the boroughs built in England by the House of Alfred, and raised a force of cavalry to meet the Magyars in the open field with some success.[124] He realized also the need to guard against collaboration between the Hungarians and the Slavic tribes who lived to the east. Thus it was that he began to concern himself with the lands of Eastern Germany. In 926 he was recognized as overlord by the Slavic Duke of Bohemia, who, prior to this time, had been under Bavarian influence.[125] This was followed in 928 by a winter campaign across the Elbe, in which he defeated the Helevians and constructed the bourg of Brunabor in Slavic territory. The Veletians, who lived between the Elbe and the Oder, and the Obodrites of Schleswig-Holstein then hastened to pay him tribute. In the next year, after the Sorbs farther south had been defeated, Henry built in their district another fortress bourg, that of Meissen. Soon afterwards, another great victory over the Slavs between the Elbe and the Saale resulted in a renewal of submission by Bohemia.[126] Then Henry, the east secure, turned north. In 934 he defeated the Swedish king, Gnupa, who was ruling part of Denmark, and added the rich trading center of Hedeby to his empire, establishing there a Saxon colony.[127] Hedeby was to remain German for the next half-century.

(Berlin 1920), pp. 1-136.

[121] Pavia was half-ruined in 924 after the Hungarian raid on Northern Italy, though it soon recovered. See R. S. Lopez, "Still Another Renaissance," *loc.cit.*, pp. 8-10.

[122] The effects of the Hungarian destruction of Strasbourg are visible as far away as Frisia. Prior to Strasbourg's suffering sack at the hands of the Magyars, its money was copied in Frisia. After it, Strasbourg money and copies are replaced in Frisia by the coinage of Cologne, which escaped damage. P. Boeles, *Friesland*, pp. 442-45.

[123] R. Lüttich, *Heinrich I der Deutsch* (Leipzig 1934), pp. 18-77.

[124] F. Lot, *L'Art militaire et les armées au moyen âge* (Paris 1946), pp. 142-44.

[125] Thietmar, *Chron.*, in *MGH Script.*, new ser., IX, 38.

[126] Widukind, *Chron. Saxon.*, I, 35, in *Script. in usum scholarum*, p. 60. See also F. Dvornik, *The Making of Central and Eastern Europe*, pp. 24-31, and J. W. Thompson, *Feudal Germany*, pp. 279-82.

[127] Widukind, *Chron. Saxon.*, I, 40, in *Script. in usum scholarum*, p. 80. Thietmar, *Chron.*, I, 17, in *MGH Script.*, new ser., IX, 34. See especially on this problem H.

Under his son, Otto, who succeeded him as King of Germany, the advance east into Slavic lands continued. One of Otto's principal lieutenants, Count Herman Billung, after an arduous campaign, forced both the Obodrites and the Wagrians, the latter living east of the Obodrites along the Baltic coast, to pay tribute. The new Danish ruler intervened in the struggle and rebuilt across the narrow peninsula the Dannevirke, which had been first constructed against Charlemagne more than a century before. Otto's forces crushed the Danish resistance however, and forced their king, Harold, to pay him tribute. He followed up his victory with the establishment of Christianity in Denmark by placing the three dioceses of Ribe, Aarhus and Schleswig (Hedeby) under the jurisdiction of the Archbishop of Hamburg. To counter this religious imperialism, Harold turned Christian himself, and made his bishoprics autonomous of German control, though he did not break his peace with Otto.[128] Meanwhile, successes to the north by Billung and another lieutenant of Otto's, Count Gero, continued German expansion between the Elbe and the Saale, until, by 939, this whole Slavic region was paying tribute and acknowledging a Christianity which was established by the Archbishop of Magdeburg.[129]

His concern with the north and northeast, however, did not keep Otto from an interest in the southeastern portion of his kingdom, though in his early years he could spare few forces to enforce his claims there. By 950 his power had compelled a reluctant Bohemia to return to Saxon allegiance, after an attack on Bavaria forced this all but independent duchy to accept him as ruler. Meanwhile, the Hungarians in 954 launched their most serious raid, which carried them through Bavaria, Franconia, the Meuse valley, Champagne, Burgundy, Northern Italy and back again to Hungary—a raid which

---

Jankuhn, *Ergebnisse und Probleme der Haithabugrabungen*, pp. 14-17. Inasmuch as there was a Frisian as well as a Saxon colony in Hedeby in this period, we might well consider it a German rather than a Scandinavian center, at least down to 983.

[128] On Otto's religious imperialism, which was but a continuation of Henry the Fowler's expansionism in a subtler form, see F. M. Fischer, "Politiker um Otto der Grossen," in *Hist. Studien*, cccxxix (Berlin 1938), 206-37, and F. Dvornik, *op.cit.*, pp. 48-51. On the attempted evangelization of Sweden by Hunni, Archbishop of Hamburg, in 936, see A. Hauck, *Kirchengeschichte Deutschlands* (Leipzig 1896), I, 58. The names of the Bishops of Hedeby, Ribe and Aarhus in 948 seem to show that they were of Frisian or Saxon origin. Later on this was not so. The Jellinge stone, of course, tells us that Harold Bluetooth made Denmark Christian, but not until 973 did he challenge Otto's power over Hedeby—unsuccessfully. H. Arbman, *Schweden*, pp. 19-21. F. E. Dahlmann, *Geschichte von Dänemark*, I, 78-93. G. Turville-Petrie, *The Heroic Age in Scandinavia*, pp. 88-93. L. Musset, *op.cit.*, pp. 82-84.

[129] Widukind, *Chron. Saxon.*, I, 17, in *Script. in usum scholarum*, pp. 84-85, 122-40.

saw Maastricht sacked and burnt. It was to be their last. For in the next year they were surprised and badly beaten at Lechfeld by a German force which consisted of Bavarian, Franconian and Swabian troops supported by a Bohemian contingent.[130] Licking their wounds, they returned to their homes on the Hungarian plain, gave up their raiding and settled down to become the Hungarians of history. Otto, with the Danes and Slavs along his borders forced to pay him tribute, the Hungarians checked and the independent duchies brought to heel, was the master at last of Germany and of Central Europe.

This, however, did not content him. In a few years he moved across the Alps into the quarreling, disorderly lands of Northern Italy, conquered them and pressed on to Rome. There he assumed the Imperial crown of Charlemagne as Emperor of the Holy Roman Empire.[131] From that time on, down to the first years of the reign of Otto III, his grandson, Germany remained peaceful, strong and united, the most important political and economic center in Northern Europe.

In Germany a certain dislocation was reflected in the economic life of the country for a period after 911, caused, no doubt, by disorders attendant upon the Hungarian incursions into the land. We know, however, that under Louis the Child (899-911) a *telonium* and the privilege of striking money was granted to Maastricht, while Huy, Dinant and Namur also possessed mints.[132] In the upper Meuse valley some economic activity also continued, since Mouzon, Verdun and Toul minted coins during the reign of Charles the Simple (898-923).[133] Between 911 and 936, however, we find little reference to these centers. One notices something of the same thing happening along the Rhine and Moselle. Between 898 and 923, Cologne, Strasbourg and Trier all possessed mints in active operation, and finds of Strasbourg money and copies made from them in Frisian coin hoards seem to show continued trade from this region to the upper Rhine.[134] In 918 there is

---

[130] Widukind, *Chron. Saxon.*, III, 8, in *ibid.*, p. 108. F. Dvornik, *op.cit.*, pp. 36-38. On the decisive battle of Lechfeld, see *Vita S. Oudalrichi*, in *MGH Script.*, IV, 377, and especially R. Lüttich, *op.cit.*, pp. 150-70. See also H. Bresslau, "Die Schlacht auf dem Lechfelde," in *Hist. Zeitschrift*, XCVII-XCVIII (1906-7), 448-62, and D. Schäfer, "Die Ungarnschlacht von 955," in *ibid.*, XCVII (1906), 538-51.

[131] On Otto's advance into Italy, see H. Holzmann, *Kaiser Otto der Grosse* (Berlin 1936), pp. 171-253; R. Cessi, *Venezia Ducale*, I, 60-83; and A. R. Lewis, *op.cit.*, pp. 187-92.

[132] *Cartulaire de St. Lambert de Liége*, ed. Bormans and Dieudonné, I, 13. Blanchet and Dieudonné, *op.cit.*, p. 380.

[133] M. Prou, *Catalogue des monnaies carolingiennes*, pp. LXXX-LXXXV.

[134] *Ibid.* On Frisian copies of Strasbourg coins, see P. Boeles, *Friesland*, pp. 440-44.

mention in our sources of merchants in Wurzburg.[135] And we learn that in 920 the Bishop of Utrecht returned to refortify his episcopal residence in this trading place. Such is the limit of our scanty information. But evidence from Hedeby and other Baltic lands shows that trade with the Rhine was more active than we would otherwise suspect. Badorf pottery, produced between Coblenz and Cologne, continued to arrive in this region without a break, as shown by archeological excavations, and so did the new Pingsdorf ware which began to be manufactured along the Rhine about 900.[136] Nor did Ulfberht swords, produced in workshops along the lower Rhine, cease to reach Scandinavia and other northern regions during these years.[137] We can assume, therefore, an economic activity along the lower Rhine and in Frisia all through the rather depressing years of the early tenth century.

When Otto I becomes ruler of the land, we notice an almost immediate upsurge of economic life. Along the Scheldt, where Ghent was last mentioned as a trading center about 875, we now hear of renewed activity and a double *portus*, one about the Abbey of St. Bavon in 966 and a new one near the Castle and St. Pierre in 941.[138] Along the lower Meuse in 935-937, Dinant and Namur were referred to as ports, too.[139] And Maastricht, sacked by the Hungarians in 954, rose from its ashes to coin money between 973 and 983.[140] We hear that by 987 it possessed a bridge across the Meuse as well.[141] Visé in 983 held a fair at which cattle, cloth, iron and metalware were sold.[142] The right to levy tolls had been accorded Dinant, Namur, Huy, Visé and Maastricht by 985.[143] Apparently trade between this Meuse valley region and the Rhinelands existed, because under Otto III we

[135] *Capitularia Reg. Franc.*, I, 123.

[136] F. Ganshof, *Les Villes entre Loire et Rhin*, p. 20.

[137] On this pottery found in unbroken sequence in Frisian sites, see P. Boeles, *Friesland*, pp. 430-38. At Hedeby, see H. Jankuhn, *Die Ausgrabungen in Haithabu 1937-39* (Berlin 1943), pp. 176-89.

[138] H. Jankuhn, "Ein Ulfberht Schwert aus der Elbe," *loc.cit.*, and his "Sechs Karten zum Handel des 10. Jahrhunderts in Westlichen Ostseebecken," in *Archeologia Geographica*, I (1950), 5-23. These Ulfberht swords, Jankuhn shows, are also found in unbroken sequence from 850 to 950 in East Prussia, Esthonia, Prague and especially along the Norwegian coast, a strong preserve of Frisian merchants from Carolingian times.

[139] *Translatio S. Eugenii*, in *Ann. Bolland*, III, 46-55. F. Rousseau, *La Meuse et le pays mosan*, pp. 69-70.

[140] *Ibid.*, pp. 71-72. H. Dannenberg, *Die deutschen Münzen der sachsischer und fränkischer Kaiserzeit* (Berlin 1876-78), pp 17-215.

[141] *Cartulaire de St. Lambert de Liége*, ed. Bormans and Dieudonné, I, 23.

[142] P. Rolland, *op.cit.*, pp. 78-79.

[143] *Ibid.*

find that the money of Cologne was copied at Maastricht, Dinant, Huy, Liége, Namur, Visé, Thuin and even Brussels.[144] On the upper Meuse, Verdun, in 985, had a merchant quarter surrounded by walls and its merchants were mentioned as trading with Spain in 949 and 953.[145]

We find equally vital developments taking place along the Rhine. Strasbourg seems to have lost its importance after its sack by the Hungarians in the first part of the century, but Cologne replaced it as a foreign trade center. Now, by the mid-tenth century, it was Cologne's coinage which was placed in Frisian coin hoards,[146] and its money was copied along the Meuse. Mainz by 949 was the home of Liutfred, a rich merchant whom Otto I sent to Constantinople on diplomatic business.[147] In 973 an Arab traveler who visited Mainz reported that silver dirhem Samanid money was in use there and spices were offered for sale.[148] Another author, writing between 966 and 967, said that when Otto I attacked Mainz in 953, it was an *urbs nobilia* and *opulenta*.[149] Worms, farther south along the Rhine, in 947 still had a colony of Frisians, probably merchants.[150] Between 972 and 994 grain merchants were spoken of as coming to Regensburg, in carts,[151] while nearby there was mention of tin, copper and lead imported from England.

Near the mouths of the Rhine, in Frisia and along the coast of Northwestern Germany we notice similar growth and economic development. In these years Thiel and Deventer succeeded to the position which Dorestad had earlier occupied.[152] Frisian trading centers like Leewarden, Bolsward and Dokkum began to coin money in the last years of the century,[153] and Stavoren in 991 was at least

[144] F. Rousseau, *La Meuse*, pp. 73-74. A. Engel and R. Serrure, *Traité de numismatique du moyen âge*, II, 563-64.
[145] *Mir. S. Bertini*, in *Acta Sanct. Boll.*, Sept., III, 597; Liudprand of Cremona, *Antapodosis*, in *Script. in usum scholarum*, p. 155; and *Vita Johannis Gorzensis*, in *MGH Script.*, IV, 369, all relate to this trade with Spain. On the fortifications of the Bourg of Verdun, see Richier, *Historia*, III, in *MGH Script.*, III, 629. Nearby Reims in 923-25 was still producing fine metalwork. Flodoard, *Hist. rem. eccl.*, IV, 19.
[146] P. Boeles, *Friesland*, pp. 444-45.
[147] Liudprand, *Antapodosis*, in *Script. in usum scholarum*, p. 153.
[148] G. Jacob, *Arabische Berichterstätter aus dem 10. Jahrhundert* (Berlin 1896), p. 31.
[149] *Vita Buionis*, in *MGH Script.*, IV, 259.
[150] *Alpertus*, in *ibid.*, p. 704.
[151] Othloni, *Vita S. Wolfkandi*, in *ibid.*, p. 537.
[152] H. Poelman, *op.cit.*, pp. 115-19.
[153] See coins dating from this period in Finnish hoards described by H. Salmo, *Deutsche Münzen in vorgeschichtlichen Funden Finnlands* (Helsinki 1948), pp. 436-44.

rich enough to be sacked by Danish pirates.[154] The merchants of Bremen were taken under the protection of the Emperor in 965,[155] while Hamburg, up to its destruction by the Slavs in 983, seems to have been an important trading center indeed.[156] Hedeby, under German control after 934, contained a colony of Saxon merchants and, in addition to coining money, possessed a Frisian colony.[157]

A similar economic development is to be found in the interior of Saxony between the Elbe and the Rhine. In 956 Otto I gave a Saxon monastery special concessions regarding tolls on merchants who were going and coming between the Rhine and the Elbe and the Saale.[158] Merseburg grew until it had a colony of merchants settled there, including some Jews.[159] Magdeburg also grew from a frontier post to a center of trading importance. Its merchants seem to have visited Bardowic, and in 975 Otto II granted them exemption from tolls at Mainz, Cologne, Thiel and Bardowic, an exemption which according to the charter goes back to the time of Otto I.[160] Bardowic, which traded with the Obodrites and Polabes and nearby Brunswick, also gained in importance in this period.[161] So did Lunéville, with its salt mines.[162] The privileges which Otto III granted Gandersheim, Magdeburg, Mainz, Cologne and Dortmund show how these centers continued to grow economically.[163] Equally important were the twenty-nine new market rights which German Emperors granted trading centers in the last years of this century.[164]

This increased commercial activity is fully reflected in German products reaching the Baltic after 950. Hedeby's excavations contain glass, arms, millstones, pottery, jewelry and rings from the Rhine-

[154] P. Boeles, *Friesland*, p. 450.

[155] *MGH Diplom. reg. et imp. Germaniae*, I, 422.

[156] P. Kletler, *Nordwesteuropas Verkehr*, pp. 102-3. For recent archeological evidence on 10th-century Hamburg, see V. Kallerman, "Die Stadtbefestingungen," in *Hammaburg*, III (1949), 15-49.

[157] G. Jacob, *Arabische Berichterstätter*, p. 33.

[158] P. Kletler, *op.cit.*, pp. 172-74.

[159] Thietmar, *Chron.*, in *MGH Script.*, III, 759.

[160] *Vita S. Adalberti Episcopi*, in *ibid.*, II, 359.

[161] W. Vogel, "Wik-orte et Wikinger," in *Hansische Geschichtsblätter*, LX (1935), 28-31.

[162] W. Reineck, *Geschichte der Stadt Luneberg* (Luneberg 1933), pp. 180-81.

[163] See the recent views of E. Ennen in "Neuere Arbeiten zur Geschichte des nordwesteuropas Stadtwesens im Mittelalter," in *Viert. für Soz- und Wirtschaft*, XXVIII (1948), 481-517.

[164] On these "market rights," see discussion in P. Kletler, *op.cit.*, pp. 135-59, and E. Ennen, *op.cit.*, pp. 490-503.

lands.[165] Birka and other Swedish sites reveal the same variety of Rhenish products and also Frisian cloth.[166] Probably the wine, salt, tin and lead which reached Hedeby in this period arrived via Frisian and Saxon intermediaries.[167] It also seems that the number of workshops along the Rhine producing fine swords increased, since we find that about 950 the Ulfberht swords had as successors weapons bearing the names of other craftsmen or production centers.[168]

Our texts provide further evidence of the Empire's external trade. The famous Toll of London of 991 reveals that men of Flanders and of Huy, Nivelles and Namur were going to trade in London. So were those referred to as "men of the Emperor," which probably means merchants from Frisia, Thiel, Deventer and other parts of Germany.[169] In the first years of the eleventh century, we hear of a guild of Frisian merchants at Sigtuna in Sweden that may, like those found at Hedeby, go back to tenth-century days.[170] Mainz, judging from Liutfred, traded with Venice and Northern Italy, while Verdun was in commercial touch with Spain. Some trade reached the Slavs in Central Europe also, probably carried on by those Jewish merchants mentioned by Thietmar as being in Merseburg, or by Ibn Jacub in 973 as trafficking with Prague.[171] Perhaps it was they who carried those Bavarian bowls produced near Regensburg to Gotland and Sweden.[172]

This foreign trade of Germany to the north, originating in the Meuse valley, the Rhinelands, Flanders, Frisia and Saxony, is amply confirmed and our knowledge even amplified by coin hoard evidence. In Frisian hoards, in the mid-Rhine region[173] and in Switzerland,[174] discovery of Samanid silver dirhems links these areas and this route with Baltic commerce, a route already made clear by Rhineland objects found in archeological sites in Scandinavia.

Even more impressive, however, are the German coins minted in

[165] H. Jankuhn, *Ergebnisse und Probleme der Haithabugrabungen*, pp. 51-59. B. Rohwer, *Friesische Handel in Mittelalter*, pp. 12-26.

[166] H. Arbman, *Birka*, pp. 1-108, and A. Geijer, *Birka*, III, 22-47, give a description of these finds.

[167] H. Jankuhn, *op.cit.*, pp. 51-54, and *Haithabu 1937-39*, pp. 157-217.

[168] H. Jankuhn, "Ein Ulfberht Schwert aus der Elbe," *loc.cit.*, pp. 137-44.

[169] F. Liebermann, *Gesetze*, I, 232.

[170] On runic evidence for this, see A. Bugge, "Altschwedische Gilden," in *Viert. für Soz- und Wirtschaft*, VI (1913), 141-44.

[171] B. Jacob, *Arabische Berichterstätter*, p. 12.

[172] H. Arbman, *Schweden und das Karolingische Reich*, pp. 110-14.

[173] G. Jacob, *op.cit.*, p. 31, tells of the Moslem traveler who found Oriental spices in Mainz and saw Samanid silver in use.

[174] On these hoards, see map in S. Bolin and J. Carlsson, *Historisk Atlas* (Malmö 1947), p. 10.

these years, from a series of hoards extending from Iceland to Finland throughout the Northern Seas. While English coins minted prior to 985 are occasional in such hoards, German ones are numerous, seeming to show that until late in the tenth century commerce from Otto's Empire to the Scandinavian north was greater in volume than that from England.[175] The definitive work on these tenth- and eleventh-century German coins, particularly those of Gotland, has still to appear, but enough is known to give some picture of German commerce during this period.

In Iceland, for instance, there exists one great find of foreign coins, the Gaulverjabaer hoard found near Reykjavík and interred about 1020. It contains about 180 Anglo-Saxon coins and about 150 German. Almost all the English ones, however, are late, dating from the time of Aethelred II. Many of the German ones—the greater part, indeed —are much earlier in date and come from Cologne (the majority), Mainz, Worms, Strasbourg, Regensburg, Huy, Verdun and Hedeby.[176] Norway's hoards show coins in even larger numbers from mints located in the region of the Meuse, the Rhinelands, Franconia, Saxony and even Swabia and Bavaria. That of Traaen, far inland from Oslo, dating from 1016, contains ten Anglo-Saxon pennies and 106 from Germany, mainly from the Rhinelands and Saxony, with two from Hedeby (940-980).[177] The slightly later hoard of Dronnegest contains 511 German, as against 363 Anglo-Saxon, coins. The German ones begin with coins minted at the time of Otto I.[178] The Josing find includes numerous Cologne pennies of Otto I's time, as well as tenth-century coins from Mainz, Worms, Strasbourg and Bavaria.[179] Another hoard from Sand near Trondelag contains 64 German coins, including early ones from Cologne, Verdun, Strasbourg and Regensburg.[180]

Danish hoards of the period repeat the pattern. Large numbers of tenth-century German coins have been discovered, always in con-

---

[175] This general point is made by N. L. Rasmusson in *Foreign Coins in Swedish Coin Finds*, p. 43. He notes that this was particularly true starting about 950.

[176] K. Eldjarn, "Gaulverjabaer Fundet," in *Nord. Numis. Arsskrift* (1948), pp. 39-62.

[177] L. B. Stevenson, "Myntfundet frä Traaen," in *Spog. og. Hist. Alfande viede Sophus Bugge Minker* (Christiania 1908), pp. 232-39.

[178] V. Ronander, "Myntfunded frä Sand," in *T.V.S. Skrifter*, No. 4 (1922), 18-27.

[179] O. A. Digre, "Myntfundet frä Donningensgt," in *Saert. av. Arst. for Det. Kgl. Norske Vidsk Silsk. Museet.* (1950), pp. 217-35.

[180] J. Peterson, "Et nyt Sølomyntfund frä Rogaland," in *Stavanger Museums Arsskrift fur 1924-25*, XVIII (1943), 108-15.

junction with Anglo-Saxon money, in hoards located around Hedeby and on the Danish islands. Of the 4,000-odd German silver pieces in these finds, about one-third were minted in the period prior to 985.[181] Gotland, which has the greatest hoards in the Baltic, furnishes even more evidence.[182] Up to the last years of the tenth century, German coins far outnumbered Anglo-Saxon. Then, for a period, we find that those from England were more numerous. Perhaps three finds from this island make this clear. At Digerakaa a hoard dating from about the year 1000 contains 1,300 silver pennies. Of these, 832 are German, mainly Otto-Adelaide pennies and Stade coins of Count Henry the Good (976-1016).[183] The Hagvats hoard, dating from about 995, has 580 German coins, as against ten English ones,[184] while that of Folhagen, five years later in date, contains 361 German coins and only four from Anglo-Saxon mints.[185]

From Finland we have even more detailed information, since German coins found in hoards there have been carefully studied and classified. They show a total of some 4,000 German silver pennies from 36 sites. About 1,000 of them were minted prior to 985. The major portion, about 750 in all, are Otto-Adelaide pennies, and another 190 are from Cologne mints. A few come from Metz and Verdun on the upper Meuse and a considerable number from Andernach, Mainz and Speyer on the upper Rhine. One is from Strasbourg and six from Regensburg.[186] Finds in Russia and in the Eastern Baltic follow the same pattern as Finnish ones.

Judging from these coin hoards, then, an active commerce linked Germany to Iceland, Norway, Denmark and the whole Baltic area prior to 985. These links were closest with the Rhine valley from Strasbourg to Frisia and also with the Meuse, Cologne being the most important center of such trade. A few other regions, Franconia, Swabia and even Regensburg in Bavaria, also traded with the north. Thus we find confirmed a commerce of which both our texts and archeology have already given indication.

To summarize, Germany in the first years of the tenth century, despite Hungarian incursions, maintained some of the commerce

---

[181] R. Skovmand, De Danske Skattefund, pp. 21-33.

[182] Gotland's 687 hoards from Viking times contain as of present count 38,000 German coins and about 21,000 Anglo-Saxon ones—not to mention some 40,000 Arabic dirhems. M. Stenberger, Die Schatzfunde Gotlands, II, 603-18.

[183] Ibid., pp. 19-20.   [184] Ibid., pp. 74-75.

[185] Ibid., pp. 21-24.

[186] H. Salmo, op.cit., pp. 337-46, with an analysis table and a map.

which she had had since Carolingian times with Scandinavia and the Baltic. After 950 she increased her trade in this direction, all the way from Iceland to Finland, with such commerce originating mainly in the Rhinelands. At the same time, a certain commercial impetus spread east from the Rhine to form new trading centers in Saxony up to the Elbe and the Saale, and revitalized the trade and economic life of the Meuse valley and even Flanders. Some commerce is found along the upper Danube as well. Such evidence makes it seem clear that though Ottonian Germany after 950 had contacts of some importance with Italy[187] and even Spain,[188] she looked north rather than south, commercially speaking. It is in Saxony, Frisia, the lower Rhinelands and the lower Meuse valley, facing the Northern Seas, that commercial growth seems clearest, while even Franconian, Swabian and Bavarian trade reached the North. Like England, the Germany of the Ottos, despite its Mediterranean connections, was essentially part of a trading area which now centered around the Northern Seas.

Scandinavia, so closely connected with England and the Germany of the Ottos, also saw changes take place during these years which separated the Viking Age from that of Svein and Canute. The chief one, from a political standpoint, was the reappearance of a strong kingdom of Denmark. In 911 there were two principal centers of power in Scandinavia: a Norwegian kingdom, united by Harold Fairhair, which had a certain authority and influence over Norse colonies in the Shetlands, Orkneys, Faroes and beyond in the Western Atlantic; and a Swedish state which included the Uppland, Gotaland, Bleckinge, Oland, some of the Danish islands and Hedeby, and also some control over Eastern Baltic lands in Courland, Samland and

[187] Trade with Italy in 911, 917 and 949 was mentioned as passing across the Alps by way of St. Gall. A. R. Lewis, *op.cit.*, p. 179. Note that the first two dates are before the great Hungarian raids which started in 924. As for Oriental spices which were found at Cambrai in this period, according to the *Polyptype of Abbot Irmirion*, II, 334, and at Mainz in 973, according to our Arab traveler (G. Jacob, *op.cit.*, p. 31), we cannot say whether they arrived via a Mediterranean Alpine route or by way of the Baltic. Since Samanid silver was also mentioned at Mainz, one may suspect the Baltic-Russian route as more probable. We also know that in the mid-9th century, according to the *Vita Rimberti*, silks reached Hamburg via the Baltic, but we cannot be sure by what route the fine silks worn by Matilda, wife of Henry the Fowler, reached Northern Germany. E. Sabbe, "L'Importation des tissus," *loc.cit.*, pp. 833-35. Again, in this period, the Baltic route seems the most probable.
[188] Only Verdun, of all Otto's domains, seems to have traded with Spain, though Otto did send Abd-ar-Rahman III an embassy to persuade him to remove the Saracen pirates from their nests at Garde Frainet and the Alps. A. R. Lewis, *op.cit.*, p. 220.

Esthonia. Gotland seems to have been independent, and Jutland was under a local dynasty allied to Norway.

This situation was changed by Henry the Fowler. His defeat of Gnupa, the Swedish king of part of Denmark, and his occupation of Hedeby appear to have broken the power of Sweden in the Western Baltic.[189] Swedish rulers were replaced here by a certain Hardecnut (Hardegan), perhaps from the Norse royal house. His son, Gorm, began to unite Denmark, according to the Jellinge Stone. But Gorm and his son and successor, Harold Bluetooth, were not very successful against the Saxon German rulers. Hedeby remained a German colony, while Denmark had to accept Christianity in 948 at the hands of the victorious Germans, and this placed the Danish bishoprics of Ribe, Aarhus and Schleswig under the control of the Archbishop of Hamburg-Bremen.[190]

During the next four decades, Harold Bluetooth gradually began to unite and strengthen his Danish kingdom. At first he did not challenge his Ottonian overlords, other than to gain control of the Danish church by turning Christian himself and checking the influence of Bremen over Danish bishoprics. Then he moved to acquire firm control over Jutland, Scania and the Danish islands which formed the heart of his realm. From this nucleus, he pushed east and west. In the Baltic he appears to have concluded a firm alliance with the rather mysterious, partly Slavic, fortress of Jomsburg, at the mouth of the Oder, near the rising trading city of Wollin. This gave him control of the South Baltic coast, at least as far as the Oder, and extending into the new rising Polish state of Miezko. Perhaps he was acting here in alliance with this Polish prince, who in these years was adding the Pomeranian coast to his kingdom.[191]

---

[189] On the runic evidence that Gnupa, or Chubna, of the Swedish royal house ruled Hedeby and some of the Danish islands up to 934, see H. Jankuhn, *Ergebnisse und Probleme der Haithabugrabungen*, pp. 14-17.

[190] A. Hauck, *Kirchengeschichte Deutschlands*, I, 58. F. Dvornik, *op.cit.*, pp. 48-51. L. Musset, *op.cit.*, pp. 82-84.

[191] On the development of a united Danish kingdom by Harold Bluetooth, see E. Arup, *Danmarks Historie*, I, 122-45; Widukind, *Chron.*, III, 65, in *MGH Script.*, III, 462; and especially S. Bollin, "Danmark och Tyskland under Harold Gormsson," in *Scandia*, LV (1931), 113-88. Harold allied himself with the Obodrites at first by marrying a daughter of Misijov, the ruler of this Slavic people. L. Musset, *op.cit.*, pp. 80-83. Most of our information on his relations with the Jomsburgvikings comes from two Sagas, the *Knytlingsaga* and the *Jomviking Saga*. Most scholars believe these freebooters were established at or near Wollin at the mouth of the Oder. However, some prefer the island of Rügen. In either case, they controlled the Oder entrance into the Baltic. On the relations between Harold and Miezko of Poland, which became close as Miezko advanced to the Baltic, see F. Dvornik, *op.cit.*, pp. 88-89.

Towards the west it was Norway which attracted the Danish king's attention, particularly the Vik region about Oslo fjord. When Harold Fairhair died in 945, Norway was filled with turmoil and civil war, caused by disputes between Harold's heirs. The two principal contenders for the Norse throne were Haakon the Good and Eric Blood-Axe. Harold Bluetooth supported Eric, who had married his sister, Gunhild. Eric was unsuccessful, however, and was driven out of the land in 948 to die in England a few years later trying to hold the kingdom of York. Relations between Norway and Denmark continued hostile for almost twenty years, until Haakon died in 966. Danish forces three times invaded the land and three times were driven out again. But Harold was nothing if not persistent. In 966 he intervened again, this time in support of his nephews, the sons of Eric Blood-Axe. When they proved incapable of governing Norway, he turned to ally himself with the most powerful of the Norse non-royal families, the Jarls of Trondheim. With the help of Jarl Haakon of this family, he at last conquered the Vik, and installed there as a puppet king Harold Grenze, a grandson of Harold Fairhair. Jarl Haakon, nominally a vassal, but actually an independent ally of the Danish king, ruled Western Norway.[192]

Successful in Norway at last, Harold felt strong enough to throw off the German yoke and retake Hedeby, the richest city in the land. Therefore, when Otto I died in 973, he attacked Germany with the support of Haakon, his Norwegian ally. This campaign proved a failure and caused Haakon and Harold to part company in 974, when the great Jarl of Trondheim rejected Danish overlordship. Harold countered by sending the Jomsburgvikings of Wollin north against his former ally. They were badly defeated in the great naval battle of Hjorunegvar, south of Nidaros. But the Vik remained Danish. Then the tide turned in Harold's favor. In 983 he joined the Slavs in their great rising against their German masters. Their victories, including the burning of Hamburg and the destruction of Ottonian frontier fortresses between the Elbe and the Oder, made it possible for him to regain Hedeby at last and add it to his kingdom.[193] Just before his death, in 986, Harold turned his attention to Sweden, using

[192] G. Turville-Petrie, *op.cit.*, pp. 115-21. L. Musset, *op.cit.*, pp. 80-82.
[193] G. Turville-Petrie, *op.cit.*, pp. 122-29. L. Musset, *op.cit.*, pp. 82-84. On the great Slavic rising of 983, see Thietmar, *Chron.*, in *MGH*, new ser., IX, 118-21, and Helmhold, *Chronicle of the Slavs*, ed. Tschan (London 1935), p. 72. On its effects on Germany, see J. W. Thompson, *Feudal Germany*, pp. 790-805.

the same strategy which had proved so successful in Norway. He supported a certain Sigtrygg as a pretender to the Swedish throne of Uppsala and backed him with a fleet, which probably included the Jomsburgvikings as a nucleus. Sigtrygg failed in his attempt, and Eric Segersall kept his Swedish throne, but this intervention in Swedish affairs foreshadowed later activities there by Canute and Svein.[194]

A strong, united, Christian kingdom of Denmark had appeared by 985, then, completely altering the political pattern in Scandinavia. This kingdom, the work of Harold Bluetooth, consisted of Jutland down to and including Hedeby, the Danish islands, Norway's Vik and Scania, and a close alliance with the formidable Jomsburgvikings and perhaps also Miezko's Poland. Only the Jarls of Trondheim and the Swedish king of Uppsala still maintained their independence. The basis of Svein's and Canute's great maritime empire had already been laid before the last years of the tenth century.

It is unfortunate that our information about these years, so full, thanks to the Sagas, on Norse and Danish political developments, is so scant concerning Sweden. We do not know what happened in Sweden between the time of King Olaf and King Gnupa, in the first years of the century, and the reign of Eric Segersall in its closing decades. It does seem clear, however, that Sweden lost, in these years, the control of the Baltic which she had previously maintained. Courland, Samland and Denmark threw off Sweden's yoke soon after 900, and Gotland remained independent, while Denmark's close alliance with the Jomsburgvikings seems to have placed southern Baltic shores under Danish influence.[195]

On the other hand, there is evidence of some continuing Swedish strength, particularly in the later years of the tenth century. Miezko, ruler of Poland, for instance, appears to have married his daughter, Gunhild, to Eric Segersall of Sweden prior to her marriage to Svein,

[194] F. Dvornik, *op.cit.*, pp. 86-89, insists that by 985 Otto III and Miezko were closely allied against Denmark and the Baltic Slavs and that Miezko gained Stettin as a result. On their relations, see *Annales Quedlinburgenses*, in *MGH Script.*, III, 66-67, and Thietmar, *Chron.*, in *MGH*, new ser., IX, 141. This policy may also have led to the marriage of Miezko's daughter to Eric Segersall of Sweden in this year.

[195] Swanstrom and Palmstierna, *Hist. de Suède*, pp. 15-16. L. Musset, *op.cit.*, p. 84. On the probable independence of Gotland from the Swedish mainland during these years, as claimed in the *Gutsaga*, see A. Bugge, *Die nordeuropäischen Verkehrswege*, pp. 236-37, and especially H. N. Sonyrwigg, *Gotland under Aldrae Medeltid* (Lund 1940), pp. 31-106. On Lettland and Courland's independence from Sweden after 900, see F. Balodis, *Det Aldsta Lettland*, pp. 144-263. B. Nerman, in *Sveriges Första Storehetstid*, pp. 177-205, probably exaggerates Uppland Sweden's power in the Baltic during these years.

son of Harold Bluetooth.[196] And the number of Swedish Varangians who entered Russia to serve in the armies of both Swiatoslav and Vladimir of Kiev shows a continuing tradition of alliance between the royal houses of Uppsala and Russia.[197] Indeed, it was to Sweden that Vladimir fled from Novgorod, when he was expelled from Russia by his brother in his early years, and from there that he gained the support to win his Kievan throne.[198] Probably by 985 Swedish monarchs had some of the political strength which was to be manifested later in the reigns of Olaf Skottkonung and Arnund Jacob.

Scandinavia, now composed of a powerful Denmark, a divided Norway and a Sweden of some stature, was much affected by the economic currents and trade growth in the Northern Seas during the tenth century. For the important trade routes which linked the lands of Northern Europe together in commerce went to Scandinavia or past its shores. These trade routes of this period are worth noting with some care. They started along the coast of Western Norway, where Halagoland, with its cod-fisheries and fur trade with the Finns and the White Sea, had some economic importance.[199] Proceeding down the coast of Norway, they branched off near the present city of Bergen. One route went west to reach Iceland and Greenland by way of the Shetlands and Faroes, or Ireland and Western England by way of the Inner Hebrides passage. Some trade may have proceeded more directly to Yorkshire and Eastern Britain from western Norse shores. A more important route, however, continued down the coast to Oslo fjord, where earlier the trading place of Skringissal had existed.[200]

[196] L. Musset, op.cit., pp. 158-60, on Gunhild, daughter of Miezko, who was the mother of Olaf Skottkonung of Sweden by her first marriage to Eric Segersall and of Canute of Denmark by her second marriage to Svein.

[197] On the close connections between the Kievan house of Rurik and Sweden, see S. F. Cross, "Medieval Russian Contacts with the West," in Speculum, x (1935), 138-41.

[198] Ibid. See also his "Yaroslav the Wise in Norse Tradition," in Speculum, IV (1929), 207-14.

[199] After sailing north to the White Sea to procure Arctic products, Ottar began his voyage south from this point. Alfred's Orosius, ed. Sweet, p. 18. Saga tradition found in the Egils Saga, VII, also speaks of important fisheries in the Lofoten Islands nearby. The cod from these fisheries along with furs were exported to England. See A. Bugge, op.cit., pp. 229-31. Here also was a trading spot, perhaps going back to the 9th century, called Bjorkey. On this trade, see L. Musset, op.cit., pp. 70-72, and R. Henning, "Die nordwesteuropäischen Pelzhandel," in Viert. für Soz- und Wirtschaft, XXIII (1930), 315-78.

[200] Ottar's voyage along the coast south described in Alfred's Orosius shows this route being used in the late 9th century, while the finds of Samanid silver scattered in

Here the route branched again. One branch proceeded down Denmark's west coast to Ribe and on to Frisia and the Rhinelands.[201] The other entered the Baltic, by way of the Kattegat, and continued past Aarhus to Hedeby.[202] Still another proceeded east from the Kattegat to skirt Scania and continue on towards Gotland, Birka and Novgorod.[203]

From Denmark's Ribe and Hedeby, particularly the latter, routes led west to England and south to the Rhinelands, Flanders and perhaps Rouen. Those from Ribe went direct; those from Hedeby went by way the Eide-Schlee passage across the Jutland peninsula.[204] In the Baltic, Hedeby was linked to routes which either passed directly along South Baltic shores to Wollin on the Oder, and on east to Truso at the mouth of the Neimen,[205] or proceeded by way of Swedish shores to Gotland, Birka, Finland and Russia.[206] From Gotland and Birka some routes led to South Baltic shores,[207] but the more important ones led to Russia via the Dvina or the Gulf of Finland. From

---

hoards along the coast, in H. Holst, *op.cit.*, pp. 56-112, show that it remained active in the 10th.

[201] This again was an old route leading to Frisia and the mouths of the Rhine. Finds of Carolingian coins dating from the early 9th century indicate that it was in use then. Finds of Ulfberht swords and German coins illustrate the same thing in the 10th. See especially H. Jankuhn, "Sechs Karten zum Handel des 10. Jahrhunderts," *loc.cit.*, pp. 7-18.

[202] Ottar followed this route in the late 9th century. Its use in the 10th is revealed by finds of Hedeby coinage and other objects from this century in the Vik region of Norway. H. Jankuhn, *op.cit.*, pp. 8-18.

[203] Little is known of this route in the 9th century, except that finds of Samanid and Abbassid silver along the Norwegian coast seem to show it to have been in operation. So, too, does the account of the battle of Haffsfjord, where it is said, in the *Saga of Harold Fairhair*, that Harold supplied his warband with "Eastern girls and silks." In the 10th century, both Samanid silver in Norse hoards and Saga tradition reveal an active connection between Norway and Russia.

[204] Adam of Bremen later speaks of Ribe as a port trading directly with England. English coins found in Danish hoards, some dating from Edward the Elder's time, show that this route was active early in this century. R. Shovmand, *op.cit.*, pp. 31-45.

[205] Again it is *Alfred's Orosius*, with its account of Wulfstan's voyage from Hedeby to Truso, that illustrates this route in operation in the late 9th century. For the 10th century, the chief proof of activity is the Hedeby coinage found in such large amounts in Poland. See H. Jankuhn, *op.cit.*, pp. 8-23.

[206] In the mid-9th century, Rimbert's *Vita Anskari* shows an active trade reaching Birka along this route. Finds of Hedeby coinage and other Hedeby manufactured objects about the Malar Sea, in Gotland and in eastern Baltic lands—as well as German coins everywhere—show it to have been even more important in the 10th century. See H. Jankuhn, *op.cit.*, pp. 8-23, on finds of Hedeby coinage, etc., and H. Salmo, *op.cit.*, and F. Balodis, *op.cit.*, pp. 88-144, on German coins in Finnish and Lithuanian coin hoards.

[207] The best proof of this route's activity in the 10th century lies in those Bavarian jars found in the Swedish Uppland and especially at Gotland. H. Arbman, *Schweden*, pp. 110-14.

there they either reached Kiev by way of Smolensk and Novgorod, or the Caspian by way of Lake Onega, Rostov and the Volga.[208]

Such routes explain the course of much of Scandinavian history in the tenth century. In general, those leading to Iceland, Ireland and Western Britain were always under Norwegian domination, while those leading to Russia and the Eastern Baltic from Gotland and Birka were Swedish-controlled. But in the center, past Denmark, lay the most vital ones, linking the two economic regions, East and West. They were subject to intense dispute, particularly the Eider-Schlee route from Hedeby to the North Sea, and the Kattegat or Skagerrak route farther north. In 911 Norway, by dominating Jutland, was in control of the Kattegat-Skagerrak passage, while Sweden, by taking Hedeby, controlled the Eider-Schlee outlet from the Baltic. When Henry the Fowler defeated the Swedes in 934 and took Hedeby, he established German control of one vital passage, the southern one, a control which Germany maintained for half a century. Meanwhile, the rising Danish kingdom of Harold Bluetooth strove through its intervention in Norway to get control of the Vik and thus complete domination of the northern route. By 966 this effort had ended in success for the Danes and a few years later, in 983, the Eider-Schlee passage and Hedeby fell to Denmark, too. Thus, by 985, Denmark could control all trade passing from East to West by way of the Baltic. In addition, through its influence at Wollin, it came into possession of a route through Poland to Russia which by-passed Swedish-controlled commercial connections in the Eastern Baltic. Denmark's long struggle with the Ottos, her stubborn intervention in Norway and her long-term alliance with the Jomsburgvikings had ended at last in success. Moreover, they led to Svein and Canute's maritime empire in the next period that we will be discussing. Until 983, however, it was the Ottos who controlled the principal route from the North Sea into the Baltic, and upon this control rested much of their political power and economic strength.

Along these vital routes there passed in the tenth century an ever-

---

[208] Both routes into Russia appear to have been active in these years. That the route leading by way of the Dvina had some importance is attested to by coin hoards in Lithuania. See F. Balodis, *op.cit.*, pp. 88-139. Coin hoards in Finland and Esthonia, as well as in Russia itself, reveal the importance of the more northern route. On this, see T. J. Arne, *La Suède et l'Orient*, pp. 91-183. In the 10th century, the northern one leading to Novgorod and the Volga was probably the more important, though the Dvina route to Polotsk and Smolensk was certainly used. See maps of coin hoards and routes into Russia in Bolin and Carlsson, *Historisk Atlas*, p. 10.

increasing volume of maritime traffic. From Western Norway, as we have shown, an important commerce linked these shores to England, Ireland and Germany. Norse traders were also rounding the North Cape to procure furs and Arctic products useful in commerce. The result of this traffic was the appearance in the Trondheim region of the town of Nidaros in the last years of the tenth century.[209] But a second and more important economic center appeared on Norway's coast, the town of Tønsberg, which succeeded to the earlier position of Skringissal on Olso fjord. This town was probably founded by Bjorn the Merchant, son of Harold Fairhair, about the middle of the tenth century.[210] It owed its existence in part to commerce from the North Sea by way of Ribe and Frisia. But probably more important was its trade which entered the Baltic by way of Kattegat and Skagerrak to reach Hedeby or pass along Swedish shores to distant Russia. We know that as early as the time of Ottar in the late ninth century, cargoes of walrus tusks, sealskins, other furs and reindeer hides were reaching Hedeby via this route. The finds of tenth-century Hedeby coinage about Oslo fjord and on Norway's west coast and even in Iceland show that such trade was increasing. So, too, does the discovery of Norwegian soapstone vessels in Hedeby excavations.[211]

But trade from Tønsberg and Olso fjord was by no means confined to Hedeby, important though it undoubtedly was. The Sagas contain much evidence of a more direct trade between Norse coasts and the Eastern Baltic and Russia. Egils in the *Egils Saga* is said to have sailed directly to Courland, where he traded for two weeks with the inhabitants before turning to piracy. Norwegian merchants traded with Novgorod, according to the *Fornmänensaga*. Olaf Tryggvasson is said to have sailed directly to Russia, whence he returned with six shiploads of silk to claim his kingdom. In the *Laxdaele Saga* we hear of a merchant called Gilli the Russian who traded in Norse and Icelandic waters. St. Olaf in his youth fled directly to Russia, where his uncle was an important official under Vladimir of Kiev.[212] And in Esthonia and Latvia archeological finds reveal a large num-

[209] L. Musset, *op.cit.*, p. 128. T. Murik, *The Story of the Nidaros*, p. 21. O. Tonning, *op.cit.*, pp. 10-11.

[210] L. Musset, *op.cit.*, p. 169. O. A. Johnsen, *Tønsbergs Historie*, I, 10-31.

[211] H. Jankuhn, *Haithabu 1937-39*, p. 161.

[212] On Saga traditions of commerce with Russia, see O. A. Johnsen, "Le Commerce et la navigation en Norvège au moyen âge," in *Revue hist.*, CLVIII (1936), 368-89, and A. Bugge, *Die nordeuropäischen Verkehrswege*, pp. 231-35. Also E. Pariset, *Historie de la soie*, II, 324-45.

ber of swords of this period of definite Norwegian workmanship.[213]

But again it is coin hoards which reinforce Saga tradition most emphatically. In Denmark the most important hoards containing Samanid silver, an evidence of contacts with Russia, are to be found in Bornholm, Zealand and Falster, which lie along the route leading to Norway rather than to Hedeby.[214] In the Vik region and along the Norwegian coasts we also find hoards which contain this Samanid silver, and these Eastern coins extend to England, Iceland, Scotland and Ireland. The most numerous finds containing dirhems are those uncovered about Oslo fjord. Two in particular, both buried about 955, were excavated at Grimstead and Tersen.[215] Evidently the ships in which Bjorn the Merchant and his partners traded with Russia reached there from this part of Norway by way of the Kattegat. Nor is coin evidence of Norway's Eastern trade limited to Samanid silver in the tenth-century hoards. Byzantine coins are also to be found there. From the Oslo region comes a find of 14 rare gold Byzantine *solidi*, minted by Romanus Lecapenus and Constantine Porphyrogenitus early in the tenth century,[216] while, scattered along the Norwegian coast as far as Rogaland, are other Byzantine silver pieces.[217]

It seems probable, however, that the commerce of Denmark was even more important than that of Norway during these years. It seems to have been concentrated in three main trading centers: Ribe, on the North Sea side of Jutland; Aarhus, on the Baltic side of the peninsula; and Hedeby, farther to the south. We know little of Ribe from our sources except that it was called a *vicus* in 860, and in 948 was the seat of one of Denmark's three bishoprics. A century later Adam of Bremen was to speak of it as an important town trading with England.[218] Remains of Hedeby money and other archeological finds around the Ribe area suggest some tenth-century trade.[219] Aarhus,

---

[213] On Norwegian weapons found in Esthonia and Latvia, dating from this period and up to 1050, see F. Balodis, *op.cit.*, pp. 200-35, and B. Nerman, *Die Verbindungen zwischen Skandinavien*, pp. 103-50.

[214] On the Kufic dirhems found in 41 hoards, see R. Skovmand, *op.cit.*, pp. 13-17.

[215] These hoards and those found nearby at Grimsby and in the Trondelag dating from the same period seem to show this trade in a graphic fashion. See H. Holst, "Die Kufiske Mynter i Solvfunnet frä Grimstead i Stokke, Vestfold," in *Nord. Numis. Arsskrift* (1936), pp. 42-52. See also for the west coast, R. Hartman, *Die Kufiske Myntfund frä Holte, Orkedolen og Herten* (Trondheim 1918), pp. 5-6.

[216] H. Holst, in *Numismatica*, VII (1928), 86-91.

[217] These silver coins include one of Basil II found in the Oslo region, one Romanus I at Traaen and one Romanus II in Rogaland. H. Holst, "Mynter i Norske Funn," *loc.cit.*, pp. 78-79.

[218] Adam of Bremen, *Descriptio Insulae Aquilonis*, I.

[219] J. Jankuhn, "Sechs Karten zum Handel des 10. Jahrhunderts," *loc.cit.*, p. 17.

along the trade route linking Hedeby and Tønsberg, was also a bishopric in 948.[220] Perhaps it, too, had grown to be a center of trade by the tenth century.

Hedeby, however, was a much more important commercial center than either of these. Already a *portus* in Carolingian times, in the tenth century it reached its apogee as the international trading center of the Baltic. Here, in its merchant quarter, were permanent colonies of Frisians and Saxons. Here Scandinavians and Slavs arrived to exchange products from all quarters of the Northern Seas. Here, between 940 and 980, it coined the only money minted in Scandinavia, the Hedeby *brachteaten* modeled after the earlier Dorestad silver pennies of Charlemagne. In Hedeby, too, by this time some industry was to be found, since pottery, weaving, goldsmithery, jewelry, and arms were being manufactured here or in the vicinity. It was the main entry point into the Baltic for glass, pottery, grain and fine weapons from the Rhinelands, cloth from Frisia, metalware, cloth and jewelry from England, even walnuts, salt and copper from Saxony—not to mention Anglo-Saxon and German money. From its northern hinterland it drew furs, wax, honey, slaves, falcons, walrus-hide rope for rigging, bone, horn and soapstone vessels. Probably silks, spices and money from Russia reached it, too.[221]

The extent of Hedeby's hinterland is revealed by finds of its products, dating from the tenth century, in scattered archeological sites all through the Baltic. These products consist of jewelry, arms and Hedeby-minted coins. Though some of these were found about Oslo fjord, as we have noted, most have been discovered in the Baltic region, which is therefore shown to be Hedeby's special trade preserve. These products reveal close contacts with Jutland, Scania and the Danish islands, and with the Malar Sea region of the Swedish Uppland, and also with Gotland, the coasts of Esthonia and the entrance to the Gulf of Finland. Such commerce simply followed the old route to Birka and Russia. However, surprisingly enough, we also find evidence of important contact during these years with Wollin[222] and

[220] Adam of Bremen, *op.cit.*

[221] On Hedeby the works of Jankuhn are definitive, particularly his description of the rise of industry there in the 10th century. See H. Jankuhn, *Ergebnisse und Probleme der Haithabugrabungen*, pp. 61-67, and *Haithabu 1937-39* (Berlin 1943). On Hedeby's imports as seen in texts and archeological finds, see *Ergebnisse und Probleme*, pp. 51-59, and *Haithabu*, pp. 161-85.

[222] Concerning Wollin, which was hardly less important than Hedeby in these years, see the contemporary account of a 10th-century Jewish traveler and his description of the port, in G. Jacob, *Arabische Berichterstätter*, pp. 29-36. For the next century, see

the Oder, leading to the headwaters of the Warta, where the new Polish state was arising. Here Hedeby coins are numerous, suggesting that it was via Hedeby, rather than such centers as Merseburg, that Poland maintained contact with the North Sea and Western Europe.[223] No wonder Harold Bluetooth coveted Hedeby, and maintained such close connections with Wollin and the Wendish coast.[224] From there a valuable commerce originated.

If Hedeby reached almost the status of a Baltic Genoa during this period, hardly less important were Sweden's two main trading centers, Birka and Gotland. Both, like Hedeby, had achieved importance in Carolingian and even Merovingian times. Both, however, present in the tenth century particular problems for the historian. During the first three quarters of this century Birka appears to have closely resembled Hedeby in its trade patterns. In its graves have been found money, jewelry, glass, arms, pottery and textiles which show that an important commerce existed with Germany and Russia.[225] Then suddenly, about 975, Birka ceased to exist. No archeological evidence of destruction in war is to be found, and there is no explanation in our sources for its disappearance.[226] All we know is that a few years later a new trading center on the Malar Sea, Sigtuna, appeared in its place some miles away, nearer the capital, Uppsala.[227]

Birka's demise can be explained in a number of ways. One is that after 950 trade with Russia, upon which Birka depended for its prosperity, dropped off sharply, since no Samanid silver minted later than 960 has been found in Baltic regions. This silver, which arrived along

---

comments of Adam of Bremen, in *Hist. Hamm. Eccl. Pont.*, II, 19. On Reric (later Lübeck), of some importance as a town between Hedeby and Wollin, see W. Vogel, "Emporium Reric," in *Festscrift Hans Koht* (Oslo 1933), pp. 85-93. See also Vogel's questioning of Wollin's existence in "Wo lag Vineta," in *Hansische Geschichtsblätter*, LXI (1936), 406-11.

[223] On the commerce of Hedeby with Poland in the 10th century, see H. Jankuhn, "Sechs Karten zum Handel des 10. Jahrhundert," *loc.cit.*, pp. 18-21.

[224] The trade of Hedeby and Wollin in this period explains their importance in the political struggle waged in these years among the Danish kings, the Ottos and Miezko of Poland. On this, see F. Dvornik, *The Making of Central and Eastern Europe*, pp. 60-90.

[225] See H. Arbman, *Birka*, and his *Schweden und des Karolingische Reich*, which sum up evidence of Birka's importance. The fact that *only* here in the whole Baltic have 9th-century Byzantine coins been found shows its early close connection with Russia. T. Arne, *La Suède et l'Orient*, pp. 61-62. On Byzantine textiles found in Birka graves, see A. Geijer, *Birka*, III, 15-52.

[226] H. Arbman, *Birka*, pp. 130-32.

[227] On the appearance and importance of Sigtuna, see E. Floderus, *Sigtuna, Sveriges Aldsta Medaltidstad* (Stockholm 1941), pp. 1-112.

a Volga-Gulf of Finland route, was vital to Sweden and therefore to Birka's economy. The objection to this theory is that there is no evidence that trade with Russia ceased about 950 or 960. In fact, German and Anglo-Saxon coin hoards in Finland and Gotland suggest that, if anything, it increased in importance down to and after the year 1000. A second possibility, and a more plausible one, is that by 970 Gotland had replaced Birka as the important trade center of Sweden, since this part of the Baltic was better located from a geographical point of view. This possibility has some merit as a theory, but a more ingenious explanation would explain Birka's demise as the result of geographical changes which took place in the Malar Sea itself, causing a lowering of the water level in the narrow estuary by which it communicated with the Baltic proper. Thus Birka's role as a trading center could be said to have ended because the water routes reaching it became unnavigable for large vessels. Isolated, it would perish, and Sigtuna, which was more fortunately located, could take its place.[228]

The disappearance of Birka seems not to have affected Gotland unfavorably. Rather its importance increased. Here have been found immense hoards, dating from these years, containing Samanid silver and coins from Ottonian Germany and Anglo-Saxon England, as well as some from Bohemia and Byzantium. Intermingled with them are jewelry and other objects of value. Judging from these hoards, Gotland was the international trading center of the Central Baltic, and much more important than Birka. Perfectly placed to tap trade going to Hedeby, Norway, Sweden's Uppland, Russia and South Baltic coasts, Gotland enjoyed a golden age of commerce such as she had not known since Vendel times or the Carolingian era.[229]

The problem presented by Gotland, then, is the opposite of Birka's disappearance as a trading center. It is, instead, how the commerce which reached its shores was handled. For in this period, as earlier, archeology shows that Gotland possessed no town or trading center

[228] For this explanation, which is an ingenious one, I am indebted to a suggestion of Prof. Store Bolin. Increases in size in this period in commercial ships as well as warcraft are a subject which needs attention. The discovery of a new site in the Malar Sea near Stockholm may throw more light on Birka's demise, when all the information on it reaches the scholarly world.

[229] See M. Stenberger, *Die Schatzfunde Gotlands*, II, on the archeological evidence. Interestingly enough, not only did the 10th century, about 950, bring a flood of German coins to Gotland, as mentioned in the text, but examination of the Stora Velinge hoard seems to show that the first half of the 10th century was the peak period for the arrival of Moslem dirhems here, too. On this, see the graph of the Stora Velinge coin-minting dates in U. S. Linder-Welin, "Ein grosser Fund Arabischer Münzen aus Stora Velinge," in *Nord. Numis. Arsskrift* (1941), p. 80.

in the ordinary sense of the word. There were, of course, other regions from which an active trade originated, like Frisia, Iceland and the Norwegian *bjorkeys*, where urbanism was either rare or non-existent. But in none of them do we find evidence of such immense wealth. Was Gotland's trade, then, like that of the Frisian *terpens* or of Iceland and Norway, in the hands of a seagoing peasantry who combined extensive commerce with an agricultural life? Did it resemble in some features New England's or Nova Scotia's mixed farming, fishing, trading pattern? Perhaps.

More plausible, however, is the possibility, suggested in a previous chapter, that Gotland was in this period, and remained until the twelfth century, a gigantic fair. According to this theory, it was a place that was centrally located and neutral, perhaps even protected by some religious pagan sanctuary, like Mecca in Arabia, where foreign merchants repaired at certain fixed times of the year to exchange their goods. Here products from the West, consisting of manufactured goods, arms, metals, salt, jewelry and money, were traded for the silks, spices, money, wax, fine honey and slaves from Russia, the Eastern Baltic and the Orient. What Gotland may have somewhat resembled, then, were the twelfth-century Fairs of Champagne, except that the routes which reached it were maritime rather than over-land. Its lack of urbanization recalls the somewhat similar situation in Champagne, even though its great wealth is proof of the important commerce of the Baltic during these years—a trade of international significance. Such an explanation is in line with the almost complete lack of any material objects, such as glass, arms, silks, textiles and pottery, found in conjunction with hoards of silver and jewelry. In this, Gotland in no sense resembles Birka, Hedeby, Gneizno or Sigtuna. The trade of this island resulted in no urbanization, then, because it was carried on by foreigners rather than native inhabitants. The Gotlanders were no more than onlookers who reaped a reward in silver and other wealth because of their location, and that was all.[230] It was by way of Gotland, however, that traffic passed from West as well as East, carried by Slavic, Norse, Frisian, German and perhaps English merchants. Unable to tap this commerce, the Swedish Uppland, so powerful in King Olaf's time, lost importance.

[230] Not until the 12th century did these *Guti*, or Gotlanders, seem to take active trading on their own account, a significant fact. Then they were to be found in England and at Novgorod and developed upon their island a trading town, Visby, largely German in its merchant composition.

All of which brings us to perhaps the most surprising changes brought by these years—those appearing along Baltic shores inhabited by Finnish, Baltic and Slavic peoples. We have noted that up to the tenth century the peoples of the Eastern Baltic from Finland to Truso in East Prussia were in general either under Swedish rule or at least under Swedish influence. Those between Denmark and East Prussia seem to have had little contact or trade of any sort with their northern Scandinavian neighbors, except for the single case of the Obodrites, whose trading place of Reric (Lübeck) was destroyed by the Danes in 809.[231] By the tenth century, however, we notice a change. The peoples of Esthonia, Courland, Livonia and Samland were no longer under Swedish influence or control.[232] And those Wends, as the Scandinavians called them, who dwelt farther west, the Pomeranians, Rani, Volinians, Wagrians and Obodrites, suddenly entered the stream of Northern Europe's political and economic life.[233] The symbol of this change, and in part its cause, were the Samanid silver dirhems that began to flow into this region, which had been isolated from the rest of Europe since the sixth century.[234] New overland routes, particularly one which passed from Kiev to the upper Danube by way of Cracow, Breslau, Prague and Regensburg, illustrate Slavic Central Europe's new importance.[235] So, too, do those routes reaching the Elbe at Magdeburg and other Ottonian frontier fortresses.[236] Thus commerce with the Baltic, and land and river routes through Poland and Bohemia, suddenly appeared in the tenth century. They help to explain the new importance of Polish and Bohemian states, and the interest in these lands shown by German monarchs, Kievan Russian rulers and Scandinavian kings who heretofore had neglected them.

Politically speaking, it was the appearance of Poland as a state

[231] W. Vogel, "Emporium Reric," *loc.cit.*, p. 133.

[232] F. Balodis, *op.cit.*, pp. 160-253.

[233] Since in 973 Ibn Jacub, writing in Moslem Central Asia, could mention Naccon, Duke of the Obodrites, it is apparent that this part of Europe was no longer remote, but had an international trade significance. See translation by G. Jacob in W. Hirsch, *Widukinds Sachsische Geschichte*, pp. 182-84, and G. Jacob, *Arabische Berichterstätter*, p. 12.

[234] On the money hoards found in Poland dating from the 10th century, most of which are of Samanid silver, see J. Kostryzewski, *Les Origines de la civilisation poloñaise*, pp. 364-89.

[235] On this route, used in 906 to reach Raffelstein on the upper Danube, see *MGH Capitularia*, II, 249-50, and G. Jacob, *op.cit.*, p. 12.

[236] See mention of Jewish merchants at Magdeburg, in *MGH Diplom.*, I, 416. For the pattern of commerce handled by Jews in these years, see J. Brutzkus, "Der Handel der westeuropäischen Juden mit dem alten Kiev," in *Zeit. für Geschichte der Juden in Deutschland*, III (1931), 219-52.

which was to prove most important. Prior to the mid-tenth century the Slavic tribes who were to make up the future Poland of the Piasts seem to have been groups of agriculturalists inhabiting lands along the middle Oder, Warta and Vistula, cultivating the soil of these rich river valleys and protected by strong places, or forts, known as *grody*. They had advanced beyond the primitive, pastoral, hunting stage of their proto-history, but were still tribal and remote from the rest of Europe.[237] Suddenly, about 962, a leader named Miezko began to unite these tribes. He built a series of new and improved *grody*, or fortresses, to protect his domains from incursions by Slavic tribes farther to the west.[238] He organized a strong standing army,[239] and, advancing towards the Oder and the Baltic, crushed the resistance of the Veletians and Pomeranians and added their tribal territories to his domains. Generally speaking, during these years he seems to have maintained an alliance with the Ottos, who were moving across the Elbe into these same regions.[240] He also appears to have maintained good relations with the Swedes and the Danes. He accepted Christianity and in 968 founded a bishopric at Poznan. Except for a short period of hostility about 970-972, he remained loyal to Otto II and III until his death. He married a German noblewoman and had his son, Boleslas Chobry, do the same, and did fealty to the Holy Roman Emperors for at least a portion of his domains which bordered on the Oder. But Miezko was no German puppet. He married one of his daughters first to Eric Segersall, King of Sweden, and then later to Svein, son of Harold Bluetooth. Thanks to these marriages, she became the mother of two of Scandinavia's most famous kings of the eleventh century, Canute of Denmark and Olaf Skottkonung of Sweden. It was probably due to these ties with Sweden and also with Denmark that Miezko was able to hold the important trading centers of Stettin and Wollin, which he occupied between 963 and 967, and Pomerania as well.[241]

---

[237] J. Kostryzewski, *op.cit.*, pp. 28-32, 102-4. R. Koebner, *The Settlement and Colonization of Europe*, pp. 57-60.

[238] On these *grody* built by Miezko, especially at Gniezno, Poznan, Lubusz and Santok, see J. Kostryzewski, *op.cit.*, pp. 103-20.

[239] *Ibid.*, pp. 505-70.

[240] On Miezko's advance west to the Oder, see Z. Wojciechowski, "Le Patrice Boleslas le Vaillant," in *Revue belge*, XXIX (1951), 42-45.

[241] On this development of Poland, see F. Dvornik, *op.cit.*, pp. 54-59, 83-84; J. Kostryzewski, *op.cit.*, pp. 543-50; and Z. Wojciechowski, *Miezko I and the Rise of the Polish State* (Gdynia 1936), pp. 1-87. See also P. Halecki, *A History of Poland* (New York 1943), pp. 10-53.

Miezko did more than expand his territory towards the west and the north. He had southern interests as well. In this direction, Cracow and the remains of White Croatia, just north of the Carpathians, were under the control of Boleslas I of Bohemia. Miezko married a daughter of Boleslas and also had marriage connections with Hungary.[242] Protected by a picked bodyguard of 3,000 men whom he paid from taxes levied upon the commerce which flowed through his kingdom, he was a ruler of importance and weight in the European scene of the late tenth century.

West of Miezko's Poland lay the principality of the Obodrites, which in 973 Ibn Jacub called one of the four major Slavic states of Central Europe. Generally speaking, it was a vassal of the Ottos, and may have carried on some trade in its port of Reric, the future Lübeck. The Obodrites, like their Slavic neighbors to the east and south, were subjected to very harsh treatment at the hands of German expansionists like Counts Gero and Billung. The result was their revolt in 983, in which they burned Hamburg and helped to check German expansion into Slavic lands.[243] However, despite this revolt, they remain rather mysterious figures whose maritime strength was increasing up to the time, in the next century, when they were to join other Wends in the great Slavic attacks on Denmark of 1043 and 1052.

East of Poland, along Baltic coasts beyond the Vistula, we find an area for which our information is almost non-existent. Truso was visited by Wulfstan in the late ninth century, but we do not know its status in the tenth. Archeology reveals that cities like Seeburg and Apolloné in Courland, Portus Semi-gallorum and Daugmalé near the mouth of the Dvina and Jersika and Trekala, farther north continued to exist throughout the period. But we know nothing of the political history of these Chud or of the Esths and Finns who lived north of them. Archeology and coin hoards show that trade passed through these regions on the way to Russia, but their level of civilization seems to have been little affected by it.[244] Saga evidence concerning Olaf Tryggvasson and Egils of the *Egils Saga* suggests that pirates and slavers were active along these shores, particularly in Esthonia.[245]

[242] J. Kostrzewski, *op.cit.*, p. 586. F. Dvornik, *op.cit.*, pp. 83-84. R. Seton-Watson, *A History of the Czechs and Slovaks* (New York 1943), pp. 20-58.

[243] F. Dvornik, *op.cit.*, pp. 55-59. J. W. Thompson, *Feudal Germany*, pp. 790-801.

[244] L. Musset, *op.cit.*, pp. 42-45. F. Balodis, *op.cit.*, pp. 140-235. B. Nerman, *Sveriges Första Storehetstid*, pp. 100-253.

[245] A. Bugge, *Die nordeuropäischen Verkehrswege*, pp. 237-40.

365

Perhaps they, like the Wends, were developing a certain sea power which they were to use in the next centuries.

South of Poland there lay the last important Slav state of Central Europe, Bohemia. It, like Poland, was a phenomenon of the tenth century, though more strongly tied to the German Empire of the Ottos than were Miezko's domains. Bohemian contingents, for example, joined German forces to turn back the Hungarians at Lechfeld in 955, and as early as the time of Henry the Fowler had accepted German overlordship.[246] Despite this vassalage, Bohemian rulers spread their dominion north and east in the course of the tenth century, until their principality included Moravia, Bohemia and lands of Southern Poland from Cracow to the borders of Ruthenia.[247] Boleslas I of Bohemia accepted Christianity and established two bishoprics in his land, one at Prague, the other farther east in Moravia.[248] His ties with Germany did not stop him from having close relations with Miezko of Poland, to whom he gave a daughter who was Miezko's first wife. Nor did Boleslas neglect his eastern borders, since we find a Bohemian princess among the many wives of Vladimir of Kiev, prior to his conversion to Christianity.[249]

Thus we see arising in the lands between Germany and Russia two strong Slavic states, both closely connected with the Holy Roman Empire of the Ottos, but maintaining interests which linked them to Scandinavia, Kievan Russia and each other as well. Both, by the end of this century, had also renounced paganism and were moving towards Christianity. Immediately east and west of these new Slavic principalities we find Slavic and Baltic peoples still tribal and pagan, but beginning to show some economic and maritime strength. North Central Europe, so long on the sidelines, was beginning to enter the mainstream of European history.

This new importance of Slavic Central Europe was closely connected with the commerce which flowed into these areas in the tenth century. We have already shown that as early as 906 Russian and Slavic traders, following a route not subject to Hungarian attack,

[246] H. Bresslau, "Die Schlacht auf dem Lechfelde," in *Hist. Zeit.*, xcvii (1906), 448-62.

[247] F. Dvornik, *op.cit.*, pp. 36-38, 268-76. These lands north of the Carpathians were the earlier White Croatian kingdom.

[248] F. Dvornik, *op.cit.*, pp. 83-135. Note that Bohemia's church was independent in this period and not under German church control.

[249] *The Primary Chronicle*, ed. Cross, p. 181.

were arriving at Raffelstein on the upper Danube.[250] Later on, trade along this route must have increased in importance, since Masudi, writing in Persia in 943, spoke of a Slavic state that he called *An Dir* (probably White Croatia), which had rich cities, numerous armaments and whose capital (probably Cracow) was visited by Moslem merchants, who brought various kinds of wares. He went on to say that near this state there was another, Al Firaz (most probably Bohemia), which had many towns, owned gold mines and had rich fields.[251] More precise is evidence given us by Ibn Jacub who, between 966 and 973, traveled along this Central European trade route. He said that it took three weeks to travel from Cracow to Prague, and that Russian, Slav, Jewish and Mohammedan merchants went there, carrying wares and money which they exchanged for slaves, tin and furs.[252] It is interesting to note that Thietmar mentioned Jewish merchants at Merseburg at about this same time. Probably the Mohammedan travelers who visited Wollin and Hedeby during these decades followed this route. So may have the camel which Miezko of Poland presented to Otto III in 986.[253] Archeological finds from tenth-century Gniezno and Birka reveal certain beads and enameled eggs which were produced in the Volynia region of the Ukraine and reached Poland and the Baltic over this route. So perhaps did certain Moslem silver dirhems, minted after 950 in more western regions of the Caliphate than Turkistan, which have been found in Polish, Swedish and Gotland hoards.[254]

Trade reaching Poland and Central Europe from the Baltic, however, seems to have been much more important than that arriving overland. There is, for instance, an almost complete lack of Samanid silver dirhems in Little Poland, in contrast to the immense hoards found in Great Poland and Pomerania. This seems to suggest that this money arrived here indirectly by way of Scandinavia and the Baltic instead of directly from Kievan Russia. This may help to explain why Miezko's principal interest was in conquering and holding Pomerania and the outlet to the Oder at Wollin and Stettin instead of regions to the south and east towards Kiev. One can infer

---

[250] *MGH Capitularia*, II, 249-50.

[251] I. Marquart, *Osteuropäische und ostasiatische Streifzüge* (Leipzig 1903), p. 102.

[252] G. Jacob, *Arabische Berichterstätter*, p. 12.

[253] *Annales Quedlinburgenses*, in *MGH Script.*, III, 66-67. See also Thietmar, *Chron.*, in *MGH*, new ser., IX, 141.

[254] H. Arbman, "Une Route commerciale pendant les Xe et XIe siècles," in *Slavia Antiqua*, V (1948), 435-38.

that commerce was essential to his state from the information, furnished us by Ibn Jacub, that the 3,000 warriors on whom he relied were paid from taxes levied upon the markets of his realm. It seems probable, therefore, that most of the spices, perfumes and textiles found in Poland in the period arrived from the East via the same Baltic routes which furnished the Samanid silver dirhems in the 90 hoards found in Greater Poland, and also in the 100 hoards in Pomerania.[255] Some trade, of course, also arrived in Poland from the West, but again it would seem that this was mainly by way of Hedeby rather than across the Elbe, since Hedeby coins are found in such large numbers in the Oder river valley and in Central Poland.[256] Some commerce also reached here via Bohemia, whose coins, minted in this period, must have passed this way to be found in hoards in Finland and on Gotland and the Swedish mainland.[257]

It is very difficult, however, to be sure just what products from Bohemia and Poland figured in commerce with the Baltic during these years, though evidence of such trade is strong indeed. It is possible that the tin, furs, and slaves which Ibn Jacub said merchants went to seek in Prague were also exported to the Baltic by way of the valleys of the Oder, Warta and Vistula. The gold mines of *Al Firaz*, probably those found active later around Liegnitz in Silesia, may also have produced some gold which was exported to Hedeby, Gotland and Sweden to pay for Eastern wares imported into Miezko's kingdom. But the large silver hoards of Poland and Pomerania seem to show a favorable balance of trade which cannot be accounted for so easily. Perhaps the most sensible solution to this problem is the following: that this portion of Europe specialized in certain products of agriculture and the forest, such as honey and beeswax, which were used in Scandinavia and exported by way of Russia to the Moslem and Byzantine East. Certainly Kostryzewski's evidence seems to show that honey was Piast Poland's principal product, and the large jars of Polish origin found at Birka and elsewhere in Sweden, ideal

---

[255] On these hoards and their distribution, see J. Kostryzewski, *op.cit.*, pp. 380-82.

[256] *Ibid.*, pp. 380-87. See also map in Bolin and Carlsson, *Historisk Atlas*, p. 10; and for the distribution of Hedeby money in Poland, H. Jankuhn, "Sechs Karten," *loc.cit.*, pp. 17-21.

[257] Most of these coins found in Gotland and elsewhere in the Baltic date from the 11th century, but in the Folhagen hoard in Gotland, dating from about 1000 A.D., we find 14 Bohemian coins of Boleslas I or II (937-999). M. Stenberger, *Die Schatzfunde Gotlands*, II, 21-24.

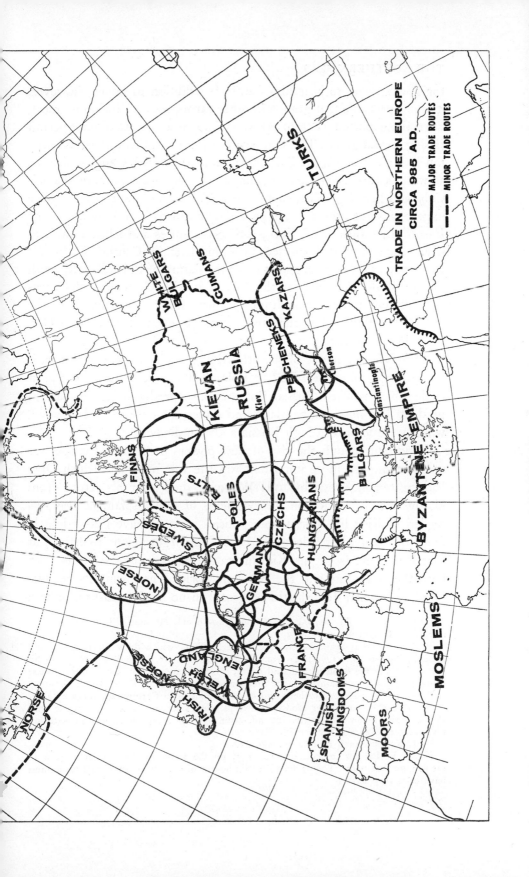

TRADE IN NORTHERN EUROPE
CIRCA 985 A.D.

—— MAJOR TRADE ROUTES
- - - MINOR TRADE ROUTES

for honey, seem to bear him out.[258] In addition to honey, however, it seems probable that grain and other farm products, including meat, were also exported north to Scandinavia, whose climate did not permit raising certain grains. The southern Baltic region, then, probably owed much of its trade via the Baltic to a demand for honey and foodstuffs, as well as furs, slaves and metals. These regions were Scandinavia's Cuba and her Argentina, supplying the bread and sweets which were in part consumed there and in part sent on to Russia and the Byzantine East.[259] In return arms, cloth, fish, glass, spices and silks, as well as silver money, were imported into this part of Central Europe.[260] Furthermore, such an explanation of the nature of Poland's trade with the north also accounts for the lack of it with Germany, which was self-sufficient in these agricultural products. Only indirectly, via Hedeby and the Baltic, did much trade reach Central Europe from Germany in this century.

As for the commerce of the other Baltic regions north of Truso, it was probably much like that of Poland. These regions had a transit trade which reached Russia. But they also produced certain natural products like horses in Samland and slaves, honey, furs and beeswax, which were valued in both Russia and Scandinavia.[261]

Important though the rise of new powers in Central Europe was in this age, even more important was the vast new state which Oleg had created in Russia by 911. When he died after his return from his unsuccessful attack on the Moslems of the Caspian, he was succeeded in Kiev by Igor, whose policies seem to have differed little from those of his predecessor. Like Oleg, Igor seems to have felt that the interests of his Kievan state required close contacts with both the Byzantine and the Moslem world. These contacts he, like Oleg, apparently felt should be based, in no small measure, upon a

[258] J. Kostryzewski, *op.cit.*, pp. 67-69, 380-89. H. Arbman, "Une Route commerciale," *loc.cit.*, pp. 435-38.

[259] The fact that Scandinavia, except for Norway, which drew on England and Ireland, imported her foodstuffs from the rich lands of the South Baltic coasts in this period explains the flood of Samanid silver, in 180 hoards, interred here during these years. It also may explain the large number of German coins in the Baltic. Germany could no longer pay for northern and eastern goods as in Carolingian times by shipping north wheat and other foodstuffs, except wine, since she could not compete with Polish grain, honey and cattle. Instead, after 950 she increasingly had to settle an unfavorable balance of trade with silver coin.

[260] J. Kostryzewski, *op.cit.*, pp. 380-85.

[261] See F. Balodis, *op.cit.*, pp. 160-235, on the trade of this region as seen in archeological remains. The 62 Latvian coin hoards of these years show that trade must have been very active.

judicious use of force. So he hired new bands of Varangian mercenaries in Scandinavia, and with 100 ships attacked Byzantine territory in Asia Minor. His forces were badly beaten by Byzantine naval flotillas in the Black Sea.[262] Two years later, however, we find him in the Caspian, where, with ships which he had brought there, he seized and held for a period the Moslem city of Berdca.[263] Masudi was sufficiently impressed by these raids to state that the Russians were the masters of the Caspian Sea. But such successes proved only temporary, and Igor's forces were compelled to retreat to their own territory. In the next year another expedition was sent against Constantinople. It traveled by land, probably because of fear of Byzantium's naval strength in the Black Sea. It resulted in a new trade treaty with Byzantium in 945.[264] While maintaining the right of Kiev's merchants to trade with Constantinople, as did the treaties of 907 and 911, it restricted them to dealing in only certain grades of fine silk cloth and contained provisions guaranteeing protection to Byzantium's trading colony in the Crimea.[265] Evidently Russia's trade with the Byzantine Empire was now put on a more strongly political basis than previously.

Igor died soon after this treaty with Constantinople, and Olga, his widow, governed the realm in peace, paying particular attention to the maintenance of good relations with the Byzantine Empire. She may even have accepted Christianity.[266] In the 960's, however, her son, Sviatoslav, succeeded to power in Kiev, and a new aggressive period began. Sviatoslav, with his zeal for war and bloodthirsty temperament, seems to have been a throwback to the Viking era. In 963 he attacked the Kazars, who had heretofore been peaceful and friendly for the most part to the Kievan state, and seized their fortress of Sarkel on the lower Don, as well as part of the Kuban. He followed this move with a campaign against the White Bulgars on the middle

[262] *Theophanes Continuator*, ed. Bonn, p. 423.

[263] B. Dorn, "Caspia," *loc.cit.*, pp. 84-108. G. Vernadsky, *Kievan Russia*, pp. 26-30.

[264] T. D. Kendrick, *History of the Vikings*, pp. 150-52. G. Vernadsky, *op.cit.*, pp. 30-32.

[265] On this trade treaty, see *The Primary Chronicle*, pp. 163-65, and R. S. Lopez, "The Silk Industry in the Byzantine Empire," in *Speculum*, XX (1945), 34-35. See also Constantine Porphyrogenitus, *De administrando imperio*, ed. Bonn, p. 71, and A. R. Lewis, *op.cit.*, p. 173.

[266] On Olga's reign, see *The Primary Chronicle*, pp. 164-75; and on her baptism in Constantinople, *Cedrenus*, ed. Bonn, II, 329, and Constantine Porphyrogenitus, *De ceremoniis*, ed. Bonn, pp. 594-97. Olga seems to have established friendly relations with the West also, especially with Otto I. *Cont. Regino Chron.*, in *MGH Script.*, I, 624, and F. Dvornik, *op.cit.*, pp. 66-70.

Volga in which he plundered their capital. Then, instigated by Byzantium, he turned west and attacked the Danubian Bulgars in the rear, thus lessening their danger to Constantinople.[267]

Sviatoslav's wars against the Kazars and White Bulgars on the middle and lower Volga apparently weakened these states and allowed the savage and nomadic Patzinaks to slip past them onto the steppes of South Russia, where they took up a position which the Magyars had held prior to their movement west into Europe. But Kiev's ruler evidently did not see the dangers of his policies. Instead, in 965, he was again attacking in the east, where he completed the fatal weakening of the Kazar state by taking and sacking its capital and principal cities, Itil and Samander.[268] Then he restlessly turned to attack Byzantium again along the lower Danube. Here he was totally unsuccessful, for his army was surrounded and captured by the Emperor John Zimisces, and he was forced to make a peace in which he gave up his Bulgarian conquests.[269] On the way back to Kiev, he and his forces were ambushed by the Patzinaks at the Dnieper rapids, and Sviatoslav himself was slain.

The bloodstained career of Sviatoslav marks, in a sense, a turning point in Kievan Russian history. His campaigns against White Bulgars and Kazars along the lower Volga resulted in a fatal weakening of these peoples and kingdoms which stood as a barrier to the expansion of nomads from Central Asia onto the steppes of South Russia, where their presence would seriously hinder Kiev's trade with both the Moslem East and Byzantium. As a result of the violence Sviatoslav had done the Kazars, the Patzinaks poured in, and he met his death at their hands. When they were followed soon after by the even more dangerous Cumans, the problem became insoluble. Sviatoslav, then, unloosed upon Russia a deluge of nomads whom neither he nor his Kievan successors were ever able to master and who brought dangers and difficulties to this Varangian state.[270]

Upon Sviatoslav's death, his realm was divided among his three sons, as was to become the Kievan custom. One, Vladimir, was given

---

[267] G. Vernadsky, *Kievan Russia*, pp. 40-49. T. D. Kendrick, *op.cit.*, pp. 152-56. F. Dvornik, *op.cit.*, pp. 95-115.

[268] G. Vernadsky, *op.cit.*, pp. 46-49. *The Primary Chronicle*, pp. 178-80. F. Dvornik, *op.cit.*, pp. 115-16. See especially D. M. Dunlop, *The History of the Jewish Kazars*, pp. 222-62.

[269] G. Schlumberger, *Jean Zimisces* (Paris 1896), pp. 113-49.

[270] On the significance of this fatal weakening of the Kazar kingdom, see A. R. Lewis, *op.cit.*, p. 232.

Novgorod and the north. A second, Yaropolk, was given Kiev. A third, Oleg, inherited lands between these two. Oleg was soon eliminated, and in 976 Yaropolk moved north and drove out Vladimir, who took refuge in Scandinavia. A few years later, leading a band of Varangian adventurers, he returned to Russia, retook his city of Novgorod, and then, marching south, captured Polotsk and Kiev.[271] His brother Yaropolk was slain, and Vladimir became the undisputed ruler of Kievan Russia. *The Primary Chronicle* relates a rather significant statement of Vladimir's concerning the Varangian mercenaries to whom he owed in part the recovery of his throne. After he had regained his kingdom, he sent a major portion of his late companions in arms to Constantinople to assist the Byzantine Emperor, Basil II, who needed support in his civil wars at home and conquests abroad. In doing so, he told Basil II, according to the *Chronicle*, "Varangians are on their way. Do not keep them in your city or they will do you as much harm as they have done here. Do not let a single one return this way."[272]

Unlike his father, Vladimir seems to have had interests which were constructive rather than destructive. He desired to establish firm contact with the Moslem East, which may have accounted for his rather inconclusive attack upon the White Bulgars in 985.[273] But his principal concern seems to have been with Byzantium. He helped Basil II, the Emperor of Constantinople, during the revolts of Bardas Skleros and Bardas Phocas, accepted Greek Orthodox Christianity for himself and his kingdom, and married a Greek princess. Under him the strong influence which Byzantium had exerted on Kiev during the time of Olga was renewed and strengthened.[274]

Vladimir was equally interested, however, in contacts with Western Europe, something which does not appear to have mattered very much to Igor, Olga and Sviatoslav. He exchanged embassies with both the Pope and the Ottos of Germany.[275] And, in 981, soon after he had gained Kiev and undisputed control of his kingdom, he led an expedition west from his capital to defeat Miezko of Poland and gain control of Premyshil, Cherwen and other towns on the trade routes leading west to Cracow and Prague.[276] He also waged cam-

[271] *The Primary Chronicle*, pp. 180-82.
[272] *Ibid.*, p. 180.   [273] *Ibid.*, p. 183.
[274] *Ibid.*, pp. 184-85. *Cedrenus*, ed. Bonn, II, 501. G. Vernadsky, *Kievan Russia*, pp. 60-65. A. R. Lewis, *op.cit.*, pp. 189-90.
[275] F. Dvornik, *op.cit.*, pp. 167-80.
[276] *The Primary Chronicle*, p. 182.

paigns against the Iatiangians and the Lithuanians and so opened routes to the Baltic by way of the Vistula and Neimen.[277] Still facing south towards the Black Sea, he understood the value of routes leading to the West more than any Kievan ruler who had preceded him, save perhaps Oleg. Owing to this, contacts were established with the strong rising states of Bohemia and Poland in Central Europe, as well as with the Baltic in the region of Samland. Under him a Russia which had communicated with Western Europe only via the Baltic, Dvina and Gulf of Finland routes established new windows to the West through Central Europe.

Such was the development of Russia between the time of the trade treaty with Constantinople in 911 and the establishment of a strong Kievan state under Vladimir by 985. Concerning its economic development we have much information, and we can divide the period into two rather definite phases, one up to the death of Sviatoslav, the other afterwards. Up to about the 960's Kiev's trade went equally to the Moslem East and Byzantium. The trade with Byzantium was carefully regulated by the trade treaties of 907, 911 and 945.[278] These treaties show that a picked group of merchants from Kiev, Chernikov and Pereslas assembled in a convoy at Kiev, and, carrying as merchandise slaves, furs, swords, honey and beeswax, descended the Dnieper and sailed along the shores of the Black Sea to Constantinople. Here they had a privileged trading status. They were given special quarters outside the city walls in which they could live for six months, while their entertainment and equipment for the long voyage home was a special charge on Byzantine officials and public funds. In return for the goods they brought, they were allowed to purchase silks, spices and wine as well as other luxury products. No other group of foreign merchants received better treatment or even equal privileges from Byzantium.[279] Probably Russian trade with the Byzantine colony of Cherson in the Crimea, though less carefully regulated by treaty, was of a similar nature.

This particular commerce with the Byzantine Empire was of great importance to Russia and no doubt the Byzantine textiles found in graves at Birka[280] and the rich Eastern wares which Miezko displayed in Poland, reached these parts of Europe by means of it.[281] So, prob-

---

[277] *Ibid.* G. Vernadsky, *op.cit.*, pp. 71-74.
[278] *The Primary Chronicle*, pp. 149-52, 163-65.
[279] R. S. Lopez, "The Silk Industry in the Byzantine Empire," *loc.cit.*, p. 152.
[280] A. Geijer, *Birka*, III, 22-47.   [281] J. Kostryzewski, *op.cit.*, pp. 378-83.

ably, did some of the silk worn by Matilda, wife of Henry the Fowler, or by the sister of Richard, Duke of Normandy.[282] It may also have been this trade which accounts for the spices which Ibn Jacub saw for sale at Mainz on his visit there in 973.[283] Certainly the Byzantine coins which we find in hoards in the Baltic in this period, like the 14 gold *solidi* discovered near Oslo or the scattered silver pieces in Norwegian, Danish, Gotland, Finnish and Swedish finds, owed their arrival there to this commerce.[284] To it also was owed the fact that the coins struck by Miezko of Poland in the late tenth century bear a Greek cross and show the influence of Byzantine monetary models.[285]

It seems probable, however, that trade with Moslem regions was more valuable to Russia than that with Byzantium, either trade carried directly by merchants who reached the mouths of the Volga on the Caspian, or that handled indirectly at first by White Bulgar or Kazar intermediaries. Moslem historians and annalists have left us some excellent pictures of this trade as it existed in the first years of the tenth century. Ibn Fadlan's account, for instance, contains a none too flattering depiction of filthy Scandinavian merchants arriving on the Volga to trade slave girls, furs and other merchandise, such as swords, for silver, gold and Eastern wares. He mentions the richness of the equipment of these traders, their gold and silver chains, and the Byzantine and Moslem silks they wore.[286] Ibn Rusta tells us of the White Bulgars and how they traded Moslem silver pieces for sable, ermine, gray squirrel and honey brought to their land by Russian merchants. He mentions the fact that the current value of a weasel fur was two dirhems.[287] Gardezi comments upon the fine weapons possessed by these Rus, their abundance of honey and the fact that they would only trade for dirhems.[288] Accounts by Masudi, who

---

[282] E. Sabbe, "L'Importation des tissus," *loc.cit.*, pp. 843-46.

[283] G. Jacob, *Arabische Berichterstätter*, p. 31.

[284] T. J. Arne, *La Suède et l'Orient*, pp. 61-62, 89-90.

[285] J. Kostryzewski, *op.cit.*, pp. 364-68, emphasizes, however, that until the 11th century Poland minted few native coins; instead, this region relied almost exclusively on Samanid and other imported silver money. See F. Dvornik, *op.cit.*, pp. 250-56, as well on this point.

[286] A. S. Cook, "Ibn Fadlan's Account of Scandinavian Merchants on the Volga in 922," in *Jour. of English and Germanic Philology*, XXII (1923), 56-63. Though Ibn Fadlan does mention in passing that these Scandinavians possessed Frankish swords, he does not emphasize them as merchandise, as Ibn Khordâdbeh did a century earlier. Mainly, from his account, they sold slaves and furs to the Moslem world.

[287] Ibn Rusta, trans. in C. Macartney, *The Magyars in the Ninth Century* (Cambridge 1930), pp. 192-94, 213-15.

[288] *Ibid.* See a summary of trade articles in G. Jacob, *Welche Handelsartikel die Araber des Mittelalters aus den nordisch-baltischen Ländern* (Berlin 1901), pp. 217-50.

shows a remarkable knowledge of the trade, habits and economies of all Central Europe as far west as Prague, round out the picture.[289] What we see is an important commerce passing through Russia to the Middle East, in which furs, honey, beeswax, slaves and arms and probably falcons and cattle were exchanged for gold, silver, silks, spices and other Eastern products. Down to about 950 or 960, the large coin hoards of Samanid silver interred in the Baltic and beyond emphasize that the balance of this trade was favorable to Europe and Russia, and that most of it was with Moslem Turkistan, where almost all of the silver dirhems were minted.[290]

Then suddenly, we notice a dramatic change in trade with the Moslem world about the time that Sviatoslav became ruler of Kiev, a change which was immediately reflected in Baltic coin hoards. No Samanid silver which was minted later than 960 arrived in the north. In its place, we find a few dirhems from Western Persia, Iraq and the Caucasus, but *not* Turkistan.[291] What seems to be shown here is an almost complete breakdown of trade with the Moslem world, particularly that which, since the late ninth century, had gone to Samanid Asia.[292] And it is interesting to note that this apparent ending of Turkistan's commerce with Russia and beyond was followed almost immediately by Sviatoslav's savage attacks upon the White Bulgars and Kazars, who had been important intermediaries in this trade. It is almost as if Kiev's ruler was blaming these peoples for the ending of a lucrative commerce. Even Vladimir's attacks upon the White Bulgars in 985 may have been an attempt to reopen Volga trade routes, still inactive.

The cause of this breakdown of Russian trade with the Middle East about the mid-tenth century has been insufficiently studied for

---

[289] I. Marquart, *op.cit.*, p. 102.

[290] N. L. Rasmusson, *Foreign Coins in Swedish Coin Finds* (London 1938), pp. 108-10.

[291] *Ibid.* On Finland's hoards with their peak period of Arabic coin imports about 950-970, see C. A. Nordman, "Schatzfunde und Handelsverbindungen in Finnlands Wikingerzeit," in *Acta Archeologia*, XIII (1942), 231-67. On the sparseness of Arabic money in Danish hoards after the 10th century, see R. Shovmand, *op.cit.*, pp. 13-15. On evidence from Norse hoards which contain no Samanid silver there minted after 949, see H. Holst, "Mynter i Norske Funn," in *Nord. Numis. Arsskrift* (1942), pp. 56-112. See also the Gotland Folhagen hoard of 1000 A.D., where the last Moslem dirhem dates from about 970, and the Oster Ryfter hoard of 1020 A.D., where the same thing is true. M. Stenberger, *op.cit.*, pp. 21-24, 63-64.

[292] Granting some time lag before Moslem coins minted in Central Asia could reach the Baltic, this would place a break in trade with Samanid Asia in the 960's or the early 970's—that is, about the time of Sviatoslav's attacks on the White Bulgars and Kazars.

anyone to venture more than a series of hypotheses. Some have felt that the arrival of the Patzinaks and Cumans in South Russia, following the fall of Kazaria in 969, lay behind a slackening of Moslem trade, and it is certain that they made commerce difficult towards the East. But perhaps one must look further. In the tenth century we find the beginnings of the Great Seljuk invasion of the Moslem world. These invasions appear to have eventually destroyed the Samanid state in Turkistan, but their first effect was to cut trade routes which linked it with China, and also with Russia and the Caspian. The advance of the Patzinaks and Cumans westwards was part of this process, since these two Turkish tribal groups were but one wing of the general advance of Turko-Asian peoples towards the West which was to continue for more than a century. The end of commerce with Turkistan on the part of Russian merchants was then the result, in part, of a Turkish invasion of Moslem Central Asia.[293]

Connected with this was another phenomenon, the shift of trade routes in the Islamic world and the Mediterranean which began as early as the last years of the ninth century. Prior to this period, the major routes between the Islamic world and China and India were those which passed by way of Iraq, by land across Central Asia, and by sea from the Persian Gulf to the Indian Ocean and beyond. There are signs that by the tenth century Iraq and Persia were no longer the great middlemen in the procuring of Eastern silks and spices. Now the important trade routes passed from Egypt and the Mediterranean via the Red Sea direct to India and China, or, if by way of Iraq, they went to Antioch and Syria on the Mediterranean. Thus Turkistan and Northern Persia, whence such Eastern wares originated in Carolingian times and even later, no longer possessed these products to trade, even if they had desired or been able to do so.[294]

Thirdly, in this same period, trade routes in the Mediterranean between the Moslem West—Spain, Sicily and North Africa—and Syria and Egypt again became important after their virtual disappearance in Carolingian times. Now via Venice or from Moslem Spain and North Africa, many products such as slaves or metals could be

[293] It was between 940 and 999 that the Turks overwhelmed the Persian Moslem Turkistan states. L. Halphen, *Les Barbares*, pp. 382-84.

[294] On this important shift of trade routes fom the Persian Gulf and Persia leading to Mesopotamia and to the Indian Ocean-Red Sea route to Egypt, see G. F. Hourani, *Arab Sea-faring in the Indian Ocean* (Princeton 1951), pp. 168-215. According to Moslem annalists, this led in the late 10th century to a tremendous decline of Bagdad and her prosperity.

imported to the Near East which earlier could only have come via Russian rivers. This was particularly true of iron, deficient in the Moslem Near East, but abundant in Spain and Tunisia.[295] In short, changing trade routes in the Mediterranean and expansion of commerce between Moslem West and Near East, the shifting of trade routes in the Indian Ocean and, finally, Turkish advances into Central Asia and South Russia itself—all had the effect of almost eliminating a commerce with the Moslem East via the Volga and Caspian, a trade which had grown from Sassanian times until 950. Such trade with the Moslem East as remained seems, from coin evidence, to have been largely by way of the Caucasus, farther to the west. While not inconsiderable, it could not replace the great Volga trade which had poured dirhems into Russia, the Baltic and Scandinavia for so long a time.

This ending of much of the commerce which had gone to the Islamic world via Russia had serious economic repercussions in the lands of Northern Europe. They will be discussed in the next chapter, but some of them already began to appear prior to 985. Kievan Russia's new interest in trade routes via Central Europe to Cracow and beyond, Vladimir's Western diplomacy as regards the Ottos, the Pope, the Poles and Bohemians, and his attempts to open trade routes towards the Baltic by way of the Niemen and Vistula, may have been but a reflection of a need to compensate for the ending of Volga trade to the East, and a resulting shift in the political and economic orientation of the Kievan state. Likewise, the rise of Poland along this new route to the Baltic and Central Europe, the demise of Birka and the growth of Gotland's importance equally show the beginnings of a new orientation of Northern Europe's commerce.

It would be wrong, however, to assume that the commerce of Kievan Russia was entirely an external and transit one and to base conclusions upon such an hypothesis. The external commerce of Russia in the tenth century was an important factor in the growth of its internal economy, but it was not as decisive as the preceding paragraphs may have made it appear. For Russia developed during these years an equally vital domestic trade, industry and agriculture. Kievan Russia herself was a vast trading area in which the south sent cattle and wheat north to the Novgorod region, in exchange for

[295] The growth of Arab trade in the Mediterranean, which began in the mid-9th century, reached its apogee in the 10th. See A. R. Lewis, *Naval Power and Trade in the Mediterranean*, pp. 132-224.

furs and other northern forest products.[296] We know that in the late tenth century Novgorod's merchants already had a chain of factories in southern Russian towns which owed their existence to this commerce. Probably internal exchange of weapons, metalware, linen and woolen cloth, furs, timber, salt, honey, wax, slaves and spices was more important to Russia than export trade. There seems to have been a merchant guild in Kiev as well as in Novgorod, and it was probably a group of guild merchants from Kiev, Chernikov and Pereslas who had the monopoly of trade with Constantinople. Russian cities like Suzdal, Novgorod, Smolensk, Chernikov, Polotsk and many others were probably in this period the largest trading centers in Europe, while their advanced commercial practices, as revealed in *The Earliest Russian Laws*, suggest a rather advanced economy. In short, by the time of Vladimir, Russia already had a vast internal market, a fact which helped to bring about some industrialization, advanced commercial practices and advanced types of economic organization.[297]

Nor was this progress confined to industry and commerce, for Russia's agricultural development also made great strides during these years. There is not space here to trace the growth of Kievan agriculture, but it is worth noting that this period saw in Russia, as in England, Ireland, Poland and the Germany of the Ottos, a continuing expansion of agricultural settlements. Much of her foreign commerce, particularly that consisting of honey and beeswax, was the result of a more intensive exploitation of natural and agricultural resources than was the case elsewhere in Slavic Europe. Perhaps it was in agriculture, as a matter of fact, that Kievan rulers were most successful. Trade with the Moslem East was a shadow of its former self by 985, that with Byzantium was later to all but disappear, but the fertile lands cleared and the agricultural riches exploited during these years were to continue to be the basis of later Russian greatness.[298]

At this point, one more factor concerning Kievan Russia needs

[296] *Kuny* and *skot* were the oldest terms for money in Russia, and a native Kievan coinage did not make its appearance until the time of Vladimir in the late 10th century. G. Vernadsky, *Kievan Russia*, pp. 121-23.

[297] On this important internal Russian trade and organization for trade, see I. M. Kulischer, *Russische Wirtschaftsgeschichte* (Jena 1923), pp. 100-18, and G. Vernadsky, *op.cit.*, pp. 116-20. See also *The Earliest Russian Laws*, trans. Vernadsky (New York 1947), pp. 29-78.

[298] On Russia's agriculture and its importance, see N. K. Chadwick, *The Beginnings of Russian History*, pp. 115-20; A. Eck, *Le Moyen Age russe* (Brussels 1932), pp. 5-33; and G. Vernadsky, *op.cit.*, pp. 99-108.

discussion: the role of Scandinavians in her economic development. There can be little doubt that the House of Rurik was almost completely Scandinavian in blood. Oleg, Igor, Olga, Sviatoslav and even Vladimir were as Scandinavian as the kings of Sweden, Norway, Dublin or York.[299] And they kept close connections with the lands from which they originated down to and past Vladimir's time. It was to Sweden, for instance, that Vladimir fled in 976 and in Scandinavia that he gathered together that band of Varangians who helped him regain his kingdom.[300] It was from the Viking north that Igor drew troops who helped him assault the Byzantine Empire and the Moslem Caspian in the 940's, and from there that Vladimir procured the mercenaries whom he sent on to Basil II. The words "Rus" or "Varyang," as used by Byzantine and Moslem writers of the period, still meant Scandinavian, and Islamic observers carefully distinguished between them and the Slavic population.[301]

Nor was this influence confined to war bands and the ruling family of Kiev. Scandinavian influence was extremely important in the commerce of Russia. The names which Constantine Porphyrogenitus gave to the rapids of the Dnieper were Scandinavian, and among the 25 known names of merchants who traded with Constantinople in 911 and 945, the majority are of Northern Viking origin also.[302] Similarly, the observations of Ibn Fadlan on Rus merchants who traded on the Volga in 920 make it evident that they, too, were Scandinavian in dress and customs.[303] And Ibn Rusta, Gardezi and Ibn Jacub clearly show that a large part of those who traded with Islam were *northern* Rus, not Slavic in origin.[304] The Scandinavian element in trade seems to have been as important as it was in warfare and government in tenth-century Russia.

If one grants this fact, one must also admit, however, that the Scandinavian element in Kievan Russia was not the only one which had influence. Slavic, Finnish and Oriental groups played almost equally vital roles. In 880-882 Oleg moved south with Finnish and Slav troops, as well as Varangians, to take Kiev and inaugurate a

---

[299] S. F. Cross, "Medieval Russian Contacts with the West," in *Speculum*, x (1935), 138-41.

[300] *The Primary Chronicle*, pp. 180-82.

[301] See the accounts of Ibn Rusta and Gardezi in *The Magyars in the Ninth Century*, pp. 192-94, 213-15, and Constantine Porphyrogenitus, *De administrando imperio*, pp. 75, 79.

[302] A. Bugge, *Nordeuropäischen Verkehrswege*, pp. 243-50.

[303] *Ibn Fadlan*, trans. Cook, pp. 56-63.

[304] Ibn Rusta and Gardezi, in *op.cit.*, pp. 192-94, 213-17. G. Jacob, *op.cit.*, p. 12.

Russian state.[305] Certainly, most of Igor's, Sviatoslav's and Vladimir's troops were drawn from the native Russian population. And there were important Slavic merchants, whose names are listed along with Scandinavian ones in the trade treaties of 911 and 945 with Byzantium,[306] and who are specifically mentioned by Gardezi[307] and Ibn Jacub.[308] Our first mention of Eastern merchants, those who traded with Raffelstein in 906, includes Slavs as well as *Rugi*, or Scandinavian Rus.[309] Nor were such Slavs the only other Russian traders. Jewish, Moslem and Turkish traders (perhaps Kazar in origin) were extremely active in this period. Ibn Jacub speaks of them at Prague at about the time of the fall of the Kazar kingdom. They seem to have moved freely throughout Russia and continued important in the land long after the tenth century.[310]

One must also emphasize that Scandinavian elements in Russia were rapidly slavicized. Rulers like Sviatoslav and Vladimir, though Norse in blood, bore Russian Slavic names. And there is evidence that the paganism of Scandinavia was not followed by Kievan rulers. Instead, prior to their conversion to Christianity, both rulers and Scandinavian merchants appear to have worshiped native Slav, Finnish and Central Asian divinities.[311] In short, the Varangian element, though vital to Kievan military, commercial and political development, rapidly became more Russian than Scandinavian. Vladimir could make use of Varangians and yet dislike them and their propensity for disorder. A Russian consciousness seems to have been already in the process of formation in the tenth century. Nor is this fact surprising, for it happened elsewhere in Northern Europe. The Scandinavian element which settled abroad in Ireland, the English Danelaw and Normandy was equally swift in its adoption of the ways, the speech, the religion and the ideas of the country of its choice. In this tendency lay the particular genius of the Scandinavians and their value to the formation of Europe.

[305] *The Primary Chronicle*, p. 146.   [306] *Ibid.*, pp. 149-52, 163-65.
[307] Gardezi, in *op.cit.*, pp. 192-94.
[308] G. Jacob, *op.cit.*, p. 12. According to Gatz, the same was true of Poland, where Slavs were the main traders. G. Gatz, *Kaffahrer, Kramer und Handelsherren* (Danzig 1942), p. 12.
[309] *MGH Capitularia*, II, 249-50.
[310] G. Jacob, *op.cit.*, p. 12. See fuller accounts in J. Rabinowitz, *Jewish Merchant Adventurers*, pp. 86-154; J. Brutzkus, "Trade with Eastern Europe, 800-1200," in *Economic History Review*, XIII (1943), 218-47; and L. Pariset, *Histoire de la soie*, II, 169-75.
[311] B. Grekov, *La Culture de la Russie de Kiev*, pp. 34-38. *The Primary Chronicle*, p. 150.

Such, then, are the features, political and economic, of the trading area which is to be found between 911 and 985 around the Northern Seas. It might be well to summarize its general character. It was a trading region which was based upon a vast, free exchange of products from Iceland, Ireland and Britain in the West to Russia in the East. It was one in which Scandinavia and the Baltic played a vital and intricate role as a clearing house, receiving industrial and agricultural goods and money from England, Ireland and Ottonian Germany in the West, importing agricultural products from Poland, Bohemia and Central Europe, and at the same time exchanging them for Eastern wares and silver money coming by way of Russia. It also saw the first steps in the formation of a Central European land trade route which would by-pass the Baltic and link West and East together directly. Up to 960, at least, Hedeby, Gotland and Novgorod were the main central links in this vast East-West exchange. After this date, Central European towns like Prague began to assume a new importance and a similar role.

In the West this economic world had few links with the Mediterranean, except by way of England and Ireland with Spain and Italy, and some via Italy with Southern Germany after 955. On the other hand, the eastern anchor of this trading area in Russia was closely connected with Byzantium and the Moslem Middle East, and this did much to stimulate the commerce of Russia, Central Europe and the Baltic.

It would be well, however, not to overestimate the importance of the Byzantine Empire and Moslem East to this great northern trading area—even to the trade of Kievan Russia itself. For the products which created and made possible the international trade of the Northern Seas in this period were native to Northern Europe for the most part—not Eastern imports. These products were the same, in general, which had figured in the international commerce of these regions since Merovingian times. They were the linen, cloth, honey and leather of Ireland; the tin, copper, lead, silver, metalware, cloth and wheat of England; the glass, cloth, arms, pottery, wine, salt and metals of the Ottonian Empire; the fish, iron, wool, furs, wood and Arctic products of Scandinavia and Iceland; the honey, wax, wheat and tin of Bohemia and Poland; the wax, honey and furs of Russia—with salt and slaves as staples of commerce everywhere. In general, England, Belgium and Western Germany were the industrial regions of this Northern European trading area, as they had been since Late Roman times. Scandinavia and Central and Eastern Europe were the agricultural regions.[312] The trade from these products, supplemented by some Eastern silver, spices and silk, had created, by the late tenth century, commercial centers in England, Ireland, along the Meuse and Rhine and upper Danube and in Saxony. Nidaros, Tønsberg, Ribe, Hedeby, Aarhus, Birka and Gotland all grew up in Scandinavia, while we find Wollin, Gneizno, Truso, Cracow and Prague in North Central Europe and many important Russian cities. Such centers as London, Dublin, Cologne, Hedeby, Wollin, Prague, Novgorod and Kiev were, by 985, much more than simple trading centers. They were already cities in the later medieval sense of the word, housing a large urban population and appearing international in the scope and the influence of their commercial activities.

Perhaps the best indication of the separation from the rest of Europe of this great northern trading area we have been describing lies in its silver coinage and lack of gold. It was silver coins from England and Germany, both based on the Carolingian penny, and dirhems of Russia and the Baltic—identical in size and weight— which tied the region together. This silver standard was separate from the gold dinars and byzants which made the Mediterranean in these years a single trading area, too. When this Mediterranean gold standard spread west and east in the tenth century to include those parts of Moslem Spain, North Africa, Iraq and Persia which had earlier been restricted to silver dirhem coinage,[313] it did not touch the north of Europe, even though the trade of the Indian Ocean was deeply affected. Judging from coin hoards, it was still Moslem silver, rather than gold, which passed north by way of Russia to the Baltic, and silver which Byzantium sent north to pay for furs, slaves, beeswax and honey brought by Varangian merchants to Constantinople. In all Scandinavian tenth-century hoards, among their thousands of silver coins we find only a handful of Byzantine and Arab gold pieces. They include the 14 Byzantine *solidi* found near Oslo,[314] and a total of 9 byzants and dinars from the Baltic, 8 of them from Gotland and Swedish hoards[315] and one from Lithuania.[316] Perhaps enough gold

[312] Although in shipbuilding, woodworking and use of metals, Scandinavia and Eastern Europe made industrial advances in this period.

[313] A. R. Lewis, *op.cit.*, pp. 168-73.

[314] On this Stromshaug hoard, a unique find of Byzantine *solidi*, see H. Holst, *Numismatica Fasc.*, VII (1928), 83-91.

[315] On the lack of gold coins in Gotland hoards from the Viking period, see M. Stenberger, *op.cit.*, pp. 683-714.

[316] F. Balodis, *Det Aldsta Lettland*, p. 166.

came from the south so that Vladimir could issue some gold coinage in the late tenth century at Kiev,[317] but even there it was not important, for Russia remained for some centuries on a silver standard for all practical purposes.

This does not mean that there was not a certain amount of gold in Northern Europe during this period. There was, just as had been true in earlier Carolingian times. In Ireland and Wales, as we have noted, gold was common and, in the form of bullion or jewelry, we find even more of it in Anglo-Saxon England. There it was coined into gold pennies by kings like Edward the Elder, Eadred and Aethelred II for special purposes. But our evidence seems to show that England's gold came from Ireland and perhaps Wales as well, and that it was essentially a local phenomenon.[318]

In Gotland's hoards we find a certain number of gold rings and other jewelry dating from this period.[319] We hear, too, of Adalbert of Prague, who complained of the *infelix aurum* which the slave trade brought to his land in the late tenth century.[320] But it seems probable that this Bohemian gold, like that found in Gotland, was a local phenomenon. Masudi mentions gold mines in Bohemia,[321] probably referring to the gold production at Liegnitz in nearby Silesia which was important in the next and subsequent centuries. It is likely that the *infelix aurum* of Adalbert came from this source. In fact, there is no evidence that the slave trade, whether with Byzantium, the Moslem East, Italy or Spain, was essentially one paid for in gold.[322] We may,

---

[317] I. M. Kulischer, *Russische Wirtschaftsgeschichte*, p. 19. But gold was still very rare in the Kievan period, when a silver standard prevailed. On Russia's *grivna*, or ring-money, in this period, see G. Vernadsky, *Kievan Russia*, pp. 121-23.

[318] See especially P. Grierson, *Carolingian Europe and the Arabs, The Myth of the Mancus*, and the articles by Blunt and Allen in *Brit. Numis. Journal*, xxv (1945-48).

[319] Gotland's Viking hoards contain a total of 108 gold bracelets, 22 gold rings and 38 *brachteates*, as well as some gold jewelry. But some, if not most, of this probably came from gold present in Scandinavia in Early Merovingian times rather than being imported in this period. M. Stenberger, *op.cit.*, pp. 513-707.

[320] M. Lombard, "L'Or mussulman de VIIe au XIe siècles," in *Annales*, II (1947), 155-56.

[321] I. Marquart, *Osteuropäische und ostasiatische Streifzüge*, p. 102.

[322] Not only are coins found in the Baltic from the Byzantine and Moslem worlds almost entirely *silver*, but so are those from Italy found in England and Ireland and the few found in French hoards. Even in Asturias, near a Moslem Spain which was on a gold standard, gold dinars are only mentioned three times in our sources, in 943, 977 and 984. On the other hand, there is abundant evidence of the use of silver dirhems or *solidos hazimas* in León and Portugal. C. Sanchez-Albornoz, "Primitiva organización monetaria de León y Castilla," in *Ann. de hist. del derecho español*, v (1928), 306-12. The so-called favorable balance of trade in *gold* which Lombard believes came from trade with the Moslem world (M. Lombard, *op.cit.*, pp. 155-58) must then be

therefore, assume that the lack of gold coinage in current use in Northern Europe reflected not only the area's separateness from the Mediterranean worlds of Islam and Byzantium, but a condition which no slave trade could adequately change during these years. In fact, the very stoppage of trade to the Moslem East at the moment it turned from a silver to a gold coinage is a most interesting phenomenon.

There was one section of the Northern Seas, however, which shared little in the trade which was so noticeable in the area from Ireland to Russia. That region consisted of France and the northwestern coast of Spain, which might almost be considered a depressed sub-area of Northern Europe for many decades. This is a most curious fact indeed. France, from 900 on, seems to have had an economy which was essentially local, matching the feudal duchies and counties into which it had disintegrated. And not a single foreign coin hoard of this period, except a few in West Britain and Ireland, contains French money. German coins and English as well are found from Iceland to Finland. So, too, are Samanid dirhems. But not French coins. Nor do we find in France dirhems, which were a symbol of Baltic connections. British and Irish merchants visited French coasts, but their trade seems to have been almost completely local during most of this tenth century, and the separate hoards of French and Samanid silver found about the Irish Sea appear to emphasize the separation of the rest of the Northern Seas from Gallic economic patterns.

That does not mean that the trading centers which existed at the time of Charles the Bald disappeared. They did not. During the reign of Charles the Simple (898-923) coins were minted in his name at Paris, St. Denis, Beauvais, Senlis, Meaux and Châlons-sur-Marne in the region about Paris, and at Autun and Mâcon in Central France.[323] Under Raoul (923-936) royal mints were in operation at Beauvais, Meaux, Paris, St. Denis, Soissons, Chartres and Etampes in the Paris area, and at Bourges, Le Puy, Angoulême and Orléans in Western France.[324] Under Louis d'Outremer we find coins minted in the king's name at Paris, Reims, Rouen, Bourges, Nevers, Mâcon and Chalon-sur-Saône.[325] But such royal coinage tells only part of

---

regarded as a myth. The gold which Northern Europe possessed in this period can only have been of *local*, not Moslem origin—with the possible exception of Kievan Russia.

[323] M. Prou, *Catalogue des monnaies carolingiennes*, pp. LXXIX-LXXXIV.
[324] *Ibid.*, pp. LXXXV-LXXXVI.   [325] *Ibid.*, pp. LXXXVI-LXXXIX.

the story. For in the tenth century, minting of money ceased to be a regalian right in France, and many feudal lords, churches and abbeys coined money of their own. At Rouen, for instance, coins minted during this period included, first, a ducal coinage of William Longsword and Richard I, and then a type copied from the royal mintage of Louis IV, which continued up until the eleventh century.[326] In Flanders the counts minted their own money at Arras, Bruges, Courtrai and Ghent throughout the tenth century.[327] The Dukes of Brittany did the same at Nantes and Rennes, particularly the latter.[328] Other baronial types were struck at Bordeaux, at Melle and in the Charente region,[329] as well as at Troyes, Clermont, Blois and Toulouse. Abbeys like St. Martial at Limoges, St. Martin of Tours, and St. Bertin at St. Omer issued their own money.[330] In Poitiers, in the Loire valley, along the Seine and in Northeastern France a very large proportion of Carolingian mints seem to have continued in operation, though not often under royal control.

One finds other signs of economic life during this period in France. Tournai, for instance, continued as a *portus* right into the tenth century. Called so in 898, it was again so mentioned in a Papal bull of 988.[331] Noyon, farther south and inland on the Ouse, was, according to Rolland, a colony of Tournai in the tenth century and in 901 possessed a fair.[332] Wissant, Guines, Quentovic and Rouen, as we have noted, all traded with England during this period, and late in the century the men of Rouen, Ponthieu and Flanders were mentioned as trading in London, those of Rouen carrying wine there.[333] As early as 963 there was mention of a fair at Châlons-sur-Marne and of one at Provins in 976,[334] perhaps a sign of a local exchange of wine for Flanders cloth, which was to grow into the Fairs of Champagne of later centuries. The part of France closest to the Rhinelands and England, then, showed some signs of economic life—though on a fairly local scale throughout the tenth century.

[326] Blanchet and Dieudonné, *Manuel de numismatique*, IV, 302-4.
[327] *Ibid.*, p. 183.   [328] *Ibid.*, pp. 122-23.
[329] M. Prou, *op.cit.*, pp. LXXXVIII-LXXXIX. Blanchet and Dieudonné, *op.cit.*, pp. 369-72.
[330] *Ibid.*, pp. 8, 334-36, 365-66.
[331] P. Rolland, *Le Problème de la continuité à Tournai*, pp. 260-63. See also *Bull. of Pope John*, XV, in *Patrologia Latina*, CXXXVI, cols. 828-30.
[332] P. Rolland, *op.cit.*, pp. 261-63. On the rebuilding of the church at Cambrai after 954, see H. Van Werweke, "Note sur le commerce de plomb," in *Mélanges Pirenne*, II, 18-33.
[333] F. Liebermann, *Gesetze*, II, 161-63.
[334] P. Rolland, *op.cit.*, pp. 278-79.

In the Loire valley one notices the same phenomenon, though Vikings disturbed this region as late as 930. In 919, for instance, St. Martin of Tours rebuilt its church. The style of this construction was imitated in Orléans in 940, and in Clermont in 947.[335] Limoges, an important spot along the pilgrim route to Compostela, seems to have been the center of some commerce by the last years of the tenth century.[336] Money struck at Rennes and Nantes was imitated by the coinage of Anjou, particularly that minted at Blois and Le Mans.[337] We find the same types of money at Bordeaux and nearby Saintes.[338] And a duke of Normandy was familiar enough with Spanish coasts to be able, in 964, to furnish Vikings at Rouen with pilots to guide them to those shores on pirate expeditions.[339] In fact, between 910 and 976 Viking raids on Asturias were almost constant.[340] France during these years was remote from the main trade currents of Northern Europe, but a certain local economic life continued along the coasts and in the interior, and even increased in intensity as the century wore on.

Coin hoards again depict this situation graphically and reveal the conditions of the time. For instance, the Saumur hoard of the early tenth century, dating from the reign of Charles the Simple, includes 2 Angers and 2 Tours deniers minted by Charles the Bald, one Tours of Charles the Fat, 2 Tours of Louis III, 56 Angers and 26 Tours of Eudes and 1,010 Melle deniers of Charles the Simple. Only coins from Melle, Tours and Angers are represented here.[341] The Evreux hoard in the Seine valley, dating from these years, is somewhat similar in character. In it are coins from Angers, Blois, Chartres, Chateaudun, Orléans, Tours, Paris and St. Denis—all local—and one each from Bourges, Reims and Le Mans, plus 14 badly made copies of the coins of Louis the Pious.[342] That of Langres, of the same general period, has one Berengar Italian silver piece, but all the rest are from the local Langres mint.[343] Another at Assebrauch in Flanders, from

---

[335] E. Mâle, *La Fin du paganisme en Gaule et les plus anciennes basiliques chrétiennes* (Paris 1950), pp. 147-50.

[336] J. Lestoquoy, "Le Commerce des œuvres d'art au moyen âye," in *Mélanges d'hist. sociale*, II (1943), 19-26.

[337] Blanchet and Dieudonné, *op.cit.*, pp. 122-23.

[338] *Ibid.*, pp. 334-36. Tours money in 970 appears to have been imitated at Toulouse as well. *Ibid.*, pp. 369-71.

[339] H. Shetelig, *The Viking History of Western Europe*, p. 140.

[340] *Ibid.*, pp. 139-40. F. Lot, *Les Invasions barbares*, pp. 160-61.

[341] E. Gariel, *op.cit.*, p. 128.   [342] *Ibid.*, pp. 128-31.

[343] This *one* Berengar Italian coin shows some contact between this section of Burgundy and Italy, probably by way of the Alpine *clusae*. *Ibid.*, pp. 131-32.

the reign of Charles the Simple, contains 139 Bruges deniers, 48 from Arras, 13 from Quentovic and 4 interlopers from St. Denis.[344]

Several somewhat later hoards reveal the same type of information. A small find at Cordre on the Loire from the reign of Louis d'Out-remer contains only money from Tours. Another from St. Tourin in Normandy has 2 coins from Blois, one from Le Mans, 2 from Vendôme, 16 from Rouen and 5 degenerate copies of the coinage of Louis the Pious.[345] Another from Central France, dating from about 950, contains 279 coins from Bourges, 266 from Melle, 35 from Nevers, 10 from Limoges, 10 from Auxerre, 5 from Le Mans, one from Blois and 65 Norman deniers.[346] Save for the Norman coins, this hoard again seems local to Western France.

Thus in coin hoards we see the essentials of tenth-century French economic history. A certain local trade existed and a certain continuation of mints is revealed. Some trade seems to have linked Rouen with the Loire valley and Flanders with the Seine. But it was all on a very small scale. Not until about 1000 was there to be a real reversal of economic tides in France, a growth of French commerce and a revival of towns. In contrast, then, to Germany, Ireland, England, Scandinavia, Central Europe and Russia, France hardly felt the trade current flowing through the Northern Seas.

Somewhat similar was the situation in Northern Spain during these years. León, beyond the mountains, was already a town with a merchant quarter and trade in Byzantine and Moslem products which arrived from the Mediterranean—even some mentioned in 938 and 1003 as coming from France.[347] Jewish merchants were the chief intermediaries in this commerce. And we find mention of Arab gold dinars in a number of Portuguese and Asturian documents dating from 943, 977 and 984. But in Galicia we discover that the money in use differed from that in León. Here are found the so-called *solidi gallicanes*, or French coins, which bear little relation to those in use in the interior farther south. Evidently, though new commercial

---

[344] *Ibid.*, pp. 133-34. The late 9th-century or early 10th-century hoard of Avignon shows the same type of localism in this part of Southern France. It contains 3 Clermont coins, one Toulouse and one Italian coin of Charles the Bold (this latter coined in Rome in conjunction with Pope John VIII during Charles' expedition there), 6 Arles and one Substantion of Carloman, one Beziers, one Uzès and one Nîmes of Charles the Fat, one *Christian Religio* type of the Bishop of Arles (perhaps 10th century) and, by the time of Charles the Simple, 44 of Arles only. *Ibid.*, pp. 147-53.

[345] *Ibid.*, pp. 147-53.

[346] *Ibid.*, pp. 153-54.

[347] C. Sanchez-Albornoz, *Estampas de la Vida en León durante el Siglo X*, pp. 11-20, 52.

388

currents were already touching this part of Spain, the same localism was prevalent as in France.[348]

There remains one more important problem to be considered in the development of Northern Europe during this period. That is the relationship between the castles and other fortifications which were to be found everywhere about the Northern Seas by 985, and the trading settlements of the time. Few questions concerning early European history have been more thoroughly debated, and few are more complex.

Perhaps it would be best to trace the rise of fortifications in Europe during this period as a preliminary step towards an answer to this problem. One thing seems certain. In Carolingian times most *wicks*, ports and *civitates* of the Carolingian Empire west of the Rhine possessed little fortification. A few centers like Utrecht[349] or frontier bourgs like those established by 805 along the Slav-Avar frontier were fortified.[350] Such a fortress was Itzehoe, which Charlemagne built between Hamburg and Hedeby to protect the frontier from the Danes.[351] These resembled the forts of the Marcher Lords of England on the Welsh frontier in the later medieval period. They probably were found in Spain and parts of the Midi, too, where we know cities like Saragossa and Barcelona in the early ninth century possessed walls.[352] But in the heart of the Carolingian Empire, neither the trading centers of the Rhinelands and Northern France nor the great abbeys and other administrative centers were fortified. In a number of cases, in centers like Reims, Beauvais, Sens and Melun, Late Roman walls, in use at the time of Gregory of Tours, had been allowed to fall into disrepair or had been pulled down.[353] In England the same thing occurred and in Ireland also. In these countries, neither monasteries nor ports were fortified by the first years of the ninth century.

Regarding Scandinavia, our information is less certain. Trading places there were few in number, and some like Gotland seem to have been fairs of the pre-urban sort rather than permanent trading com-

---

[348] *Ibid.*, p. 38, and C. Sanchez-Albornoz, *Primitiva organizacion monetaria en León y Castilla*, pp. 306-16.

[349] C. W. Werbist, *Saint Willibrod* (Louvain 1939), pp. 99-102.

[350] The Capitulary of Thionville in 805 suggests that these bourgs were frontier posts controlling trade with the Slavs and Avars.

[351] H. Shetelig, *op.cit.*, pp. 106-7.

[352] On Spanish fortifications, see R. Buckler, *Harunul'-Rashid and Charles the Great* (Cambridge, Mass., 1931), pp. 8-17.

[353] F. Vercauteren, *Belgique Secunde*, pp. 370-71. The same is true of Tournai, according to P. Rolland, *op.cit.*, pp. 256-58.

munities. At both Birka and Hedeby a fortress or castle existed, it is true, but in either case there is little evidence that the entire trading community was fortified.[354]

In the Slavic world to the east, however, quite a different situation existed in Carolingian times. This was a land covered with *grody*, or fortresses, to which the population could retire in time of attack. The proto-historic *grody* of Poland have been most carefully studied, and they reveal that the region between the Oder and the Vistula was dotted with such fortifications to protect the peasant population who lived in them or in their shadow.[355] We find from archeology that the same situation prevailed in Esthonia and Latvia during this period.[356] In Russia, as well, such fortresses abounded and the Scandinavian name for Russia was *Guardrike*, or land of the *grody*. To regard more than a few of these *grody*, like Novgorod, Kiev or Smolensk, for example, as towns would be an error. Most were simple places of rural, tribal refuge in time of danger. In the Slavic east by the ninth century all trading places were fortified, but all fortifications were by no means trading places. In a sense, then, Slavic Europe resembled later medieval patterns of defense much more than it did the other European lands to the west.

It was the period of Viking assaults which began to change the fortification pattern of Western Europe. At first, except in those coastal regions where Charlemagne built naval defenses, there is little evidence of fortifications being established. Abbeys like Armagh, Lindisfarne and Noirmoutier and ports like Quentovic, Dorestad and Canterbury were completely unprepared for raiders, who arrived without warning by sea and departed before hastily raised bands of local warriors could oppose them. Neither Irish tribal governments nor Anglo-Saxon kings nor Carolingian monarchs could at first discover an effective method of dealing with such attacks.

Soon the Vikings inaugurated a new phase. They began to construct permanent fortified camps on islands just offshore, at the mouths of rivers or elsewhere. From these fortresses they could raid into the interior, and there they could retreat when local resistance to their plundering became dangerous. Apparently Ireland was the first to

[354] H. Arbman, *Birka*, and H. Jankuhn, *Haithabu 1937-39*, show by archeological evidence the relatively peaceful and unfortified nature of both these centers in Carolingian times.

[355] J. Kostrzewski, *op.cit.*, pp. 102-4.

[356] On the archeological evidence, see F. Balodis, *op.cit.*, pp. 126-63, which discusses such typical *grody* as Apolloné, Seeburg, Grobina, etc., in eastern Baltic regions.

see this sort of fortification: Dublin, built by Thorgisl in 831.[357] Soon many more were constructed along French and English shores. Sheppey and Thanet at the mouth of the Thames were occupied by 851,[358] and other islands at the mouths of the Loire, Garonne, Charente, Seine and Somme a little later. The Scandinavian invaders may have gotten the idea of such fortresses from their Slavic neighbors or they may have developed them independently as an answer to certain raiding problems which they encountered in Western Europe. At any rate, the use of these fortified camps made the Vikings especially formidable foes, since they were difficult to capture. Charles the Bald discovered this when he attempted to take the Viking fortress of Oisella on the Seine in 862,[359] and so did Anglo-Saxon monarchs again and again. Finally, in the great Danish invasion of England in 865-878 and the subsequent large-scale Viking attack on the Low Countries in 879-892, the Scandinavian freebooters brought their techniques of fortifying camps to a new level of perfection. In the Netherlands they transformed Asseult, Louvain, Ghent and Courtrai into fortresses which proved extremely difficult to take,[360] as were their camps on the Seine and Loire.[361] In England, too, it was the fortresses built by Gudrum's Danish army which helped to make Alfred's defense of Wessex and the reconquest of his kingdom so difficult a task.[362] For many years the Danish Five Boroughs of the Midlands stood as a barrier to Anglo-Saxon advances north in the tenth century,[363] while York's fortifications proved of such value to the Danes that Aethelstan, when he conquered it in 927 but proved too weak to hold it, carefully pulled down the city's walls and dismantled its fortifications.[364]

If the Vikings first discovered the value of such forts in Europe, their victims were not long in recognizing the advantages which they

[357] J. Ryan, "Pre-Norse Dublin," in *Proc. of Royal Soc. of Antiq. of Ireland*, L (1949), 64-65.

[358] R. Hodgkin, *History of the Anglo-Saxons*, II, 517-18.

[359] T. D. Kendrick, *History of the Vikings*, pp. 209-10.

[360] See H. Vander Linden, "Les Normands à Louvain," in *Revue hist.*, CXXIV (1924), 64-81. F. L. Ganshof, *Les Origines du Comté de Flandre*, pp. 17-20.

[361] On these *Dani* in Western Gaul, see L. Auzias, *L'Aquitaine carolingienne*, pp. 285-328.

[362] On these Danish fortified camps, see F. Stenton, *Anglo-Saxon England*, pp. 250-67.

[363] A. Mawrer, "The Redemption of the Five Boroughs," in *Eng. Hist. Review*, XXXVIII (1903), 551-56.

[364] F. Stenton, *op.cit.*, pp. 352-53. William of Malmesbury, *Gesta regum*, in *Roll Series*, I, 148.

possessed. The first organized governmental attempt to build a fort-ress seems to have been the bridge at Pîtres which Charles the Bald built and fortified in order to deny the Vikings the use of the Seine.[365] Soon afterwards, around 867 or 868, local magnates were constructing castles in the Charente region to protect this district from Viking invaders.[366] By 885-886 Paris was protected by walls. In Flanders and Northern France we find similar fortifications at Bruges in 879, Cambrai soon after 881, Arras soon after 883, Langres in 887, Tournai in 898, St. Omer in 891 and Huy in 895.[367] The castles at Ghent and Antwerp, once supposed to date no earlier than the tenth century, are now shown by archeology to have been earlier, probably representing the occupation and use of fortifications originally constructed by the Vikings. Everywhere the story is the same. Trading centers like those mentioned above, abbeys like Monteuil-sur-Mer, bishops' residences like Utrecht, which was fortified about 920, show the trend of the times.[368] By 950 France and the Low Countries were covered with fortifications, either newly built fortresses or older Roman works, such as those used at Cologne. They served as centers to protect the inhabitants of a certain area, or they represented protection for an abbey or the residence of a king or high churchman.

We find this process going on in England, too, starting in the last years of the ninth century. As Alfred reconquered his land, he es-tablished fortresses, called boroughs, in the areas he took from the Danes. Some were new, others were established settlements like London, Rochester, Canterbury or Winchester, where walls were now built. As his successors, Aethelfrida of Mercia, Edward the Elder, Aethelstan, Edmund and Eadred, reconquered the Danelaw, they continued this practice.[369] By 959, England, like France and the Low Countries, was covered with fortifications. English fortresses, however, differed from those of France in being planned and organ-ized by a central government. They remained under royal control and were placed under the power of a public official. By Aethelstan's

---

[365] F. Lot, "Le Pont de Pîtres," in *Le Moyen Age*, XI (1905), 217-31.

[366] Ademar de Chabannes, *Chron.*, III, 19, ed. Chavannon (Paris 1897), p. 137.

[367] See the excellent account of the building of castles in the Low Countries in F. L. Ganshof, *Etudes sur le développement des villes entre Loire et Rhin*, pp. 11-20. See also F. Vercauteren, "Comment s'est-on defendu contre les invasions normandes?" in *Annales du XXXᵉ Congrès de la fed. hist. de Belgique* (1936), pp. 219-57.

[368] F. L. Ganshof, *op.cit.*, p. 20.

[369] F. Stenton, *op.cit.*, pp. 300-86. See also C. Stephenson, *Borough and Town*, and J. Tait, *The Medieval English Borough*.

time each one of them had a mint.[370] But the general result was similar to that found in France.

In Ireland much the same thing happened. There, in the interior, by the late ninth century, fortresses were also established, particularly around abbeys like Glendalough.[371] The round towers of Ireland, so long considered a mystery, are now believed by Petrie to have been built as protection against the Vikings in the same period.[372] Nor were such fortifications constructed by the native Irish alone. Viking settlers at various coastal points like Limerick, Wexford and Waterford built fortifications that matched those of Dublin.[373] All through the tenth century and later they helped to perpetuate Viking power in the island.

In Germany, the tenth century saw a similar movement under way. Henry the Fowler, under the impetus of Hungarian and Slavic raids, and to hold his Slavic conquests in Eastern Germany, began to build bourgs in Saxony and Thuringia. This work was continued by his successors. Sometimes old Roman walls served as the nucleus of such fortifications, as at Strasbourg or Trier. Sometimes, as at Brunabor or Magdeburg, new ones were constructed.[374] By 960, at any rate, the Ottonian Empire, like England, France and Ireland, was dotted with fortresses. But Germany resembled England, and differed from France and Ireland, in the fact that it was the central power of the ruler which lay behind such fortifications. Except in Eastern Marcher districts, he maintained control over them, establishing the mints and markets they contained and the regulations under which they functioned.

Even farther to the east the fortress impetus continued. Miezko of Poland, in the late tenth century, built a special new type of *grody* along his Elbe frontiers to protect them from Germans or hostile Slavic enemies, and to keep a firm hold on valuable trading places like Stettin.[375] Nor were Danish rulers of the period unaware of the advantages of fortresses. The revived Dannevirke of Harold Blue-

---

[370] *The Laws of Aethelstan*, II, 14, in C. Attenborough, *The Earliest English Laws*, p. 135.

[371] L. Price, *Féilsgribhinn Eóirin Mhic Néill* (Dublin 1950), pp. 7-17.

[372] P. J. Noone, *Glendalough and the Seven Churches* (Kilmartin Hill, Ireland, 1950).

[373] J. Ryan, *Pre-Norse Dublin*, pp. 67-78.

[374] Oman, *The Art of War*, pp. 118-29. F. Lot, *L'Art militaire et les armées au moyen âge*, pp. 142-44.

[375] J. Kostryzewski, *op.cit.*, pp. 104-12, analyzes evidence from excavations on specially constructed *grody* at Gniezno, Poznan, Lubusz and Santok.

tooth, Hedeby's tenth-century walls and the fortress pirate center of Jomsburg, near Wollin, all illustrate the value they attached to such defenses.[376] Even in Russia in the late tenth century Vladimir was stimulated to build *grody* to protect his lands to the south from Patzinak attacks.[377] Apparently in Poland these *grody* were under an official appointed by the ruler, called a *zupan*, with powers much like those exercised by the port-reeve in England or Ottonian castellans. He not only commanded the castle garrison but regulated markets and governed the surrounding district in the monarch's name.[378] Probably the same system prevailed in Russia. And in Norway, in the late tenth century, we find established settlements under the control of a similar royal official.[379] By 950 Northern Europe was a land of fortresses, either based on older Roman or Slavic fortifications or completely new foundations.

What was the relationship between these fortresses and the growing commercial centers of this period? Was castle or bourg or borough the nucleus about which the later towns of Europe grew? Here we must beware of hasty generalizations. Certainly these fortifications exerted an influence upon both older and newer settlements, upon *wicks*, ports and the like in Northern Europe. They furnished protection in an age when it was much needed. In certain areas like England, Germany, Scandinavia and the Slavic East, they served as administrative centers, where coins were minted and where justice was dispensed. To a lesser extent this was true of fortresses in France and the Low Countries. Such activities increased the economic importance of such centers and may have helped commercial development. Some fortresses, like certain ones in Ireland, or Bruges in Flanders,[380] or a number of boroughs, bourgs and *grody* in England,[381] Germany[382] and Poland,[383] may have been the germ from

---

[376] Thietmar, *Chron.*, I, 17. H. Jankuhn, *Ergebnisse und Probleme der Haithabugrabungen*, pp. 12-31.

[377] G. Vernadsky, *Kievan Russia*, pp. 73-74.

[378] J. Kostryzewski, *op.cit.*, pp. 112-28.

[379] On these *gjardkeri*, see O. Tønning, *op.cit.*, pp. 11-13.

[380] Bruges seems to have arisen in this period with a castle as a nucleus which was built by the Counts of Flanders about 879 or earlier. F. L. Ganshof, "Iets over Brugge gerunde de preconstitutionale periode," in *Niederlandsche Historie-Bladen*, I (1938), 281-85.

[381] See J. Tait, *op.cit.*, pp. 17-153, and C. Stephenson, *op.cit.*, pp. 81-206, on the development of English boroughs into towns. Also R. Darlington, "The Early History of English Towns," in *History*, XXIII (1938), 163-67.

[382] On Germany, E. Ennen, "Neuere Arbeiten zur Geschichte des nordwesteuropas Stadtwesens im Mittelalter," in *Viert. für Soz- und Wirtschaft*, XXXVIII (1949),

which the later towns grew. In certain other cases, like Ghent[384] and Southampton,[385] we find the Carolingian *portus* moved to a location nearer the newly erected fortress.

But just as often it was the *portus*, or trading center, which preceded the fortification, as at Tours, Orléans, Maastricht, Verdun, Poitiers, Cologne, London, Worms, Mainz, Winchester and Hedeby. And it is equally important to note how few of the many tenth-century fortresses ever developed into urban centers at all.[386] It was agricultural growth, industry and trade that created the towns and the embryos of towns by the tenth century, not fortifications or governmental activities carried on in such places. The presence of fortresses in certain natural trade locations helped the process along in some cases, but they did not—indeed, they could not—cause trading settlements to form in the Europe of this period. This was done by economic forces far beyond the power of rulers of this period either to create or to control.

If this be doubted, a bit of tenth-century evidence from England may prove decisive. The powerful Aethelstan, who built many boroughs, established a single pure coinage for his realm and, being interested in economic matters, attempted to control the trade of his realm. Perhaps in so doing he was trying to increase his revenues from taxes levied on commerce. At any rate, in one of his early laws he directed that *all* trade of more than a few pennies in value would take place in a royal borough or *portus* under the supervision of a king's official, the port-reeve.[387] Yet this proved a failure almost at once, for a later enactment allowed free trade, under certain minimum conditions,

---

sums up the latest theories and research.

[383] J. Kostryzewski, *op.cit.*, pp. 110-14, makes it clear that all later Polish towns had a *grody* as their original nucleus.

[384] On the establishment of a second *portus* at Ghent near the castle, see "De Twee opoolgente gentsche 'portus,'" in *Hand. Soc. Emil. Brugge*, II (1939), 37-41.

[385] On the move of Southampton from the original *portus* at Hamwith to a new location near the castle between 900 and 1086, see M. Maitland-Miller, "Southampton Excavations," in *Hampshire Field Club Proceedings*, XVIII (1950), 2. Maitland-Miller believes, however, that some of old Hamwith continued its existence near the Church of St. Mary at the older location.

[386] This was particularly true in Poland and among the Baltic Slavs, where the Obodrites had 53 *grody* and the Lucicians 95 in all. J. Kostryzewski, *op.cit.*, p. 106. It is also true in England, where only *ports* became commercially important—not *all* boroughs. J. Tait, *op.cit.*, pp. 30-46. Also we know that the round towers of Ireland almost never developed into urban centers. Nor did many castles in France and Germany either.

[387] *Laws of Aethelstan*, II, 12, in C. Attenborough, *Earliest English Laws*, p. 135.

in districts outside these boroughs,[388] a proviso that his successor Edgar repeated in later laws with some modification.[389] Economic growth could, it seems, be helped by borough centers of tenth-century England, but it could neither be restricted to them nor controlled through them.

To summarize, the development of fortresses and other fortified areas in Northern Europe was an outgrowth of Viking and Hungarian raids, governmental policies of rulers like Miezko and Vladimir and the rising feudalism of a land like France. It was not a decisive element for or against the great economic growth which we have been viewing in Northern Europe during this period. Like the forts which dotted our American West during our advance to the Pacific, some fortresses helped to create economic and commercial growth, some had little influence upon it, and some may even have hindered it. It is not to such fortresses, nor to the feudal lords, churchmen or monarchs who erected them, that we must turn for the causes of the rise of towns and town embryos in tenth-century Europe. Rather it was the improved agriculture, the increased shipping and the international trade routes which, from 911 to 985, laid the basis of future economic progress.

[388] *Laws of Aethelstan*, IV, 2, in *ibid.*, p. 147.
[389] *Laws of Edgar*, IV, 5, in *ibid.*, p. 163.

7. The Danish Sea Empire and the Kievan Kingdom, A.D. 985-1043

THE YEARS from 911 to 985, following the period of Viking assaults, had been quiet ones around the Northern Seas. Perhaps the naval strength developed by the House of Alfred in England accounts for this lull in maritime conflict. The slow process of integration of Scandinavians into the life of the lands where they settled—in France, England, Ireland and Russia—may have absorbed all Viking energies. Perhaps the peaceful growth and economic progress of these decades left little room or need for Scandinavian warlike activity. Certainly strong monarchies in Norway and in Sweden in the first years of the tenth century, and in Denmark, Kiev and Poland a little later, provided few opportunities for Viking onslaughts. At any rate, it would seem that up to 980 such piratical activities, even such naval actions as occurred, were of minor consequence. Kievan monarchs launched one great naval raid in the Black Sea and a second in the Caspian. Several naval battles were fought off Norway's coasts as a new Denmark arose. English, Irish and Anglo-Danish flotillas maneuvered in the Irish Sea and off Yorkshire. But the general tenor of maritime activities was commercial, not aggressive, except in areas of the Eastern Baltic and along the western shores of Spain and France, where some Viking traditions lingered and where no strong governments existed to keep order. It might have seemed that the integration and absorption of Scandinavia, the Baltic region and Central Europe into a European world would take place rapidly and without further difficulty.

That, however, was not to be. Suddenly, in the 980's, we find a new wave of piratical attacks, a return to Viking days in the Northern Seas. Scandinavians returned to the pattern of their freebooting past, sailing west again from Norway, Denmark and Sweden to harry the coasts of England and Ireland, to raid the shores of Christian and Moslem Spain and to voyage on west of Iceland as far as the coasts of North America. From Sweden new bands of warriors pushed east to join Kievan rulers in a last attack on Constantinople and a last raid on Moslem Sarkland. In the Baltic, the Wends along its south shore rose to destroy German political power east of the Elbe and took to the sea, joining Swedish, Norse and Danish fleets in internecine conflicts. Their power was not broken until their great assault on Denmark in 1042-1043. In short, the Viking Age began again, and lasted for sixty years before it vanished forever. And in its final surge it created a vast maritime empire for the Kings of Denmark, Svein and Canute, which stretched from Samland and Sweden to the shores of the Irish Sea and came close to uniting all the regions of Europe which earlier Viking fleets had dominated. This naval empire proved ephemeral, but it showed that the Viking spirit was not dead in the tenth century, but merely slumbering and awaiting an opportunity to burst forth.

It would be an error, however, to view these years as a mere repetition of the time when Hastings, Bjorn Ironsides, Rollo and Ragnar Hairybreeks roamed the Northern Seas. Men like Olaf Tryggvasson, Thorkel or Jarl Eric resembled their Viking predecessors, but not completely. The difference seems to lie in the fact that their piratical activities were not haphazard or individualistic, as had earlier been the case. They were often the result of the plans of two shrewd, able rulers, Svein and Canute, who harnessed such piracies to help them build a strong empire and for whom maritime raids were but part of an over-all political strategy. Olaf Tryggvasson, St. Olaf and Harold Hardraada seem to have been equally capable of using Viking activities as a means to an end—as a step towards the greater political objective of establishing themselves upon the throne of a united Norway. Behind the new Viking façade of these years, then, there seems to have been more of the spirit of a Harold Fairhair present than that of the sons of Ragnar Ladbrok. Or perhaps, despite all, there was something of a spirit of order using the forces of aggression for its own different purposes. Already we sense a spirit that later we call Norman, a spirit which was to lead a William of Normandy or a Roger Guiscard to use force and chaos to create strong, organized, integrated political units. The last gasp of Viking aggressiveness in the Northern Seas contained within itself a developing, orderly tendency which led to a better future for Northern Europe.

It was perhaps a combination of special factors, caused by political disorders, which recreated the Viking era about 980. It began in England, when a Viking force from Ireland and the Isle of Man seized and ravaged the town of Chester. At the same time another pirate band, perhaps from Denmark, raided Hampshire and the Isle of Thanet. In the next year descents were made along the coasts of Devon and Cornwall, and in 982 both London and Portland in Dorset were raided. Five years later Watchet in the Bristol Channel was attacked.[1] All these raids, which were small-scale affairs, except for the attack on Chester, may have originated from Norman ports across the Channel. For there Viking mercenaries had found employment in local feudal struggles in France and some had even been sent on to Spain by the Duke of Normandy when their usefulness to him had ended.[2] Or they may have been the result of disturbances in Ireland, about 980, which saw Dublin conquered by the High King of Ireland. This forced a number of Norse out of the land who took to freebooting in order to gain a livelihood.[3]

At any rate, it seems clear that Aethelred, King of England, blamed the Norman duke for such Viking activities, and particularly for keeping Norman ports open to pirates, where they could dispose of booty taken in England. His protests were more than verbal, for in 988 he sent his fleet to Norman shores. By 991, with Papal help, peace was made between England and Normandy, and the duke agreed to cease offering encouragement to the raiders.[4]

At the same time, along the German-Danish border an upheaval was beginning. Otto II was in Italy, and no strong ruling hand directed German affairs. When word reached the north of Otto's great defeat at Cape Stilo in Italy and of his death in 983 soon after, a major Slavic uprising took place between the Elbe and the Oder. It is hard not to see the hand of Harold Bluetooth of Denmark in this rising, which caused Hedeby to pass into his control, while Slavic Obodrites sacked and burned Hamburg. Though cooperation between Miczko of Poland and the young Otto III had, by 985, limited the effects of this Slavic revolt, the lands east of the Elbe were lost to Germany for more than a century.[5]

Harold of Denmark, however, does not appear to have been satisfied with the mere gaining of Hedeby. Still allied with the Wends,

[1] T. D. Kendrick, *History of the Vikings*, pp. 257-61. F. Stenton, *Anglo-Saxon England*, pp. 370-75. Actually the primary source for this period is the *Anglo-Saxon Chronicle* in its various versions.

[2] F. Shetelig, *Introduction to the Viking History of Western Europe*, p. 140.

[3] J. Ryan, "Pre-Norman Dublin," in *Proc. of Royal Soc. of Antiq. of Ireland*, L (1949), 19-35. H. Shetelig, *op.cit.*, pp. 70-72.

[4] Richard of Normandy is referred to in a contemporary source as "Richard, Duke of the Pirates." Richer, *Liber quartor historiacum*, ed. Waitz, p. 186. See also F. Stenton, *op.cit.*, pp. 372-74, on the agreement between Duke Richard and Aethelred II about ending this kind of assistance to raiders of English shores.

[5] F. Dvornik, *The Making of Central and Eastern Europe*, pp. 55-59. Z. Wojcie-chowski, *Miezko I and the Rise of the Polish State*, pp. 88-97. For sources, see *Annales Quedlin-burgenses*, in *MGH Script.*, III, 66-67, and Thietmar, *Chron.*, in *MGH Script.*, new ser., IX, 41.

he went on to the Viking-Wend pirate fortress of Jomsburg, near Wollin, and from there, in 986, launched an attack on Sweden with a fleet which supported Styrrborn, a pretender to the throne of Uppsala. This attack was beaten off by Eric Segersall, the Swedish monarch, and it was probably about this time that he wedded Gunhild, daughter of Miezko of Poland—a marriage that may have strengthened a Swedish-Polish alliance against Danish-Wendish aggression. At this point Harold Bluetooth died, and his son Svein succeeded him. But the troubles Harold had provoked did not end with him.[6] In 990 a large Swedish force sailed south and ravaged Denmark, probably in revenge for Danish intervention in Sweden in 986.[7] Thus along Danish, Swedish and Wendish coasts in the Baltic we find unstable political conditions, and a period of disorder which recreated that atmosphere in which Viking piratical activities naturally flourished.

The good sense and ability of Otto III, Miezko, Eric Segersall and Svein kept piratical raids and upheavals from spreading farther in the Baltic after 990. But a byproduct of these Wendish-Swedish-Danish disorders suddenly linked them with England. In 991 Olaf Tryggvasson, scion of the House of Harold Fairhair of Norway, commanding a large fleet which included certain Swedish Viking ships that had just been engaged in attacking Denmark, sailed west to continue raiding in England.[8] No doubt word had reached him of the successful raids along English coasts of 980-987. Perhaps some of his ships had even participated in these attacks. Certainly Olaf was aware of the weakness and unpopularity of Aethelred II, who ruled Anglo-Saxon Britain. His fleet stopped along the way in Frisia to raid Stavoren and then proceeded on to England.[9]

Olaf Tryggvasson's force was no small raiding band, like those which had been harrying English shores for a decade. It was almost a full-scale army. It raided along the coast and then advanced inland into East Anglia to seek more plunder. There it was met by forces led by the valiant Byrhtnoth, Earldorman of this portion of England. In the battle which followed at Maldon, Byrhtnoth was slain, fighting

[6] J. Kostryzewski, *Les Origines de la civilisation polonaise*, p. 586. Svanstrom and Palmstierna, *Hist. du Suède*, pp. 16-17. L. Musset, *Les Peuples scandinaves*, p. 82.

[7] L. Musset, *op.cit.*, p. 85.

[8] G. Turville-Petrie, *The Heroic Age in Scandinavia*, pp. 130-38. See also the *Saga of Olaf Tryggvasson* for his early days in Russia and as a pirate in the Eastern Baltic. See Svanstrom and Palmstierna, *op.cit.*, pp. 13-14, on the Swedish contingent in this force.

[9] P. Boeles, *Friesland*, pp. 449-50.

bravely to the last.[10] This Viking victory failed, however, to raise in King Aethelred any military spirit or zeal for resistance. Instead he preferred to negotiate a trade treaty with Olaf and pay him and his men the huge sum of 22,000 pounds of gold and silver as a Danegeld.[11] Aggression against England had proved effective and most rewarding—a fact that was not lost on interested parties in Scandinavia.

Meanwhile Svein was setting his Danish house in order. He ended hostilities with Sweden and formed a firm alliance with the young King Olaf Skottkonung, who probably succeeded his father, Eric, at about this time. To cement this alliance and to re-establish good relations with his Polish neighbors as well, Svein married Olaf's mother Gunhild, who was also the sister of Boleslas Chobry, the new ruler of Poland. She soon bore Svein a son, the famous Canute, who was therefore the half brother of Sweden's king and nephew of Poland's ruler.[12] Nor did the diplomacy of Svein neglect the victorious Olaf Tryggvasson, who returned to Scandinavia laden with English booty and Danegeld. He gave him his sister Thyri in marriage, though he kept up close relations with the Jarls of Lade, Denmark's allies and viceroys on Norway's west coast.[13] With Sweden, Poland, Norway and the Wendish coasts, especially Jomsburg, firmly allied to him, Svein was ready to turn his attention to England and to exploit the rich possibilities it represented.

Knowledge of Svein's intentions apparently reached Britain, for in 992 a strong fleet was mustered to protect its shores. It may have been due to these naval preparations that in 993 only Northumbria suffered raids. Here Lindsey and the town of Bamborough were attacked, but the richer and more populous portions of England suffered no damage.[14]

By 994, however, Svein was ready and sailed to England with a large naval flotilla of 94 ships and some 2,000 fighting men—some of whom were under the command of his brother-in-law, Olaf

---

[10] See E. D. Laborde, *Bryhtnoth and Maldon* (London 1936), and E. Gordon, *The Battle of Maldon* (Cambridge 1937).

[11] F. Stenton, *op.cit.*, pp. 374-76. On the trade treaty between Olaf and Aethelred II, see *Laws of the Kings of England*, ed. Robertson, pp. 56-60.

[12] J. Kostryzewski, *op.cit.*, p. 586. L. Musset, *op.cit.*, pp. 156-57.

[13] J. Turville-Petrie, *op.cit.*, pp. 135-36. Thyri, Svein's sister, was half Slavic by birth, since their mother had been a daughter of the Duke of the Obodrites. She had been married first to a certain Burizlaf of Wendland (Boleslas, a Pomeranian prince?), according to the *Saga of Olaf Tryggvasson*.

[14] T. D. Kendrick, *op.cit.*, pp. 263-64. F. Stenton, *op.cit.*, pp. 376-77.

Tryggvasson. It is possible that Svein may have announced this invasion of England as a claim to the English throne, for we learn that some of the English were willing to accept him as king.[15] Certainly it was more than a simple raid. At any rate, the Danish fleet sailed to London, where it was beaten off, and then plundered the coasts of Essex, Kent, Sussex and Hampshire. Here the Viking allies, Svein and Olaf, quarreled and, after extorting 16,000 pounds of Danegeld from Aethelred in return for deserting his ally and leaving England in peace, Olaf sailed away to Norway with his ships. Svein, with the remainder of the expedition, plundered Wales and the Isle of Man and returned to Denmark.[16]

Olaf's desertion of Svein and his return to Norway were not without purpose. As a successful sea-king, loaded with money and plunder and possessing a formidable flotilla, he saw an opportunity to gain Norway for himself. So he sailed to Nidaros, and there killed Jarl Haakon of Lade, the Danish viceroy of this coast. Within a short time he had become king of all Norway from the Vik to the Arctic Circle and seems also to have exercised some control over distant Iceland. Jarl Haakon's sons and their partisans fled to Denmark.[17]

Any further plans Svein might have had against England now had to be dropped, since a new, hostile Norway loomed to his north. Furthermore, he may have had a falling-out with both his wife, Gunhild, and his Polish ally, since we learn from the *Knutlingsaga* that about this time Canute's mother fled with him to Jomsburg, and the young boy was raised in this curious Viking fortress.[18]

But attacks on England still continued. In 997 new pirate fleets appeared along the south shore and raided Devon, Cornwall, Somerset and South Wales. In the next year they plundered the coasts of Dorset and Hampshire. In 999 they attacked Kent. Then, copying the tactics of their Viking predecessors, they occupied the Isle of Wight as a base of operations.[19] They may also have been given cooperation by the Norman duke, Richard, across the Channel, who allowed them the use of his ports as places to sell their booty and outfit their expeditions, as in 988. There seems little doubt that this ruler had suspiciously close Viking connections. It was he, for instance, who was able

[15] D. Whitelock, *Anglo-Saxon Wills*, pp. 44, 148-49.

[16] T. D. Kendrick, *op.cit.*, pp. 264-65. F. Stenton, *op.cit.*, p. 377.

[17] L. Musset, *op.cit.*, pp. 165-67. G. Turville-Petrie, *op.cit.*, p. 140.

[18] L. Musset, *op.cit.*, pp. 156-58. See the *Knutlingsaga* on his youth among the Jomsburgvikings, and L. M. Larson, *Canute the Great* (New York 1912), pp. 5-87.

[19] T. D. Kendrick, *op.cit.*, pp. 167-68. F. Stenton, *op.cit.*, pp. 378-79.

to procure the release, after a three-year captivity, of the Viscountess of Limoges, who had been captured by Vikings in raids along France's west coast.[20]

Meanwhile Svein in Denmark was relieved of his great adversary, Olaf Tryggvasson. The latter, in 1000, perhaps in the hope of establishing a successful naval alliance with Wendish shores, and particularly with the Jomsburgvikings and even Poland, sailed south into Danish waters with a small fleet. On his return home to Norway he was surprised off Rugen by a joint Dano-Swedish armada which included vessels of the Norse Jarls of Lade, Olaf's sworn enemies. In the battle which followed, one of the most famous in Scandinavian tradition, Olaf, though outnumbered, fought valiantly to the end on the decks of his Long Serpent, and then plunged into the sea to meet his death. Norway resumed her Danish allegiance, and the Jarls of Lade returned victorious to their west coast as viceroys ruling in Svein's interest.[21]

With his hands free, Svein conciliated his old allies, the Jomsburgvikings, and returned to English waters. He appears to have wintered in Normandy, probably with the assent of Duke Richard. The next year he invaded England with large forces, marching inland to win the battle of Alton, plundering Devon and burning Peignton. Aethelred was glad to purchase peace at the price of another 24,000 pounds of silver. But he realized the danger of his position all too well. To keep Normandy from serving any longer as a base for Danish and other assaults on Britain, he married Emma, sister of Duke Richard—a marriage to have fateful consequences for England.[22] And then, in 1003, he ordered the massacre of every Dane in his kingdom—the typical revenge of a weak man. According to tradition, one of Svein's sisters was among the victims.[23]

Svein was meanwhile preparing a large-scale invasion of Britain, with a huge fleet and army which included Danes, Norwegians and Swedes, each in a separate division under national leaders.[24] The

[20] F. Lot, *Les Invasions barbares*, pp. 147-48, and *Les derniers Carolingiens*, pp. 346-51.

[21] This battle of Svolder took place near the Oder, rather than off Denmark where Adam of Bremen in *Gesta Hamm. Eccl. Pont.*, II, 40, locates it. Concerning it, in addition to the *Saga of Olaf Tryggvasson*, see Brøgger and Shetelig, *The Viking Ships*, pp. 225-28.

[22] F. Stenton, *op.cit.*, pp. 379-80. T. D. Kendrick, *op.cit.*, p. 168.

[23] *Cartulary of St. Frideswides*, ed. Wigram, pp. 2-9. William of Malmesbury, *Gesta regum*, in *Roll Series*, I, 207.

[24] On the Swedes who took part in these attacks on England, see runic evidence in Svanstrom and Palmstierna, *op.cit.*, pp. 13-14.

great camps excavated at Trelleborg in North Jutland and Aggers-
borg in Zealand probably represent the mustering places for this expedition of Svein and for certain later ones of his son, Canute.[25] It
seems clear indeed that this invasion was not merely a Danish one. It
was a Scandinavian affair with Norse, Swedish and Danish forces led
by Denmark's king. And it was the most formidable invading force to
attack England since the great Danish invasion of 965-978, which it
much resembled.

In 1003 the Danes landed on the south coast of England and, concentrating upon Wessex, raided inland as far as Winchester and Salis-
bury, both of which they plundered. In 1004 they were in East
Anglia, where they sacked both Thetford and Norwich. In 1006 they
ravaged the southeast, concentrating upon Kent and the seizure of
Sandwich. The Isle of Wight again served them as a base and as
winter quarters. Aethelred was forced to purchase peace for an even
larger sum than before, 36,000 pounds, before the Danish host withdrew in 1007.[26]

At last the Anglo-Saxon monarch did what he should have done
much earlier, which was to concentrate upon naval defenses instead
of attempting to bribe his enemies with Danegelds that only encouraged them to greater aggression. Therefore, in 1008 the country
was divided into 310 districts, each being taxed to pay for the building
and upkeep of one naval vessel of 60 oars and its crew. However,
part of this new fleet, stationed at Sandwich, was mishandled and
almost at once 80 vessels were lost in a mutiny and storm. The rest
were sailed by their crews to London, where the ships were abandoned. England again lay defenseless in the path of the Viking
storm.[27]

It was not long in arriving. Svein stayed in Denmark, but in 1009
he sent Thorkell, a loyal ally and chief of the Jomsburgvikings, to
England, with a large force. Thorkell, off Sandwich, was joined by a
Norwegian flotilla commanded by Olaf Haroldson, of the Norse
royal family, whose early years as a Viking adventurer much resemble
those of his kinsman, Olaf Tryggvasson. Together, Olaf and Thorkell forced Canterbury and Kent to pay them off with a Danegeld
of 3,000 pounds of gold and silver. They next sacked East Anglia.

---

[25] On the excavations which revealed these large fortified camps, see P. Norland,
"Trelleborg," in *Nordiske Fortidsminder*, IV (Copenhagen 1848), 1.

[26] F. Stenton, *op.cit.*, pp. 380-81. T. D. Kendrick, *op.cit.*, pp. 168-69.

[27] On this fleet and the method of raising it, see W. L. Clowes, *Royal Navy*, I,
19, and F. Stenton, *op.cit.*, pp. 424-25.

Then, under the leadership of Olaf, they attacked London. The city stood firm and they were beaten off. The desperate Aethelred raised a huge sum of 45,000 pounds of silver as a Danegeld, and purchased, in 1012, the services of both leaders and the 45 ships they controlled, receiving a promise from them that they would help him defend his realm.

The next year Svein arrived again in Britain with a large army. Thorkell, despite his oath to Aethelred, immediately joined him. Olaf stayed loyal to his English master. Svein began by attacking in the north and the Midlands, where the predominantly Danish population submitted to him. Then he marched south, and before long only London still held out against him. Olaf fled to Normandy, and he was soon followed by Aethelred when London surrendered to the Danish king in 1014. Svein had won England at last.[28]

But at the very moment of his greatest triumph Svein died. Anglo-Saxon hopes revived. Aethelred returned to England, aided now by the sound generalship of his son, Edmund Ironside, who became the symbol about which English resistance rallied. But the Danes did not give up. In 1015, Canute arrived in Britain with a large force of 200 ships, including many contributed by Haakon, the Norse Jarl of Lade. Canute landed in Southwest England and Eadric, the Saxon Earldorman of West Mercia, went over to him with 40 ships. Northumbria submitted. But Aethelred's death left Edmund un-hampered by his unworthy father, and the war went on as London stood firm. Finally, in 1017 Edmund died, and Canute was universally accepted as England's king. After thirty-eight years of attacks England at last was in the hands of a Danish conqueror.[29]

Canute at once proved himself an able and constructive ruler of Britain. He married Emma of Normandy, Aethelred's widow, and, after levying a large Danegeld in 1018, used this money to pay off his Viking warriors and relieve his new kingdom of their presence. They sailed away, to trouble England no more.[30] Probably some, unable to give up a life of plunder, joined Irish Norse Vikings who were expelled from Ireland after Clontarf in 1016 and sailed to

[28] F. Stenton, op.cit., pp. 381-86. T. D. Kendrick, op.cit., pp. 270-72. On St. Olaf's early years, see Saga traditions in Johnsen and Helgason, Saga Olafs Konungs hins helga, 1 (Oslo 1930), 1-156, which is the definitive work.

[29] F. Stenton, op.cit., pp. 381-87. T. D. Kendrick, op.cit., pp. 272-73.

[30] F. Stenton, op.cit., pp. 392-94. Thietmar, Chron., IX, 7. L. M. Larson, Canute the Great, pp. 83-106.

Aquitaine. At any rate, in 1018, Viking bands ravaged[31] western French shores and were repelled only with great difficulty.

While Canute was busy completing his conquest of England, a new foe of his maritime empire appeared. This was Olaf Haroldson, known to history as St. Olaf. As we have mentioned, Olaf had fled from England to Normandy in 1013, when Aethelred's cause seemed hopeless. There he apparently accepted Christianity and may have taken part in the great Viking raid on Spain in 1015-1016. At any rate, as a successful sea-king he sailed in 1016 to the shores of Norway. There he found that much of the strength of the Jarls of Lade was with Canute in England, and so little opposition could be offered him. He easily conquered Norway, and Jarl Eric of Lade fled to England, where Canute compensated him with large grants of land. Olaf became King of Norway, as Olaf Tryggvasson had twenty years earlier.[32]

Canute at first did little to counter Olaf's successful assumption of power in Norway. He was too busy consolidating his own position in England. Besides he found that Denmark also demanded his attention. In 1019, on the death of his brother, whom he had left there as viceroy, Canute was forced to return to his Danish kingdom. Once there, he began to mend his diplomatic fences in the Baltic. He appears to have re-established close ties with the Jomsburgvikings, in whose fortress he had spent his youth, and to have strengthened his alliance with his nephew, Boleslas, ruler of Poland. In 1020 he also seems to have sent an expedition to Samland which, according to Saxo Grammaticus, paid him tribute at this time. Danish interests and alliances in the Baltic had been advanced east to the borders of Kievan Russia.[33]

Perhaps it was Canute's activity in the Baltic which accounted for the changed attitude of Sweden. Up to this time Canute's half brother, Olaf Skottkonung, had been a very loyal ally of Denmark and had sent a large Swedish contingent to aid Svein in his invasions of England. He had become a Christian and had brought from England Anglo-Saxon missionaries, who began the conversion of this pagan

[31] Ademar de Chabannes, *Chron.*, ed. Chavannon, pp. 166-67, 177. Perhaps these were in large part the same Viking fleets which plundered Spanish coasts, too, in 1016 and 1026. H. Shetelig, *Viking History of Western Europe*, p. 140.

[32] See *Saga Olafs Konungs hins helga*, I-II, on these years of Olaf's power in Norway. Also G. Turville-Petrie, *op.cit.*, pp. 142-58.

[33] L. Musset, *op.cit.*, pp. 160-62. F. Stenton, *op.cit.*, pp. 394-96. Henry of Huntington, *Hist. Angliae*, in *Patrologia Latina*, ed. Migne, CXCV, cols. 917-18.

land.[34] But perhaps he began to view the powerful Danish empire with concern when England was added to it. At any rate, he balanced off his Danish friendship by marrying one daughter to Canute's sworn enemy, St. Olaf of Norway, in 1019, and another to Yaroslav of Kiev, who controlled nearby Novgorod. When Canute increased his Baltic possessions in 1020, then, he found himself faced by an increasingly hostile Sweden. One might say that two alliance systems faced each other in the Baltic and Scandinavia: Denmark and Poland, backed by the Wends, against Norway, Sweden and Russia. By 1022, when Olaf Skottkonung died and was succeeded by his son, Arnund Jacob, the break with Denmark became an open breach.

In 1026 Canute was ready to act. He gathered together a large fleet and sailed against Sweden, where, at Holy River, he met a large joint Norse-Swedish armada under Arnund and Olaf of Norway. The ensuing battle seems to have been a rather decisive victory for Canute, since it was followed by St. Olaf's abandonment of his ships and return to Norway overland by way of Sweden, and by Canute's annexation of the Swedish southern province of Bleckinge. Norse Sagas, however, fail to give Canute credit for this victory.[35] It even seems probable that Arnund Jacob had to do homage to Canute for his Swedish kingdom, since coins were struck at Sigtuna in this period bearing Canute's name and referring to him as King of Sweden.[36]

With Sweden neutralized or conquered, Canute turned his attention to Norway. In 1028 he gathered together a large fleet and sailed to Norway with the exiled Jarls of Lade, Olaf's bitter enemies. In advance, however, he made sure of success, according to Saga tradition, by scattering bribes freely among Norse magnates. Olaf was beaten almost without a battle. He fled to Russia, where he was welcomed by Yaroslav, and shortly thereafter returned to Norway to meet his death at the hands of Norse partisans of Canute. With his passing, Canute's maritime empire, stretching from the Irish Sea to Samland, seemed at last secure.[37]

Canute then proceeded to buttress his dominions with alliances. He had long been on particularly friendly terms with his nephew,

[34] L. Musset, op.cit., p. 172; G. Turville-Petrie, op.cit., pp. 159-60; and especially B. Nerman, Sveriges Första Storhetstid, pp. 206-20.
[35] On the battle, see F. Stenton, op.cit., pp. 400-1, and Brøgger and Shetelig, The Viking Ships, p. 228.
[36] L. Musset, op.cit., p. 161.
[37] G. Turville-Petrie, op.cit., pp. 160-64, and especially Saga Olafs Konungs, for traditions on his last days.

Boleslas Chobry, who ruled Poland and controlled Central Europe from the Baltic to Moravia. But in 1027 Boleslas died and his state relapsed into disorder. Canute, however, kept a firm grip on South Baltic coasts, since from Florence of Worcester we hear of a certain Wrytsliof Dux, a Wendish tribal leader whom Canute had as a guest in England in 1026.[38] Perhaps, as Dvornik believes, even before Boleslas' death Canute was encroaching upon Polish Pomerania. At any rate, a year later he turned to Germany, and in 1027 married his daughter to Henry, the son of Emperor Conrad, and at last received formal recognition of his empire's ownership of Schleswig and Hedeby, which had been in Danish hands since 983.[39] Then, as the most powerful ruler of Northern Europe, he went on a pilgrimage to Rome, where he was well received by the Papal court.[40] He returned to die in England in 1035, leaving an empire buttressed by a friendly Germany and composed of a contented England, a powerful Denmark, and a conquered Norway and possessing great influence in the Baltic.

Canute's empire, however, was not destined to last for long after his death. Perhaps even before 1035 Samland had broken away, since it appears to have been independent when Adalbert of Prague visited it.[41] And Danish influence over Wend shores of the South Baltic also apparently crumbled when Poland disintegrated after 1027. Norway soon followed. Svein, one of Canute's sons, had been placed over the land as viceroy by his father. He ruled harshly and badly, so that when Magnus the Good, son of St. Olaf, arrived in Norway from Russia in 1035, he was welcomed as king. Svein was driven out and died soon afterwards.[42] There remained two other sons of Canute, Harold Harefoot and Hardicanute. Harold, who ruled England, died in 1040 just before his brother Hardicanute could invade his realm. And Hardicanute's death followed in 1042.[43] England returned to the House of Alfred, and Edward the Confessor, who was the son of Aethelred and Emma, peacefully ascended the throne. In Denmark,

---

[38] Florence of Worcester, *Chron.*, ed. Thorpe, I, 199. F. Dvornik, *op.cit.*, pp. 227-30, on Canute's relations with Poland and Pomerania.

[39] Adam of Bremen, *Gesta Hamm. Eccl. Pont.*, II, 54.

[40] On Canute's trip to Rome and the privileges he secured there, see J. Tait, *The Medieval English Borough*, p. 119.

[41] *Passio S. Adalberti*, in *Fontes rerum Bohem.* (Prague 1870), I, 231-33.

[42] G. Turville-Petrie, *op.cit.*, p. 164. L. Musset, *op.cit.*, p. 170.

[43] T. D. Kendrick, *op.cit.*, p. 273. On Flanders' role in the last days of Canute's sons, see P. Grierson, "The Relations Between Flanders and England," in *Trans. of Royal Hist. Soc.*, XXI (1941), 90-95.

Magnus of Norway invaded the land, and, after crushing a great Wendish invasion in 1042-1043, added it to his realm.[44] Only Sven Estridsen, Canute's nephew, remained of a royal house which five years before had ruled a huge maritime Danish empire, and he was to contend for years before he could regain his Danish realm from Magnus. The Danish maritime empire begun by Harold Bluetooth and completed by Svein and Canute had vanished by 1043 and with it ended the Viking Age in Northern Europe.

Beyond Canute's empire in the Western Atlantic lay Ireland which, in the middle of the tenth century, despite Irish native resistance, was largely controlled by the Norse settlers in the seaport towns. As early as 968, when the native Irish took Limerick, the tide began to turn.[45] In 980, Dublin, the center of Norse power in the island, had been captured by Maelsechniall and was forced to pay tribute.[46] In 996, again, the High King levied tribute upon the Dublin Norse.[47] Gradually, however, Brian Boru replaced the High King as the leader of Irish native forces. In 1000 he took Dublin, and in 1002 became High King himself.

It would be wrong, however, to view relations between the native Irish and the Norse settlers who had their center in Dublin as uniformly unfriendly. More generally, in fact, there was rather close collaboration between them. Brian Boru himself had close marriage ties with the Norse settlers of the land, for he married the mother of Sictric III, King of Dublin. And in the year 1000 an Irish source speaks of the King of Ulster as having "a fleet at Lough Aran and a marriage alliance with the King of the Galls."[48] In 1002 Brian Boru even appears to have taken part in the Danish Viking raids on England, for he is said to have crossed the Irish Sea and levied tribute from the Scots, Welsh and Saxons.[49] Perhaps this means he shared in the Danegelds of the period.

Some of the same Viking fleets, however, which afflicted English shores at the time of Svein and Canute also attacked Ireland. Under this new influx of invaders, some, at least, of the Norse settlers threw off the native Irish yoke that Brian Boru and Maelsechniall had fast-

---

[44] T. D. Kendrick, *op.cit.*, pp. 180-83.
[45] *Wars of the Gaedhil with the Gael*, pp. 79-81.
[46] J. Ryan, "Pre-Norse Dublin," *loc.cit.*, pp. 19-23.
[47] J. Young, "A Note on the Norse Occupation of Ireland," *loc.cit.*, p. 14.
[48] H. Shetelig, *The Viking History of Western Europe*, pp. 76-77. J. Young, *op.cit.*, pp. 28-32. *Book of Rights*, p. 249.
[49] H. Shetelig, *op.cit.*, p. 77.

ened upon them, and challenged Irish power. The result was the great battle of Clontarf, which Brian fought just outside Dublin against these invaders. There is, however, some question as to whether or not this battle was an all-out Irish-Norse battle, as has often been claimed. Brian had some Norse mercenaries or "auxiliaries" in his Irish forces. And Sictric of Dublin, far from fighting against the native Irish, appears to have been neutral. The outcome, however, was a great Irish victory which drove the invaders from the island, though Brian himself perished in the battle. We hear no more of Viking assaults on Ireland, which was thus spared the fate of England.[50]

The native Norse settlers were not expelled as a result of this battle. They continued to hold Dublin and other towns along the coast. They continued also to launch regular raids across the Irish Channel into Wales, perhaps to procure slaves.[51] But they became fervent Christians in the eleventh century; indeed, King Sictric of Dublin actually visited Rome as a pilgrim at about the same time as Canute's visit to the Eternal City.[52] Though he was captured by the King of Meath in 1027, he and his family continued in control of Dublin until 1052, when the King of Leinster at last annexed the city to his realm.[53] And, even then, Norse settlers continued to dominate Irish seaports and Irish foreign trade right down to the end of the eleventh century.[54] Despite Brian Boru and his victory at Clontarf, the fate of the Norse in Ireland was not expulsion from the island, but integration and assimilation into Irish life and Irish civilization.

Farther north in the Hebrides, Orkneys, Shetlands, Faroes and distant Iceland these years seem to have been quiet ones. All remained relatively unaffected by the bitter struggles that took place in Norway, except for a short period around 1022, when the Jarls of the Orkneys, of the Thorfin family, who were dominant in these waters and allied to the Jarls of Lade, defeated a fleet sent against them by St. Olaf.[55] Only with difficulty was Olaf able to command obedience here, though tradition does hold that he exercised some sort of control over Iceland for a short period.[56]

[50] *Wars of the Gaedhil with the Gael*, p. 169. F. Lot, *op.cit.*, pp. 178-79. T. D. Kendrick, *op.cit.*, pp. 290-98.
[51] B. G. Charles, *Old Norse Relations with Wales*, pp. 33-35.
[52] H. Shetelig, *op.cit.*, p. 78.
[53] *Annals of Four Masters*, anno 1052.
[54] T. D. Kendrick, *op.cit.*, pp. 297-99.
[55] A. W. Brøgger, *Ancient Emigrants*, pp. 150-57.
[56] J. S. Clouston, *A History of Orkney* (Kirkwall 1932), pp. 73-134.

Iceland's chief importance, however, does not lie in its relationship with Norway or in its intervention in Norse affairs. Rather, the major events which took place there were the introduction of Christianity and Icelandic expansion towards the west. This westward expansion had already, by 985, taken an Icelandic colony to Greenland's shores. Fifteen years later, a second colony was established somewhat farther north than the original settlement of Eric the Red. At about the same time, Leif Ericson made his famous voyage of discovery to the North American continent, and established on its shores, for a short period, a remote Viking colony.[57] By 1043, then, Icelanders had pushed west to Greenland and on to North America, whither for some centuries they were to sail to procure timber. The rest of Europe was aware of this discovery since Adam of Bremen tells us of Vinland in his writings.[58]

During these years from 985 to 1043, events in Ireland or in the more remote Norse colonies of the Atlantic had very little effect on the growth and destinies of Canute's naval empire, the principal power in the Northern Seas. To the east, however, lay Kievan Russia, and it was the rulers of this state who, more than any others, rivaled Svein and Canute in power and who did much to make their task difficult. Under Yaroslav and Valdimir, Kievan Russia became a most powerful state, not only in the East, but also in the effect of their policies upon Central Europe, the Baltic and Scandinavia.

In the last chapter, we noted how Vladimir regained his principality of Novgorod and, about 980, went on to become sole ruler of the Kievan state. We have seen how, in 985, he attacked the White Bulgars in an attempt to reopen the lucrative Volga trade routes, and how he paid particular attention to his Byzantine connections, marrying a Greek princess and accepting Greek Orthodox Christianity. We have seen that he also opened connections with the West by conquering the cities of the Red Ukraine, expanding into Lithuania to clear the Vistula and Niemen routes to the Baltic. His embassies to the Pope and the Ottos also show the Western interests he cultivated during his reign.

Until his death Vladimir followed similar policies. There can be little doubt that Byzantine connections proved decisive in influencing Russia's future destiny, and that it was Vladimir who did much to

[57] E. Reman, *The Norse Discoveries and Explorations in America* (Berkeley, Calif., 1949), gives the best account based on the Vinland Sagas.
[58] Adam of Bremen, *Gesta Hamm. Eccl. Pont.*, IV, 38.

foster them. But he continued to pay close attention to the West. When Miezko of Poland, between 987 and 990, seized Cracow and Silesia from Bohemia and thus interposed his state between Kiev and Western markets, Vladimir entered into friendly relations with him. He married one of his sons, Yaropolk, to a daughter of Boleslas Chobry, Miezko's successor in Poland, and a daughter to Casimir I, one of Boleslas' heirs. He may even have married another one of his daughters, Predslava, to Miezko himself in his last years. Thus Vladimir bound himself by marriage alliances to the powerful Piast family. Nor did he neglect Central European areas south of Poland, for we find him marrying another daughter to Ladislas, King of Hungary.[59]

The Kievan ruler also maintained Scandinavian interests throughout his reign. Though he feared Varangian ferocity, he welcomed Olaf Tryggvasson when the latter fled Norway in his youth and gave him a high position in his realm. He also kept in close touch with Sweden's royal family and one of his wives (of the pagan period) was certainly a Swede.[60] Indeed, it seems possible that he expanded Russia's power for a period from Novgorod west towards the Baltic, since the *Primary Chronicle* tells us that the Chud paid him tribute.[61] As important as the connections were which he maintained with Constantinople, his interest in the West via the Baltic and Central Europe seem to have been almost more important.

When Vladimir died in 1015, the division of his realm illustrated the triple orientation of the Russia of his day. One son, Mstislav, of whom we know very little, inherited Chernikov and Tmutorakan, near the Crimea, and thus held that portion of Russia which had connections with Byzantium via the Crimea, and with the Moslem East by way of the Caucasus and the White Bulgars of the Volga. A second, Sviatopolk, who had married a Polish princess, inherited Kiev and with it Russian interest in Central Europe. The third, Yaroslav, was given Novgorod, which faced Scandinavia and the Baltic.

What followed was almost a repetition of the events which had taken place in Vladimir's early days. Civil war broke out between the

---

[59] *The Primary Chronicle*, p. 182. F. Dvornik, *op.cit.*, pp. 250-55. See also B. Leib, "The Kiev State and Western Europe," in *Trans. of Royal Hist. Soc.*, XXIX (1947), 278-315.

[60] S. F. Cross, "Medieval Russian Contacts with the West," in *Speculum*, X (1935), 138-40. B. Grekov, *La Culture de la Russie de Kiev*, pp. 47-51. *The Primary Chronicle*, p. 181.

[61] *The Primary Chronicle*, p. 182. G. Vernadsky, *Kievan Russia*, pp. 64-65.

three brothers. In the ensuing conflict, Sviatopolk was supported by Polish arms, and Yaroslav, who had married the Swedish Princess Ingrid, by Sweden. Though Sviatopolk had some initial successes, in 1021 Yaroslav defeated him and his Polish allies and gained complete control of Kiev and Novgorod.[62] He was less successful, however, in efforts to dislodge his brother Mstislav, and only when the latter died in 1036 did Chernikov, Tmutorakan and the southeast come under his control. From then on, until his death in 1054, he ruled a united Kievan realm.[63]

Like his predecessors, Yaroslav was well aware of the importance of connections with Byzantium and the Moslem East, particularly when, after 1036, he held Southern Russia. He therefore appears to have waged war, with some success, against the nomadic Patzinaks who threatened his communications with the south and like his father, Vladimir, he raised fortresses against them.[64] In 1043 he sent Kievan Russia's last great naval expedition against Constantinople, though without much success, it is true.[65] It must have also been with Yaroslav's blessing that in 1040-1042 his old allies, the Swedes, launched the last great Varangian expedition against the Moslem East, attacking distant Moslem Sarkland in a vain attempt to reopen the route to the riches of the Middle East.[66] He also married his son, Vsebolod, to a Byzantine princess.[67]

But the evidence seems to show that Yaroslav was much more interested in the West than in the East—even more than his father Vladimir had been. After defeating the Polish forces of Boleslas Chobry, who had intervened in Kievan affairs, he went on to reconquer the Red Ukraine from Poland, with its important cities of Premysl and Cherven.[68] Then, in 1029, he intervened directly in Piast affairs, supporting first Bezprym and then later Casimir the Renovator in

[62] G. Vernadsky, op.cit., pp. 74-77; and, for sources, The Primary Chronicle, pp. 212-22, and Thietmar, Chron., in MGH Script., new ser., IX, 486-88, 528-32.

[63] G. Vernadsky, op.cit., pp. 77-79.

[64] The Primary Chronicle, pp. 222-24. M. Hrudevsky, History of the Ukraine (New Haven 1941), pp. 76-101.

[65] G. Vernadsky, op.cit., p. 82. On relations with Constantinople, see also B. Leib, Rome, Kiev et Byzance au XIe siècle (Paris 1924).

[66] On the runes found in Sweden which show evidence of this last Swedish attack on the Moslem East, see T. J. Arne, "Austr i Karusm och Särklandnamnet," in Fornvännen, xv (1947), 290-305. This may have coincided with the failure of the 11th-century trade treaty with the White Bulgars to produce much trade. On this treaty and references to it (in Russian), see G. Vernadsky, op.cit., p. 126.

[67] B. Leib, op.cit., pp. 213-19.

[68] The Primary Chronicle, p. 225.

their struggles to control Poland. Indeed, Casimir's victory over his enemies in 1039 marked the height of Kievan influence in Central Europe, since this Piast ruler owed his throne to the help of his brother-in-law, Yaroslav.[69] Nor did Yaroslav's interest in the West stop here, for we know he married two of his sons to German noblewomen, one daughter to Andrew, King of Hungary, and another to Henry I of France.[70] His marriage alliances, then, reveal European interests which extend as far west as Paris.

If anything, Yaroslav's relations with Scandinavia seem to have had even greater importance to him. He himself had married a daughter of Olaf Skottkonung of Sweden, and he seems to have kept the Swedish connection intact. For instance, his attack on Esthonia in 1030 and his founding of the city of Dorpat appear to have been coordinated with Swedish attacks on this coast between 1030 and 1040.[71] He, like his father, seems to have appreciated the value of holding this section of the Eastern Baltic. And it may have been this interest which led him towards enmity with Canute, who in 1020 was reaching out in this direction. At any rate, Yaroslav from this time on, or even earlier, gave assistance and comfort to Canute's enemies in Norway. To Russia St. Olaf fled in his youth, as Olaf Tryggvasson had done before him. There, according to the Sagas, he was raised by an uncle who was a captain in Yaroslav's guard of Scandinavians.[72] Later, in 1029, when he was driven out of Norway by Canute, he sought refuge at Yaroslav's court and left his son, Magnus, behind when he returned to Norway to meet his death in 1031. Four years later, it was from Russia that Magnus sailed to Norway and assumed his father's throne.[73] Even Harold Hardraada, after serving in Yaroslav's bodyguard and marrying a daughter of his in 1042, owed his Norwegian throne in 1047 to assistance given him by Kiev's ruler.[74] If the House of Canute failed to hold its maritime empire, and even had difficulty in holding Denmark after Canute's death, this was in no small meas-

---

[69] On this period of disorder in Poland and Yaroslav's intervention there, see F. Dvornik, op.cit., pp. 223-35.

[70] S. F. Cross, "Yaroslav the Wise in Norse Tradition," in Speculum, IV (1929), 190-97.

[71] L. Villecourt, L'Esthonie (Paris 1932), p. 14. L. Musset, op.cit., pp. 172-73. S. F. Cross, "Yaroslav the Wise," loc.cit., pp. 242-47.

[72] On these episodes, see Saga Olafs Konungs hins helga, and S. F. Cross, "Medieval Russian Contacts with the West," loc.cit., pp. 137-43.

[73] S. F. Cross, "Yaroslav the Wise in Norse Tradition," loc.cit., pp. 143-45, and The Saga of Magnus the Good.

[74] S. Blondel, "The Last Exploits of Harold Sigurdsson in Greek Service," in Classica et Medievalia, II (1939), 1-26.

ure due to the hostility of Yaroslav of Kiev. A power in the Baltic, allied to Swedish, Norse and Polish ruling families, linked to Germany and even France, he had until his death great influence in Northern European affairs.

But this influence did not survive the death of Kiev's great ruler in 1054. Russia was divided among his successors, and none of them proved powerful enough to reunite the realm, as he and his father Vladimir had done.[75] Though Western connections were maintained, and Kiev recovered some power in the late eleventh and early twelfth centuries, its days of decisive influence in Northern Europe were over. Like those of Canute, his great rival, Yaroslav's dominion and influence ended with his death and with them died an age in Northern Europe.

Between Russia and the Danish empire, the two greatest Northern powers of this era, lay Sweden, Poland, Bohemia and Germany. They also played important roles in the political scene. First, let us examine Sweden. We know a little more of Swedish history in this period than we do for the preceding decades. Under three able monarchs, Eric, Olaf and Arnund Jacob, the Swedish state had a significant part in Northern European affairs. After 990, her rulers at first worked in close concert with Svein and Canute, assisting in the conquest of England and allying their house with Canute's Polish allies, for Olaf was not only Canute's half brother, but the brother-in-law of Boleslas Chobry of Poland as well, and he married his son, Arnund Jacob, to one of Boleslas' daughters. During this period Sweden made much progress, coining her first money, and, under Olaf Skottkonung, as his name reveals, levying taxes for the first time upon the land. It seems possible that Eric Segersall played the same role in Sweden that Harold Fairhair had done in Norway and Harold Bluetooth in Denmark, beginning the transformation of his realm from an archaic, loosely held Scandinavian pagan monarchy to a more centralized state. Under Olaf the conversion of Sweden, initiated a century and a half before by St. Anskar, received a new impetus and Sweden began to enter the family of European Christian nations.[76]

The reign of Arnund Jacob coincided with a certain change in Sweden's orientation. Though Sweden had helped Vladimir to regain his throne in Russia in 980-987, in general her policies had been pro-Danish. Now she began to oppose the great Canute and, by marriage

[75] F. Dvornik, op.cit., pp. 258-61.
[76] B. Nerman, Sveriges Första Storhetstid, pp. 206-29.

and political ties, Arnund associated himself closely with the Norway of St. Olaf and the Kievan Russia of his kinsman, Yaroslav. Anglo-Saxon influence in the Swedish church, heretofore dominant, was replaced by German influences from Hamburg. And Sweden not only supported St. Olaf's two attempts to seize Norway, but appears to have cooperated with Yaroslav in Courland, and to have aided in the last great Varangian raid toward the Moslem East. At first this policy proved disastrous. Sweden lost the Bleckinge to Denmark, and for a period after 1026 had to accept Danish overlordship. But when, after 1035, the Danish empire of Canute disintegrated, Arnund Jacob ended up on the winning side. Curiously enough, however, Sweden suffered the fate of Russia and Denmark. Arnund Jacob was the last great monarch of the Uppsala line. With his death the power of these kings, which went back to Vendel times, passed to a certain Stenkil, who represented a new Vestergotland family. And Sweden entered a period of disorder and darkness from which she was not to emerge until the next century.[77]

In Central Europe, during most of this period, Piast Poland was the leading power. As we showed in the last chapter, by 985 Miezko had carved out of Slavic Europe a sizable united realm in the region between the Oder and the Vistula. Accepting Christianity, and basing his power on strong fortifications and a sizable mercenary army, he had expanded his realm to the Oder, seized Pomerania and for certain periods of time held the cities of the Red Ukraine which dominated overland trade routes to Kiev. He was generally closely allied with Denmark and Sweden, though friendly also to the Ottos of Germany. After 985 he conquered Cracow and Silesia from Bohemia, and thus controlled a realm which stretched from the Carpathians to the Baltic.[78]

In 992 Miezko's son, Boleslas the Valiant, succeeded him and continued his father's policies. Boleslas kept up his father's policy of friendship with Denmark, at least until late in his reign, and, except for a short period, maintained friendly relations with Kiev. With Germany he had a more stormy relationship. But he appears to have gained recognition of his independence from Otto III, to have established close contacts with the Papacy and to have held at bay the Emperor Henry of Germany when the latter tried to increase his authority over Poland. He expanded his state northeast towards Samland

[77] L. Musset, op.cit., pp. 172-73. B. Nerman, op.cit., pp. 229-39.
[78] Z. Wojciechowski, *Miezko I and the Rise of the Polish State*, pp. 52-73.

and south to the borders of Hungary, at the expense of Bohemia.[79]

Unfortunately Miezko's immediate successors, who followed him upon the throne after 1027, had little of his ability. Both Miezko II and Bezprym were too weak to hold Piast conquests together, and for twelve years Poland was torn by factional strife, backed alternately by Germany, Russia and Bohemia. Finally, in 1039 Casimir the Renovator recovered some of the power lost by his immediate predecessors by regaining Pomerania and reconquering Silesia and Cracow from Bohemia. But Casimir was largely under Kievan influence, and after his death Poland, like Sweden, underwent a period of disintegration and disorder from which she was not to emerge until the next century.[80]

A few words will suffice for Bohemia and for Hungary. Bohemia in 985 was a relatively weak state. She remained so during most of this period, being dominated by her stronger neighbors. She had a brief period of glory under Boleslas II when she conquered Poland, but it was only momentary. By 1043 she came definitely under German influence and remained so for many, many decades.[81]

On the other hand, in this period Hungary definitely increased in importance. After their defeat at Lechfeld by Otto I in 955, the Hungarians ceased to be a menace to their neighbors. Under able rulers, Hungary settled down, accepted Christianity and began to assume the form of a more stable, centralized kingdom. About the year 1000, under King Stephen, she began to expand until she controlled the whole Hungarian plain and lands extending south to the Adriatic. She later took Slovakia from Bohemia and checked efforts of Henry II of Germany to reduce her to vassal status. By 1043 she had become the strongest state in Central Europe, with her great days ahead of her.[82]

East of these new Slavic realms lay Germany, which had been so powerful at the time of Otto I. Under Otto III, however, it had lost much of its political leadership and importance in Northern Europe. It was still strong enough to remain all but untouched by the Viking-

[79] J. Kostryzewski, *op.cit.*, pp. 15-16. Z. Wojciechowski, "Le Patrice Boleslas le Vaillant," in *Revue belge*, XXIX (1951), 219-44. F. Dvornik, *op.cit.*, pp. 141-66.

[80] F. Dvornik, *op.cit.*, pp. 218-35.

[81] *Ibid.*, pp. 226-35. For the sources on the conquest of Poland by Boleslas II of Bohemia, see Cosmas Pragensis, *Chron.*, in *MGH Script.*, new ser., II, 82-95. On final German overlordship at the time of Henry II, see *ibid.*, pp. 95-100.

[82] On this early period in Hungarian development, see D. Csudy, *Arpad und die Arpaden* (Budapest 1908), pp. 1-73.

like attacks of the Scandinavians on England, but Otto III did not regain the lands lost to the Slavs between Elbe and Oder in the great rising of 983. Instead, he concentrated his attention on Italy, where his dream of a revived Roman Empire had full sway, and contented himself with a Central European policy which tied Poland, Bohemia and Hungary very loosely into a Holy Roman Empire.[83] His successors, Henry II and Conrad II, however, appear to have shared neither his interest in Italy nor his lofty Imperial conceptions. Able but limited in their outlook, these rulers contented themselves with following a narrow conception of German interests, attempting to maintain their authority in Germany and to increase it towards the Slavic East. In both aims they were, on the whole, successful, except in regard to Hungary. And in the vassalage they imposed upon Poland and Bohemia and other Slavic lands to the east of the Oder, they laid the basis for the German *Drang nach Osten* of the twelfth century.[84]

Still farther west lay France and the Christian kingdoms of Northern Spain, the last region of Northern Europe to be considered. Shortly after 985 the French monarchy at last came under the control of the Capetian family. But up to 1043, and long afterwards, it remained a weak control indeed. For the Capetian Kings of France by the year 1000 had authority over only the church and their own Isle-de-France domains. On the other hand, if the French monarchy was weak, this period saw various parts of the land gain strength. Gradually, rulers like the Counts of Flanders and Anjou and the Dukes of Normandy, Brittany and Aquitaine began to consolidate their power and authority on a local scale, preparing the way for later development.[85] In Christian Spanish states, too, we find in the early eleventh century, after Al-Mansor's final assaults northwards, the beginnings of a Christian advance beyond the Tagus which was to lead to the Reconquista.[86] France and Spain, particularly the former, were by 1043 moving slowly but surely towards that political, economic and cultural leadership which they were to assume in the Late Middle Ages.

[83] F. Dvornik, *op.cit.*, pp. 161-66.

[84] *Ibid.*, pp. 230-35.

[85] The fundamental work is still F. Lot, *Les derniers Carolingiens*. On Normandy, see C. Haskins, *The Normans in European History*, pp. 1-95. On Flanders, see F. L. Ganshof, *La Flandre sous les premiers comtes*. On Eastern France, R. Poupardin, *Le Royaume de Bourgogne (888-1026)*. There is no good modern study of the development of feudal Brittany, Aquitaine or Toulouse in this period.

[86] On this change in Spain, see R. Altimira, *Historia de España*, I (Barcelona 1900), 206-68, and R. Menéndez-Pidal, *The Cid and His Spain* (New York 1934), pp. 106-400.

How, then, can we sum up the years in Northern Europe from 985 to 1043? It was an age which at first saw a continuation of earlier trends, with one new development: the temporary linking of Anglo-Saxon England, Norway and Denmark in the maritime empire of Svein and Canute—an empire that was also the reflection of a last outburst of Viking aggressive energy. In Canute's time this empire was balanced by a Germany of considerable strength and an even more powerful Kievan Russia, while Sweden, Poland and Hungary, newly arisen in Central Europe, continued their growth and development under able monarchs. Ireland far to the West finally conquered—or, rather, absorbed—its Norse invaders and colonists.

But Canute's empire did not prove strong enough to endure. By 1043 it had disintegrated. Norway and Sweden emerged again under national monarchs, while Denmark seemed destined to fall into Norse hands, for a time at least, as Magnus the Good conquered the land. But disintegration did not stop with Canute's empire. It affected the kingdoms of his neighbors and his enemies as well. After the death of Yaroslav, Kievan Russia fell apart. So did Poland and Sweden after the reigns of Casimir and Arnund Jacob, respectively. Only Hungary and Germany remained strong states in the last half of the eleventh century. In fact, by the mid-century point, one can feel the stirring of new forces in all Northern Europe. As the Viking period ended, this new Europe began to take shape, and it was not the Europe of Canute and Yaroslav. Mighty as their realms and their power had been, they represented the past, an older order of things. The new was appearing in Normandy, Flanders, France and the Rome of a slowly reviving Papacy.

During these years in which the Danish empire of Canute and Kievan Russia were ascendant in Northern Europe, the economic growth which we noted earlier as a feature of the tenth century continued in Ireland, England, Germany and most of Scandinavia and the Baltic. To these regions we can now add France and Northern Spain, which began to move from a local commerce to one which was more integrated with the stream of trade that moved through the Northern Seas of Europe. The Garonne, the Loire, the Seine and the Scheldt began to carry commerce which flowed into a wider European maritime trading area.

We can see this new economic growth most clearly in the Meuse valley and in Flanders. We noted in our last chapter how, in the late tenth century, the Meuse trading places continued their earlier economic importance and, by the reign of Otto III, were all coining money copied after that of Cologne.[87] In the early eleventh century their economic quickened. In addition to the tenth-century bridge at Maastricht, we now find new ones being built of stone at Liége between 1025 and 1038, and at Huy, Givet, Visé and Namur soon afterwards.[88] In 1007 Dinant was referred to as an *emporium*.[89] The metalware of this region was still its principal industry, and no doubt this explains the presence of merchants from this region at both London and Cologne, the great international trading cities of the period, where they could purchase the tin and copper which they needed in their manufacture of brass and bronze. This probably accounts for the mention of men of Huy, Liége and Nivelles in the Toll of London of 991-1001,[90] and for the fact that Cologne coins were copied by Meuse mints. Probably Walloon merchants were already going in numbers to Cologne and the Rhinelands to procure copper and wine, as we know they did later in the century.[91]

Farther west in Flanders, the slight development of commerce visible at Ghent and Tournai in the tenth century blossomed into new economic life. Cloth towns at Arras, St. Omer, Ghent, Douai, Ypres and Lille, so important later, were already beginning to take on form and substance. At Cambrai in 1001, for instance, we hear that merchants were active.[92] Tournai in 1010 was referred to as a wealthy trading center,[93] and three years later, in 1013, we learn of a merchant of this town carrying wool to sell in Ghent, where a fair was found as early as 1003.[94] Apparently Tournai also trafficked in cut stone, which was shipped down the Scheldt to Ghent and even farther.[95] Arras, according to a *telonium* of 1024, possessed a number of merchants who seem to have represented the same patrician families found in there in the ninth century.[96] The same *telonium* reveals wine reaching the town by land in carts during this period.[97] Wine was also to

[87] F. Rousseau, *La Meuse*, pp. 72-73.

[88] *Ibid.*, pp. 82-84.

[89] P. Rolland, *Le Problème de la continuité à Tournai*, p. 277.

[90] F. Liebermann, *Gesetze*, II, 161-63.

[91] F. Rousseau, *op.cit.*, pp. 90-92, and "L'Expansion Wallone et Lorraine vers l'est," in *Les Dialectes belgo-romains*, II (1937), 188-91.

[92] F. Vercauteren, *Belgique Secunde*, p. 463.

[93] *Acta Sanct. Boll.*, April 1, p. 885.

[94] *Vita Macharii*, in *MGH Script.*, XV, 616.

[95] F. Vercauteren, *op.cit.*, p. 464.

[96] R. Doehaerd, "Note sur l'histoire d'un ancien empôt, le tonlieu d'Arras," in *Bull. de l'Acad. d'Arras*, XVI (1943-46), 217-43.

[97] *Cartulaire de Guiman d'Arras*, ed. Van Drival, p. 167.

be found in Abbeville in 997,[98] and a little later was said to be a common drink at St. Omer.[99] The wine at Arras probably came from Champagne or the Ouse valley, and that at Abbeville and St. Omer by sea from Rouen, whose merchants were at this time shipping it for sale to London as well. In 1036 we find English cheese at St. Omer.[100] Apparently the cloth industry, earlier mainly domanial in manufacture, was now moving from the countryside to the new urban centers.[101] And perhaps already that specialization in this industry was beginning to take place that caused Ghent to send its cloth eastward, St. Omer and the surrounding region to send it to England, and Arras to send it to the south towards central France.

Along the coast we notice similar economic growth. Bruges had earlier had some importance as a mint and center of administration for the Counts of Flanders. Now, in 1010, it was called a *portus*[102] and, according to the *Economium Emmae* in 1037, an international trading center.[103] Here and at nearby Arensburg, Wissant and Boulogne a new Flemish maritime tradition was taking form, one to be heard from later in the century. Already it was strong enough so that in 1039 or 1040 Hardicanute could raise in Bruges a fleet of some 60 ships to aid him in his claim to the English throne.[104]

As Flanders and the Meuse valley increased the scope of their economic life, Brabant, between the two, could not help but be affected also, though to a lesser degree. A new route, replacing the older Chaussée de Brunehaut, now linked Bruges and Ghent with Cologne. And to this road Brussels probably owed its early growth and the fact that in Otto III's time it was already coining money modeled on that of the Rhineland.[105] Sea and river traffic reaching this region was, however, probably more important. To it was due Antwerp's rise in this early eleventh century, and the fact that merchants from St. Trond and Gembloux were visiting London. Certainly, in 1050 St. Trond was known to English sailors.[106]

[98] R. Doehaerd, *L'Expansion économique belge*, p. 38.
[99] H. Pirenne, "Les Vins de France au moyen âge," *loc.cit.*, p. 231.
[100] R. Doehaerd, *op.cit.*, p. 39.
[101] H. Laurent, *La Draperie des Pays-Bas en France et dans la Méditerranée* (Paris 1935), pp. 26-29.
[102] F. L. Ganshof, "Iets over Brugge gerunde de preconstitutionale periode" in *Nieder Hist.*, I (1938), 284. *Ex mirac. S. Bavonis*, in *MGH Script.*, xv, 597.
[103] *Cnutonis regis gesta*, in *ibid.*, XII, 523-24.
[104] P. Grierson, "The Relations Between Flanders and England," *loc.cit.*, pp. 101-2.
[105] F. Rousseau, *La Meuse*, pp. 72-73.
[106] Stepelinus, *Mirac. S. Trudonis*, II, 74, in *MGH Script.*, xv, 827-28.

We have noted that this commercial growth of Belgian towns was linked to London on one side and to Cologne on the other, while some contacts had been established with the Ouse valley to the south as well. It does seem clear, however, that the major impetus to growth came from commerce flowing north rather than south. This is made evident by coin hoards discovered in various parts of Northern Europe dating from these years. Coins of Meuse mints later than 985 in date, for example, have been found in hoards in Norway, Denmark, the Swedish mainland, Gotland, Poland, Russia, Finland and Iceland. Two examples from opposite sides of the Scandinavian world will suffice to illustrate this fact. In the Icelandic hoard of Gaulverjabaer dating from about 1020 we find, amongst a number of German coins, pennies from Huy and Verdun.[107] In Finnish hoards are an even larger number of coins minted along the Meuse between 983 and 1039. They include coins from Toul, Metz, Verdun and Epinal on the upper Meuse, but more from its lower reaches: 16 from Huy, 15 from Liége, 9 from Namur, 7 from Maastricht, 4 from Thuin, 4 from Stavelot, 3 from Visé and one from Dinant.[108]

The money of Flanders is not so widespread in its incidence in northern coin hoards as that of the Meuse valley, but in Finnish hoards of the period there are four coins from Brussels and five from Flanders.[109] Other finds in Russia, Sweden and Courland contain money minted by Count Baldwin IV prior to 1035,[110] and in the Norwegian Foldoy hoard of 1060 we find coins from Brussels as well.[111] It is clear that the impetus to trade growth which caused the development of these Belgian towns came not only from Cologne and London but from the entire northern portion of Europe extending from Iceland to Russia.

Belgium was stimulated by contacts and commerce to England, the Rhinelands and the North during this period, but so were other parts of France. We have already noted that men from Rouen and

---

[107] K. Eldjarn, "Gaulverbajaer Fundet," in *Nord. Numis. Arsskrift* (1948), pp. 39-50.

[108] This seems to represent new trade going to this part of Europe, since no coins minted prior to 983 have been found in Finnish hoards. H. Salmo, *Deutsche Münzen in vorgeschichtlichen Funden Finnlands* (Helsinki 1948), pp. 337-41.

[109] Again it is only starting with this period that we begin to find such coins in Finnish hoards. H. Salmo, *op.cit.*, pp. 339-41.

[110] R. Doehaerd, *op.cit.*, pp. 28-31. On Mosan money in Baltic regions, including Poland, see F. Rousseau, "L'Expansion Wallone," *loc.cit.*, pp. 191-92.

[111] This hoard contains money struck in Flanders and at Brussels, Celles, Liége, Huy and Dinant. A. W. Brøgger, "Et Myntfunde frä Folden," in *Aarbrøger*, XI (1910), 239-82.

Pontieu traded with London, that terminus of North Sea trade, which shows that commerce from the north already had reached the Seine valley. There is other evidence of this as well. Tournai, in this period, apparently had contacts with Limoges along the routes which led from Flanders to the Shrine of St. James of Compostela,[112] while Verdun merchants still traded with Moslem Spain.[113] And there is, of course, that wine reaching Arras from the south in 1024, already mentioned. France's economic life was beginning to merge with that of the rest of Europe.

Nor was this trade confined to French regions near Flanders. The commercial life of the Loire and Garonne regions also felt a new impetus. Between 997 and 1014, the church of St. Martin of Tours was rebuilt a second time since 900 and much enlarged.[114] Money at Rennes and Nantes minted after 990 imitated the style of Blois and Anjou, which seems to indicate a certain new Loire trade.[115] At Bordeaux, Duke William of Aquitaine began to rebuild the monastery of St. Croix and a new cathedral. To help pay for this construction we find Count Sancho-William of Gascony in 1029-1036 contributing one-third of a *telonium* levied at Bais on the Garonne.[116] In 1040 Agen reopened its mint and again began coining money,[117] while the Bordeaux coinage of these years was minted at Saintes and throughout the Charente region.[118]

This new Garonne economic activity and that about Bordeaux and Saintes was certainly connected with maritime activity on the Atlantic, but it may also have been connected with new trade reaching France from Italy over the passes, or *clusae*, of the Alps near Geneva. In the first years of the eleventh century we hear of Alpine colporteurs at Asti and Aosta,[119] now that Moslem pirates from Fraxinentum no longer interfered with Alpine commercial traffic. Though our first record of Italian merchants in France dates from 1076, perhaps commerce was already coming north from Italy over Alpine routes.[120]

[112] J. Finot, "Le Commerce entre la France et la Flandre au moyen âge," in *Ann. du Comité flamande de France*, XXI (1893), 312.

[113] E. Sabbe, "Quelques types de marchands," in *Revue belge*, XIII (1934), 183-84.

[114] This same style is found during this period at Clermont, Limoges and Toulouse on pilgrim routes leading to Santiago de Compostela. E. Mâle, *La Fin du paganisme en Gaule et les plus anciennes basiliques chrétiennes* (Paris 1950), pp. 147-50.

[115] Blanchet and Dieudonné, *Manuel de numismatique française*, IV, 2-23.

[116] P. Courtreault, *La Cathédrale de Bordeaux* (Paris 1935), pp. 7-8.

[117] Blanchet and Dieudonné, *op.cit.*, pp. 218-24.

[118] *Ibid.*, p. 215.

[119] J. Tyler, *The Alpine Passes*, p. 91.

[120] Jaffé, *Regestum*, II, 115, 132, 146.

Even the old sea routes from Rouen to the Garonne and Spain seem to have been again in operation, since as early as 964 we hear of pilots of Rouen capable of guiding a Viking fleet to Asturias, while Duke Richard of Normandy in 1003 seems to have been able to secure the release of a Viscountess of Limoges whom Vikings had seized as a captive on one of their raids on Western France.[121] No wonder we hear of French money in Galicia all through the tenth century and afterwards,[122] and of French products in León in 1003.[123] In 1043 the maritime traffic from Spain and Western France mentioned later in the Laws of Oleron was apparently already in existence.

If French commerce and economic life were growing and merging with that of the Northern Seas in this period, even more development was taking place in England. The motive behind Svein's and Canute's conquest of the land seems clearly to have been its wealth, which made it a tempting prize. We have already mentioned that it furnished 165,000 pounds of gold and silver to the invaders in Danegelds alone, between 991 and 1018.[124] When we recall that, in the whole of the ninth century, Carolingian France under similar circumstances furnished only 45,000 pounds of Danegelds, we begin to realize the greater prosperity of Anglo-Saxon England under Aethelred. During the reign of Aethelred, England had 75 mints which coined money of the realm.[125] The new mints of this period are interesting because their location shows where the economy of the land was quickening. Earlier, in the tenth century, mints were generally located in Central Wessex, Kent, East Anglia and the Midlands. Now under Aethelred, and during the reign of Canute, we find a whole series of new mints established in the Cinq Ports towns of Hastings, Hythe and Romney,[126] while Domesday Book reveals that Dover and the other Cinq Ports were of enough economic importance to have freedom from tolls in all England.[127] We find other new mints in the far west at Totnes, Taunton, Wilton and Bristol.[128] Chester still carried on trade with Ireland and in the mid-eleventh century was

[121] F. Lot, *Les Invasions barbares*, p. 147.
[122] C. Sanchez-Albornoz, "Primitiva organizacíon monetaria de León y Castilla," *loc.cit.*
[123] C. Sanchez-Albornoz, *Estampas de la Vida en León durante el Siglo X*, p. 52.
[124] G. C. Brooke, *English Coins*, pp. 66-67.
[125] *Ibid.*, p. 65.
[126] On these mints, which are represented by coins of Aethelred II and Canute found in Norse hoards, see H. Holst, "Mynter i Norske Funn," *loc.cit.*, pp. 101-6.
[127] J. Tait, *The Medieval English Borough*, pp. 120-26.
[128] H. Holst, *op.cit.*, pp. 101-6.

importing furs, probably from Dublin,[129] while Cardiff and Swansea also appear to have had an active trade.[130] Gloucester was now an important center for the production of iron.[131] Perhaps the most significant index of the growing commerce of the land is the number of moneyers in various trade centers at the time of Edward the Confessor (1042-1066). There were 20 in London, 25 in York, 9 in Lincoln and Winchester, 8 in Chester, 7 in Canterbury and Oxford, 6 in Thetford, Gloucester and Worcester, 5 in Hereford and 4 or 5 in Ipswich and Norwich.[132]

London was still the greatest trading place in England, attracting foreign merchants from Germany, Flanders, the Meuse Valley and France.[133] It seems also to have had a good-sized Scandinavian merchant colony, which after 1015 was apparently concentrated in Southwark, on the other side of the Thames from London proper.[134] York, which was filled with Danish traders, was only a little less important than London.[135] Thetford continued to prosper as a pottery center, and its six moneyers of 1042 reveal how swiftly it recovered from its two plunderings by the Danes, in 1004 and 1010.[136] Salt was produced and sold at Droitwich on a more than local scale,[137] while the tin mines of Cornwall never ceased production judging from coins of Aethelred and Harold Harefoot that have been found there.[138] Nor did operations cease in the silver and lead mines of the Mendips and the Midlands, where most of the silver which was paid out in Danegelds was produced.[139] A money economy was so normal even in country districts that in Central Wessex, prior to the Norman conquest, the king drew his revenues from his manors in the form of cash rather than kind.[140]

[129] Domesday Book, I, 262.
[130] T. D. Kendrick, op.cit., pp. 326-27. A. H. Williams, An Introduction to the History of Wales, pp. 154-58.
[131] Domesday Book, I, 162. This section of Domesday also mentions trade in timber on the Wye.
[132] G. C. Brooke, English Coins, pp. 69-71.
[133] F. Liebermann, Gesetze, I, 232.
[134] A. Bugge, "The Norse Settlements in the British Isles," in Trans. of Royal Soc., IV (1921), 191-95. O. Johnsen, op.cit., pp. 389-90.
[135] F. Stenton, "York in the Eleventh Century," in Yorkshire Historical Tracts, VIII (London 1927).
[136] G. Knocker and R. Hughes, "Anglo-Saxon Thetford," loc.cit., pp. 5-6.
[137] Domesday Book, I, 172.
[138] H. O. Hencken, The Archeology of Cornwall, pp. 263-64.
[139] O. Davies, Roman Mines in Europe, pp. 158-64.
[140] R. L. Poole, The Exchequer in the Twelfth Century (Cambridge 1947), pp. 27-31.

Equally interesting is evidence of a number of guilds in this pre-Conquest England. We hear of them at Canterbury, Dover, Cambridge, London and Winchester. Since some of these guilds are referred to as *Cneuhts* guilds, there has been a tendency to regard a portion of them, at least, as social rather than economic in origin and function. However, it should be pointed out that in Anglo-Saxon England commerce was not necessarily carried on by servile or semi-servile classes as was the case in France. England in this period rather resembled Scandinavia, with which it was linked politically, and where both kings and nobles engaged in commercial activities. When we consider that it was said that "the merchant who makes three voyages overseas at his own expense becomes a *Cneuht*," we realize the essentially economic as well as social function of a *Cneuhts* guild. The Cambridge guild, for instance, was probably active in the export of the famous *opus angliscum* to the Continent.[141]

This foreign trade of England was important enough for it to be specifically recognized in the treaty of 991 made by Aethelred with Olaf Tryggvasson, then a Viking sea-king raiding British shores whose activities interfered with English merchant shipping. This treaty provided that Olaf's men would not molest either Anglo-Saxon or foreign vessels when they were in English ports, and that if English ships were wrecked in native waters, the crews would be allowed to carry freely such merchandise as they could save to the nearest borough. In foreign ports or along foreign shores, protection was also to be granted English traders and they were to be free from pirate molestation.[142]

The foreign trade which Aethelred felt worth securing by a special treaty with Viking raiders was in this period a most important one, indeed. Particularly active was the trade from Wales and West Britain to Ireland, as had been the case earlier. The growth of seaports like Bristol, Totnes, Cardiff, Swansea and Chester seem to make this clear. So does the fact that when in 1000 Sictric III, King of Dublin, minted the first Irish coins, he copied Anglo-Saxon silver pennies and even employed certain English moneyers to put his mint into operation.[143] Such trade accounts for the 120 Welsh horses which

---

[141] W. Cunningham, *The Growth of English Industry and Commerce*, 5th ed., I, 129-30. C. Gross, *The Guild Merchant*, I, 186; II, 37. See also E. Coornaert, *Les Gildes médiévales*, pp. 45-46.

[142] *Laws of the Kings of England*, ed. Robertson, pp. 56-60.

[143] W. O'Sullivan, "The Earliest Irish Coinage," in *Proc. of Royal Soc. of Antiq. of Ireland*, LI (1950), 90-157.

were in the possession of Olaf, King of Dublin, when he was captured by the Irish in 1023.[144] It also explains the presence of Irish coins as well as English ones in the Inchkenneth hoard buried in the Hebrides about the year 1000.[145] And to it, no doubt, is owed the Dano-Irish Dublin money and two stamped gold bars in the somewhat later Halton Moor hoard of Lancashire, which also contains 860 Anglo-Saxon pennies minted by the rulers of England from Aethelstan through Canute.[146]

We have already noted the trade between London and Germany, Flanders and France shown in the Toll of 991-1001, as well as trade connections with St. Omer, St. Trond, Thiel and Gembloux established before 1043. To these we should add the sudden appearance of Dover, Hastings, Hythe and Romney as mints and trading places under Aethelred and Canute.[147] These Cinq Ports could only have owed their existence to a new and more active cross-Channel traffic. Trade also went from England to western French and Spanish coasts. We know this from the Roncevalles hoard of English pennies found in Spain,[148] which was mentioned in the last chapter, and from the fact that both the Inchkenneth hoard of the Hebrides and the Halton Moor hoard of Lancashire contained French deniers of a type minted in Western France.[149] Canute's own close relations with Duke William of Aquitaine may have reflected his desire to stimulate this valuable commerce, for he was always eager to extend the trade of his kingdom.[150]

The most important feature of England's trade during this period was her commerce with Scandinavia and the Baltic, which appears to have increased immensely in volume, particularly after England

[144] J. Ryan, *Pre-Norse Dublin.*

[145] This hoard contains one coin of Sictric III of Dublin as well as a set of English pennies minted by Anglo-Saxon kings of the 10th century through Aethelred II.

[146] In addition to 860 Anglo-Saxon coins from Aethelstan through Canute, this hoard has in it two stamped gold bars which probably came from Ireland. See analyses by R. Taylor-Combe, in *Archeologia*, XVIII (1907), 199-223. For other evidence of gold in England in this period, see *Laws of Canute*, II, 710-11, which required heirs of the great nobles of England to pay 50 gold *mancusi* to the king to claim their inheritance.

[147] H. Holst, *op.cit.*, pp. 101-6, on the appearance of these coins in Norwegian coin hoards.

[148] Mateu Y. Lopis, "El hallazzo de 'pennies' ingleses en Roncesvalles," in *Principe de Viana*, XI (1950), 201-10.

[149] See notes 145 and 146 above. Those found at Halton Moor are definitely from the west of France. R. Taylor-Combe, in *Archeologia*, XVIII (1907), 199-223.

[150] Ademar de Chabannes, *Chron.*, p. 163.

became part of Canute's maritime empire. It must be emphasized, however, that though Danish conquest stimulated the exchange of goods with this part of Europe, a valuable commerce was already in existence before Canute became England's king. The massacre of all Danes in England by Aethelred II in 1003 suggests that many Scandinavians, whom we later find at London,[151] York and Chester in great numbers, were already carrying on trade with Britain. So, too, does the fact that the first coins minted in Scandinavia by Jarl Eric in Norway, by Svein in Denmark and by Olaf Skottkonung in Sweden were obviously copies of Anglo-Saxon money, made some time before Danish conquest of the land.[152] We have already mentioned Saga evidence of Norse trade with England by Sigurd and Hough at the time of Olaf Tryggvasson's reign in Norway.[153] Between 1020 and 1030 we also hear of the Norwegian trader, Thor Hind, who brought furs and skins to England which he exchanged for wheat and cloth.[154] Even Swedish rune stones show connections between Britain and this part of the Baltic.[155]

Again, however, it is numismatic evidence from Scandinavia which best reveals the scope and extent of England's contacts in this period. Much of the money found in Norse, Swedish, Danish and Gotland coin hoards of this time reflects, of course, not trade so much as the immense Danegelds which Aethelred II paid to Svein and Canute, and the bribes which the latter scattered so lavishly along the coasts of Norway in his struggle with St. Olaf. But there can be little doubt that much of it represents a genuine trade, particularly in Canute's time and during the reigns of his sons. The amount of Anglo-Saxon money found in this region is really astounding. In Danish hoards over 5,000 Anglo-Saxon silver pennies have been discovered, more than 90 per cent of which were minted during this period.[156] In Norwegian hoards the figure is 2,600 coins,[157] in Gotland 19,000,[158] in Finland 2,000,[159] and thousands more have been unearthed in

---

[151] William of Malmesbury, *Gesta regum*, in *Roll Series*, I, 207.

[152] F. Stenton, *op.cit.*, pp. 529-30.

[153] *Heimskringla, The Saga of Olafs Tryggvasson*, LX, pp. 241-42.

[154] A. Bugge, *Die nordeuropäischen Verkehrswege*, p. 23. *The Saga of Olafs Tryggvasson*, pp. 310-15.

[155] Svanstrom and Palmstierna, *op.cit.*, p. 14.

[156] R. Skovmand, *De Danske Skattefund*, pp. 17-21.

[157] H. Holst, *op.cit.*, pp. 56-101.

[158] M. Stenberger, *Die Schatzfunde Gotlands*, II (see tables at end of volume). See also the summary of S. Bolin, in "Gotlands Vikingatidsskatter och Världshandeln," in *Ur Boken om Gotland* (Visby 1945), pp. 135-37.

[159] C. A. Nordman, *Anglo-Saxon Money Found in Finland* (Helsinki 1928), pp.

hoards on the Swedish mainland, in Russia, Courland and Poland. Even in remote Iceland a single hoard of the year 1020 contains 179 Anglo-Saxon pennies out of a total of 360 coins.[160] At least 80 per cent of the coins in all of them are Anglo-Saxon pennies minted by Aethelred and the Danish monarchs of Britain. What in the period prior to 985 had been a mere trickle of Anglo-Saxon coins to the Baltic, Norway and Iceland had now become a positive flood. Like earlier ones, later Norwegian, Swedish and Danish coins—those of St. Olaf, Canute and Arnund Jacob—continued to be modeled upon those of England,[161] and in Sweden Anglo-Saxon moneyers appear to have been imported, just as in Ireland.[162] Perhaps this explains why Canute's reign was such a popular one in England, for under him, the area in which Britain's products and her merchants held sway extended from Ireland to Finland. In these years, even more than in the earlier tenth century, Anglo-Saxon England was the great trading nation of the Northern Seas. No wonder Aethelred II and Edward the Confessor, alone of European monarchs, possessed a gold coinage!

Nor did England's commerce stop with Northern Europe. Again we have evidence of connections with Italy. When Canute, in 1027, went on his pilgrimage to Rome, he made sure to obtain for English merchants on their way to Italy exemption from tolls from both Conrad II of Germany and Rudolf III of Burgundy.[163] Evidently both the South German passes and the *clusae* leading to Italy from the upper Rhone were being used by Anglo-Saxon merchants and pilgrims now, as earlier. Perhaps they had even increased in number, since Canute appears to have set up new and special hospices for them in the Holy City.[164]

Probably the best description of England's commerce comes from a contemporary source. Writing in the early years of the eleventh century, the Abbot of Wareham said that Anglo-Saxon merchants went overseas to procure purple cloth and silk, precious gems and gold, various fine clothes, wine, olive oil and Oriental spices and glass, and that this brought prosperity to the land.[165] If we added to this list the

---

1-193. Of mainland Swedish hoards, two from Bleckinge are typical: one at Ederstade contains 238 Anglo-Saxon coins and 38 imitations; the other from Hjortsberga contains 480 Anglo-Saxon coins.

[160] K. Eldjarn, "Gaulverjabaer Fundet," in *Nord. Numis. Arsskrift* (1948).

[161] H. Shetelig, *Scandinavian Archeology*, pp. 274-75.

[162] F. Stenton, *op.cit.*, p. 530.   [163] Mansi, *Collectio consilium*, XIX, 499.

[164] D. Whitelock, *The Beginnings of English Society* (London 1952), p. 123.

[165] R. S. Lopez, "Relations anglo-byzantines," *loc.cit.*, p. 153.

furs, fish and northern products of Scandinavia and the Baltic, we would have a picture of England's import trade during this period. For, from the Abbot's list, Anglo-Saxon England imported Oriental wares from the Baltic or Italy, gold from Ireland, wine, glass and fine cloth from Flanders and the Rhinelands, and wine and olive oil from France and Spain. In exchange, Britain traded abroad its silver, lead, iron, tin, wheat, cheese, honey, horses, fine cloth and metalware, and exported much silver coin. Not until long after the Norman Conquest was England again to reach the level of economic prosperity she attained in these years.

As England's trade increased during this period, so did that of nearby Ireland and the more remote Norse islands of the Western Atlantic. The gradual increase of native Irish strength in Ireland which began about 980 and culminated in Brian Boru's victory at Clontarf does not appear to have interfered with the land's growing prosperity. We have already noted that it was in this period, about 1000, that Sictric III, King of Dublin, coined the first money in Ireland's history. The great cathedral which he built shows the growth of this port.[166] So, too, do the riches which its seizure in 1016 provided its Irish conquerors.[167] Its wealth was specially commented on in Scandinavian Sagas. Not all of its trade went to England and Wales, though they were, no doubt, Ireland's principal customers. The *Eyrbryggya Saga* mentions early eleventh-century trade with Norway,[168] and Irish coins that have been found in the Hebrides and Norway show the routes this traffic followed.[169] Nor did it stop here, for Irish money in Gotland and Finnish hoards suggests that Irish commerce continued all the way to Russia.[170] We find it extending south to France as well, for Dublin, in the early eleventh century, agreed to furnish tribute in the form of 150 barrels of wine a year.[171] Its contacts even extended to Rome, where Olaf Curan of Dublin went on a

---

[166] J. Young, "A Note on the Norse Occupation of Ireland," *loc.cit.*, pp. 32-33.

[167] *The Wars of the Gaedhil with the Gael*, pp. 160-76.

[168] *Eyrbrygga Saga*, XXIX, LXV. A. Bugge, *op.cit.*, pp. 274-75.

[169] The Sand hoard of circa 1020 on Norway's west coast contains 3 Irish coins. V. Ronander "Myntfundet frä Sand," in *T.V.S. Skrifter*, IV (1921), 81-97. The Dronningenst hoard of 1035 also has in it 3 Dublin coins of Sictric. O. A. Digre, "Myntfundet frä Dronningenst," in *Saert. av Arrst. Selsk Museet*, XXI (1950), 163-72.

[170] The Oster Ryfter hoard of 1020 in Gotland contains 11 Irish coins. M. Stenberger, *op.cit.*, pp. 63-64. So do later ones like that found at Kvarna. In Finland, Irish coins are found in hoards discovered at Nousiamen, Lieto, Parmio, Drottingholm, Palkone, Haltula, Asitkola and Kunjijoki. C. A. Nordman, *op.cit.*, pp. 30-172.

[171] A. Bugge, *op.cit.*, p. 273. *Annals of Ulster*, II, 89.

pilgrimage in 1027.[172] Ireland, like England, was in these years the center of a trade which extended over all the Northern Seas, to Iceland, Norway, Novgorod, England, France and Italy.

The same is true of Iceland and even Greenland. Iceland continued the commerce with Ireland, Norway ond England which we noted in the last chapter.[173] Now Greenland joined the trade picture. We hear, for instance, of an Icelander who traveled about Scandinavia in this period with a polar bear which he had brought back from distant Arctic shores.[174] And in 1035-1040 there was a voyage, attested to by Adam of Bremen, of Frisian adventurers sailing to Greenland to trade.[175] Adam in 1070 even mentioned Norse Vinland, the Greenlanders' colony in North America.[176] And there is ample evidence that Greenland exported walrus ivory to England and the Continent all through the eleventh century.[177] Even this remote portion of the Atlantic world contributed its share to the commerce of the period.

England's and Ireland's expanding commerce was matched during this period by that of Germany. If the Meuse and Flanders felt an increased trade impetus about the year 1000, so did the Rhinelands and the rest of Germany. As in England, we see this process most clearly in the establishment of new mints. In the Rhinelands, in addition to older centers like Cologne, Mainz, Trier and Strasbourg, the towns of Worms, Wurzburg, Basel, Andernach and Duisberg reveal their new importance by minting silver money. At the mouths of the Rhine, Utrecht, Deventer and Thiel expanded their economic life, and so did a number of other centers in Frisia, such as Gronigen, Leer, Stavoren, Hamland, Jever, Emden and some others, all of which coined money during these years—most of them for the first time. Farther east in Lower Saxony the great Slavic uprisings of 983 no doubt caused serious dislocation, yet early eleventh-century mints were in operation at Thietmar, Merseburg, Hildersheim, Quellenburg, Stade, Hamburg, Bardowic and Magdeburg, as well as at Erfurt in Thuringia and at Soest and Dortmund in Westphalia. To the south in Swabia we find new mints at Breisach, Esslingen, Willingen, Zurich and Constance.[178] Mainz in 1049 was reported to be a city of

[172] H. Shetelig, *The Viking History of Western Europe*, p. 78.
[173] *Origines Islandicae*, II, 27-32. O. Tønning, *op.cit.*, pp. 14-26.
[174] L. Musset, *op.cit.*, pp. 219-20.
[175] H. S. Lucas, "Medieval Economic Relations Between Flanders and Greenland," in *Speculum*, XII (1937), 167-181.
[176] Adam of Bremen, *Gesta Hamm. Eccl. Pont.*, IV, 38.
[177] H. S. Lucas, *op.cit.*, p. 174. O. Tønning, *op.cit.*, pp. 26-27.
[178] On these mints, see H. Dannenberg, *Die deutschen Münzen der sachsischen*

great importance,[179] while, as we have noted, Thiel traded with England. Already the twenty-nine market rights given German towns by Otto III were inadequate for the economic needs of growing German towns.

The location of these new mints and trading places in Germany followed the general pattern of development which we noted in the earlier Ottonian period. They illustrated the general orientation northward of German commerce and economic life, since it was in Frisia and Saxony that the majority of them were located. But there also seems to have been a subsidiary growth of mints on the upper Rhine and upper Danube, which shows a growing, strong economic connection with Italy via the Alpine passes, and some trade overland towards Poland and Bohemia.[180] The Germany of Otto III, Henry II and Conrad II revealed a continuation and intensification of earlier German trade patterns.

It seems clear, for instance, that in these years Saxon and Frisian merchants were most active in Germany's trade with the Baltic and the Scandinavian North. We have already noted that between 1035 and 1045 a Frisian expedition sailed from the Weser to Greenland.[181] And we know that in the early years of the eleventh century a Frisian guild was active in Sigtuna, the successor to Birka in the Malar Sea region of Sweden.[182] Throughout Scandinavia we continue to find in archeological sites of this period glass, pottery and arms from Rhineland workshops—some of them perhaps new ones.[183] By the late eleventh century we even hear of Flanders cloth in Novgorod.[184]

Again, however, it is coin hoards which provide us with our principal evidence. In finds dating from these years, Anglo-Saxon coins generally are more numerous than German ones. But nevertheless the number of German pennies found in hoards from Iceland to Finland shows that the commerce from the Holy Roman Empire to the

---

und fränkischen Kaiserzeit, I-II (Berlin 1876-1905). More useful is H. Salmo, *Deutschen Münzen in vorgeschichtlichen Funden Finnlands* (Helsinki 1948).

[179] *Translatio S. Servatii*, in *MGH Script.*, XII, 90.

[180] On the increase of trade crossing the Alps to and from Italy in this period, see A. R. Lewis, *op.cit.*, p. 233. On the fact that there was not too much direct trade between Germany and Poland, and that mainly via Bohemia, see J. Kostryzewski, *op.cit.*, pp. 387-89.

[181] H. Lucas, *op.cit.*, p. 174.

[182] A. Bugge, "Altschwedische Gilden," *loc.cit.*, pp. 141-44.

[183] H. Jankuhn, "Ein Ulfberht Schwert aus der Elbe," *loc.cit.*, pp. 137-43. F. Balodis, *op.cit.*, pp. 212-34. B. Nerman, *Sveriges Första Storhetstid*, pp. 170-80.

[184] H. Pirenne, "Draps de Ypres à Novgorod au commencement du XIIe siècle," in *Revue belge*, IX (1930), 183-215.

north did not slacken. The Iceland hoard of 1020, which we have described a number of times, contains 107 German coins, including, of those minted during this period, 23 from Cologne and 12 from Frisia.[185] In Norway, 2,500 German coins have been discovered, of which the larger proportion date from these years. They include money minted in Andernach, Duisburg, Echternach, Cologne, Remagen and Trier in the middle Rhinelands; Mainz, Spire, Worms, Wurzburg and Strasbourg on the upper Rhine; Thiel, Deventer, Utrecht, Bolsward, Dokkum, Emden, Groningen, Jever, Leeuwarden, Stavoren and Zwolle in Friesland and at the Rhine mouths; and Corvey, Dortmund, Halberstadt, Hildesheim, Lüneburg, Münster, Soelst, Bamburg and Erfurt in Saxony and Central Germany. Even coins from Augsburg, Regensburg, Constance and Salzburg are represented. We find money from 52 German mints in all.[186]

From Denmark a large proportion of the 4,000 German coins, perhaps 60 per cent, are from this same distribution of mints,[187] while perhaps half of Gotland's 38,000 German coins were minted in the period 985-1043.[188] Swedish mainland and Finnish hoards contain the same type of distribution from the same mints as those found in Norwegian hoards—suggesting that it was via Saxony and Frisia that German trade reached the Scandinavian and Baltic North.[189] German coins in northern coin finds, then, illustrate a continued traffic north more remarkable in some ways than that of Anglo-Saxon England in this period, since neither Danegelds nor political connections can have accounted for the presence of this money in Northern Europe. No wonder that when St. Olaf or Arnund Jacob wished to combat Anglo-Saxon influences in their churches and states, they turned so naturally to Hamburg and Germany.[190] For Saxon and Frisian merchants made economic and cultural ties between Scandinavia and Germany almost as important as those with England.

To this German and English trade, as well as to that with the Baltic, was owed the continued growth of Norway's *bjorkeys* into more fully developed trading centers. We have already shown how

---

[185] K. Eldjarn, *op.cit.*, pp. 39-62.   [186] H. Holst, *op.cit.*, pp. 106-7.
[187] R. Skovmand, *op.cit.*, pp. 8-25.
[188] M. Stenberger, *Die Schatzfunde Gotlands*, II, 632-715.
[189] On these German coins in Finland, see H. Salmo, *op.cit.*, especially pp. 337-44. These coins in the early 11th century did not, however, reach the Baltic via the Oder and Central European land routes. As in the 10th century, they followed sea routes from Frisia and Saxony.
[190] T. Wilson, *History of the Church and State in Norway* (London 1903), p. 78. B. Nerman, *op.cit.*, pp. 229-39. L. Musset, *op.cit.*, pp. 172-73.

Tønsberg developed on Oslo fjord about the middle of the tenth century and how Nidaros was important enough by 996, at the time of Olaf Tryggvasson, to have reached urban status. In the early eleventh century they continued to develop, and to them a third primitive town was added in St. Olaf's time, Sarpsborg on the other side of Oslo fjord from Tønsberg.[191]

The Sagas speak of Norway's trade to Ireland and Iceland from this coast, and two coin hoards of the early eleventh century tend to confirm these traditions. In the Jossing hoard of Rogaland, dating from 1017-1018, are three coins of Sictric III of Dublin, and the same number are found in the Dronningenst find, which goes back to 1035.[192] There are also several Ommiad Spanish coins in these hoards which probably arrived via Ireland.[193]

But it does seem probable that trade with the Baltic reaching Norway, perhaps from as far away as Russia, was more important than that to Norse colonies in the Atlantic. We have many Saga references to such connections, particularly those which tell of Olaf Tryggvasson's youthful stay in Russia and of St. Olaf's flight to Kiev's court after his expulsion from Norway by Canute in 1028.[194] These political connections seem, however, to have included economic contacts as well. From the *St. Olaf Saga* we learn of a great seafarer who made regular merchant voyages to and from Russia,[195] while the six vessels which Olaf Tryggvasson brought back with him from his stay in Kiev seem to have been loaded with much fine silk.[196] No doubt this silk, like that worn by Magnus, Canute and St. Olaf, was of Russian origin. So, probably, was that given to St. Olaf by Astrid of Sweden.[197]

Lest this be considered mere tradition, in Norway we have some coin evidence of such trade during this period with the East and the Baltic. In the Oslo region we find one Byzantine coin minted by Basil II (976-1025) and on the west coast at Norge one of Romanus III (1028-34)[198] as well as a number of eleventh-century Kufic dir-

---

[191] *Ibid.*, p. 169.

[192] V. Ronander, *op.cit.*, pp. 93-97. O. A. Digre, *op.cit.*, pp. 163-68.

[193] H. Shetelig, "Arabiske Mynter frä Vestlandet," in *Oldtiden*, III (1913), 28-51.

[194] On these contacts with Russia, see S. F. Cross, "Medieval Russian Contacts with the West," and "Yaroslav the Wise in Norse Tradition," in *Speculum*, IV (1929), 207-14, and X (1935), 138-41.

[195] *St. Olafs Saga*, LXIV. On the continuance of an important fur trade with the White Sea region in this period see *ibid.*, CXXXIII, and A. Bugge, *op.cit.*, pp. 230-31.

[196] E. Pariset, *Histoire de la soie*, II, 324-40.   [197] *Ibid.*

[198] H. Holst, "Mynter i Norske Funn," *loc.cit.*, pp. 56-112. In addition, in Rogaland we find three imitations of Byzantine 10th-century coins.

hems in other places.[199] These may have come from Russia.[200] More normal, judging from coin evidence, was the trade with Baltic Swedish coasts and Denmark's shores as far as Wollin. Such commerce would account for the fact that the Dronningenst hoard of 1035 contains nine Swedish coins of Olaf Skottkonung and Arnund Jacob (994-1034) and two Bohemian ones minted between 999 and 1035.[201] To it we may owe the single Swedish penny of the Sand hoard of Trondelag, which dates from 1020,[202] and the coins from Bohemia, Hungary and numerous Baltic mints of Canute, Hardicanute and Magnus the Good which are found in the later Foldoy hoard of 1060.[203]

The trade reaching Norway via Kattegat and Skagerrak seems to have accounted, in part at least, for a similar urban growth apparent by the early eleventh century in Denmark. About 1100 we find Lund appearing in Scania, probably founded by Canute.[204] Nearby, in Jutland and on the islands, were Alborg, Viborg, Roskilde and Odense —all of which possessed mints for coining money under Canute, Hardicanute and Magnus the Good (1015-1043).[205] The appearance of new trading places and mints in these years in Denmark illustrates a certain shift in trade from the Eider-Schlee route, across the Jutland peninsula, to the more northern Kattegat-Skagerrak passage. Hedeby continued as a trading center down to 1043, and so did Ribe, and they both possessed mints.[206] However, new economic life was not found here, but farther north. Nor are these new mints the only proof of this fact. Coin hoards in Denmark, dating from 1016-1050, show the same thing. The major part of them have been discovered in North Jutland, Zealand and Scania, and few about Hedeby.[207] Even agricultural developments in Denmark reveal this new economic orientation, for in the eleventh century it was in Jutland, Zealand and Scania and

[199] H. Holst, op.cit., pp. 72-91.

[200] As proof of this direct connection between Norway and Russia, we find in a Sogne hoard one of Yaroslav's Russian coins. H. Holst, op.cit., p. 79. At the other end of the Baltic in Finland, one hoard also contains 2 rare Norwegian coins minted by St. Olaf. C. A. Nordman, op.cit., p. 10.

[201] O. A. Digre, op.cit., pp. 95-96.

[202] V. Ronander, op.cit., pp. 165-68.

[203] A. W. Brøgger, "Et Myntfund frä Foldøen," loc.cit., pp. 239-51.

[204] L. Musset, op.cit., p. 95. E. Lundberg, "Lunds stadsplan pâ 1000-talet," in Formannen, XXXVII (1942), 390-98.

[205] The Foldoy hoard of 1060 contains certain coins minted in Lund as well as some from these other centers—all dating from the early 11th century. A. W. Brøgger, op.cit., pp. 256-73.

[206] Magnus the Good was still coining money at Hedeby and Ribe between 1042 and 1047. A. W. Brøgger, op.cit., pp. 279-82.

[207] R. Shovmand, op.cit., pp. 146-82.

about Norway's Vik that a beginning was being made in clearing the heavy forest and increasing agricultural production.[208] In the tenth century, as we have shown earlier, the Kattegat-Skagerrak route was of some importance in commerce between the Baltic and North Sea, but less so than the Eider-Schlee route to Hedeby. In the eleventh century, the reverse was apparently true, and Hedeby began to lose importance. Probably larger ships made the deep-water northern route the more practical one.[209]

This new orientation of trade past Danish shores, however, explains more than Hedeby's gradual decline. It helps to illustrate why Svein and Canute were so persistent in their determination to dominate Norway's Vik region, and why Olaf Tryggvasson or Magnus the Good should concern themselves with Danish and Western Baltic affairs. For though Denmark and Southern Norway might be politically separate, the Kattegat-Skagerrak route ensured an economic inseparability that led ruler after ruler to try to translate it into political fact.

Farther east in the Baltic lay Sweden, which under Olaf Skottkonung and Arnund Jacob also engaged in Baltic commerce. It still received silks from Russia, and archeological evidence from Sigtuna reveals that it was also trading with Wollin and Central European regions, as had been the case earlier.[210] Sigtuna's Frisian guild likewise suggests a commerce which reached the Rhinelands and Germany, while the existence of other Swedish guilds, shown by rune stones, suggests some early eleventh-century quickening of economic life.[211]

Uppland Sweden was not, however, as important in a commercial sense in this period as it had been earlier, and Sigtuna does not appear to have been on a par with earlier Birka as a trade center. Rather it was Gotland which in these years became the center of Eastern Baltic commerce, diverting trade away from the Swedish mainland. This island,

---

[208] L. Musset, *op.cit.*, pp. 174-75.

[209] It seems probable that it was not destruction in war but the fact that it was bypassed by the commerce of the period that caused the decline of Hedeby, as it had earlier ended Birka's importance. Thus the role played by larger commercial vessels which carried goods directly into the Baltic rather than by way of the Eider-Schlee passage was the decisive factor by 1050.

[210] H. Arbman, "Une Route commerciale au Xe et XIe siècles," in *Slavia Antiqua*, v (1948), 435-38, points out that much of the beads, enameled eggs, combs and pottery found at Sigtuna resemble those found in excavations at Gniezno in Poland. These and certain other objects from Southern Russia must have reached Sigtuna via the Oder and Stettin or Wollin.

[211] A. Bugge, "Altschwedische Gilden," *loc.cit.*, pp. 142-44.

judging by coin evidence, enjoyed a trade which in the early eleventh century was as prosperous as it had been in the late tenth. This is, of course, reflected in the thousands of Anglo-Saxon and German coins found in Gotland's hoards which we have already mentioned. It is also shown, however, by the presence of over 1,000 Danish coins and the large amount of Byzantine, Polish, Czech and even Hungarian minted silver pieces. Gotland's essential separation from the Swedish mainland is also clearly revealed by the fact that in its 687 coin hoards there are but 115 Swedish minted coins, compared with 36,000-odd German, 19,000 Anglo-Saxon, 1,050 Danish, and over 400 Byzantine coins.[212] Gotland was the trade center of the Baltic but evidently little of what reached it was destined for Sweden itself.

Even more interesting is what the Gotland hoards of this period tell us concerning the arrival of Arabic silver dirhems in the Baltic. No Samanid silver money minted as late as 985 is found in Gotland hoards, as we have earlier emphasized.[213] Thus, trade by way of the Volga to Gotland and Sweden from the Moslem East must have been non-existent by the beginnings of this period. Some Moslem dirhems of a later date are found in these hoards, however, representing a sprinkling of coins from Islamic mints in Western Persia and Iraq which probably arrived here by way of the Caucasus and Central Europe, following approximately the same trade paths as the 400 Byzantine coins.[214] However, it is apparent that by 1043 even this trickle of commerce with the Moslem world had ended, since no Moslem coins at all reached Gotland that were minted later than the first years of the eleventh century.[215] Here certainly lies the clue to the decadence of the trade of the Swedish mainland, which apparently depended on this Volga river trade for its supplies of silver to

---

[212] M. Stenberger, *Die Schatzfunde Gotlands*, II, 211-562. The limited nature of Sweden's trade across the Baltic and into Russia is further revealed by examination of Finnish coin hoards dating from the early 11th century. We find in these hoards hundreds of English and German coins, even Irish ones in 8 finds, but very few Swedish minted ones. In fact, only 7 Swedish coins have been found here, as compared with 33 Danish, for instance. C. A. Nordman, *op.cit.*, pp. 8-25.

[213] M. Stenberger, *op.cit.*, pp. 570-703. S. Bolin, *Gotlands Vikingatidsskatter*, pp. 5-27.

[214] Arbman believes all these late Moslem dirhems reached the Baltic by way of Poland and Central Europe. But there seems little reason to doubt that some of these more Western Kufic coins, like a few late Byzantine ones, also arrived by way of Novgorod or the Dvina route. H. Arbman, "Une Route commerciale au Xᵉ et XIᵉ siècles," *loc.cit.*, pp. 435-38.

[215] S. Bolin, *op.cit.*, pp. 8-17. N. L. Rasmusson, "Foreign Coins in Swedish Coin Finds," *Trans. of International Num. Congress* (1938), pp. 130-42.

maintain its economic life. And this no doubt is why, in 1040-1042, Swedes tried once more to stimulate this commerce by launching their final raid on Western Sarkland in Central Asia.[216] It was a vain attempt. For though Gotland continued to serve as a center for the exchange of wares in the Baltic into the late eleventh and twelfth centuries, Sweden after 1043 entered a period of economic decline and darkness which was to last for almost a century. No longer linked to the traffic reaching the Caspian, its economy and commerce, which had grown fat on this trade since the seventh century, simply withered away. In 1070 Adam of Bremen could speak of Sweden as an almost unknown land and give us details of its life, such as the existence of Birka, which, while true of the previous century, had little to do with the world of Olaf Skottkonung and Arnund Jacob which had immediately preceded his own.[217]

If Sweden began to decline as an economic center of international importance in this period, not so Kievan Russia, to which trade streams from the Baltic via Gotland, Finland and Novgorod continued to flow. In the last years of the tenth century and the first years of the eleventh, Kiev was probably at the peak of its prosperity and unusually precocious in its economic life as compared with the most advanced regions of Western Europe. When the Polish forces of Boleslas Chobry, for instance, took Kiev early in the eleventh century, they found it a city of eight markets and forty churches.[218] The famous Kievan church of Hagia Sophia and that of Saint Saverin in Chernigov show the great material wealth and high degree of artistic skill available in Russia during this period—perhaps second only to that of Byzantium.[219] The *Russian Primary Laws* continue to reveal an advanced economy, in which the population of the cities was organized into *verv*, or guilds and partnerships were normal business arrangements and money was made available for loans at interest by the prince and important merchants. Storage space for merchandise was available, and bankruptcy was legally permissible. Judged on the basis of

[216] On this last expedition, see T. J. Arne, *Austr i Karusum och Särklandnammet*, pp. 290-305.

[217] Adam of Bremen, *Gesta Hamm. Eccl. Pont.*, IV, 21-27, contains a long account which seems to describe 11th-century Sweden. Yet it is obviously archaic in nature and probably represents Adam's incorporation into his narrative of an earlier description of Sweden by Archbishop Hunni who visited the Malar Sea region in 934-936.

[218] Thietmar, *Chron.*, in *MGH Script.*, new ser., IX, 50.

[219] B. Grekov, *La Culture de la Russie de Kiev*, pp. 6-8.

the commercial provisions of its laws, Kiev was at this time in advance of the simpler societies of the West.[220]

On the other hand, there is little evidence that Russia's important internal trade and agriculture had, by the early eleventh century, given rise to as much industry as we find in Western Europe. We do find in Kiev a large quarter which appears to have occupied itself with the making of objects of iron. Woodworking of various sorts and the weaving of flax into linen cloth were also of some importance. But in contrast to the diversified industries of Belgium, England and the Rhinelands, Kievan Russia in this period seems to have been curiously backward and to have concerned itself largely with commerce in primary products like grain, salt, cattle, furs and honey which came from its farms and forests.[221]

Perhaps this relative lack of industry, compared with what was to be found in Western Europe, Byzantium and Islam, explains why Russia's foreign trade was so important to her. Upon it she relied for manufactured goods—cloth, silks, glassware, spices, even metals. Much came from the Islamic and Byzantine worlds and the rest via the Baltic and Central Europe from the West. Some of the imported Oriental wares she was accustomed to ship to the Baltic and Central Europe to pay for Western products, while some at least of the furs, slaves, honey, wax and arms which paid for her imports from Constantinople and the Middle East came from the West also.

Perhaps this is why after 985, despite her prosperity, Russia faced a certain economic crisis. When the Volga ceased to bring commerce from the Moslem East, and the streams of Moslem Samanid dirhems dried up, she had lost her most valued export market for her raw materials and an important source of Eastern products, too. Now she no longer needed extra supplies of Baltic furs, wax, honey and slaves. She had all she required for trade with Byzantium and the Moslem Caucasus within her own territory. She began instead to have a surplus of her own to be shipped West. Gotland probably continued to be important in this traffic, transmitting Western wares to Novgorod and Russian products to the West. But Sweden, with no Russian need for the goods she produced, suddenly found herself on the economic sidelines.[222]

[220] G. Vernadsky, *Kievan Russia*, pp. 118-20, 140-44. See also *Medieval Russian Laws*, trans. Vernadsky (New York 1947), pp. 1-221.
[221] G. Vernadsky, *Kievan Russia*, pp. 99-116. J. Kulischer, *Russische Wirtschaftsgeschichte*, pp. 100-5.
[222] Vernadsky notes that the same raw materials were imported into or exported

The full effects of this change and reorientation of Kiev's external trade were not, however, fully apparent, except in Sweden, pior to 1043 or even 1056. For Russia under Yaroslav and Mstislav kept two routes open to her vital Eastern trade areas. One was that to the Crimea and Constantinople. Up to 1043 Yaroslav's attacks on this city seem to show that its trade was still important. Evidence of this is also seen in the Byzantine coins found in Baltic and Norwegian coin hoards and the silks and Eastern wares that continued to reach Central Poland and the North from Russia.[223] Russian control of Tmutorakan in this period also allowed her to reach Moslem Caucasus regions, free of Turkish domination, down to the end of Yaroslav's reign, as Scandinavian coin evidence in the form of early eleventh-century Moslem silver dirhems from this region indicates.[224] But when Yaroslav died in 1056, or perhaps earlier, despite that last Swedish expedition to Sarkland in 1040-1042, even this trade ended. Cumans and Patzinaks in South Russia finally severed Kiev's connections with both the Black Sea and the Caspian, and Russia, in large part the product of this trade, disintegrated.[225] Not until the twelfth century was she again to enjoy an important trade with Eastern lands and then on a much smaller scale than before 1043.

The gradual closing of routes leading to the Moslem East and the diminution of Russian trade to Byzantium as well may have been responsible for the increasing importance of trade from Kiev to Central Europe along routes which went back to the tenth century. One of these routes reached Poland and then swung north, by way of the Warta and Oder, to the Baltic via Gniezno and Wollin. Probably this route accounts for the archeological discovery of certain objects produced in Kievan Russian in early eleventh-century sites such as Gniezno, Lund and Sigtuna, and perhaps to it are owed certain Moslem coins of the same period found in Norwegian, Danish,

---

from Russia during this period, depending upon the market, this being especially true of furs, wax and honey. G. Vernadsky, op.cit., pp. 118-19. He does not, however, give any explanation for this fact.

[223] N. L. Rasmusson, op.cit., pp. 130-42, points out that a scattering of these coins continued to reach the Baltic as late as 1070.

[224] On finds of these rare dirhems from the domains of the Marawids, Buwayids and Okalids, see M. Stenberger, op.cit., pp. 115-638; N. L. Rasmusson, op.cit., pp. 136-42; and S. Bolin, Gotlands Vikingatidskatter, pp. 11-23.

[225] Perhaps 1040 saw the end of Moslem dirhem imports into the Baltic, and these last expeditions of the Russians against Constantinople in 1043 and of the Swedes to Turkestan in 1042 were a reaction to this trade stoppage.

Swedish and Gotland coin hoards.[226] From this route also Boleslas gained the wealth of which Otto III found evidence when he visited Poland in 998.[227]

The routes continued on to Prague, as Ibn Jacub revealed in 966-973, and we find in eleventh-century Bohemian graves many objects of Kievan origin: buttons, fine jewelry and such.[228] Exactly what was shipped back to Russia is doubtful, but it seems very unlikely that in this period it was the slaves and furs which had been articles of earlier commerce. Probably the tin of Bohemia, the copper of Saxony and arms and other manufactured German wares formed the basis of this traffic. So, too, did salt, the prohibition of whose export caused a crisis in Kiev.[229] But by the late eleventh century, if not before, furs, instead of being imported into Russia, were being exported over this route to Southern Germany.[230] In short, in the eleventh century, trade with Russia over Central European routes gradually increased, while that reaching her via the Baltic seems to have remained steady or been reduced in volume.[231]

Here the political divisions of Russia, as noted earlier, seem to show the economic foreign trade interest of the land. We noted that at the time of Vladimir's early youth Russia was divided into a Kiev under Yaroslav, and a Novgorod under Vladimir, with a domain of Oleg in between. After Vladimir had eliminated his rivals and taken Kiev, Russia stayed united until his death in 1015. Again, the three-fold division appeared—Yaroslav in Novgorod, Sviatopolk in Kiev and Mstislav in Tmutorakan—until Yaroslav in 1036 finally succeeded in uniting Russia again. Each of these regions represented a different foreign trade interest: Novgorod with the Baltic, Kiev with Central Europe and Tmutorakan with the Moslem and Byzantine East. After Yaroslav's death in 1056, they were again to reassert themselves, as Russia's economy declined and each area felt the attraction of the

[226] H. Arbman, op.cit., pp. 436-38.

[227] J. Kostryzewski, op.cit., pp. 565-70.

[228] J. Schanril, Die Vorgeschichte Böhmens und Mährens (Berlin 1928), pp. 288-315.

[229] G. Vernadsky, op.cit., pp. 99-108.

[230] For instance, furs worth 100 marks were shipped west from Kiev to South Germany in the late 11th century to help raise money to build a monastery at Regensburg. F. Dvornik, op.cit., pp. 250-52.

[231] Vernadsky believes an increase in commerce with the West more than compensated for the losses suffered in losing Byzantine and Moslem markets for Russian goods. G. Vernadsky, op.cit., pp. 118-19. On this trade, see also J. Kulischer, op.cit., pp. 118-40, and L. Goetz' survey in Deutsch-russische Handelsgeschichte des Mittelalters (Hamburg 1916), pp. 1-83.

foreign economic region to which it was tied by commerce. The existence of these separate regions up to 1043, however, provides proof of the importance of foreign trade and commerce to the Kievan state, until Patzinaks and Cumans attacked and changing trade routes began to produce a different, more local, agrarian economy.

Between Germany, Scandinavia and Russia lay a vast area of the Baltic and Central Europe over which the trade which linked these regions passed. Here, during at least the first four or five decades of this period, there is evidence of prosperity, as elsewhere in Northern Europe. Baltic trade routes of an international sort, for instance, may have by-passed Sweden, but they continued to reach Finland and the Eastern Baltic, probably by way of Gotland. The many hoards of German silver coins in Finland show approximately the same distribution of mints as those in Gotland and seem much the same in character, being mixed with large numbers of Anglo-Saxon pennies minted by Aethelred II, Canute and Canute's sons and successors.[232] In Courland we find over 1,000 German and Anglo-Saxon coins minted during this period in coin hoards of a similar type.[233] We also find in Esthonian sites examples of fine swords from the Rhinelands, showing a continuation of this trade.[234] Subjected to alternating Russian, Swedish and Danish influences, and in Samland even some influence from Poland, down to about 1030 this area continued to furnish honey, wax, slaves, and horses to Western traders and to Russia, and to serve as an intermediary region via the Gulf of Finland, the Dvina and the Niemen between Russia and the West.

There is even some evidence that these Baltic peoples began in this period to develop a certain maritime tradition and sea power of their own, which enabled them to trade with Gotland and other Baltic ports on their own account. For the two great Wendish attacks upon Denmark—that of 1043, which Magnus of Norway defeated, and that of 1050, which Sven Estridsen smashed—both contained contingents from the the peoples of the Eastern Baltic.[235] Perhaps,

[232] H. Salmo, *op.cit.*, pp. 217-42. C. A. Nordman, *Anglo-Saxon Coins Found in Finland*, pp. 1-30.

[233] F. Balodis, *Det Aldsta Lettland*, pp. 200-35.

[234] On swords and other weapons from Sweden and Southern Norway found in Esthonia down to about 1050 A.D., see B. Nerman, *Die Verbindungen zwischen Skandinavien und das Ostbalticum*, pp. 173-80. See also H. Jankuhn, "Ein Ulfberht Schwert aus der Elbe," *loc.cit.*, pp. 133-38.

[235] The pirates of Courland are mentioned as attacking Norwegian-held Denmark in *The Saga of Magnus the Good*, XXIII, and *The Saga of Harold Hardraada*, XL. See also L. Musset, *op.cit.*, pp. 240-45. On Karelian fleets from Finland late in this

by 1043, the maritime, piratical skill of Baltic Slavs, Esths and Finns which so impressed Adam of Bremen about 1070 had already been manifested in these northern waters.

In Central Europe, Poland, at least down to 1027, also showed a growth continuous since Miezko's time. Under Boleslas Chobry, for instance, at least six of its *grody* achieved definitive urban status. Of these, Wollin, Stettin, Gniezno and Cracow were the most important.[236] Both Miezko and Boleslas Chobry coined money in this period, like their neighbors in Scandinavia, Russia, Germany and Bohemia.[237] Along the trade routes that linked their land to Russia, the Baltic, Bohemia and Germany flowed the commerce which we have been discussing. Introducing Christianity to their realm, building political alliances with their neighbors, the Poles were beginning to be integrated into the economic life and culture of Northern Europe in this period.

After 1027, however, this period of unity and relative prosperity appears to have been severely compromised. The collapse of Canute's naval empire seems to have been foreshadowed by the earlier disintegration of that of his Central European Slavic ally. After twelve years of conflict, in 1039, Casimir the Renovator reorganized Poland, but a certain lack of economic unity became apparent, as Pomerania, facing the Baltic, began to pull away from the Central Polish Warta heartland. Its Wendish princes regained their independence and formed a slavic world of Baltic pirates which was to continue until the days of German expansion into these regions during the twelfth century.[238]

Farther south, Bohemia seems to have enjoyed much the same type of continued economic growth as Poland. She engaged in an active trade with Germany to the west, and Russia to the east, as we have shown. Her rulers, too, coined silver in this period, thus entering the money economy of Northern Europe,[239] while Prague became an

---

period, see V. Normanin, "Finnlands Handel mit Skandinavien unter Forntiden," in *Nordiske Kultur*, XVI (1933), 215-47.

[236] J. Kostryzewski, *op.cit.*, pp. 127-28.

[237] *Ibid.*, pp. 366-68. Poland's native coinage did not become abundant until late in the century, according to Kostryzewski. Barter and foreign coins were mainly used.

[238] On these years, see F. Dvornik, *op.cit.*, pp. 218-35, and S. Ketryzinski, "The Introduction of Christianity and the Early Kings of Poland," in *Cambridge History of Poland* (1950), I, 36-40.

[239] On this Bohemian coinage which began to be minted some decades earlier than that of Poland, see K. Turnewald, *Česká a Moravská denáry a brachtéaty* (Prague 1949), pp. 16-106.

even more important trading center than it had been when Ibn Jacub visited it in the tenth century. Bohemian commerce did not pass only along Central European trade routes, since coin hoards in the Baltic and in Norway reveal that some traffic, at least, went north through Poland to reach the more remote portions of Northern Europe.[240]

Even more interesting is the growth and economic development of Hungary. Up to 955 this land had been inhabited by Magyars whose major occupation appears to have consisted of raiding their neighbors. By 985 this had changed, and Hungary began to be economically connected with its neighbors by trade. A new commerce flowed north from Hungary across Poland to the Baltic, as is shown by the presence of large numbers of Hungarian coins in early eleventh-century Polish hoards,[241] and by the discovery of similar silver pieces in Gotland and Finland.[242] Similarly, an important trade began to reach Kiev, which may help to account for the marriage alliances which linked Hungarian kings with Kiev's ruling family in this period.[243] Moreover, Hungarians began, in these decades, to trade down the Danube with Constantinople, renewing a commerce which had not existed since the days of Attila in the fifth century, except for a brief ninth-century interlude. In 1026 Richard of St. Vannes and a group of pilgrims followed this route on their way to Constantinople and the Holy Land.[244] Hungary at last began to be affected by the commerce which flowed across Europe from the Baltic to Constantinople, and from the Adriatic to the North Sea.

[240] Judging from coins found in Scandinavian and Baltic hoards, this Bohemian trade to the Baltic did not become important until about 1000 A.D., since it is only in hoards buried after this date that we find money minted by Bohemian rulers. As examples of such coins, we find one Bohemian piece in an Icelandic hoard of 1020 (K. Eldjarn, *op.cit.*, pp. 39-62), and one in a Norwegian hoard of 1060 (A. W. Brøgger, "Et Myntfund frä Foldøen," *loc.cit.*, pp. 239-82). There are also 4 coins in the Digerakra hoard and 4 in the Sigsawe hoard from Gotland. M. Stenberger, *op.cit.*, pp. 19-20, 108-10. Each of the Nousanien, Lieto and Rosio hoards of Finland, dating from 1040-50, has one Bohemian coin also. C. A. Nordman, *op.cit.*, pp. 5-10.

[241] Hungarian coins, minted in this period, have been found in 50 hoards in Poland. J. Kostryzewski, *op.cit.*, pp. 372-74.

[242] Hungarian coins, judging from evidence based on coin hoards, appear to have begun arriving in the Baltic about 1040. We find one Hungarian coin in the Foldoy hoard in Norway, which dates about 1060. A. W. Brøgger, *op.cit.*, pp. 239-71. And others are found in the Gotland Digerakra and Gerete hoards. M. Stenberger, *op.cit.*, pp. 19-20, 59-60. There is even one Hungarian coin in the Lieto Finnish hoard of 1050. C. A. Nordman, *op.cit.*, p. 5.

[243] B. Lieb, "The Kiev State and Western Europe," in *Trans. of Royal Hist. Soc.*, XXIX (1949), 83-172.

[244] Dezso Pais, "Les Rapports franco-hongrois sous le règne des Arpad," in *Revue des études hongroises*, I (1937), 16.

The economy of Northern Europe, then, from 985 to 1043 in general saw a continuation of earlier trends. Canute's maritime empire, the Russia of Vladimir and Yaroslav, the Poland of Miezko and even the Hungary of Stephen and Andrew all contributed to this development. Almost everywhere in England, Ireland, Belgium, Germany, Poland, Norway, Denmark and Russia we find an appearance and growth of towns and an increase in the number of markets and mints. Everywhere throughout the lands of Northern Europe money was coined by the rulers. Yaroslav could marry his daughter to a king of France, and Olaf and Magnus could set forth from faraway Kiev to win a Norse kingdom. Canute in England could concern himself with the affairs of distant Samland, and an Icelander could know the streets of distant Constantinople. France and Spain in the West and Hungary in the East were now linked to the commerce of the Northern Seas, which extended from Greenland to Kiev and from Finland to Aquitaine and which allowed Anglo-Saxon princes to seek refuge at the court of Magyar rulers in Central Europe.

To this interdependence, mingling and growth of the economies of the lands around the Northern Seas, one should add a new feature, the beginning of a tendency on their part to merge with the economy of the Mediterranean to the south. In some parts of Europe, we have noticed this prior to 985. It became stronger in the late tenth and early eleventh centuries. More and more traffic now began to use the Alpine passes from Venice and Northern Italy into Southern Germany. Arms, hawks, slaves and other Northern products reached the Po river valley, while spices and other Oriental wares reached Constance in increased amounts.[245] Nor was this traffic confined to Germany. The *clusae* to France, so long closed by Moslem freebooters, began to take on new life, as Canute gained privileges of toll exemption for his English merchants going to Italy, and Alpine colporteurs at Asti began to carry their burdens through the Mount Geneva and Little St. Bernard passes towards Geneva.[246] A new maritime traffic from the Mediterranean began to stir along the shores of the Midi, and to flow up the Rhone towards the north, and west towards the Garonne valley[247]—meeting commerce from the Atlantic moving more freely inland from Bordeaux, Tours and Paris. Spain, both in

[245] A. R. Lewis, *op.cit.*, p. 223.
[246] J. Tyler, *Alpine Passes*, p. 91. Mansi, *Collectae consilium*, XIX, 499.
[247] On these new signs of life in the regions about Montpellier and Genoa, see A. R. Lewis, *op.cit.*, pp. 220-22.

445

Catalonia and Asturias, added her products to the surge towards the North,[248] while the Hungarians began to serve as intermediaries in a traffic moving between Byzantium and the Baltic via the Danube.[249] New groups of pilgrims reached Rome, Constantinople and the Holy Land by way of Alpine passes, the Danube and Russian rivers.[250] Harold Hardraada could serve in the Varangian guard of Constantinople and die a king of Norway. Adventurers from Normandy who were now appearing in Southern Italy took the first steps towards the formation of the Norman kingdom of Two Sicilies,[251] while others, going to Spain, began to reinforce the Spanish Christian kings who were beginning their long Reconquista.[252] Though still profoundly northern in its commerce and economic life, Europe beyond the Mediterranean began to mingle with the commerce and life of its blue waters.

And where new trade centers grew in this period, we find about them agrarian growth, too, much more important than that of Carolingian and Ottonian times. In England, the forest was pushed back about the new borough mints of Aethelred and Canute, and new land was won for cultivation, until by 1050 the face of the country resembled that of later medieval England.[253] In Flanders, the rising towns marked a movement to continue Carolingian draining of the marshes and establishment of new polders.[254] In France, clearing of

[248] On Catalonia in this period, see J. M. Fort, "Origines del regimen municipal de Cataluña," in *Ann. de hist. del derecho español*, XVI (1938), 171-89. On Northwestern Spain, see C. Sanchez-Albornoz, *Estampas de la vida en León*, pp. 13-257, and L. Valdiavellano, "El mercado, apuntes para sur estudio in León," in *Ann. de hist. del derecho español*, VIII (1931), 231-42.

[249] Hungary's new role as an intermediary between Mediterranean Italy and Dalmatia, Byzantium, Russia and the Baltic needs additional study. It was one of the major changes which took place in Central Europe during this period. Perhaps in part it was the result of Byzantium's defeat of the Bulgars and her advance to the Danube during the first years of the 11th century.

[250] As an example of such large pilgrim groups, that of Richard of St. Vanne is important. See *Hugonis chron.*, in *MGH Script.*, VIII, 393, and *Gesta epis. Verdun*, in *ibid.*, p. 394.

[251] Amari, *Storia di Mussulmani*, new ed., III, 30-41. C. Haskins, *The Normans in European History*, pp. 198-203, has also an excellent résumé of Norman penetration into Southern Italy. See also A. R. Lewis, *op.cit.*, pp. 234-35.

[252] Ademar, *Chron.*, in *MGH Script.*, IV, 104-5, mentions French feudal adventurers in Catalonia. See E. Lévi-Provençale, *L'Espagne mussulmane*, p. 458, on their use as mercenary soldiers by Almansor. On the beginnings of the Reconquista in the early 11th century, see R. Dozy, *Recherches sur l'histoire et la littérature en Espagne*, II, 103-96.

[253] F. Stenton, *op.cit.*, pp. 276-86. C. Fox, *The Archeology of the Cambridge Region*, pp. 90-206.

[254] F. Ganshof, *La Flandre sous les premiers comtes*, pp. 7-52, gives a description of this process in this part of the Netherlands.

waste and forest was resumed in Normandy, in the Isle-de-France, in Picardy and the Loire valley, though more slowly in the west.[255] In Northern Spain the same thing happened. In Germany, along the upper Danube and around the new trade centers of Saxony, forests disappeared. About Polish towns[256] and in Kievan Russia virgin land was broken by the plow,[257] while in Norway's Vik and Denmark's Jutland, Scania and Zealand the primeval forest was cleared.[258] Everywhere, as in past eras, agrarian and urban development went hand in hand, remaking the face of Europe and increasing the already substantial gains of earlier years. And it was this agricultural growth which provided the food to feed the population of the rising urban centers.

The character of the commerce of Northern Europe did not change during this period, though its extent did. As earlier, we find furs, fish, iron and northern wares provided by Scandinavia; wool, *wadmal*, furs and walrus ivory from Iceland and Greenland; wheat, honey, metals and cloth from England; gold, linen, wheat and honey from Ireland; glass, arms, metals, cloth, pottery, wine and metalware from Germany and the Low Countries; honey, wax, and wheat from Poland; furs, honey and wax from Finland and the Baltic; tin from Bohemia; linen flax, wax, furs from Russia; and wine and olive oil from France and Spain. Salt was produced in many localities in Western France, England, Germany, Poland and Northern Russia and was traded everywhere. Slaves, too, were a staple article of commerce originating in Wales, Scandinavia and Slavic lands, and were sent south[259] along with furs and arms to Moslem lands by way of France, Venice and Russia—though the slave trade seems to have been less important in this period than earlier.

From the East by way of Russia, Italy and Spain still came fine

---

[255] M. Bloch, *Les Caractères originaux de l'histoire rurale française*, pp. 14-17. R. Koebner, "The Colonization and Settlement of Europe," in *Cambridge Econ. History of Europe*, I, 63-66.

[256] On agrarian expansion and advance in Eastern Germany in this period, see R. Koebner, *op.cit.*, pp. 66-70. On the same process in Poland, J. Kostryzewski, *op.cit.*, pp. 28-29.

[257] G. Vernadsky, *Kievan Russia*, pp. 99-110.

[258] L. Musset, *op.cit.*, pp. 174-75.

[259] The slave trade seems to have declined in Europe by the early 11th century. Nevertheless it still had some importance in Wales, Ireland and Scandinavia. See B. Charles, *Old Norse Relations with Wales* (Cardiff 1934), pp. 34-37, and E. Bromberg, "Wales and the Medieval Slave Trade," in *Speculum*, XVII (1942). On the sale of English slaves to Scandinavia by Canute's sister, see William of Malmesbury, *Gesta regum*, in *Roll Series*, I, 245. On slaves still to be found in Russia, *The Earliest Russian Laws*, p. 28.

silks, spices and luxury articles, now made available almost every-where. International trading centers like London, Cologne, Got-land, Kiev, Novgorod, Dublin and Bruges continued to grow. In general, the Rhine, Meuse, Scheldt and Thames regions of the West were industrial in character, while the North and East remained agricultural. Contact with the Mediterranean had still not become the determining factor in Northern Europe's trade.

Already, though, important changes that forecast further ones were apparent in Northern Europe's trade patterns. One was the growth of trade routes overland by way of Hungary and Poland which linked Northern and Western Europe directly to Russia and Byzantium. The other was the severance of routes to the Caspi-an, Sea of Azov and Black Sea from Kievan Russia. By 1043 trade between these regions had all but ceased to exist and, to replace this loss, Russia turned west to trade goods she had earlier sent east. As this happened, the Varangian routes from the Baltic led no farther east than Novgorod, not to Bagdad and Samarkand. The Swedes suffered first from this change and then the delicate balance of com-merce in the Baltic was affected as Poland and then the Kievan state disintegrated. Trade began to flow to Venice, to Genoa and to the Rhone from the East, instead of to the Volga, the Don, the Dnieper and the Baltic.[260] Gradually the center of gravity of Northern Europe's economic life began to shift south and west again. The age of Novgorod, of Kiev, of Wollin, of Prague as great centers of Eastern trade was coming to an end. That of Venice, Genoa, Mar-seilles and Barcelona was beginning. The end of Canute's empire, of the Kievan Russia of Yaroslav and of Boleslas Chobry's strong Piast Poland heralded the future grandeur of France, Flanders and Angevin England.

We now turn to the question of the naval power and ships which characterized this last flowering of Scandinavian power in the age of Svein and Canute. One of the chief characteristics of this period is the appearance of organized naval power at last upon the Northern Seas. In England the professional navy which Alfred had founded and Aethelstan and Edgar so carefully preserved was continued by Aethelred. Unfortunately, under incompetent leadership and the pressure of Danish attacks this force was mismanaged and helped England little. But we can see the outlines of a national English

[260] On the basic factors behind this change, see A. R. Lewis, *op.cit.*, pp. 183-258.

navy in the system which Aethelred tried too late to establish—a system in which each part of the land paid a portion of the cost of building and maintaining one naval vessel, and in which other shipping could be impressed into service if the occasion warranted.[261]

In Denmark, on the other hand, the same system was used with more success. The establishment of naval districts, each required to furnish ships and crews upon the summons of the sovereign, helped to account for the successes gained by Svein and Canute.[262] And this system did not exist only in Denmark. It was found in Norway, too, where since the days of Haakon the Good a similar coastal defense system had been in operation.[263] Traces of it can also be found in Sweden, where the *roslagen* system was in current use.[264] The great fleets of Svein and Canute, of Olaf Tryggvasson, St. Olaf and Magnus of Norway, of Swedish kings like Arnund Jacob, were nationally organized flotillas, in a new sense of the word. And when Canute took England, he strengthened the Anglo-Saxon system he found there and continued to maintain a strong fleet manned by professional seamen.[265]

The great naval battles which took place in this period, such as that off Rügen in which Olaf Tryggvasson perished, or of Holy River, where Canute smashed Norse and Swedish naval power, seem thus to represent the modern naval tradition of organized fleets in combat, rather than the old Viking individualism.[266] The Jomsburgvikings, until their destruction by Magnus of Norway in 1043, do recall something of the older pirate past, but they were the exception which proves the rule. In general, in this age we see an emergence of national navies which presages modern times. Only along Wendish and East Baltic

[261] See W. L. Clowes, *The Royal Navy*, I, 19, on the raising of this fleet. On the continuance of this system into the 12th century, see F. Liebermann, *Gesetze*, II, 638, and D. Whitelock, *Anglo-Saxon Wills*, p. 52. See also F. Stenton, *Anglo-Saxon England*, pp. 424-26. It thus seems probable that England had the first regular navy in Western Europe since Charlemagne's time.

[262] E. Boll, *Leding* (Christiania 1920).

[263] Tradition assigns the beginnings of Norway's system of musterships to the reign of Haakon the Good about 950. Thus it was the earliest organized naval force found in Scandinavia. Since Haakon was raised in England at Aethelstan's court, it seems probable that he copied the already existing Anglo-Saxon naval organization in some respects. But it should be emphasized that the Norse musterships were for defense only. See Brøgger and Shetelig, *The Viking Ships*, pp. 227-29.

[264] S. Tunberg, "Roden och roslagen," in *Svensk Hist. Tidskrift*, LXVIII (1949), 73-83.

[265] On Canute's strong navy, see W. L. Clowes, *op.cit.*, p. 19, and F. Stenton, *op.cit.*, pp. 406-7, 424-26. See also L. Larson, *Canute the Great*, pp. 78-103.

[266] For accounts of tactics used in these naval battles, see Brøgger and Shetelig, *op.cit.*, pp. 223-33, and W. L. Rogers, *Naval Warfare Under Oars* (Annapolis 1931), pp. 71-89.

coasts did something of the freebooting tradition continue into the next period.

Still another interesting feature of this age is the size of the warships in use. In the late ninth and tenth centuries it was Anglo-Saxon England which inaugurated the great ships that were to be used later. By the time of Canute what we find are large *drekkars*, or dragon ships, carrying 60 oars to a side and perhaps as many as 400 or 500 men. Not until the twelfth and thirteenth centuries were such large craft again to be constructed in Northern European waters. And they seem to have hardly lasted past the mid-eleventh century themselves, for we know that it was in much smaller vessels that William the Conqueror crossed the English Channel. With the passing of the great *drekkars*, the Viking Age ended in the Northern Seas.[267]

It would not be proper, however, to view the maritime activities of this period solely in terms of national fleets and the huge warships possessed by Scandinavian monarchs and leaders. For they were not the only mariners or ships then in use in Northern Europe. As earlier, Frisian vessels traded everywhere relatively undisturbed, even traveling as far as Greenland,[268] while on the coast of Flanders a new maritime strength was appearing about Bruges which was to become of great importance in the late part of the century.[269] England continued to possess important shipping, as did Normandy, whose merchants now visited London. Both the Irish and Norse of Ireland used the sea, as before, while from distant Iceland and Greenland Scandinavian

---

[267] Perhaps the 10th-century ship presented to Aethelstan by Harold Fairhair was a *drekkar*. Otherwise we must assume that the new class of warships began in Scandinavia with the construction of Olaf Tryggvasson's "Crane" in 995. See Brøgger and Shetelig, *op.cit.*, pp. 191-92. Canute, however, built similar ships in England and also probably in Denmark. F. Stenton, *op.cit.*, pp. 406-7. As a matter of fact, the building of these huge ships falls into two periods: the first between 995 and 1063 (Olaf Tryggvasson through Harold Hardraada); and the second from 1182 to 1263, when even larger *drekkars* were launched in Norway and Denmark. Brøgger and Shetelig, *op.cit.*, pp. 186-223.

[268] The Bayeux Tapestry shows clearly that the ships used by William the Conqueror were small ones. But they seem to have been of Scandinavian design and type and clinker-built. As a matter of fact, all along the coast of France, even beyond Normandy, there was much Scandinavian influence exerted on French ships during these years. See A. May, "French Sea-Terms of Northern Origin," in *Mariners Mirror*, XXVI (1940), 145-57.

[269] Adam of Bremen, *Gesta Hamm. Eccl. Pont.*, IV, 39-40. On the Frisian *kogge*, see Brøgger and Shetelig, *op.cit.*, pp. 236-37. On the other hand, it seems probable that Flemish ships resembled those of Normandy, which they joined in sailing to conquer England in 1066. On the growth of a new naval power in Flanders by 1039-1040, see P. Grierson, "The Relations Between Flanders and England," *loc.cit.*, pp. 90-95.

mariners traveled to North America.[270] On western Gallic, and northern Spanish coasts and in Brittany native maritime skills flourished,[271] and in the Baltic Slavs, Esths, Balts and Finns became hardy and dangerous naval opponents of Scandinavian shipping.[272] Galician, Breton, Norman, Flemish, Frisian, English, Irish and Slav mariners roamed the seas with the Scandinavians and helped to account for the growth of trade and commerce of this period. And to these peoples rather than to the Scandinavians was to belong the future Atlantic commerce of Northern Europe.

We now turn to our final problem, that of the organization which lay behind the commerce and industry of this period in Northern Europe—who the merchants were and how they organized their activities. These are most difficult questions to answer. No single type of organization was found in the eleventh century, any more than in Carolingian times. We still find, for instance, individuals in Frisia, Iceland and Scandinavia who were partly peasants and partly merchants.[273] We also find highly developed partnerships in Kievan Russia, where the earliest Russian laws refer to temporary associations of merchants.[274] And in Norway we learn of looser merchant associations formed for the duration of a certain period of time or series of trading ventures.[275] Equally common seems to have been the practice of individual merchants trading on their own account.[276]

But gradually, in this period, we also see the emergence of a newer, more permanent type of association—the merchant guild. It had its roots in practices going back to Carolingian times or even before, in those early fraternal organizations found throughout the Teutonic

---

[270] The *knorrs* were the ships used for voyages to Iceland, Greenland and America. Brøgger and Shetelig, *op.cit.*, pp. 233-35.

[271] We would like to know more of the ship-types which were used along western French and Galician Spanish coasts in this period. We know they were formed into a navy off Galicia late in the century. Were they, as seems probable, still modeled on the *barca*?

[272] Wendish (Baltic Slavic) ships, which met the finest Norse vessels on even terms during these years, were probably modeled along the same lines. At least those of the Jomsburgvikings were, even though these pirates were probably predominantly Slavic. On such Slavic ships, see the conjectures of R. Bruchner, *Histoire de la culture polonaise*, pp. 188-92, and H. Falk, "Altnordisches Seewesen," in *Wörter und Sachen*, IV (1912), 88-104. Kostrzewski believes the Wends were seamen as skilled as the Scandinavians. J. Kostrzewski, *op.cit.*, pp. 357-62.

[273] O. Tønning, *op.cit.*, pp. 14-26. L. Musset, *op.cit.*, pp. 250-52.

[274] G. Vernadsky, *Kievan Russia*, pp. 119-20.

[275] O. Tønning, *op.cit.*, pp. 3-4.

[276] O. A. Johnsen, "Le Commerce et la navigation en Norvège au moyen âge," in *Revue hist.*, CLXXXVIII (1936), 394-95. The career of Godric late in the century, examined with such care by Vogel and Pirenne, is also an example of this.

world—featuring a common guild banquet, various charitable functions and so forth. It is possible that even in the eleventh century Anglo-Saxon guilds were largely social.[277] What was new was the transformation of this fraternal organization into a permanent merchant guild, continuing its social functions, but primarily economic in purpose. The Frisian guilds at Sigtuna,[278] the merchant guilds of Novgorod and other Russian centers,[279] and the guild of merchants who traveled from Thiel to trade in England[280] all represented this new type of organization. So, too, did those we find at St. Omer in Flanders,[281] at Cambridge, Canterbury and Winchester in England[282] and at Najera and León in Asturias.[283] They were new, permanent groups of merchants bound together for trade purposes. In Flanders, soon after 1043, they were to extend beyond single towns to form *hansas*.[284] They had great economic advantages over individual merchant adventurers and partnerships in that they allowed a pooling of capital on a permanent basis. This and their institutional existence gave them strength and unity. In relation to the simpler free merchant individualism of Scandinavia, for instance, the Flemish guilds, which have been carefully studied, represented an economic advance. They were thus superior to earlier ways of conducting commerce. And they gave tremendous impetus to economic growth in the regions where they were strongest, in the lands of the Continent between the Seine and the Rhine and across the Channel in England. It was to them, as much as to manufacturing skill or maritime commerce, that this portion of Europe was to owe its future economic progress.

Closely linked to the rise of merchant guilds, we find still a second phenomenon, the movement of industry from domains or abbeys in the countryside to the newly rising towns. Again, this was not an

---

[277] G. Gross, *The Guild Merchant*, I, 191.

[278] On the Frisians at Hedeby, see G. Jacob, *Arabische Berichteratätter*, p. 33. At Sigtuna, A. Bugge, "Altschwedische Gilden," in *Viert. für Soz- und Wirtschaft*, VI (1913), 141-44. For Norse guilds at Trondheim late in the century, see O. A. Johnsen, *op.cit.*, p. 394.

[279] G. Vernadsky, *op.cit.*, p. 146.

[280] *MGH Script.*, IV, 718.

[281] G. Espinas and H. Pirenne, "Les Coutumes de la gilde marchande de Saint-Omer," in *Le Moyen Age*, XIV (1901), 159-96. Almost as old is that of Arras. See E. Coornaert, "Les Gildes médiévales," *loc.cit.*, pp. 43-45.

[282] E. Coornaert, *op.cit.*, pp. 45-46.

[283] R. S. Lopez, "Still Another Renaissance," in *American Hist. Review*, LVII (1951), 3-15.

[284] F. L. Ganshof, *La Flandre*, pp. 65-67. It must be emphasized, however, that the *Hansa* of London did not appear until the 12th century.

entirely new phenomenon. By Carolingian times the glass, pottery and arms industries of the Rhinelands and the cloth industry of Flanders were probably only partly domanial. Now, however, this trend increased, as export industries discovered the advantages to be derived from association with merchant guilds in the rising trading centers. By the early eleventh century, in Flanders and in the Meuse valley, as well as in Germany and England, manufacture of pottery, cloth, arms, metalware and glassware was located in towns, not in the countryside.[285]

It seems probable that the reason for this shift of industry to urban centers lies in the growth of artisan guilds, which began to appear in this period in towns like Arras.[286] This may also have been true in England and in Kievan Russia.[287] At any rate, such artisan guilds served as a spur to increased productivity and therefore were reflected in greater urban wealth.

In short, the early eleventh century saw the development of a new organization of commerce and industry, the guilds, in areas as widely separated as León and Kiev. They were based on earlier organizations and were still in the process of evolution, but they gave a superior economic system to the regions where they were most numerous: the Low Countries, Germany, England and perhaps Russia. Under their impetus, new towns and old trading places grew even more rapidly than before, matching the improved agriculture and expanding commerce of the times.

It must not be assumed, however, that other forms of economic organization disappeared just because guilds were arising, for they certainly did not. Much domanial industry no doubt continued in the countryside.[288] As late as the thirteenth century, the part-time peasant and trader pattern continued in Frisia and Scandinavia. In the eleventh, individual merchant adventurers and trading partnerships continued to carry on commerce. Advanced and less-advanced methods of doing business continued side by side. Servile peasants carried domanial goods and wine long distances to be used by abbeys and

[285] D. Whitelock, *The Beginnings of English Society*, pp. 132-33. F. L. Ganshof, *La Flandre*, pp. 64-65. R. Doehaerd, *op.cit.*, pp. 27-30.

[286] E. Coornaert, *op.cit.*, pp. 208-9.

[287] G. Vernadsky, *Kievan Russia*, pp. 143-46. D. Whitelock, *op.cit.*, pp. 132-33. G. Unwin, *The Guilds and Companies of London*, pp. 44-48.

[288] M. Bloch, "Economie-nature ou économie-argent," in *Ann. d'hist. sociale*, 1 (1939), 7-16.

feudal nobles,[289] at the same time that free guild merchants were doing so in a free money economy. The earliest Russian laws reveal that slaves and free servants were often present in the same households.[290] As earlier, the principal feature of Western European life was its infinite variety of economic levels and economic systems. More advanced agriculture, urbanization and guild economies were found side by side with a domanial system. Only the important first steps had been taken, but they were steps which by the early eleventh century had carried Europe far beyond the levels it had reached in Carolingian and Ottonian times.

Such, then, was the state of the lands around the Northern Seas by the mid-eleventh century. The Northern European trading area of Carolingian and Viking times had expanded as better agrarian production and new urban centers appeared everywhere. The volume of commerce had grown steadily, until not a single area from Ireland to the Black Sea had failed to be affected by it. Everywhere in Europe, coins minted by the local governments had expanded the area of a true money economy. These coinages were on the whole identical in type and weight and so acceptable everywhere. And now, by way of Spain, the Rhone, Venice and the Black Sea this Northern European trade world began to mingle more freely with that of the Mediterranean. A common money system and international trade routes had been established, as well as merchant and craft guilds, while industry began to move into the new towns—particularly in the West. Ships continued to improve, and navigation had become so superior that Frisian and Scandinavian vessels did not fear to travel into the wide expanses of the North Atlantic as far as Greenland and beyond. There was hardly a people or district about the Northern Seas which by this time had not developed a maritime tradition and a hardy race of sailors and fishermen. Economically, politically, even morally, Northern Europe was ready by 1043 to turn south to the Mediterranean and to challenge Byzantium and Islam in the age soon to arise, the age of the Crusades.

[289] H. Van Werweke, "Comment les abbayes belges se procuraient-ils du vin au moyen âge?" in *Revue belge*, II (1923), 236-47.
[290] G. Vernadsky, *op.cit.*, pp. 334-37.

8, The Emergence of Europe,
A.D. 1043-1100

ANY CHANGES took place in Northern Europe between the end of Canute's empire and the period of the First Crusade. Anglo-Saxon England was conquered by the Norman Duke William and became closely linked with a French, Continental destiny. Norway and Denmark were finally separated into two national monarchies. The Holy Roman Empire of Germany engaged in its great quarrel over investitures with the Papacy, a struggle which left it weaker and more disunited as the twelfth century dawned. Poland and Sweden practically ceased to exist as states for a century, and Russia, once so powerful, relapsed into disunity. Most of the Baltic became a Slavic sea. Important changes, then, disturbed and, for decades, disrupted the vast trading area of Northern Europe which had extended from Ireland to Novgorod and from London to Nidaros and which had until this period grown so steadily in size and importance.

An even more important change, however, lay behind these events. It was the merging of Northern and Southern Europe, the mixing and mingling of that life which had developed around the waters of the North with that which was touched by the waters of the Mediterranean. This had begun as early as the first decades of the eleventh century, but it was after 1043 that we find it culminating in a new Europe. Normans in Southern Italy and Sicily, Western French feudal lords in Spain, Italian merchants in France, Papal intervention in Germany, Flemish, Brabançon and English pirates in the Mediterranean, great numbers of pilgrims from Scandinavia and Iceland in Rome and the Holy Land, adventurers from all over Europe reaching Constantinople—all these marked a new era. The symbol, the proof, of it was, of course, the First Crusade. This movement in which the North and the Mediterranean—English, French, Scandinavian, German, Italian and Byzantine—joined in a common purpose began a new period for Europe. When the King of Norway, Sigurd the Jerusalem-farer, traveled by sea around Spain to Palestine, when King Eric of Denmark could do the same by way of Russia and Constantinople, a new age had been born. A Europe had come into being as the result of the interfertilization of North and South, and of Viking and feudal lord mingling with Italian merchant. The dream of Charlemagne and Otto III was becoming a reality, soon to be embodied in Papal Rome's leadership of the entire West. In the next century, at the Fairs of Champagne, in the cities of Southern Germany and South-western France, even in Hungary, these two streams of commerce were to meet and produce that European international trade which characterized the later Middle Ages.

The outcome of this age was not, however, immediately apparent in the changes which occurred in the North Sea and Baltic during these decades. The end of Canute's empire saw a certain disorder, a certain political fragmentation take place, for this great Danish ruler had no successor in the Northern Seas. England by 1042 had reverted to Edward the Confessor, the issue of Aethelred's marriage, in his old age, with Emma of Normandy. Edward thus represented the blood of Alfred of Wessex's line of kings which had produced so many strong English monarchs in the tenth century. Having spent his youth in exile with his Norman relatives, however, he came to the throne more Norman than English in sentiment. Thus he favored Normans in his Anglo-Saxon realm, and under him we find a beginning of that Norman penetration of the land which was to culminate in its conquest by William in 1066.

Worse still, Edward, though worthy and kind, was weak and incapable as a king. The chief power in the realm was not in his hands but belonged to the powerful Earl Godwin of Wessex. This latter owed his position to Canute rather than Edward and had great ambitions for himself and his family. Since Edward was childless, the House of Godwin strove throughout his reign to solidify its position so that it could take over the kingship upon his death. What we have, then, in England in this period is a situation not unlike that which the Merovingians faced with their powerful Carolingian Mayors of the Palace, or which later Carolingian rulers of France faced with their Capetian rivals. Hence the disorder and the civil strife which paralyzed effective government in England, down to Edward's death in 1065. Had he been a more competent ruler, more truly popular with his subjects, he might have been able to control Godwin and his sons. As it was, England drifted into an anarchy from which William of Normandy alone was to derive profit. For he, like Godwin, was a party to the triangle, patiently waiting until the death of his kinsman, Edward, would deliver into his hands the rich prize which England represented.

In Scandinavia also the situation was complicated by struggles over thrones. Upon Canute's death in 1035, Norway had passed to Magnus, son of St. Olaf. When Canute's sons perished one by one, only a nephew, Svein Estridson, of the line of Harold Bluetooth, was left with a valid claim to the land. So Magnus of Norway hastened south to conquer Denmark. Svein, backed by Wendish fleets, resisted with but little success, until Magnus' death in 1047 gave him an opportunity to regain his kingdom. But this did not bring peace. Magnus was succeeded on the throne of Norway by Harold Hardraada, an adventurer with much of the Viking in his makeup, who continued to attack Denmark in the hope of adding it to his kingdom and began to cast covetous eyes on England as well.[1]

Finally, still another power was vitally concerned with the situation developing in England and in Scandinavia. That was Flanders. Her counts controlled a rich principality with a growing economy and a maritime commerce which reached both Scandinavia and Britain in this period. They could not be indifferent to the struggle going on in Britain between Edward and the House of Godwin, or unaware of William of Normandy's ambitions. Nor could they help but be concerned with the long battle fought by Norse kings to take and hold Denmark and with Norse ambitions in the North Sea.[2]

This was the basic political background against which events in England and the North Sea evolved after Edward ascended the English throne in 1042. Upon his accession to power, he found it wise to follow the lead of the House of Godwin, then his principal supporters. This family, who owed their position to Canute, naturally threw their support and that of England behind Svein Estridson in his struggle with Magnus over Denmark. And since Henry III, Emperor of Germany, had married a daughter of Canute, he supported Svein also. On the other hand, relations between England and Flanders after 1042 appear to have been strained. We do not know all the reasons for this hostility, but it seems possible that in part it was the result of Edward's resentment at the aid Flanders gave his rivals for the English throne when Emma made her visit there in 1037-1038. Perhaps it rested also on a rivalry between London and Bruges over

[1] L. Musset, Les Peuples scandinaves, pp. 160-70. G. Turville-Petrie, The Heroic Age in Scandinavia, pp. 160-64. The basic sources of our knowledge of these years are the traditions in The Saga of Magnus the Good and The Saga of Harold Hardraada, both in Snorri Sturluson's Heimskringla.

[2] On the relations between Flanders and Anglo-Saxon England, see P. Grierson, "The Relations Between Flanders and England Before the Norman Conquest," in Trans. of the Royal Hist. Soc., XI (1941), 97-105.

trade in this part of the North Sea. At any rate, by 1045 Normandy, England, Germany and Denmark were lined up in opposition to Flanders and Norway.

In 1045 the English fleet was stationed at Sandwich for fear that Magnus of Norway, who had won victories in Denmark, would follow them up with an attack upon England. In the next year an even larger defensive force was gathered there. Therefore, when Svein Estridson asked for 50 ships to support him, England dared not provide them. In the following year Magnus died, and Svein was able to recover his Danish kingdom without English help. But Harold Hardraada, Magnus's successor, continued attacking Denmark, and again Svein asked for help. This time Edward apparently dispatched ships to Denmark's assistance. In revenge, in 1048, a raiding force of 25 Norse vessels attacked Sandwich and plundered Sussex and the Isle of Wight. Flanders opened her ports to these raiders and allowed them to sell their booty there.[3] Edward was so incensed at Flemish unfriendliness that he was glad to join his allies, the Danes, in a blockade of the coast of Flanders during a time when Baldwin, the Count, was fighting his overlord, Henry III of Germany.[4] Thanks to this blockade, Baldwin was forced to submit in a humiliating fashion to the Holy Roman Emperor. He blamed his defeat on Edward, and from this time was his persistent foe, and England's as well.

An opportunity for Baldwin arose the following year, when Edward, tired of the domineering Earl Godwin and his policies, drove him and his family into exile. They immediately sought out Edward's enemies. Godwin collected a small naval force in Flanders, no doubt with the Count's assistance. He was joined by vessels which his son, Harold, raised in Ireland. Edward was unprepared. In 1049 and 1050 he had, for reasons of economy, progressively weakened the fleet which he had inherited from Canute's reign, entrusting naval defense to levies from the general shore area of the Cinq Ports. What was left of the royal fleet, about 50 ships, became stormbound and put in to London, where the crews abandoned the vessels. The naval levies which Edward raised at Pevensey, Romney, Hythe, Folkstone and Dover, instead of fighting Godwin and Harold, joined them. The unmanned royal warships in London could not be used to defend the city. When Godwin arrived, he was unopposed and the city capitulated

[3] *Anglo-Saxon Chronicle*, ed. Plummer, p. 165. Florence of Worcester, *Chron.*, ed. Thorpe, I, 199.

[4] *Anglo-Saxon Chronicle*, pp. 166-67. Florence of Worcester, *Chron.*, I, 201.

to him. Edward had no choice but to return him to power, and during the rest of his reign was practically a prisoner of the House of Godwin.[5]

As Edward's reign moved towards its close, ominous forces gathered about England. Godwin had died, but his able son, Harold, inherited his position and an ambition to be Edward's successor as King of England. Harold's violent brother, Tostig, was equally ambitious, and across the Channel Duke William of Normandy was also determined to follow his cousin, Edward, upon the English throne. Still a fourth ambitious man, Harold Hardraada, King of Norway, was eyeing this rich realm whose throne was soon to be vacant. England had few allies. Denmark was friendly to her and to Harold, who was connected with the Danish royal house by marriage, but Germany, with Emperor Henry III dead, was not at the moment a force which could be depended upon. Harold and England thus faced a hostile Normandy, an unfriendly Flanders and a threatening Norway, with only faraway Denmark a potential ally. And even Tostig, Harold's brother, was at odds with him.

Of those ready to take advantage of this situation, William of Normandy was the most thoroughly prepared. Having made himself undisputed master of his own duchy, he married Matilda, daughter of England's enemy Count Baldwin of Flanders. This marriage and a large money payment secured for him the support, or at least the benevolent neutrality, of his father-in-law. He had a large fleet of transport vessels constructed and with the Pope's blessing gathered his expeditionary force together on the Channel coast across from England.[6] In Norway, Harold Hardraada prepared an expedition, too. Upon the death of Edward, Harold was chosen king of an England which faced two dangerous and redoubtable opponents.[7]

It was the state of England's naval defenses which made the situation particularly ominous. The weaknesses of 1051-1052 remained and England in 1065 could be defended only by hastily raised levies of ships, instead of by a standing navy. In that year, the inadequacy

[5] F. Stenton, *Anglo-Saxon England*, pp. 558-60.

[6] On Flanders' attitude towards William's plans and hopes and Count Baldwin's passive assistance, see G. H. George, "The Contributions of Flanders to the Conquest of England," in *Revue belge*, v (1926), 81-97. On William's payment of 300 marks to Baldwin in 1066, see B. D. Lyon, "The Money Fief Under the English Kings," in *Eng. Hist. Review*, CCLIX (1950), 178.

[7] On the tremendous naval preparations of Harold Hardraada for his invasion, see Brøgger and Shetelig, *The Viking Ships*, pp. 228-29.

of Anglo-Saxon naval power was fully revealed. Tostig, whom Harold had driven from the land, appeared with a raiding force off the south coast. Since most of his men were Flemings, it seems probable that Baldwin of Flanders had helped him to gather this force, though they may also have represented assistance given him by William of Normandy. Tostig raided Sussex with impunity and then occupied the naval base at Sandwich, where part of the royal fleet joined him. Harold at last mustered sufficient naval levies to proceed against him, and Tostig, with 60 ships, sailed north along the east coast. Defeated at Lindsay, he continued north to Scotland and then, with part of his flotilla, proceeded to Norway, where he joined his brother's other dangerous opponent, Harold Hardraada of Norway.[8]

This advance warning of his plight appears to have spurred Harold into naval action. In the spring of 1066 he mobilized a large fleet off the Isle of Wight, where he could watch and counter any moves by William, whom he judged to be the more dangerous of his foes. This fleet, however, composed as it was of hastily assembled levies, could not long be kept together and it soon began to disintegrate. Harold then attempted to move it to London, where more supplies were probably available. Instead, he lost many ships on the voyage and little naval strength remained when his maritime levies reached the Thames. As in the case of Edward the Confessor fifteen years earlier, he found himself without naval defenses.[9]

The King of Norway, Harold Hardraada, was the first to take advantage of the situation. Not only did Harold have no fleet, but he himself was in South England with his army poised to watch any move from Normandy. So Harold Hardraada, with Tostig, landed in Yorkshire, where he defeated the local forces of Earls Morcar and Edwin and took York. Harold of England marched north, and in the battle of Stamford Bridge won a great victory. Harold Hardraada and Tostig were slain and their invading army hacked to pieces. The Norwegian threat had been met and mastered.[10]

But Harold's absence in the north and his lack of any fleet gave William his opportunity. He landed unopposed on the shores of England. He occupied the port of Hastings as a beachhead and, drawing up his forces, awaited his Saxon enemy. Harold was not long in arriv-

[8] Ordericus Vitalus, *Hist. eccl.*, ed. Prevost, II, 120-23. Gaimer, *L'Estoire des Engles*, in *Roll Series*, I, 219. F. Stenton, *op.cit.*, pp. 577-78.

[9] F. Stenton, *op.cit.*, pp. 578-79.

[10] *Ibid.*, pp. 580-83.

ing, for by forced marches he brought his tired army south from Yorkshire, and hastily pushed forward to meet William's mounted Norman French array. In the battle of Hastings which followed, he perished fighting bravely. Without opposition, William moved north to London, where he was accepted as king. Though many years of fighting remained before he could completely crush opposition to his rule, William had gained a kingdom. Anglo-Saxon England had ended and Norman England begun.[11]

What seems particularly significant during these years of Edward the Confessor and Harold is the weakness of England's naval establishment. It was this weakness which had made Edward so powerless to deal with Godwin in 1050-1051. It was the same feebleness upon the sea which made the brave resistance of Harold against Tostig, Harold Hardraada and William of Normandy so fruitless in 1065-1066, and which all but ensured his defeat at Hastings. These Anglo-Saxon rulers forgot what Alfred, Aethelstan, Edgar and Canute seem to have understood—that a strong fleet was England's real defense against her enemies. They paid for it by losing dominance of the land, allowing control to pass to an alien Norman monarch and Norman-French aristocracy who remade England according to their own desires and in their own interest. Had Edward the Confessor not blundered in 1049-1050 by all but disbanding the royal fleet, had the House of Godwin not acquiesced in this policy, the history of England might have been very different. Undependable naval levies, even those from regions like the Cinq Ports, which apparently specialized in providing such forces, could not take the place of a standing navy.[12] In failing to appreciate this fact, Edward the Confessor and the House of Godwin prepared the way for the ruin of Anglo-Saxon England and the success of its Norman conquerors.

William's conquest of Britain did not, however, end the maritime dangers which faced his realm. Denmark had played no role in the crucial months that saw Harold slain and England conquered. But now Svein, who was related by marriage to Godwin's house and who

[11] There are many fine accounts of this decisive battle. Among the more interesting is that found, with maps, in J. A. Williamson, *The Evolution of England* (2nd ed., Oxford 1950), pp. 65-75.

[12] Dover, Sandwich and Romney owed ship service of fifteen days, according to Domesday, but one cannot be sure of what was owed by Hastings, Hythe and Rye. Perhaps the Cinq Ports organization in its final form was actually a 12th-century development. See F. W. Brooks, "Cinq Ports," in *Mariners Mirror*, xv (1929), 143-49.

was relieved of danger from Norway by Harold Hardraada's death, determined to take a hand in the game. His opportunity came when William found Yorkshire in revolt against him in 1069. Svein sent a large joint Norse-Danish fleet to assist the rebels there and in 1070 came himself with additional ships. William was forced to buy him off with a large Danegeld before he could crush the Yorkshire risings with great cruelty in 1072.[13] But Svein did not give up his ambitions in England, and in 1074 sent another fleet of 200 ships to raid the coasts of William's realm.[14]

To this Danish-Norse hostility was added that of Flanders. Flemish hostility was not at first apparent. William had married Count Baldwin's daughter and made an agreement whereby he paid his father-in-law 300 marks a year for his help and friendship. To this aid he probably owed much of his early successes in Britain. In 1071, however, Baldwin V was replaced as Count by his brother, Robert the Frisian. Robert was a remarkable man, indeed. As a second son, full of ambition, he realized he could not succeed to Flanders. So he took to the sea and in Frisia became a pirate sea-king—hence his name. He seems to have raided English coasts in conjunction with the Danish attacks of Svein there in 1069-1071. In this latter year he seized Flanders from William's father-in-law. He then married a daughter to Canute, son of Svein of Denmark. Under him Flanders turned from friendship with Norman England to outright hostility, and until 1086 William faced a dangerous maritime alliance of Flanders and Denmark directed against his shores. In fact, in this year Canute of Denmark was actually preparing a vast armada, by means of which, with Flemish help, he hoped to conquer England, when William's death brought disorder to the land.[15] Canute's assassination ended this threat to Britain, but not until 1093 did Robert the Frisian, his ally, make peace, upon payment again at Rouen of the 300-mark subsidy which his predecessor had received from the Norman king.[16] And as late as 1095 Norse trading ships were still being plundered by the English when they ventured into British waters.[17]

It is this state of affairs—namely, this hostility with Denmark, and

[13] F. Stenton, *op.cit.*, pp. 594-97.

[14] L. Musset, *op.cit.*, pp. 160-61.

[15] *Ibid.*, pp. 161-65. F. L. Ganshof, *La Flandre sous les premiers comtes*, pp. 63-90. See especially C. Verlinden, "Le Chroniqueur Lambert de Hersfeld et les voyages de Robert le Frison," in *Revue belge*, x (1931), 209-15.

[16] William of Malmesbury, *Gesta regum*, in *Roll Series*, I, 478-79. See also B. D. Lyon, *op.cit.*, pp. 176-81.

[17] *Placita Anglo-Normanni*, ed. Stubbs, p. 67.

then Flanders and at times Norway—which explains why for twenty-five years William and his successor, William Rufus, paid so much attention to naval affairs. William I raised fleets which protected his coasts and were used in 1071 against Earl Morcar in Yorkshire, in 1072 against Scotland, and which raided the Continent (probably Flanders) in 1073. He seems to have reconstituted a standing navy by the end of his reign, based on the old Anglo-Saxon system. With such a navy William Rufus was able to defeat his brother, Robert, in Normandy in 1087, and to raid Scotland successfully in 1091.[18] And it probably was this force which helped to bring peace at last to English shores in 1091 or 1093, after twenty-five years of conflict.

One further naval struggle took place in the Northern Seas around England at this time. In Norway, in 1093, Magnus Barelegs succeeded his father, Olaf the Peaceful, from whom he differed profoundly. A Viking type like his grandfather, Harold Hardraada, he conceived the project of adding to his realm the independent Norse settlements in the Shetlands, Orkneys, Hebrides and Isle of Man and perhaps Ireland as well. In 1098-1099 he launched a great expedition to the west to take these islands, and in the process raided Wales. Here, however, English forces came to help the Welsh and forced his retirement. In 1102, he again took the offensive, this time concentrating upon Ireland, which he hoped to conquer for his half-Celtic son, Sigurd. There he died in 1103, and with his passing ended those disorders which had for so long a time afflicted this portion of the Northern Seas.[19] Henceforth, it was towards the Holy Land that Scandinavian monarchs were to direct their attention, rather than towards the British Isles. The six decades of naval attacks, maritime struggles and disorder which marked the period 1043-1103 had ended, leaving a strong Flanders, a stronger England and the national monarchies of Denmark and Norway at peace with one another, ready for the important developments which the twelfth century was to bring.

If naval events which took place around Britain in this period make a consecutive, orderly narrative, that is not true of French waters. Here maritime events are obscure, indeed. It seems probable, however, that echoes of the quarrels taking place around Britain reached beyond Normandy to western French and Spanish shores. Certain espisodes in the career of Robert the Frisian seem to make this clear. He, the

[18] W. L. Clowes, *The Royal Navy*, I, 88-90. *Roger of Hoveden*, ed. Saville, p. 265, on use of navy by William Rufus.
[19] L. Musset, *op.cit.*, pp. 168-70.

implacable enemy of England, is also said to have led several naval
expeditions to Spanish coasts and even into the Mediterranean. Several
things make this probable.[20] First is the fact that, by the time of the
First Crusade, Flemish and Brabançon pirates were already located
on the coasts of Cilicia in Asia Minor.[21] These freebooters must have
arrived in the Mediterranean via Atlantic routes. Second, when Sigurd,
King of Norway, in the first decades of the twelfth century wished
to go on pilgrimage to the Holy Land, he sailed there directly by
way of England and the Strait of Gilbraltar.[22] Thus there seems
nothing unusual in Robert the Frisian's following such routes by
sea to the south, and in fact it seems clear that they were well known.
Perhaps the fleets that the Spanish kings of Galicia built in this period
provided additional security for those who chose to follow them.

Our information concerning what took place in the Baltic during
this period is equally fragmentary in nature. But it seems that, like
England, this area was disturbed by conflict and maritime struggles.
One cause of this lay in the attempt of Magnus and Harold Hardraada
to take Denmark, and Svein Estridson's long struggle to keep it. In
the conflicts which followed, the Wends and Jomsburgvikings appear
to have supported Svein. Magnus, who held all Denmark for a
period of years, according to Saga evidence, crushed the Jomsburgvikings in 1043 and destroyed their pirate fortress. He also defeated
the Wends at Lireskolide in the same year. Again in 1050-1051, when
his successor, Harold Hardraada, invaded Denmark, the Wends were
defeated near Hedeby and this trading center was destroyed in the
fighting.[23] It was replaced, according to Adam of Bremen, by the
less important Schleswig, which lay slightly north of it.[24] Then in
1066 Harold Hardraada was slain in Britain, and Svein at last was
secure in his Danish realm. He apparently maintained friendly relations with the nearby Wends, but we hear nothing of Danish conquest

[20] C. Verlinden, op.cit., seems to have some doubts as to the authenticity of some of
these expeditions.
[21] On these pirates in the *Eastern* Mediterranean, see C. Cahen, *La Syrie du nord
au temps des croisades* (Paris 1940), pp. 208-23. W. L. Clowes, *The Royal Navy*,
p. 94.
[22] L. Musset, op.cit., pp. 170-71. On this and other voyages from Scandinavia to
Byzantium and the Holy Land in this period, see P. Riart, *Expéditions et Pèlerinages
des Scandinaves en Terre Sainte* (Paris 1869), pp. 1-85. See also H. Midbar, *Historia
de projectione danorum, in Hierosolyman* (Oslo 1941), pp. 1-174.
[23] L. Musset, op.cit., pp. 242-45.
[24] Adam of Bremen, *Gesta Hamm. Eccl. Pont.*, II, 19.

464

of this South Baltic shore until the time of Waldemar in the early thirteenth century.[25]

If wars between Denmark and Norway account for a part of the disorders that afflicted the Baltic in these decades, the disintegration of Piast Poland helps to explain much of the remainder. We have already noted how Poland was in disorder for more than a decade after the death of Boleslas the Valiant in 1027 and how Casimir the Renovator, with Russian assistance, regained his realm. Not until 1047, however, was he strong enough to recapture Pomerania along the Baltic. And after his death in 1058 it broke away from the Polish kingdom again. For the rest of the eleventh century, Pomerania and other Wend Baltic shores as far as the Oder remained pagan and tribal, a domain of pirates whose raids Adam of Bremen has described for us as a source of constant disorders in this inland Northern Sea.[26]

Even more obscure seems to have been the fate of the lands of the Eastern Baltic that stretched from the Niemen to the Gulf of Finland. Canute's efforts to hold Samland did not even survive his last days, and Swedish expeditions in this direction from 1030 to 1040 seem to have proved equally abortive. Perhaps Yaroslav's attempts were more successful, at least in Esthonia, and some Russian hegemony about the Gulf of Finland, which protected trade routes passing from Gotland to Novgorod, may have lasted as late as 1106.[27] But, in general, the Finns, Esths, Cours and Balts of these coasts seem, in this period, to have been independent, pagan, tribal peoples possessing some pirate strength but little organization or civilization. They, like the Wends, were so to remain until the days of German intervention into Baltic affairs in the next century.[28]

[25] On the Slavic character of these shores in the 12th century, see Helmhold, *Chronicle of the Slavs*, I, 2.

[26] A. B. Boswell, "The Twelfth Century—From Growth to Division, 1079-1202," in *Cambridge History of Poland*, I, 43-44. S. Ketryzinski, "Introduction of Christianity and the Early Kings of Poland," in *ibid.*, pp. 36-42. Judging from both coin evidence from Baltic hoards and Adam of Bremen's testimony, Wollin remained an active port. On this coast of Poland, see also G. Vernadsky, *Kievan Russia*, pp. 318-32.

[27] Almost no objects of Swedish origin have been found in Russian sites dating later than the middle of the 11th century. See T. J. Arne, *La Suède et l'Orient*, p. 61. But Esthonia was still dominated by Yaroslav in 1030, if not later (L. Villecourt, *L'Esthonie*, p. 14), and routes to Novgorod via Finland and Gotland stayed active, judging by coin hoard evidence.

[28] L. Musset, *op.cit.*, pp. 42-43, 240-45. Can it be that Karelian and Balt pirates destroyed Gotland's status as a great fair by the late 11th century and that the large number of coin hoards found there dating from these years were buried owing to this new insecurity caused by pirate raids? On these hoards, see tables in M. Stenberger, *Die Schatzfunde Gotlands*, II.

Had Sweden been stronger in this period, she might have filled this Baltic power vacuum created by Polish, Danish and Russian weakness. But, following the death of Arnund Jacob in 1054, she too entered a period of decline. We know that a certain Stenkil of Vestergotland succeeded to the power of the old royal house of Uppsala about 1060. We also know that as a Christian he faced a certain amount of pagan hostility. That, however, is approximately the limit of our information. Sweden issued no coins in this period and the names of her monarchs are unknown to us. Even Adam of Bremen reveals an amazing ignorance of Sweden which can only be the result of its isolation from its neighbors in Denmark. His picture of a pagan Sweden, rich and mysterious, possessing a great shrine at Uppsala and a prosperous port at Birka, in touch through trade with the outside world, must be regarded either as fanciful or as a use of archaic material a century out of date to cover up his own ignorance. Birka had ceased to exist for almost a hundred years when he wrote, and it is doubtful that paganism at Uppsala survived in such fashion in a land where Christianity had spread under kings like Olaf Skottkonung, Arnund Jacob and Stenkil. All we can truly say of political events in Sweden is that they are obscure and remain so until new and more ordered life appears there in the mid-twelfth century.[29]

By the late eleventh century, then, most of the lands around the Baltic had changed from a region in which a series of strong monarchies—Denmark, Poland, Sweden and Russia—held sway into a European backwater. Denmark kept some influence, and a trade route continued to flow from Danish shores to Gotland and on to Novgorod, both of which maintained some economic life and political importance. But Sweden and eastern and southern Baltic shores relapsed into political obscurity. Wends, Balts and Cours possessed sufficient naval power to intervene in Denmark in 1043 and 1051. But otherwise they reverted to paganism, always strong amongst them, and were divided into tribes and confederacies whose organization is unknown to us. So they remained on the borders of European civilization until the next century.[30]

[29] Adam of Bremen, in *Gesta Hamm. Eccl. Pont.*, IV, 21-27, gives a curious picture of Sweden in these years which makes one distrust all his information concerning lands about the Eastern Baltic. Adam's views can be corrected only by archeological and numismatic evidence for the period 1050-1150, which is still too slight. What little has been discovered seems to point to a Sweden which remained Christian, but was remote and isolated from the rest of Northern Europe.

[30] This may account for the gap in Swedish art forms between the Viking and the

The same disorder and political disintegration which we see around the Baltic in the period spread to Kievan Russia as well. With the death of Yaroslav in 1054, the unity of Kiev ended for many decades. Perhaps what followed was a mere division of Russia into politico-economic regions such as we have described as occurring earlier after Sviatoslav's and Vladimir's deaths. But this time no successor arose to reunite these regions into a single realm. Kiev and its ruler maintained a certain predominance over other parts of Russia, but could not achieve an effective political control. Quarreling amongst themselves, the heirs of the House of Rurik were not able to deal even with dangers caused by nomadic Cumans, who raided on the very outskirts of Kiev and Pereslas and severed connections between Russia and the Black and Caspian Seas. Some contacts were, however, maintained with the West, which represented a certain continuation of the policies of Yaroslav. A marriage was arranged between Vladimir Monomarch, grandson of Yaroslav, and Gytha of England, who was the daughter of Harold and a niece of Svein Estridson of Denmark. This seems to show a continued Kievan interest in Baltic contacts. Vladimir's sister also married, first, Henry of Nordmark, and then Henry IV of Germany, which indicates similar interest in Central Europe. Even some Byzantine connections are suggested by Vsebolod's marriage to a Greek princess. But, in general, through the years of the late eleventh century, Kievan Russia's contacts with both the West and Byzantium were relatively fewer and less important than had been the case earlier.[31] This was not to change until the early twelfth century, in the time of Sviatopolk II, who broke the power of the Cumans and reopened the routes to the Black Sea. He married one of his daughters to Hungary's king in 1104, and another to the King of Poland in 1102, thus re-establishing contacts along the overland routes across Central Europe. Until this time, however, Kievan Russia was not an important factor in European affairs.[32]

---

medieval period and for the primitiveness which reigned along the Baltic shores from Lübeck to Esthonia when German merchants penetrated these regions in force in the next century.

[31] S. F. Cross, "Yaroslav the Wise in Norse Tradition," in *Speculum*, IV (1929), 207-14. B. Lieb, *Rome, Kiev et Byzance au XIe siècle*, pp. 92-186. G. Vernadsky, *Kievan Russia*, pp. 83-86. On the German menace as late as 1094, see *The Primary Chronicle*, p. 270.

[32] The revival of Baltic trade with Russia on a larger scale in the 12th century seems to have coincided with a reopening of trade routes from Kievan Russia to Central Asia and Constantinople by Sviatopolk and his immediate successors. On this ruler and his achievements, see G. Vernadsky, *op.cit.*, pp. 85-95. This revived Eastern trade did not, however, match that of the 10th century in importance.

The same political weakness noticeable in Russia, Poland and the Baltic is to be found even in Germany, which, up to the death of Henry III in 1054, had been a strong state. Henry left a young heir, Henry IV, during whose years of minority the land was wracked with disorder. When he assumed full power, an even worse situation arose, the investiture controversy with Gregory VII. Unable to win a victory over the Papacy by force of arms, Henry lived to see his realm rent by divisions, with a nobility more and more able to defy Imperial authority and a church upon which he could no longer depend. By 1100 Germany had begun to move from strength towards weakness. Its rulers, once the most powerful in Europe, began to manifest the powerlessness which characterized them in the early twelfth century and later.[33]

Let us sum up the political developments which took place in Northern Europe during the period from 1043 to 1100. In the East, Russia moved from unity to division, while Poland, Sweden and Baltic lands fell on evil days, and even Germany developed weaknesses. In the West, a weak England coveted by the House of Godwin and the King of Norway fell instead into the hands of William of Normandy. Rather than bringing peace, however, this touched off a series of maritime struggles between England and its Flemish, Danish and Norwegian neighbors that did not end until the death of Magnus Barelegs in 1103. By then, a strong England and the well-integrated national states of Denmark and Norway were at last at peace, while in France the first steps towards the centralized realm of the later Capetians were about to be taken. The center of power in Northern Europe had again begun to move, this time south and west. Now, between the Thames, the Rhine and the Loire, a region linked to the Mediterranean as well as to the Northern Seas was beginning to produce the new European civilization of the High Middle Ages.

This age of transition between the end of Canute's empire and the First Crusade had important effects upon the economy of Northern Europe. And it must be particularly emphasized that it also saw a certain interruption in the economic advance which, as we have noted in previous chapters, had gone on almost continuously from 900 to 1050 A.D. In England, in parts of the Baltic and in Eastern Europe this was not an age of growth but of economic stagnation and even retrogression. On the other hand, in Spain, France, Norway and

[33] G. Meyer, *Jahrbücher des deutschen Reichs unter Heinrich IV und Heinrich V* (Leipzig 1890-1909), is the fundamental study of these reigns.

most of the German Empire economic advance continued, while in some regions like Iceland, Ireland and Denmark few changes from the conditions existing in 1043 can be discerned. In other words, these years in the lands about the Northern Seas saw uneven growth and decay taking place simultaneously in various parts of Northern Europe. Uniformity had ceased to be the normal pattern.

England's economic life during this period presents some particular problems. This kingdom in the early eleventh century showed evidence of being the center of an important international commerce. Under William I and William II this ceased to be true. Perhaps the first steps in this change began before the Norman Conquest, during the reign of Edward the Confessor, when difficulties with Flanders began to limit trade with the Continent. At any rate, the Laws of Edward the Confessor which state that only Britons, Saxons, Jutes, Picts and Scots have a right to live in England seem to be directed against the foreign merchants who were so numerous in Canute's day. If they were enforced, they may have caused a serious diminution of commerce.[34] It is interesting to note, for instance, that in 1049-1050 Edward the Confessor abandoned a standing navy and dismissed the house carls, or king's bodyguard. This was due, according to Stenton, to a need for economy.[35] Such financial stringency, unknown in Canute's time, may reflect a certain lessening of prosperity.

On the other hand, down to 1066 other indications of English wealth abound. Edward continued to coin gold, the last monarch to do so for many years.[36] The number of moneyers in principal English trading centers like London, York, Thetford, Chester, Winchester, Lincoln and Canterbury, much greater than in Aethelstan's time, points to continued economic progress.[37] So, too, do the large number of Anglo-Saxon coins minted during Edward's reign which we find in coin hoards in Denmark, Norway, Sweden, Finland and the island of Gotland.[38] And evidence from the Continent shows that trade with Flanders, the Meuse, the Rhinelands and Normandy continued.

[34] F. Liebermann, *Gesetze*, I, 658.

[35] F. Stenton, *op.cit.*, pp. 425-26. W. L. Clowes, *The Royal Navy*, I, 19. See the rather perplexing account of this affair in the *Anglo-Saxon Chronicle E*, anno 1047. On Edward's remission of taxes and perhaps the Danegeld, see the *Anglo-Saxon Chronicle D*, anno 1050.

[36] D. Allen and G. Blunt, in *British Numis. Journal*, XXV (1945-48). For other references to gold in this period, see D. Whitelock, *Anglo-Saxon Wills*, p. 71, 185; 81, 192; 89, 201.

[37] G. C. Brooke, *English Coins*, pp. 68-69.

[38] N. L. Rasmusson, "Foreign Coins in Swedish Coin Finds," in *Trans. of Int. Num. Congress* (1938), pp. 138-42.

Important economic changes, however, followed William's conquest of England—changes which some historians have underestimated, since they have been more interested in the strong political system he established in his newly won kingdom than in its economic results. These alterations produced checks to the economic growth of the land which continued down to 1100. They had two causes: first, certain internal changes brought about by William; and, second, the difficulties in the North Sea which we have already noted.

In its effect upon the internal affairs of England, the Norman conquest differed substantially from that by the Danes a half-century before. It is true that Canute, as King of England, brought in many Danish officials, and it is also probable that the Danish population of the land increased substantially during his reign. But he did nothing to change the structure and life of the Anglo-Saxon society which he found there. He acted like just another Saxon monarch, and native families like the House of Godwin rose to positions of high importance under him. After his death and that of his sons, an Anglo-Saxon king like Edward the Confessor could succeed him almost without incident and even feel bound to the Denmark from which Canute had come.

With William it was otherwise. He completely replaced the Anglo-Saxon nobility, as soon as practicable, with one recruited from his Norman, French and Flemish knights. He imposed upon the land an alien, Norman feudal system. He encouraged the migration to England of large numbers of French and Flemish merchants, who took up residence in the towns and boroughs of England. In short, despite his conscious preservation of much of the military, legal, administrative and financial systems of the Anglo-Saxon past, his conquest represented a serious rearrangement of English life in all its phases, and resistance to his rule in Yorkshire and the north caused him at times to resort to savage and damaging repression.[39]

[39] On these changes, see F. Stenton, *The First Century of English Feudalism* (Oxford 1932). But to get a contemporary sense of the shock of William's conquest on Anglo-Saxon society, see the comments by the writers of the *Anglo-Saxon Chronicle* upon the deaths of William and his son, William Rufus. "The king sold his land on very hard terms . . . as hard as he could . . . and did not care how sinfully the reeves had got it from poor men, nor how many unlawful things they did. But the more just laws were talked about, the more unlawful things were done . . . certainly in his time people had much oppression and very many injuries" (*Anglo-Saxon Chronicle E*, anno 1087). And on William II: "Because of his avarice he was always harassing this nation with military service and unjust taxes so that in all his days justice was in abeyance. . . . All that was hateful to God and to just men was customary in this country in this time" (*ibid.*, anno 1100).

Were this all, it would be enough to explain a dislocation in England's economic life sufficient to have had detrimental effects. But in addition, as we have shown, William's relations with the lands which lay across the North Sea were hostile. This was particularly true of Denmark, which sent fleets to harry English shores with regularity for almost twenty years, and which was preparing a full-scale naval assault on the land as late as 1086. Nor were relations much better with Norway, right down to the death of Magnus Barelegs in 1103. Until 1100, then, continuous hostility existed between Norman England and Scandinavia and the Baltic.[40]

Relations between Flanders and England were not much better. For a brief time after the conquest, between 1066 and 1071, William enjoyed the support of Flemish counts to whom he was related by marriage. Some Flemish nobility who accompanied his forces even received wide fiefs in England. In 1071, however, Robert the Frisian became Count of Flanders in place of William's friendly kinsman. For the next twenty years he proved a redoubtable foe. Connected by marriage to the Danish royal house, he had a hand in all William's maritime difficulties. As late as 1086 he promised 600 ships to Canute of Denmark for his proposed expedition against Britain. Nor did the Flemish nobility in England prove reliable. The revolt of Eustache of Boulogne showed the Norman king the lack of wisdom in putting confidence in those in his entourage who came from Flanders. Not until William Rufus made peace with Count Robert at Dover in 1093 and renewed England's subsidy to Flanders did a new day dawn in Anglo-Flemish relations.[41]

These facts help to explain England's lack of economic growth in these years. They explain, for instance, why York had 25 moneyers whom we know of by name during the twelve-year reign of Edward the Confessor, but only 22 in the next 71 years (1066-1137).[42] They help to explain why Thetford, which had six moneyers and an important pottery production, should by the late eleventh century have given so little evidence of urban life.[43] They explain why Wil-

[40] L. Musset, op.cit., pp. 160-61. On Danish preparations to attack England, see the Anglo-Saxon Chronicle E, anno 1087.

[41] F. L. Ganshof, La Flandre, pp. 80-102. See also C. Verlinden, op.cit., pp. 235-37. The principal source again is the Anglo-Saxon Chronicle. See Anglo-Saxon Chronicle D, anno 1071; A.S. Chron. E, anno 1075; A.S. Chron. D, anno 1079; A.S. Chron. E, anno 1085. On the final peace with Flanders in 1903, see William of Malmesbury, Gesta regum, I, 478-79.

[42] F. Stenton, York in the Eleventh Century.

[43] G. Knocker and R. Hughes, "Anglo-Saxon Thetford," loc.cit., pp. 8-9.

liam coined no gold, and why the clearing of the English forests, which continued unchecked right up to 1050, should have ceased. Under him, in this Early Norman period, some regions which had been agricultural, like the New Forest, actually returned to woodland.[44] Indeed, it even seems possible that his introduction into England of the Continental feudal and manorial systems was more than political. Was it not perhaps the reflection of a certain new economic localism in the land, like that which we have seen in France in the early ninth and tenth centuries, where feudalism also took root? And it seems probable that the immense fund of information on England found in Domesday Book more nearly reflects the contemporary depressed land of 1086 than it does earlier economic conditions.[45]

It is evidence from across the North Sea, however, which makes clearest how England's commerce declined. Between 1066 and 1095 we have no evidence of any direct trade between Norway and England, until in this latter year we hear of William Rufus compensating captains of Norse trading vessels for losses incurred when their ships were plundered in English waters.[46] Norwegian coin hoards show this lack of trade even more dramatically. Late eleventh-century coin hoards contain much Frisian and German money, but not a single English coin minted later than the reign of Edward the Confessor.[47] Under Olaf Kyrre, English influence in the Norwegian Church, so vital earlier, is replaced by that of Hamburg.[48]

We notice the same thing in Denmark and the Baltic. Direct evidence of Dano-English trade is limited to a remark, perhaps archaic, in which Adam of Bremen mentions Ribe as a port which was two days' sailing time from England and which shipped horses there.[49] But again, as in Norway, while Danish, Swedish, Gotland and Finnish coin hoards of the period contain masses of money from Frisia and

---

[44] F. Stenton, *Anglo-Saxon England*, pp. 288-89.

[45] This may explain why Stephenson, who relied so much on the Domesday Survey, found so little urbanism in England in this period. C. Stephenson, *Borough and Town*, pp. 130-266. It is also worth noting that it was in Eastern England, which relied so much on trade with Scandinavia and Flanders, that there was most Domesday evidence of urban decay—for instance, at Lincoln, Torksey and probably York. See Lady Stenton's admirable summary of this evidence in D. Stenton, *English Society in the Early Middle Ages* (London 1951), pp. 169-71.

[46] *Placita Anglo-Normanni*, ed. Stubbs, p. 67.

[47] Yet a few coins of Edward the Confessor have been found in Norwegian hoards. H. Holst, "Mynter i Norske Funn," in *Nord. Numis. Arsskrift* (1943), pp. 101-6.

[48] L. Musset, *op.cit.*, pp. 169-70.

[49] Adam of Bremen, *Descript. Insulae Aquilones*, 1.

Germany, they contain practically no Anglo-Saxon coins minted during the reigns of William I and William II. In Denmark, for instance, only two hoards contain such coins, in contrast to the flood of Anglo-Saxon money minted by Canute and Edward the Confessor.[50] Obviously, trade with Denmark and the Baltic in these years was but a trickle.

The same thing seems to have been true of trade with Flanders. Earlier in the century we have much evidence of important commerce between Flanders and England. But except for one mention of English trade reaching Wissant in 1068[51]—and this was during the short period of good Flemish-English relations—we hear nothing of such commerce again until after 1093. Flemish merchants are found in France, they go to Cologne and Coblenz, their coins are found in the Baltic, but there is little evidence of their presence in England during these decades. Contacts were not renewed until the reign of William Rufus, and it is only the twelfth century that we hear of a Flemish *hanse* of London trading in England.[52]

It seems possible that William himself deliberately discouraged commerce with these neighbors to the east. He may have invoked the Laws of Edward the Confessor, which gave the right to live in England only to Irish, Scots, Welsh and English, and thus denied his ports to Flemish and Scandinavian merchants.[53] At any rate, early in the twelfth century we learn that foreign merchants could stay only forty days in England, and Norwegian traders were restricted to London, though Danes could travel more freely.[54] Is this an echo of William's policies? It seems entirely probable.

On the other hand, there is no evidence of any limitation on English trade towards the south and the west. William's coins were copied by Irish moneyers, which seems to point to a continued trade,[55]

---

[50] R. Shovmand, *op.cit.*, pp. 17-21. One hoard in Gotland, that found at Kvarna, dating from about 1080, contains coins struck by William the Conqueror. M. Stenberger, *op.cit.*, pp. 50-51. In other hoards, no coins later than those of Edward the Confessor are to be found. In Finland, according to Nordman, only one hoard, that of Hamalina (circa 1100), contains such money—in this case, one coin of William II.

[51] *Ex chronico centulensi sive S. Richardii*, in Bouquet, *op.cit.*, XI, 133.

[52] E. Coornaert, *Les Gildes médiévales*, pp. 228-31.

[53] F. Liebermann, *Gesetze*, I, 658.

[54] *Ibid.*, p. 575. In the Domesday Survey at Chester the fact is mentioned that only those ships "having the King's peace" may trade there. Others would suffer confiscation of ship and goods. This suggests some type of trade controls. *Domesday Book*, I, 262b.

[55] Some disturbance came from raids launched on West England from Ireland by Harold's sons in 1069. *Anglo-Saxon Chronicle D*, anno 1069. But afterwards relations with the Irish seem to have been peaceful. On Irish coins which copied

as does evidence of a traffic in slaves to Dublin from Welsh and western English ports.[56] Judging from the evidence to be found in Domesday Book, there seems to have been a vitality in Western Britain not found elsewhere, which may have resulted from this trade by way of Chester and Bristol.[57]

Trade with France also remained important and may even have increased in volume. It was the French Laws of Oleron which influenced maritime provisions found in the Laws of William, perhaps written down towards the end of his reign,[58] as the Norman Laws of Bretaille became the models for English *villes neuves*. It was Dover and other Cinq Ports towns just opposite France which had a freedom of tolls in all England.[59] A Frenchman, William of Poitiers, in 1070 mentioned *opus angliscum*, or fine English cloth. Certainly the links between England and France were closer than had been true for some centuries.[60]

England under her first Norman kings, then, was certainly less prosperous than earlier, and what economic vitality she appeared to have linked her to Ireland and France rather than to Flanders, Scandinavia and the Baltic. Only after the accession of Henry I, a monarch married to a Saxon princess, do we find a return to a more normal commercial intercourse between England and Flanders, Norway and Denmark. Then Britain again became the center of international Northern European commerce which she had previously been under Canute.[61] But in some ways the break with Scandinavia and the Baltic that took place from 1066 to 1100 proved permanent. German, Frisian and Flemish merchants who dealt in these markets without English competition for almost half a century did not lose them afterwards. They maintained a commerce which was to culminate in the Hanseatic League.

William's English ones, see W. O. Sullivan, "The Earliest Irish Coinage, in *Proc. of Royal Soc. of Antiq. of Ireland*, LXXIX (1949), 100-77.

[56] E. Bromberg, *Wales and the Medieval Slave Trade*, pp. 267-69.

[57] *Domesday Book*, I, 262b; 162a; 172a, on trade of Chester, Gloucester and Droitwich.

[58] L. A. Senegaleia, "Medieval Sources of English Maritime Law," in *Mariners Mirror*, XXV (1940), 12.

[59] On the freedom from tolls enjoyed by London merchants in 1121-1122, which probably went back to at least the 11th century, see *Charter of Henry I*, in *Monastican Anglicanum*, VI, 157. On similar privileges of Dover, see J. Tait, *op.cit.*, pp. 118-19.

[60] *Gesta Guillelmi ducis Normaniae regis angliae*, in *MGH Script.*, XI, 103.

[61] This change lies as the economic underpinning of the next century's cultural revival that we call the Twelfth Century Renaissance.

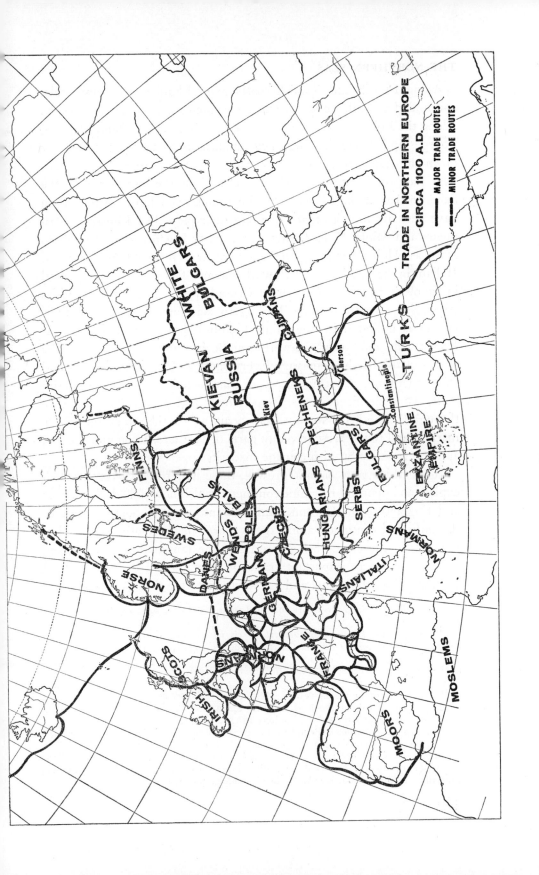

TRADE IN NORTHERN EUROPE
CIRCA 1100 A.D.

▬▬▬ MAJOR TRADE ROUTES
- - - - MINOR TRADE ROUTES

WHITE BULGARS

KIEVAN RUSSIA

CUMANS

Kherson

PECHENEGS

Kiev

TURKS

BYZANTINE EMPIRE

Constantinople

BULGARS

SERBS

HUNGARIANS

CZECHS

POLES

BALTS

FINNS

SWEDES

WENDS

DANES

NORSE

GERMANY

NORMANS

ITALIANS

SCOTS

IRISH

NORMANS

FRANCE

MOORS

MOSLEMS

Along French and Spanish coasts from Flanders to Compostela, and inland as well, we see increasing economic activity in these years. Along the Loire, centers like Tours, Blois, Angers, Le Mans, Orléans, Bourges and Nantes assumed new importance as trade flowed freely down the river and along roads leading to Bordeaux and Toulouse. The Fair of Lendit in Paris began to link the commerce of the Seine to that of the Loire.[62] Pilgrim routes from Belgium to Galicia gave new life to cities that lay along their path, like Limoges, Périgueux and Saintes.[63] The same new activity began to link France to Italy as Alpine passes again became active. By 1076 we learn of Italians in the Isle-de-France,[64] while money of Poitou was to be found in Savoy by the time of the First Crusade.[65] On the Garonne and its tributaries a new commerce leading to Narbonne and the Mediterranean is indicated by the mints established during these years at Rodez, Albi and Auch,[66] as well as at Beziers and Melgueil near the shores of the Mediterranean.[67] Everywhere in Central, Southern and Western France new churches were constructed and new monasteries built, as economic currents from North and South flowed freely through the land. In Northwestern Spain we see the same thing. New markets and towns arose in many parts of Navarre, León and Castile, and a new native Spanish coinage made its appearance.[68]

It was this new economic growth, these new trade currents, which explain an important maritime commerce which now linked Normandy and England to the Garonne and Charente regions. Some commerce certainly had continued along these shores in the tenth century, but now in the late eleventh it gave rise to the famous Laws of Oleron, which describe an important trade in wine carried by Bretons and Normans from Bordeaux and La Rochelle to the Strait of Dover and

[62] J. Levillain, "Essai sur les origines du Lendit," in *Revue hist.*, CLV (1927), 241-76.
[63] J. Bedier, *Les Légendes épiques*, III (Paris 1912), 115-23. P. Courtreault, *Pour l'histoire de Bordeaux et du Sud-Ouest* (Bordeaux 1934), pp. 14-37.
[64] Jaffé, *Regestum*, II, 15, 132, 146.
[65] Blanchet and Dieudonné, *Manuel de numismatique*, IV, 372-73.
[66] *Ibid.*, pp. 371-72.
[67] *Ibid.* Concerning the money of Melgueil of this period, which included some gold dinars modeled on those of Moslem Spain, see C. De Vic and J. Vaisette, *Histoire générale de Languedoc* (Toulons 1883), V, 346.
[68] C. Sanchez-Albornoz, "Primitiva organizacion monetaria de León y Castilla," *loc.cit.*, pp. 14-16. On the growth of trade and commerce at Barcelona which led to the writing-down of her laws in this period, see C. Poumaride *Les Usages de Barcelona* (Paris 1907), pp. 58-62. On the improvement in this region's economic conditions in this period, see A. R. Lewis, *op.cit.*, pp. 274-78.

as far as England's east coast. Perhaps the Laws were written down in the twelfth century, but they reflect conditions as they existed in this period as well.[69]

Flanders was similarly connected with France by land and water commercial routes. Merchants of Tournai followed the pilgrim routes as far as Limoges.[70] Others from Flanders were arriving in Laon as early as 1066 to exchange their woolens for wine, beginning that exchange which was to grow later into the great Fairs of Champagne,[71] for we learn in 1070 and 1090 that May and September fairs were already found in this part of France.[72] Sea traffic is also shown by the wine which reached St. Omer in 1083[73] and the expeditions of Robert the Frisian already alluded to.[74] After 1093, peace with England no doubt increased the volume of this traffic, but already in this period Flanders was beginning at last to integrate her commerce with that arriving from the Mediterranean lands of Italy and Southern France. It seems probable, however, that prior to the twelfth century, Flemish trade was still largely oriented towards the North and East, rather than towards France and England.[75] It is at Coblenz in 1070, for instance, that we hear of merchants of Ghent coming to buy wine,[76] and slightly later it is an archdeacon of Trier, Winric, who reveals a familiarity with Flemish cloth in his *Conflectus ovis et lini*.[77] And only in the last years of the eleventh century do we find mention of English trade, at Tournai about 1090, in St.

[69] These laws mention mainly Bordeaux, La Rochelle and the coasts of Brittany and Normandy. To Pardessus they seem Norman in origin. J. Pardessus, *Collection des lois maritimes anterieures au XVIIIe siècle* (Paris 1828), I, 229-36. For a more recent account which accepts Pardessus' 11th-century date, see L. A. Senigaleia, "Medieval Sources of English Maritime Law," in *Mariners Mirror*, XXVI (1940), 11-13.

[70] P. Rolland, "Le Problème de la continuité à Tournai," in *Ann. d'hist. écon. et sociale*, VIII (1933), 265-67.

[71] M. Prou, *Recueil des actes de Phillipe I, roi de France* (Paris 1921), p. 82. See also R. Doehaerd, "Laon, capitale du vin," in *Annales*, V (1950), 86-97.

[72] P. Rolland, *op.cit.*, p. 64.

[73] H. Pirenne, "Les Coutumes de la gilde-marchande de Saint-Omer," in *Le Moyen Age*, LI (1907), p. 192.

[74] C. Verlinden, "Le Chroniqueur Lambert de Hersfeld et les voyages de Robert le Frison," in *Revue belge*, X (1931), 151-77. Robert apparently visited both Byzantium and the Holy Land between 1086 and 1090.

[75] F. L. Ganshof, *La Flandre*, pp. 67-68.

[76] K. Hohlbaum, *Hansisches Urkundenbuch*, I, 3-4. F. Rousseau, *La Meuse*, pp. 90-91.

[77] A. Van de Vijver and C. Verlinden, "L'Auteur et la portée du conflictus ovis et lini," in *Revue belge*, XII (1933), 59-81.

Trond at about the same time.[78] By the twelfth it had resulted in the famous Hanse of London.[79]

The beginnings of more Flemish commerce with France by land and sea, and of continued trade with the Rhinelands did not exhaust the scope of Flanders' trade in this period. As earlier, an important commerce linked this region with the Baltic and even distant Novgorod.[80] It is this commerce which explains the growth of Bruges and the marriage and political alliances linking Count Robert the Frisian with the Danish royal house.[81] In contrast to the lack of English coins in Scandinavian and Baltic coin hoards, those of Flanders are found in Norway, Denmark, Gotland and Finland in about the same proportion as earlier in the eleventh century.[82] Finnish hoards contain coins minted during this period in Flanders, but none from Theil, which suggests that Bruges was now the great seaport of this region trading with the Baltic.[83] No wonder we find mention of Flemish cloth in Novgorod in the late eleventh and early twelfth centuries!

The commerce of the Meuse valley was equally important during these years, though we now hear nothing of its merchants going to London. Elsewhere, however, there is much evidence of increased international contacts. In a *telonium* of Coblenz we learn of merchants of Huy, Dinant and Namur in 1073 and 1104.[84] In 1103 they were mentioned as carrying cloth, wool, tin and perfumes to the three great fairs held at this city, and even proceeding on to Saxony and Dortmund in search of copper.[85] These Walloons had a special quarter of their own at Cologne and thus represented the second oldest foreign merchant colony in the city—the Frisian being older.[86] Prob-

---

[78] *Chron. S. Andreae castri cameracensis*, in *MGH Script.*, VII, 542. C. Piot, *Cartulaire de l'abbaye de St. Trond*, I, 28. *Mirac. S. Micberti*, in *MGH Script.*, VIII, 520.

[79] E. Coornaert, *op.cit.*, pp. 228-31.

[80] H. Pirenne, "Draps d'Ypres à Novgorod," in *Revue belge*, IX (1930), 233-45. A. Eck, "À propos des draps d'Ypres à Novgorod," in *ibid.*, X (1931), 591-94.

[81] R. Doehaerd, *op.cit.*, pp. 28-32. *Anglo-Saxon Chronicle D*, anno 1079, and *E*, anno 1085.

[82] For example, the Norwegian Foldoy hoard of circa 1060 contains money minted in Flanders. A. W. Brøgger, "Et myntfund frä Foldøen," in *Aarbrøger* (1910), pp. 239-82. The same is true of Finland, where Flanders money has also been found. H. Salmo, *op.cit.*, pp. 337-41.

[83] *Ibid.*

[84] K. Hohlbaum, *op.cit.*, pp. 3-4.

[85] R. Rousseau, *La Meuse*, pp. 90-92.

[86] K. Heusen, *Topographie der Stadt Köln im Mittelalter*, I, 56-65. F. Rousseau, "L'Expansion Wallone et Lorraine vers l'est," in *Les Dialectes belgo-romains* (Liége 1937), pp. 188-91.

ably they were already penetrating as far east as Poland and the Upper Danube, where they are mentioned in the next century.[87]

From numismatic evidence we also gain information as to the wide commercial connections between the Meuse region and Northern and Eastern Europe. The coins of this area, particularly those of Count Albert III of Namur (1064-1102), have been found in hoards of Norway, Denmark and Sweden, and one in Poland, dating from the end of the century, also contains money from Meuse towns.[88] So do those of late eleventh-century Finland, where we find money minted in Bouillon, Maastricht, Liége, Celles, Namur and Dinant— coins of the latter two centers being particularly numerous.[89] Even more than Flanders, the Meuse valley now had an important commerce with Northern and Eastern Europe.

Similar contacts between the rest of Germany and the coasts of Scandinavia and the Baltic are revealed by late eleventh-century coin hoards. Coins from mints in Frisia, Saxony, the Rhinelands, Franconia, Thuringia and even Swabia and Bavaria continue to be found in hoards in Norway, Denmark, Sweden, Gotland and Finland. In Finland, coins from Frisia and the lower Rhine seem particularly numerous, especially ones minted at Mainz, Worms, Cologne, Utrecht, Deventer, Groningen, Erfurt, Goslar and Gittelde.[90] Coins from Goslar and Gittelde are of particular interest, when found in this faraway part of the Baltic, since their mints were not in operation until after 1043.[91] On the other side of the Scandinavian world, in the Foldoy hoard of Norway, dating from 1060, a similarly wide variety of German mints is represented, 30 in all. Of its German coins, 80 come from the Rhinelands, 77 from Franconia, 49 from Frisia, 35 from Saxony, 7 from Bavaria and 6 from Swabia.[92] In Gotland we

---

[87] R. Doehaerd, *L'Expansion économique Belge*, pp. 39-41.

[88] F. Rousseau, *op.cit.*, pp. 191-92. On such coins found in Russia as well, see F. Rousseau, "Les Monnaies mosanes des XIe et XIIe siècles découvertes en Russie," in *Namuricum*, IX (1932), 161-79. On those found in a Polish late 11th-century hoard, see R. Graetens, *Der Fund von Ludwigisce. Ein Schatz deutsches und Skandinavischer Denaredes XI Jahrhundert* (Halle 1934), pp. 23-29.

[89] Those minted in this period in the Meuse region and found in Finnish hoards include one coin from Bouillon, one from Liége, one from Maastricht, 5 from Celles, 21 from Dinant and 28 from Namur. H. Salmo, *op.cit.*, pp. 337-41.

[90] There are 320 coins minted in Frisia dating from this period found in Finnish hoards, as well as 157 from Franconia and 114 from Saxony. H. Salmo, *op.cit.*, pp. 338-40.

[91] No doubt it was the opening of the Harz silver mines which gave rise to these new mints, and accounted for the presence of 45 Goslar pennies and 61 from Gittelde in Finnish hoards. *Ibid.*, pp. 340-41.

[92] A. W. Brøgger, *op.cit.*, pp. 239-52.

also gain some information from these hoards. One hoard, that of Kvarna, circa 1080, contains 181 Anglo-Saxon pennies, including a very few minted as late as the time of William the Conqueror, but 933 German ones, mainly from the late eleventh century.[93] Two rare Swedish hoards, dating from about 1070 and interred in Smaland to Kexas and Torlop, contain, respectively, 86 German and 7 Anglo-Saxon coins, and 122 German and only 19 Anglo-Saxon pennies. The German coins are mainly from Frisian mints, which suggests that the Frisian guilds and trade colony that were found in Sigtuna as early as the first years of the eleventh century were still the most important merchant group trading with Sweden.[94]

In fact, coin evidence seems to show that in this, as earlier, the Frisians and Saxons were the principal traders who linked Scandinavia and the Baltic with Western Europe, though some Norwegian and Danish merchants may have traded directly with Utrecht, too.[95] It is no wonder that Norway's church dropped its Anglo-Saxon ties and established connections with Hamburg after 1066, for it was German commerce and German merchants that were important in Norwegian waters. Already, as coin hoards reveal, that German domination of Norway's external trade with Western Europe which in the next century formed a subject dealt with in the *Saga of King Sverre* was firmly established.[96] And these coin hoards, particularly those in Finland, also appear to show that the important German merchant colony in Novgorod of the twelfth century had late eleventh-century beginnings. German domination of the Baltic trade route did not begin with the rise of Lübeck in the 1130's. It had earlier origins.

It must not be thought, however, that it was only by way of the Baltic that German merchants and merchandise reached Russia. Land routes, particularly those which originated in Regensburg in Bavaria, were of almost equal importance. They accounted for the presence of

[93] M. Stenberger, *Die Schatzfunde Gotlands*, II, 50-51.

[94] G. H. Rundquist, "Tva silverskatter från Vikingatiden i Smolansk jord (Keixas och Torlapsfynden)," in *Hyltén Cavallins-föreningen för Hambygdskunsk Arsbok* (1945), pp. 49-96, and "Tva silverskatter från vikingatiden i Smolansk jord," in *Nord. Numis. Arsskrift* (1946), pp. 35-74. A somewhat earlier immense hoard from Hjortsberga (Bleckinge), dating from about 1060, has 3,414 German coins and 480 Anglo-Saxon coins in it.

[95] Some of these German coins found in this period in the Baltic may, however, have reached there by way of the Oder, Poland and Wollin and Stettin.

[96] L. Musset, *op.cit.*, pp. 169-76. The later *Saga of King Sverre* emphasizes the role of German merchants, who carried wine to Norway and exported fish and butter in return for it. Probably they did so in the 11th century, too.

German colonies of merchants in both Kiev and Smolensk during these years.[97] For instance, when funds were needed to build an abbey at Regensburg, they were raised in part in Kiev by a gift of furs which were then brought back to Germany and sold.[98] No doubt it was this type of trade and contact that brought about the matrimonial alliances between Kiev and German rulers and nobles in these years.

This continuation of German trade with Norway, the Baltic and Russia, coupled with a growing commerce with Hungary and, south across the Alps, with Italy, explains not only the continued growth of new and old German towns, but the contrast between her economy and that of Norman England. For Germany was linked in these years by overland and maritime routes to most of Northern, Southern and Eastern Europe. Her political life might falter, but her economic progress continued unchecked.

Hungary, to the southeast of Germany, also shows continued economic growth as a center of trade routes which were now active north to Poland and the Baltic, west to Germany, and east to Kievan Russia and Byzantium. We find during these years a merchant colony of Hungarians at Constantinople.[99] We find large amounts of Hungarian coins north of the Carpathians in Polish coin hoards.[100] We even find a scattering of them in hoards like that of Foldoy in Norway, Geretse and Kvarna in Gotland and at Luto in Finland.[101] And close relations continued to be maintained with Russia, as we know from Hungarian marriage alliances with Kiev's rulers.[102]

On the other hand, our evidence seems to show less growth in Poland and Bohemia. Scattered Bohemian coins in Scandinavian and Finnish hoards suggest that some commerce continued north from Prague along the Oder route which had been so active in the tenth century.[103] And it is also true that Kievan objects found in eleventh-century Bohemian graves, as well as certain Bohemian saints revered

[97] G. Vernadsky, *Kievan Russia*, pp. 118-19.

[98] F. Dvornik, *The Making of Central and Eastern Europe*, pp. 249-50.

[99] W. Heyd, *Histoire du commerce*, II, 82-84.

[100] These hoards in Poland, which contain 11th-century Hungarian money, number 50 in all. J. Kostryzewski, *op.cit.*, pp. 272-73.

[101] On the Foldoy hoard, see A. W. Brøgger, *op.cit.*, pp. 239-71. On Gotland hoards, M. Stenberger, *op.cit.*, pp. 13-602. On Finland's hoards, C. A. Nordman, *op.cit.*, pp. 1-193.

[102] B. Lieb, "The Kiev State and Western Europe," in *Trans. of Royal Hist. Soc.*, XXIX (1949), 63-122.

[103] See N. A. Rasmusson, *op.cit.*, on such coins.

in Russia, suggest that trade did continue.[104] Yet it seems possible that such contacts were less important than earlier.

The same is true of Poland after the death of Casimir in 1058. About Poland's economy we know little, except that some transit trade from Hungary and Bohemia passed through it on the way to the Baltic.[105] By 1102 it had re-established contacts with the Kiev of Sviatopolk II and seems to have traded with Russia by sending its salt there as an export.[106] Most evidence, however, suggests that this commerce was less important than it had been in the great days of Miezko and Boleslas.

As for Kievan Russia, we can speak with much less authority as regards its economic status in these years than we could for the earlier period. We have noted that Russia, by way of Novgorod and the Baltic, and by way of Kiev and Central Europe, maintained connections with Western Europe. Novgorod seems to have had a particularly active commerce and by the early twelfth century had diverted the Norwegian fur trade of the White Sea into her own hands.[107] Her merchants and ships traveled west to Wollin, and probably Gotland as well, at the time of Adam of Bremen.[108] Kiev, as we have noted, had a western trade with Hungary, Bohemia, Poland and Germany.

It seems probable, however, that this trade was not as profitable as it had been earlier, since Russia's agrarianism and economic localism continued to increase in these years. Cut off by the Cumans from effective contact with the Black and Caspian Seas until about 1102, Russia was unable to procure the spices, silks and other Eastern wares which she had formerly had in such abundance and had shipped to the West to pay for imports, and which had attracted so many Western merchants. Now her exports going west from Novgorod and Kiev and Smolensk seem to have consisted largely of those natural products, like furs, wax, flax and linen goods, which were to be her mainstay during the years of the Hanseatic League and the Late Middle

[104] J. Schanderl, *Die Vorgeschichte Böhmens und Mährens* (Munich 1929), pp. 288-316.

[105] J. Kostryzewski, *op.cit.*, pp. 345-67.

[106] G. Vernadsky, *op.cit.*, pp. 92-93.

[107] On the end of Norway's fur trade with the White Sea and Novgorod's trade ascendancy over this region, see O. A. Johnsen, *Le Commerce et la navigation en Norvège au moyen âge*, pp. 388-89.

[108] G. Vernadsky, *op.cit.*, pp. 331-32. Adam of Bremen, *Gesta Hamm. Eccl. Pont.*, II, 19.

Ages.[109] Though still rich, she had ceased by 1100 to play a very important political and economic role in Northern Europe.

There remains a consideration of the economic life of Scandinavia and those lands of the Western Atlantic settled by the Norse. Probably Norway developed most during these years. By 1043 three towns had already reached urban status along Norwegian coasts: Tønsberg and Sarpsburg on Oslo fjord, and Nidaros on the west coast. Under Harold Hardraada, Oslo joined these two southern towns as a trading center of some importance. Then, at the time of his son, Olaf Kyrre, we find Bergen appearing on the west coast below Nidaros. Finally, in the first years of the twelfth century, Konghelle on the Skagerrak also attained urban status.[110] By 1130 Oderic Vitalis could speak of these six—Nidaros, Bergen, Tønsberg, Oslo, Sarpsburg and Konghelle—as the towns then existing in Norway.[111] Other signs of economic life are to be found in the abundant silver coinage that Harold Hardraada minted at Hamar and Nidaros, which circulated widely.[112]

Though Frisian and German merchants appear to have controlled a most important trade to Norwegian shores, this commerce was not the only reason for Norway's economic development in this period. Trade was active to the west as well, which may have replaced in some ways the loss of English markets. Bergen and Nidaros were the centers for trade with Ireland, Groenland, the Faroes, Orkneys, Shetlands and the lands about the Irish seas.[113] Some Icelanders seem to have traded with Rouen and Utrecht in this period, but it seems probable that most western Norse colonies traded more directly with Norway.[114] We learn from the Sagas, for instance, that Harold Hardraada, because of a famine in Norway, at one time forbade grain shipments to Iceland and then relented and allowed four ships to sail there.[115] And from a description of a Norse ship in the contemporary poem, *Tristan and Isolde*, we learn what products such a vessel would normally carry. In the poem, the Norwegian trading vessel has on

[109] G. Vernadsky, *op.cit.*, pp. 118-20. L. Goetz, *Deutsche-russische Handelsgeschichte des Mittelatters*, pp. 80-116.

[110] L. Musset, *op.cit.*, p. 169.   [111] *Odericus Vitalis*, ed. Prevost, IV, 27.

[112] O. A. Johnsen, *op.cit.*, p. 198.

[113] O. Tønning, *op.cit.*, pp. 14-26. The lack of coin hoards found in Norway which date from the *late* 11th century is probably due to peace which, the *Olaf Kyrre Saga* tells us, prevailed in Norway during the reign of this monarch.

[114] O. Tønning, *op.cit.*, pp. 16-18, 75-76. O. A. Johnsen, *op.cit.*, pp. 197-99.

[115] On this prohibition, see *Harold Hardraadas's Saga*, pp. 40-45, and O. Tønning, *op.cit.*, pp. 20-23.

board a cargo for the Continent consisting of gray and white furs, hawks, falcons, dried fish, whale oil and sulphur.[116] Probably some of this cargo, particularly the sulphur and falcons, were of Icelandic origin transshipped from Norway. Islands nearer than Iceland, like the Orkneys, seem to have had equally close contacts with Norway, which accounts for the close alliance which existed between Jarl Thorfin of Orkney and Harold Hardraada, and for Magnus Barelegs' determination to add these islands and Ireland as well to his realm.[117]

The chief trade reaching Oslo fjord in this period, seems, from coin hoard evidence, to have been with Utrecht and other German ports. But some commerce, as earlier, went to the Baltic by way of Denmark and beyond. In the Foldoy hoard of 1060, for instance, we find Danish coins minted at Odensee, Roskilde, Viborg, Hedeby and Lund, with those of Lund the most numerous. This hoard also includes one Hungarian and one Bohemian coin and one minted by the Byzantine Emperor Michael VI (1056-57), all of which must have arrived here by way of the Baltic.[118] It would seem, however, that there was now little of that direct trade with Novgorod and Russia which we noted in the earlier period, and that Norway's Baltic commerce was carried on by Danish and German intermediaries. The reason for suggesting this is that not a single Norse coin of this period has been found in Gotland and Finnish coin hoards, though Danish ones are by no means rare.[119] Perhaps this lack of direct connection explains why Norse traders abandoned the fur trade of the White Sea to Novgorod merchants in this period.

Denmark was even more important as a trading center than Norway, since her location gave her control of the entrances and exits to the Baltic. In addition to a flourishing trade with Utrecht and other German ports, and with Bruges as well, she had some connections, though probably slight, with England.[120] She also was an important intermediary on Baltic routes to Gotland. In Gotland's hoards,

---

[116] *Tristan and Isolde*, ed. Baume, XVIII.

[117] L. Musset, *op.cit.*, pp. 210-11. J. Clouston, *A History of Orkney*, gives fuller information, much of it based on Saga traditions.

[118] A. W. Brøgger, *op.cit.*, pp. 252-53. This seems to be the latest 11th-century coin hoard found in Norway.

[119] See again M. Stenberger, *op.cit.*, on Gotland hoards, and H. Salmo, *op.cit.*, on Finnish ones. One Byzantine coin minted by Michael VI (1056-57) which reached Norway may represent direct contact between Norway and Russia after 1043. But it is the only evidence of such connection. H. Holst, *op.cit.*, p. 103.

[120] Coin hoards show that there was some trade, though not much, with England at the time of William I and William II. R. Shovmand, *op.cit.*, pp. 18-21.

for instance, we find a total of 1,543 Danish coins, the largest single number of Western coins, except for those from Germany and England.[121] She also had some connection with the Swedish mainland, since both the Småland hoards of Torlop and Kiexas contain Danish money.[122] So do contemporary ones in Finland.[123] Danish merchants traded with Eastern Baltic lands as well, for we learn that at the time of Svein Estridson they were trading cloth for furs in Samland, and that a certain Christian merchant arrived from Courland at the Danish court whom the king loaded with presents.[124] We also know from the Sagas that this Danish monarch maintained contact with Wendish shores, which, since certain Kievan Russian objects have been found not only at Lund but at Gniezno, evidently maintained contact with Central Europe.[125]

On the other hand, Adam of Bremen's account of Baltic trade in this period seems very confusing indeed. He speaks of important commerce carried on by Slavic and Russian ships which reached Hedeby. Since Hedeby was not in existence after 1051, this seems impossible, and even its successor, Schleswig, is shown by coin evidence and archeology to have had little importance.[126] He also mentions Ribe as a thriving port trading with England. Yet archeology and coin hoards of the late eleventh century seem to indicate this to be rather unlikely, since trade with England was slight. We have already noted that his statements about Birka and Sweden are completely out of line with the facts. Nor does he mention any of the new centers which we know, from coin evidence, to have been important in this period: Lund, Viborg, Odensee, Roskilde and Aalborg. A possible explanation of all this is that Adam's account has nothing to do with the late eleventh-century Baltic, but is an accurate description of its trade in the early or middle years of the tenth century. What has gone

---

[121] M. Stenberger, *Die Schatzfunde Gotlands*, II, especially tables at end of volume.

[122] The Kiexas hoard has 24 Danish minted coins and the Torlaps hoard 49 of them, as opposed to 86 and 122 German coins, respectively. G. H. Lindquist, *op.cit.*, pp. 83-91. Several somewhat earlier Bleckinge hoards have a similar proportion of Danish minted silver pieces.

[123] Danish money of this period is found in the following Finnish hoards: at Nousianen, 5 coins; at Lieto, 18; at Parmio, one; at Drottingholm, one; at Rasio, one; at Nastola, one; at Kurijoki, one; and at Kursanshove, 5. H. Salmo, *op.cit.*, pp. 1-39.

[124] Adam of Bremen, *Gesta Hamm. Eccl. Pont.*, I, 62. On trade between Denmark and Wollin, see *ibid.*, II, 19. And on commerce to Bornholm, see *ibid.*, IV, 16. See also L. Musset, *op.cit.*, pp. 242-45.

[125] H. Arbman, "Une Route commerciale au Xe et XIe siècles," *loc.cit.*, pp. 435-38.

[126] On this decline and disappearance of Hedeby, see H. Jankuhn, *Haithabu 1937-39* (Berlin 1943), pp. 180-97, which shows an end of German imported pottery here about 1050.

under his name, then, is possibly an earlier account which he incorporated into his narrative. It may have been originally composed by the Archbishop of Hamburg, Hunni, who, we know, visited Sweden in the late tenth century. If this be so, it explains anomalies which have bothered Scandinavian scholars for decades.[127] All we can say from other evidence is that Denmark traded with Finland, Gotland, Sweden, Courland, Samland and Wend coasts in this period, with her most important trade going to Gotland on the main route towards Novgorod and Russia.

This brings us to the question of Gotland and the Eastern Baltic. A certain amount of coin evidence shows that trade continued to reach Denmark, Gotland and Finland from Courland, Samland and Wendish shores, since the Bohemian and Hungarian money minted in this period which we find in coin hoards could only have arrived there by way of these coasts.[128] Kievan Russian objects which archeology has discovered at Lund, Sigtuna and Gniezno similarly seem to suggest a continuation of earlier trade by way of Wollin and the Oder to Central Europe and beyond.[129] It is probable that such traffic was limited, however, and that the Cour and Slavic pirates whom Adam of Bremen mentions as a menace to navigation were already in control of these shores. By the early twelfth century, Helmhold could speak of these shores as inhabited by a primitive, simple people with little instinct for trade, pagan and far removed from the main currents of Western civilization.[130]

Sweden presents much the same picture, from the little we know of it in this period. It contains late eleventh-century coin hoards which show that some commerce was maintained with the Western European world and Denmark—a trade probably carried on then, as earlier, by Frisian merchants.[131] Archeology also seems to prove

---

[127] Ribe is mentioned as trading with England in Adam of Bremen, *Descrip. Insulae Aquilonis*, 1, but what money reached Denmark from England in this period is not found in this vicinity but rather in the Danish islands and Scania. R. Shovmand, *op.cit.*, pp. 18-21. While it is probable that some of Adam of Bremen's information on Denmark is contemporary, most of it is not. For questions as to Wollin's existence in this period, see W. Vogel, "Wo lag Vineta?" *loc.cit.*, pp. 217-21.

[128] See Chapter VII on this coin evidence. Also H. Salmo, *op.cit.*, and C. A. Nordman, *op.cit.*, for Finland; and M. Stenberger, *op.cit.*, for Gotland. Little trade, however, judging from coin hoard evidence, reached Sweden after 1050.

[129] H. Arbman, *op.cit.*, pp. 435-38, shows that Lund and Sigtuna had some connection with Poland via Wollin and Stettin.

[130] Helmhold, *Chronicle of the Slavs*, 1, 2.

[131] On Sigtuna and its fortunes, see E. Floderus, *Sigtuna Sveriges äldsta Medeltidstad*, pp. 1-156.

that for a time after 1043 Sigtuna survived as a trading center. Then, like Birka, Sigtuna simply disappeared, and Sweden entered a general period of economic isolation and decline from which she was not to emerge until the middle of the next century.

On the other hand, Gotland, like Finland, continued to enjoy a large measure of economic life, right up to 1100. Her coin hoards show much contact with Denmark, Germany and other regions about the Baltic.[132] Perhaps in this period, as earlier, the island continued to serve as a fair for the entire region. But it seems more likely that her role was one of an intermediary along main routes leading to Finland and Novgorod.[133] At any rate, by the early twelfth century Gotland began to change into a more normal trading center with a large town growing up at Viborg. Soon we begin to hear of *Guti*, or Gotlanders, trading with England[134] and with Novgorod on their own account.[135] Gotland, like the rest of the Baltic, entered a new era.

What seems to have been the economic trend is the following: An important commercial route continued to exist all through the period from Denmark and the Kattegat-Skagerrak entrance into the Baltic to Finland and Russia by way of Gotland. Along this route the main trade of the Baltic passed. But for at least some decades other commerce of a minor nature was carried on with Sweden and southern and eastern Baltic coasts. Gradually, however, this subsidiary trade lost importance, until by 1100 it had all but ceased, leaving the main Gotland-Novgorod route the only one still in operation. Gotland's days as a great Baltic fair ended, and in the twelfth century she began, like other Baltic shores, to enter upon a new destiny, one which was tied up with an aggressive German expansion into the lands beyond the Elbe and those about the Baltic Sea.

As these changes took place in the Baltic, an even more important transformation was occurring in the economy of all Northern Europe. This was the merging of the trade, the politics and the culture of the

---

[132] The particularly catholic mixture of coins found in Gotland from the 10th and early 11th centuries continues for these years, too. M. Stenberger, *op.cit.*, pp. 230-56. There is, however, no sign of a town there until after 1000.

[133] The similarity between the coin hoards of Finland and Gotland makes this a strong probability. So does the fact that such hoards differ from those found on the Swedish mainland north of Danish-controlled Bleckinge. On this trade, see L. Musset, *op.cit.*, p. 249, and S. F. Cross, "Medieval Russian Contacts with the West," in *Speculum*, X (1935), 142-43.

[134] F. Liebermann, *Gesetze*, I, 658.

[135] On this 12th-century trade with Russian Novgorod, see L. Goetz, *op.cit.*, pp. 14-54, and G. Vernadsky, *Kievan Russia*, pp. 335-37.

lands around the Northern Seas with those of the Mediterranean. We have seen how, earlier in the eleventh century, new trade flowed across the Alpine passes from France, and the Rhone valley, which had been quiescent since the days of Louis the Pious, began to be filled with new economic activity. By the late eleventh century this commerce had grown in importance. From Adriatic Venice and Lombardy an increasing number of merchants and their wares were reaching Southern Germany, the upper Rhine valley and even Hungary.[136] We again find Italian traders in Northern France.[137] From Provence trade flowed up the Rhone towards Champagne, where fairs were again arising,[138] and towards Bordeaux by way of the Garonne valley.[139] Traders and pirates sailed into the Mediterranean by way of Spanish Atlantic coasts. Down the Danube went others who re-opened a route from Hungary to Byzantium.[140] Even Kiev re-established contact with Constantinople about 1102.[141] By way of Spain, Narbonne, Montpellier and Marseilles, along Alpine passes to Genoa, Pisa and Venice, and by Danube and Dnieper to Byzantium, the life of Northern Europe began to mingle with that of the South. Normans in Southern Italy and Sicily, Cluniac monks and feudal adventurers in Spain, Western pirates and adventurers in the Eastern Mediterranean[142] all represent this new development.

Symbolic of this surge southwards was the great pilgrim traffic to the Holy Land which grew steadily throughout the eleventh century. Newly converted Scandinavians hastened to Rome and the Holy Land.[143] So, too, did Norman knights like Richard of St. Vannes[144] or Frenchmen like Lietbud of Cambrai or Flemings like Robert the Frisian.[145] After having been isolated for some centuries from the main currents of the Moslem and Byzantine Mediterranean world, Northern Europe, now a relatively highly developed region, sent forth its sons again to the South.

[136] A. R. Lewis, op.cit., p. 248.   [137] Jaffé, Regestum, II, 115, 132, 146.
[138] A. R. Lewis, op.cit., p. 247.
[139] Y. Renouard, "Voies de communication entre Méditerranée et Atlantique," in Mélanges Louis Halphen, pp. 590-94.
[140] It is certainly significant that most of those who went to Constantinople on the First Crusade followed this route.
[141] B. Lieb, Rome, Kiev et Byzance au XIe siècle.
[142] R. Doehaerd, op.cit., pp. 29-32.
[143] P. Riart, Expéditions et pèlerinages des Scandinaves en Terre Sainte, pp. 1-85. H. Midbar, Historia de projectione danorum in Hierosolyman, pp. 1-174.
[144] D. Pais, "Les Rapports franco-hongrois sous le règne des Arpad," in Revue des études hongroises, I (1923), 121-53.
[145] R. Doehaerd, op.cit., pp. 29-31.

The general mixture of commerce, military adventure and pious pilgrimage had fused by the end of the century into what we call the the First Crusade. This crusading movement, exalting the power of the Papacy, using trader, pilgrim and adventure in a new way in the service of religion, had by the twelfth century produced that medieval Europe in which Italian and Fleming, Roman and Parisian, German, Scandinavian, English, Spaniard and Slav were merged together in a new and greater unity. By the time King Sigurd of Norway sailed into the Mediterranean wearing the Crusader's cross, and King Eric of Denmark traveled through the Baltic and Russia to Constantinople on the same errand, this new age had dawned. Vikings had turned into Crusaders and the era of Canute had become that of Urban II and St. Bernard. The death in Ireland of Magnus Barelegs, the last Viking, marked the passing of an age. His son, traveling to Jerusalem as a Crusader, marked the beginning of another.

Conclusion

THE Northern European world which had emerged by 1100 and began then to mingle with the Mediterranean to form what we know as Europe was, as we have shown in these chapters, the product of an involved history and of many complex and varied forces. No single cause, no simple series of changes produced the commerce, the agriculture, the trading centers, the variety of ships and the economic organization which had developed in the lands around the Northern Seas by the time of the First Crusade. If these pages do nothing else, it is the author's hope that they will serve to show the complexity of the forces at work, the difficulties involved in generalizations and the tremendous problems that still remain to be solved by historians dealing with these centuries.

A study of these years, however, does lead to certain conclusions. Perhaps the most important is that Northern Europe emerged as a result of a slow growth in which all of its peoples participated and to which each made important contributions. Roman and German, Irish and Anglo-Saxon, Frisian and Carolingian Frank, Scandinavian and Slav, Russian, Pole, Fleming, Saxon, Norman and Frenchman, each took the lead, in one period or another, as mariner, merchant and clearer of the waste. The making of Northern Europe in these centuries was a cooperative venture in which every group of people from the Urals to Greenland and from the Alps, Pyrenees and Danube to the frozen waters of the North made great—nay, indispensable—contributions.

In the second place, it seems evident that this process of development was neither constant nor uniform in all the lands around the Northern Seas. Often it was halting in some regions, and at times it was attended by actual declines. In general, the periods of growth were the Late Roman Empire, Early Merovingian times, the age of Louis the Pious, and the tenth and early eleventh centuries. Those of decline were the period of the German invasions, Late Merovingian times, the late ninth century and the last years of the eleventh century. But periods of decline proved less important in the long run than those of growth, and always held within them the seeds of an even greater development. The history of these years in Northern Europe, then, is like that of a forest. Individual trees perish, but the forest itself continues to grow without ceasing.

Finally, the history of these years reveals how false is the concept of those who see in the early period of Northern European development a Dark Age, from which peoples emerged only gradually from the depression into which the barbarian Germans had plunged a Roman world. Far from being a period of darkness, of numb waiting for a new day to dawn, these centuries reveal themselves as full of expansion, development and hope. The Northern European world of 1100, even that of 900, was more advanced than the Romano-barbarian world from which it had sprung. Its newly cleared fields, its growing towns, its maritime trade had expanded the area of civilization far beyond that of the Pax Romana, and laid a healthy basis for future growth. The making of Northern Europe, then, is not the story of a painfully evolving barbarism, but of a steadily expanding civilization.

Index